HERITAGE CLASSICS:
A Collection of
Essential Wisdom

By Katie Parrott Trudgeon

For JP, whom God made larger than other men so that I, and thousands of others, could see further from atop his mighty shoulders. Thanks for the magnificent view.

TABLE OF CONTENTS

PART ONE – CLASSICAL FOUNDATIONS

CHAPTER 1 – ANCIENT GREECE

CHAPTER 2 – ANCIENT ROME

PART TWO—MEDIEVAL METAMORPHOSIS

CHAPTER 3—EARLY MIDDLE AGES

CHAPTER 4—THE HIGH MIDDLE AGES

CHAPTER 5—THE LATE MIDDLE AGES AND PIONEERS OF A NEW AGE

PART THREE—REVOLUTIONS OF THE MIND

CHAPTER 6—THE RENAISSANCE

CHAPTER 7—PROTESTANT REFORMATION

CHAPTER 8—SCIENTIFIC REVOLUTION

CHAPTER 9—THE AGE OF DISCOVERY AND CONQUEST

PART FOUR—TYRANNY AND TRIUMPH

CHAPTER 10—THE AGE OF ABSOLUTISM

CHAPTER 11—THE ENLIGHTENMENT AND THE AMERICAN REVOLUTION

CHAPTER 12—THE FRENCH REVOLUTION

PART FIVE — CONFLICT AND CONQUEST

CHAPTER 13 — THE INDUSTRIAL AGE

CHAPTER 14 — THE AGE OF IMPERIALISM

CHAPTER 15 — WORLD WAR I

CHAPTER 16—TOTALITARIANISM AND WORLD WAR II

INTRODUCTION

Becoming a Historical Detective

I have never understood why everyone in the world does not love history as much as I do. To me, history is full of the most wildly fantastic stories of courage and triumph, love and hate, joy and despair. The true stories of the past far surpass anything fictional that I have ever seen or read in terms of drama, wisdom and emotion. So why is it that for so many, history is a mystery?

Many of us, maybe you, see history as a collection of random dates, people and events that took place a long time ago that has little to no connection to our lives today. How could people who lived 3000 years ago possibly help us solve our modern day problems? How could wars that were fought with spears and arrows guide us on decisions of war in the 21st century? For far too many of us, the answer is "They can't." But I propose that this disconnect from history is because people do not know how to read it correctly. The purpose of this book is to help you study and understand history in a deeply meaningful way and to connect you with the timeless humanness we share across the ages. History's mysteries are easily solved if you have the right tools to begin the quest.

All great treasure hunters have a collection of tools to help them unearth their discoveries. Explorers had ships, compasses and courage. Paleontologists have picks, shovels, sieves and luck. Treasure hunters have a map but X seldom, if ever, marks the spot. Historians have words. Words are our primary tool for unlocking the secrets of the past. We also, thanks to archaeologists, have artifacts like pottery, ruins of buildings and burial sites. But it is the words written down by people long, long ago that transport us back to the past. But just like other great seekers who must know which tools to trust, we must know how to read the words of the past carefully and ask lots of questions along the way. That is what we are going to learn to do together.

This book is a collection of stories or pieces of stories that have been written over the last 3000 years. These historical stories, because they were written during different eras of the past, are called "primary sources." This is just a fancy way of saying that these documents are like journals you may keep. They were about the author—him or herself—or at least about the time they were alive. So they are much more likely to be reliable than things someone wrote about those people hundreds or even thousands of years after their lives. And they are definitely more interesting.

As you work your way through this book, I ask you to keep a few things in mind that might help you see history differently:

1. Think of the author as a regular person, writing you a letter. Try to imagine what they might look like. The authors of the documents in this book were as real as you or me. They were also as smart, as kind, as opinionated and as flawed. Thinking of authors as ordinary people helps me connect personally to what they have written.

2. Ask yourself what the author was feeling as he or she wrote. Human life seems to have changed very much over time but human emotion has not changed. Like you, these authors felt love, heartache, fear, insecurity, arrogance, forgiveness and grief. As

1

you read the documents in each section, ask yourself what the author was feeling when he or she was writing. Each of the documents in this collection has a deep emotional element to it. Part of your detective work is to figure out what the motivating emotion was in each case. And the distance of time will start to melt away.

How To Read and Analyze a Primary Source

As I have already stated, a *primary source* is a document or physical object which was written or created during the time under study. These sources were present during an experience or time period and offer an inside view of a particular event.   A *secondary source* interprets and analyzes primary sources. These sources are usually written after the time of study by people who did not experience the events first-hand.

In this book, we will be exploring primary sources and ,as we work through this book together, there are specific steps you will be asked to follow as you read:

Step One: The first step is identifying the source or author and determining if he or she is a trustworthy source. For each document, look up the author and determine who he is and if his work qualifies as a primary source based on the facts you find.

Step Two: Each of the documents starts with a set of "Reading and Discussion" questions. You should read over these questions and then read the entire document over once.

Step Three: As you read, you should annotate your document, which simply means to mark your document with highlighting, notes, comments and questions that will be helpful in your analysis. Annotating helps you to be an active reader. And do not worry about whether you are "doing it right." Different readers have different annotation styles. I personally use lots of stars, arrows and exclamation points and phrases like "YES!" or "This is key." Also mark any words or passages that are unclear so you can go back over those. I usually use a simple "?" or "???????" if it is a concept that has completely stumped me. Mark up your text in any way that works best for you as long it easily guides you back to important sections and main ideas.   During this step, DO NOT stop to answer any of the questions. That part comes later.

Step Four: Once you have read and annotated the entire document, go back to any words or sections that were unclear. Look up any vocabulary that you are unfamiliar with or reread tricky passages for more clarity. Make sure before you move to answering the questions that you understand the document well. It sometimes helps to write a short one-paragraph summary or ask yourself if you could easily tell your mom the key points of what you just read. If you cannot do either of those things, you should read the passage again.

Step Five: Finally, upon completing a thorough reading, you are ready to begin working on the reading and discussion questions. Though some of the questions for each document are strictly factual questions, most ask for your opinion on or interpretation of what you have read. This requires some deep thinking. There are many sides to every story and many ways to interpret those stories. Your job here is as interpreter, and it takes serious work to decide for yourself what you think and how you assign meaning to what you have read. It's detective work, remember?

What is Western Civilization?

When I ask my students on the first day of class "What is Western Civilization?" the first answer I always get is "Civilization that is in the west." And I am always happy to say that this is a correct answer! But for our purposes it is not entirely satisfactory. Since the earth is a sphere, west is a relative location. For people in Japan, China is western, and for people in Saudi Arabia, Africa is west, right? (Look at a map if you have to!) So when we study Western Civilization we must first decide where west is for us. For our studies, Western Civilization is the European world and all the places shaped by European influence, especially the Americas (for reasons we will discuss later). Western Civilization began on the shores of the Mediterranean Sea in Greece. For the last five thousand years, ideas that were born on the mainland and the hundreds of islands of Greece have been spreading across continents and oceans and have impacted the lives of billions of people.

It is tricky to assign a specific date to the beginning of Western Civilization, since it was an offshoot of non-western culture that had been born earlier in places like Egypt and Mesopotamia. As early as 10,000 BCE, an agricultural revolution took place that caused nomadic people in the modern day Middle East to settle down into the first communities. Those communities grew over time into a large population of people and became the Fertile Crescent civilization of Mesopotamia. As Mesopotamians progressed and as populations grew, those people spread out and colonized new places like Egypt and Phoenicia. And for 7000 years after the birth of Mesopotamia, knowledge and innovation spread further west until it reached the shores of Greece in the west and places like China and India in the east. In around 3000 BCE, those seeds of knowledge from the Fertile Crescent grew into Western Civilization. As I said, we do not know the day, month or year that Western Civilization began but we do know generally when it started. Since historians like the use of neat round numbers to mark the start and end of things, we will use the date 3000 BCE as the year our Western story began.

For five thousand years Western Civilization, our civilization, has thrived and spread to the far reaches of the planet. That sounds like a very, very long time and it is. The power and influence of Western Civilization is impressive. But it is important to keep everything in perspective. According to scientists, the earth was created 4.6 billion years ago. Humans have walked the earth for about 2.7 million years. Our ancestors spent most of that time as nomadic hunters and gatherers who focused almost entirely on survival and the creation of the most basic shelter and weapons. It was not until 12,000 years ago that we settled into the first civilizations in the Fertile Crescent. And as we have already discussed, our Western Civilization has been around for roughly 5000 years. Imagine that on a timeline if you can. And then insert yourself onto that timeline and consider your place in history for a moment. Or another way of visualizing the history of earth is to think of it as a clock. If the existence of earth is represented in a 24-hour period, humans have been a part of the story only the last few seconds before midnight at the end of that very, very long day. This should help us to keep our story in proper perspective.

Every human being has but a moment in time when you consider things on the scale of "big history." Since history is simply the study of past events, everything is history, from the creation of the universe and the earth to the founding of modern nations and the events that happened in your life last week. And everything is part of the same story. Though it is hard to imagine, you and I are connected to people who lived thousands, or even hundreds of thousands of years ago. It is sometimes hard to find value or interest in things that happened to people a long, long time ago in places that are very far away until you consider that their story is your story. You might be surprised to learn how much your life is shaped by men whose names you do not yet know and which can barely pronounce—men like Cliesthenes, Thucydides, Archimedes, Hippocrates, Copernicus and Montesquieu. Too few people understand that the present would not be possible without the past. But my hope is that you will not be among those people. I hope that you will come to understand that the story of Western Civilization is the story of giants of intellect, whose colossal ideas and immense courage have created the world we live in today.

Now that we know where our Western Civilization is and when it started, we must look at the word civilization. What does it mean to be civilized? You may think that any large population of people makes up a civilization, and you would be partly right. But there is much more to civilization that being part of a group. A group of people who live in the same geographic area and who have relationships with one another is a society, but not necessarily a civilization.   In order to be a civilization, a group or society of people must have five things: technology; specialized workers; cities as centers of trade; a system of writing; and complex institutions. So what does that mean?   Basically, it means that societies must be highly organized in order to win "civilized" status. Let's look at each characteristic of civilization specifically so that in our studies we will be able to recognize a civilization when we see one and to notice when and if civilization falls apart.

Technology. In the world we live in today, it is impossible not to know what technology is in the modern sense, but how does it lead to the creation of civilizations and what is it beyond smart phones, laptops and the internet? Technology is, quite simply, an invention or tool that is used to make life easier or to solve problems. Long before the computer, there was technology. Simple machines like levers, pulleys and inclined planes are all technology. A wheel, a metal axe, a triangular sail and a loom are all technology. Technology is any invention that allows society to move forward and improve. It allows us to work more efficiently and create better products of our labor. Perhaps most importantly, it gives people the time and freedom to develop specific skills and become specialized workers, which in turn makes trade possible.

Specialized Workers. In the beginning, every family hunted for their own food, built their own shelters, made their own clothes. Every hour of the day was spent meeting the most basic needs of human survival. Then something really important happened. People learned to farm and to use animals in the labor of planting and harvesting crops. You might be asking, "Who cares?" But something as basic as the planting and harvesting of crops probably changed the way humans live more than any other single event in history. Farming is important because it allowed people to stay in one place. They got to lay down roots, build houses and begin to form societies with other people. And over time, people got so good at farming that many farmers had extra food that could be traded with their neighbors. Before long, a single family no longer had to grow apples and harvest wheat and raise chickens in order to feed themselves.

Let's look at the following scenario to see how specialized workers and trade evolve in non-nomadic societies. Because farmer A had more apples than he needed, he traded them to Farmer B for chickens and eggs because Farmer B was excellent at raising healthy chickens. Farmer C too could now stop growing apples and raising chickens because he had a surplus of wheat that he could trade with Farmers A and B for apples and chickens. You get the idea. And raising only chickens, or growing only wheat or apples takes much less time than doing all three and so for the first time in history, people had free time. Imagine at this same time that Farmer A got his hands on the simplest of tools. . . a metal needle. He had been trying for years to sew the family's clothes with a wooden needle and the needle was constantly breaking. He wasted hundreds of hours getting new needles every time one broke. But a metal needle, which would not break easily, was a technological wonder to Farmer A, who could now sew six pairs of trousers in the time it had taken to sew one with a wooden needle. This is how technology leads to innovation and specialization. Farmer A shared his new technology with his friends and soon they were all making more clothes than their families could wear in a lifetime. So they decided to divide their labor and each person specialized in making only a certain garment. Overtime, this small society no longer has single families meeting all of their own needs. Instead it had apple farmers, chicken ranchers, wheat growers, hat makers, cobblers and seamstresses. When a society has ample food supplies and free time to develop special skills, the result is specialized workers or specialists.

Cities as Centers of Trade. Specialized workers who are really good at their jobs create products that people want. There will always be one hat maker or basket weaver whose products stand out above the rest. And because it is impractical to walk from one village to another in search of each particular product you desire, people began coming together in a central meeting place to exchange or trade their products. First people came together at an established time for market days and then returned to their homes. But eventually people moved closer and closer to these market centers for the ease of doing business. It made more sense to live where you could buy and sell products easily than it did to make a long journey regularly. And out of economic necessity, cities were born as centers of trade.

A System of Writing. When you are trading pants for apples with your next-door neighbor, it is easy to remember what quantities were exchanged and what products were asked for or promised for next month. A simple verbal exchange of the business details was all that was needed to complete the business deal. But in newly emerging cities, hundreds or even thousands of merchants might be exchanging their goods on a single day and the volume of products exchanged could be quite large. It would be very difficult to remember that you gave 12 pairs of pants to the wine merchant who promised you 20 casks of wine after the grape harvest and that you had ordered 60 axes from the blacksmith which would be ready for pickup next week in exchange for enough trousers for all 18 of his employees. Without a system of writing, increasingly complex business transactions would be almost impossible to keep straight. And so written language was created.

Complex institutions. A complex institution is simply any organization which is created to provide structure and order to a society. As very large trade cities emerged, the first thing that was necessary was government and a justice system. When lots of people live together, there must be rules or laws to govern those people, to ensure their business transactions are fair and to keep people safe. A government is a complex institution, as are banks, schools, armies, and religious organizations. The more advanced a civilization is, the more complex institutions it will have.

Civilization, in a nut shell, is a society of people that is organized for efficiency and progress. And Western Civilization is actually a collection of highly organized, progressive civilizations who built on the successes and learned from the failures of earlier civilizations to bring us into the present day. The civilizations of the past, it is important to remember, stumbled a lot along the way, and sometimes had really, really terrible ideas. They made horrible decisions, failed to consider all the information and fell flat on their faces. The story of Western Civilization is as much a story about the failures of humankind as it is about success. To me, this is what makes Western Civilization a beautiful story. Over and over, men and women failed. But they never stopped trying. And the collective efforts of generations of men and women who refused to give up is the story of us. It is a remarkable story that I am so very eager for you to know.

PART ONE–
CLASSICAL FOUNDATIONS

If you look up the word "classic" in the dictionary, many definitions come up, including *of the first or highest quality; of enduring interest, quality, or style.* Another definition, though, is *of or relating to ancient Greek and Roman culture.* When we talk about the classical foundations of the Western world, we are talking about cultural influences of the highest quality and enduring in interest and style. These cultural influences are Greek and Roman. Many of the ideas that we think of today as new American ideas are actually very, very old Greek and Roman ideas, from our running water and indoor plumbing to our representative democracy. There is an old saying that "All roads lead to Rome." For Western Civilization, this is absolutely true. In this book, we will travel back to our past to understand the present and the roads we will travel are Roman. The Romans *literally* built the roads that united the world but they also created enduring pathways of thoughts, inventions and ways of life that lead from very ancient times to the present day. And the Romans actually got many of their ideas from the Greeks.

Isaac Newton, the father of physics, said of his achievements, "If I have seen further than others, it is because I have stood on the shoulders of giants." This was Newton's way of paying respect to the sometimes forgotten men who came before him whose ideas paved the way for his discoveries. He did what he did because of what had been done before. He had a sturdy foundation on which to build. The same is true for our current progress. The ancients Greeks and Romans were giants of intellect, innovation and invention. Only by standing on their shoulders have we seen ourselves so far along the road of human progress. Having a deep understanding of our classical past is essential to understanding the world around us.

CHAPTER 1—
ANCIENT GREECE (3000 to 323 BCE)

<u>GUIDING QUESTIONS</u>
- What is meant by the statement, "The Greeks were the thinkers?"
- What values were shared by all Greeks?
- What lessons can we learn from the collapse of Greece?
- What can we learn about the values of the Greeks through their writing?
- How is our modern human story connected to the story of the Greeks?
- What was the Greek idea of "honor?"
- What is "hubris" and how did it influence Greek literature and thought?

Western Civilization as we know it is a mix of influences from dozens of cultures over thousands of years but the cultures of classical Greece and Rome are the foundation upon which the Western world was built. Our journey through the history of the Western world begins on the shores of the Mediterranean Sea in Greece five millennia ago.

Ancient Greece, contrary to popular belief, was not one place with one set of ideas, one type of government and one value system. It was a collection of hundreds of city-states separated by geographical obstacles that made unity among the Greek peoples impossible even if they had wanted to be unified—which they did not. But all Greeks shared a few key characteristics—they cherished honor and duty, learning and ingenuity. They despised cowardice and also something called hubris, or excessive pride. They were all fiercely independent and they all shared a deep pride in their "Greek-ness." The Greeks were innovators and inventors. The Greeks were the thinkers in the ancient world and their ideas shape every facet of life in the West today.

The earliest known Greek peoples were the Minoans (2700 to 1500 BCE), who inhabited the Mediterranean island of Crete. The Minoans had a system of writing, sophisticated temples and palaces, running water, a complex government structure and a highly organized navy. The Minoans were also highly cultured, emphasizing art, athletics and drama and had one of the first known theaters. Their religion laid the foundations for the pantheon of Greek gods and goddesses that make up Greek mythology today. The Minoan civilization ended abruptly and mysteriously, but most think the island of Crete was devastated by a major natural disaster like an earthquake, a tsunami or a volcanic eruption. The other dominant early Greek civilization was a people known as the Mycenaeans (1900 to 1100 BCE).

Unlike the culturally and artistically advanced Minoans, the Mycenaeans were a warrior society and were most likely the main aggressors in the Trojan War, as passed down to us in Homer's *Iliad*. The Trojan War was an epic clash between the ancient city-state of Troy and a number of other Greek civilizations, including Mycenae. Troy was ultimately destroyed during the Trojan War, and the only details we have of that event are found in artifacts and the colorful details, perhaps partly factual, included in the *Iliad*. What is certain is that, after the Trojan War in roughly 1100 BCE, Greek civilization stood still and a period called the Greek Dark Ages began which lasted for nearly 300 years.

The term "Dark Ages" is most often associated with the period in Medieval Europe after the fall of Rome which you will learn about later. However, the first documented "Dark Ages" were in Greece after the Trojan War. The term "Dark Ages" refers to a standstill in civilization or a period of stagnation where learning and innovation cease and ignorance and barbarism rule. How do historians know there was a period of Dark Ages in Greece between 1100 and 800 BCE? Because they have found *nothing* from that 300 year period. No pottery, no buildings, no written records, no signs of trade. In history, during times of progress and stability, people leave countless thousands of hints as to their existence. They build temples. They write books. They build ships for trade or conquest. They keep business records or important laws on clay tablets. They build irrigation channels, fortresses, burial shrines and temples, the ruins of which can be studied by future generations. But in times of upheaval, disaster, war and chaos, nothing is created. When mere survival is a struggle, people have time for nothing else, least of all education, arts or sophisticated building projects.

To date, historians and archaeologists have unearthed no artifacts, records or other signs of civilized existence in Greece from the period between 1100 and 800 BCE. What happened to Greece during that time? There are numerous theories but no definitive answer. Perhaps a natural disaster completely devastated the region again like the event that destroyed the Minoan culture. But more likely the Greek city-states were weakened by the Trojan War or similar conflict and were overwhelmed by an invasion of a warlike group from northern Greece called the Dorians. Whatever the cause for the standstill, there is no sign of progress and culture in Greece for these dark 300 years after 1100 BCE.

Despite disagreements about what caused the Greek Dark Ages, we know for sure that they had come to an end by 800 BCE because as of that date there were books. How it is that books alone, and just two of them in this case, can signal the rebirth of culture, progress and civilization as a whole? Because someone had the time to write them! Writing great works of literature is a luxury one cannot afford in times of turmoil. The two books in question that date back to 800 BCE are two of the greatest works of literature in history— *The Iliad* and *The Odyssey*, both of which are credited to the blind bard, Homer. Both books were epic poems which means they are long poems about heroes' journeys. But they were much more than that. They served as the only written chronicle of early Greek history, even if many of the events were fictional. In these two works we learn much about the ancient Greeks--their religious beliefs, their style of government and warfare, their idea of heroism, honor and a life well-lived. *The Iliad* and *The Odyssey* also foreshadow the brilliance of the Greek mind that is to be fully revealed in the centuries after the darkness.

Between 800 and 500 BCE, Greek city-states were becoming a dominant force in the ancient world. They expanded and conquered vast amounts of territory in the Mediterranean and Aegean Seas and they built an immense trade network spanning the whole known world. Two of the most powerful Greek city-states were Sparta and Athens and they could not have been more different. Sparta was one of the most militaristic civilization in history. Every Spartan boy served in the military from the age of seven to the age of 30. They ate, slept, trained, lived and died with their fellow soldiers and they were taught to be tough as nails by sleeping on the cold floor, eating tasteless Spartan stew and wearing little clothing even in the deep winter. Today, if a person lives a Spartan existence, that means their lives are "marked by simplicity, frugality, or avoidance of luxury and comfort." Because male Spartan citizens spent their lives in the military, Sparta was supported by a huge population of slaves. Women in Sparta enjoyed far more freedoms and privileges than women anywhere else in the ancient world. They received a solid education and were encouraged to be physically fit. They could own property and they ran Spartan society when the men were away at war. It will not be until modern times that women would again enjoy as many rights as the women of Sparta.

Sparta's opposite in Greece and its primary enemy was the city-state of Athens. Athens was also politically and militarily powerful but unlike Sparta, the Athenians placed a high value on art, education, architecture, theater and all types of cultural refinement. It is Athens that most people think of when they imagine ancient Greece. The Athenians built great temples to their many gods, the most famous of which is the Parthenon, which still sits atop the Acropolis in Athens today. It was in Athens that democracy was born. After centuries of being ruled by cruel and corrupt kings, a Greek named Cleisthenes was the architect of Athenian democracy in 508 BCE. The Greek word "demokratia" literally means "people power." The political system of democracy in Athens was the first time in history when a large group of citizens participated in how they were governed. In a democracy, direct participation of the citizen was required. Democracy can only work if citizens exercise their duty to vote. In addition to allowing male citizens to vote on laws, the Greeks also invented the modern judicial system, based on the concept of trial by jury.

The Greeks invented democracy partly to grant all citizens a say in government but they also believed that democracy was the only way to check absolutism, or all the power of a nation being controlled by one man or group. This fear of absolutism will be a driving force in events in Western history into the modern era. By the time of the decline of Greece as a whole, dozens of other city-states had also become democracies, and people through the ages have fought for the same freedoms in government that the citizens of Athens enjoyed 2500 years ago.

The birth of democracy in Athens helped to make her a super-power and a dangerous rival to the already dominant Spartans. A 50-year war between Athens and Sparta would ultimately lead to their mutual downfalls but for a period between 499 and 449 BCE the two fought as allies with other Greek city-states in to defeat the million-man army of the Persian Empire and the Persian Emperor Xerxes. Persia was a rapidly growing empire in modern-day Turkey and the Middle East. The Persians were among the first groups to practice imperialism, or the act of conquering and ruling vast territories. In 547 BCE the Persians conquered the Greek territory of Ionia and had plans to conquer the rest of Greece. Persia was ruled by emperors who were often tyrants, though some Persian rulers ruled with surprising tolerance.

The Persian Emperor Cyrus the Great practiced a policy called assimilation, which meant that once conquered people accepted his authority and agreed to pay taxes to the Persian Empire, they were granted privileges of citizenship and could keep their religious beliefs and most other elements of their lifestyle before conquest. This was a smart policy because many regions agreed to Persian conquest without war. But the Greeks, who treasured their honor and their independence above all things, vowed never to submit to a foreign empire.

Athens and Sparta were among the first of the Greeks to decide they would fight the seemingly unbeatable million-man army of Emperor Xerxes, the son of Cyrus the

Great. The details of the Persian War have become the stuff of legend. It was during the Persian War that the marathon was born, after a Greek runner named Pheidippides ran 26 miles from the town of Marathon to Athens to deliver the news that the Persians had been defeated in an importantly battle. Immediately after delivering the message Pheidippides died. The 26-mile race was added to the Olympic games to commemorate his sacrifice. The Persian War was also the conflict where the mighty 300 Spartan warriors held off Xerxes' massive army for three days in order to allow the other Greek city-states time to prepare for invasion. All the Greek city-states ultimately joined the fighting and the Greeks were miraculously victorious in driving the Persians out of Greece in 449 BCE. Athens and Sparta fought together when their common "Greek-ness" was threatened by Persian imperialism. But once Persia had been defeated it became clear that the Mediterranean world was not big enough for these two powerful rivals.

Just eighteen years after the Greek defeat of the Persians, Athens and Sparta were at war in a conflict that would mark the beginning of the end of Greek power. This conflict, known as the Peloponnesian War, lasted from 431 to 404 BCE. The cause of the war was a simple power struggle. Sparta believed that Athens was exercising too much power in Greece and was practicing the same types of imperialist policies that had caused the Persian Wars less than two decades earlier. Sparta gathered a group of allies to stop Athenian aggression and Athens gathered its own group of powerful friends. A long, bloody war followed for the next 27 years. Though Sparta and her allies were the technical victors (in part because of a deadly plague that struck Athens), the Peloponnesian War had no real winner. Every city-state in Greece that fought in the war was economically and physically devastated by almost 30 years of fighting. Greece as a whole was so weakened that it never recovered.

In less than 100 years after the end of the Peloponnesian War, ancient Greece was no more. By 350 BCE, the city-states of Greece were being conquered by King Phillip of Macedonia, a small kingdom just north of Greece. Phillip was an ambitious ruler who extended his kingdom into Asia before his death in 336 BCE. He left his throne to his even more ambitious son, who would become known as Alexander the Great. Alexander, who was educated by the great Greek philosopher Aristotle, is one of the greatest military commanders in history. In just thirteen short years, Alexander conquered and ruled the largest empire that the world had ever seen. His territory stretched from Greece, into north Africa and across the modern Middle East. He accomplished all of this by the age of 32.

In addition to being a brilliant commander, Alexander was a capable and broad-minded leader. He believed that his empire would thrive best if it had a shared culture. He required his officers, who were Greek, to marry women in the eastern regions he conquered in order to create a literal "marriage of East and West." He appointed Persians, Greeks and Egyptians into powerful positions equally. He adopted some eastern cultural practices while retaining many Greek customs. The result of this union of west and east was a new culture known as Hellenistic Culture. Unfortunately, Alexander died an untimely death before his vision could be fully realized. Because he did not have an heir and did not appoint a successor before his death, the empire he had fought so long to conquer was greedily divided among his generals who lacked Alexander's leadership abilities and vision. Greece fell steadily into decline and by 200 BCE what had been the fiercely independent city-states of Greece would all be part of the new and mighty Republic of Rome.

Though the great civilizations of ancient Greece have been gone for more than 2000 years, no other civilization before or since more constantly shapes and defines our modern existence than ancient Greece. As you may recall, the Greeks gave us the Olympics, the alphabet, architecture, literature and drama. But most importantly, the ancient Greeks gave us great *ideas*. The ancient Greeks, and the Athenians in particular, were "the thinkers" who pondered timeless questions about life, the universe and the meaning of existence. They wondered about the mysteries of nature and the universe and provide us with incredibly sophisticated answers. The achievements of the Greek mind were astonishing. Philosophy, which literally means "the love of wisdom," was created by great Greek minds like Socrates, Plato and Aristotle. Philosophy is the study of the fundamental nature of knowledge, reality, and existence. The Greek philosophers were the first to try to explain human behavior and the cosmos with reason and logic instead of with religion and a multitude of gods. They pondered timeless questions about the relationship between good and evil, about the reasons for the order of the universe, the true nature of beauty and love and the ideal form of government. They challenged people to *think* and *seek answers*. They encouraged us and still encourage us to be constantly searching for truth and virtue and to live our lives thoughtfully, morally and deliberately. The ancient Greeks were also mathematicians, astronomers, scientists and engineers. The accomplishments of the Greeks in every field of study would not be matched until the 1700s. There has never been an era before or since with such a concentration of brilliant, innovative thinkers.

Finally, the Greeks were the first to recognize the importance of their achievements and contributions to the human race and so they created history. History is a continuous, systematic narrative or story of past events about a particular group, country, period or person. Greek historians like Herodotus and Thucydides were the first people to record significant events of their own lifetimes and to rediscover the stories of other important ancient civilizations including the Persians and the Egyptians. The creation of history marks a crucial moment in the evolution of human thought. For the first time with the Greeks, human actions were not simply done and then forgotten. The Greeks realized that human accomplishments--their accomplishments--were impressive and deserved to be remembered. They recognized that without knowledge of the past, there would be no building blocks for the future. Greek historians wrote the opening chapters of the human story which continues on into this moment. It is through these stories that we are all connected.

Homer, *The Iliad*, 800 BCE

Reading and Discussion Questions

1. Define "honor." What do you think Homer is telling us here about the Greek sense of "honor?"
2. Who is depicted as "honorable" in the portion of the story below?
3. Who is not honorable? Why?
4. Did you find any examples of "hubris" in your reading? Explain.
5. Is there a clear hero in this part of the story? Explain.
6. What did you learn about Greek culture and values from your reading? Explain at least three things about the Greeks that you understand better after your reading.

The Iliad is the first known work of Western literature. It is believed to have been a story told and passed down orally for generations before it was finally written down. It was told by poets in a specific rhythm and verse and it is the story of the legendary Trojan War. The Trojan War was fought between the Greeks (Achaeans) and the Trojans. As Homer tells it, Troy was the richest civilization in the ancient world and it was also very peaceful. The Greek city-states, including Mycenae, envied the wealth of Troy but never had a reason to invade because of Troy's peaceful nature. They found their reason, however, when the young Trojan prince, Paris, fell in love with and abducted the wife of a very powerful Greek. The woman's name was Helen and she is known to have had "a face that launched a thousand ships." Helen was married to the king of Sparta, Menelaus and Menelaus was the brother of the king of all the Greeks, Agamemnon. When Paris abducted Helen and took her back to Troy, Menelaus and Agamemnon gathered all their allies and declared war on Troy.

For eleven years the war raged between the Trojans and the Greeks. In the story of the Iliad, Homer introduces us to hundreds of fantastic, colorful characters and he uses them to explore Greek values like honor, duty and a very important Greek idea called hubris. Hubris is defined as "god-like" pride and was viewed as the greatest of all sins by the Greeks. In the following passages from the Iliad, we learn the story of five central characters to the Iliad. We will meet Paris who is, of course, the Trojan prince who abducts Helen. We also meet Paris' brother, Hector. Paris and Hector's father is Priam, King of Troy. On the other side of the story we meet Achilles, the bravest and most celebrated of the Greek soldiers and Menelaus, the husband of Helen who feels his honor was harmed when his wife was taken from him. In Book III and Book XXII, we see the fate of the Iliad's central characters and we learn a lot about the Greek code of ethics. In Book XXIV, we see a human moment between King Priam and wrathful Achilles and learn more about honor and the sacredness of burial rituals for the Greeks.

Book III -- Paris, Menelaus, and Helen

In an attempt to avoid an all-out war, an agreement is reached for Paris (a.k.a. Alexander) to fight Menelaus is single combat to resolve their dispute. In the middle of combat, the gods intervene and the battle between the two is unfinished.

Once troops had formed in ranks under their own leaders,
Trojans marched out, clamouring like birds, like cranes
screeching overhead, when winter's harsh storms drive them off,
screaming as they move over the flowing Ocean,
bearing death and destruction to the Pygmies,
launching their savage attack on them at dawn.*
Achaeans came on in silence, breathing ferocity,
determined to stand by each other in the fight.   10

They advanced at full speed out across the plain.
The two armies moved in close towards each other.
Then godlike Paris stepped out, as Trojan champion,
on his shoulders a leopard skin. He had bow and sword.
Brandishing two bronze-tipped spears, he challenged
the best men in the whole Achaean force to fight—
a single combat, to the death. War-loving Menelaus
noticed Alexander striding there, his troops   20
bunched up in ranks behind him, and he rejoiced,
like a famished lion finding a large carcass—
antlered stag or wild goat—and devouring it at once,
though fierce young hunters and swift dogs attack.

So Menelaus was pleased to see Paris there,
right before his eyes. Menelaus had in mind
taking revenge on the man who'd injured him.
At once Menelaus jumped from his chariot,
down to the ground, his weapons in his fists.
When godlike Alexander saw Menelaus there,   30
among the fighters at the front, his heart sank.
He moved back into the ranks, among his comrades,
avoiding death. Just as a man stumbles on a snake
in some mountainous ravine and gives way, jumping back,
his limbs trembling, his cheeks pale, so godlike Paris,
afraid of Menelaus, slid back into proud Trojan ranks.
Seeing this, Hector went at Alexander, insulting him:

"Despicable Paris, handsomest of men,
but woman-mad seducer. How I wish
you never had been born or died unmarried.   40
That's what I'd prefer, so much better
than to live in shame, hated by others.
Now long-haired Achaeans are mocking us,
saying we've put forward as a champion
one who looks good, but lacks a strong brave mind.
Was this what you were like back on that day

14

you gathered up your faithful comrades,
sailed sea-worthy ships across the ocean,
went out among a foreign people,
and carried back from that far-off land   50
a lovely woman linked by marriage
to warrior spearmen, thus bringing on
great suffering for your father and your city,
all your people—joy to your enemies
and to yourself disgrace? And can you now
not face Menelaus? If so, you'd learn
the kind of man he is whose wife you took.
You'd get no help then from your lyre, long hair,
good looks—Aphrodite's gifts—once face down,
lying in the dirt. Trojans must be timid men.   60
If not, for all the evil things you've done
by now you'd wear a garment made of stones."

To Hector godlike Paris then replied:
"Hector, you're right in what you say against me.
Those complaints of yours are not unjustified.
Your heart is tireless, like a wood-chopping axe
wielded by a craftsman cutting timber for a ship.
The axe makes his force stronger. Your mind's like that—
the spirit in your chest is fearless. But don't blame me
for golden Aphrodite's lovely gifts.   70
Men can't reject fine presents from the gods,
those gifts they personally bestow on us,
though no man would take them of his own free will.

You want me now to go to battle.
Get others to sit down—Trojans and Achaeans.
Put me and war-loving Menelaus
in their midst to fight it out for Helen,
all her property. The one who triumphs,
comes off victorious, the better man,
let him take all the goods and lead her home,   80
as his wife. Let others swear a solemn oath,
as friends, either to live on in fertile Troy
or to return to horse-breeding Argos,
land of the lovely women of Achaea."

Achaeans and Trojans were elated, full of hope
that wretched war would end. They pulled the chariots back
into the ranks, climbed out, disarmed, and placed their weapons
next to each other on the ground, with little room
between both groups.

[A priest made an offering to the gods and announced the decision for one-on-one combat.]

15

"Paris and war-loving Menelaus   280
are going to fight it out with their long spears
over the woman. The man who wins,
who comes off the victor, gets the woman
and her property. The others will all swear
an oath of friendship, a binding one—
we will live in fertile Troy, they in Argos,
where horses breed, and in Achaea,
land of lovely women."

So they prayed. Hector of the flashing helmet
turned his eyes to one side and shook out the lots.
Alexander's token fell out immediately.
The troops sat down in their respective places,
by their high-stepping horses and their inlaid armour.
Paris, husband to Helen with the lovely hair,
hoisted his fine armour on his shoulders. On his shins,
he clipped leg armour fitted with silver ankle clasps.
Then he put around his chest the body armour
belonging to his brother Lycaon. It fit him well.   370
On his shoulder he looped his bronze, silver-studded sword,
his huge strong shield. On his handsome head he put
a fine helmet with nodding horse-hair plumes on top,
full of menace. Then he picked out a brave spear
which fit his grip. Menelaus prepared himself as well.

When the two men, standing on each side with their troops,
had armed themselves, they strode out to the open space
between the Trojans and Achaeans, staring ferociously.
As horse-taming Trojans and well-armed Achaeans
gazed at the two men, they were overcome with wonder.   380
The two men approached each other over measured ground,
brandishing their spears in mutual fury.
Alexander was the first to hurl his spear.
It struck Menelaus' shield, a perfect circle,
but the bronze did not break through, the point deflected
by the powerful shield. Then Menelaus, Atreus' son,
threw in his turn. First he made this prayer to Zeus:

"Lord Zeus, grant I may be revenged on this man,
who first committed crimes against me,
lord Alexander. Let him die at my hands,   390
so generations of men yet to come
will dread doing wrong to anyone
who welcomes them into his home as friends."

Menelaus then drew back his long-shadowed spear,
and hurled it. It hit the son of Priam's shield,
a perfect circle. The heavy spear pierced through it,
went straight through the fine body armour, through the shirt
which covered Alexander's naked flesh.

16

But Paris twisted to the side, evading a black fate.
Pulling out his silver-studded sword, the son of Atreus   400
raised it and struck the crest of Paris' helmet.
But the sword shattered into three or four pieces,
falling from his hand. The son of Atreus, in vexation,
looked up into wide heaven, crying out:

        "Father Zeus,
what god brings us more trouble than you do?
I thought I was paying Alexander
for his wickedness, but now my sword
has shattered in my fist, while from my hand
my spear has flown in vain. I haven't hit him."

As Menelaus said these words, he sprang forward,   410
grabbing the horse hair crest on Paris' helmet,
twisting him around. He began dragging Paris off,
back in the direction of well-armed Achaeans.
The fine leather strap stretched round Paris' soft neck,
right below his chin, was strangling him to death.
At that point Menelaus would have hauled back Paris
and won unending fame, if Aphrodite, Zeus' daughter,
had not had sharp eyes. Her force broke the ox-hide strap,
leaving Menelaus clutching in his massive hands
an empty helmet. Whipping it around, Menelaus   420
hurled the helmet in among well-armed Achaeans.
His loyal companions retrieved it. He charged back,
with his bronze spear, intent on killing Alexander.
But Aphrodite had snatched Paris up—for a god
an easy feat—concealed him in a heavy mist,
and placed him in his own sweetly scented bedroom.

Helen, child of Zeus,
who bears the aegis, sat down. With eyes averted,
she began to criticize her husband:

        "You've come back from the fight. How I wish   480
you'd died there, killed by that strong warrior
who was my husband once. You used to boast
you were stronger than warlike Menelaus,
more strength in your hands, more power in your spear.
So go now, challenge war-loving Menelaus
to fight again in single combat.
I'd suggest you stay away. Don't fight it out
man to man with fair-haired Menelaus,
without further thought. You might well die,
come to a quick end on his spear."   490

Replying to Helen, Paris said: Wife,
don't mock my courage with your insults.
Yes, Menelaus has just defeated me,

17

but with Athena's help. Next time I'll beat him.
For we have gods on our side, too. But come,
let's enjoy our love together on the bed.
Never has desire so filled my mind as now,
not even when I first took you away
from lovely Lacedaemon, sailing off
in our sea-worthy ships, or when I lay with you   500
in our lover's bed on the isle of Cranae.
That's how sweet passion has seized hold of me,
how much I want you now."

                    Paris finished speaking.
He led the way to bed. His wife went, too.
The two lay down together on the bed.

Atreus' son paced through the crowd, like a wild beast,
searching for some glimpse of godlike Alexander.
But no Trojan nor any of their famous allies
could reveal Alexander to warlike Menelaus.
If they'd seen him, they had no desire to hide him.   510
For they all hated Paris, as they hated gloomy death.
Agamemnon, king of men, addressed them:

"Listen to me, Trojans, Dardanians, allies—
victory clearly falls to war-loving Menelaus.
So give back Argive Helen and her property,
compensate us with a suitable amount,
something future ages will all talk about."

As he finished speaking, the other Achaeans cheered.

Book XXII--The Death of Hector

*Because of Paris' cowardice and the intervention of the gods on his behalf, the war
between the Trojans and the Greeks begins. The war rages on for years, with no side
getting the upper hand, again as a result of the intervention of the gods. In one battle,
Hector kills Achilles' best friend, Patroclus, which sends Achilles into a rage. Achilles
vows to destroy Hector and get revenge for his friend's death. The scene that follows is
the battle between Hector and Achilles. Before heading out to battle, Hector's father,
King Priam, begs Hector not to fight Achilles because Priam knows Hector will die in
battle.*

The old man,
hands outstretched, appealed to Hector's sense of pity:
"Hector, my dear son, don't stand out there alone,
facing that man with no one else to help you,
or you will quickly meet your death, slaughtered
by Peleus' son, who's much more powerful.   50
Don't be obstinate. If only the gods
would love Achilles just as much as I do,
then dogs and vultures would soon gnaw at him

as he lay there.

Come here, my child,
inside the walls, so you can help to save
Trojan men and women. Don't give that man,
Achilles, great glory. He'll take
your own dear life. Have pity on me, too.
Though full of misery, I still can feel.
Father Zeus will kill me with a cruel fate
on the threshold of old age, once I've seen
so many dreadful things—my sons butchered,
my daughters hauled away, their houses ransacked,   80
their little children tossed down on the ground
in this murderous war, my daughters-in-law
led off captive in hard Achaean hands.

In the end, I'll be ripped by ravenous dogs,
in front of my own doors when some man strikes me
with his sharp bronze or throws his spear in me,
robbing my limbs of life—the same dogs I raised
at home beside my table to guard the doors.
They'll drink my blood, then lie there at the gates,
their hearts gone mad. When a young man dies in war   90
lying there cut down by sharp bronze, that's all right.
Though dead, he shows us his nobility.
But when the dogs disfigure shamefully
an old man, chewing his grey head, his beard,
his sexual organs, that's the saddest thing
we wretched mortals see."

But Hector's heart
would not budge. He stood awaiting huge Achilles,
who was getting closer. Just as a mountain snake
waits for some man right by its lair, after eating
poison herbs so that a savage anger grips him,
as he coils beside his den with a fearful glare—
that's how Hector's dauntless heart would not retreat.
But then he leaned his bright shield up against the wall   120
where it jutted out, and, with a groan, spoke up,
addressing his courageous heart:

                    "What do I do?
If I go through the gates, inside that wall,
Polydamas will be the first to blame me,
for he told me last night to lead the Trojans
back into the city, when many died,
once godlike Achilles rejoined the fight.
But I didn't listen. If I'd done so,
things would have been much better. As it is,
my own foolishness has wiped out our army.   130
Trojan men will make me feel ashamed—

19

so will Trojan women in their trailing gowns.
I'm afraid someone inferior to me
may say, 'Hector, trusting his own power,
destroyed his people.'

        That's what they'll say.
For me it would be a great deal better
to meet Achilles man to man, kill him,
and go home, or get killed before the city,
dying in glory. But what would happen,
if I set my bossed shield and heavy helmet   140
to one side, leaning my spear against the wall,
and went out to meet noble Achilles,
just as I am, promising that Helen,
along with all the goods shipped here to Troy
by Alexander in his hollow ships,
the origin of our hostilities,
would be given to the sons of Atreus,
to take away with them—in addition,
to give the Achaeans an equal share
of all this city holds.

But why's my dear heart having this debate?
If I went out to meet him in that way,
he'd show me no respect. He wouldn't pity me.
Once I'd set aside my armour, he'd kill me
on the spot, unarmed, like some woman.
There's no way I can bargain with him now,   160
like a boy and girl chatting by some rock
or oak tree, as they flirt with one another.
No, it's better to clash in battle right away.
We'll see which one wins victory from Zeus."

[Hector decides to fight and faces Achilles]

"I'll no longer try to run away from you,
son of Peleus, as I did before, going   310
three times in flight around Priam's great city.
I lacked the courage then to fight with you,
as you attacked. But my heart prompts me now
to stand against you face to face once more,
whether I kill you, or you kill me.
So come here. Let's call on gods to witness,
for they're the best ones to observe our pact,
to supervise what we two agree on.
If Zeus grants me the strength to take your life,
I'll not abuse your corpse in any way.   320
I'll strip your celebrated armour off,
Achilles, then give the body back again
to the Achaeans. And you'll do the same."

20

Swift-footed Achilles, with a scowl, replied:
"Hector, don't talk to me of our agreements.
That's idiotic, like a faithful promise
between men and lions. Wolves and lambs
don't share a common heart—they always sense
a mutual hatred for each other.
In just that way, it's not possible for us,   330
for you and me, to be friends, or, indeed,
for there to be sworn oaths between us,
till one or other of us falls, glutting Ares,
warrior with the bull's hide shield, on blood.
You'd best remember all your fighting skills.

With these words, he hefted his long-shadowed spear,
then hurled it. However, anticipating the throw,
splendid Hector saw it coming and evaded it
by crouching down, so the bronze spear flew over him,
then struck the ground.

            "You missed, godlike Achilles. So it seems   350
you learned nothing from Zeus about my death,
although you said you had. That was just talk.
You were telling lies to make me fear you,
so I might forget my strength and courage.
Well, with your spear you won't be striking me
in my back as I run away in fear.
You'll have to drive it through my charging chest,
as I come right at you, if a god permits.
Now, see if you can cope with my bronze point.
I hope you get this whole spear in your flesh.   360
This war would then be easier on Trojans
with you dead, for you're their greatest danger.

With these words, Hector balanced his long-shadowed spear,
then threw it. It struck the shield of Peleus' son,
right in the centre. That spear didn't miss its mark.
But it bounced some distance off the shield. Hector,
angry that the spear had flown from his hand and missed,
stood dismayed, for he had no substitute ash spear.
So he shouted out, calling to Deïphobus,
who carried a white shield, asking him with a yell   370
to pass him his long spear. But Deïphobus
was nowhere to be seen. Then Hector in his heart
saw everything so clearly—he said:

            "This is it, then.
The gods are summoning me to my death.
There's no escape. For a long time now,
this must have been what Zeus desired,   380
and Zeus' son, the god who shoots from far,
and all those who willingly gave me help

21

in earlier days. So now I meet my fate.
Even so, let me not die ingloriously
without a fight, but in some great action
which those men yet to come will hear about."

Hector finished speaking. He pulled out his sharp sword,
that strong and massive weapon hanging on his thigh,
gathered himself, then swooped like some high-flying eagle
plummeting to the plains down through the murky clouds   390
to seize a tender lamb or cowering rabbit—
that's how Hector charged, brandishing his sharp sword.

As Hector charged, noble Achilles struck him,   410
driving the spear point through his tender neck.
But the heavy bronze on that ash spear did not cut
his windpipe, so he could still address Achilles
and reply to him. Hector fell down in the dust.
Lord Achilles then cried out in triumph:

"Hector,
I've drained strength from your limbs—now dogs and birds
will tear you into miserable pieces."

His strength fading, Hector of the shining helmet
answered Achilles: "By your life, I beg you,
by your knees, your parents—don't let dogs eat me.
No, you should accept
all the bronze and gold you might desire,
gifts my father and lady mother give you,
if you'll send my body home again,   430
so Trojans and Trojans' wives can bury me,
with all the necessary funeral rites."

Scowling at Hector, swift-footed Achilles then replied:
"Don't whine to me, you dog, about my knees
or parents. I wish I had the heart and strength
to carve you up and eat you raw myself
for what you've done to me. So there's no one
who'll keep the dogs from going at your head,
not even if they bring here and weigh out
a ransom ten or twenty times as much,   440
with promises of more, or if Priam,
son of Dardanus, says he'll pay your weight
in gold. Not even then will your mother
set you on a funeral bed and there lament
the son she bore. Instead, the dogs and birds
will eat you up completely."

His life slipped out,
flying off to Hades, mourning his fate to have to leave
such youthful manliness. Over dead Hector,

godlike Achilles
pulled his bronze spear from the corpse, set it aside,
and stripped the blood-stained armour from the shoulders.
Then the rest of Achaea's sons came running up.
They gazed at Hector's stature, his handsome body.
They came up close and wounded Hector.

Then on noble Hector's corpse
he carried out a monstrous act. He cut through
the tendons behind both feet, from heel to ankle,
threaded them with ox-hide thongs, and then tied these
onto his chariot, leaving the head to drag behind.
He climbed up in his chariot, brought on the splendid armour,
then lashed his horses. They sped off eagerly,   500
dragging Hector. A dust cloud rose above him,
his dark hair spread out round him, and Hector's head,
once so handsome, was covered by the dust, for Zeus
had given him to his enemies to dishonour
in his own native land. So all his head grew dirty.

Book XXIV--Achilles and Priam

*In Greek tradition, a body must receive a proper funeral and burial rites in order to be
welcomed into the afterlife. By disrespecting Hector's body and refusing to return it to
his family for burial, Achilles is interfering with the will of the gods. In this passage,
King Priam goes to Achilles to beg for the return of his son. He brings with him a
huge ransom of treasure to offer to Achilles.*

Priam climbed from his chariot to the ground.
The old man went directly in the hut
where Achilles, dear to Zeus, usually sat.   580
He found Achilles there, with only two companions,
sitting some distance from him—warrior Automedon
and Alcimus, offshoot of the war god Ares—
busy attending him. He'd just completed dinner.
He'd had food and drink, but the table was still there.
The men did not see great Priam as he entered.
He came up to Achilles, then with his fingers
clasped his knees and kissed his hands, those dreadful hands,
man-killers, which had slain so many of his sons.
Just as sheer folly grips a man who in his own land   590
kills someone, then runs off to a land of strangers,
to the home of some rich man, so those who see him
are seized with wonder—that's how Achilles then
looked on godlike Priam in astonishment.
The others were amazed. They gazed at one another.
Then Priam made his plea, entreating:

"Godlike Achilles,
remember your own father, who's as old as me,
on the painful threshold of old age.

23

It may well be that those who live around him
are harassing him, and no one's there   600
to save him from ruin and destruction.
But when he hears you're still alive,
his heart feels joy, for every day he hopes
he'll see his dear son come back home from Troy.
But I'm completely doomed to misery,
for I fathered the best sons in spacious Troy,
yet I say now not one of them remains.

I had fifty when Achaea's sons arrived—
nineteen born from the same mother's womb,
others the women of the palace bore me.   610
Angry Ares drained the life of most of them.
But I had one left, guardian of our city,
protector of its people. You've just killed him,
as he was fighting for his native country.
I mean Hector. For his sake I've come here,
to Achaea's ships, to win him back from you.
And I've brought a ransom beyond counting.
So Achilles, show deference to the gods
and pity for myself, remembering
your own father. Of the two old men,   620
I'm more pitiful, because I have endured
what no living mortal on this earth has borne—
I've lifted up to my own lips and kissed
the hands of the man who killed my son."

Priam finished. His words roused in Achilles
a desire to weep for his own father. Taking Priam's hand,
he gently moved him back. So the two men there
both remembered warriors who'd been slaughtered.
Priam, lying at Achilles' feet, wept aloud
for man-killing Hector, and Achilles also wept   630
for his own father. The sound of their lamenting filled the house.

When godlike Achilles had had enough of weeping,
when the need to mourn had left his heart and limbs,
he stood up quickly from his seat, then with his hand
helped the old man to his feet, feeling pity
for that grey head and beard. Then Achilles spoke—
his words had wings:

                    "You unhappy man,
your heart's had to endure so many evils.
How could you dare come to Achaea's ships,   640
and come alone, to rest your eyes on me,
when I've killed so many noble sons of yours?
You must have a heart of iron. But come now,
sit on this chair. Though we're both feeling pain,
we'll let our grief lie quiet on our hearts.

For there's no benefit in frigid tears.
That's the way the gods have spun the threads
for wretched mortal men, so they live in pain,
though gods themselves live on without a care.
On Zeus' floor stand two jars which hold his gifts—   650
one has disastrous things, the other blessings.
When thunder-loving Zeus hands out a mixture,
that man will, at some point, meet with evil,
then, some other time, with good.

You must endure it all,   680
without a constant weeping in your heart.
You achieve nothing by grieving for your son.
You won't bring him to life again, not before
you'll have to suffer yet another evil."

Old godlike Priam then answered Achilles:
"Don't make me sit down on a chair, my lord,
while Hector lies uncared for in your huts.
But quickly give him back, so my own eyes
can see him. And take the enormous ransom
we've brought here for you. May it give you joy.   690
And may you get back to your native land,
since you've now let me live to see the sunlight."

With an angry look, swift-footed Achilles snapped at Priam:
"Old man, don't provoke me. I myself intend
to give you Hector.
So don't agitate my grieving heart still more,
or I might not spare even you, old man,
though you're a suppliant here in my hut.
I could transgress what Zeus has ordered."

Achilles spoke. The old man, afraid, obeyed him.
Then Peleus' son sprang to the door, like a lion.   710
Then from the polished wagon they brought in
that priceless ransom for Hector's head, leaving there
two cloaks and a thickly woven tunic, so Achilles
could wrap up the corpse before he gave it back
for Priam to take home. Achilles then called out,   720
ordering his servant women to wash the body,
and then anoint it, after moving it away,
so Priam wouldn't see his son, then, heart-stricken,
be unable to contain his anger at the sight.
Servants washed the corpse, anointed it with oil,
and put a lovely cloak and tunic round it.
Achilles himself lifted it and placed it on a bier.
Then together he and his companions set it   730
on the polished wagon.

25

Old godlike Priam

then asked Achilles: "If you're willing
for me to give lord Hector a full burial,
then, Achilles, as a personal favour,
there is something you could do for me.
We'll mourn Hector for nine days in our home.   820
On the tenth day we'll have his funeral.
Then there'll be a banquet for the people.
On the eleventh, we'll make his burial mound.
The twelfth day, if we must, we'll go to war."

Swift-footed Achilles then said to Priam:
"All right, old Priam, things will be arranged
as you request. I'll suspend the fighting
for the length of time you've asked for."

Thucydides, Pericles' Funeral Oration, *Peloponnesian War*, 430 BCE

Reading and Discussion Questions

1. Define "eulogy."
2. What types of privileges does Pericles highlight that he says make Athens superior to all others?
3. Some consider this speech "a eulogy of Athens herself." Explain how that statement might be true.
4. Which line from the speech is most admirable/powerful to you?

This famous eulogy was given by the Athenian leader Pericles after the first battles of the Peloponnesian War. Funerals after such battles were public rituals and Pericles used the occasion to make a classic statement of the value of democracy. This speech was recorded by the Greek historian Thucydides. Thucydides was one of the first political historians and he recorded events in history to shine a light on the human motivations behind political acts.

For our system of government does not copy the systems of our neighbors: we are a model to them, not they to us. Our constitution is called a democracy, because power rests in the hands not of the few but of the many. Our laws guarantee equal justice for all in their private disputes; and as for the election of public officials, we welcome talent to every arena of achievement, nor do we make our choices on the ground of class but on the grounds of excellence alone. And as we give free play to all in our public life, so we carry the same spirit into our daily relations with one another. We have no black looks or angry words for our neighbor if he enjoys himself in his own way, and we even abstain from little acts of churlishness; that, though they do no mortal damage, leave hurt feelings in their wake.

Open and tolerant in our private lives, in our public affairs we keep within the law. We acknowledge the restraint of reverence; we are obedient to those in authority and to the laws, especially to those that give protection to the oppressed and those unwritten laws of the heart whose transgression brings admitted shame. Yet ours is no workaday city

26

only. No other city provides so many recreations for the spirit—contests and sacrifices all the year round, and beauty in our public buildings to cheer the spirit and delight the eye day by day. Moreover, the City is so large and powerful that all the wealth of all the world flows in to her, so that our own Attic products seem no more familiar to us than the fruits of the labors of other nations. . . .

So too with education. The Spartans toil from early childhood in the laborious pursuit of courage, while we, free to live and wander as we please, march out nonetheless to face the selfsame dangers. Here is the proof of my words: when the Spartans advance into our country, they do not come alone but with all their allies; but when we invade our neighbors we have little difficulty as a rule, even on foreign soil, in defeating men who are fighting for their own homes. Moreover, no enemy has ever met us in our full strength, for we have our navy to look after at the same time that our soldiers are sent on service to many scattered possessions; but if our enemies chance to encounter some portion of our forces and defeat a few of us, they boast that they have driven back our whole army, or, if they are defeated, that the victors were in full strength. Indeed, if we choose to face danger with an easy mind rather than after rigorous training, and to trust rather in our native manliness than in state-sponsored courage, the advantage lies with us; for we are spared all the tedium of practicing for future hardships, and when we find ourselves among them we are as brave as our plodding rivals. Here as elsewhere, then, the City sets an example that deserves admiration.

We are lovers of beauty without extravagance, and lovers of wisdom without effeminacy. Wealth to us is not mere material for vainglory but an opportunity for achievement; and we think poverty nothing to be ashamed of unless one makes no effort to overcome it. Our citizens attend both to public and private duties and do not allow absorption in their own affairs to diminish their knowledge of the City's business. We differ from other states in regarding the man who keeps aloof from public life not as "private" but as useless; we decide or debate, carefully and in person all matters of policy, and we hold, not that words and deeds go ill together, but that acts are foredoomed to failure when undertaken undiscussed. For we are noted for being at once most adventurous in action and most reflective beforehand.

Other men are bold in ignorance, while reflection will stop their going forward. But the bravest are surely those who have the clearest vision of what lies before them, glory and danger alike—and yet go forth to meet it. In doing good, too we are the exact opposite of the rest of mankind. We secure our friends not by accepting favors but by granting them. And so this makes friendship with us something that can be counted on; for we are eager, as creditors, to cement by continued kindness our relation to our friends. If they do not respond with the same warmth, it is because they feel that their services will not be given spontaneously but only as repayment of a debt. We are alone among mankind in doing men benefits, not on calculation of self-interest, but in the fearless confidence of freedom. . . .

In a word, I say our City as a whole is an education to Greece, and that our citizens yield to none, man by man, for independence of spirit, many-sidedness of attainment, and complete self-reliance in limbs and brain. . . .

Plutarch, The Ancient Customs of the Spartans, *Parallel Lives*, c. 100 CE

Reading and Discussion Questions
Based on what you learned about Athens in Pericles' funeral oration and the reading below about Sparta, compare Athens to Sparta. Focus specifically on:

1. each city-states' emphasis on education, arts and other "refinements."
2. each city-states' government.
3. each city-states' military policies.

The description below of Sparta is written by the famous Roman historian, Plutarch. Plutarch was actually raised in Greece and later became a Roman citizen, so he had a dual cultural background. Perhaps this is what influenced him to write his primary work, a book called Parallel Lives. *In it, Plutarch compares great Romans to great Greeks to see what they had in common as far as character, integrity and honor. He compared their flaws also. Parallel Lives is one of the only glimpses we have into the psychology of the men of the ancient world. The excerpts below are taken from "The Life of Lycurgus," who was the famous Spartan who reformed Spartan society and brought it the laws that defined it as a civilization.*

On Mealtime
To each one of those who comes in to the public meals the eldest man says, as he points to the doors, "Through these no word goes out."

A thing that met with especial approval among them was their so-called black broth, so much so that the older men did not require a bit of meat, but gave up all of it to the young men. It is said that Dionysus, the despot of Sicily, for the sake of this bought a slave who had been a Spartan cook, and ordered him to prepared the broth for him, sparing no expense; but when the king tasted it he spat it out in disgust; whereupon the cook said, "Your Majesty, it is necessary to have exercised in the Spartan manner, and to have bathed in the Eurotas, in order to relish this broth."

The Spartans, after drinking in moderation at their public meals, go away without a torch. In fact, they are not permitted to walk with a light either on this route or on any other, so that they may become accustomed to travelling in darkness at night confidently and fearlessly.

On Education
They learned to read and write for purely practical reasons; but all other forms of education they banned from the country, books and treatises being included in this quite as much as men. All their education was directed toward prompt obedience to authority, stout endurance of hardship, and victory or death in battle.

Young Men
They always went without a shirt, receiving one garment for the entire year, and with unwashed bodies, refraining almost completely from bathing and rubbing down.
The young men slept together, according to division and company, upon pallets which they themselves brought together by breaking off by hand, without any implement, the

tops of the reeds which grew on the banks of the Eurotas. In the winter they put beneath their pallets, and intermingled with them, the plant called lycophon, since the material is reputed to possess some warming qualities.

Moreover, the young men were required not only to respect their own fathers and to be obedient to them, but to have regard for all the older men, to make room for them on the streets, to give up their seats to them, and to keep quiet in their presence. As the result of this custom each man had authority, not as in other states over his own children, slaves, and property, but also over his neighbour's in like manner as over his own, to the end that the people should, as much as possible, have all things in common, and should take thought for them as for their own. When a boy was punished by anybody, if he told his father, it was a disgrace for his father, upon hearing this, not to give him another beating.

The boys steal whatever they can of their food, learning to make their raids adroitly upon people who are asleep or are careless in watching. The penalty for getting caught is a beating and no food. For the dinner allowed them is meagre, so, through coping with want by their own initiative, they may be compelled to be daring and unscrupulous.

This was the object of the starvation diet. It was meagre both for the reasons given and purposely that the youth should never become accustomed to being sated, but to being able to go without food; for in this way, the Spartans thought, the youth would be more serviceable in war if they were able to carry on without food, and they would be more self-controlled and more frugal if they lived a very considerable time at small expense. And to put up with the plainest diet, so as to be able to consume anything that came to hand, they thought made the youths' bodies more healthy owing to the scanty food, and they believed that this practice caused the bodies, repressed in any impulse towards thickness and breadth, to grow tall, and also to make them handsome; for a spare and lean condition they felt served to produce suppleness, while an overfed condition, because of too much weight, was against it.

It was not allowed them to go abroad, so that they should have nothing to do with foreign ways and undisciplined modes of living. Lycurgus also introduced the practice of banning all foreigners from the country, so that these should not filter in and serve to teach the citizens something bad.

The selling of anything was not permitted; but it was their custom to use the neighbours' servants as their own if they needed them and also their dogs and horses, unless the owners required them for their own use. And in the country, if anyone found himself lacking anything and had need of it, he would open an owner's storehouse and take away enough to meet his need, and then replace the seals and leave it.

They used to make the Helots drunk and exhibit them to the young as a deterrent from excessive drinking.

They did not attend either comedy or tragedy, so that they might not hear anyone speak either in earnest or in jest against the laws.

The boys in Sparta were lashed with whips during the entire day at the altar of Artemis Orthia, frequently to the point of death, and they bravely endured this, cheerful and proud, vying with one another for the supremacy as to which one of them could endure being beaten for the longer time and the greater number of blows. And the one who was victorious was held in especial repute. This competition is called 'The Flagellation,' and it takes place each year.

One of the noble and blessed privileges which Lycurgus appears to have secured for his fellow-citizens was abundance of leisure. In fact it was not permitted them to take up any menial trade at all; and there was no need whatever of making money, which involves a toilsome accumulation, nor of busy activity, because of his having made wealth wholly unenvied and unhonoured. The Helots tilled the soil for them, paying a return which was regularly settled in advance. There was a ban against letting for a higher price, so that the Helots might make some profit, and thus be glad to do the work for their masters, and so that the masters might not look for any larger return.

Plato, The Apology of Socrates, *Dialogues, c. 430 BCE*

Reading and Discussion Questions
1. What has Socrates been accused of and why?
2. Why does Socrates think that the Athenians would be harming themselves rather than harming Socrates if they put him to death?
3. Why does Socrates think that, "an unexamined life is not worth living?"
4. Why does Socrates say there is reason to believe that death is a good?
5. What do you think it says of the Athenians that they killed Socrates?

Plato was a philosopher and mathematician in ancient Greece who is considered to be the most influential thinker in Western philosophy. He founded a school called The Academy in Athens which turned out such notable students as Aristotle among many others. Plato was the student of Socrates and his Dialogues is a collection of conversations, many of which involve Socrates. It is often said that all modern work in philosophy is "but a footnote to Plato." He has influenced areas as far reaching as politics, metaphysics, math, ethics and religion. In "Apology," Plato recounts the events, believed to be factual surrounding the trial and death of his mentor, Socrates.

Socrates' Defense

I will begin at the beginning, and ask what the accusation is which has given rise to this slander of me. What do the slanderers say? They shall be my prosecutors, and I will sum up their words in an affidavit. "Socrates is an evil-doer, and a curious person, who searches into things under the earth and in heaven, and he makes the worse appear the better cause; and he teaches the aforesaid doctrines to others."

I dare say, Athenians, that someone among you will reply, "Why is this, Socrates, and what is the origin of these accusations of you: for there must have been something strange which you have been doing?" Men of Athens, this reputation of mine has come of a certain sort of wisdom which I possess. If you ask me what kind of wisdom, I reply, such wisdom as is attainable by man, for to that extent I am inclined to believe that I am wise. My friend, Chaerephon, went to the oracle at Delphi and boldly asked the oracle to tell him whether there was anyone wiser than I was, and the Pythian prophetess answered that there was no man wiser.

When I heard the answer, I said to myself, What can the god mean? and what is the interpretation of this riddle? for I know that I have no wisdom, small or great. What can he mean when he says that I am the wisest of men? And yet he is a god and cannot lie; that would be against his nature. After a long consideration, I at last thought of a method of trying the question. I reflected that if I could only find a man wiser than myself, then I might go to the god with a refutation in my hand. I should say to him, "Here is a man who is wiser than I am; but you said that I was the wisest." Accordingly I went to one who had the reputation of wisdom, and observed to him - and the result was as follows: When I began to talk with him, I could not help thinking that he was not really wise, although he was thought wise by many, and wiser still by himself; and I went and tried to explain to him that he thought himself wise, but was not really wise;

and the consequence was that he hated me, and his enmity was shared by several who were present and heard me. So I left him, saying to myself, as I went away: Well, although I do not suppose that either of us knows anything really beautiful and good, I am better off than he is - for he knows nothing, and thinks that he knows. I neither know nor think that I know. In this latter particular, then, I seem to have slightly the advantage of him. Then I went to another, who had still higher philosophical pretensions, and my conclusion was exactly the same. I made another enemy of him, and of many others besides him.

he notes that the men in repute were all foolish, but the "inferior" were wise

The result of my mission was just this: I found that the men most in repute were all but the most foolish; and that some inferior men were really wiser and better. I will tell you the tale of my wanderings and of the "Herculean" labors, as I may call them, which I endured only to find at last the oracle irrefutable.

There is another thing: - young men of the richer classes, who have not much to do, come about me of their own accord; they like to hear the pretenders examined, and they often imitate me, and examine others themselves; there are plenty of persons, as they soon enough discover, who think that they know something, but really know little or nothing: and then those who are examined by them instead of being angry with themselves are angry with me: This confounded Socrates, they say; this villainous misleader of youth! - and then if somebody asks them, Why, what evil does he practise or teach? they do not know, and cannot tell; but in order that they may not appear to be at a loss, they repeat the ready-made charges which are used against all philosophers about teaching things up in the clouds and under the earth, and having no gods, and making the worse appear the better cause; for they do not like to confess that their pretence of knowledge has been detected - which is the truth: and as they are numerous and ambitious and energetic, and are all in battle array and have persuasive tongues, they have filled your ears with their loud and inveterate calumnies.

Someone will say: And are you not ashamed, Socrates, of a course of life which is likely to bring you to an untimely end? To him I may fairly answer: There you are mistaken: a man who is good for anything ought not to calculate the chance of living or dying; he ought only to consider whether in doing anything he is doing right or wrong - acting the part of a good man or of a bad.

Strange, indeed, would be my conduct, O men of Athens, if I say, now, when, as I conceive and imagine, God orders me to fulfil the philosopher's mission of searching into myself and other men, I were to desert my post through fear of death, or any other fear.

31

Men of Athens, I honor and love you; but I shall obey God rather than you, and while I have life and strength I shall never cease from the practice and teaching of philosophy, exhorting anyone whom I meet after my manner, and convincing him, saying: O my friend, why do you who are a citizen of the great and mighty and wise city of Athens, care so much about laying up the greatest amount of money and honor and reputation, and so little about wisdom and truth and the greatest improvement of the soul, which you never regard or heed at all? Are you not ashamed of this? And if the person with whom I am arguing says: Yes, but I do care; I do not depart or let him go at once; I interrogate and examine and cross-examine him, and if I think that he has no virtue, but only says that he has, I reproach him with undervaluing the greater, and overvaluing the less. And this I should say to everyone whom I meet, young and old, citizen and alien, but especially to the citizens, inasmuch as they are my brethren. For this is the command of God, as I would have you know; and I believe that to this day no greater good has ever happened in the state than my service to the God.

For I do nothing but go about persuading you all, old and young alike, not to take thought for your persons and your properties, but first and chiefly to care about the greatest improvement of the soul. I tell you that virtue is not given by money, but that from virtue come money and every other good of man, public as well as private. This is my teaching, and if this is the doctrine which corrupts the youth, my influence is ruinous indeed. But if anyone says that this is not my teaching, he is speaking an untruth.

For if you kill me you will not easily find another like me, who, if I may use such a ludicrous figure of speech, am a sort of gadfly, given to the state by the God; and the state is like a great and noble steed who is tardy in his motions owing to his very size, and requires to be stirred into life. I am that gadfly which God has given the state and all day long and in all places am always fastening upon you, arousing and persuading and reproaching you. And as you will not easily find another like me, I would advise you to spare me.

The jury finds Socrates guilty and condemns him to death.

Socrates' Comments on his Sentence
I do not now repent of the manner of my defense, and I would rather die having spoken after my manner, than speak in your manner and live. . . The difficulty, my friends, is not in avoiding death, but in avoiding unrighteousness, for that runs faster than death.

Let us reflect--we shall see that there is great reason to hope that death is a good, for one of two things: - either death is a state of nothingness and utter unconsciousness, or, as men say, there is a change and migration of the soul from this world to another. Now if you suppose that there is no consciousness, but a sleep like the sleep of him who is undisturbed even by the sight of dreams, death will be an unspeakable gain; for eternity is then only a single night.

But if death is the journey to another place, and there, as men say, all the dead are, what good, O my friends and judges, can be greater than this? If indeed when the pilgrim arrives in the world below, he is delivered from the professors of justice in this world, and finds the true judges who are said to give judgment there, Minos and Rhadamanthus and Aeacus and Triptolemus, and other sons of God who were righteous in their own life, that pilgrimage will be worth making. What would not a man give if he might converse with Orpheus and Musaeus and Hesiod and Homer? Nay, if this be true, let me die again and again. I, too, shall have a wonderful interest in a place where I can converse with Palamedes, and Ajax the son of Telamon, and other heroes of old, who have suffered death through an unjust judgment; and there will be no small pleasure, as I think, in comparing my own sufferings with theirs. Above all, I shall be able to continue my search into true and false knowledge; as in this world, so also in that; I shall find out who is wise, and who pretends to be wise, and is not. What would not a man give, O judges, to be able to examine the leader of the great Trojan expedition; or Odysseus or Sisyphus, or numberless others, men and women too! What infinite delight would there be in conversing with them and asking them questions! For in that world they do not put a man to death for this; certainly not. For besides being happier in that world than in this, they will be immortal, if what is said is true.   Wherefore, O judges, be of good cheer about death, and know this of a truth - that no evil can happen to a good man, either in life or after death.

Plato, *The Republic*, 380 CE

Reading and Discussion Questions

1. What type of ruler does Plato say we need?
2. What traits does Plato say that a philosopher-king will have? Explain four.
3. In the Allegory of the Cave, explain the experience of the people in the cave. What do they see? What do they do all day?
4. What happens to the one prisoner when he is released from his chains? How does his perception of reality and truth change?
5. What happens when the freed prisoner returns to the cave? What is the nature of his relationship to the other prisoners once he returns?
6. What lesson is Plato trying to teach the reader with this story?

Plato was an Athenian aristocrat and disciple of Socrates and he based his philosophy on Socrates' teachings. Plato was greatly affected by the decline of Athenian politics as a result of the Peloponnesian War. The rule of Athens by corrupt politicians, flawed decision making and the condemnation and death of Socrates convinced Plato that Athenian democracy was a failure.

In The Republic, *Plato proposed organizing government in harmony with the needs of human nature. He believe that society should be organized into three classes: 1. People who are driven by a desire for food, wealth and gratification should be farmers, tradesmen, or artisans; 2. People who are naturally courageous and energetic should be soldiers; and 3. The select few who have wisdom and understanding—the philosophers—should be the rulers.*

In Plato's ideal government, the wisest would rule and the people would have no power to participate in political decision-making. The people would give up influence for the security of wise leadership and the state would guarantee an educational system that produced good citizens who were obedient to the state.

Below are two excerpts from Plato's Republic. The first is an exchange between Socrates and a man named Glaucon where Plato lays out his ideas for the qualities that a philosopher-king should possess. The second excerpt is one of Plato's most famous, called "The Allegory of the Cave." In it, Plato is trying to demonstrate that the masses have no clear understanding of reality or of truth. Most people, according to Plato, are like prisoners shackled in darkness who only see shadows of reality. Only a very few people ever see the truth as it really is and it is these few, Plato tells us, who should be given political power.

On the Nature of the Philosopher-King

[SOCRATES] Unless either philosophers become kings in their countries or those who are now called kings and rulers come to be sufficiently inspired with a genuine desire for wisdom; unless that is to say, political power and philosophy meet together ... there can be no rest from troubles. There is no other way of happiness either for the state or for the individual....

Now ... we must, I think, define ... whom we mean by these lovers of wisdom who, we have dared to assert, ought to be our rulers. Once we have a clear view of their character, we shall be able to defend our position by pointing to some who are naturally fitted to combine philosophic study with political leadership, while the rest of the world should accept their guidance and let philosophy alone.

[GLAUCON] Yes, this is the moment for a definition....

[S] ... One trait of the philosophic nature we may take as already granted: a constant passion for any knowledge that will reveal to them something of that reality which endures for ever and is not always passing into and out of existence. And, we may add, their desire is to know the whole of that reality; they will not willingly renounce any part of it as relatively small and insignificant.

[G] True.

[S] Is there not another trait which the nature we are seeking cannot fail to possess truthfulness, a love of truth and a hatred for falsehood that will not tolerate untruth in any form?

[G] Yes, it is natural to expect that.

[S] It is not merely natural, but entirely necessary that an instinctive passion for any object should extend to all that is closely akin to it; and there is nothing more closely akin to wisdom than truth. So the same nature cannot love wisdom and falsehood; the genuine lover of knowledge cannot fail, from his youth up, to strive after the whole of truth.

[G] I perfectly agree.

[S] Now we surely know that when a man's desires set strongly in one direction, in every other channel they flow more feebly, like a stream diverted into another bed. So when the current has set towards knowledge and all that goes with it, desire will abandon those pleasures of which the body is the instrument and be concerned only

34

with the pleasure which the soul enjoys independently-if, that is to say, the love of wisdom is more than a mere pretense. Accordingly, such a one will be temperate and no lover of money; for he will be the last person to care about the things for the sake of which money is eagerly sought and lavishly spent.

[G] That is true.

[S] Again, in seeking to distinguish the philosophic nature, you must not overlook the least touch of meanness. Nothing could be more contrary than pettiness to a mind constantly bent on grasping the whole of things, both divine and human.

[G] Quite true.

[S] And do you suppose that one who is so high-minded and whose thought can contemplate all time and all existence will count this life of man a matter of much concern?

[G] No, he could not.

[S] So for such a man death will have no terrors.

[G] None.

[S] A mean and cowardly nature, then, can have no part in the genuine pursuit of wisdom.

[G] I think not.

[S] And if a man is temperate and free from the love of money, meanness, pretentiousness, and cowardice, he will not be hard to deal with or dishonest. So, as another indication of the philosophic temper, you will observe whether, from youth up, he is fair-minded, gentle, and sociable.

[G] Certainly.

The Allegory of the Cave

[S] Next, said I, here is a parable to illustrate the degrees in which our nature may be enlightened or unenlightened. Imagine the condition of men living in a sort of cavernous chamber underground, with an entrance open to the light and a long passage all down the cave. Here they have been from childhood, chained by the leg and also by the neck, so that they cannot move and can see only what is in front of them, because the chains will not let them turn their heads. At some distance higher up is the light of a fire burning behind them; and between the prisoners and the fire is a track with a parapet built along it, like the screen at a puppet-show, which hides the performers while they show their puppets over the top.

[G) I see, said he.

[S) Now behind this parapet imagine persons carrying along various artificial objects, including figures of men and animals in wood or stone or other materials, which project above the parapet. Naturally, some of these persons will be talking, others silent.

[G] It is a strange picture, he said, and a strange sort of prisoners.

[S] Like ourselves, I replied; for in the first place prisoners so confined would have seen nothing of themselves or of one another, except the shadows thrown by the fire-light on the wall of the Cave facing them, would they?

[G] Not if all their lives they had been prevented from moving their heads.

[S] And they would have seen as little of the objects carried past.

[G] Of course.

[S] Now, if they could talk to one another, would they not suppose that their words referred only to those passing shadows which they saw?
[G] Necessarily.

[S] And suppose their prison had an echo from the wall facing them? When one of the people crossing behind them spoke, they could only suppose that the sound came from the shadow passing before their eyes.

[G] No doubt.

[S] In every way, then, such prisoners would recognize as reality nothing but the shadows of those artificial objects.

[G] Inevitably. . . .

[S] Now consider what would happen if their release from the chains and the healing of their unwisdom should come about in this way. Suppose one of them were set free and forced suddenly to stand up, turn his head, and walk with eyes lifted to the light; all these movements would be painful, and he would be too dazzled to make out the objects whose shadows he had been used to see. What do you think he would say, if someone told him that what he had formerly seen was meaningless illusion, but now, being somewhat nearer to reality and turned towards more real objects, he was getting a truer view? Suppose further that he were shown the various objects being carried by and were made to say, in reply to questions, what each of them was. Would he not be perplexed and believe the objects now shown him to be not so real as what he formerly saw?

[G] Yes, not nearly so real.

[S] And if he were forced to look at the firelight itself, would not his eyes ache, so that he would try to escape and turn back to the things which he could see distinctly, convinced that they really were clearer than these other objects now being shown to him?

[G] Yes.

[S] And suppose someone were to drag him away forcibly up the steep and rugged ascent and not let him go until he had hauled him out into the sunlight, would he not suffer pain and vexation at such treatment, and, when he had come out into the light, find his eyes so full of its radiance that he could not see a single one of the things that he was now told were real?

[G] Certainly he would not see them all at once.

[S] He would need, then, to grow accustomed before he could see things in that upper world. At first it would be easiest to make out shadows, and then the images of men and things reflected in water, and later on the things themselves. After that, it would be easier to watch the heavenly bodies and the sky itself by night, looking at the light of the moon and stars rather than the Sun and the Sun's light in the day-time.
[G] Yes, surely.

[S] Last of all, he would be able to look at the Sun and contemplate its nature, not as it appears when reflected in water or any alien medium, but as it is in itself in its own domain.

[G] No doubt.

[S] And now he would begin to draw the conclusion that it is the Sun that produces the seasons and the course of the year and controls everything in the visible world, and moreover is in a way the cause of all that he and his companions used to see.
[G] Clearly he would come at last to that conclusion.

[S] Then if he called to mind his fellow prisoners and what passed for wisdom in his former dwelling place, he would surely think himself happy in the change and be sorry for them. They may have had a practice of honouring and commending one another, with prizes for the man who had the keenest eye for the passing shadows and the best memory for the order in which they followed or accompanied one another, so that he could make a good guess as to which was going to come next. Would our released prisoner be likely to covet those prizes or to envy the men exalted to honour and power in the Cave? Would he not feel like Homer's Achilles, that he would far sooner "be on earth as a hired servant in the house of a landless man" or endure anything rather than go back to his old beliefs and live in the old way?

[G] Yes, he would prefer any fate to such a life.

[S] Now imagine what would happen if he went down again to take his former seat in the Cave. Coming suddenly out of the sunlight, his eyes would be filled with darkness. He might be required once more to deliver his opinion on those shadows, in competition with the prisoners who had never been released, while his eyesight was still dim and unsteady; and it might take some time to become used to the darkness. They would laugh at him and say that he had gone up only to come back with his sight ruined; it was worth no one's while even to attempt the ascent. If they could lay hands on the man who was trying to set them free and lead them up, they would kill him.

[G] Yes, they would.

[S] Every feature in this parable, my dear Glaucon, is meant to fit our earlier analysis. The prison dwelling corresponds to the region revealed to us through the sense of sight, and the firelight within it to the power of the Sun. The ascent to see the things in the upper world you may take as standing for the upward journey of the soul into the region of the intelligible; then you will be in possession of what I surmise, since that is what you wish to be told.

Heaven knows whether it is true; but this, at any rate, is how it appears to me. In the world of knowledge, the last thing to be perceived and only with great difficulty is the essential Form of Goodness. Once it is perceived, the conclusion must follow that, for all things, this is the cause of whatever is right and good; in the visible world it gives birth to light and to the lord of light, while it is itself sovereign in the intelligible world and the parent of intelligence and truth. Without having had a vision of this Form no one can act with wisdom, either in his own life or in matters of state....

Aristotle, *Politics*, 340 BCE

Reading and Discussion Questions

1. What is Aristotle's view on property ownership and why? Should property be owned privately or collectively and why?
2. How does Aristotle define a "citizen" and what relationship does the individual have to the community to the whole?
3. What three types of governments does Aristotle describe in Book III? Explain each.
4. What is tyranny and how is it related to monarchy? What is oligarchy and how is it related to aristocracy? What is democracy and how is it related to polity?
5. What is the function of the state, according to Aristotle? Specifically, what are the six needs of humans and of society that the state must meet?
6. What is the role of education in supporting the state?

Aristotle was an ancient philosopher and scientist who has deeply influenced Western thought on everything from science and religion, to government and education. Aristotle was a student of Plato at The Academy and he founded his own school called the Lyceum. Aristotle was also the personal tutor of Alexander the Great, for Aristotle was widely renowned in his own lifetime as the greatest mind in the Mediterranean world. Below are excerpts from two of Aristotle's works, of which there are dozens. The first selection is from Politics, *in which Aristotle discusses what type of government will allow citizens to achieve the greatest degree of happiness. He analyzes the appropriate function of "the state" and the responsibilities of "the citizen" in relation to the state.*

Book I:
Our purpose is to consider what form of political community is best of all for those who are most able to realize their ideal of life. Three alternatives are conceivable: The members of a state must either have (1) all things or (2) nothing in common, or (3) some things in common and some not. That they should have nothing in common is clearly impossible, for the constitution is a community, and must at any rate have a common

place—one city will be in one place, and the citizens are those who share in that one city. But should a well ordered state have all things, as far as may be, in common, or some only and not others?

* * * * *

Property should be in a certain sense common, but, as a general rule, private; for, when everyone has a distinct interest, men will not complain of one another, and they will make more progress, because every one will be attending to his own business. And yet by reason of goodness, and in respect of use, 'Friends,' as the proverb says, "will have all things common." Even now there are traces. For, although every man has his own property, some things he will place at the disposal of his friends, while of others he shares the use with them. Again, how immeasurably greater is the pleasure, when a man feels a thing to be his own; for surely the love of self is a feeling implanted by nature and not given in vain, although selfishness is rightly censured.

No one, when men have all things in common, will any longer set an example of generosity; for generosity consists in the use which is made of property. [Common ownership has the] appearance of goodness and equality; men are easily induced to believe that in some wonderful manner everybody will become everybody's friend, especially when some one is heard denouncing the evils now existing in states, suits about contracts, convictions for perjury, flatteries of rich men and the like, which are said to arise out of the possession of private property. These evils, however, are due to a very different cause—the wickedness of human nature.

Book III:
He who would inquire into the essence and attributes of various kinds of governments must first of all determine "What is a state?" A state is composite, like any other whole made up of many parts; these are the citizens, who compose it. It is evident, therefore, that we must begin by asking, who is the citizen, and what is the meaning of the term? . . . . He who has the power to take part in the deliberative or judicial administration of any state is said by us to be a citizens of that state; and, speaking generally, a state is a body of citizens sufficing for the purposes of life.

Like the sailor, the citizen is a member of a community. Now, sailors have different functions, for one of them is a rower, another a pilot, and a third a look-out man...Similarly, one citizen differs from another, but the salvation of the community is the common business of them all. This community is the constitution; the virtue of the citizen must therefore be relative to the constitution of which he is a member.

First, let us consider what is the purpose of a state, and how many forms of government there are by which human society is regulated. We have already said, in the first part of this treatise, . . . that man is by nature a political animal. And therefore, men, even when they do not require one another's help, desire to live together; not but that they are also brought together by their common interests in proportion as they severally attain to any measure of well-being.

The words constitution and government have the same meaning, and the government, which is the supreme authority in states, must be in the hands of one, or of a few, or of the many. The true forms of government, therefore, are those in which the one, or the few, or the many, govern with a view to the common interest; but governments which rule with a view to the private interest, whether of the one or of the few, or of the many, are perversions. Of forms of government in which one rules, we call that which regards the common interests, *monarchy*; that in which more than one, but not many, rule, *aristocracy* (and it is so called, either because the rulers are *the best men*, or because they have at heart *the best interests* of the state and of the citizens). But when the citizens at large administer the state for the common interest, the government is called a *polity*. And there is a reason for this use of language.

Of the above-mentioned forms, the perversions are as follows: of monarchy, *tyranny*; of aristocracy, *oligarchy*; of polity, *democracy*. For tyranny is a kind of monarchy which has in view the interest of the monarch only; oligarchy has in view the interest of the wealthy; democracy, of the needy: none of them the common good of all. Tyranny, as I was saying, is monarchy exercising the rule of a master over the political society; oligarchy is when men of property have the government in their hands; democracy, the opposite, when the indigent, and not the men of property, are the rulers....Then ought the good to rule and have supreme power?

Book VII:

Now it is evident that the form of government is best in which every man, whoever he is, can act best and live happily....If we are right in our view, and happiness is assumed to be virtuous activity, the active life will be the best, both for every city collectively, and for individuals. In what remains the first point to be considered is what should be the conditions of the ideal or perfect state; for the perfect state cannot exist without a due supply of the means of life...

Let us then enumerate the functions of a state: First, there must be food; secondly, arts, for life requires many instruments; thirdly, there must be arms, for the members of a community have need of them, and in their own hands, too, in order to maintain authority both against disobedient subjects and against external assailants; fourthly, there must be a certain amount of revenue, both for internal needs, and for the purposes of war; fifthly, or rather first, there must be a care of religion which is commonly called worship; sixthly, and most necessary of all there must be a power of deciding what is for the public interest, and what is just in men's dealings with one another. These are the services which every state may be said to need. A state then should be framed with a view to the fulfillment of these functions. There must be farmers to procure food, and artisans, and a warlike and a wealthy class, and priests, and judges to decide what is necessary and expedient.

Now, since we are here speaking of the best form of government, i.e., that under which the state will be most happy (and happiness, as has been already said, cannot exist without virtue), it clearly follows that in the state which is best governed and possesses men who are just absolutely, and not merely relatively to the principle of the constitution.

Book VIII:

The citizen should be molded to suit the form of government under which he lives. And since the whole city has one end, it is manifest that education should be one and the same for all, and that it should be public, and not private. Neither must we suppose that any one of the citizens belongs to himself, for they all belong to the state, and are each of them a part of the state, and the care of each part is inseparable from the care of the whole. The customary branches of education are in number four; they are---(1) reading and writing, (2) gymnastic exercises, (3) music, to which is sometimes added (4) drawing. Of these, reading and writing and drawing are regarded as useful for the purposes of life in a variety of ways, and gymnastic exercises are thought to infuse courage. Concerning music a doubt may be raised.---in our own day most men cultivate it for the sake of pleasure, but originally it was included in education, because nature herself, as has been often said, requires that we should be able, not only to work well, but to use leisure well; for, what ought we to do when at leisure? Clearly we ought not to be amusing ourselves, for then amusement would be the end of life. But if this is inconceivable, we should introduce amusements only at suitable times, and they should be our medicines, for the emotion which they create in the soul is a relaxation, and from the pleasure we obtain rest.....

Aristotle, *Nicomachean Ethics*, 340 BCE

Reading and Discussion Questions
1. What are the three types of life that Aristotle says men may choose to pursue?
2. Which type of life does Aristotle say leads to the most happiness and why?

The following reading is from Aristotle's book Nichomachean Ethics, *in which Aristotle analyzes the key to a happy life, which he connects to living virtuously. Aristotle believed that virtuosity and wisdom could be learned through daily practice and the development of virtue and wisdom as habits, not unlike brushing your teeth or making your bed. We practice doing things that we want to be good at and Aristotle said the habits we should practice continuously were the exercise of virtue and the pursuit of wisdom in order to live a happy life.*

In view of the fact that all knowledge and every pursuit aims at some good, there is very general agreement; for both the general run of men and people of superior refinement say that it is happiness, and identify living well and doing well with being happy. To judge from the lives that men lead, most men seem (not without some ground) to identify the good, or happiness, with pleasure; which is the reason why they love the life of enjoyment. For there are, we may say, three prominent types of life---a life of leisure and enjoyment, a political life, and thirdly the contemplative life. The answer to the question we are asking is plain: Happiness lies in virtuous activity, and perfect happiness lies in the best activity, which is contemplative. Contemplation is preferable to war or politics or any other practical career, because it allows leisure, and leisure is essential to happiness. Practical virtue brings only a secondary kind of happiness; the supreme happiness is in the exercise of Reason, for Reason, more than anything else, *is* man. Man cannot be *wholly* contemplative, but in so far as he is so he shares in the divine life. The activity of God, which surpasses all others in blessedness, must be contemplative. And that all these attributes belong most of all to the philosopher is manifest. He, therefore, is the dearest to the gods. And he who is will presumably be also the happiest; so that in this way too the philosopher will more than any other be happy.

CHAPTER 2—
ANCIENT ROME (753 BCE to 476 CE)

GUIDING QUESTIONS
- What does it mean that the Romans were the "doers?"
- What ideas on law and government did we get from Rome?
- What is SPQR and how is it connected to Rome's success?
- Why did the Roman Republic collapse?
- Why did the Roman Empire fall?
- What things make up Rome's legacy in the modern world?
- Can Rome's collapse serve as a warning to us in the modern world?

When you mention "Rome" almost everyone has an image come to mind. Some may see a gladiatorial combat, or the Colosseum. Others may imagine Julius Caesar being stabbed by his best friends or the mighty battles of the Roman legions. Maybe you see Christian Rome with the Pope in his pointy hat or St. Peter's Cathedral. Rome is different things to different people. But what is Rome, really? Rome is one of the greatest civilizations in history. This is true in part because of her ability to reinvent herself as necessary. Rome was first a city. Then it became a monarchy. When monarchy became corrupt, Rome became a republic. And finally Rome was a great empire before falling to ashes after more than 1200 years as a dominant force in the ancient world.

Unlike the Greeks, who have beautiful, whimsical and heroic stories about the origins of their people, the Roman origin stories are much less romantic. You may know the story of Romulus and Remus, two brothers who were raised by wolves and who believed it was their destiny to found a great city. They each built their own city because they could not agree to rule together and because Remus would not admit his brother's city was superior, Romulus murdered him by shoving him of the walls of his city, which came to be known as Rome. Romulus became the first king of Rome. The king needed subjects to rule over and in order to populate his city and have subjects, he promised protection to criminals and outcasts who had been chased out of their own communities. Rome was originally a city of outlaws. Consequently, no respectable women would come to Rome willingly and so to fix this problem, the Roman men abducted women from the neighboring town and made them their wives. This story is known as The Rape of the Sabine Women and it has been immortalized by artists for centuries.

This was Rome's founding story. It is an immoral and ruthless story. It is also a tough, honest story about power and necessity. The spirit of the ancient Romans is really captured in these founding stories. They did not necessarily have time for *nice* because they were interested in what was *necessary*. Romans liked things that *worked*. If these things were also pretty or pleasant, fine. But for Romans, the only valuable things were things with purpose.

Romulus founded the city of Rome in 753 BCE and for the next 250 years, Rome was a monarchy. The period from 753 to 509 BCE was known as the Age of Kings. There were seven kings of Rome and each of them was as corrupt, ruthless and immoral as

Romulus, Rome's first king. There was no law in Rome except what the king said was the law. As a result, the laws changed a lot from one king to the next and the people had no protections or rights in government. In 509 BCE, Rome was under the rule of a particularly nasty tyrant named Tarquinius Superbus. Superbus was corrupt and had many corrupt children, including his son Sextus Tarquinius. As you will read in the story of the Rape of Lucretia, Sextus stole the virtue of Rome's most honorable woman and in order to avenge her death, Romans declared they would never be ruled by kings again. In the year 509 BCE, the Roman Republic was born.

The Republic was an adaptation to the Greek invention of democracy, and was just one example of how Romans borrowed Greek ideas and called them Roman. After the Peloponnesian War, Greece was steadily in decline and was ultimately conquered or assimilated by Rome. As the Roman Republic grew and came into contact with Greeks and Greek culture, they saw and seized on a great opportunity. Founding a new civilization takes time and imagination and the Latins (or Romans as they will come to be known) realized they could save a lot of time and energy by taking Greek ideas, renaming them and calling them Roman. This saved them the energy of having to invent their own culture, religion and philosophy. If the Greeks were the great thinkers, the Romans were the "doers." The Romans liked things that had a function and a purpose. They were more concerned with efficiency than beauty. They built aqueducts, invented concrete and united their empire with a modern system of roads. They liked the idea of people's participation in government *in theory* but decided democracy was too time-consuming and impractical for such practical people. So they created a new form of government, the Republic, which was a practical adaptation of democratic ideals.

The Roman Republic lasted 500 years through the belief that if the Senate and the people of Rome were united, there was nothing that could not be achieved. This belief in the Senate and the People of Rome was represented by the letters SPQR, and it adorned every Roman street sign and sewer cover as well as the shoulder of every Roman legionnaire. The Roman Republic is the model for our own nation's republic and it was a balance of two principles—1. People should have a voice in government; and 2. There should be many safeguards in place to make sure no one man ever holds all the power. Under the Republic, we are given the first Western code of law, called the Twelve Tables. Citizens had certain protections under the law for the first time in history and they, in turn, worked, fought, learned, paid for the maintenance and success of their Republic. The Roman army conquered territory from France to India. And during the height of the Republic every soldier was a volunteer who fought proudly and honorably in service of Rome. It was true that when the people and the government in Rome were united, the world was theirs for the taking. SPQR.

By the year 60 BCE, the Romans had conquered most of the known world. Citizens grew very wealthy as a result of these great victories and enjoyed the luxuries in their lives. They became complacent. Many were no longer as eager to fight and possibly die for their way of life. They would rather be fed and entertained. Roman citizens had forgotten that they owed their successes to the work and sacrifice of their ancestors and believed they were simply born into greatness. It became tiresome rather than honorable to serve in the army or participate in government. As fewer people sought education and public service, politicians became corrupt and self-serving.

43

Great military leaders like Julius Caesar became celebrities who won great political power with the support of the masses. Caesar threw great parties and sponsored elaborate gladiatorial games and the people loved him for it. He was what is known as a *demagogue*, a politician who wins support by telling people what they want to hear. Caesar also made a number of very popular reforms in Rome that won even more affection from the people. But as he pleased the people with one hand, he was stealing power from them with the other. A handful of Senators in Rome feared that Caesar intended to make himself king, with the people's support. Remembering that the Republic had been founded to prevent the rise of a king or tyrant, these senators decided that in order for the Republic to live, Caesar must die. On March 15th of 44 BCE, Caesar was murdered in the Roman Senate by at least three dozen of his friends. And they hoped that the Republic had been saved.

But after Caesar's death it became clear that it was not Caesar who was killing the Republic. It was the people. Gone were the days of unity and SPQR. Every man worked for his own enrichment and not the welfare of his neighbor. They wanted someone to follow rather than helping in the leading. It was easier to most to hand over their power to a demagogue who would tell them pretty lies and keep them entertained and unburdened by the responsibility of governing.

After Caesar's death, there was a long civil war between Caesar's best friends, Mark Antony and Octavian, over who would rule Rome. Ultimately Octavian prevailed and in 27 BCE he became Caesar Augustus, the first emperor of the new Roman Empire. Romans eagerly gave over their power to one man who considered himself a god. For the next 200 years, Rome's former greatness propelled the empire forward. The period from 27 BCE to 180 CE is called the Pax Romana or Roman Peace. It was a period of relative stability and the Roman Empire continued to expand. The empire was lead by a handful of wise emperors and under good leadership, Rome flourished. But under bad leadership, Rome grew increasingly weak and vulnerable.

But by 200 C.E, Rome, though still very powerful, was very sick. Corruption, disease and complacency had infected Rome and the Romans. And her neighbors could sense her weakness. For centuries Rome had conquered and ruled over a diverse group of people throughout the Mediterranean world. And when Romans treated their subjects fairly, there was peace. But when Roman leaders mistreated their subjects and neglected to manage their far away provinces efficiently, resentful tribes, like the Gauls and the various Germanic tribes, began looking to take back the land they believed was rightfully theirs.

In around 300 CE, a new threat emerged that would result in the final collapse of the western Roman Empire. A group of nomadic warriors called the Huns began migrating near Roman borders and many of Rome's neighbors sought protection within the borders of the empire. When the Roman rulers refused to let its desperate neighbors into the empire for safety, those groups instead fought their way in by force. These events were collectively known as the Barbarian Invasions, because the Romans viewed all their neighbors as barbarians, or far less civilized and refined then they themselves were. Wave after wave of barbarian invasion weakened Rome and ate away chunks of her territory until, in 476 CE, the Roman Empire collapsed.

"Why didn't anyone do anything to stop this disaster" you may be asking? Many rulers, seeing the decline of Rome, did things to try to stabilize the empire or even revive it after its collapse.   In 285 CE, the empèror Diocletian realized that the empire had grown too big to be ruled by just one man and so he created a "tetrarchy" or a government of four co-emperors.   He hoped this solution would result in the more efficient management of the empire but it did not.   Political leaders, including emperors, were under-qualified and corrupt. Without good leadership, an empire cannot survive. Some good rulers did try to return Rome to its former glory but each realized Rome was sick beyond saving. The cancer that had infected Rome could not be cured.

The Rape of Lucretia, 509 BCE

Reading and Discussion Questions

1. Who is Lucretia and what virtue does she represent in this story?
2. What virtues does this story put forth for Roman society through the example of Lucretia?
3. Why would this story have mattered to Romans?

The last king of Rome was known as Tarquinius Superbus, and he, his sons and his army were battling a neighboring tribe. They were talking one night over wine about which of their wives was the most virtuous. They could not agree but a friend of the king, Tarquinius Conlatinus, demanded his wife was by far the most virtuous so they went to meet her and find out for themselves. Here is the story as given to us by the great Roman historian, Livy.

One day when the young men were drinking at the house of Sextus Tarquinius, after a supper where they had dined with the son of Egerius, Tarquinius Conlatinus, they fell to talking about their wives, and each man fell to praising his wife to excess. Finally Tarquinius Conlatinus declared that there was no need to argue; they might all be sure that no one was more worthy than his Lucretia. "Young and vigorous as we are, why don't we go get out horses and go and see for ourselves what our wives are doing? And we will base our judgement on whatever we see them doing when their husbands arrive unannounced." Encouraged by the wine, "Yes, let's go!" they all cried, and they went on horseback to the city. Darkness was beginning to fall when they arrived and they went to the house of Conlatinus. There, they found Lucretia behaving quite differently from the daughters-in-law of the King, whom they had found with their friends before a grand feast, preparing to have a night of fun. Lucretia, even though it was night, was still working on her spinning, with her servants, in the middle of her house. They were all impressed by Lucretia's chaste honor. When her husband and the Tarquins arrived, she received them, and her husband, the winner, was obliged to invite the king's sons in. It was then that Sextus Tarquinius was seized by the desire to violate Lucretia's chastity, seduced both by her beauty and by her exemplary virtue. Finally, after a night of youthful games, they returned to the camp.

Several days passed. Sextus Tarquinius returned to the house of Conlatinus, with one of his companions. He was well received and given the hospitality of the house, and maddened with love, he waited until he was sure everyone else was asleep. Then he took up his sword and went to Lucretia's bedroom, and placing his sword against her left breast, he said, "Quiet, Lucretia; I am Sextus Tarquinius, and I have a sword in my hand. If you speak, you will die." Awakening from sleep, the poor woman realized that she was without help and very close to death. Sextus Tarquinius declared his love for her, begging and threatening her alternately, and attacked her soul in every way. Finally, before her steadfastness, which was not affected by the fear of death even after his intimidation, he added another menace. "When I have killed you, I will put next to you the body of a nude servant, and everyone will say that you were killed during a dishonorable act of adultery." With this menace, Sextus Tarquinius triumphed over her virtue, and when he had raped her he left, having taken away her honor.

Lucretia, overcome with sorrow and shame, sent messengers both to her husband at Ardea and her father at Rome, asking them each to come "at once, with a good friend, because a very terrible thing had happened." Spurius Lucretius, her father, came with Publius Valerius, the son of Volesus, and Conlatinus came with Lucius Junius Brutus; they had just returned to Rome when they met Lucretia's messenger. They found Lucretia in her chamber, overpowered by grief. When she saw them she began to cry. "How are you?" her husband asked. "Very bad," she replied, "how can anything go well for a woman who has lost her honor? There are the marks of another man in your bed, Conlatinus. My body is greatly soiled, though my heart is still pure, as my death will prove. But give me your right hand in faith that you will not allow the guilty to escape. It was Sextus Tarquinius who returned our hospitality with enmity last night. With his sword in his hand, he came to take his pleasure for my unhappiness, but it will also be his sorrow if you are real men." They promised her that they would pursue him, and they tried to appease her sorrow, saying that it was the soul that did wrong, and not the body, and because she had had no bad intention, she did no wrong. "It is your responsibility to see that he gets what he deserves," she said. "I will absolve myself of blame, and I will not free myself from punishment. No woman shall use Lucretia as her example in dishonor." Then she took up a knife which she had hidden beneath her robe, and plunged it into her heart, collapsing from her wound; she died there amid the cries of her husband and father.

Brutus, leaving them in their grief, took the knife from Lucretia's wound, and holding it all covered with blood up in the aid, cried, "By this blood, which was so pure before the crime of the prince, I swear before you, O gods, to chase the King Lucius Tarquinius Superbus, with his criminal wife and all their offspring, by fire, iron, and all the methods I have at my disposal, and never to tolerate Kings in Rome evermore, whether of that family of any other."

47

Roman Law and *The Twelve Tables*, 450 BCE

Reading and Discussion Questions

1. What was the purpose of the Twelve Tables?
2. How did Roman law protect the rights of individuals?
3. Which laws restricted the freedoms of individuals?
4. How does this list of laws compare to those of our society today? Are there any that are similar to our laws?
5. What three laws seem unfair or tyrannical? Explain your choices.

The Romans were one of the most legally-minded people in history. The development of their law was one of Rome's greatest and most enduring achievements. Roman law formed during the Republic was adapted to serve the needs of the Empire. When the Empire declined, it was incorporated into the legal system of the Middle Ages, where it became the model for Western law codes until the 20th Century.

The earliest Roman law was religious law and it was written by Roman priests. Disputes between individuals were decided by the king was also a judge. The king's judgments were called jus, and they were first codified in the Twelve Tables in 450 BCE.

The Twelve Tables were strict and harsh but they worked to maintain law and order during the Age of Kings and the early days of the Republic. But as the Republic grew, more laws were eventually needed to smoothly administer Rome's rapidly growing territory.

We inherit many fundamental legal ideas from the Romans, including the belief that men should not be accused anonymously of a crime, that they should not be penalized for what they think, that they should be considered innocent until he is proven guilty. The purpose of justice, in the Roman view, was to give every man that which is his own. One of the most important steps in ensuring a successful and long-lasting civilization is the organization and publication of it laws. This ensures that all people know what the law is and will, therefore, abide by it. About 450 BCE, the Romans codified their laws and inscribed them on twelve bronze tables which were set up in the Roman Forum. These Twelve Tables were the basis of all later Roman law, and through it, of the legal system of much of the Western world. Below are excerpts from the Twelve Tables.

TABLE III:

1. In the case of an admitted debt of awards made by a court, 30 days shall be allowed for payment.

2. In default of payment, after these 30 days of grace have elapsed, the debtor may be arrested and brought before the magistrate.

3. Unless the debtor discharge the debt, or someone come forward in court to guarantee payment, the creditor may take the debtor away with him and bind him with

thongs and fetters the weight of which shall be fifteen pounds, or less if the creditor wishes . . .

5. In default of settlement of the claim, the debtor may be kept in bonds for 60 days. In the course of this period he shall be brought before the judge on three successive market days, and the amount of the debt shall be publicly declared. After the third market day the debtor may be punished with death or sold beyond the Tiber.

TABLE IV:

1. Monstrous or deformed offspring may be put to death by the father.

2. The father shall, during his who life, have absolute power over his children. He may imprison his son, or scourge him, or keep him working in the fields in fetters {chains}, or put him to death, even if the son held the highest offices of state . . .

TABLE V:
1. All women shall be under the authority of a guardian.

2. The provisions of the will of a paterfamilias [head of the household] concerning his property and the tutelage [support] of his family, shall have the force of law.

TABLE VI:
1. The legal effect of every contract, and of every conveyance shall rest upon the declarations made in the transaction.

2. Any one who refuses to stand by such contractual declarations shall pay a penalty of double damages.

TABLE VII: . . .
7. Holders of property along a road shall maintain the road to keep it passable; but if it be passable, anyone may drive his beast or cart across the land wherever he chooses.

TABLE VIII:
1. Whoever publishes a libel—that is today writes falsely imputed [intending] crime or immorality to anyone—shall be beaten to death with clubs . . .

3. For breaking a bone of a freeman, the fine shall be 300 asses; of a slave, 150 asses ..

12. A person committing burglary in the night may be lawfully killed.

13. A thief in the daytime may not be killed unless he carried a weapon . . . .

23. Perjurers and false witnesses shall be hurled from the Tarpeian Rock . . . .

26. Seditious [conspiratorial, rebellious] gatherings in the city during the night are forbidden.

Polybius, The Roman Constitution, *The Histories, c. 200 BCE*

Reading and Discussion Questions
1. Polybius said, "nearly the whole world fell under the power of Rome in less than fifty-three years." Based on your reading, how did that happen?
2. Identify the three branches or parts of the Roman government and be able to explain at least three powers of each part.
3. How are the powers listed above for each branch of government checked by the other branches? List specific examples.

In 167 B.C., Rome, interfering in the squabbles of Greece, took one thousand hostages from the Achaean League. One of these hostages was Polybius, a Greek historian and a member of an influential Greek family. In Rome, Polybius became friends with several powerful Romans and came to admire the new power of Rome. His Histories *tells the story of the newly emerging superpower. He proposed to explain, "in what manner and under what kind of constitution it came about that nearly the whole world fell under the power of Rome in somewhat less than fifty-three years, an event certainly without precedent."*

I am aware that some will be at a loss to account for my interrupting the course of my narrative for the sake of entering upon the following disquisition on the Roman constitution. But I think that I have already in many passages made it fully evident that this particular branch of my work was one of the necessities imposed on me by the nature of my original design; and I pointed this out with special clearness in the preface which explained the scope of my history. I there stated that the feature of my work which was at once the best in itself, and the most instructive to the students of it, was that it would enable them to know and fully realize in what manner, and under what kind of constitution, it came about that nearly the whole world fell under the power of Rome in somewhat less than fifty-three years - an event certainly without precedent. . .

Of the Greek republics, which have again and again risen to greatness and fallen into insignificance, it is not difficult to speak, whether we recount their past history or venture an opinion on their future. For to report what is already known is an easy task, nor is it hard to guess what is to come from our knowledge of what has been. But in regard to the Romans it is neither an easy matter to describe their present state, owing to the complexity of their constitution; nor to speak with confidence of their future, for our inadequate acquaintance with their peculiar institutions in the past whether affecting their public or private life. It will require then no ordinary attention and study to get a clear and comprehensive conception of the distinctive features of this constitution. . . . .

As for the Roman constitution, it had three elements, each of them possessing sovereign powers; and their respective share of power in the whole state had been regulated with such a scrupulous regard to equality and equilibrium, that no one could say for certain, not even a native, whether the constitution as a whole were an aristocracy or democracy or despotism. And no wonder: for if we confine our observation to the power of the Consuls we should be inclined to regard it as despotic; if on that of the Senate, as aristocratic; and if finally one looks at the power possessed by the people it would seem a clear case of a democracy. What the exact powers of these several parts were and still, with slight modifications, are, I will now state.

The Consuls, before leading out the legions, remain in Rome and are the supreme masters of the administration. All other magistrates, except the Tribunes, are under them and take their orders. They introduce foreign ambassadors to the Senate: bring matters requiring deliberation before it; and see to the execution of the decrees. If, again, there are any matters of state which require the authorization of the people, it is their business to see to them, to summon the popular meetings, to bring the proposals before them, and to carry out the decrees of the majority. In the preparation for war also, and in a word in the entire administration of a campaign, they have all but absolute power. It is competent to them to impose on the allies such levies as they think good, to appoint the military tribunes, to make up the roll for soldiers and select those that are suitable. Besides they have absolute power of inflicting punishment on all who are under their command while on active service; and they have authority to expend as much of the public money as they choose, being accompanied by a quaestor who is entirely at their orders. A survey of these powers would in fact justify our describing the constitution as despotic, a clear case of royal government. Nor will it affect the truth of my description if any of the institutions I have described are changed in our time or in that of our posterity and the same remarks apply to what follows.

The Senate has first of all control of the treasury, and regulates the receipts and disbursements alike. For the quaestors cannot issue any public money for the various departments of the state without a decree of the Senate, except for the service of the Consuls. The Senate controls also what is by far the largest and most important expenditure, that, namely, which is made by the censors every lustrum' for the repair or construction of public buildings; this money cannot be obtained by the censors except by the grant of the Senate. Similarly all crimes committed in Italy requiring a public investigation, such as treason, conspiracy, poisoning, or willful murder, are in the hands of the Senate. Besides, if any individual or state among the Italian allies requires a controversy to be settled, a penalty to be assessed, help or protection to be afforded, all this is the province of the Senate. Or again, outside Italy, if it is necessary to send an embassy to reconcile warring communities or to remind them of their duty, or sometimes to impose requisitions upon them, or to receive their submission, or finally to proclaim war against them, this too is the business of the Senate. In like manner, the reception to be given to foreign ambassadors in Rome and the answers to be returned to them, are decided by the Senate. With such business the people have nothing to do. Consequently, if one were staying at Rome when the Consuls were not in town, one would imagine the constitution to be a complete aristocracy; and this has been the idea entertained by many Greeks, and by many kings as well, from the fact that nearly all the business they had with Rome was settled by the Senate.

After this one would naturally be inclined to ask what part is left for the people in the constitution, when the Senate has these various functions, especially the control of the receipts and expenditure of the exchequer; and when the Consuls, again, have absolute power over the details of military preparation and an absolute authority in the field? There is, however, a part left the people, and it is a most important one. For the people is the sole fountain of honor and of punishment; and it is by these two things and these alone that dynasties and constitutions and, in a word, human society are held together: for where the distinction between them is not sharply drawn both in theory and practice, there no undertaking can be properly administered, as indeed we might

51

expect when good and bad are held in exactly the same honor. The people then are the only court to decide matters of life and death; and even in cases where the penalty is money, if the sum to be assessed is sufficiently serious, and especially when the accused have held the higher magistracies.

Again, it is the people who bestow offices on the deserving, which are the most honorable rewards of virtue. It has also the absolute power of passing or repealing laws; and, most important of all, it is the people who deliberate on the question of peace or war. And when provisional terms are made for alliance, suspension of hostilities, or treaties, it is the people who ratify them or the reverse.

These considerations, again, would lead one to say that the chief power in the state was the people's, and that the constitution was a democracy.

Such, then, is the distribution of power between the several parts of the state. I must now show how each of these several parts can, when they choose, oppose or support each other.

The Consul, then, when he has started on an expedition with the powers I have described, is to all appearance absolute in the administration of the business in hand; still he has need of the support both of people and Senate, and, without them, is quite unable to bring the matter to a successful conclusion. For it is plain that he must have supplies sent to his legions from time to time; but without a decree of the Senate they can be supplied neither with grain, nor clothes, nor pay, so that all the plans of a commander must be futile if the Senate is resolved either to shrink from danger or hamper his plans. And, again, whether a Consul shall bring any undertaking to a conclusion or no depends entirely upon the Senate: for it has absolute authority at the end of a year to send another Consul to supersede him, or to continue the existing one in his command. Again, even to the successes of the generals the Senate has the power to add distinction and glory, and on the other hand to obscure their merits and lower their credit. For these high achievements are brought in tangible form before the eyes of the citizens by what are called "triumphs." But these triumphs the commanders cannot celebrate at all, unless the Senate concurs and grants the necessary money. As for the people, the Consuls are pre-eminently obliged to court their favor, however distant from home may be the field of their operations; for it is the people, as I have said before, that ratifies or refuses to ratify terms of peace and treaties; but most of all because when laying down their office they have to give an account of their administration before it. Therefore in no case is it safe for the Consuls to neglect either the Senate or the good will of the people.

As for the Senate, which possesses the immense power I have described, in the first place it is obliged in public affairs to take the multitude into account, and respect the wishes of the people; and it cannot put into execution the penalty for offenses against the republic which are punishable with death, unless the people first ratify its decrees. Similarly, even in matters which directly affect the Senators, for instance in the case of a law diminishing the Senate's traditional authority, or depriving Senators of certain dignities and offices, or even actually cutting down their property, even in such cases the people have the sole power of passing or rejecting the law. But most important of all is the fact that, if the Tribunes interpose their veto, the Senate not only are unable to pass a decree, but cannot even hold a meeting at all, whether formal or informal. Now, the Tribunes are always bound to carry out the decree of the people, and above all

52

things to have regard to their wishes: therefore, for all these reasons, the Senate stands in awe of the multitude and cannot neglect the feelings of the people.

In like manner the people on its part is far from being independent of the Senate, and is bound to take its wishes into account both collectively and individually. For contracts too numerous to count are given out by the censors in all parts of Italy for the repairs or construction of public buildings; there is also the collection of revenue from many rivers, harbors, gardens, mines, and land; everything, in a word, that comes under the control of the Roman government. And in all these the people at large are engaged; so that there is scarcely a man, so to speak, who is not interested either as a contractor or as being employed in the works. For some purchase the contracts from the censors for themselves; and others go partners with them; while others again go security for these contractors, or actually pledge their property to the treasury for them. Now over all these transactions the Senate has absolute control. It can grant an extension of time; and in case of unforeseen accident can relieve the contractors from a portion of their obligation, or release them from it altogether if they are absolutely unable to fulfill it. And there are many details in which the Senate can inflict great hardships, or, on the other hand, grant great indulgences to the contractors; for in every case the appeal is to it. But the most important point of all is that the judges are taken from its members in the majority of trials, whether public or private, in which the charges are heavy. Consequently, all citizens are much at its mercy, and being alarmed at the uncertainty as to when they may need its aid, are cautious about resisting or actively opposing its will. And for a similar reason men do not rashly resist the wishes of the Consuls, because one and all may become subject to their absolute authority on a campaign.

The result of this power of the several estates for mutual help or harm is a union sufficiently firm for all emergencies, and a constitution than which it is impossible to find a better. For whenever any danger from without compels them to unite and work together, the strength which is developed by the State is so extraordinary that everything required is unfailingly carried out by the eager rivalry shown by all classes to devote their whole minds to the need of the hour, and to secure that any determination come to should not fail for want of promptitude; while each individual works, privately and publicly alike, for the accomplishment of the business in hand.

Sallust, Moral Deterioration, *Catiline Conspiracy, 63 BCE*

Reading and Discussion Questions
1. Identify and explain five reasons why the Roman Republic thrived, according to Sallust.
2. What virtues made the Roman Republic great, according to Sallust?
3. What has caused the deterioration of Rome, according to the author?
4. What things have the Romans come to value at the time of this writing?

Most people assume that the problems in ancient Rome began during the Imperial period, after the assassination of Julius Caesar in 44 BCE. But Rome had grown sick well before it became an empire. The following passage, from the Roman historian Sallust, was written nearly 20 years before Caesar's assassination and the birth of the Roman Empire. Sallust discusses very clearly the things that had made the Roman Republic succeed and also observed well before anyone else what was causing its collapse.

Since the occasion has arisen to speak of the morals of our country, the nature of my theme seems to suggest that I go farther back and give a brief account of the institutions of our forefathers in peace and in war, how they governed the commonwealth, how great it was when they bequeathed it to us, and how by gradual changes it has ceased to be the noblest and best, and has become the worst and most vicious.

The city of Rome, according to my understanding, was at the outset founded and inhabited by Trojans, who were wandering about in exile under the leadership of Aeneas and had no fixed abode; they were joined by the Aborigines, a rustic folk, without laws or government, free and unrestrained. After these two peoples, different in race, unlike in speech and mode of life, were united within the same walls, they were merged into one with incredible facility, so quickly did harmony change a heterogeneous and roving band into a commonwealth. But when this new community had grown in numbers, civilization, and territory, and was beginning to seem amply rich and amply strong.

They had a constitution founded upon law, which was in name a monarchy; a chosen few, whose bodies were enfeebled by age but whose minds were fortified with wisdom, took counsel for the welfare of the state. These were called Fathers, by reason either of their age or of the similarity of their duties. Later, when the rule of the kings, which at first had tended to preserve freedom and advance the state, had degenerated into a lawless tyranny, they altered their form of government and appointed two rulers with annual power, thinking that this device would prevent men's minds from growing arrogant through unlimited authority.

Good morals were cultivated at home and in the field; there was the greatest harmony and little or no avarice; justice and probity prevailed among them, thanks not so much to laws as to nature. Quarrels, discord, and strife were reserved for their enemies; citizen vied with citizen only for the prize of merit. They were lavish in their offerings to the gods, frugal in the home, loyal to their friends. By practicing these two qualities, boldness in warfare and justice when peace came, they watched over themselves and their country.

But when our country had grown great through toil and the practice of justice, when great kings had been vanquished in war, savage tribes and mighty peoples subdued by force of arms, then Fortune began to grow cruel and to bring confusion into all our affairs. Those who had found it easy to bear hardship and dangers, anxiety and adversity, found leisure and wealth, desirable under other circumstances, a burden and a curse. Hence the lust for money first, then for power, grew upon them; these were, I may say, the root of all evils. For greed destroyed honor, integrity, and all other noble qualities; taught in their place insolence, cruelty, to neglect the gods, to set a price on everything. Ambition drove many men to become false; to have one thought locked in the breast, another ready on the tongue; to value friendships and enmities not on their merits but by the standard of self-interest, and to show a good front rather than a good heart. At first these vices grew slowly, from time to time they were punished; finally, when the disease had spread like a deadly plague, the state was changed and a government second to none in equity and excellence became cruel and intolerable.

But at first men's souls were hurt less by greed than by ambition — a fault, it is true, but not so far removed from virtue; for the noble and the base alike long for glory, honor, and power, but the former mount by the true path, whereas the latter, being destitute of noble qualities, rely upon craft and deception. Avarice implies a desire for money, which no wise man covets; steeped as it were with noxious poisons, it renders the most manly body and soul effeminate; it is ever unbounded and insatiable, nor can either plenty or want make it less.

As soon as riches came to be held in honor, when glory, dominion, and power followed in their train, virtue began to lose its lustre, poverty to be considered a disgrace, blamelessness to be termed malevolence. Therefore as the result of riches, luxury and greed, united with insolence, took possession of our young manhood. They pillaged, squandered; set little value on their own, coveted the goods of others; they disregarded modesty, chastity, everything human and divine; in short, they were utterly thoughtless and reckless.

Cicero, Justifying the Assassination of Julius Caesar, 44 BCE

Reading and Discussion Questions
1. What, according the Cicero, is "the blackest of all crimes?"
2. Did Caesar violate the Roman constitution with his actions? Explain.
3. Think back to the story of the Rape of Lucretia. How might that story have influenced the men who assassinated Caesar?
4. From the Roman perspective, was Caesar's murder justified?
5. Why do you think Cicero, the author, was murdered? Can you make any comparisons between his life and death and that of Socrates?

Marcus Tullius Cicero was a Roman philosopher, lawyer, politician and orator. He was an outspoken critic of the corruption of the late Roman Republic and wrote about the roots of this corruption and the ways to return Rome to its former power and virtue. Much of what Cicero said and wrote was politically unpopular and he was killed in 43 CE. His severed hands and head were put on display in the Roman Forum as an example of what happens when you criticize powerful men. Cicero believed that Julius Caesar was an example of the lack of virtue that had taken hold in Rome. He and many other influential Romans feared that Caesar aimed to establish himself as the king of Rome. The very word king was unacceptable to patriotic Romans, who remembered their early history and the corruption of Rome's many kings before the founding of the Republic. On March 15, 44 BCE, Caesar was slain by some sixty senators, who acted, they said, to restore the liberty of the Roman people. Cicero did not participate in the assassination. The excerpt below is from Cicero's On Duties and explains why, in Cicero's opinion, Caesar had to die.

Our tyrant deserved his death for having made an exception of the one thing that was the blackest crime of all. Why do we gather instances of petty crime - legacies criminally obtained and fraudulent buying and selling? Behold, here you have a man who was ambitious to be king of the Roman People and master of the whole world; and he achieved it! The man who maintains that such an ambition is morally right is a madman; for he justifies the destruction of law and liberty and thinks their hideous and detestable suppression glorious. But if anyone agrees that it is not morally right to be kind in a state that once was free and that ought to be free now, and yet imagines that it is advantageous for him who can reach that position, with what remonstrance or rather with what appeal should I try to tear him away from so strange a delusion? For, oh ye immortal gods! can the most horrible and hideous of all murders - that of fatherland - bring advantage to anybody, even though he who has committed such a crime receives from his enslaved fellow-citizens the title of "Father of his Country?" Expediency, therefore, must be measured by the standard of moral rectitude, and in such a way, too, that these two words shall seem in sound only to be different but in real meaning to be one and the same.

What greater advantage one could have, according to the standard of popular opinion, than to be a king, I do not know; when, however, I begin to bring the question back to the standard of truth, then I find nothing more disadvantageous for one who has risen to that height by injustice. For can occasions for worry anxiety, fear by day and by night, and a life all beset with plots and perils be of advantage to anybody?

Virgil, *The Aeneid*, 19 BCE

<u>Reading and Discussion Questions</u>

1. What is Jupiter's prophecy to Aeneas?
2. How is Augustus introduced to the reader in Book I? What imagery or mood is conjured when Virgil writes about Augustus?
3. Briefly summarize Aeneas' version of events at the end of the Trojan War, including the story of the Trojan Horse. What finally happens to Troy? And in what manner does Aeneas escape?
4. Why do you think Virgil spends so much time talking about events in Troy when this is a story about the founding of Rome?
5. Why do you think Virgil included the story of Dido, queen of Carthage, in his epic? What does Aeneas and Dido' relationship represent in terms of their two civilizations?

The Aeneid is a Latin epic poem completed by the famous Roman poet, Virgil, in 19 CE. It was commissioned by Augustus to give Rome and the Romans a founding story they could be proud of. During the reign of Augustus, the only explanation the Romans had about their founding was that their founder, Romulus, was a murderer who had been raised by a wolf and who had populated their city with thieves, rapists and other undesirables. Augustus, who was the master of self-promotion, wanted an origin story that better promoted his own greatness and so he had one created. The Aeneid is one of the first massive works of propaganda, which is ideas or materials created to help the cause of a specific person, or group, usually political. The Aeneid at once gave Romans a lineage and a history they could be proud of and simultaneously promoted Augustus as the part-divine descendant of a Greco-Roman hero.

The Aeneid is the story of a hero, Aeneas, who was a minor character in Homer's Iliad and whose mother is the Roman goddess Venus. It is almost a Roman sequel to the Greek epic The Iliad and is another great example of how the Romans took things that were Greek, adapted them and called them Roman. Aeneas' story begins where the Iliad ends, in the flames of the destroyed city of Troy. The Aeneid's plot reads as the final part of the story of the Trojan War and of Aeneas' fleeing from the burning city. But it quickly becomes very Odyssey-esque in that Aeneas wanders for ten years, having adventures and misadventures along the way, before finally landing in Latium (Italy), or the land of the Latins. There he founds the city of Alba Longa which is ruled by a monarchy. Romulus was, according to the story, a descendant of the great Alban kings descended from Aeneas, thus the heroic story of Aeneas and the less heroic story of Romulus and Remus were happily linked.

In the passages below, we learn the story of what happened to Troy, including the story of the Trojan Horse, which was an invention of Virgil and not Homer, as is commonly believed. Along his journey, Aeneas finds refuge in the city of Tyre, which is the capital of the newly founded kingdom of Carthage in North Africa. Aeneas has a short but dramatic romance with the Dido, the Queen of Carthage. The romance ends in tragedy and the story seems to be a poetic device for explaining the age-old hatred between Rome and Carthage which culminated in the Punic Wars. The Aeneid creates a very Roman hero in Aeneas, who is often torn between emotion and duty but always does what duty commands. Duty is a sacred Roman virtue. The Aeneid is viewed by some as a lesser version of the works of Homer but it was literature that served a purpose beyond art. It was intended to glorify Augustus by suggesting that he was the descendant of the great Alban kings and of Aeneas himself, and therefore divine. Augustus wanted his memory and his legacy to be immortalized and The Aeneid is in many ways, a timeless monument to his eternal greatness.

BOOK ONE

BkI:1-11 Invocation to the Muse

I sing of arms and the man, he who, exiled by fate,
first came from the coast of Troy to Italy, and to
Lavinian shores – hurled about endlessly by land and sea,
by the will of the gods, by cruel Juno's remorseless anger,
long suffering also in war, until he founded a city
and brought his gods to Latium: from that the Latin people
came, the lords of Alba Longa, the walls of noble Rome.
Muse, tell me the cause: how was she offended in her divinity,
how was she grieved, the Queen of Heaven, to drive a man,
noted for virtue, to endure such dangers, to face so many
trials? Can there be such anger in the minds of the gods?

BkI:257-296 Jupiter's Prophecy

'Don't be afraid, Cytherea [Aeneas' mom], your child's fate remains unaltered:
You'll see the city of Lavinium, and the walls I promised,
and you'll raise great-hearted Aeneas high, to the starry sky:
No thought has changed my mind. This son of yours
will wage a mighty war in Italy, destroy proud peoples,
and establish laws, and city walls, for his warriors,
until a third summer sees his reign in Latium, and
three winter camps pass since the Rutulians were beaten.
But the boy Ascanius, surnamed Iulus now (He was Ilus
while the Ilian kingdom was a reality) will imperially
complete thirty great circles of the turning months,
and transfer his throne from its site at Lavinium,
and mighty in power, will build the walls of Alba Longa.

Here kings of Hector's race will reign now
for three hundred years complete, until a royal priestess,
Ilia, heavy with child, shall bear Mars twins.
Then Romulus will further the race, proud in his nurse
the she-wolf's tawny pelt, and found the walls of Mars,
and call the people Romans, from his own name.
I've fixed no limits or duration to their possessions:
I've given them empire without end. Why, harsh Juno
who now torments land, and sea and sky with fear,
will respond to better judgement, and favour the Romans,
masters of the world, and people of the toga, with me.

From this glorious source a Trojan Caesar will be born,
who will bound the empire with Ocean, his fame with the stars,

Augustus, a Julius, his name descended from the great Iulus.
You, no longer anxious, will receive him one day in heaven,
burdened with Eastern spoils: he'll be called to in prayer.
Then with wars abandoned, the harsh ages will grow mild:
White haired Trust, and Vesta, Quirinus with his brother Remus
will make the laws: the gates of War, grim with iron,
and narrowed by bars, will be closed: inside impious Rage will roar
frighteningly from blood-stained mouth, seated on savage weapons,
hands tied behind his back, with a hundred knots of bronze.'

BkI:372-417 She Directs Him to Dido's Palace
Aeneas encounters a stranger along his journey, and he speaks to her:

'O, if I were to start my tale at the very beginning,
and you had time to hear the story of our misfortunes,
Vesper would have shut day away in the closed heavens.
A storm drove us at whim to Libya's shores,
sailing the many seas from ancient Troy,
if by chance the name of Troy has come to your hearing.
I am that Aeneas, the virtuous, who carries my household gods
in my ship with me, having snatched them from the enemy,
my name is known beyond the sky.
I seek my country Italy, and a people born of Jupiter on high.
I embarked on the Phrygian sea with twenty ships,
following my given fate, my mother, a goddess, showing the way:
barely seven are left, wrenched from the wind and waves.
I myself wander, destitute and unknown, in the Libyan desert,
driven from Europe and Asia.'

BkI:464-493 The Frieze
[Aeneas comes to a temple of Juno in the city of Tyre, the capital of Carthage (modern day Libya) with a mural depicting the Trojan War and the destruction of Troy. Aeneas weeps. He meets the queen of Carthage, named Dido.]

So he speaks, and feeds his spirit with the insubstantial frieze,
sighing often, and his face wet with the streaming tears.
For he saw how, here, the Greeks fled, as they fought round Troy,
chased by the Trojan youth, and, there, the Trojans fled,
with plumed Achilles pressing them close in his chariot.
Not far away, through his tears, he recognizes Rhesus's
white-canvassed tents, that blood-stained Diomede, Tydeus's son,
laid waste with great slaughter, betrayed in their first sleep,
diverting the fiery horses to his camp, before they could eat
Trojan fodder, or drink from the river Xanthus.
Elsewhere Troilus, his weapons discarded in flight,
unhappy boy, unequally matched in his battle with Achilles,
is dragged by his horses, clinging face-up to the empty chariot,
still clutching the reins: his neck and hair trailing
on the ground, and his spear reversed furrowing the dust.
Meanwhile the Trojan women with loose hair, walked
to unjust Pallas's temple carrying the sacred robe,

59

mourning humbly, and beating their breasts with their hands.
The goddess was turned away, her eyes fixed on the ground.
Three times had Achilles dragged Hector round the walls of Troy,
and now was selling the lifeless corpse for gold.
Then Aeneas truly heaves a deep sigh, from the depths of his heart,
as he views the spoils, the chariot, the very body of his friend,
and Priam stretching out his unwarlike hands.
He recognised himself as well, fighting the Greek princes,
and the Ethiopian ranks and black Memnon's armour.
Raging Penthesilea leads the file of Amazons,
with crescent shields, and shines out among her thousands,
her golden girdle fastened beneath her exposed breasts,
a virgin warrior daring to fight with men.

[*Aeneas and his men are welcomed into Tyre by Dido and the Tyrhinian people. A
feast is held in their honor and during their first meeting, Dido falls madly in love with
Aeneas. She is under a spell by Cupid, who pierced her heart with an unquenchable
love for Aeneas. At the feast for Aeneas, Dido asks Aeneas to tell everyone his story.*]

BOOK TWO

BkII:1-56 The Trojan Horse: Laocoön's Warning
They were all silent, and turned their faces towards him intently.
Then from his high couch our forefather Aeneas began:
'O queen, you command me to renew unspeakable grief,
how the Greeks destroyed the riches of Troy,
and the sorrowful kingdom, miseries I saw myself,
and in which I played a great part.

'After many years have slipped by, the leaders of the Greeks,
opposed by the Fates, and damaged by the war,
build a horse of mountainous size, through Pallas's divine art,
and weave planks of fir over its ribs:
they pretend it's a votive offering: this rumour spreads.
They secretly hide a picked body of men, chosen by lot,
there, in the dark body, filling the belly and the huge
cavernous insides with armed warriors.
Tenedos is within sight, an island known to fame,
rich in wealth when Priam's kingdom remained,
now just a bay and an unsafe anchorage for boats:
they sail there, and hide themselves, on the lonely shore.
We thought they had gone, and were seeking Mycenae
with the wind. So all the Trojan land was free of its long sorrow.

The gates were opened: it was a joy to go and see the Greek camp,
the deserted site and the abandoned shore.
Here the Dolopians stayed, here cruel Achilles,
here lay the fleet, here they used to meet us in battle.
Some were amazed at virgin Minerva's fatal gift,
and marvel at the horse's size: and at first Thymoetes,
whether through treachery, or because Troy's fate was certain,

urged that it be dragged inside the walls and placed on the citadel.
But Capys, and those of wiser judgement, commanded us
to either hurl this deceit of the Greeks, this suspect gift,
into the sea, or set fire to it from beneath,
or pierce its hollow belly, and probe for hiding places.

The crowd, uncertain, was split by opposing opinions.
Then Laocoön rushes down eagerly from the heights
of the citadel, to confront them all, a large crowd with him,
and shouts from far off: 'O unhappy citizens, what madness?
Do you think the enemy's sailed away? Or do you think
any Greek gift's free of treachery? Is that Ulysses's reputation?
Either there are Greeks in hiding, concealed by the wood,
or it's been built as a machine to use against our walls,
or spy on our homes, or fall on the city from above,
or it hides some other trick: Trojans, don't trust this horse.
Whatever it is, I'm afraid of Greeks even those bearing gifts.'

So saying he hurled his great spear, with extreme force,
at the creature's side, and into the frame of the curved belly.
The spear stuck quivering, and at the womb's reverberation
the cavity rang hollow and gave out a groan.
And if the gods' fate, if our minds, had not been ill-omened,
he'd have incited us to mar the Greeks hiding-place with steel:
Troy would still stand: and you, high tower of Priam would remain.

[The Trojans decide to accept the gift of the horse.]

BkII:228-253 The Horse Enters Troy

Then in truth a strange terror steals through each shuddering heart,
and they say that Laocoön has justly suffered for his crime
in wounding the sacred oak-tree with his spear,
by hurling its wicked shaft into the trunk.
"Pull the statue to her house", they shout,
"and offer prayers to the goddess's divinity."

We breached the wall, and opened up the defences of the city.
All prepare themselves for the work and they set up wheels
allowing movement under its feet, and stretch hemp ropes
round its neck. That engine of fate mounts our walls
pregnant with armed men. Around it boys, and virgin girls,
sing sacred songs, and delight in touching their hands to the ropes:
Up it glides and rolls threateningly into the midst of the city.

BkII:254-297 The Greeks Take the City

And now the Greek phalanx of battle-ready ships sailed
from Tenedos, in the benign stillness of the silent moon,
seeking the known shore, when the royal galley raised
a torch, and Sinon, protected by the gods' unjust doom,
sets free the Greeks imprisoned by planks of pine,
in the horses' belly. Opened, it releases them to the air,

and sliding down a lowered rope, Thessandrus, and Sthenelus,
the leaders, and fatal Ulysses, emerge joyfully
from their wooden cave, with Acamas, Thoas,
Peleus's son Neoptolemus, the noble Machaon,
Menelaus, and Epeus who himself devised this trick.
They invade the city that's drowned in sleep and wine,
kill the watchmen, welcome their comrades
at the open gates, and link their clandestine ranks.

[Then Hector spoke to Aeneas in a dream and said:]

"Ah! Son of the goddess, fly, tear yourself from the flames.
The enemy has taken the walls: Troy falls from her high place.
Enough has been given to Priam and your country: if Pergama
could be saved by any hand, it would have been saved by this.
Troy entrusts her sacred relics and household gods to you:
take them as friends of your fate, seek mighty walls for them,
those you will found at last when you have wandered the seas."

[Aeneas gathers his family and close friends and he tells them of Hector's message. They did not want to abandon the city because they were brave. They stayed and fought in defense of the castle and there was a great battle. Aeneas and his companions fought bravely but the palace was overrun with Greeks. King Priam was killed by Achilles and Troy was overcome with despair. Troy had been defeated. Having fought bravely, Aeneas gathered the rest of his friends and family, including his son and father, and they fled the city. Aeneas' wife was killed before she could escape with them.]

BkII:796-804 Aeneas Leaves Troy
And here, amazed, I found that a great number of new
companions had streamed in, women and men,
a crowd gathering for exile, a wretched throng.
They had come from all sides, ready, with courage and wealth,
for whatever land I wished to lead them to, across the seas.
And now Lucifer was rising above the heights of Ida,
bringing the dawn, and the Greeks held the barricaded
entrances to the gates, nor was there any hope of rescue.
I desisted, and, carrying my father, took to the hills.

BOOK FOUR

BkIV:1-53 Dido and Anna Discuss Aeneas
But the queen, wounded long since by intense love,
feeds the hurt with her life-blood, weakened by hidden fire.
The hero's courage often returns to mind, and the nobility
of his race: his features and his words cling fixedly to her heart,
and love will not grant restful calm to her body.

[Dido discusses her feelings with a friend, Anna, who has this to say, encouraging Dido in her feelings]

"The Trojan ships made their way here with the wind,
with gods indeed helping them I think, and with Juno's favour.
What a city you'll see here, sister, what a kingdom rise,
with such a husband! With a Trojan army marching with us,
with what great actions Punic glory will soar!

BkIV:54-89 Dido in Love
By saying this she inflames the queen's burning heart with love
and raises hopes in her anxious mind, and weakens her sense
of shame. First they visit the shrines and ask for grace at the altars:
they sacrifice chosen animals according to the rites,
to Ceres, the law-maker, and Phoebus, and father Lycaeus,
and to Juno above all, in whose care are the marriage ties:
Dido herself, supremely lovely, holding the cup in her hand,
pours the libation between the horns of a white heifer
or walks to the rich altars, before the face of the gods,
celebrates the day with gifts, and gazes into the opened
chests of victims, and reads the living entrails.

Ah, the unknowing minds of seers! What use are prayers
or shrines to the impassioned? Meanwhile her tender marrow
is aflame, and a silent wound is alive in her breast.
Wretched Dido burns, and wanders frenzied through the city,
like an unwary deer struck by an arrow, that a shepherd hunting
with his bow has fired at from a distance, in the Cretan woods,
leaving the winged steel in her, without knowing.
She runs through the woods and glades of Dicte:
the lethal shaft hangs in her side.

*[Aeneas appears to share Dido's love and the two plan to be married, and to rule her
kingdom together. But as usual, the gods meddle in human affairs and Jupiter sends
the messenger god, Mercury, to remind Aeneas that he is destined for greater things.]*

BkIV:219-278 Jupiter Sends Mercury to Aeneas
Mercury challenged him at once: "For love of a wife
are you now building the foundations of high Carthage
and a pleasing city? Alas, forgetful of your kingdom and fate!
The king of the gods himself, who bends heaven and earth
to his will, has sent me down to you from bright Olympus:
he commanded me himself to carry these words through
the swift breezes. What do you plan? With what hopes
do you waste idle hours in Libya's lands? If you're not stirred
by the glory of destiny, and won't exert yourself for your own
fame, think of your growing Ascanius, and the expectations
of him, as Iulus your heir, to whom will be owed the kingdom
of Italy, and the Roman lands." So Mercury spoke,
and, while speaking, vanished from mortal eyes,
and melted into thin air far from their sight.

BkIV:279-330 Dido Accuses Aeneas
Aeneas, stupefied at the vision, was struck dumb,

63

and his hair rose in terror, and his voice stuck in his throat.
He was eager to be gone, in flight, and leave that sweet land,
shocked by the warning and the divine command.
Alas! What to do? With what speech dare he tackle
the love-sick queen? What opening words should he choose?
And he cast his mind back and forth swiftly,
considered the issue from every aspect, and turned it every way.

This seemed the best decision, given the alternatives:
he called Mnestheus, Sergestus and brave Serestus,
telling them to fit out the fleet in silence, gather the men
on the shore, ready the ships' tackle, and hide the reason
for these changes of plan. He in the meantime, since
the excellent Dido knew nothing, and would not expect
the breaking off of such a love, would seek an approach,
the tenderest moment to speak, and a favourable means.
They all gladly obeyed his command at once, and did his bidding.
But the queen sensed his tricks (who can deceive a lover?)
and was first to anticipate future events, fearful even of safety.
That same impious Rumour brought her madness:
they are fitting out the fleet, and planning a journey.
Her mind weakened, she raves, and, on fire, runs wild
through the city.

Of her own accord she finally reproaches Aeneas in these words:
"Faithless one, did you really think you could hide
such wickedness, and vanish from my land in silence?
Will my love not hold you, nor the pledge I once gave you,
nor the promise that Dido will die a cruel death?
Even in winter do you labour over your ships, cruel one,
so as to sail the high seas at the height of the northern gales?
Why? If you were not seeking foreign lands and unknown
settlements, but ancient Troy still stood, would Troy
be sought out by your ships in wave-torn seas?

Is it me you run from? I beg you, by these tears, by your own
right hand (since I've left myself no other recourse in my misery),
by our union, by the marriage we have begun,
if ever I deserved well of you, or anything of me
was sweet to you, pity this ruined house, and if
there is any room left for prayer, change your mind.
The Libyan peoples and Numidian rulers hate me because of you:
my Tyrians are hostile: because of you all shame too is lost,
the reputation I had, by which alone I might reach the stars.
My guest, since that's all that is left me from the name of husband,
to whom do you relinquish me, a dying woman?
Why do I stay? Until Pygmalion, my brother, destroys
the city, or Iarbas the Gaetulian takes me captive?
If I'd at least conceived a child of yours
before you fled, if a little Aeneas were playing
about my halls, whose face might still recall yours,

I'd not feel myself so utterly deceived and forsaken."

BkIV:331-361 Aeneas Justifies Himself
She had spoken. He set his gaze firmly on Jupiter's
warnings, and hid his pain steadfastly in his heart.
He replied briefly at last: "O queen, I will never deny
that you deserve the most that can be spelt out in speech,
nor will I regret my thoughts of you, Elissa,
while memory itself is mine, and breath controls these limbs.

I'll speak about the reality a little. I did not expect to conceal
my departure by stealth (don't think that), nor have I ever
held the marriage torch, or entered into that pact.
If the fates had allowed me to live my life under my own
auspices, and attend to my own concerns as I wished,
I should first have cared for the city of Troy and the sweet relics
of my family, Priam's high roofs would remain, and I'd have
recreated Pergama, with my own hands, for the defeated.
But now it is Italy that Apollo of Grynium,
Italy, that the Lycian oracles, order me to take:
that is my desire, that is my country. Jupiter himself,
(I swear it on both our heads), has brought the command
on the swift breeze: I saw the god himself in broad daylight
enter the city and these very ears drank of his words.
Stop rousing yourself and me with your complaints.
I do not take course for Italy of my own free will."

*[Dido was overcome with grief and begged Aeneas to stay but he would not betray the
will of the gods. Aeneas and his companions ready the ships and depart. Heartbroken
and humiliated, Dido resolves to die. She begins making preparations for her death
and funeral, grieving the loss of Aeneas all the while.]*

BkIV:584-629 Dido's Curse
And now, at dawn, Aurora, leaving Tithonus's saffron bed,
was scattering fresh daylight over the earth.
As soon as the queen saw the day whiten, from her tower,
and the fleet sailing off under full canvas, and realised
the shore and harbour were empty of oarsmen, she
struck her lovely breast three or four times with her hand,
and tearing at her golden hair, said: "Ah, Jupiter, is he to leave,
is a foreigner to pour scorn on our kingdom? Shall my Tyrians
ready their armour, and follow them out of the city, and others drag
our ships from their docks? Go, bring fire quickly, hand out the
weapons, drive the oars! What am I saying? Where am I?
What madness twists my thoughts? Wretched Dido, is it now
that your impious actions hurt you? The right time was then,
when you gave him the crown. So this is the word and loyalty
of the man whom they say bears his father's gods around,
of the man who carried his age-worn father on his shoulders?

Couldn't I have seized hold of him, torn his body apart,

and scattered him on the waves? And put his friends to the sword,
and Ascanius even, to feast on, as a course at his father's table?
True the fortunes of war are uncertain. Let them be so:
as one about to die, whom had I to fear? I should have set fire
to his camp, filled the decks with flames, and extinguishing
father and son, and their whole race, given up my own life as well.
O Sun, you who illuminate all the works of this world,
and you Juno, interpreter and knower of all my pain,
and Hecate howled to, in cities, at midnight crossroads,
you, avenging Furies, and you, gods of dying Elissa,
acknowledge this, direct your righteous will to my troubles,
and hear my prayer. If it must be that the accursed one
should reach the harbour, and sail to the shore:
if Jove's destiny for him requires it, there his goal:
still, troubled in war by the armies of a proud race,
exiled from his territories, torn from Iulus's embrace,
let him beg help, and watch the shameful death of his people:
then, when he has surrendered, to a peace without justice,
may he not enjoy his kingdom or the days he longed for,
but let him die before his time, and lie unburied on the sand.

This I pray, these last words I pour out with my blood.
Then, O Tyrians, pursue my hatred against his whole line
and the race to come, and offer it as a tribute to my ashes.
Let there be no love or treaties between our peoples.
Rise, some unknown avenger, from my dust, who will pursue
the Trojan colonists with fire and sword, now, or in time
to come, whenever the strength is granted him.
I pray that shore be opposed to shore, water to wave,
weapon to weapon: let them fight, them and their descendants."

BkIV:630-705 The Death of Dido
Then Dido grew restless, wild with desperate purpose,
rolling her bloodshot eyes, her trembling cheeks
stained with red flushes, yet pallid at approaching death,
rushed into the house through its inner threshold, furiously
climbed the tall funeral pyre, and unsheathed
a Trojan sword, a gift that was never acquired to this end.
Then as she saw the Ilian clothing and the familiar couch,
she lingered a while, in tears and thought, then
cast herself on the bed, and spoke her last words:
"Reminders, sweet while fate and the god allowed it,
accept this soul, and loose me from my sorrows.
I have lived, and I have completed the course that Fortune granted,
and now my noble spirit will pass beneath the earth.
I have built a bright city: I have seen its battlements,
avenging a husband I have exacted punishment
on a hostile brother, happy, ah, happy indeed
if Trojan keels had never touched my shores!"
She spoke, and buried her face in the couch.
"I shall die un-avenged, but let me die," she cried.

"So, so I joy in travelling into the shadows.
Let the cruel Trojan's eyes drink in this fire, on the deep,
and bear with him the evil omen of my death."
She had spoken, and in the midst of these words,
her servants saw she had fallen on the blade,
the sword frothed with blood, and her hands were stained.

Augustus, *The Deeds of the Divine Augustus*, 14 CE

Reading and Discussion Questions
1. Define "dictator." According to Augustus, was he a dictator?
2. In your opinion, was Augustus a dictator?
3. What do you think Augustus was trying to achieve by writing this document?
4. What do you think of the accomplishments of Augustus? Explain.

Before Julius Caesar was assassinated, he named his nephew, Octavian, as his heir since he had no legitimate male children. But power did not pass easily to Octavian and Rome was plunged into a violent civil war between Octavian and Marc Antony, who had been Caesar's best friend. The civil war raged on for more than a decade until 27 BCE, when Octavian was victorious. After he assumed power in Rome, he changed his name from Octavian to Caesar Augustus. At the end of his life, he recorded the deeds for which he wanted to be remembered. They were inscribed on two bronze pillars in Rome, to be read by all Romans.

2. I drove the men who slaughtered my father [Caesar] into exile with a legal order, punishing their crime, and afterwards, when they waged war on the state, I conquered them in two battles.

3. I often waged war, civil and foreign, on the earth and sea, in the whole wide world, and as victor I spared all the citizens who sought pardon. As for foreign nations, those which I was able to safely forgive, I preferred to preserve than to destroy. About five hundred thousand Roman citizens were sworn to me. I led something more than three hundred thousand of them into colonies and I returned them to their cities, after their stipend had been earned, and I assigned all of them fields or gave them money for their military service. I captured six hundred ships in addition to those smaller than triremes.

5. When the dictatorship was offered to me, both in my presence and my absence, by the people and senate, I did not accept it.

9. The senate decreed that vows be undertaken for my health by the consuls and priests every fifth year. In fulfillment of these vows they often celebrated games for my life; several times the four highest colleges of priests, several times the consuls. Also both privately and as a city all the citizens unanimously and continuously prayed at all the shrines for my health.

10. By a senate decree my name was included in the Saliar Hymn, and it was sanctified by a law, both that I would be sacrosanct for ever. I was unwilling to be high priest in the place of my living colleague; when the people offered me that priesthood which my father had, I refused it.

67

15. I paid to the Roman plebs, HS 300 per man from my father's will and in my own name gave HS 400 from the spoils of war when I was consul for the fifth time (29 BCE); furthermore I again paid out a public gift of HS 400 per man, in my tenth consulate (24 BCE), from my own patrimony; and, when consul for the eleventh time (23 BCE), twelve doles of grain personally bought were measured out.

18. When the taxes fell short, I gave out contributions of grain and money from my granary and patrimony, sometimes to 100,000 men, sometimes to many more.

20. I rebuilt the Capitol and the theater of Pompey, each work at enormous cost, without any inscription of my name. I rebuilt aqueducts in many places that had decayed with age, and I doubled the capacity of the Marcian aqueduct by sending a new spring into its channel. I completed the Forum of Julius and the basilic which he built between the temple of Castor and the temple of Saturn, works begun and almost finished by my father. When the same basilica was burned with fire I expanded its grounds and I began it under an inscription of the name of my sons, and, if I should not complete it alive, I ordered it to be completed by my heirs. Consul for the sixth time (28 BCE), I rebuilt eighty-two temples of the gods in the city by the authority of the senate, omitting nothing which ought to have been rebuilt at that time. Consul for the seventh time (27 BCE), I rebuilt the Flaminian road from the city to Ariminum and all the bridges except the Mulvian and Minucian.

22. Three times I gave shows of gladiators under my name and five times under the name of my sons and grandsons; in these shows about 10,000 men fought. Twice I furnished under my name spectacles of athletes gathered from everywhere, and three times under my grandson's name. I celebrated games under my name four times, and furthermore in the place of other magistrates twenty-three times. Twenty-six times, under my name or that of my sons and grandsons, I gave the people hunts of African beasts in the circus, in the open, or in the amphitheater; in them about 3,500 beasts were killed.

23. I gave the people a spectacle of a naval battle, in the place across the Tiber where the grove of the Caesars is now, with the ground excavated in length 1,800 feet, in width 1,200, in which thirty beaked ships, biremes or triremes, but many smaller, fought among themselves; in these ships about 3,000 men fought in addition to the rowers.

24. Silver statues of me-on foot, on horseback, and standing in a chariot-were erected in about eighty cities, which I myself removed, and from the money I placed golden offerings in the temple of Apollo under my name and of those who paid the honor of the statues to me.

25. I restored peace to the sea from pirates. In that slave war I handed over to their masters for the infliction of punishments about 30,000 captured, who had fled their masters and taken up arms against the state. All Italy swore allegiance to me voluntarily, and demanded me as leader of the war which I won at Actium; the provinces of Gaul, Spain, Africa, Sicily, and Sardinia swore the same allegiance.

26. I extended the borders of all the provinces of the Roman people which neighbored nations not subject to our rule. I restored peace to the provinces of Gaul and Spain,

likewise Germany, which includes the ocean from Cadiz to the mouth of the river Elbe. I brought peace to the Alps from the region which is near the Adriatic Sea to the Tuscan, with no unjust war waged against any nation.

27. I added Egypt to the rule of the Roman people.

28. I founded colonies of soldiers in Africa, Sicily, Macedonia, each Spain, Greece, Asia, Syria, Narbonian Gaul, and Pisidia, and furthermore had twenty-eight colonies founded in Italy under my authority, which were very populous and crowded while I lived.

34. In my sixth and seventh consulates (28-27 BCE), after putting out the civil war, having obtained all things by universal consent, I handed over the state from my power to the dominion of the senate and Roman people. And for this merit of mine, by a senate decree, I was called Augustus. After that time, I exceeded all in influence, but I had no greater power than the others who were colleagues with me in each magistracy.

35. When I administered my thirteenth consulate (2 BCE), the senate and Equestrian order and Roman people all called me father of the country, and voted that the same be inscribed in the vestibule of my temple, in the Julian senate-house, and in the forum of Augustus.

Tacitus, On Augustus, *The Annals*, 66 CE

Reading and Discussion Questions
1. According to Tacitus, was Augustus a dictator? Why or why not?
2. How does Tacitus' description of Augustus compare with the way Augustus describes himself?

Tacitus was a Roman senator and historian whose two major works were Annals *and* Histories. *In both works he tried to record the details of the reign of Roman emperors after Augustus. He began* Annals, *however, with his perspective on the events of Augustus' reign.*

Rome at the outset was a city state under the government of kings: liberty and the consulate were institutions of Lucius Brutus. Dictatorships were always a temporary expedient. Augustus, who, under the style of "Prince," gathered beneath his empire a world outworn by civil broils. But, while the glories and disasters of the old Roman commonwealth have been chronicled by famous pens, and intellects of distinction were not lacking to tell the tale of the Augustan age, until the rising tide of *sycophancy* deterred them, the histories of [Augustus and his heirs], were falsified through cowardice while they flourished, and composed, when they fell, under the influence of still rankling hatreds. Hence my design, to treat a small part (the concluding one) of Augustus' reign without anger and without partiality.

When the killing of Brutus and Cassius had disarmed the Republic; when Pompey had been crushed in Sicily, and, with Lepidus thrown aside and Antony slain, even the Julian party was leaderless but for the Caesar; after laying down his triumviral title and proclaiming himself a simple consul content with tribunician authority to safeguard the commons, he first won over the armies with riches, the people by cheapened corn, the world by the promises of peace, then step by step began to make his ascent and to unite in his own person the functions of the senate, the magistracy, and the legislature. Opposition there was none: the boldest spirits had succumbed on stricken fields or by proscription-lists; while the rest of the nobility found a cheerful acceptance of slavery the smoothest road to wealth and office, and, as they had thriven on revolution, stood now for the new order and safety in preference to the old order and adventure. Nor was the state of affairs unpopular in the provinces, where administration by the Senate and People had been discredited by the feuds of the magnates and the greed of the officials, against which there was but frail protection in a legal system for ever deranged by force, by favoritism, or (in the last resort) by gold.

It was thus an altered world, and of the old, unspoilt Roman character not a trace lingered. Equality was an outworn creed, and all eyes looked to the mandate of the sovereign — with no immediate misgivings, so long as Augustus in the full vigour of his prime upheld himself, his house, and peace.

Seneca, *What is the Principal Thing In Life?*, 50 CE

Reading and Discussion Questions
1. What is Seneca's opinion of rulers and conquerors like Alexander the Great?
2. What is the key to a happy life, according to Seneca?
3. Do you agree or disagree with his ideas for a happy life? Explain.

Lucius Annaeus Seneca was a Roman philosopher and statesman during the early Roman Republic. He was a Stoic philosopher. Stoics believed that negative emotions were responsible for bad judgment and emphasized trying to live a life in harmony with nature. Seneca wrote several books and hundreds of essays or letters called Epistolae, in which he contemplated questions like "What is a life well lived?" He was forced to commit suicide by the emperor Nero for supposedly conspiring in an assassination plot against the emperor. Below is an excerpt from Seneca's writings in which he analyzed how we should live our lives meaningfully.

Some writers have wasted their efforts in narrating the doings of foreign kings, and in telling, as the case may be, the sufferings or the cruelties of nations. Surely it is wiser to try to end ones own ills than to record for a coming generation the ills of others. How much better to make one theme the works of the gods than the robberies of Philip, or Alexander, or the other conquerors who earned their fame by the destruction of mankind ! Such men were as truly scourges of humanity as a flood by which a whole plain has been inundated, or a conflagration by which the greater part of its living creatures has been burnt up.

How much better is it to inquire what ought to be done than what has been done, and to teach those who have entrusted their state to fortune that nothing she gives is stable, but that all her gifts are more fickle than the very air ! For she cannot rest, her delight is to match sadness with joy, and to mingle smiles with tears. Therefore in the day of prosperity let no man exult, in the day of adversity let no man faint : the successions of fortune alternate. Why should you boast yourself? The wave meantime bears you aloft on its crest ; but where it may strand you, you cannot tell. Its end will be of its own

70

choice, not of yours. Or why, again, do you despond ? You have been carried down to the nadir ; now is the chance of rising again. Adversity alters for the better, success for the worse.

What, I ask, then, is the principal thing in human life ? Not to have filled the seas with fleets, nor to have planted the standard of the nation on the shores of the Red Sea, nor, when land has been exhausted, to have wandered for the injury of others over the Ocean in quest of the unknown. Rather it is to have grasped in mind the whole universe, and to have gained what is the greatest of all victories, the mastery over besetting sins. There are hosts of conquerors who have had cities and nations under their power, but a very few who have subdued self. What is the principal thing ? I say again. To raise the soul above the threats and promises of fortune ; to consider nothing as worth hoping for. What is the principal thing ? To be able to endure adversity with joyful heart ; to bear whatever betide just as if it were the very thing you desired to happen. For you would have felt it your duty to desire it, had you known that all things happen by God s decree.

Tears, complaints, lamentation, are rebellion. What is the principal thing ? A heart in face of calamity resolute and invincible ; an adversary, yea, a sworn foe, to luxury ; neither anxious to meet nor anxious to shun peril ; a heart that knows how to fashion fortune to its will without waiting for her ; which can go forth to face ill or good dauntless and unembarrassed, paralyzed neither by the tumult of the one nor the glamour of the other. What is the principal thing ? Not to admit evil counsel into the heart, and to lift up clean hands to heaven ; to seek for no advantage which some one must give and some one lose in order that it may reach you ; to pray a prayer that no one will envy for purity of heart ; as for other blessings which are highly esteemed by the world, even should some chance bring them to your home, to regard them as sure to depart by the same door by which they entered.

What is the principal thing ? To lift ones courage high above all that depends upon chance ; to remember what man is, so that whether you be fortunate, you may know that this will not be for long ; or whether you be unfortunate, you may be sure you are not so if you do not think yourself so.

The principal thing is to have life on the very lips, ready to issue when summoned. This makes a man free, not by right of Roman citizenship, but by right of nature. He is the true freeman who has escaped from bondage to self. That slavery is constant, from it there is no deliverance ; it presses us day and night alike, without pause, without respite. To be a slave to self is the most grievous kind of slavery ; yet its fetters may easily be struck off, if you will but cease to make large demands upon yourself, if you will cease to seek a personal reward for your services, and if you will set clearly before you your nature and your time of life, even though it be the bloom of youth ; if you will say to yourself, Why do I rave, and pant, and sweat ? Why do I ply the earth ? why do I haunt the forum ? Man needs but little, nor needs that little long.

Seneca, On Gladiators, 50 CE

<u>Reading and Discussion Questions</u>
1. Do the gladiatorial games contribute to or take away from the pursuit of a happy life, according to Seneca?
2. Do you think gladiatorial games contributed to or took away from the pursuit of happiness for the Romans?

The spectacle of gladiatorial combat was initiated by wealthy Romans over 250 years before the birth of Christ as a part of the ceremonies held to honor their deceased relatives. Later, these games became separate events sponsored by Rome's leading citizens in order to enhance their prestige. With the decline of the Republic and the rise of the Empire, gladiator games were appropriated by the emperor. The primary purpose of these life-or-death duels was to entertain the multitude of spectators that jammed the arena.

The Roman philosopher Seneca took a dim view of gladiatorial contests and the spectacle that accompanied them. Interestingly, his criticism is not based on revulsion at the butchery he witnesses, but because the display is boring and therefore unworthy of the attention of a well-reasoned man. In a letter to a friend, he describes what he saw in the arena during the reign of Emperor Caligula:

There is nothing so ruinous to good character as to idle away one's time at some spectacle. Vices have a way of creeping in because of the feeling of pleasure that it brings. Why do you think that I say that I personally return from shows greedier, more ambitious and more given to luxury, and I might add, with thoughts of greater cruelty and less humanity, simply because I have been among humans?

The other day, I chanced to drop in at the midday games, expecting sport and wit and some relaxation to rest men's eyes from the sight of human blood. Just the opposite was the case. Any fighting before that was as nothing; all trifles were now put aside - it was plain butchery.
The men had nothing with which to protect themselves, for their whole bodies were open to the thrust, and every thrust told. The common people prefer this to matches on level terms or request performances. Of course they do. The blade is not parried by helmet or shield, and what use is skill or defense? All these merely postpone death.

In the morning men are thrown to bears or lions, at midday to those who were previously watching them. The crowd cries for the killers to be paired with those who will kill them, and reserves the victor for yet another death. This is the only release the gladiators have. The whole business needs fire and steel to urge men on to fight. There was no escape for them. The slayer was kept fighting until he could be slain.

'Kill him! Flog him! Burn him alive!' (the spectators roared) 'Why is he such a coward? Why won't he rush on the steel? Why does he fall so meekly? Why won't he die willingly?" Do not, my Lucilius, attend the games, I pray you. Either you will be corrupted by the multitude, or, if you show disgust, be hated by them. So stay away."

72

Marcus Aurelius, *The Meditations*, 167 CE

Reading and Discussion Questions
1. What is Aurelius' opinion of how to live a good life?
2. What arguments does Aurelius offer to help people accept death? How persuasive do you find them?
3. How does his philosophy emphasize the independence of the individual? Does this emphasis on the individual result in selfishness?

The emperor Marcus Aelius Aurelius Antoninus was the ruler of the Roman Empire from 161-180 CE. His death marked the end of the peaceful and prosperous period in Rome called the Pax Romana. After Aurelius' death, Rome was ruled by one tyrant after another until its final collapse in 476 CE. As Emperor, Aurelius was often at war with the neighboring Germanic tribes but he was also a social reformer who worked for the improvement of the lives of the poor, slaves, and convicted criminals. He was a fierce opponent of Christianity, because he felt that the religion threatened the values that had made Rome great. Aurelius was not entirely original in his ideas and his Meditations were most likely a journal never meant for publication. But his writings reflect well the ideas of Stoicism, a life philosophy prevalent in both Greece and Rome. Stoics believed that with wisdom and understanding came a release from suffering and fear. The possession of virtue was the ideal kind of happiness to Stoics.

Book Four:

Men seek retreats for themselves, houses in the country, at the seashore, and in the mountains; and you tend to desire such things very much. But this is a characteristic of the most common sort of men, for it is in your power whenever you will to choose to retreat into yourself. For nowhere either with more quiet or more freedom from trouble does a man retreat than into his own soul, particularly when he has within him such thoughts that by looking into them he is immediately perfectly tranquil; and I affirm that tranquility is nothing other than the proper ordering of the mind.

Do not act as if you were going to live ten thousand years. Death hangs over you. While you live, while it is in your power, be good.

How much trouble he avoids who does not look to see what his neighbor says or does or thinks, but only to what he does himself, that it may be just and pure; or as Agathon says, do not consider the depraved morals of others, but cling to the straight and narrow path without deviating from it.

He who has a powerful desire for posthumous fame does not consider that every one of those who remember him will himself also die very soon; then again also they who have succeeded them, until the whole remembrance shall have been extinguished as it is transmitted through men who foolishly admire and then perish. But suppose that those who will remember are even immortal, and that the remembrance will be immortal, what good will this do you?

Constantly regard the universe as one living being, having one substance and one soul; and observe how all things have reference to one perception, the perception of this one

73

living being; and how all things act with one movement; and how all things are the cooperating causes of all things which exist; observe too the continuous spinning of the thread and the structure of the web.

You are a little soul carrying about a corpse, as Epictetus used to say. Time is like a river made up of the events which happen, and a violent stream; for as soon as a thing has been seen, it is carried away, and another comes in its place, and this will be carried away too.

Think continually how many physicians are dead after often fretting over the sick; and how many astrologers after predicting with great pretensions the deaths of others; and how many philosophers after endless discourses on death or immortality; how many heroes after killing thousands; and how many tyrants who have used their power over men's lives with terrible insolence as if they were immortal; and how many cities are entirely dead, so to speak, Helice and Pompeii and Herculaneum, and innumerable others. Add to the total all whom you have known, one after another. One man after burying another has been laid out dead, and another buries him: and all this in a short time. To conclude, always observe how ephemeral and worthless human things are, and what was yesterday a little mucus to-morrow will be a mummy or ashes. Pass then through this little space of time in the way of nature, and end your journey in contentment, just as an olive falls off when it is ripe, blessing nature who produced it, and thanking the tree on which it grew.

Be like the cliff against which the waves continually break, but which stands firm and tames the fury of the water around it.

Book Five:
The best way of avenging yourself is not to become like the wrongdoer.

Most of the things which ordinary people admire have to do with objects of the most general kind, those which are held together by cohesion or natural organization, such as stones, wood, fig trees, vines, olives. But those which are admired by men who are a little more reasonable have to do with the things which are held together by a living principle, such as flocks and herds. Those which are admired by men who are still more enlightened are the things which are held together by a rational soul, not however a universal soul, but rational so far as it is a soul skilled in some art, or expert in some other way, or simply rational so far as it possesses a number of slaves. But he who values a rational soul, a universal soul which is fitted for political life, values nothing else except this; and above all things he keeps his soul in a condition and in activities suitable to reason and social life, and he cooperates in this with those who are of the same kind as himself.

So keep yourself simple, good, pure, serious, free from pretense, a friend of justice, a worshipper of the gods, kind, affectionate, strenuous in performing all proper acts. Strive to be the sort of person which philosophy wishes to make of you. Revere the gods and help others. Life is short. There is only one fruit of this earthly life: a pious disposition and social acts.

He who has seen present things has seen all, both everything which has taken place from all eternity and everything which will be for time without end; for all things are of one kin and of one form.

74

Ammianus Marcellinus, Luxury of the Rich in Rome, *400 CE*

Reading and Discussion Questions
1. What does the author say Romans valued most about during the time he was writing?
2. What were things that Romans valued earlier in their history, according to this passage?
3. What can you learn about the decline and fall of the Roman Empire from this passage? Be able to discuss at least three things.

The following account of the problems in the Roman Empire was written only about a generation before the Visigoth king Alaric plundered Rome in 410 CE. The historian Ammianus Marcellinus observed Rome on a visit and saw the city as full of emptiness, shallowness, and as lacking of any real culture.

Rome is still looked upon as the queen of the earth, and the name of the Roman people is respected and venerated. But the magnificence of Rome is defaced by the inconsiderate levity of a few, who never recollect where they are born, but fall away into error and licentiousness as if a perfect immunity were granted to vice. Of these men, some, thinking that they can be handed down to immortality by means of statues, are eager after them, as if they would obtain a higher reward from brazen figures unendowed with sense than from a consciousness of upright and honorable actions; and they are even anxious to have them plated over with gold!

Others place the summit of glory in having a couch higher than usual, or splendid apparel; and so toil and sweat under a vast burden of cloaks which are fastened to their necks by many clasps, and blow about by the excessive fineness of the material, showing a desire by the continual wriggling of their bodies, and especially by the waving of the left hand, to make more conspicuous their long fringes and tunics, which are embroidered in multiform figures of animals with threads of divers colors.

Others again, put on a feigned severity of countenance, and extol their patrimonial estates in a boundless degree, exaggerating the yearly produce of their fruitful fields, which they boast of possessing in numbers, from east and west, being forsooth ignorant that their ancestors, who won greatness for Rome, were not eminent in riches; but through many a direful war overpowered their foes by valor, though little above the common privates in riches, or luxury, or costliness of garments.

Those few mansions which were once celebrated for the serious cultivation of liberal studies, now are filled with ridiculous amusements of torpid indolence, reechoing with the sound of singing, and the tinkle of flutes and lyres. You find a singer instead of a philosopher; a teacher of silly arts is summoned in place of an orator, the libraries are shut up like tombs, organs played by waterpower are built, and lyres so big that they look like wagons! and flutes, and huge machines suitable for the theater. The Romans have even sunk so far, that not long ago, when a dearth was apprehended, and the foreigners were driven from the city, those who practiced liberal accomplishments were expelled instantly, yet the followers of actresses and all their ilk were suffered to stay; and three thousand dancing girls were not even questioned, but remained unmolested along with the members of their choruses, and a corresponding number of dancing masters.

On account of the frequency of epidemics in Rome, rich men take absurd precautions to avoid contagion, but even when these rules are observed thus stringently, some persons, if they be invited to a wedding, though the vigor of their limbs be vastly diminished, yet when gold is pressed in their palm they will go with all activity as far as Spoletum! So much for the nobles. As for the lower and poorer classes some spend the whole night in the wine shops, some lie concealed in the shady arcades of the theaters. They play at dice so eagerly as to quarrel over them, snuffing up their nostrils, and making unseemly noises by drawing back their breath into their noses;---or (and this is their favorite amusement by far) from sunrise till evening, through sunshine or rain, they stay gaping and examining the charioteers and their horses; and their good and bad qualities. Wonderful indeed it is to see an innumerable multitude of people, with prodigious eagerness, intent upon the events of the chariot race!

Ammianus Marcellinus, Description of the Huns, 415 CE

Reading and Discussion Questions
   1. Who are the Huns?
   2. Describe their lifestyle. How do they eat? Sleep? Work? Fight?
   3. What can you learn about how the Huns led to Rome's collapse, from this reading?

The historian Ammianus Marcellinus chronicled the life of the rich in Rome, Roman lifestyle and the collapse of the Roman Empire. In the reading below, Marcellinus wrote about the Huns, a savage tribe of Asian nomads who were one of the primary causes of Rome's final collapse.

The people called Huns, slightly mentioned in the ancient records, live beyond the Sea of Azov, on the border of the Frozen Ocean, and are a race savage beyond all parallel.

At the very moment of their birth the cheeks of their infant children are deeply marked by an iron, in order that the usual vigor of their hair, instead of growing at the proper season, may be withered by the wrinkled scars; and accordingly they grow up without beards, and consequently without any beauty, like eunuchs, though they all have closely knit and strong limbs and plump necks; they are of great size, and bow-legged, so that you might fancy them two-legged beasts, or the stout figures which are hewn out in a rude manner with an axe on the posts at the end of bridges.

They are certainly in the shape of men, however uncouth, but are so hardy that they neither require fire nor well-flavored food, but live on the roots of such herbs as they get in the fields, or on the half-raw flesh of any animal, which they merely warm rapidly by placing in between their own thighs and the back of their horses.

They never shelter themselves under roofed houses, but avoid them. Nor is there even to be found among them a cabin thatched with reed; but they wander about, roaming over the mountains and the woods, and accustom themselves to bear frost and hunger and thirst from their very cradles. And even when abroad they never enter a house

76

unless under the compulsion of some extreme necessity; nor, indeed, do they think people under roofs as safe as others.

They wear linen clothes, or else garments made of the skins of field-mice; nor do they wear a different dress out of doors from that which they wear at home; but after a tunic is once put round their necks, however much it becomes worn, it is never taken off or changed till, from long decay, it becomes actually so ragged as to fall to pieces.

They are nearly always on horseback, their horses being ill-shaped, but hardy; and sometimes they even sit upon them like women if they want to do anything more conveniently. There is not a person in the whole nation who cannot remain on his horse day and night. On horseback they buy and sell, they take their meat and drink, and there they recline on the narrow neck of their steed, and yield to sleep so deep as to indulge in every variety of dream.

And when any deliberation is to take place on any weighty matter, they all hold their common council on horseback. They are not under the authority of a king, but are contented with the irregular government of their nobles, and under their lead they force their way through all obstacles.

Sometimes, when provoked, they fight; and when they go into battle, they form in a solid body, and utter all kinds of terrific yells. They are very quick in their operations, of exceeding speed, and fond of surprising their enemies. With a view to this, they suddenly disperse, then reunite, and again, after having inflicted vast loss upon the enemy, scatter themselves over the whole plain in irregular formations; always avoiding the fort or an entrenchment.

And in one respect you may pronounce them the most formidable of all warriors, for when at a distance they use missiles of various kinds, tipped with sharpened bones instead of the usual points of javelins, and these bones are admirably fastened into the shaft of the javelin or arrow; but when they are at close quarters they fight with the sword, without any regard for their own safety; and often while their antagonists are warding off their blows they entangle them with twisted cords, so that, their hands being fettered, they lose all power of either riding or walking.

None of them plough, or even touch a plough handle; for they have no settled abode, but are homeless and lawless, perpetually wandering with their wagons, which they make their homes; in fact, they seem to be people always in flight. Their wives live in these wagons, and there weave their miserable garments; and here, too, they sleep with their husbands, and bring up their children till they reach the age of puberty; nor, if asked, can any one of them tell you where he was born, as he was conceived in one place, born in another at a great distance, and brought up in another still more remote.

In truces they are treacherous and inconstant, being liable to change their minds at every breeze of every fresh hope which presents itself, giving themselves up wholly to the impulse and inclination of the moment; and, like brute beasts, they are utterly ignorant of the distinction between right and wrong. They express themselves with great ambiguity and obscurity; have no respect for any religion or superstition whatever; are immoderately covetous of gold; and are so fickle and irascible that they very often, on the same day that they quarrel with their companions without any provocation, again become reconciled to them without any mediator.

77

In this way, through the turbulent zeal of violent people, the ruin of the Roman Empire was brought on. This, at all events, is neither obscure nor uncertain that the unhappy officers who were entrusted with the charge of conducting the multitude of the barbarians across the river, though they repeatedly endeavored to calculate their numbers, at last abandoned the attempt as hopeless; and the man who would wish to ascertain the number might as well - as the most illustrious of poets says - attempt to count the waves in the African Sea, or the grains of sand tossed about by the zephyrs.

PART TWO—
MEDIEVAL METAMORPHOSIS

The era between the fall of Rome and the rise of the Renaissance is called the Middle Ages because it was in between, or in the middle of, two great eras. But there were three distinct periods of that era that all had distinct characteristics. The first period, known as the Early Middle Ages or the Dark Ages, was the period between 500 and 1000 CE when Rome had collapsed, the ancient world had ended and Europe was consumed by ignorance, fear and death. This period in Western Europe is considered one of the bleakest in history. Only one other time, during the Greek Dark Ages, did civilization seem to stagnate so completely. The second period is known as the High Middle Ages and it lasted from 1000 to 1300 CE. This was a period where life stabilized in much of Europe, as law, order and even some degree of education returned. It was also the period of the Crusades, however, which increased global conflict substantially. Finally came the Late Middle Ages from 1300 to 1500. This was a period of crisis and also rebirth. Plague and war devastated the population during this era but the people of Europe rebounded from tragedy with a renewed will to live and to live well.

Many people wrongly assume that the Middle Ages was all gloom and doom and stagnation. But I like to think of the Middle Ages as a period of metamorphosis, much like the period when a caterpillar withdraws into his cocoon. No immediately visible change is happening but in the seeming stillness, a complete transformation is underway. Just as a caterpillar is not immediately remade into a butterfly, so too the greatness of Rome was not immediately remade into the Renaissance. This often underestimated period of evolution and painful reinvention happened during the Middle Ages.

CHAPTER 3—
THE EARLY MIDDLE AGES (500 to 1000 CE)

GUIDING QUESTIONS

- How "dark" were the Dark Ages? In what ways were they dark?
- How did the Christian Church achieve almost total control of its subjects during this period?
- Why was Islam an attractive alternative to some Christians during this time?
- How did the Viking invasions impact the future of Europe?
- How did feudalism lead to a new civilization in Europe?
- What were the four influences, groups or institutions that created the new culture of Medieval Europe?

In 476 CE, the Roman Empire lay in ashes and Western Europe was overrun by Germanic tribes whom the Romans has simply called "barbarians." Though the tribes of Germania were considered uncivilized or barbaric by the Greeks and Romans, they each had a distinct culture, language and religion that would help reshape Western Europe. As the twelve major tribes and dozens of lesser tribes of Germania sought refuge from the Huns, they settled all over Europe and north Africa. Many of the places they settled would later bare their names. Tribes called the Finns, the Swedes, the Norse and the Franks brought their names to places we now know as Finland, Sweden, Norway and France. The people who the Romans considered barbarians became the fathers of all the nations of Europe.

By 500 CE, Europe was transforming into something new, though for the people living then it must have felt much more like an end than a beginning. Education, law and order, trade and other institutions that are central to the notion of being "civilized" had disappeared. But new ways of life were slowly emerging. Roman traditions were being replaced by or intermingled with traditions of Germanic peoples. And the Christian Church sought to fill the void left after Rome's collapse by becoming both a religious and a political super-power. For the next five hundred years, the Christian Church tried to ensure, and nearly succeeded in ensuring, that the only thought in Europe was Christian thought, the only law was Christian law and the only government was a Christian government.

Civilization in Western Europe collapsed almost completely after 476 CE but it is important to realize that this collapse was not a global one. Nor did the stagnation consume all of what had been the Roman Empire. In an attempt to bolster the failing empire, Rome was divided into two parts in 395 CE, with the hope that if Rome had two emperors and two sets of governments, stability might be returned to the realm. The empire was divided into eastern and western regions. The Eastern Roman Empire was known as the Byzantine Empire and had its capital in Constantinople. The Western Roman Empire was still ruled from Rome. The split did provide some protection to Rome's legacy in the long run because only the Western Roman Empire fell prey to barbarian invasions in the 300s and 400s CE. The Byzantine Empire survived nearly a thousand years longer than the Western Roman Empire and as a result, much of the culture of Rome and also of ancient Greece was preserved for the future in great Byzantine cities like Constantinople and Alexandria.

During the first 100 years of the Dark Ages or early Middle Ages, it seemed that the power of the Christian Church was unstoppable. Most of the "barbarian tribes" of Germania converted to Christianity either willingly or "by the sword." Many tribes adopted Christianity as their official religion by 600 CE. Church leaders convened countless meetings to create a Christian government along the lines of Roman government before the collapse. They deliberately and carefully planned how the church could also become the state. Clergymen were assigned specific jurisdictions, or regions of control. In the same way that a mayor ruled over a town or a governor ruled over a state or province, Christian bishops were given large territories called dioceses, while priests were given smaller jurisdictions called parishes. In 590 CE, the pope even declared that he had his own empire called Christendom, which was a borderless kingdom of all Christians. This meant that wherever in the world there was a Christian, the Church had power. The creation of Christendom marked the beginning of the politicization of the Christian Church that would dominate Western history into the modern era.

During the Early Middle Ages, the church took over every aspect of life for Medieval Europeans. Towns were physically built with a very large church in the center and the church building served as meeting hall, school and social gathering place. It also served as the courthouse and the clergy served as judges. The Roman system of law and order was replaced by a new Christian justice system, based on the belief that God would spare the innocent and punish the guilty. One of the more bizarre practices of the Middle Ages was the practice of "trial by ordeal," where a person accused of a crime (usually against the church) would be forced to undergo a physical ordeal or torture to determine his innocence or guilt. A simple example of trial by ordeal was holding an accused person's hand over a candle flame. If the person's flesh burned, they were found guilty of their crime because God did not protect them from harm. If their flesh did not burn, they were deemed innocent because they had received God's protection. You might imagine that almost every person accused of a crime was found guilty under these circumstances. Trial by ordeal was a very effective tool in ensuring obedience among Medieval Christians but it was not the only tool at the disposal of church officials.

In order to further ensure that clergy had all the power that government officials in other eras had enjoyed, they were given three unchallengeable tools to rule over Europeans in the Middle Ages. The first tool the church used was excommunication, which was to be expelled from the Christian community. If you were excommunicated, it meant that God no longer recognized you as a Christian soul and you therefore had no chance of going to Heaven. Priests and other clergy actively exercised the power of excommunication. Clergymen also had the power to issue interdicts, which were mass excommunications. These were most often used to persuade a leader of a town to submit to church authority by threatening to not only excommunicate the leader but his entire community. Finally, the church had the power of Papal Infallibility, which meant that the authority and the word of clergy was unchallengeable. Clergymen were viewed during this era as the direct spokesmen for God and consequently, their word was as good as divine law. The tool of papal infallibility was grossly abused by corrupt clergy who took advantage of their immense power to pursue selfish and often very un-Christian motives. With these tools in hand and a very organized government-like structure in place, the religion that was only a small sect during most of the Roman Empire seemed poised to dominate the world by 600 CE. That is, until the new religion of Islam was founded in Arabia by 622 CE by a man named Muhammad, which shook the Christian establishment to its core.

In the beginning, Islam was not seen as so different from Christianity. It was also an Abrahamic religion that believed in the Old Testament and Jesus as a prophet. Islam and Christianity shared many of the same basic beliefs. And yet Islam promised a simpler path to salvation through the Five Pillars in a time when the path to Heaven through Christianity was increasingly unclear in the minds of many western Christians. As a result, Islam became a powerful rival to Christianity, both politically and spiritually. Within 100 years of its founding, Islam had become the dominant religion throughout the Middle East, northern Africa and Spain and was threatening Christian supremacy as far into Europe as France. Christians and Muslims had their first military clash in France in 732 CE. This clash was known as the Battle of Tours and it foreshadowed much more deadly confrontations to come in the Crusades (1095-1290 CE), which resulted in the deaths of between 9 and 12 million people over 200 years. Much of the history of the Middle Ages is really the story of the battle for souls between these two faiths.

Islam was not the only challenge Christian Europeans faced in the 8th and 9th centuries, however. In 800 CE, a new group of fearsome raiders from Scandinavia threatened the stability in Europe once more. The Vikings, as they were known, were exploring, invading and colonizing territory across Europe and as far west as Minnesota in the United States by the end of the 8th century and would not be stopped for 200 years. It was a Viking named Leif Erikson, and not Christopher Columbus, who was the first European to discover the Americas and Erikson did it more than 500 years before Columbus. Makes you rethink the purpose of Columbus day, huh?

The Vikings were known for their terrifying style of attack but also for their advanced seafaring technology, the centerpiece of which was their longboat. Viking longboats could sail across vast oceans but could also navigate up the shallowest rivers, making the Vikings among history's greatest nautical engineers. Like the Huns before them, Viking raids became the stuff of legend. But unlike the Huns, who caused people to disperse and live far distances apart from each other, Viking invasions actually caused people to come back together. Some consider the Vikings the "saviors of western civilization" because, by seeking safety in numbers, the people of Western Europe created a system of defense that would be the basis of the new society in Europe--Feudalism.

Feudalism, though often thought of as an accidental and random response to Viking brutality, may have actually been the creation of one man named Charlemagne. Charlemagne was a great conqueror, a great administrator and a great ruler. But even great rulers need methods for winning powerful subjects to their favor. Charlemagne, and his line of French kings, called Carolingians, began a practice of giving land in exchange for political support. This exchange of land became known as Feudalism. In around 800 CE, Charlemagne was able to create the first stable and unified kingdom in Europe. Like Justinian before him, Charlemagne dreamed of reviving the greatness of the Roman Empire. He so closely modeled his kingdom after Rome that he called it the Holy Roman Empire. He tried to copy Roman building styles, organized his kingdom based on the Roman model and thought of himself as one of the long line of Roman emperors. The only difference was that Charlemagne's was a purely and strictly Christian empire, though he himself did not always lead with a perfect Christian example.   Later historians would observe about the kingdom he created that "it was neither holy, nor Roman, nor an empire." It was, however, the first attempts of western Europeans at civilized life after Rome.

The feudal system which was influenced by Charlemagne became the arena in which we witness great strides in philosophy, commerce, education, literature, and politics. This is the world of knights and ladies, popes and emperors, lords and vassals, and other important players on the Medieval stage. The Medieval town or manor was where these dramas originated but by later in the Middle Ages, great castles and chateaus became the ornate stages for Medieval life. Many of these great castles and impenetrable walled cities of Europe still stand today.

So what was "Dark" about the Dark Ages? The darkness of this period was not a physical darkness but an intellectual darkness. Much of the work of Greece and Rome was destroyed during the waves of barbarian invasions.   And even more was confiscated by the Christian church. As we have discussed, the Christian Church during this era had one singular mission which was to make the world Christian. Non-Christian thought, including science and philosophy, was considered an impediment to this goal. Consequently, the works of Plato, Archimedes, Hippocrates and countless other ancient geniuses simply disappeared. Immediately after the fall of Rome, people still whispered of the works of the ancients, but after a few generations, the memory of Greek and Roman wisdom was erased almost completely.   Ancient ideas were replaced by the ideas of one well-meaning Christian monk named St. Augustine, whose writings would define European life for a thousand years.

Augustine of Hippo was a Roman Christian monk who wrote a book called *The City of God* in 410 CE. During that time, Rome was in the midst of the Barbarian Invasions, and life was scary. Augustine tried to comfort Christians who were being blamed for Rome's collapse. He shifted the blame to pagan Romans, arguing that their immoral lives and their focus on earthly pleasures was the cause of Rome's troubles. He said that men sometimes have to choose between earthly and heavenly happiness and that too much happiness on earth, the City of Man, could decrease one's chances of eternal happiness in Heaven, the City of God. He urged Christians to accept that there may be suffering on earth and to know their reward awaits them after their death. Augustine's writings were misinterpreted, as most Europeans were illiterate during the Middle Ages and learned of Augustine's writings through word-of-mouth. They accepted as truth the misrepresentation of what Augustine wrote by clergy who either distorted his writings for their own advantage or wrongly retold the story the way it had been inaccurately told to them. People believed that Augustine said Christians *must* suffer, instead of Christians *may* suffer, during their earthly lives. It was also accepted as true that any pleasure on earth was a sin that would be judged after death. The catastrophic result of this misinformation was that Christians were paralyzed by fear. They shunned pleasure, free-thinking and self-expression. Religion and life-after-death consumed Medieval Christian life. Consequently, there was virtually no progress, education or ingenuity for more than 500 years. The Augustinian view taught that focus on self meant taking focus away from God and was therefore a sin.   Most Europeans during the early Middle Ages lacked the education to ever question this point of view and even those few who might have questioned it dared not speak up. Through the exercise of powerful tools and a new worldview, the Christian Church had quite literally put the fear of God in people so completely that the darkness of ignorance and blind obedience enslaved Europeans for five centuries.

PRIMARY SOURCES—EARLY MIDDLE AGES

Tacitus, *Germania*, 98 CE

Reading and Discussion Questions
1. Define "barbarian."
2. Based on your reading, were the Germanic people "barbarians?"
3. What criticisms do you find about Rome in this reading?
4. What do you think Tacitus' opinion of the Germanic people is? Explain.
5. How do you think Tacitus would compare Romans to the Germanic tribes?

Just beyond the borders of the Roman Empire was a region called Germania. During all of Rome's history, the mighty Roman army was never able to conquer Germania, in which there were dozens of distinct Germanic tribes. Because those tribes did not speak Latin like the Romans and because they had different customs and lifestyles, the Romans called the Germanic people "barbarians." Tacitus, an important Roman historian, wrote the most detailed early description of the Germanic tribes at the end of the first century CE. He also provides a useful sketch of Roman culture and its strengths and weaknesses, during his lifetime.

Physical Characteristics.
For my own part, I agree with those who think that the tribes of Germany are free from all taint of intermarriages with foreign nations, and that they appear as a distinct, unmixed race, like none but themselves. Hence, too, the same physical peculiarities throughout so vast a population. All have fierce blue eyes, red hair, huge frames, fit only for a sudden exertion. They are less able to bear laborious work. Heat and thirst they cannot in the least endure; to cold and hunger their climate and their soil inure them.

Government. Influence of Women.
They choose their kings by birth, their generals for merit. These kings have not unlimited or arbitrary power, and the generals do more by example than by authority. If they are energetic, if they are conspicuous, if they fight in the front, they lead because they are admired. But to reprimand, to imprison, even to flog, is permitted to the priests alone, and that not as a punishment, or at the general's bidding, but, as it were, by the mandate of the god whom they believe to inspire the warrior. They also carry with them into battle certain figures and images taken from their sacred groves. And what most stimulates their courage is, that their squadrons or battalions, instead of being formed by chance or by a fortuitous gathering, are composed of families and clans. Close by them, too, are those dearest to them, so that they hear the shrieks of women, the cries of infants. They are to every man the most sacred witnesses of his bravery-they are his most generous applauders. The soldier brings his wounds to mother and wife, who shrink not from counting or even demanding them and who administer food and encouragement to the combatants.

Punishments. Administration of Justice.
In their councils an accusation may be preferred or a capital crime prosecuted. Penalties are distinguished according to the offense. Traitors and deserters are hanged on trees; the coward, the unwarlike, the man stained with abominable vices, is plunged

into the mire of the morass with a hurdle put over him. This distinction in punishment means that crime, they think, ought, in being punished, to be exposed, while infamy ought to be buried out of sight- Lighter offenses, too, have penalties proportioned to them; he who is convicted, is fined in a certain number of horses or of cattle. Half of the fine is paid to the king or to the state, half to the person whose wrongs are avenged and to his relatives.

Marriage Laws.

Their marriage code, however, is strict, and indeed no part of their manners is more praiseworthy. Almost alone among barbarians they are content with one wife, except a very few among them, and these not from sensuality, but because their noble birth procures for them many offers of alliance.

Very rare for so numerous a population is adultery, the punishment for which is prompt, and in the husband's power. Having cut off the hair of the adulteress and stripped her naked, he expels her from the house in the presence of her kinsfolk, and then flogs her through the whole village. The loss of chastity meets with no indulgence; neither beauty, youth, nor wealth will procure the culprit a husband. No one in Germany laughs at vice, nor do they call it the fashion to corrupt and to be corrupted.

They receive one husband, as having one body and one life, that they may have no thoughts beyond, no further-reaching desires, that they may love not so much the husband as the married state. To limit the number of children or to destroy any of their subsequent offspring is accounted infamous, and good habits are here more effectual than good laws elsewhere.

Sermon on the Mount & Olivet Discourse, *The Bible*, 80 CE

Reading and Discussion Questions
1. Summarize Jesus teachings about: How to treat your enemy; the accumulation of wealth; Judging others; Generosity; Anxiety
2. In the Olivet Discourse, Jesus is very clear about eternal punishment and reward. He first speaks to those who he separates on his right. What have those people done and what is their reward?
3. Next he speaks to those on his left. What have those people done and what happens to them?
4. What is Jesus trying to teach his disciples in the Olivet Discourse about how to live a Godly life?

The Bible *is a collection of texts that consists of two books, the Old Testament and the New Testament. The Old Testament is the first, older part of the Bible and is based on the lives and writings of ancient Israelites. The Old Testament is the central part of the Hebrew Bible. The New Testament is the story of Jesus, of the apocalypse and of the last judgment. It is the basis of the fundamental beliefs in Christianity and it is belief in the New Testament which is the major difference between Christians and Jews.*

The first four books of the New Testament are the books of Matthew, Mark, Luke and John. Together these books are called The Gospels. It is in The Gospels that we learn most about Jesus during his life and it is also here that we hear most directly from Jesus himself about how his followers should live.

Two of the most famous of Jesus' teachings come from the Book of Matthew. They are the "Sermon on the Mount" and "The Olivet Discourse" and in both, Jesus is teaching his disciples about the principles of living a virtuous and Christian life. He is trying to clarify to his audience of followers exactly what the Ten Commandments mean and to show them what Christian behavior looks like. The Book of Matthew was written in approximately 70 CE during the reign of the Roman Emperor Vespasian.

Sermon on the Mount

5 Now when Jesus saw the crowds, he went up on a mountainside and sat down. His disciples came to him, 2 and he began to teach them.

He said:
3 "Blessed are the poor in spirit,
 for theirs is the kingdom of heaven.
4 Blessed are those who mourn,
 for they will be comforted.
5 Blessed are the meek,
 for they will inherit the earth.
6 Blessed are those who hunger and thirst for righteousness,
 for they will be filled.
7 Blessed are the merciful,
 for they will be shown mercy.
8 Blessed are the pure in heart,
 for they will see God.
9 Blessed are the peacemakers,
 for they will be called children of God.
10 Blessed are those who are persecuted because of righteousness,
 for theirs is the kingdom of heaven.
11 "Blessed are you when people insult you, persecute you and falsely say all kinds of evil against you because of me. 12 Rejoice and be glad, because great is your reward in heaven, for in the same way they persecuted the prophets who were before you.

Murder
21 "You have heard that it was said to the people long ago, 'You shall not murder,[a] and anyone who murders will be subject to judgment.' 22 But I tell you that anyone who is angry with a brother or sister[b][c] will be subject to judgment. And anyone who says, 'You fool!' will be in danger of the fire of hell.

Adultery
27 "You have heard that it was said, 'You shall not commit adultery.'[e] 28 But I tell you that anyone who looks at a woman lustfully has already committed adultery with her in his heart. 29 If your right eye causes you to stumble, gouge it out and throw it away. It is better for you to lose one part of your body than for your whole body to be thrown into hell.

Divorce

31 "It has been said, 'Anyone who divorces his wife must give her a certificate of divorce.'[f] 32 But I tell you that anyone who divorces his wife, except for sexual immorality, makes her the victim of adultery, and anyone who marries a divorced woman commits adultery.

Eye for Eye

38 "You have heard that it was said, 'Eye for eye, and tooth for tooth.'[h] 39 But I tell you, do not resist an evil person. If anyone slaps you on the right cheek, turn to them the other cheek also. 40 And if anyone wants to sue you and take your shirt, hand over your coat as well. 41 If anyone forces you to go one mile, go with them two miles. 42 Give to the one who asks you, and do not turn away from the one who wants to borrow from you.

Love for Enemies

43 "You have heard that it was said, 'Love your neighbor[i] and hate your enemy.' 44 But I tell you, love your enemies and pray for those who persecute you, 45 that you may be children of your Father in heaven. He causes his sun to rise on the evil and the good, and sends rain on the righteous and the unrighteous. 46 If you love those who love you, what reward will you get? Are not even the tax collectors doing that? 47 And if you greet only your own people, what are you doing more than others? Do not even pagans do that? 48 Be perfect, therefore, as your heavenly Father is perfect.

Giving to the Needy

6 "Be careful not to practice your righteousness in front of others to be seen by them. If you do, you will have no reward from your Father in heaven.

2 "So when you give to the needy, do not announce it with trumpets, as the hypocrites do in the synagogues and on the streets, to be honored by others. Truly I tell you, they have received their reward in full. 3 But when you give to the needy, do not let your left hand know what your right hand is doing, 4 so that your giving may be in secret. Then your Father, who sees what is done in secret, will reward you.

Fasting

16 "When you fast, do not look somber as the hypocrites do, for they disfigure their faces to show others they are fasting. Truly I tell you, they have received their reward in full. 17 But when you fast, put oil on your head and wash your face, 18 so that it will not be obvious to others that you are fasting, but only to your Father, who is unseen; and your Father, who sees what is done in secret, will reward you.

Treasures in Heaven

19 "Do not store up for yourselves treasures on earth, where moths and vermin destroy, and where thieves break in and steal. 20 But store up for yourselves treasures in heaven, where moths and vermin do not destroy, and where thieves do not break in and steal. 21 For where your treasure is, there your heart will be also.

24 "No one can serve two masters. Either you will hate the one and love the other, or you will be devoted to the one and despise the other. You cannot serve both God and money.

Do Not Worry

25 "Therefore I tell you, do not worry about your life, what you will eat or drink; or about your body, what you will wear. Is not life more than food, and the body more than clothes? 26 Look at the birds of the air; they do not sow or reap or store away in barns, and yet your heavenly Father feeds them. Are you not much more valuable than they? 27 Can any one of you by worrying add a single hour to your life[n]?

28 "And why do you worry about clothes? See how the flowers of the field grow. They do not labor or spin. 29 Yet I tell you that not even Solomon in all his splendor was dressed like one of these. 30 If that is how God clothes the grass of the field, which is here today and tomorrow is thrown into the fire, will he not much more clothe you— you of little faith? 31 So do not worry, saying, 'What shall we eat?' or 'What shall we drink?' or 'What shall we wear?' 32 For the pagans run after all these things, and your heavenly Father knows that you need them. 33 But seek first his kingdom and his righteousness, and all these things will be given to you as well. 34 Therefore do not worry about tomorrow, for tomorrow will worry about itself. Each day has enough trouble of its own.

Judging Others

7 "Do not judge, or you too will be judged. 2 For in the same way you judge others, you will be judged, and with the measure you use, it will be measured to you.
3 "Why do you look at the speck of sawdust in your brother's eye and pay no attention to the plank in your own eye? 4 How can you say to your brother, 'Let me take the speck out of your eye,' when all the time there is a plank in your own eye? 5 You hypocrite, first take the plank out of your own eye, and then you will see clearly to remove the speck from your brother's eye.

The Narrow and Wide Gates

13 "Enter through the narrow gate. For wide is the gate and broad is the road that leads to destruction, and many enter through it. 14 But small is the gate and narrow the road that leads to life, and only a few find it.

The Olivet Discourse

31 "When the Son of Man comes in his glory, and all the angels with him, he will sit on his glorious throne. 32 All the nations will be gathered before him, and he will separate the people one from another as a shepherd separates the sheep from the goats. 33 He will put the sheep on his right and the goats on his left.

34 "Then the King will say to those on his right, 'Come, take your inheritance, the kingdom prepared for you since the creation of the world. 35 For I was hungry and you gave me something to eat, I was thirsty and you gave me something to drink, I was a stranger and you invited me in, 36 I needed clothes and you clothed me, I was sick and you looked after me, I was in prison and you came to visit me.'

37 "Then the righteous will answer him, 'Lord, when did we see you hungry and feed you, or thirsty and give you something to drink? 38 When did we see you a stranger and invite you in, or needing clothes and clothe you? 39 When did we see you sick or in prison and go to visit you?' 40 "The King will reply, 'Truly I tell you, whatever you did for one of the least of these brothers and sisters of mine, you did for me.'

41 "Then he will say to those on his left, 'Depart from me, you who are cursed, into the eternal fire prepared for the devil and his angels. 42 For I was hungry and you gave me nothing to eat, I was thirsty and you gave me nothing to drink, 43 I was a stranger and you did not invite me in, I needed clothes and you did not clothe me, I was sick and in prison and you did not look after me.'

44 "They also will answer, 'Lord, when did we see you hungry or thirsty or a stranger or needing clothes or sick or in prison, and did not help you?'

45 "He will reply, 'Truly I tell you, whatever you did not do for one of the least of these, you did not do for me.' 46 "Then they will go away to eternal punishment, but the righteous to eternal life."

St. Augustine, *City of God*, 410 CE

Reading and Discussion Questions
1. Define the following terms: "scripture," "doctrine," "theology."
2. Why must the virtuous suffer? There are two reasons.
3. Explain three qualities or characteristics of the earthly city.
4. Explain three qualities or characteristics of the city of God.
5. Is this work by Augustine scripture, doctrine or theology? Explain.
6. How did Augustine's work influence Christian thinking about life?

Amidst the chaos and death that characterized life in Rome during the barbarian invasions, Romans desperately sought an explanation for what had happened to their empire. Pagan Romans blamed the Christians for creating a division and a lack of loyalty in Rome. One of the greatest philosophers in history named Augustine of Hippo, had a different explanation. Augustine was alive during the barbarian invasions and the Visigoth sack of Rome in 410 A.D. He said that it was pagan immorality and not Christian piety that was to blame for the collapse of the Roman Empire. He wrote all these ideas in his masterpiece, The City of God. In his book, Augustine also tried to comfort Christians during their time of suffering by saying that Christians had always suffered and would always suffer, in this world. But he also said that good and faithful Christians would win an eternal end to suffering in Heaven—the City of God. Augustine's writings had such a profound impact on Christians of his time that his views became the prevailing world-view for the next 1000 years.

On Accusations that Christians Were to Blame

Those murderers (barbarians) who everywhere else showed themselves pitiless came to our churches, their furious rage for slaughter was bridled, and their eagerness to take prisoners was quenched. Thus escaped multitudes who now reproach the Christian religion, and blame Christ for the ills that have befallen their city; but the preservation of their own life—a boon which they owe to the respect entertained for Christ by the barbarians—they attribute not to our Christ, but to their own good luck. They ought rather, had they any right perceptions, to attribute the severities and hardships inflicted by their enemies, to that divine providence which is wont to reform the depraved manners of men by chastisement, and which exercises with similar afflictions the righteous and praiseworthy,—either translating them, when they have passed through the trial, to a better world, or detaining them still on earth for ulterior purposes. And they ought to attribute it to the spirit of these Christian times, that, contrary to the

89

custom of war, these bloodthirsty barbarians spared them for Christ's sake.

Therefore ought they to give God thanks, and with sincere confession flee for refuge to His name, that so they may escape the punishment of eternal fire. For of those whom you see insolently and shamelessly insulting the servants of Christ, there are numbers who would not have escaped that destruction and slaughter had they not pretended that they themselves were Christ's servants. Yet now, in ungrateful pride and most impious madness, and at the risk of being punished in everlasting darkness, they perversely oppose that name under which they fraudulently protected themselves for the sake of enjoying the light of this brief life.

Why the Virtuous Must Suffer
There seems to me to be one principal reason why the good are punished along with the wicked, when God is pleased to visit with punishments the bad manners of a community. They are punished together, not because they have spent an equally corrupt life, but because the good as well as the wicked love this present life; while they ought to hold it cheap, that the wicked, being admonished and reformed by their example, might lay hold of life eternal. Lastly, there is another reason why the good are punished—the reason which Job's case exemplifies: that the human spirit may be proved, and that it may be shown with what strength of faith, and with how pure a love, it clings to God.[2]

Of the Nature of the Two Cities, the Earthly and the Heavenly.
The two cities have been formed by two loves: the earthly city by the love of self, even to the contempt of God; the heavenly city by the love of God, even to the contempt of self. The former, in a word, glories in itself, the latter in the Lord. For the one seeks glory from men; but the greatest glory of the other is God, the witness of conscience. The one lifts up its head in its own glory; the other says to its God, "Thou art my glory, and the lifter up of mine head."[1] In the one, the princes and the nations it subdues are ruled by the love of ruling; in the other, the princes and the subjects serve one another in love, the latter obeying, while the former take thought for all. The one delights in its own strength, represented in the persons of its rulers; the other says to its God, "I will love Thee, O Lord, my strength."[2]

And therefore the wise men of the one city, living according to man, have sought for profit to their own bodies or souls, or both, and those who have known God "glorified Him not as God, neither were thankful, but became vain in their imaginations, and their foolish heart was darkened; professing themselves to be wise,"—that is, glorying in their own wisdom, and being possessed by pride,—"they became fools, and changed the glory of the incorruptible God into an image made like to corruptible man, and to birds, and four-footed beasts, and creeping things." For they were either leaders or followers of the people in adoring images, "and worshipped and served the creature more than the Creator, who is blessed for ever."[3] But in the other city there is no human wisdom, but only godliness, which offers due worship to the true God, and looks for its reward in the society of the saints, of holy angels as well as holy men, "that God may be all in all."[4]

The End of the Wicked
But, on the other hand, they who do not belong to this city of God shall inherit eternal misery, which is also called the second death, because the soul shall then be separated from God its life, and therefore cannot be said to live, and the body shall be subjected

to eternal pains. And consequently this second death shall be the more severe, because no death shall terminate it. For in this life, when this conflict has arisen, either pain conquers and death expels the feeling of it, or nature conquers and health expels the pain. But in the world to come the pain continues that it may torment, and the nature endures that it may be sensible of it; and neither ceases to exist, lest punishment also should cease. Now, as it is through the last judgment that men pass to these ends, the good to the supreme good, the evil to the supreme evil, I will treat of this judgment in the following book.

Three Documents on the Spread of Christianity, 400 - 800 CE

After Christianity was made the official religion of the Roman Empire in 386 CE, church leaders tried in every way possible to spread Christianity. Sometimes it was spread through missionary work, sometimes through conquest and sometimes through the use of physical punishment. Between 400 and 800, the vast majority of the Germanic tribes were "Christianized." Below, you will find excerpts from three documents that all deal with different methods of conversion.

1. St. Augustine, On the Correction of the Donatists, 417 CE

Reading and Discussion Questions
 1. According to Augustine, how are men better led to God — by teaching or fear?
 2. What do you think is the meaning of the phrase, "He that spares the rod hates his son?" Do you agree or disagree with it?
 3. Explain the story of Paul and how Augustine uses it to justify the use of punishment in bringing people to God.
 4. How does Augustine compare heretics to wandering sheep? What should a shepherd do to wandering sheep?

The early years of Christianity were challenging. For centuries before the laws of Constantine and Theodosius, which made Christianity first a legal and then the official religion of the empire, Christians were brutally persecuted. After Christianity was made legal, however, the question for church leaders was what to do with pagans and other minority Christian sects whose practices were causing problems for the established Church. One of those minority sects was a group called the Donatists. In the following letter from St. Augustine to a friend, he debates the question of what to do with the Donatists, who were considered "heretics." Specifically, he debates whether or not physical punishment is appropriate for punishing and "reforming" heretics.

21. It is indeed better (as no one ever could deny) that men should be led to worship God by teaching, than that they should be driven to it by fear of punishment or pain; but it does not follow that because the former course produces the better men, therefore those who do not yield to it should be neglected. For many have found advantage (as we have proved, and are daily proving by actual experiment), in being first compelled by fear or pain, so that they might afterwards be influenced by teaching, or might follow out in act what they had already learned in word.

91

But, moreover, holy Scripture has both said concerning the former better class, "There is no fear in love; but perfect love casts out fear;" 1 John 4:18 and also concerning the latter lower class, which furnishes the majority, "A servant will not be corrected by words; for though he understand, he will not answer." Proverbs 29:19 In saying, "He will not be corrected by words," he did not order him to be left to himself, but implied an admonition as to the means whereby he ought to be corrected; otherwise he would not have said, "He will not be corrected by words," but without any qualification, "He will not be corrected." For in another place he says that not only the servant, but also the undisdained son, must be corrected with stripes, and that with great fruits as the result; for he says, "You shall beat him with the rod, and shall deliver his soul from hell;" Proverbs 23:14 and elsewhere he says, "He that spares the rod hates his son."

22. For who can possibly love us more than Christ, who laid down His life for His sheep? John 10:15 And yet, after calling Peter and the other apostles by His words alone, when He came to summon Paul, who was before called Saul, subsequently the powerful builder of His Church, but originally its cruel persecutor, He not only constrained him with His voice, but even dashed him to the earth with His power; and that He might forcibly bring one who was raging amid the darkness of infidelity to desire the light of the heart, He first struck him with physical blindness of the eyes. If that punishment had not been inflicted, he would not afterwards have been healed by it. But opponents of this view [and defenders of heretics like the Donatists] will say: Is man not at liberty to believe or not believe? Towards whom did Christ use violence? Whom did He compel? Here they have the Apostle Paul. Let them recognize in his case Christ first compelling, and afterwards teaching; first striking, and afterwards consoling. For it is wonderful how he who entered the service of the gospel in the first instance under the compulsion of bodily punishment, afterwards labored more in the gospel than all they who were called by word only; 1 Corinthians 15:10 and he who was compelled by the greater influence of fear to love, displayed that perfect love which casts out fear.

23. Why, therefore, should not the Church use force in compelling her lost sons to return, if the lost sons compelled others to their destruction? Although even men who have not been compelled, but only led astray, are received by their loving mother with more affection if they are recalled to her bosom through the enforcement of terrible but salutary laws, and are the objects of far more deep congratulation than those whom she had never lost. Is it not a part of the care of the shepherd, when any sheep have left the flock, even though not violently forced away, but led astray by tender words and coaxing blandishments, to bring them back to the fold of his master when he has found them, by the fear or even the pain of the whip, if they show symptoms of resistance?

26. God in His great mercy, knew how necessary was the terror inspired by these acts, and a kind of medicinal inconvenience for the cold and wicked hearts of many men.

* * * * * *

2. Bede, Letter from Pope Gregory I, 601 CE

Reading and Discussion Questions
1. What was Pope Gregory's advice on what to do with pagan temples? Should they be destroyed? Why or why not?
2. What was Pope Gregory's advice on what to do about animal sacrifices? Should they be stopped? Why or why not?
3. Do you agree or disagree with Pope Gregory's advice on how to deal with pagans and their practices? Explain.

Pope Gregory I was the leader of the Christian Church from 590 to 604 CE and his primary mission was spreading Christianity and creating a Christian empire called Christendom. In the following letter below, he sends advice to one of his clergymen in Britain about how to get the English people to convert to Christianity.

Howbeit, when Almighty God has led you to the most reverend Bishop Augustine, our brother, tell him what I have long been considering in my own mind concerning the matter of the English people; to wit, that the temples of the idols in that nation ought not to be destroyed; but let the idols that are in them be destroyed; let water be consecrated and sprinkled in the said temples, let altars be erected, and relics placed there. For if those temples are well built, it is requisite that they be converted from the worship of devils to the service of the true God; that the nation, seeing that their temples are not destroyed, may remove error from their hearts, and knowing and adoring the true God, may the more freely resort to the places to which they have been accustomed.

And because they are used to slaughter many oxen in sacrifice to devils, some solemnity must be given them in exchange for this, as that on the day of the dedication, or the nativities of the holy martyrs, whose relics are there deposited, they should build themselves huts of the boughs of trees about those churches which have been turned to that use from being temples, and celebrate the solemnity with religious feasting, and no more offer animals to the Devil, but kill cattle and glorify God in their feast, and return thanks to the Giver of all things for their abundance; to the end that, whilst some outward gratifications are retained, they may the more easily consent to the inward joys.

For there is no doubt that it is impossible to cut off every thing at once from their rude natures; because he who endeavours to ascend to the highest place rises by degrees or steps, and not by leaps. Thus the Lord made Himself known to the people of Israel in Egypt; and yet He allowed them the use, in His own worship, of the sacrifices which they were wont to offer to the Devil, commanding them in His sacrifice to kill animals, to the end that, with changed hearts, they might lay aside one part of the sacrifice, whilst they retained another; and although the animals were the same as those which they were wont to offer, they should offer them to the true God, and not to idols; and thus they would no longer be the same sacrifices.

* * * * * *

3. Einhard, Charlemagne's Forced Conversion of Saxons, 830 CE

Reading and Discussion Questions
1. Who is Charlemagne and what was he trying to accomplish during his reign?
2. Who are the Saxons?
3. According to Einhard, why did Charlemagne's war with the Saxons last more than 30 years?
4. Do you agree or disagree with Charlemagne's methods for converting the Saxons to Christianity? Explain.

During the period of the Germanic Migrations, dozens of tribes settled all over Europe and north Africa. One of those tribes was a group called the Franks, who settled in what is today northern France. Between their original settlement of the area in 486 and the year 806 CE, the Franks had captured vast territory in western and central Europe by conquering their neighbors. One of their most fearsome foes was another tribe called the Saxons, with whom the Franks were at war from 772 to 806. The Franks were led to victory in the war with the Saxons by their king, Charles the Great, or Charlemagne. Charlemagne's victory over the Saxons was not just a victory for the Franks but for Christianity as well. Charlemagne was a Christian king who vowed to create the first unified Christian kingdom through conquering and converting all the pagan tribes of Germania. By his death in 815, he had largely accomplished his mission. The Frankish historian Einhard gives us a complete chronicle of Charlemagne's life and conquests, including his conversion of the Saxon tribes to Christianity, often under threat of death.

No war ever undertaken by the Frank nation was carried on with such persistence and bitterness, or cost so much labor, because the Saxons, like almost all the tribes of Germany, were a fierce people, given to the worship of devils, and hostile to our religion, and did not consider it dishonorable to transgress and violate all law, human and divine. Then there were peculiar circumstances that tended to cause a breach of peace every day. Except in a few places, where large forests or mountain ridges intervened and made the bounds certain, the line between ourselves and the Saxons passed almost in its whole extent through an open country, so that there was no end to the murders, thefts and arsons on both sides. In this way the Franks became so embittered that they at last resolved to make reprisals no longer, but to come to open war with the Saxons.

Accordingly war was begun against them, and was waged for thirty-three successive years with great fury; more, however, to the disadvantage of the Saxons than of the Franks. It could doubtless have been brought to an end sooner, had it not been for the faithlessness of the Saxons. It is hard to say how often they were conquered, and, humbly submitting to the King, promised to do what was enjoined upon them, without hesitation the required hostages, gave and received the officers sent them from the King. They were sometimes so much weakened and reduced that they promised to renounce the worship of devils, and to adopt Christianity, but they were no less ready to violate these terms than prompt to accept them, so that it is impossible to tell which

came easier to them to do; scarcely a year passed from the beginning of the war without such changes on their part. But the King did not suffer his high purpose and steadfastness - firm alike in good and evil fortune - to be wearied by any fickleness on their part, or to be turned from the task that he had undertaken, on the contrary, he never allowed their faithless behavior to go unpunished, but either took the field against them in person, or sent his counts with an army to wreak vengeance and exact righteous satisfaction.

At last, after conquering and subduing all who had offered resistance, he took ten thousand of those that lived on the banks of the Elbe, and settled them, with their wives and children, in many different bodies here and there in Gaul and Germany. The war that had lasted so many years was at length ended by their acceding to the terms offered by the King; which were renunciation of their national religious customs and the worship of devils, acceptance of the sacraments of the Christian faith and religion, and union with the Franks to form one people.

Two Accounts of the Viking Invasions, 800-900 CE

Reading and Discussion Questions
1. Describe the nature of the Viking raid on Lindesfarne.
2. There were dozens of accounts of the Lindesfarne raid similar to the one you read. How do you think people reacted to these stories? How would you have reacted?
3. Based on your understanding of Part 2 of your reading (Viking Invasion of France), were the Vikings irrational and always prone to violence? Explain.

The Vikings, also known as Norsemen, Northmen or Danes, were seafaring north Germanic people who raided, traded, explored, and settled in wide areas of Europe, Asia, and the North Atlantic islands from about 800 to 1000 CE. The Vikings employed wooden longships with wide, shallow hulls, allowing navigation in rough seas or in shallow river waters. The Vikings were excellent sailors and fearsome warriors. This combination allowed the Vikings to travel as far east as Constantinople and Russia, as far west as Iceland, Greenland and Minnesota. This period of Viking invasions and expansion, known as the Viking Age, was one of the most important eras in shaping the new civilization that was emerging in Europe by 1000 CE.

1. Raid of Lindesfarne
The Vikings were exploring western Europe and beyond prior to 800 CE but the first documented Viking attack was in 793 CE in England at the Christian monastery at Lindesfarne. Perhaps the most vivid account of the events of that day came through Simeon of Durham, a twelfth century historian, who working through locally written sources, produced a compelling account:

"In the same year the pagans from the northern regions came with a naval force to Britain like stinging hornets and spread on all sides like fearful wolves, robbed, tore and slaughtered not only beasts of burden, sheep and oxen, but even priests and deacons, and companies of monks and nuns. And they came to the church of Lindisfarne, laid everything waste with grievous plundering, trampled the holy places with polluted steps, dug up the altars and seized all the treasures of the holy church. They killed some of the brothers, took some away with them in fetters, many they drove out, naked and loaded with insults, some they drowned in the sea... "

"Lo, it is nearly 350 years that we and our fathers have inhabited this most lovely land, and never before has such terror appeared in Britain as we have now suffered from a pagan race, nor was it thought that such an inroad from the sea could be made. Behold, the church of St. Cuthbert spattered with the blood of the priests of God, despoiled of all its ornaments; a place more venerable than all in Britain is given as a prey to pagan peoples."

2. Viking Invasion of France
Perhaps the one of the most intriguing texts produced along these lines was written by the Northumbrian Alcuin, living with Charlemagne in France at the time of the raid.

"The Northmen came to Paris with 700 sailing ships, not counting those of smaller size which are commonly called barques. At one stretch the Seine was lined with the vessels for more than two leagues, so that one might ask in astonishment in what cavern the river had been swallowed up, since it was not to be seen. The second day after the fleet of the Northmen arrived under the walls of the city, Siegfried, who was then king only in name but who was in command of the expedition, came to the dwelling of the illustrious bishop. He bowed his head and said: "Gauzelin, have compassion on yourself and on your flock. We beseech you to listen to us, in order that you may escape death. Allow us only the freedom of the city. We will do no harm and we will see to it that whatever belongs either to you or to Odo shall be strictly respected." Count Odo, who later became king, was then the defender of the city. The bishop replied to Siegfried, "Paris has been entrusted to us by the Emperor Charles, who, after God, king and lord of the powerful, rules over almost all the world. He has put it in our care, not at all that the kingdom may be ruined by our misconduct, but that he may keep it and be assured of its peace. If, like us, you had been given the duty of defending these walls, and if you should have done that which you ask us to do, what treatment do you think you would deserve?" Siegfried replied. "I should deserve that my head be cut off and thrown to the dogs. Nevertheless, if you do not listen to my demand, on the morrow our war machines will destroy you with poisoned arrows. You will be the prey of famine and of pestilence and these evils will renew themselves perpetually every year." So saying, he departed and gathered together his comrades."

"In the morning the Northmen, boarding their ships, approached the tower and attacked it [the tower blocked access to the city by the so-called "Great Bridge," which connected the right bank of the Seine with the island on which the city was built. The tower stood on the present site of the Châtelet]. They shook it with their engines and stormed it with arrows. The city resounded with clamor, the people were aroused, the bridges trembled. All came together to defend the tower. There Odo, his brother Robert, and the Count Ragenar distinguished themselves for bravery; likewise the courageous Abbot Ebolus, the nephew of the bishop. A keen arrow wounded the prelate, while at his side the young warrior Frederick was struck by a sword. Frederick died, but the old man, thanks to God, survived. There perished many Franks; after receiving wounds they were lavish of life.

At last the enemy withdrew, carrying off their dead. The evening came. The tower had been sorely tried, but its foundations were still solid, as were also the narrow bays which surmounted them. The people spent the night repairing it with boards. By the next day, on the old citadel had been erected a new tower of wood, a half higher than the former one. At sunrise the Danes caught their first glimpse of it. Once more the latter engaged with the Christians in violent combat. On every side arrows sped and blood flowed. With the arrows mingled the stones hurled by slings and war-machines; the air was filled with them. The tower which had been built during the night groaned under the strokes of the darts, the city shook with the struggle, the people ran hither and thither, the bells jangled. The warriors rushed together to defend the tottering tower and to repel the fierce assault. Among these warriors two, a count and an abbot [Ebolus], surpassed all the rest in courage. The former was the redoubtable Odo who never experienced defeat and who continually revived the spirits of the worn-out defenders. He ran along the ramparts and hurled back the enemy. On those who were secreting themselves so as to undermine the tower he poured oil, wax, and pitch, which, being mixed and heated, burned the Danes and tore off their scalps. Some of them died; others threw themselves into the river to escape the awful substance. . .

Beowulf, c. 800 CE

Reading and Discussion Questions
1. Write a description or draw a picture of Grendel.
2. What impact did Grendel have on the kingdom of the Danes?
3. Why does Beowulf say he has come?
4. How will Beowulf fight Grendel?
5. Describe or draw the battle between Beowulf and Grendel.
6. Beowulf is considered a great hero. Why? Describe qualities that he has that might have been considered heroic.
7. By studying Beowulf as a Medieval hero, what can we learn about the values of Medieval times?

Beowulf is the oldest known work of English literature and is considered a masterpiece of epic poetry, along the lines of the Iliad *or the* Aeneid. *Its author is unknown. Beowulf is significant both because of its literary genius and for the history and culture it reveals. Beowulf is a more than 3000-line poem that uses alliteration, rather than rhyming verse, to set the rhythm of the poem. It is written in Old English and is an important tool in tracking the evolution of the English language which was in its early development around the time* Beowulf *was written.*

Beowulf is a poem named for its main character, who is a heroic warrior from modern-day Sweden. Beowulf comes to Denmark to help its king, Hrothgar, defeat a terrible monster that is killing and eating all of Hrothgar's subjects. In a great adventure story, Beowulf crosses the sea, Viking-style, and slays the monster Grendel (and Grendel's mom) and returns home a hero. He is so beloved in his own homeland that he is made king of his people. But long into his reign, his own country is terrorized by a dragon and Beowulf sacrifices his own life to slay the dragon and save his kingdom. He is said to have the strength in his grip of 30 men and fears nothing. He is all grit, and brute strength and courage and he is the embodiment of the Medieval hero.

Beowulf gives it reader a detailed look at life in Medieval Scandinavia during the time of the Vikings. It also offers a unique perspective of both Christian and pagan life during the 9th century. The narrator of the poem is Christian and tells the story from a Christian viewpoint, but the reader also learns about pagan rituals, practices and everyday lifestyle in Scandinavia in exquisite detail. Yet it is clear from the tone of the narrator that there is a general condemnation of non-Christians during this time and

Beowulf's narrative voice seems to hint that the non-Christian subjects of the work might have "had it coming," so to speak.

Beowulf is the great epic of the Middle Ages, and marks an important historical moment, much like the Iliad did in ancient Greece. For 500 years between 500 and 1000 CE, Europe was believed to be almost entirely immersed in intellectual darkness. The chaos of Rome's collapse left the western world reeling and reorganizing, often violently. The Dark Ages are judged as being almost entirely devoid of cultural achievement or advancement. And while this was true to a large degree, there was Beowulf. And that has to make us wonder what was happening in England in around 800 CE that made penning this great work possible. That is certainly a question worth pondering.

Grendel Terrorizes Heorot Hall

So times were pleasant for the people there
Until finally one, a fiend out of Hell,   100
Began to work his evil in the world.
Grendel was the name of this grim demon
Haunting the marches, marauding round the heath
And the desolate fens; he had dwelt for a time
In misery among the banished monsters,
Cain's clan, whom the creator had outlawed
And condemned as outcasts. For the killing of Abel
The Eternal Lord had exacted a price:
Cain got no good from committing that murder
Because the Almighty made him anathema   110
And out of the curse of his exile there sprang
Ogres and elves and evil phantoms
And the giants too who strove with God
Time and again until He gave them their final reward.

So, after nightfall, Grendel set out
For the lofty house, to see how the Ring-Danes
Were settling into it after their drink,
And there he came upon them, a company of the best
Asleep from their feasting, insensible to pain
And human sorrow. Suddenly then   120
The God-cursed brute was creating havoc:
Greedy and grim, he grabbed thirty men
From their resting places and rushed to his lair,
Flushed up and inflamed from the raid,
Blundering back with the butchered corpses.

Then as dawn brightened and the day broke
Grendel's powers of destruction were plain:
Their wassail was over, they wept to heaven
And mourned under morning. Their mighty prince,
The storied leader, sat stricken and helpless,   130
Humiliated by the loss of his guard,
Bewildered and stunned, staring aghast
And the demon's trail, in deep distress.

He was numb with grief, but got no respite
For one night later the merciless Grendel
Struck again with more gruesome murders.
Malignant by nature, he never showed remorse.
It was easy then to meet with a man
Shifting himself to a safer distance
To bed in the bothies, for who could be blind   140
To the evidence of his eyes, the obviousness
Of that hall-watcher's hate? Whoever escaped
Kept a weather-eye open and moved away.

So Grendel ruled in defiance of right,
One against all, until the greatest house
In the world stood empty, a deserted wall stead.
For twelve winters, seasons of woe,
The lord of the Shieldings suffered under
His load of sorrow; and so, before long,
The news was known over the whole world.   150

Sad lays were sung about the beset king,
The vicious raids of Grendel,
His long and unrelenting feud,
Nothing but war; how he would never
Parley or make peace with any Dane
Nor stop his death-dealing nor pay the death-price.
No counsellor could ever expect
Fair reparation from those rabid hands.
All were endangered; young and old
Were hunted down by that dark death-shadow   160
Who lurked and swooped in the long nights
On the misty moors; nobody knows
Where these reavers from Hell roam on their errands.

So Grendel waged his lonely war,
Inflicting constant cruelties on the people,
Atrocious hurt. He took over Heorot,
Haunted the glittering hall after dark,
But the throne itself, the treasure-seat,
He was kept from approaching; he was the Lord's outcast.

These were hard times, heart-breaking   170
For the prince of the Shieldings; powerful counselors,
The highest in the land, would lend advice,
Plotting how best the bold defenders
Might resist and beat off sudden attacks.
Sometimes at pagan shrines they vowed
Offering to idols, swore oaths
That the killer of souls might come to their aid
And save the people. That was their way,
Their heathenish hope; deep in their hearts
They remembered Hell. The Almighty Judge   180

99

Of good deeds and bad, the Lord God,
Head of the Heavens and High King of the World,
Was unknown to them. Oh, cursed is he
Who in time of trouble had to thrust his soul
In the fire's embrace, forfeiting help;
He has nowhere to turn. But blessed is he
Who after death can approach the Lord
And find friendship in the Father's embrace.

So that troubled time continued, woe
That never stopped, steady affliction   190
For Halfdane's son, too hard an ordeal.
There was panic after dark, people endured
Raids in the night, riven by terror.

After many years, word reached Beowulf of the terror that Grendel was wreaking on Herorot. He felt it his duty to try and slay the beast.]

Beowulf Comes to Denmark
The hero arose, surrounded closely
By his powerful thanes. A party remained   400
Under orders to keep watch on the arms;
The rest proceeded, lead by their prince
Under Heorot's roof. And standing on the hearth
In webbed links that the smith had woven,
The fine-forged mesh of his gleaming mail shirt,
Resolute in his helmet, Beowulf spoke:
"Greetings to Hrothgar. I am Hygelac's kinsman,
One of his hall-troop. When I was younger,
I had great triumphs. Then news of Grendel,
Hard to ignore, reached me at home: 410
Sailors brought stories of the plight you suffer
In this legendary hall, how it lies deserted,
Empty and useless once the evening light
Hides itself under Heaven's dome.
So every elder and experience councilman
Among my people supported my resolve
To come here to you, King Hrothgar,
Because all knew of my awesome strength.
They had seen me boltered in the blood of enemies
When I battled and bound five beasts,   420
Raided a troll-nest and in the night-sea
Slaughtered sea-brutes. I have suffered extremes
And avenged the Geats (their enemies brought it
Upon themselves, I devastated them).

Now I mean to be a match for Grendel,
Settle the outcome in a single combat.
And so, my request, O king of Bright-Danes,
Dear prince pf the Shieldings, friend of the people
And their ring of defense, my one request

Is that you won't refuse me, who have come this far,   430
The privilege of purifying Heorot,
With my own men to help me, and nobody else.

I have heard moreover that the monster scorns
In his reckless way to use weapons;
Therefore, to heighten Hygelac's fame
And gladden his heart, I hereby renounce
Sword and the shelter of the broad shield,
The heavy war-board: hand-to-hand
Is how it will be, a life-and-death
Fight with the fiend. Whichever one death fells   440
Must deem it a just judgment by God.
If Grendel wins, it will be a gruesome day;
He will glut himself on the Geats in the war-hall,
Swoop without fear on that flower of manhood
As on others before. Then my face won't be there
To be covered in death; he will carry me away
As he goes to ground, gorged and bloodied;
He will run gloating with my raw corpse
And feed on it alone, in a cruel frenzy,
Fouling his moor-nest. No need then   450
To lament for long or lay out my body:
If the battle takes me, send back
This breast-webbing that Weland fashioned
And Hrethel gave me, to Hygelac.
Fate goes ever as fate must."

[After several days of preparing and waiting for the arrival of Grendel at Herorot, the beast finally arrives and the battle begins.]

Beowulf Slays Grendel

In off the moors, down through the mist-bands   710
God-cursed Grendel came greedily loping.
The bane of the race of men roamed forth,
Hunting for a prey in the high hall.
Under the cloud-murk he moved towards it
Until it shone above him, a sheer keep
Of fortified gold. Nor was that the first time
He had scouted the grounds of Hrothgar's dwelling---
Although never in his life, before or since,
Did he find harder fortune or hall-defenders.
Spurned and joyless, he journeyed on ahead   720
And arrived at the bawn. The iron-braced door
Turned in its hinge when his hand touched it.
Then his rage boiled over, he ripped open
The mouth of the building, maddening for blood,
Pacing the length of the patterned floor
With his loathsome tread, while a baleful light,
Flame more than light, flared from his eyes.
He saw many men in the mansion, sleeping,

101

A ranked company of kinsmen and warriors
Quartered together. And his glee was demonic,   730
Picturing the mayhem: before morning
He would rip life from limp and devour them,
Feed on their flesh: but his fate that night
Was due to change, his days of ravening
Had come to an end.

          Mighty and canny,
Hygelac's kinsman was keenly watching
For the first move the monster would make.
Nor did the creature keep him waiting
But struck suddenly and started in:
He grabbed and mauled a man on his bench,   740
Bit into his bone-lappings, bolted down his blood
And gorged on him in lumps, leaving the body
Utterly lifeless, eaten up
Hand and foot. Venturing closer,
his talon was raised to attack Beowulf
Where he lay on the bed: he was bearing in
With open claw when the alert hero's
Comeback and armlock forestalled him utterly.
The captain of evil discovered himself
In a handgrip harder than anything   750
He had ever encountered in any man
On the face of the earth. Every bone in his body
Quailed and coiled, but he could not escape.
He was desperate to flee to his den and hide
With the devil's litter, for in all his days
He had never been clamped or cornered like this.
Then Hygelac's trusty retainer recalled
His bedtime speech, sprang to his feet
And got a firm hold. Fingers were bursting,
The monster back-tracking, the man overpowering.   760
The dread of the land was desperate to escape,
To take a roundabout road and flee
To his lair in the fens. The latching power
In his fingers weakened; it was the worst trip
The terror-monger had taken to Heorot.
And now the timber trembled and sang,
A hall-session that harrowed every Dane
Inside the stockade: stumbling in fury,
The two contenders crashed through the building.

The hall clattered and hammered, but somehow   770
Survived the onslaught and kept standing:
It was handsomely structured, a sturdy frame
Braced with the best of blacksmith's work
Inside and out. The story goes
That as the pair struggled, mead benches were smashed
And sprung off the floor, gold fittings and all.

Before then, no Shielding elder would believe
There was any power or person on earth
Capable of wrecking their horn-rigged hall
Unless the burning embrace of fire   780
Engulf it in flame. Then an extraordinary
Wail arose, and bewildering fear
Came over the Danes. Everyone felt it
Who heard that cry as it echoed off the wall,
A God-cursed scream and strain of catastrophe,
The howl of the loser, the lament of the hell-serf
Keening his wound. He was overwhelmed,
Manacled tight by the man who of all men
Was foremost and strongest in the days of this life.

But the earl troop's leader was not inclined   790
To allow his caller to depart alive:
He did not consider that life of much account
To anyone anywhere. Time and again,
Beowulf's warriors worked to defend
Their lord's life, laying about them
As best they could with their ancestral blades.
Stalwart in action, they kept striking out
On every side, seeking to cut
Straight to the soul. When they joined the struggle
There was something they could have not known at the time,   800
That not blade on earth, no blacksmith's art
Could ever damage their demon opponent.
He had conjured the harm from the cutting edge
Of every weapon. But his going away
Out of the world and the days of his life
Would be agony to him, and his alien spirit
would travel far into fiends' keeping.

Then he who had harrowed the hearts of men
With pain and affliction in former times
And had given offense also to God   810
Found that his bodily powers had failed him.
Hygelac's kinsman kept him helplessly
Locked in a handgrip. As long as either lived
He was hateful to the other. The monster's whole
Body was in pain, a tremendous wound
Appeared on his shoulder. Sinews split
And the bone-lappings burst. Beowulf was granted
The glory of winning; Grendel was driven
Under the fen banks, fatally hurt,
To his desolate lair. His days were numbered,   820
The end of his life was coming over him,
He knew it for certain; and one bloody clash
Had fulfilled the dearest wishes of the Danes.

The man who had lately landed among them,
Proud and sure, had purged the hall,
Kept it from harm; he was happy with his night-work
And the courage he had shown. The Geat captain
Had boldly fulfilled his boast to the Danes:
He had healed and relieved a huge distress,
Unremitting humiliations,   830
The hard fate they'd been forced to undergo,
No small affliction. Clear proof of this
Could be seen in the hand the hero displayed
High up near the roof: the whole of Grendel's
Shoulder and arm, his awesome grasp.

CHAPTER 4 –
THE HIGH MIDDLE AGES (1000 to 1500 CE)

GUIDING QUESTIONS
- How did the events of the Late Middle Ages lay the foundations for a rebirth of European society?
- In what ways did people win rights in government during this period? In what ways did people lose rights?
- What is collective learning? When and where was it happening in Medieval Europe and what was its impact?
- Explain the two events that caused the Christian Church to lose power during this period.
- What was the positive byproduct of the Crusades, as discussed in your reading?

The period known as the Middle Ages lasted 1000 years. As we have already discussed, there was seemingly little or no progress in Western Europe during this period, especially when compared to the achievements of the Greeks and the Romans who had dominated the Mediterranean world during ancient times. The Medieval period was a time or regrouping, reorganizing and reinventing. All the institutions that had dominated Europe under Roman rule vanished and along with them, culture and knowledge were also largely wiped from memory. People in Medieval Europe had to literally relearn how to be civilized. They had to create *new* institutions, find *new* leaders, create *new* industries and form *new* nations. They had to start over. And yet they did have a faint echo of the past from which they could learn. If Medieval Europeans looked very closely and listened very carefully, they could hear and see the legacy of Greece and Rome around them. Many Europeans lived in the shadow of old Roman aqueducts and temples or near Roman roads or fortifications. They knew that people before them had done great things. And they began to wonder "Why not us?"

This question—"Why not us?"—was very powerful. In the first centuries after Rome's collapse, the answer to the question was probably, "Because life is hard and we lack the knowledge or the time to do what the Romans did." But after the chaos of the migrations had waned and after the Viking invasions stopped, these Roman monuments still loomed. And new generations asked again, as they looked at great structures like the Pont du Gard, Hadrian's Wall and the Arles Amphitheater, "Why not us?" By 1000 CE, there was a small spark of optimism and belief in the human spirit. This was a huge departure from the resignation and helplessness of the Dark Ages. Now when people asked "Why not us?" the answer was more likely something like "Well, maybe."

The Medieval castles and Romanesque churches of this period show us that people were taking risks and pushing boundaries of the known and the possible. By the end of the Middle Ages, known as the Late Medieval period, the question was no longer the self-pitying "Why not *us*?" but a much more confident "Why *not* us?" By 1350, the confidence in human ability had been reborn and Medieval Europeans once again believed in their ability to accomplish great things.

For most of the 500 year period of the early Middle Ages, there was little in the way of "civilization." Only in the kingdom of the Franks and in Anglo-Saxon England did we find elements of civilization, including cities as trade centers, common written language and complex institutions like government and businesses. Even in these places, civilized life was simple. But in 1000 CE, the foundations of future great civilizations were laid in response to Viking invasions. For nearly 200 years (800 to 1000 CE) the Scandinavian raiders pillaged and colonized freely throughout Europe and North America. And for most of that time, the people of Medieval Europe could muster no adequate defense against Viking raids. The reason they were defenseless is they were largely "uncivilized," in the sense that they were not unified, they lived in small, widely spread communities and they had no common language for effective communication even if travel over long distances had been possible. They were isolated, and it became evident that isolation made people vulnerable. So over time, people sought safety in numbers. Communities of increasing size formed by 1000 CE, thanks in large part to feudalism.

Feudalism, or the feudal system, is a military and political system based on the exchange of land. In the feudal system, a landowner gave away portions of his land, called fiefs, to others in exchange for taxes, military service and advice. The exchange of land in feudalism created a system of mutual benefit. The large landowner or lord was better able to defend his realm from Vikings or other invaders because of the defensive support promised to him by those to whom he gave land. The men who received land from a lord were called vassals. And vassals, in addition to becoming landowners, got the benefit of the organization of the lord's community as well as a safe haven created by the lord in his castle. Castles of the Middle Ages were created as a last line of defense. If invaders succeeded in pillaging the countryside and the estates of the lord's vassals, the entire community could seek refuge within the lord's walls. Civilization was reborn in this way and this is why, in a way, the Vikings saved civilization.

In the feudal system, the relationship between lord and vassal was sacred. Each man took his responsibilities to the other very seriously and usually pledged his life in honor of that bond. But relationships in the feudal system could be very complicated. A person could be both a lord and a vassal. If a man were given a very large piece of land by a lord, he became a vassal and served his lord with defense and taxes. But that man could himself divide his large estate into smaller estates or fiefs and give those away, thus becoming a lord himself. Men were given different titles depending on the size of their lands. A duke was someone who owned a very large estate, sometimes the size of a state. A count was also someone who owned a large fief, called a county. A baron owned a slightly smaller but still sizable territory, and so on down the ladder of nobility. The lowest noble is a knight. He is a landowner whose territory is too small to be further subdivided and therefore knights, by definition, cannot be lords. Knights are the ones that are primarily responsible for the defense of the first lord's realm. The higher nobility, though also responsible for defense, served as advisors on the first lord's council. These councils served as a sort of executive cabinet through which the fiefdom was run. Over time, very powerful first lords consolidated many realms into their territory. Their fiefdoms became kingdoms and very powerful first lords became kings. This is how the kingdoms of Europe were born.

With all the fighting and counseling that was going on among the nobles, someone had to do the work of farming and feeding the community. So who did this work? Nobles were far too busy and too important for physical labor and so the feudal system relied on the labor of serfs. Serfs were similar to slaves except that they were paid a small wage and they were not owned by anyone. But serfs were bound to their fiefs and to their lords and could not leave the fief where they were born except in very rare instances. The serfs planted the crops, harvested the wheat, ground the flour, baked the bread, slaughtered the livestock, cured the bacon. They also tended the noble households, served them three meals a day and looked after noble children. The feudal system and the lives of the feudal nobility would not have been possible without serfs and yet the serfs had no rights as individuals. They were able to keep a small portion of the grain they grew and the meat they butchered for themselves but this was the only privilege they enjoyed. Serfs lived with the livestock because livestock was actually more valuable than the serfs themselves. And so the serfs slept with the animals to make sure that the animals remained safe during the night.

One of the defining characteristics about the High Middle Ages was the rigid and unchangeable structure of the social classes. There were three classes of Medieval society and you were destined to die in the same class of society that you were born into. The first class of people is the clergy. Clergy, as we know, are officials of the church from monks and parish priests all the way up to the pope himself. People could choose to join the clergy and often second sons of nobles, who had no chance of inheriting money or title, joined the clergy because it was their only opportunity for influence. The second class in Medieval society was the nobility. Nobles or nobility are landowners. The biggest landowners were kings, and the lowest landowners were knights. But all nobles, regardless of rank, were important and were the only group recognized and protected by the laws of society. The third class of society in the Middle Ages was "everybody else." This category was mainly comprised of serfs although there were a handful of free peasants in this group as well. The vast majority of the Medieval population was part of the third class, and yet the largest group enjoyed the fewest protections or privileges under the law. Estimates vary widely on what percentage of the population were serfs and peasants but they probably comprised no less than 80% of the population until the 1350s.

Despite the rigidity of the feudal class structure, the feudal system was responsible for the reemergence of culture and civilized life in western Europe. Throughout history, great moments of innovation and progress have happened when large numbers of people come together. This phenomenon is called *collective learning*. Here is how David Christian, creator of The Big History Project, explains collective learning— "Each of us is pretty smart, but all that makes up human culture is not the product of individual geniuses. Instead, all the many different things that express the astonishing creativity of our species were slowly built up over time as millions of individuals shared and combined their ideas and experiences over many generations." In other words, when people get together and share ideas, great things happen. And in the High and Late Middle Ages, people came out of their rural isolation into communities of increasing size and complexity, and new ideas came with them. Those ideas were shared and grew over time.

Nowhere is the impact of collective learning in the Middle Ages seen more clearly than in the evolution of the cathedral. In the Early Middle Ages beginning in the reign of Charlemagne, Romanesque architecture was born. The first great churches of Europe were constructed then. Romanesque architecture represented an important moment in the growth of the Medieval mindset because by about 800 CE, Christian Europeans were trying to do something both meaningful and beautiful. Having lived in the shadow of Roman ruins for centuries, Medieval Christians started trying to copy the style of Roman churches, hence the name "Romanesque." And by the end of the Romanesque period, many churches were indeed quite sophisticated and beautiful. With the knowledge they had at the time, Romanesque churches were a great achievement. But these churches will be dwarfed by the grandeur, symmetry and beauty of the Gothic cathedrals that come to dominate the late Medieval landscape.

During the High Middle Ages secular, or non-religious thought, deed or action was still viewed with skepticism, which is why there are no significant works of non-Christian literature or art until the eve of the Renaissance. Construction sites of the great cathedrals, then, became the main breeding ground for collective learning and innovation. The work on these sites was done in the name of God; therefore, creative collaboration was permissible. While working on these divine projects, something powerful and profoundly *human* was also happening on these sacred building sites—innovation, knowledge, progress and hope. The rise of the great spires of Chartres Cathedral and Notre Dame mirror the resurrection of civilized life in Europe. The very reemergence of Western Civilization is tied to the craftsmanship and vision enshrined in Europe's great cathedrals. Lives improved and the hopes and dreams of Medieval Europeans rose with every brick, buttress, arch and spire.

The confidence gained during the construction of the great cathedrals ultimately seeped into other aspects of life. People took risks in other arenas. Kings during the later years of the Middle Ages began to exercise absolute, and often abusive, power over their subjects. Over time, people grew tired of these abuses. In 1215, the nobles of England united to demand protections under the law and threatened the overthrow of the English King John if their demands were not met. The result of this ultimatum was the document called the Magna Carta, which is the basis of much western law today. Not since the Plebeians in ancient Rome threatened revolt over abuses of power had people been willing to fight for rights in government. For the first time in 700 years, the power of a king was limited by the rule of law. The drafting of the Magna Carta marked a pivotal point in the human struggle against the tyranny of absolutism in the western world.

People during the High Middle Ages challenged other positions of authority as well. As you know, Medieval popes and other clergy exercised tremendous power over the uneducated masses in Europe. They controlled whether or not people had access to God and therefore they controlled their eternal destinies. But two events substantially diminished the all-consuming power of the Christian Church during this period. The first was the split of the Church in 1054, known as the Great Schism. By 1000 CE, Christians in the Byzantine Empire were practicing Christianity differently than those in Western Europe. Their sermons were delivered in Greek instead of Latin and Byzantine priests could marry, unlike Western priests. Most importantly, though, Byzantine Christians used religious images called icons in their worship. This was a practice forbidden by the Western church because it was thought to violate the commandment forbidding the worship of false idols. The pope in Rome tried to enforce Western standards in Byzantium but Byzantine Christians felt no sense of obligation to the pope and refused to comply. Byzantine Christians followed the leadership of a figure called the patriarch, who was kind of like a vice-pope who led the Eastern churches. Seeing that resolution between Eastern and Western Christians was impossible, in 1054 Byzantine Christians declared themselves a separate branch of Christianity, called the Christian Orthodox Church. The Western Church then became known as the Catholic Church. This was a devastating blow to the power of the pope, since the split caused him to lose nearly half of his subjects in the "break up." By the end of the 11th century, the Catholic Church would be desperate for ways to regain the power that had been lost as a result of the split. That opportunity presented itself in Byzantium roughly 20 years after the split in 1054.

As we have discussed, Islam had been rapidly expanding into traditionally Christian territory since roughly 650 CE. By 1075, Islam was on the verge of conquering the Byzantine Empire. Sensing that they would be unable to defend themselves without support, the Byzantine Emperor Alexius Comnenus sent repeated pleas to Pope Urban II in Rome to send troops. Urban refused. He was still bitter about the split many years earlier and was in no mood to help, until he saw the Byzantine crisis as an opportunity. In 1095, Pope Urban agreed to send troops to aid Christian brethren in their fight against Muslims *if* the Byzantine emperor and the patriarch agreed to dissolve the Orthodox Church and return to the leadership of the pope. Having no choice but to accept or forfeit his empire to Muslim invaders, Comnenus reluctantly accepted the pope's proposal. The war that followed between Christians and Muslims is known as The Crusades.

The Crusades were a series of nine "holy wars," fought over control of Byzantium and the Holy Land in particular. They lasted nearly 200 years and resulted in the deaths of between nine million and twelve million people. In order to get Christian troops to join him on Crusade, Pope Urban II preyed on the ignorance of most Christians and said that Christ, through Biblical scripture, commanded them to kill Muslims. Urban promised immediate forgiveness for sins for anyone who participated in the Crusades and instant entrance into Heaven. These promises were too good to refuse and hundreds of thousands of Christian Europeans took up arms in the Crusades. There was no clear winner of the Crusades, and Christians and Muslims are still fighting over the Holy Land today, nearly 1000 years later. The human toll of the Crusades was devastating but they did have one small positive result, which was the decline in the power of the Catholic Church and the pope. While on Crusade, Christians realized that Muslims were not monsters like they had been told. Crusaders began to question whether or not everything they had been told by the church was true. Before the Crusades, Christians willingly and blindly followed Church commands. After the Crusades, Christians were much less willing to blindly follow the authority of the pope. They began to question and to think for themselves for the first time in more than 500 years, and just as the Catholic Church had feared it would be, questioning and free-thinking was dangerous. It was dangerous, even deadly, for the unquestionable and all-encompassing power of the pope and Roman Catholicism.

A demand for free-thinking and access to education led to one of the greatest advances of the High Middle Ages--the birth of the university. Since the time of Charlemagne, churches and monasteries served as schools for clergy and for children of wealthy nobles. Education there was often limited to reading and interpreting the Bible and might have included basic arithmetic. The year 1088 marked a huge leap forward in the pursuit of knowledge in the establishment of the University of Bologna. The University of Paris was established in 1119. In England the University of Oxford and the University of Cambridge were established between 1150 and 1225. Powerful collective learning happened in the university setting and great works of classical masters, including Plato and Aristotle, were rediscovered. This knowledge from the past helped illuminate the path to the future.

Peace and Truce of God, *975 to 1000 CE*

Reading and Discussion Questions
1. What was happening in western Europe around 1000 CE that made the Peace and Truce of God necessary?
2. Define "anathema."
3. Looking at documents A and B, what types of behaviors were prohibited?
4. What was the punishment for breaking the laws established in these documents?
5. Do any of the laws established in sources A and B resemble laws in the western world today? Which ones?

As we discussed in our unit on the Early Middle Ages, Charlemagne was able to achieve a high level of peace and stability during his reign but things fell apart again shortly after his death. Later Carolingian kings of Charlemagne's line utterly failed to maintain order. In around 1000 CE, feudalism and the Medieval manor system developed and brought with it its own level of order and stability. And yet by the late 1000s, warfare was rampant.

Powerful feudal lords envied other powerful feudal lords. Envy and greed are powerful motivators and feudal lords began warring for control of territory. In the feudal system, each lord had knights to defend his realm, originally from Vikings and other raiders. But by 1000 CE the Viking threat had subsided and the knights in Europe became restless. Knights are trained to fight and when the foreign enemies disappeared, they began looking for local foes with which to do battle. Feudal lords were all too happy to give the knights an outlet for their aggressions by warring with a rival lord and his fiefdom. After 1000 CE violence among knights in Western Europe was rampant. The bloodshed and loss of life became so bad that a series of meetings and protests were convened to find a solution to the problem. These meetings resulted in a series of documents that are collectively known as The Peace and Truce of God.

Early on, these peace assemblies resembled something more like a religious festival where people gathered to see Passion Plays, pay homage to sacred relics and pray for peace. But out of these gatherings came doctrines, oaths and decrees that would evolve into some of the first Medieval law. Over time, powerful lords and kings recognized these cries for peace presented an opportunity to exercise control. They realized they could make laws to control people. And the laws that they made, in cooperation with church officials, are together known as the Peace and Truce of God. They were especially powerful because they combined church authority with secular authority. For instance, the punishment for any act of violence was excommunication from the church. To be excommunicated from the church is to be separated from God and from life in Heaven in the hereafter. It was incredibly dangerous for a non-religious leader to have such tremendous religious power.

The specifics of the laws themselves that are known as the Peace and Truce of God are interesting because they give us a good idea of the turmoil in Europe around 1000 CE and how religious and secular officials tried to win control. They are even more important because they represent the first efforts of the Middle Ages to establish widespread law and order. And a number of law enforcement institutions take shape during this period which are a fundamental element in the birth of Western Civilization. Every region, province or fiefdom would have had its own version of laws relating to The Peace and Truce of God. The following are two such examples.

A. The Peace of God from the Synod of Charroux

This decree was issued by the Synod Charroux, a church governing body in France, in A.D. 989.

1. Anathema [1] against those who break into churches. If anyone breaks into or robs a church, he shall be anathema unless he makes satisfaction.

2. Anathema against those who rob the poor. If anyone robs a peasant or any other poor person of a sheep, ox, ass, cow, goat, or pig, he shall be anathema unless he makes satisfaction.

3. Anathema against those who injure clergymen. If anyone attacks, seizes, or beats a priest, deacon, or any other clergyman, who is not bearing arms (shield, sword, coat of mail, or helmet), but is going along peacefully or staying in the house, the sacrilegious person shall be excommunicated and cut off from the church, unless he makes satisfaction, or unless the bishop discovers that the clergyman brought it upon himself by his own fault.

B. Truce for the Bishopric of Terouanne (1063)

Drogo, bishop of Terouanne, and count Baldwin [of Hainault] have established this peace with the cooperation of the clergy and people of the land.

Dearest brothers in the Lord, these are the conditions which you must observe during the time of the peace which is commonly called the truce of God, and which begins with sunset on Wednesday and lasts until sunrise on Monday.

1. During those four days and five nights, no man or woman shall assault, wound, or slay another, or attack, seize, or destroy a castle, burg, or villa, by craft or by violence.

2. If anyone violates this peace and disobeys these commands of ours, he shall be exiled for thirty years as a penance [2], and shall make compensation for the injury which he committed. Otherwise he shall be excommunicated by the Lord God and excluded from all Christian fellowship.

3. All who associate with him in any way, who give him advice or aid, or hold converse with him shall be under excommunication [3]until they have made satisfaction.

4. If any violator of the peace shall fall sick and die before he completes his penance, no Christian shall visit him or move his body from the place where it lay, or receive any of his possessions.

5. In addition, brethren, you should observe the peace in regard to lands and animals and all things that can be possessed. If anyone takes from another an animal, a coin, or a garment, during the days of the truce, he shall be excommunicated unless he makes

111

satisfaction. If he desires to make satisfaction for his crime, he shall first restore the thing which he stole or its value in money, and shall do penance for seven years within the bishopric. If he should die before he makes satisfaction and completes his penance, his body shall not be buried or removed from the place where it lay, unless his family shall make satisfaction for him to the person whom he injured.

6. During the days of the peace, no one shall make a hostile expedition on horseback, except when summoned by the count, and all who go with the count shall take for their support only as much as is necessary for themselves and their horses.

7. All merchants and other men who pass through your territory from other lands shall have peace from you.

8. You shall also keep this peace every day of the week from the beginning of Advent to the octave of Epiphany, and from the beginning of Lent to the octave of Easter, and from the feast of Rogations [the Monday before Ascension Day] to the octave of Pentecost.

10. If anyone has been accused of violating the peace and denies the charge, he shall take the communion and undergo the ordeal of hot iron. If he is found guilty, he shall do penance within the bishopric for seven years.

The Crusades and the Notion of the Holy War, 800-1000 CE

Reading and Discussion Questions
1. Define "heathen." Define "indulgence."
2. According to numbered sources A and B below, what happens to Christians who die in battle against non-believers?
3. In Document C, what is the problem the author is asking for help with?
4. What does the author of Document C say people should do "If we love God and wish to be recognized as Christians?" There are two things.
5. Is the request the author is making consistent with your understanding of the teachings of the Bible? Why or why not?

The Crusades were not the first "holy war." Dating all the way back to the sixth century, the Christian Church had been at war with "heathens." There was some question about what happened to a Christian soul who died in a war for God. By the ninth century, the church had taken a clear position on acts of violence by Christians against non-Christians. The following sources show us exactly what that position was.

A. **Forgiveness of Sins for those who Die in Battle with the Heathen, Pope Leo IV, 847 CE**

To the Frankish Army
Now we hope that none of you will be slain, but we wish you to know that the kingdom of heaven will be given as a reward to those who shall be killed in this war. For the Omnipotent knows that they lost their lives fighting for the truth of the faith, for the preservation of their country, and the defense of Christians. And therefore God will give then, the reward which we have named.

112

B. Indulgence for Fighting the Heathen, Pope John VIII, 878 CE

Given to the bishops of France

You have modestly expressed a desire to know whether those who have recently died in war, fighting in defense of the church of God and for the preservation of the Christian religion and of the state, or those who may in 'the future fall in the same cause, may obtain indulgence for their sins. We confidently reply that those who, out of love to the Christian religion, shall die in battle fighting bravely against pagans or unbelievers, shall receive eternal life. For the Lord has said through his prophet: "In whatever hour a sinner shall be converted, I will remember his sins no longer." By the intercession of St. Peter, who has the power of binding and loosing in heaven and on the earth, we absolve, as far as is permissible, all such and commend them by our prayers to the Lord.

C. Call for a Crusade, Gregory VIII, 1074 CE

We hereby inform you that the bearer of this letter, on his recent return from across the sea [from Palestine], came to Rome to visit us. He repeated what we had heard from many others, that a pagan race had overcome the Christians and with horrible cruelty had devastated everything almost to the walls of Constantinople, and were now governing the conquered lands with tyrannical violence, and that they had slain many thousands of Christians as if they were but sheep. If we love God and wish to be recognized as Christians, we should be filled with grief at the misfortune of this great empire [the Greek] and the murder of so many Christians.

But simply to grieve is not our whole duty. The example of our Redeemer and the bond of fraternal love demand that we should lay down our lives to liberate them. "Because he has laid down his life for us: and we ought to lay down our lives for the brethren," [1 John 3:16]. Know, therefore, that we are trusting in the mercy of God and in the power of his might and that we are striving in all possible ways and making preparations to render aid to the Christian empire [the Greek] as quickly as possible. Therefore we beseech you by the faith in which you are united through Christ in the adoption of the sons of God, and by the authority of St. Peter, prince of apostles, we admonish you that you be moved to proper compassion by the wounds and blood of your brethren and the danger of the aforesaid empire and that, for the sake of Christ, you undertake the difficult task of bearing aid to your brethren [the Greeks].

113

Pope Urban II, Speech at Council of Clermont, 1095 CE

Reading and Discussion Questions

1. In two to three sentences, explain your reaction to this speech.
2. Is this speech consistent with what you understand about the Bible as it relates to murder and forgiveness for sins? Explain your answer.
3. What is the Pope asking people to do? Why?
4. If you were in the audience listening to this speech in 1095, would you have done what the Pope asked? Why or why not?
5. What about this speech might people have found convincing?

In 1095, Alexios I Komnenos, the Byzantine emperor, wrote Pope Urban II, and asked for aid from the west against Muslim armies, who taken nearly all of Asia Minor under their control. At the Council of Clermont, Urban addressed a great crowd and urged all to go to the aid of the Greeks and to recover the Holy Land and other Byzantine territory from the rule of the Muslims. Below is Pope Urban II's speech calling for the beginning of the Crusades.

"Most beloved brethren: Urged by necessity, I, Urban, by the permission of God chief bishop and prelate over the whole world, have come into these parts as an ambassador with a divine admonition to you, the servants of God. I hoped to find you as faithful and as zealous in the service of God as I had supposed you to be. But if there is in you any deformity or crookedness contrary to God's law, with divine help I will do my best to remove it. If you wish to be the friends of God, gladly do the things which you know will please Him. You must especially let all matters that pertain to the church be controlled by the law of the church."

"Although, O sons of God, you have promised more firmly than ever to keep the peace among yourselves and to preserve the rights of the church, there remains still an important work for you to do. Freshly quickened by the divine correction, you must apply the strength of your righteousness to another matter which concerns you as well as God. For your brethren who live in the east are in urgent need of your help, and you must hasten to give them the aid which has often been promised them. For, as the most of you have heard, the Turks and Arabs have attacked them and have conquered the territory of Romania [the Greek empire] as far west as the shore of the Mediterranean and the Hellespont, which is called the Arm of St. George. They have occupied more and more of the lands of those Christians, and have overcome them in seven battles. They have killed and captured many, and have destroyed the churches and devastated the empire. If you permit them to continue thus for awhile with impurity, the faithful of God will be much more widely attacked by them. On this account I, or rather the Lord, beseech you as Christ's heralds to publish this everywhere and to persuade all people of whatever rank, foot-soldiers and knights, poor and rich, to carry aid promptly to those Christians and to destroy that vile race from the lands of our friends. I say this to those who are present, it meant also for those who are absent. Moreover, Christ commands it.

"All who die by the way, whether by land or by sea, or in battle against the pagans, shall have immediate remission of sins. This I grant them through the power of God with which I am invested. O what a disgrace if such a despised and base race, which worships demons, should conquer a people which has the faith of omnipotent God and is made glorious with the name of Christ! With what reproaches will the Lord overwhelm us if you do not aid those who, with us, profess the Christian religion! Let those who have been accustomed unjustly to wage private warfare against the faithful now go against the infidels and end with victory this war which should have been begun long ago. Let those who for a long time, have been robbers, now become knights. Let those who have been fighting against their brothers and relatives now fight in a proper way against the barbarians. Let those who have been serving as mercenaries for small pay now obtain the eternal reward. Let those who have been wearing themselves out in both body and soul now work for a double honor. Behold! on this side will be the sorrowful and poor, on that, the rich; on this side, the enemies of the Lord, on that, his friends. Let those who go not put off the journey, but rent their lands and collect money for their expenses; and as soon as winter is over and spring comes, let hem eagerly set out on the way with God as their guide."

Pope Leo III, *On the Misery of the Human Condition, 1195 CE*

Reading and Discussion Questions
1. What is the nature of humans, according to Pope Leo III? Why is man like this?
2. In your opinion, why did the Pope write this? How might it be useful for the church to embrace an attitude like this about humans and human behavior?

In 1195, Pope Innocent III wrote a book called De Miseria Condicionis Humane *(On the Misery of the Human Condition). It represented the prevailing view of the Catholic Church at the time about the nature of man as sinful and base. In his book, Leo discusses many questions about religion, man and the afterlife and paints a very grim picture of all three topics. The following excerpt represents the prevailing attitudes about life during the Middle Ages.*

Who therefore will give my eyes a fountain of tears so that I may bewail the miserable beginning of the human condition, the culpable progress of human behavior, the damnable ending of human dissoluteness. With tears I might consider what man is made of, what man does, what man will be. Man is indeed formed from earth, conceived in sin, born to pain. He does depraved things that are unlawful, shameful things that are indecent, vain things that are unprofitable. He becomes fuel for the fire, food for worms, a mass of putridness. I shall show this more clearly; I shall analyze more fully. Man is formed of dust, of clay, of ashes: what is more vile, from the filthiest sperm. He is conceived in the heat of desire, in the fervor of the flesh, in the stench of lust: what is worse, in the blemish of sin. He is born to labor, fear, sorrow: what is more miserable, to death. He does depraved things by which he offends God, offends his neighbors, offends himself. He does vain and shameful things by which he pollutes his fame, pollutes his person, pollutes his conscience. He does vain things by which he neglects serious things, neglects profitable things, neglects necessary things. He will become fuel for the inextinguishable fire that always flames and burns; food for the immortal worm that always eats and consumes; a mass of horrible putridness that always stinks and is filthy.

Magna Carta, 1215 CE

Reading and Discussion Questions
1. Why was the Magna Carta written?
2. What laws does the Magna Carta make about: Women? Taxation? Treatment when accused of a crime or brought to trial? The relationship of church and state? Explain laws in relation to each topic.
3. What ideas from the Magna Carta have been specifically adopted by our own government?
4. Why do you think the Magna Carta is considered one of the most influential documents in Western history?

In 1215, England was ruled by a self-serving and cruel ruler named King John. John was the younger brother of King Richard "the Lion Heart," who was a beloved king and a great conqueror. Richard won the adoration of the English people by first leading the King's Crusade in the Middle East and then by conquering much land in France for England. Richard was killed in battle and his weak and incompetent brother John took the throne. John was desperate to prove he was as great a king as his brother and tried to continue his brother's conquests in France. But unlike Richard who won battle after battle, John lost . . . a lot. The more he lost, the more eager he became for the next military campaign and so he raised armies—and taxes—to prove his worth. Over time, the English people grew tired of paying John's increasingly excessive taxes and many refused to pay more. When they refused, John threw them in jail, confiscated their property and denied justice or a fair trial to those he imprisoned. He was a tyrant in every sense of the word. In 1215, the English nobles had had enough and drafted a document that would become the cornerstone of western law, known as the Magna Carta or "Great Charter."

The Magna Carta consisted of 63 different provisions or laws that they wanted the king to agree to, and they included everything from marriage and inheritance law to property rights and rules of taxation. John reluctantly signed the Magna Carta in 1215 to avoid being dethroned. While the Magna Carta is important for each of the new laws it established in England, it is more important for what the document, as a whole, did for the first time in modern European history. The Magna Carta established "the rule of law," which means that there is a uniform law of the land and even the king is not above it. This was a landmark moment in the evolution of government and justice because for the first time since the Roman Empire, there was law greater than the power of the king. The Magna Carta has been the model for legal protections in government across the globe and was one of the main influences on the founders of the United States when they crafted a new government in the 1780s. Below are excerpts from the famous document.

JOHN, by the grace of God King of England, Lord of Ireland, Duke of Normandy and Aquitaine, and Count of Anjou, to his archbishops, bishops, abbots, earls, barons, justices, foresters, sheriffs, stewards, servants, and to all his officials and loyal subjects, Greeting.

FIRST, THAT WE HAVE GRANTED TO GOD, and by this present charter have confirmed for us and our heirs in perpetuity, that the English Church shall be free, and shall have its rights undiminished, and its liberties unimpaired. This freedom we shall observe ourselves, and desire to be observed in good faith by our heirs in perpetuity.

TO ALL FREE MEN OF OUR KINGDOM we have also granted, for us and our heirs for ever, all the liberties written out below:

(6) Heirs may be given in marriage, but not to someone of lower social standing. Before a marriage takes place, it shall be' made known to the heir's next-of-kin.

(7) At her husband's death, a widow may have her marriage portion and inheritance at once and without trouble. She shall pay nothing for her dower, marriage portion, or any inheritance that she and her husband held jointly on the day of his death. She may remain in her husband's house for forty days after his death, and within this period her dower shall be assigned to her.

(8) No widow shall be compelled to marry, so long as she wishes to remain without a husband. But she must give security that she will not marry without royal consent, if she holds her lands of the Crown, or without the consent of whatever other lord she may hold them of.

(12) No `scutage' or `aid' (tax) may be levied in our kingdom without its general consent.

(17) Ordinary lawsuits shall not follow the royal court around, but shall be held in a fixed place.

(20) For a trivial offence, a free man shall be fined only in proportion to the degree of his offence, and for a serious offence correspondingly, but not so heavily as to deprive him of his livelihood.

(35) There shall be standard measures of wine, ale, and corn (the London quarter), throughout the kingdom. Weights are to be standardized similarly.

(38) In future no official shall place a man on trial upon his own unsupported statement, without producing credible witnesses to the truth of it.

(39) No free man shall be seized or imprisoned, or stripped of his rights or possessions, or outlawed or exiled, or deprived of his standing in any other way, nor will we proceed with force against him, or send others to do so, except by the lawful judgment of his equals or by the law of the land.

(40) To no one will we sell, to no one deny or delay right or justice.

(45) We will appoint as justices, constables, sheriffs, or other officials, only men that know the law of the realm and are minded to keep it well.

117

(54) No one shall be arrested or imprisoned on the appeal of a woman for the death of any person except her husband.

(60) All these customs and liberties that we have granted shall be observed in our kingdom in so far as concerns our own relations with our subjects. Let all men of our kingdom, whether clergy or laymen, observe them similarly in their relations with their own men.

(61) SINCE WE HAVE GRANTED ALL THESE THINGS for God, for the better ordering of our kingdom, and to allay the discord that has arisen between us and our barons, and since we desire that they shall be enjoyed in their entirety, with lasting strength, for ever, we give and grant to the barons the following security:
The barons shall elect twenty-five of their number to keep, and cause to be observed with all their might, the peace and liberties granted and confirmed to them by this charter.

(63) IT IS ACCORDINGLY OUR WISH AND COMMAND that the English Church shall be free, and that men in our kingdom shall have and keep all these liberties, rights, and concessions, well and peaceably in their fullness and entirety for them and their heirs, of us and our heirs, in all things and all places for ever.

CHAPTER 5—
LATE MIDDLE AGES & PIONEERS OF A NEW AGE
(1300 to 1500 CE)

GUIDING QUESTIONS
- How was life changing in Europe by 1300?
- What were the three crises that impacted Europe in the 1300s and what was the impact of each?
- How did the Black Death help to usher in a new era in Europe?
- How did Aquinas, Dante, Petrarch and Giotto each help to transform the way people thought and lived their lives?

By 1300, the people of Europe hoped and even believed that the worst of their suffering was over. As you read in the High Middle Ages, civilization was reemerging. Cities became centers of trade, the feudal system became the basis for secular government and the Catholic Church seemed to be loosening its stranglehold over Medieval Christians. Education was increasing and with it, free thought. There might be, many people came to believe, a light at the end of the long dark tunnel. But the period known as the Late Middle Ages (1300-1500) proved that tunnel was much longer and darker than had previously been imagined.

By 1300 the suffering in Europe was not yet at an end. In fact, a combination of rebellion, plague and war during the 14th century brought Europe to the brink of collapse. The Middle Ages are usually not thought of as an important time for people's struggle for rights in government and an end to oppression; and yet, in the 1300s, we see the first signs of future rebellions stirring among the peasants and the middle class. It is true that the feudal system brought stability and commerce to European civilizations. But the feudal system is made up of rigid and inflexible social classes and feudal society is run by the nobility. In Medieval Europe, those who owned land mattered and had rights, and those who did not own land did not. The vast majority of people in England and France did not own land and were growing increasingly resentful of the wealth and privilege of the upper class. Between 1300 and 1380, there were several dozen, if not hundreds of small uprisings both in rural and urban areas. The targets of these rebellions was not the king or queen but the nobles, with whom peasants and the working class had the most contact. Most of these rebellions were put down with swift brutality, including public executions of the rebels. This conflict between social classes that began brewing as early as the 1300s will eventually erupt into full-blown revolutions across Europe.

As the lower classes battled against their noble lords and masters, France and England were immersed in a war for control of Europe. This conflict, known as the Hundred Years' War, lasted 116 years and settled the rivalry between England and France for a time. Since the 11th century, English kings had controlled substantial territory in France. Very ambitious English kings, including Richard the Lionheart and his cowardly brother King John, waged frequent wars in France to increase British land. The war began in 1337 and for the next 116 years, the French fought to push the English out of France for good. The war raged on until 1453 and for much of the long, bloody conflict England seemed the obvious winner. But thanks to the leadership, and some would say the miraculous acts, of Joan of Arc, the French orchestrated a shocking turnaround and chased the English out of France for good.

The human and physical impact of the war was substantial. About one million people died as a result the war and while most of those deaths were on the battlefield. tens of thousands died of starvation. The physical devastation of towns and cities in France was also enormous. Overall, the major impact of the Hundred Years' War was that it began the crumbling of the feudal system. The majority of the people who died were peasants. Fewer peasants meant a smaller workforce to support the Medieval feudal manor. Though the war changed the feudal system and European society, it was a much more deadly enemy—the Black Death—that caused truly radical change.

The bubonic plague, or the Black Death as it was called, struck Europe in 1347. In terms of the loss of human life, the Black Death is the biggest catastrophe in history. It is estimated that, out of a population of 80 million people in Europe in 1347, roughly 60% (or 48 million people) died of the plague. The impact of this disease on Europe is immeasurable. It was a turning point in history. In many places, the plague caused the final collapse of the feudal system since the peasant class was hit the hardest by the plague. As you have read, feudalism cannot survive without the laborers. As old institutions crumbled, old customs and beliefs were abandoned. Survivors of the Black Death looked for new ways of understanding life and the world around them. Many new ideas were born during the years after the plague and many old ideas from the classical past were unearthed and learned anew. This demand for knowledge both old and new resulted in a rebirth for the people of Western Europe called the Renaissance.

Adversity is defined as a state or instance of serious or continued difficulty or misfortune. Adversity is the thing in life that humans are almost genetically programmed to avoid. But adversity in life is inevitable and many great minds suggest that the way we deal with adversity shows us the depth of our character. Many people have laid down and given up in the face of adversity in history. But far more people fight through it and find great courage and strength to overcome hard times. The period of the late Middle Ages is one of my favorites because the Medieval Europeans refused to surrender to their suffering. An unfathomable portion of the population of Europe had died during the 1300s. There was virtually no family that had not been touched by tragedy. But rather than wallowing in despair, they chose to live. And because they did not give up, an era of unparalleled intellectual, cultural and religious progress followed from their misery.

In the early 1300s, a Florentine poet named Francesco Petrarch was one of those people who would not accept the misery of the past as his only option for the future. He had a lot to feel hopeless about, as almost everyone he had ever loved, including his entire family, was killed by the plague. But Petrarch did not give up. Petrarch was one of the greatest students ever of the classics. He wrote hundreds of letters and poems that remembered the greatness of the Greeks and Romans. He wrote to Cicero, Seneca and other Stoics, as well as Homer and other great Greek thinkers. Petrarch deeply lamented the darkness of his age because he knew how much more was possible and had been achieved in the past. He called on people in his writings to awaken from their stupor and live the way God had intended. Francesco Petrarch was the inventor of a new worldview called Humanism. His ideas led to revolutions in every facet of life.

Petrarch wrote poems like the *Epistolae Metrica* that said aloud what people across Europe had likely been feeling for ages.

Living, I despise what melancholy fate
has brought us wretches in these evil years.
Long before my birth time smiled and may again,
for once there was, and yet will be, more joyful days.
But in this middle age time's dregs
sweep around us, and we beneath a heavy
load of vice. Genius, virtue, glory now
have gone, leaving chance and sloth to rule.
Shameful vision this! We must awake or die!

Petrarch believed humans were *powerful*, not helpless. He believed human achievements must be *celebrated*, not suppressed. And he believed that life should be deeply *savored*, not squandered. He asked over and over and over again, Why can't we have happiness here on earth and in the hereafter? And the answer that came back faintly at first and then louder over time was, "*We can.*"

Petrarch was a pioneer of a new age, but there were others. During the High Middle Ages, Europeans were exposed to the ideas of Aristotle at newly emerging universities. This changed everything, including the life and writings of a man called Thomas Aquinas. Aristotle, who was a Greek and therefore a "pagan," was a huge influence on the writings of Aquinas, who was a monk and a theologian and is now a saint. Aquinas was deeply religious but still was able to embrace the wisdom of classical genius like Aristotle. In his greatest work, *Summa Theologica*, Aquinas tried to prove the existence of God, which had before been considered fundamentally unprovable. Using some of the arguments of Aristotle, Aquinas used reason instead of faith to prove God. This was a huge leap forward in western philosophy and in church ideas. Very carefully, Aquinas forged new ground by marrying classical wisdom and church teachings. This was an idea that even a century before would have been considered an act of heresy and punished harshly. Aquinas' success paved the way for others to use reason and rational thinking to answer other big questions about life and the cosmos.

As people gradually gained knowledge through collective learning and rational thinking, they also gained *courage*. Authors like Dante Alighieri shook the establishment to its core by writing the epic poem, *The Divine Comedy*. Dante's book is considered a crucial bridge between the Middle Ages and the emerging Renaissance and is one of the greatest works of world literature. Dante, who wrote the *The Divine Comedy* in the early 14th century, was wise to keep his subject matter religious. He tells a story of a man's journey from hell to heaven, from sin to redemption. It is the essential religious journey. But Dante's story was also wildly imaginative. Most of the images he paints in his writing have no basis in the Bible but are pure fantasy. *The Divine Comedy* forged new ground by interpreting, rather than merely reciting, the Bible and Biblical stories. It shocked audiences then and it continues to captivate them today.

Big changes sometimes happen in hundreds or thousands of tiny ways. The actions of a handful of courageous men in a time when self-expression was forbidden absolutely transformed human existence. By daring to say, think and write something new, these pioneers ushered in a new age, a new way of thinking and finally, a new way of living.

PRIMARY SOURCES – THE LATE MIDDLE AGES & PIONEERS OF A NEW AGE

Thomas Aquinas, *Summa Theologica*, 1270 CE

<u>Reading and Discussion Questions</u>
1. What are the three objections to the existence of God that Aquinas explains and how does he respond to each objection?
2. Explain each of the five proofs that Aquinas puts forth that he says explain the existence of God and try to identify what the science is that he uses in each of his proofs.
3. In what way are the ideas of Aquinas different from other Medieval thought? Why might they be considered a bridge to a new era in history?

Thomas Aquinas (1225 to 1274) was a Catholic priest and theologian from Italy who wrote Summa Theologica, *a 3000-page work that attempted to answer the fundamental questions of the Christian faith. He is one of the most influential thinkers in Western history. Aquinas was as devout a Catholic as there ever was and in many ways he embodied the Medieval ideal of religion as life. Aquinas devoted his life to supporting the church, defending the faith and recruiting new followers to Catholicism. It is for this reason that Aquinas was made a saint by the Catholic Church. But the ideas in* Summa Theologica *represent a subtle but profoundly important shift in thinking and laid the groundwork for future intellectual revolutions.*

Summa Theologica *is a massive work, and it tackles questions in three areas: the nature of God, the nature of man, and the nature of Christ. That may not sound at all revolutionary but the very fact that Aquinas' work was asking questions and providing answers was groundbreaking. Since the birth of the Christian Church, asking questions about religion was forbidden and getting answers was an impossibility. So Aquinas' works signaled a radical shift in thinking. What was even more radical for the time was that Aquinas was heavily influenced in his own writings by non-Christians. He obsessively read Plato and Aristotle and most of his ideas about the cosmos and man's place in it, as well as his relationship to a higher power, were influenced by pagan philosophers. For centuries before* Summa Theologica, *only one answer had ever been given to the question "How do we know God exists?" The answer was "because the Bible says it is so." But Aquinas' work marked the first time logic and scientific proofs were used to explain God's existence. In the Middle Ages, "proof" was a forbidden concept. Faith, or believing something when there is no proof, was the main Medieval virtue. Aquinas' proofs of God and of other big questions from the Bible mark the birth of scientific thinking in an era when science was still strictly forbidden.*

Whether God exists.

It is objected (1) that God does not exist, because if one of two contradictory things is infinite, the other will be totally destroyed; that it is implied in the name God that there is a certain infinite goodness: if then God existed, no evil would be found. But evil is found in the world; therefore it is objected that God does not exist. Again, that what can be accomplished through a less number of principles will not be accomplished through more. It is objected that all things that appear on the earth can be accounted for through other principles, without supposing that God exists, since what is natural can be traced to a natural principle, and what proceeds from a proposition can be traced to the human reason or will. Therefore that there is no necessity to suppose that God exists. But as against this note what is said of the person of God (Exod. III., 14) I am that I am. Conclusion. There must be found in the nature of things one first immovable Being, a primary cause, necessarily existing, not created; existing the most widely, good, even the best possible; the first ruler through the intellect, and the ultimate end of all things, which is God.

I answer that it can be proved in five ways that God exists.

The first and plainest is the method that proceeds from the point of view of motion. It is certain and in accord with experience, that things on earth undergo change. Now, everything that is moved is moved by something; nothing, indeed, is changed, except it is changed to something which it is in potentiality. Moreover, anything moves in accordance with something actually existing; change itself, is nothing else than to bring forth something from potentiality into actuality. Now, nothing can be brought from potentiality to actual existence except through something actually existing: thus heat in action, as fire, makes fire-wood, which is hot in potentiality, to be hot actually, and through this process, changes itself. The same thing cannot at the same time be actually and potentially the same thing, but only in regard to different things. What is actually hot cannot be at the same time potentially hot, but it is possible for it at the same time to be potentially cold. It is impossible, then, that anything should be both mover and the thing moved, in regard to the same thing and in the same way, or that it should move itself. Everything, therefore, is moved by something else. If, then, that by which it is moved, is also moved, this must be moved by something still different, and this, again, by something else. But this process cannot go on to infinity because there would not be any first mover, nor, because of this fact, anything else in motion, as the succeeding things would not move except because of what is moved by the first mover, just as a stick is not moved except through what is moved from the hand. Therefore it is necessary to go back to some first mover, which is itself moved by nothing—and this all men know as God.

The second proof is from the nature of the efficient cause. We find in our experience that there is a chain of causes: nor is it found possible for anything to be the efficient cause of itself, since it would have to exist before itself, which is impossible. Nor in the case of efficient causes can the chain go back indefinitely, because in all chains of efficient causes, the first is the cause of the middle, and these of the last, whether they be one or many. If the cause is removed, the effect is removed. Hence if there is not a first cause, there will not be a last, nor a middle. But if the chain were to go back infinitely, there would be no first cause, and thus no ultimate effect, nor middle causes, which is admittedly false. Hence we must presuppose some first efficient cause—which all call God.

The third proof is taken from the natures of the merely possible and necessary. We find that certain things either may or may not exist, since they are found to come into being and be destroyed, and in consequence potentially, either existent or non-existent. But it is impossible for all things that are of this character to exist eternally, because what may not exist, at length will not. If, then, all things were merely possible (mere accidents),

123

eventually nothing among things would exist. If this is true, even now there would be nothing, because what does not exist, does not take its beginning except through something that does exist. If then nothing existed, it would be impossible for anything to begin, and there would now be nothing existing, which is admittedly false. Hence not all things are mere accidents, but there must be one necessarily existing being. Now every necessary thing either has a cause of its necessary existence, or has not. In the case of necessary things that have a cause for their necessary existence, the chain of causes cannot go back infinitely, just as not in the case of efficient causes, as proved. Hence there must be presupposed something necessarily existing through its own nature, not having a cause elsewhere but being itself the cause of the necessary existence of other things---which all call God.

The fourth proof arises from the degrees that are found in things. For there is found a greater and a less degree of goodness, truth, nobility, and the like. But more or less are terms spoken of various things as they approach in diverse ways toward something that is the greatest, just as in the case of hotter (more hot) which approaches nearer the greatest heat. There exists therefore something that is the truest, and best, and most noble, and in consequence, the greatest being. For what are the greatest truths are the greatest beings, as is said in the Metaphysics Bk. II. 2. What moreover is the greatest in its way, in another way is the cause of all things of its own kind (or genus); thus fire, which is the greatest heat, is the cause of all heat, as is said in the same book (cf. Plato and Aristotle). Therefore there exists something that is the cause of the existence of all things and of the goodness and of every perfection whatsoever---and this we call God.

The fifth proof arises from the ordering of things for we see that some things which lack reason, such as natural bodies, are operated in accordance with a plan. It appears from this that they are operated always or the more frequently in this same way the closer they follow what is the Highest; whence it is clear that they do not arrive at the result by chance but because of a purpose. The things, moreover, that do not have intelligence do not tend toward a result unless directed by some one knowing and intelligent; just as an arrow is sent by an archer. Therefore there is something intelligent by which all natural things are arranged in accordance with a plan---and this we call God.

In response to the first objection, then, I reply what Augustine says; that since God is entirely good, He would permit evil to exist in His works only if He were so good and omnipotent that He might bring forth good even from the evil. It therefore pertains to the infinite goodness of God that he permits evil to exist and from this brings forth good.

My reply to the second objection is that since nature is ordered in accordance with some defined purpose by the direction of some superior agent, those things that spring from nature must be dependent upon God, just as upon a first cause. Likewise, what springs from a proposition must be traceable to some higher cause which is not the human reason or will, because this is changeable and defective and everything changeable and liable to non-existence is dependent upon some unchangeable first principle that is necessarily self-existent as has been shown.

Dante Alighieri, *The Divine Comedy*, 1265 CE

1. In Canto I, what happens to Dante? Where is he? What animals does he encounter? Who does he meet?
2. In Canto XII, what is the Phlegethon? Who does Dante encounter there?
3. How are the sinners being punished in Canto XII, specifically? Does this punishment represent poetic justice? Explain.
4. In Canto XXVIII, what sinners do Virgil and Dante encounter?
5. Who is Bertrand de Born and what was his sin? How was he punished in accordance with his sin?
6. In Canto XXVIII, who is the sinner Dante meets that is split open from chin to groin? Why is this sinner punished in this way?
7. Describe or draw a picture of Lucifer, based on the description in Canto XXXIV.
8. Who are the three sinners in Lucifer's mouth and what, specifically were their sins? Why are they being punished in this way?
9. How do Dante and Virgil finally exit the Inferno? Where are they headed?
10. What do you believe Dante's message is to his reader, based on your understanding of what you have read?

Dante Alighieri (1265 – 1321), the author of The Divine Comedy, *was an Italian poet living in Florence during the Late Middle Ages. Dante spent the last thirteen years of his life writing the epic poem, which is considered one of the great masterpieces of world literature. The work was completed in 1321 and is a critical bridge between the Middle Ages and the Renaissance. Like other men of the age, Dante was a devout Catholic and wrestled with questions about God, the afterlife, sin and salvation. He explored all of those questions in* The Divine Comedy. *In that way, Dante's work is quintessentially Medieval. But the way Dante explored those questions was imaginative and daring, which are hallmarks of the Renaissance.*

The Divine Comedy, *like earlier epics including the* Iliad *and the* Aeneid, *is an adventure story of a hero who has embarked upon a great journey. Dante is the hero and protagonist of his own story. His journey takes him through the depths of Hell, atop the mountain of Purgatory and finally face-to-face with God in Heaven. Dante's poem is a trilogy, or a work in three parts, and the poem is divided by the parts of his journey—Inferno (Hell), Purgatory and Paradise (Heaven). His work is an allegory, which is a story that uses symbols or metaphors to teach a lesson, and in the* Divine Comedy, *Dante's journey through Hell and into Heaven is a metaphor for the journey from sin to redemption. The* Divine Comedy *is meant to scare the reader back onto the straight and narrow by creating vivid pictures of how sins are punished. In the spirit of the Middle Ages, Dante's work is literally scary as hell.*

Beyond the fantastic voyage of his pilgrim, however, Dante's work is revolutionary for its use of language and of imagination. The Divine Comedy *was the first book of any substance to be written in the common man's language, which for Dante was Italian. All previous "great" works were written in Latin, the language of scholars. Dante wanted common people to be able to read his book and so he wrote it in their* language. Dante's work was also groundbreaking because the details he wrote about Heaven and Hell were entirely made up. At the time when Dante wrote The Divine Comedy, self-expression was forbidden and interpretation of the Bible was a sin. Dante did both in his work. The Bible says almost nothing about what Heaven and Hell look like or how sinners were punished. Dante's work is overflowing with graphic descriptions of each circle of Hell, grotesque punishments for each sin and even real people being punished for those sins. The level of detail in The Divine Comedy paints a vivid picture of Dante's journey so that we, as the reader, all become pilgrims. As dark and terrifying as Hell is, Paradise is equally awe-inspiring. The Divine Comedy is a powerful tool for directing Christians in how they should live, but it also became a powerful tool for change. It was a wild work of imagination, the likes of which had not been known in Europe for more than 500 years. And it became an inspiration for others who sought more freedom to express themselves, to explore their passions, to ask questions and to find answers.

CANTO I—The Three Beasts, Virgil

Halfway through the journey we are living
I found myself deep in a darkened forest,
For I had lost all trace of the straight path.

Ah how hard it is to tell what it was like,
5   How wild the forest was, how dense and rugged!
To think of it still fills my mind with panic.

So bitter it is that death is hardly worse!
But to describe the good discovered there
I here will tell the other things I saw.

10   I cannot say clearly how I entered there,
So drowsy with sleep had I grown at that hour
When first I wandered off from the true way.

But when I had reached the base of a hill,
There at the border where the valley ended
15   That had cut my heart to the quick with panic,

I looked up at the hill and saw its shoulder
Mantled already with the planet's light
That leads all people straight by every road.

With that my panic quieted a little
20   After lingering on in the lake of my heart
Through the night I had so grievously passed.

And like a person who with panting breath
Struggles ashore out of the wide ocean
Only to glance back at the treacherous surf,

25 Just so my mind, racing on ahead,
 Turned back to marvel at the pass no one
 Ever before had issued from alive.

 After resting awhile my worn-out body,
 I pressed on up the wasted slope so that
30 I always had one firm foot on the ground.

 But look! right near the upgrade of the climb
 Loomed a fleet and nimble-footed leopard
 With coat completely covered by dark spots!

 He did not flinch or back off from my gaze,
35 But blocking the path that lay before me,
 Time and again he forced me to turn around.

The hour was the beginning of the morning,
 And the sun was rising with those stars
 That first attended it when divine Love

40 Set these lovely creations round in motion,
 So that the early hour and the pleasant season
 Gave me good reason to keep up my hopes

 Of that fierce beast there with his gaudy pelt.
 But not so when — to add now to my fears —
45 In front of me I caught sight of a lion!

 He appeared to be coming straight at me
 With head held high and furious for hunger,
 So that the air itself seemed to be shaking.

 And then a wolf stalked, ravenously lean,
50 Seemingly laden with such endless cravings
 That she had made many live in misery!

 She caused my spirits to sink down so low,
 From the dread I felt in seeing her there,
 I lost all hope of climbing to the summit.

55 And just as a man, anxious for big winnings,
 But the time comes instead for him to lose,
 Cries and grieves the more he thinks about it,

 So did the restless she-beast make me feel
 When, edging closer toward me, step by step,
60 She drove me back to where the sun is silent.

 While I was falling back to lower ground,
 Before my eyes now came a figure forward
 Of one grown feeble from long being mute.

When I saw him in that deserted spot,
65   "Pity me!" I shouted out to him,
"Whoever you are, a shade or living man."

"Not a man," he answered. "Once a man,
Of parents who had come from Lombardy;
Both of them were Mantuans by birth.

70   "I was born late in Julius's reign
And dwelt at Rome under the good Augustus
In the period of false and lying gods.

"A poet I was, and I sang of the just
Son of Anchises [Aeneas]who embarked from Troy
75   After proud Ilium was burned to ashes.

"But why do you turn back to so much grief?
Why not bound up the delightful mountain
Which is the source and font of every joy?"

"Are you then Virgil and that wellspring
80   That pours forth so lush a stream of speech?"
Shamefacedly I responded to him.

"O glory and light of all other poets,
May the long study and the profound love
That made me search your work come to my aid!

85   "You are my mentor and my chosen author:
Alone you are the one from whom I have taken
The beautiful style that has brought me honor.

"Look at the beast that drove me to turn back!
Rescue me from her, celebrated sage,
90   For she causes my veins and pulse to tremble."

"You are destined to take another route,"
He answered, seeing me reduced to tears,
"If you want to be clear of this wilderness,

"Because this beast that forces you to cry out
95   Will not let anyone pass by her way
But harries him until she finally kills him.

110   "I think and judge it best for you, then,
To follow me, for I will be your guide,
Directing you to an eternal place

115 "Where you shall listen to the desperate screams
And see the spirits of the past in torment,
As at his second death each one cries out;

"And you shall also see those who are happy
Even in flames, since they hope to come,
120 Whenever that may be, among the blessed.

"If you still wish to ascend to the blessed,
A soul worthier than I shall guide you:
On my departure I will leave you with her.

"For the Emperor who rules there above,
125 Since I lived in rebellion to his law,
Will not permit me to enter his city.

"Everywhere his kingdom comes: there he reigns,
There his heavenly city and high throne.
Oh happy the one elected to go there!"

130 And I said to him, "Poet, I entreat you,
By the God whom you have never known,
So may I flee from this and from worse evil,

"Lead me to the place you just described
That I may come to see Saint Peter's gate
135 And those you say are deeply sorrowful."

Then he moved on and I walked straight behind.

CANTO XII — The Violent, Phlegethon

The place where we had come to clamber down
The bank was mountainous, and what was there
So grim all eyes would turn away from it.

Just like that rockslide on this side of Trent
5 That struck the flank of the Adige River —
Either by an earthquake or erosion —

Where, from the mountaintop it started down
To the plain below, the boulders shattered so,
For anyone above they formed a path,

10 Such was the downward course of that ravine;
And at the brink over the broken chasm
There lay outspread the infamy of Crete

129

That was conceived within the bogus cow;
And when he saw us, he bit into himself,
15   Like someone whom wrath tears up from inside.

My clever guide cried out to him, "Perhaps
You believe that this is the Duke of Athens
Who in the upper world contrived your death?

"Go off, you beast! this man does not approach
20   Instructed by your sister but comes here
In order to observe your punishments."

Just as the bull breaks loose right at that moment
When he has been dealt the fatal blow
And cannot run but jumps this way and that,

25   So I saw the Minotaur react —
And my quick guide called out, "Run for the pass!
While he's raging is our chance to get down!"

And so we made our way down through the pile
Of rocks which often slid beneath my feet
30   Because they were not used to holding weight.

I pushed on, thinking, and he said, "You wonder,
Perhaps, about that wreckage which is guarded
By that bestial rage I just now quelled.

"Now you should know that the other time
35   I journeyed here below to lower hell,
These boulders as yet had not tumbled down:

"But for certain, if I recall correctly,
It was shortly before He came who took
From Dis the great spoils of the topmost circle

40   "That this deep loathsome valley on all sides
Trembled so, I thought the universe
Felt love, because of which, as some believe,

"The world has often been turned back to chaos.
And at that instant this ancient rock split up,
45   Scattering like this, here and elsewhere.

"But fasten your eyes below — down to the plain
Where we approach a river of blood boiling
Those who harm their neighbors by violence."

O blind cupidity and rabid anger
50   Which so spur us ahead in our short life
Only to steep us forever in such pain!

130

I saw a broad ditch bent into a bow,
As though holding the whole plain in its embrace,
Just as my guide had explained it to me.

55   Between the ditch and the foot of the bank
Centaurs came running single-file, armed
With arrows as they hunted in the world.

Seeing us descend, they all pulled up,
And from their ranks three of them moved forward
60   With bows and with their newly selected shafts.

And from afar one shouted, "To what tortures
Do you approach as you climb down the slope?
Answer from there, or else I draw my bow."

My master said, "We will make our response
65   To Chiron there who hovers at your side —
To your own harm, your will was always rash."

Then he nudged me, and said, "That is Nessus,
Who died for the lovely Dejanira
By taking his own revenge upon himself;

70   "And in the middle, staring at his chest,
Is mighty Chiron, who tutored Achilles;
The last is Pholus, who was so full of frenzy."

Thousands on thousands march around the ditch,
Shooting at any soul that rises up
75   Above the blood more than its guilt allows.

When we drew near to these fleet-footed beasts,
Chiron took an arrow and with its notch
Parted his shaggy beard back from his jaws,

And when he had uncovered his huge mouth,
80   Said to his companions, "Have you noticed
How that one there behind stirs what he touches?

"A dead man's feet would not cause that to happen!"
And my good guide, now standing at the chest
Where the two natures fuse together, answered,

85   "He is indeed alive, and so alone
That I must show him all the somber valley.
Necessity not pleasure brings him here.

"A spirit came from singing alleluia
To commission me with this new office:
90   He is no robber nor I a thieving soul.

"But by the power by which I move my steps
Along this roadway through the wilderness,
Lend us one of your band to keep by us

"To lead us where we two can ford across
95   And there to carry this man on his back,
For he is not a spirit who flies through air."

Chiron pivoted around on his right breast,
Saying to Nessus, "Go back and guide them — if
Another troop challenges, drive them away!"

100   So with this trusted escort we moved on
Along the bank of the bubbling crimson river
Where boiling souls raised their piercing cries.

There I saw people buried to their eyebrows,
And the strong centaur said, "These are tyrants
105   Who wallowed in bloodshed and plundering.

"Here they bewail their heartless crimes: here lie
Both Alexander and fierce Dionysius
Who brought long years of woe to Sicily;

"And there with his head of jet-black hair
110   Is Azzolino; and that other blond one
Is Opizzo d'Este, who in the world

"Actually was slain by his own stepson."
With that I turned to the poet, who said,
"Now let him be your first guide, I your second."

115 A little farther on, the centaur halted
Above some people who appeared to rise
Out of the boiling stream up to their throats.

He pointed to one shade off by himself,
And said, "In God's own bosom, this one stabbed
120   The heart that still drips blood upon the Thames."

Then I saw others too who held their heads
And even their whole chests out of the stream,
And many of them there I recognized.

So the blood eventually thinned out
125   Until it scalded only their feet in it;
And here we found a place to ford the ditch.

132

"Just as you see, this side, the boiling brook
Grow gradually shallower," the centaur said,
"So I would also have you understand

130 "That on the other side the riverbed
Slopes deeper down from here until it reaches
Again the spot where tyranny must grieve.

"Heavenly justice there strikes with its goads
That Attila who was a scourge on earth
135 And Pyrrhus and Sextus, and forever milks

"The tears, released by boiling blood from both
Rinier of Corneto and Rinier Pazzo
Who waged such open warfare on the highways."

Then he turned back and once more crossed the ford.

Notes

12 The Minotaur, born of Pasiphae the queen of Crete who used a wooden cow to seduce a bull, was half man and half bull. Theseus (l. 17) slew him with the help of Ariadne, half-sister to the beast. The Minotaur appears here as an example of violence in the seventh circle.

40 Again Christ's harrowing of hell is alluded to. The crucifixion was marked by a great earthquake.

47 The river of blood is the Phlegethon.

56 The centaurs were half men and half horse; their leader was Chiron. The centaur Nessus (l. 67) tried to rape Dejanira, but was killed by her husband Hercules. Before dying, Nessus gave her a poisoned shirt for Hercules; it destroyed him.

98 Nessus now carries Dante on his back along the riverbank and across the boiling shallows to the other side (l. 126).

107 Alexander the Great or the tyrant Alexander of Pherae (368-359 B. C.). Dionysius of Syracuse was a fifth-century tyrant.

110 Azzolino da Romano (1194-1259) and Opizzo II d'Este (d. 1293) were two brutal Italian tyrants.

119 Guy de Montfort, to avenge his father's death, murdered Henry, nephew of Henry III of England, in 1271.

134 Attila the Hun, who ruled from 433 to 453, was called the Scourge of God.

135 This Pyrrhus may be either the son of Achilles, a fighter in the Trojan war, or the king of Epirus (318-272 B. C.) who battled against the Romans. Sextus is probably the son of Pompey the Great; he became a pirate.

137 Rinier of Cometo and Rinier Pazzo were two notorious highwaymen of Dante's day.

CANTO XXVIII
The Sowers of Discord, Bertrand de Born

Who could ever, even in straight prose
And after much retelling, tell in full
The bloodletting and wounds that I now saw?

Each tongue that tried would certainly trip up
5 Because our speaking and remembering
Cannot comprehend the scope of pain.

Were all those men gathered again together
Who once in the fateful land of Apulia
Mourned the lifeblood spilled by the Trojans,

133

10   And those who shed their blood in the long war
       In which the spoils were a mound of golden rings,
       As Livy has unerringly informed us,

       And those also who felt the painful gashes
       In the onslaught against Robert Guiscard,
15   And those others whose bones are still stacked up

       At Ceperano where all the Apulians
       Turned traitors, and those too from Tagliacozzo
       Where old Alardo conquered without weapons,

       And those who show their limbs run through and those
20   With limbs hacked off — they all could not have matched
       The ninth pocket's degraded state of grief.

       Even a cask with bottom or sides knocked out
       Never cracked so wide as one soul I saw
       Burst open from the chin to where one farts.

25   His guts were hanging out between his legs;
       His pluck gaped forth and that disgusting sack
       Which turns to shit what throats have gobbled down.

       While I was all agog with gazing at him,
       He stared at me and, as his two hands pulled
30   His chest apart, cried, "Look how I rip myself!

       "Look at how mangled is Mohammed here!
       In front of me, Ali treks onward, weeping,
       His face cleft from his chin to his forelock.

       "And all the others whom you see down here
35   Were sowers of scandal and schism while
       They lived, and for this they are rent in two.

       "A devil goes in back here who dresses us
       So cruelly by trimming each one of the pack
       With the fine cutting edge of his sharp sword

40   "Whenever we come round this forlorn road:
       Because by then our old wounds have closed up
       Before we pass once more for the next blow.

       "But who are you, moping upon that ridge
       Perhaps to put off facing the penalty
45   Pronounced on you by your own accusations?"

       "Death has not yet reached him, nor guilt led him
       To the torture here," — my master answered,
       "But, to offer him the full experience,

                           134

"I who am dead am destined to guide him
50 From circle to circle down here into hell,
And, as surely as I speak to you, it's true."

More than a hundred, when they heard him, halted
Inside the ditch to peer at me in wonder,
Forgetting their torments for the moment.

55 "Tell Brother Dolcino then, you who perhaps
Shortly shall see the sun, to arm himself
With food — unless he wants to follow me

"Here promptly — so that the weight of snow
Does not bring victory to the Novarese
60 Who otherwise would not find winning easy."

With one foot lifted in the air to go,
Mohammed addressed these words to me,
Then set the foot back on the ground and left.

Another sinner with his throat lanced through
65 And with his nose carved off up to the eyebrows
And with only a single ear remaining

Stopped with the rest to stare in amazement,
And, before they could, he opened wide his windpipe,
Which on the outside looked bright red, and said,

70 "O you whom guilt does not condemn and whom
I have seen in the land of Italy,
Unless a strong resemblance now deceives me,

"Remember Pier da Medicina should you
Ever return to view the gentle plain
75 Which slopes from Vercelli to Marcabò,

"And make known to the two best men of Fano,
To Messers Guido and Angiolello,
That, unless our foresight here be worthless,

"They shall be thrown overboard from their ship
80 And sunk with stones near La Cattolica
Through the treachery of a felon tyrant.

"Between the islands of Cyprus and Majorca
Neptune never saw a crime more heinous
By raiding pirates or the ancient Argives.

135

85   "That one-eyed traitor — who rules over the city
       On which someone here with me would prefer
       That he had never fed his single sight —

       "Shall first arrange for them a parley with him,
       Then act to make sure that they will not need
90   Vows or prayers against Focara's headwinds."

       And I told him, "If you want me to carry
       News of you above, point out and tell me
       Who is the one who rues sighting the city?"

       At that he gripped a hand upon the jaw
95   Of his companion and forced his mouth agape,
       Shouting, "Here's the one, but he doesn't talk!

       "This chap in exile submerged all the doubts
       Of Caesar, boasting that one well prepared
       Can only suffer loss by hesitation."

100   Oh how flabbergasted he appeared to me,
       With his tongue slashed in his throat — Curio,
       Who once had been so resolute in speaking!

       And one who had both of his hands chopped off,
       Raising up his stumps in the smut-filled air
105   So that the blood besmeared and soiled his face,

       Cried out, "You will also remember Mosca
       Who said, alas, 'What's done is dead and gone!'
       That sowed the seed of trouble for the Tuscans!"

       And I added, "— and for your kinsfolk, death!"
110   With that the sinner, sorrow heaped on sorrow,
       Scurried away like one gone mad with grief.

       But I stayed there to inspect that muster
       And spied something that I should be afraid
       To tell of on my own without more proof,

115   Had I not the assurance of my conscience,
       The good companion heartening a man
       Beneath the breastplate of its pure intention.

       I saw for sure — and still I seem to see it —
       A body without a head that walked along
120   Just as the others in that sad herd were walking,

       But it held the severed head by the hair,
       Swinging it like a lantern in its hand,
       And the head stared at us and said, "Ah me!"

Itself had made a lamp of its own self,
125 And they were two in one and one in two:
How can that be? He knows who so ordains it.

When it was right at the base of the bridge,
It raised up full length the arm with the head
To carry closer to us words, which were:

130 "Now you see the galling punishment,
You there, breathing, come visiting the dead:
See if you find pain heavier than this!

"And so that you may bring back news of me,
Know that I am Bertran de Born, the one
135 Who offered the young king corrupt advice.

"I made the son and father rebel foes.
Achitophel with his pernicious promptings
Did no worse harm to Absalom and David.

"Because I severed persons bound so closely,
140 I carry my brain separate (what grief!)
From its life-source which is within this trunk.

"So see in me the counterstroke of justice."

Notes

24 See the fate of Judas in Acts 1:18, "he burst open and his guts spilled out."

31 Mohammed (d. 632), the founder of Islam, with his son-in-law Ali appears here in the ninth pouch with the sowers of schism.

55 Fra Dolcino in 1300 headed the Apostolic Brothers, an outlawed religious sect that was forcibly suppressed; he was burned at the stake in 1307.

73 Pier da Medicina, driven from Romagna in 1287, intrigued among its rulers to turn them against themselves.

76 Malatestino of Rimini, to acquire Fano for himself, invited Angiolello da Carignano and Guido del Cassero, two of the town's leaders, to meet him at La Cattolica, a cape between the two towns, and had them drowned off the headland of Focara. The city (ll. 85 and 93) is Rimini.

97 Curio is said by the Roman poet Lucan to have urged Caesar to cross the Rubicon, declaring war on the Republic in 49 B.C. The spot is near Rimini.

106 Mosca dei Lamberti suggested that one of the Buondelmonti be murdered rather than beaten; the act resulted in the strife between Ghibellines and Guelphs. See Paradiso XVI, l. 135, and note.

118 The headless body is that of Bertran de Born (1140-1215), a knight and Provençal troubadour, who was believed to have instigated a quarrel between Henry II of England and his son.

137 Achitophel supported Absalom in his rebellion against his father King David (2 Samuel 15-17).

CANTO XXXIV
Lucifer, Judecca

"'The Banners of the King of Hell Advance'
Closer to us," my master said; "so look
Straight ahead and see if you can spot them."

Just as when a thick fog starts to settle
5 Or when evening darkens all our hemisphere,
Far-off a windmill appears to be rotating,

137

So I thought I saw such a structure there.
Then out of the wind I stepped back behind
My guide, because there was no other shelter.

10   I was now — and with fear I set it down
In verse — where the shades were wholly sealed
And yet showed through below like straws in glass.

Some of them lie flat, some stand upright,
One on his head and one upon his soles;
15   Another, like a bow, bends face to foot.

When we had made our way so far forward
That my master sensed it time to show me
The creature who was once so beautiful,

He took a step aside and made me stop;
20   "Look at Dis," he said, "look at the place
Where you must arm yourself with steadfastness."

How faint and frozen, reader, I grew then
Do not inquire: I shall not write it down,
Since all my words would be too few and weak.

25   I did not die and still I did not live.
Think for yourself — should you possess the talent —
What I became, robbed of both life and death!

The emperor of the kingdom of despair
Rose up from mid-chest out of the sheer ice;
30   And I come closer to a giant's height

Than giants match the size of his huge arms:
See now how large the whole of him must be
If it's proportionate to that one part!

Were he once as beautiful as now he's ugly
35   (And yet he raised his fist against his Maker!)
Well may all our grief come down from him!

Oh how much wonder was it for me when
I saw that on his head he had three faces:
One in front — and it was fiery red —

40   And two others, which joined onto this one
Above the center of his shoulder blades,
And all three came together at his crown.

138

The right face seemed halfway white and yellow
While the left one looked the color of the race
45   That lives close to the source of the Nile.

Beneath each face there sprouted two large wings,
Suitably massive for such a bird of prey:
I never sighted sails so broad at sea.

They had no feathers but looked just like a bat's,
50   And he kept flapping these wings up and down
So that three winds moved out from in around him:

This was the cause Cocytus was all iced.
With six eyes he wept, and from his three chins
Dripped down the teardrops and a bloody froth.

55   In each mouth he mashed up a separate sinner
With his sharp teeth, as if they were a grinder,
And in this way he put the three through torture.

For the one in front, the biting was as nothing
Compared to the clawing, for at times his back
60   Remained completely stripped bare of its skin.

"That soul up there who suffers the worst pain,"
My master said, "is Judas Iscariot —
His head within, he kicks his legs outside.

"Of those other two, with their heads hung down,
65   The one who hangs from the black snout is Brutus:
Look how he writhes and mutters not a word!

"That other one is Cassius, who seems brawny.
But nightfall rises once again, and we now
Must take our leave, since we have seen the whole."

70   As he requested, I held him round the neck,
And then he waited the right time and place,
And when the wings spread open wide enough

He caught firm hold of Satan's shaggy flanks.
Downward from shock to shock he climbed below
75   Between the matted hair and frozen crust.

When we were at the point at which the thigh
Revolves, right where the hip widens out,
My guide, by straining and agonizing effort,

Turned his head round to where his legs had been
80   And grabbed the hair, like a man climbing up,
So that I thought we'd headed back to hell!

"Hold tight! these are the only stairs to take us
Out of this sin-filled hole," said my master,
Panting, like a man worn out, for breath.

85   Then he squeezed through the crevice of a rock
And raised me up onto its rim to sit,
And afterward reached me with one wary step.

I lifted up my eyes, thinking I'd see
Lucifer as I had left him — instead
90   I found him with his legs suspended upward!

And if at that time I became confused
Let dull minds judge: those who do not see
What point it was that I must just have passed.

"Stand up!" my master said, "Up on your feet!
95   The way is long and the path strenuous.
The sun once more turns back to middle tierce."

It was no palace hall, the place where we
Had come, but a natural stone cavern
With scanty lighting and a treacherous floor.

100   "Before we uproot ourselves from this abyss,
My master," said I when I stood up straight,
"Talk to me a bit to clear my error:

"Where is the ice? And how can he be fixed
Upside-down like that? And how in so short time
105   Has the sun moved from dusk to morning?"

And he told me, "You picture yourself still
On the other side of center where I caught
The hair of the vile worm that pierced the earth.

"You were there as long as I climbed downward.
110   When I turned myself round you passed the point
To which all weight on every side pulls down.

"And now you come under the hemisphere
Opposite that which domes the vast dry land:
There, beneath its pinnacle of sky,

115   "The Man, sinless in birth and life, was slain.
Your feet stand on a little sphere, a spot
That marks the other side of Judecca.

"Here it is morning when it is evening there,
And he whose hair supplied our ladder down
120 Is still stuck fast, as he was from the first.

"He fell down straight from heaven on this side,
And the land, which once had bulged out here,
In fright at his fall cloaked itself with sea

"And rushed up toward our hemisphere; perhaps,
125 What you see on this side, to flee from him,
Left this space vacant here and spurted upward.

"Below, as far away from Beelzebub
As the limit of his tomb, there is a place
Which is known not by sight but by the sound

130 "Of a small stream that courses down this way
Along the hollow of a rock it wore
Away with winding flow and trickling fall."

Along that hidden path my guide and I
Started out to return to the bright world.
135 And without a thought for any resting-stops,

We bounded up, he first and I second,
Until, through a round opening, I saw
Some of the lovely things the heavens hold:

From there we came out to see once more the stars.

Notes

1 Vexilla regis prodeunt inferni: the opening line, quoted in Latin by Dante, is a slightly parodied version of a sixth-century hymn by Fortunatus. The pilgrims reach the fourth zone of Cocytus which is called Judecca (l. 117) for the traitor Judas.

20 Dis is another name that Dante uses for Lucifer. He is also addressed as Satan in l. 73.

34 Lucifer (a word derived from Latin, meaning "bearer of light") was beautiful before he rebelled against God.

61 The sinners in the three mouths of Lucifer are Judas Iscariot, the apostle who betrayed Christ,center, and Brutus and Cassius (ll. 65-67), left, who conspired to assassinate Julius Caesar.

67 Cassius looks brawny because, with his skin chewed away, the muscles are exposed.

68 It is the evening of Holy Saturday. When the poet passes the center point of the earth, it will be twelve hours earlier (l. 96).

112 Lucifer fell headfirst from heaven through the southern hemisphere. All the land on that side of the globe rushed to the north, except for a mound caused by the impact of his fall: the Mount of Purgatory.

130 The stream of Lethe runs down from the Garden of Paradise on the top of purgatory.

141

Giorgio Vasari, Giotto, *Lives of the Artists*, 1320 CE

<u>Reading and Discussion Questions</u>
1. When and how were Giotto's talents as an artist discovered?
2. What was the origin of the phrase "You are rounder than the O of Giotto," and what did it mean? What did it say about Giotto as an artist?

In 1550, an author named Giorgio Vasari wrote a book entitled Lives of the Most Excellent Painters, Sculptors and Architects, commonly refereed to simply as Lives. In his six-part book, Vasari provides exquisite biographies of more than 100 of the greatest artists of the Renaissance, most of whom were from Florence. Vasari's Lives is considered the textbook on Renaissance art history, as it chronicles the details of each artist's life, explanations of the techniques used by each and a little gossip thrown in to add flavor to the narrative. One of the first artists for whom Vasari wrote a biography was Giotto di Bondone, known as Giotto. Giotto was a pioneer in painting and all later great Renaissance masters, including Michelangelo himself, credit Giotto with reinventing painting as an art form. Specifically, Giotto was a master of fresco painting.

The word "fresco" means "fresh" and fresco painting is the technique of painting on wet plaster. Fresco was an ancient art form revived and mastered by Giotto in the early 1300s. Fresco paintings required great skill and knowledge of the artist's materials, and Giotto was a dedicated student of the science of frescos. When completed, frescos had the benefit of lasting a very long time, because the dried plaster became part of the wall on which it was painted. Well-crafted frescos absorbed a tremendous amount of paint and the depth of color iN a great fresco was mesmerizing. Giotto's blues were especially powerful and once you see a Giotto blue, you will not likely forget it. Beyond the artistic technique that Giotto became famous for, Giotto did something else that was even more innovative. He tried to paint the subjects of his paintings realistically. This may not seem like a big deal but it is a big step towards Humanist attitudes that will define the Renaissance. He wanted humans to look like humans and to be beautiful. Before Giotto, artists were much more concerned with conveying the Biblical message in a painting than they were with its realism. Medieval paintings look almost like cartoons, because they were not meant to be beautiful. They were meant to teach a lesson. As a painter in the Middle Ages, Giotto's paintings were all religious and never strayed from the task of teaching viewers important religious ideas. But his paintings were also artistically beautiful, powerful and realistic. Giotto's subtle but revolutionary innovations in painting altered the art world perhaps more than any other painter of the early Renaissance era.

Now in the year 1276, in the country of Florence, about fourteen miles from the city, in the village of Vespignano, there was born to a simple peasant named Bondone a son, to whom he gave the name of Giotto, and whom he brought up according to his station. And when he had reached the age of ten years, showing in all his ways though still childish an extraordinary vivacity and quickness of mind, which made him beloved not only by his father but by all who knew him, Bondone gave him the care of some sheep. And he leading them for pasture, now to one spot and now to another, was constantly driven by his natural inclination to draw on the stones or the ground some object in nature, or something that came into his mind. One day Cimabue [a famous Florentine art teacher], going on business from Florence to Vespignano, found Giotto, while his sheep were feeding, drawing a sheep from nature upon a smooth and solid rock with a pointed stone, having never learnt from any one but nature. Cimabue, marvelling at him, stopped and asked him if he would go and be with him. And the boy answered that if his father were content he would gladly go. Then Cimabue asked Bondone for him, and he gave him up to him, and was content that he should take him to Florence.

There in a little time, by the aid of nature and the teaching of Cimabue, the boy not only equalled his master, but freed himself from the rude manner of the Greeks, and brought back to life the true art of painting, introducing the drawing from nature of living persons, which had not been practised for two hundred years; or at least if some had tried it, they had not succeeded very happily. Giotto painted among others, as may be seen to this day in the chapel of the Podestà's Palace at Florence, Dante Alighieri, his contemporary and great friend, and no less famous a poet than Giotto was a painter.

After this he was called to Assisi by Fra Giovanni di Muro, at that time general of the order of S. Francis, and painted in fresco in the upper church thirty-two stories from the life and deeds of S. Francis, which brought him great fame. It is no wonder therefore that Pope Benedict sent one of his courtiers into Tuscany to see what sort of a man he was and what his works were like, for the Pope was planning to have some paintings made in S Peter's. And one morning going into the workshop of Giotto, who was at his labours, he showed him the mind of the Pope, and at last asked him to give him a little drawing to send to his Holiness. Giotto, who was a man of courteous manners, immediately took a sheet of paper, and with a pen dipped in red, fixing his arm firmly against his side to make a compass of it, with a turn of his hand he made a circle so perfect that it was a marvel to see it Having done it, he turned smiling to the courtier and said, "Here is the drawing." But he, thinking he was being laughed at, asked, "Am I to have no other drawing than this?" "This is enough and too much," replied Giotto, "send it with the others and see if it will be understood." The messenger, seeing that he could get nothing else, departed ill pleased, not doubting that he had been made a fool of. However, sending the other drawings to the Pope with the names of those who had made them, he sent also Giotto's, relating how he had made the circle without moving his arm and without compasses, which when the Pope and many of his courtiers understood, they saw that Giotto must surpass greatly all the other painters of his time. This thing being told, there arose from it a proverb which is still used about men of coarse clay, "You are rounder than the O of Giotto,".

So the Pope made him come to Rome, and he painted for him in S. Peter's, and there never left his hands work better finished.

143

Francesco Petrarch, *Letters*, 1345 CE

Reading and Discussion Questions

1. Look up and define the word "lament." Are Petrarch's letters "laments" or something different? Explain.
2. Petrarch's letters are emotional. What does he feel so passionately about?
3. Choose one person from the past (no longer living) to whom you would like to write a letter in the style of Petrarch.

Francesco Petrarch was an Italian writer and poet and is considered the father of Humanism. He was born in Florence, Italy at the end of the Middle Ages (1304 to 1374). He was a voracious student of the history of ancient Greece and Rome and was insatiable in his consumption of classical literature. His rediscovery of works of classical geniuses is credited with causing the Renaissance. Petrarch spent his life search for lost books, letters and manuscripts from ancient Greeks including Homer, Plato, Aristotle, Euripides and Sophocles. He poured over the thousands of letters and manuscripts by great Roman historians and philosophers like Seneca, Marcus Aurelius, Cicero, Livy and countless others. He deeply regretted the loss of so much wisdom from the classical past and dedicated his life to rediscovering it and exposing others to lost knowledge. He wrote thousands of letters where he expressed his regret for the present and his hope for the future.

Letter to Titus Livy

I should wish (if it were permitted from on high) either that I had been born in thine age or thou in ours; in the latter case our age itself, and in the former I personally should have been the better for it. I should surely have been one of those pilgrims who visited thee. For the sake of seeing thee I should have gone not merely to Rome, but indeed, from either Gaul or Spain I should have found my way to thee as far as India.

As it is, I must fain be content with seeing thee as reflected in thy works not thy whole self, alas, but that portion of thee which has not yet perished, notwithstanding the sloth of our age. We know that thou didst write one hundred and forty-two books on Roman affairs. With what fervor, with what unflagging zeal must thou have labored; and of that entire number there are now extant scarcely thirty.

Oh, what a wretched custom is this of willfully deceiving ourselves! I have said " thirty," because it is common for all to say so. I find, however, that even from these few there is one lacking. They are twenty-nine in all, constituting three decades, the first, the third, and the fourth, the last of which has not the full number of books. It is over these small remains that I toil whenever I wish to forget these regions, these times, and these customs. Often I am filled with bitter indignation against the morals of today, when men value nothing except gold and silver, and desire nothing except sensual, physical pleasures. If these are to be considered the goal of mankind, then not only the dumb beasts of the field, but even insensible and inert matter has a richer, a higher goal than that proposed to itself by thinking man. But of this elsewhere.

It is now fitter that I should render thee thanks, for many reasons indeed, but for this in especial : that thou didst so frequently cause me to forget the present evils, and transfer me to happier times. As I read, I seem to be living in the midst of [famous or heroic Romans] the Cornellii Scipiones Africani, of Laelius, Fabius Maximus, Metellus, Brutus and Decius, of Cato, Regulus, Cursor, Torquatus, Valerius Corvinus, Salinator, of Claudius, Marcellus, Nero, Aemilius, of Fulvius, Flaminius, Attilius, Quintius, Curius, Fabricius, and Camillus. It is with these men that I live at such times and not with the thievish company of today among whom I was born under an evil star. And Oh, if it were my happy lot to possess thee entire, from what other great names would I not seek solace for my wretched existence, and forgetfulness of this wicked age! Since I cannot find all these in what I now possess of thy work, I read of them here and there in other authors, and especially in that book where thou art to be found in thy entirety, but so briefly epitomized that, although nothing is lacking as far as the number of books is concerned, everything is lacking as regards the value of the contents themselves.

To Marcus Tullius Cicero

O great father of Roman eloquence! not I alone but all who deck themselves with the flowers of Latin speech render thanks unto you. It is from your well-springs that we draw the streams that water our meads. You, we freely acknowledge, are the leader who marshals us; yours are the words of encouragement that sustain us; yours is the light that illumines the path before us. In a word, it is under your auspices that we have attained to such little skill in this art of writing as we may possess. . . .

You have heard what I think of your life and your genius. Are you hoping to hear of your books also; what fate has befallen them, how they are esteemed by the masses and among scholars? They still are in existence, glorious volumes, but we of today are too feeble a folk to read them, or even to be acquainted with their mere titles. Your fame extends far and wide; your name is mighty, and fills the ears of men; and yet those who really know you are very few, be it because the times are unfavourable, or because men's minds are slow and dull, or, as I am the more inclined to believe, because the love of money forces our thoughts in other directions. Consequently right in our own day, unless I am much mistaken, some of your books have disappeared, I fear beyond recovery. It is a great grief to me, a great disgrace to this generation, a great wrong done to posterity. The shame of failing to cultivate our own talents, thereby depriving the future of the fruits that they might have yielded, is not enough for us; we must waste and spoil, through our cruel and insufferable neglect, the fruits of your labours too, and of those of your fellows as well, for the fate that I lament in the case of your own books has befallen the works of many another illustrious man.

Now, in conclusion, you will wish me to tell you something about the condition of Rome and the Roman republic: the present appearance of the city and whole country, the degree of harmony that prevails, what classes of citizens possess political power, by whose hands and with what wisdom the reins of empire are swayed, and whether the Danube, the Ganges, the Ebro, the Nile, the Don, are our boundaries now, or in very truth the man has arisen who 'bounds our empire by the ocean-stream, our fame by the stars of heaven,' or 'extends our rule beyond Garama and Ind,' as your friend the Mantuan has said. Of these and other matters of like nature I doubt not you would very gladly hear. Your filial piety tells me so, your well-known love of country, which you cherished even to your own destruction. But indeed it were better that I refrained. Trust me, Cicero, if you were to hear of our condition today you would be moved to tears, in whatever circle of heaven above, or Erebus below, you may be dwelling. Farewell, forever.

PART THREE—
REVOLUTIONS OF THE MIND

When most people hear the word *revolution*, they imagine angry groups who have taken up arms in a struggle against tyrants. Americans, in particular, think of our *revolution* as the event that won us our freedom from oppressive British rule. Armed revolution, as we see it, made our way of life possible. Similar stories are true of nations all over the world.

It surprises my students to learn that the word *revolution* simply means "radical change." While many radical changes in the world are achieved through armed rebellion, I would argue that a great many more powerful changes are caused by revolutions of the mind. Changing minds changes history, and it is usually the radical changes in the way we think that lead to radical changes in the way we act and in the things we are willing to fight for.

As you have read, in the Late Middle Ages, some people were radically altering the way they thought about education, religion, art and the human condition. These people were called Humanists. They believed deeply in the power of humans to make positive changes in the world. Humanists came in many shapes and sizes. Humanists are artists, scientists, philosophers and rulers. The qualities Humanists have in common are a deep love of wisdom, a respect for the achievements of the past and a desire to improve the future. Humanists were revolutionaries, because they dreamed of and caused radical changes in the world around them.

The period of European history between 1450 and 1600 is more revolutionary than any other time in history because everything about life was radically changed. And these changes were caused by ideas, not weapons. The Renaissance, the Protestant Reformation, the Scientific Revolution and the Age of Discovery were all revolutions which radically changed the human experience forever. And they were all caused by the power of our ideas, not the might of our armies.

CHAPTER 6—
THE RENAISSANCE (1350 to 1550 CE)

GUIDING QUESTIONS
- Why was Florence the birthplace of a new age?
- In what ways was the Renaissance a "rebirth?"
- What things were different in Renaissance Europe than in Medieval Europe?
- What was the role of the Medici family in starting the Renaissance?
- What is the role of the "rebel" in starting the Renaissance? Is it a good or a bad thing to be a "rebel?"
- The attitudes of Renaissance Humanism spread into many other areas. What other areas of life were changed by this new attitude?

Of all the marvelous periods in history, the Renaissance is my favorite. I am accused by my students of saying this about every period in history but truly, I love the Renaissance the most. It was a beautiful age when brilliant people did beautiful and brilliant things that defy understanding. More than any other moment in time, the Renaissance demonstrates the power of humans and reveals the depths of human potential. It is impossible for me to fully put into words the awe-inspiring feats of the Renaissance.

I have been on several occasions, absolutely and utterly paralyzed by the power of the works of the Renaissance. That same paralysis returns to me now as I try to put into words for you the genius of this age. There simply are no words. It is my hope that, though my words are brief, my love of the Renaissance will nonetheless be transmitted here. The Renaissance cannot be studied through text only. It must be experienced. No words could ever make you feel the cold dampness of the Sistine Chapel or make you understand what Michelangelo's blue looks like. For me, there is no blue but his blue. In a thousand words I could not describe what it feels like to understand the fall of man by standing in front of Hieronymous Bosch's Garden of Earthly Delights or what it is like to feel both damned and redeemed in the same moment. Trying to *tell* you what perfect genius looks, smells, sounds and feels like would be the same as sending you back into Plato's cave. Asking you to take my word for what the Renaissance feels like is no better than shackling you in the cave again and asking you to take the shadows on the wall as the truth. Therefore, I only undertake to teach you the history of this period and to explain the reasons why such brilliance flourished during this time in history. The awe of the period you simply have to experience for yourself.

For 900 years after the fall of Rome, Europe was stagnant. Intellectual darkness enshrouded the continent and, as Petrarch said "Genius, virtue, glory now have gone, leaving chance and sloth to rule." The light of the classical world seemed to have been extinguished and fear and hopelessness prevailed. By 1300, as we have seen, there were glimmers of light in the works and ideas of a few brave pioneers but overall, Medieval Europe was under the total control of the Catholic Church and was still mired in darkness. But in around 1400, a flood of light rushed forth and ushered in a new age. That light came from the city-state of Florence.

148

Every age has a place which is its beacon of light. During ancient times, the cities of Athens and Rome were the centers of learning and innovation. During the Middle Ages, feudal cities like Paris and London were the main sites of progress. But in the 1400s, when the rest of Europe was still immersed in Medieval monotony and obedience, a city-state on the Italian peninsula called Florence was far ahead of its time. Florence had an advantage over other places in Europe in 1400 partly because of its geography. It is located on the northern part of the Italian peninsula and it became an important stopping point on the trade route between Europe and the Middle East. Florence also had a lot more political freedom than other places like France and England in the late Middle Ages because Florence was a small, independent city-state and not a massive kingdom. This meant that Florence had a small, progressive government that did not answer to kings and long established traditions. Florence had the freedom to make the rules that suited them when they suited them. Italy will not be a unified nation until 1871. Until that time, the Italian peninsula remained a collection of independent, and often rivaling, city-states, of which Florence was the wealthiest and most powerful.

Florence was also unique in that it had something today we call the middle class, which was unheard of in Medieval times. The people in the great kingdoms of Europe still lived under the rigid social structure of the feudal system, with only two classes of people—those who had land and power, and everybody else. But in Florence, a robust merchant (or middle) class developed centuries before its it did elsewhere. Florence had a vibrant trade market, skilled craftsmen, shop keepers and business owners, which meant that Florence also had considerable wealth. The combination of an independent, open-minded government and wealthy citizens made Florence a perfect breeding ground for a new era, which we know as the Renaissance.

The Renaissance literally means "rebirth" and most people know that. But far fewer people know what, exactly, was reborn. The term re-birth means that something had been resurrected that existed in the world before and so the Renaissance was not the birth of something entirely new. Instead, it was a rediscovery or rebirth of knowledge, art and culture from classical Greece and Rome. It was Petrarch's dream come true! In thousands of letters, Petrarch lamented the loss of wisdom of the past and longed for a day when people remembered things like *The Iliad*, *The Odyssey*, the ideas of the Stoics and the virtues of the Greeks. He wanted others to appreciate the perfect symmetry of Greek sculpture and the eternal beauty of Roman frescoes. Largely because of Petrarch's lamentations and his thousands of poems and letters, people did wake up and open their eyes to the beauty of the past. But at first this daring exploration of the past only happened in Florence. The rest of Europe was still too afraid of such boldness.

In the 1400s, the Catholic Church still had a strong hold on Medieval Christians. The only approved literature was Christian literature and the only acceptable art was Christian art. And these rules made the works of Greece and Rome forbidden because they were pagan. But Florence from the beginning was more rebellious than the rest of Europe. Florence had an independent government and a wealthy and diverse population comprised of different classes, races and religions. This was the recipe for very progressive thinking. Florentines were bold enough to read forbidden works when others were not. In fact, the very fact that something was forbidden was what made it interesting!

One rebellious Florentine helped to kick-start the Renaissance more than any other. His name was Cosimo di Medici. Cosimo was the son of the wealthiest banker in Florence, Giovanni di Medici. Most of the money that flowed through Europe's trade markets was managed by the Medici bank. Even the pope kept his money in the Medici bank, which is what earned them the label of "God's bankers." Cosimo was in many ways a stereotypical son of a rich man. He went to the best schools, had rich friends and sought grand adventures. The kinds of adventures Cosimo sought were treasure hunting expeditions and the treasures he hunted were manuscripts, sculptures and other priceless artifacts from the past. Cosimo was a great fan of Petrarch and a lover of history himself. He was familiar with the accomplishments of the past and he organized groups of treasure hunters to hunt down lost manuscripts of everyone from Plato and Aristotle to Pythagoras, Archimedes and many pre-Christian mystics. He was not constrained by the rules that controlled most people. "Pagan" to him meant "forbidden" which meant "fun." When a treasure hunt paid off for Cosimo, he would have a large party at his family palace to unveil his latest discovery. Invitations to Cosimo's parties were the hottest tickets in town. It was in this way that the classical past was reborn. Over time, people were not content simply to marvel at the great works of the past. They were inspired to create new works that would mark their own greatness in a new age.

The Renaissance was a cultural and artistic revolution inspired by Humanism. Humanism is a life philosophy where humans and human achievement are celebrated rather than suppressed. Humanism is the opposite attitude of Augustine's advice to live for the afterlife. Humanists lived for and savored the here and now. Renaissance Humanists shared several key characteristics. First, they believed in living life to the fullest and cultivating their many talents. The goal of every Humanist was to be a Renaissance man, or one who could dance as well as he painted, debate intelligently, write eloquently and defend virtue in all his actions. Humanists believed that by making themselves all that they could be personally, they could make the world better. Second, they all had a broad education in the classics. The word Humanist comes from the Greek *Humanitas*, which means scholarship or education in the liberal arts. Humanists pursued education in the traditional classical areas of logic, literature, history, rhetoric (speech), philosophy and the arts. Third, they were realists and, in their methodical thinking, they were scientists of sorts. They wanted to understand how things really worked and they believed that all things could be understood scientifically--even politics and society. They refused to believe anything, including religion, based on faith alone and demanded reasons or logic in everything. Fourth, Humanists believed everything could be understood by studying the natural world. They studied nature, they painted nature, the philosophized about nature and they reveled in nature. And they viewed humans as a part, perhaps the greatest part, of nature and wanted to understand and celebrate every element of human creation.

During the Renaissance, arts of all types flourished—painting, architecture, sculpture, literature, philosophy. The Renaissance is most well known because of men like Michelangelo and Leonardo da Vinci but there were hundreds of other geniuses also crafting brilliant masterpieces during the late 1400s and early 1500s in Florence. Dozens of art schools, many of which were funded by the Medici family, sought out the best talent to work for them. For the Medici family, art was much more than something pretty to look at and admire. For the Medici, art was power. Long before there were billboards, pop-up ads, political campaigns and reality shows to promote popular brands and powerful people, there was art. The Medici family used art as propaganda. They commissioned domes which defied gravity that were widely known to have been commissioned by the Medici and they sponsored public murals depicting themselves in scenes from the *Bible*. Nearly every great palace and town square housed something paid for by the Medici family and this was a very effective display of their power and wealth. The Medici family revived many old Roman ideas, the most important of which was that one could achieve near immortality through monumental works of art.

Thanks to the Medici family, Florence was a hotbed of creative activity and wealth in the 1400s but it was not without conflict. The Medici were the most powerful family in Florence but there were many rival families who resented Medici influence, and Medici corruption. Florence was the scene of political conspiracies, assassinations and violent seizures of power by warring private armies. A keen observer of human nature and of political realities was a man named Niccolo Machiavelli. Machiavelli was a low-level government bureaucrat who worked for different sides of powerful rival families in Florence and learned what it took to win and keep power. What he observed went against everything that Plato believed, that the wisest and most virtuous among us should rule. Machiavelli, as a Humanist, had no interest in "should" or fantasies of rulers in a perfect world. Machiavelli was interested in the reality of politics and the reality that he saw was that usually the most ruthless, calculating and charismatic man wins.

Machiavelli wrote his observations in his book, *The Prince*, in 1513. He studied living rulers and politicians, including the Medici family's most dangerous rival, the Borgia family, and reached the conclusion that, in politics, nice guys usually finish last. Machiavelli is very controversial and his writings were rejected as overly cynical at the time they were written. Machiavelli looked at the cold facts about politics and what he presented was more truth than audiences at the time, and some people today, could handle. Machiavelli is considered the father of political science because he analyzed politics and government for what they really were instead of what they should be. In other words, he studied politics scientifically. His ideas may not be popular but most people today agree that they are difficult to dispute, because the evidence he presented is convincing. Just as the great painters, sculptors and architects of the Renaissance pushed boundaries and challenged accepted norms, Machiavelli and a host of other writers stirred up controversy through the power of the written word. Over time, the courage of self-expression that was born in Florence spread as people got word of the radical cultural revolution that had been born there.

By 1500, the contagious Humanist spirit spread throughout Europe. France, Belgium, England were soon swept up by the Renaissance and its radical new attitudes. The spread of the Renaissance beyond the Italian states is called the Northern Renaissance. Northern Renaissance painters included men like Jan van Eyck, Albrect Durer, Hieronymous Bosch and Hans Holbein the Younger but most people are more familiar with the writers of the Northern Renaissance. Renaissance attitudes and art spread to England and inspired works by Thomas More, Christopher Marlow and the great William Shakespeare. The spread of the ideas of Humanist Florence were aided tremendously by what many consider the most important invention in modern history—the printing press. In 1455, Johannes Gutenberg invented the movable type press, and the world changed almost instantaneously. Ideas that took years to spread before the press now spread overnight. Ideas and techniques in art and architecture could be spread rapidly, as could new books. But the printing press impacted far more than the spread of artistic ideas. It changed everything.

Humanism and the printing press were a revolutionary combination that overhauled every aspect of the status quo in less than 200 years. Art and artistic expression were the first areas revolutionized by Humanism, but every facet of life was soon transformed by this new attitude. Thanks in part to the groundbreaking work of Thomas Aquinas in the late Middle Ages, scientific thinking was also radically reimagined in what became known as the Scientific Revolution. Leonardo da Vinci is most well known as an artist but he is also considered the Father of Modern Science. More than any other, da Vinci was the ideal Renaissance man. He had an insatiable, childlike curiosity and he was fascinated by the natural world. He wanted to understand the inner workings of everything, from human anatomy to the function of plants and the efficiency of weaponry. Much of his art is in fact just his sketches of his experiments. Da Vinci showed the world what humans were capable of and what they were capable of was astounding. The great Renaissance orator, Pico de Mirandolla, best captured the essence of the Renaissance and the pursuit of all great Renaissance Humanists, to be all that we were divinely created to be—"With freedom of choice and with honor, as the maker and molder of thyself, thou mayest fashion thyself in whatever shape thou shalt prefer." You can be, do or make anything you want because that is what you were made for. Has there ever been a greater expression of optimism and hope for the future than that? It is little wonder that an era inspired by these sorts of feelings produced works of genius for which there are simply no words.

PRIMARY SOURCES – THE RENAISSANCE

Pico della Mirandola, Oration on the Dignity of Man, 1486 CE

Reading and Discussion Questions
1. According to Pico, why is man "the most fortunate of creatures?"
2. What was God's dilemma when he created man, according to this speech?
3. What picture does Pico paint about human capabilities and the ability of man to shape his future? Is it a hopeful or hopeless picture? Explain.
4. Compare this speech with the excerpt from *On the Misery of the Human Condition* from the High Middle Ages. How are these two viewpoints on human life different? Do they have anything in common? Do these viewpoints help you better to understand the periods in which they were written? Explain your answer.

The Oration on the Dignity of Man is a famous speech made in 1486 by Pico della Mirandola, an Italian scholar and philosopher. Pico was a devoted Humanist and a student of the classics. He devoted his life to learning and lecturing on the things he had learned. His speech, The Oration on the Dignity of Man, is considered the perfect articulation of Renaissance attitudes. It is the embodiment of the Humanist philosophy and represents the final transformation from gloomy and limiting Medieval ideas about life and human capabilities to a new era when nothing was impossible in the realm of human achievement.

I have read in the records of the Arabians, reverend Fathers, that Abdala the Saracen, when questioned as to what on this stage of the world, as it were, could be seen most worthy of wonder, replied: "There is nothing to be seen more wonderful than man." In agreement with this opinion is the saying of Hermes Trismegistus: "A great miracle, Asclepius, is man." But when I weighed the reason for these maxims, the many grounds for the excellence of human nature reported by many men failed to satisfy me -- that man is the intermediary between creatures, the intimate of the gods, the king of the lower beings, by the acuteness of his senses, by the discernment of his reason.

Admittedly great though these reasons be, I have come to understand the reason why man is the most fortunate of creatures and consequently worthy of all admiration and a rank to be envied not only by brutes but even by the stars and by minds beyond this world. It is a matter past faith and a wondrous one. Why should it not be? For it is on this very account that man is rightly called and judged a great miracle and a wonderful creature indeed . . . .

. . . God the Father, the supreme Architect, had already built this cosmic home we behold, the most sacred temple of His godhead, by the laws of His mysterious wisdom. The region above the heavens He had adorned with Intelligences, the heavenly spheres He had quickened with eternal souls, and the excrementary and filthy parts of the lower world He had filled with a multitude of animals of every kind. But, when the work was finished, the Craftsman kept wishing that there were someone to ponder the plan of so great a work, to love its beauty, and to wonder at its vastness. Therefore, when everything was done (as Moses and Timaeus bear witness), He finally took thought concerning the creation of man.

God took man as a creature of indeterminate nature and, assigning him a place in the middle of the world, addressed him thus: "Neither a fixed abode nor a form that is thine alone nor any function peculiar to thyself have we given thee, Adam, to the end that according to thy longing and according to thy judgment thou mayest have and possess what abode, what form, and what functions thou thyself shalt desire. The nature of all other beings is limited and constrained within the bounds of laws prescribed by Us. Thou, constrained by no limits, in accordance with thine own free will, in whose hand We have placed thee, shalt ordain for thyself the limits of thy nature. We have set thee at the world's center that thou mayest from thence more easily observe whatever is in the world. With freedom of choice and with honor, as though the maker and molder of thyself, thou mayest fashion thyself in whatever shape thou shalt prefer. Thou shalt have the power to degenerate into the lower forms of life, which are brutish. Thou shalt have the power, out of thy soul's judgment, to be reborn into the higher forms, which are divine."

Giorgio Vasari, Michelangelo and Leonardo Da Vinci, *Lives of the Artists*, 1550 CE

Reading and Discussion Questions
1. Read and annotate the stories of both Michelangelo and Leonardo and then explain: A. The circumstances in which both Michelangelo and Leonardo were discovered as artists; B. The art forms in which both men excelled; C. The specific projects which are detailed by Vasari.
2. Compare Vasari's descriptions of Michelangelo and Leonardo. For whom do you think Vasari had a deeper affection? For whom did he have more respect as an artist? Explain your answers.
3. Overall, who do you think Vasari believed was the greater human being? Explain your answer.

In 1550, Giorgio Vasari wrote the book that became the foundation of modern art history. Its full title is Lives of the Most Excellent Painters, Sculptors and Architects, from Cimabue to Our Times. *It is usually referred to as simply Vasari's* Lives. *In the six-volume work, Vasari chronicles the lives and accomplishments of more than 100 of the most influential artists from the 1300s to the 1500s. You have already read Vasari's account of Giotto di Bondone, who is considered one of the pioneers of modern painting. The following passages are excerpts from Vasari's biographies of Michelangelo Buonarotti and Leonardo da Vinci. You will notice the extreme praise that Vasari heaps on both men, and he is verging on excessive in the superlatives and accolades he uses to describe them. Vasari knew both Michelangelo and da Vinci personally, while he only knew about many of the other artists through reputation and viewing their works. He uses words like "the divine Michelangelo" and talks about the almost God-like genius of da Vinci. The reader is left wondering whether Vasari exaggerated the accounts of the two Renaissance masters or if it is possible that they truly were as brilliant and gifted as Vasari would have us believe.*

While industrious and choice spirits, aided by the light afforded by Giotto and his followers, strove to show the world the talent with which their happy stars and well-balanced humours had endowed them, and endeavoured to attain to the height of knowledge by imitating the greatness of Nature in all things, the great Ruler of

154

Heaven looked down and, seeing these vain and fruitless efforts and the presumptuous opinion of man more removed from truth than light from darkness, resolved, in order to rid him of these errors, to send to earth a genius universal in each art, to show single-handed the perfection of line and shadow, and who should give relief to his paintings, show a sound judgment in sculpture, and in architecture should render habitations convenient, safe, healthy, pleasant, well-proportioned, and enriched with various ornaments. He further endowed him with true moral philosophy and a sweet poetic spirit, so that the world should marvel at the singular eminence of his life and works and all his actions, seeming rather divine than earthy.

In the arts of painting, sculpture and architecture the Tuscans have always been among the best, and Florence was the city in Italy most worthy to be the birthplace of such a citizen to crown her perfections. Thus in 1474 the true and noble wife of Ludovico di Lionardo Buonarotti Simone, said to be of the ancient and noble family of the Counts of Canossa, gave birth to a son in the Casentino, under a lucky star. The son was born on Sunday, 6 March, at eight in the evening, and was called Michelangelo, as being of a divine nature, for Mercury and Venus were in the house of Jove at his birth, showing that his works of art would be stupendous.

Michelangelo grew up in a town three miles from Florence, on family property inherited from his ancestors, a place full of rocks and quarries which are constantly worked by stonecutters and sculptors who are mostly natives. There Michelangelo was put to nurse with a stonecutter's wife. Thus he once said jestingly to Vasari: "What good I have comes from the pure air of your native Arezzo, and also because I sucked in chisels and hammers with my nurse's milk." In time Ludovico had several children, and not being well off, he put them in the arts of wool and silk. Michelangelo, who was older, he placed with Maestro Francesco da Urbino to school. But the boy devoted all the time he could to drawing secretly, for which his father and seniors scolded and sometimes beat him, thinking that such things were base and unworthy of their noble house.

At this time Lorenzo de' Medici the Magnificent ruled Florence. Lorenzo, who loved painting and sculpture, was grieved that no famous sculptors lived in his day to equal the great painters who then flourished, and so he resolved to found a school. Accordingly he asked the tutor of the local art school if he had any youths in his shop inclined to this he should send them to the garden, so that he might see them at work. The tutor elected among others Michelangelo as being the best.

Michelangelo was working on a sculpture of an old man and had opened its mouth and made the tongue and all the teeth. On seeing this, Lorenzo jestingly said, for he was a pleasant man, "You ought to know that the old never have all their teeth, and always lack some." Michelangelo took him seriously in his simplicity, and so soon as he was gone he broke out a tooth and made the gum look as if it had fallen out. He anxiously awaited the return of Lorenzo, who, when he saw Michelangelo's simplicity and excellence, laughed more than once, and related the matter to his friends as a marvel. He returned to help and favour the youth, and sending for his father, Ludovico, asked him to allow him to treat the boy as his own son, a request that was readily granted. Accordingly Lorenzo gave Michelangelo a room in the palace, and he ate regularly at table with the family and other nobles staying there. He remained in the house for four years until after the death of Lorenzo in 1492.

MICHELANGELO THE SCUPLTOR

On the death of Lorenzo Michelangelo returned home, much grieved at the loss of that great man and true friend of genius. Buying a large block of marble, he made a Hercules of four braccia, which stood for many years in the Strozzi palace, and was considered remarkable. For S. Spirito in Florence Michelangelo made a wooden crucifix, put over the lunette above the high altar to please the prior, who gave him suitable rooms, where he was able, by frequently dissecting dead bodies, to study anatomy, and thereby he began to perfect his great design....

During his stay in Rome he made such progress in sculpture that his conceptions were marvellous, and he executed difficulties with the utmost ease, frightening those who were not accustomed to see such things, for when they were done the works of others appeared as nothing beside them. Thus the cardinal of St. Denis, called Cardinal Rohan, a Frenchman, desired to leave a memorial of himself in the famous city by such a rare artist, and got him to do a marble Pieta. The rarest artist could add nothing to its design and grace, or finish the marble with such polish and art, for it displays the utmost limits of sculpture. Among its beauties are the divine draperies, the foreshortening of the dead Christ and the beauty of the limbs with the muscles, veins, sinews, while no better presentation of a corpse was ever made. The sweet air of the head and the harmonious joining of the arms and legs to the torso, with the pulses and veins, are marvellous, and it is a miracle that a once shapeless stone should assume a form that Nature with difficulty produces in flesh. Michelangelo devoted so much love and pains on this work that he put his name on the girdle crossing the Virgin's breast, a thing he never did again. One morning he had gone to the place to where it stands and observed a number of Lombards who were praising it loudly. One of them asked another the name of the sculptor, and he replied, "Our Gobbo of Milan." Michelangelo said nothing, but he resented the injustice of having his work attributed to another, and that night he shut himself in the chapel with a light and his chisels and carved his name on it.

It brought him great renown, and though some fools say that he has made the Virgin too young, they ought to know that spotless virgins keep their youth for a long time, while people afflicted like Christ do the reverse, so that should contribute more to increase the fame of his genius than all the things done before.

Some of Michelangelo's friends wrote from Florence urging him to return, as there was an infamous and colossal chunk of marble that was to be given away for a commission and his friends did not want a lesser artist to ruin it. Michelangelo on returning tried to obtain it, although it was difficult to get an entire figure without pieces, and no other man except himself would have had the courage to make the attempt, but he had wanted it for many years, and on reaching Florence he made efforts to get it. It was nine braccia high, and unluckily one Simone da Fiesole had begun a giant, cutting between the legs and mauling it so badly that he abandoned it, and it had rested so abandoned for many years. Michelangelo examined it afresh, and decided that it could be hewn into something new while following the attitude sketched by Simone, and he decided to ask the wardens and Soderini for it. They gave it to him as worthless, thinking that anything he might do would be better than its present useless condition.

Accordingly Michelangelo made a wax model of a youthful David holding the sling to show that the city should be boldly defended and righteously governed, following

David's example. He began it in the opera, making a screen between the wall and the tables, and finished it without anyone having seen him at work. The marble had been hacked and spoiled by Simone so that he could not do all that he wished with it, though he left some of Simone's work at the end of the marble, which may still be seen. This revival of a dead thing was a veritable miracle.

All the colossal statues of antiquity do not compare with it in proportion and beauty. The legs are finely turned, the slender flanks divine, and the graceful pose unequalled, while such feet, hands and head have never been excelled. After seeing this no one need wish to look at any other sculpture or the work of any other artist.

MICHELANGELO PAINTS THE SISTINE CHAPEL

After the Pope had returned to Rome, and when Michelangelo had finished the statue, Bramante, the friend and relation of Raphael and therefore ill-disposed to Michelangelo, seeing the Pope's preference for sculpture, schemed to divert his attention, and told the Pope that it would be a bad omen to get Michelangelo to work on his tomb, as it would seem to be an invitation to death. He persuaded the Pope to get Michelangelo, on his return, to paint the vaulting of the Sistine Chapel. In this way Bramante and his other rivals hoped to confound him, for by taking him from sculpture, in which he was perfect, and putting him to colouring in fresco, in which he had had no experience, they thought he would produce less admirable work than Raphael. Thus, when Michelangelo returned to Rome, the Pope was disposed not to have the tomb finished for the time being, and asked him to paint the vaulting of the chapel. Michelangelo tried every means to avoid it, and recommended Raphael, for he saw the difficulty of the work, knew his lack of skill in coloring, and wanted to finish the tomb.

But the more he excused himself, the more the impetuous Pope was determined he should do it. At length, seeing that the Pope was resolute, Michelangelo decided to do it. Impressed by the greatness of the task before him, Michelangelo sent to Florence for help, resolving to prove himself superior to those who had worked there before, and to show modern artists the true way to design and paint. The circumstances spurred him on in his quest of fame and his desire for the good of art. When he had completed the cartoon designs, he waited before beginning to colour them in fresco until some friends of his, who were painters, should arrive from Florence, as he hoped to obtain help from them, and learn their methods of fresco-painting, in which some of them were experienced. He made them begin some things as a specimen, but perceiving their work to be very far from his expectations, he decided one morning to destroy everything which they had done, and shutting himself up in the chapel he refused to admit them, and would not let them see him in his house. This jest seemed to them to be carried too far, and so they took their departure, returning with shame and mortification to Florence.

Michelangelo then made arrangements to do the whole work singlehanded. His care and labour brought everything into excellent train, and he would see no one in order to avoid occasions for showing anything, so that the most lively curiosity was excited. Pope Julius was very anxious to see his plans, and the fact of their being hidden greatly excited his desire. But when he went one day he was not admitted. This led to the disturbance already referred to, when Michelangelo had to leave Rome. Michelangelo has himself told me that, when he had painted a third of the vault, a certain mouldiness began to appear one winter when the north wind was blowing. This was because the

Roman lime, being white and made of travertine, does not dry quickly enough, and when mixed with pozzolana, which is of a tawny colour, it makes a dark mixture. If this mixture is liquid and watery, and the wall thoroughly wetted, it often effloresces in drying. This happened here, where the salt effloresced in many places, although in time the air consumed it. In despair at this, Michelangelo wished to abandon the work but the pope would not allow it. When he had finished half, the Pope, who sometimes went to see it by means of steps and scaffolds, wanted it to be thrown open, being an impatient man; unable to wait until it had received the finishing-touches. Immediately all Rome flocked to see it, the Pope being the first, arriving before the dust of the scaffolding had been removed.

Altogether Michelangelo received 3000 crowns from the Pope for this work, and he must have spent twenty-five on the colours. The work was executed in great discomfort, as Michelangelo had to stand with his head thrown back, and he so injured his eyesight that for several months he could only read and look at designs in that posture. I marvel that Michelangelo endured the discomfort. However, he became more eager every day to be doing and making progress, and so he felt no fatigue, and despised the discomfort.

O, happy age O, blessed artists who have been able to refresh your darkened eyes at the fount of such clearness, and see difficulties made plain by this marvellous artist! His labours have removed the bandage from your eyes, and he has separated the true from the false which clouded the mind. Thank Heaven, then, and try to imitate Michelangelo in all things.

Michelangelo thereafter returned to the happier art of sculpture and also did much work in architectural design, but little painting. In 1533, more than 20 years after completing the Sistine Chapel ceiling, Pope Paul III desired Michelangelo to come to him in Rome and paint the walls of the Sistine Chapel. The pope wished that he should paint the Last Judgment and Lucifer driven out of heaven for his pride, for which many years before he had made sketches and designs.

Michelangelo refused the pope's request, saying he was bound by obligations on other works. But the Pope in anger cried out, "I have desired this for thirty years, and now that I am Pope I will not give it up. I am determined that you shall serve me." Michelangelo thought of departing from Rome, but fearing the greatness of the Pope, and seeing him so old, thought to satisfy him with words. And the Pope came one day to his house with ten cardinals, and desired to see all the statues Michelangelo was working on, and they appeared to him miraculous, particularly the Moses. And when he saw the cartoons and drawings for the chapel, the Pope urged him again to come into his service. Michelangelo, since he could do no other, resolved to serve Pope Paul.

When Michelangelo had completed about three quarters of the work, Pope Paul went to see it, and Messer Biagio da Cesena, the master of the ceremonies, was with him, and when he was asked what he thought of it, he answered that he thought it not right to have so many naked figures in the Pope's chapel. This displeased Michelangelo, and to revenge himself, as soon as he was departed, he painted him in the character of Minos with a great serpent twisted round his legs. Nor did Messer Biagio's entreaties either to the Pope or to Michelangelo himself, avail to persuade him to take it away.

When this Last Judgment was uncovered, he was seen to have vanquished not only all the painters who had worked there before, but even to have surpassed his own work on the ceiling. He laboured at this work eight years, and uncovered it in the year 1541, on Christmas Day, I think, to the marvel of all Rome, or rather all the world; and I who went that year to Rome was astounded.

Afterwards he painted for Pope Paul the Conversion of S. Paul and the Crucifixion of S. Peter. These were the last pictures he painted, at the age of seventy-five, and with great fatigue, as he told me; for painting, and especially working in fresco, is not an art for old men. But his spirit could not remain without doing something, and since he could not paint, he set to work upon a piece of marble, to bring out of it four figures larger than life, for his amusement and pastime, and as he said, because working with the hammer kept him healthy in body. It represented the dead Christ, and was left unfinished, although he had intended it to be placed over his grave.

In all his spare time Michelangelo worked almost every day at that stone of which we have spoken before, with the four figures, but now he broke it, either because the stone was hard or because his judgment was now so ripe that nothing he did contented him. His finished statues were chiefly made in his youth; most of the others were left unfinished, for if he discovered a mistake, however small, he gave up the work and applied himself to another piece of marble. He often said this was the reason why he had finished so few statues and pictures.

About a year before his death, Vasari, seeing that Michelangelo was much shaken, prevailed upon the Pope to give orders concerning the care of him, and concerning his drawings and other things, in case anything should befall him. In the presence of his physician and other friends, in perfect consciousness, he made his will in three words, leaving his soul in the hands of God, his body to the earth, and his goods to his nearest relations, charging his friends when passing out of this life to remember the sufferings of Jesus Christ; and so, on the seventeenth day of February, at twentyt-three o'clock of the year 1564, he expired to go to a better life.

Michelangelo's imagination was so perfect that, not being able to express with his hands his great and terrible conceptions, he often abandoned his works and destroyed many of them. I know that a little before his death he burnt a great number of drawings and sketches. It should appear strange to none that Michelangelo delighted in solitude, being as it were in love with art. Nevertheless he held dear the friendship of many great and learned persons, among whom were many cardinals and bishops.

In his manner of life he was most abstemious, being content when young with a little bread and wine while at his work, and until he had finished the Last Judgment he always waited for refreshment till the evening, when he had done his work. Though rich he lived poorly, never taking presents from any one. He took little sleep, but often at night he would rise to work, having made himself a paper cap, in the middle of which he could fix his candle, so that he could have the use of his hands.

He had a most tenacious memory; he could remember and make use of the works of others when he had only once seen them; while he never repeated anything of his own, because he remembered all he had done. He felt very strongly against those who had done him an injury, but he never had recourse to vengeance.

His conversation was full of wisdom and gravity, mixed with clever or humorous sayings. Many of these have been noted down, and I will give some. A friend of his was once talking to him about death, and saying that he must dread it very much because he was so continually laboring in his art; but he answered, "All that was nothing, and if life pleased us, death was a work from the hand of the same Master, and ought not to displease us."

Certainly he was sent into the world to be an example to men of art, that they should learn from his life and from his works; and I, who have to thank God for felicity rare among men of our profession, count among my greatest blessings that I was born in the time when Michelangelo was alive, and was counted worthy to have him for my master, and to be treated by him as a familiar friend.

* * * * * *

Giorgio Vasari, "Leonardo da Vinci" *Lives*, 1550 CE

The greatest gifts are often seen, in the course of nature, rained by celestial influences on human creatures; and sometimes, in supernatural fashion, beauty, grace, and talent are united beyond measure in one single person, in a manner that to whatever such an one turns his attention, his every action is so divine, that, surpassing all other men, it makes itself clearly known as a thing bestowed by God (as it is), and not acquired by human art. This was seen by all mankind in Leonardo da Vinci, in whom, besides a beauty of body never sufficiently extolled, there was an infinite grace in all his actions; and so great was his genius, and such its growth, that to whatever difficulties he turned his mind, he solved them with ease. In him was great bodily strength, joined to dexterity, with a spirit and courage ever royal and magnanimous; and the fame of his name so increased, that not only in his lifetime was he held in esteem, but his reputation became even greater among posterity after his death.

Truly marvellous and celestial was Leonardo, the son of Ser Piero da Vinci; and in learning and in the rudiments of letters he would have made great proficience, if he had not been so variable and unstable, for he set himself to learn many things, and then, after having begun them, abandoned them. Thus, in arithmetic, during the few months that he studied it, he made so much progress, that, by continually suggesting doubts and difficulties to the master who was teaching him, he would very often bewilder him. He gave some little attention to music, and quickly resolved to learn to play the lyre, as one who had by nature a spirit most lofty and full of refinement: wherefore he sang divinely to that instrument, improvising upon it. Nevertheless, although he occupied himself with such a variety of things, he never ceased drawing and working in relief, pursuits which suited his fancy more than any other. Ser Piero, having observed this, and having considered the loftiness of his intellect, one day took some of his drawings and carried them to Andrea del Verrocchio, who was much his friend, and besought him straitly [sic] to tell him whether Leonardo, by devoting himself to drawing, would make any proficience. Andrea was astonished to see the extraordinary beginnings of Leonardo, and urged Ser Piero that he should make him study it; wherefore he arranged with Leonardo that he should enter the workshop of Andrea, which Leonardo did with the greatest willingness in the world.

And he practised not one branch of art only, but all those in which drawing played a part; and having an intellect so divine and marvellous that he was also an excellent geometrician, he not only worked in sculpture, making in his youth, in clay, some heads of women that are smiling, of which plaster casts are still taken, and likewise some heads of boys which appeared to have issued from the hand of a master; but in architecture, also, he made many drawings both of ground-plans and of other designs of buildings; and he was the first, although but a youth, who suggested the plan of reducing the river Arno to a navigable canal from Pisa to Florence. He made designs of flour-mills, fullingmills, and engines, which might be driven by the force of water; and since he wished that his profession should be painting, he studied much in drawing after nature, and sometimes in making models of figures in clay, over which he would lay soft pieces of cloth dipped in clay, and then set himself patiently to draw them on a certain kind of very fine Rheims cloth, or prepared linen; and he executed them in black and white with the point of his brush, so that it was a marvel, as some of them by his hand, which I have in our book of drawings, still bear witness; besides which, he drew on paper with such diligence and so well, that there is no one who has ever equalled him in perfection of finish; and I have one, a head drawn with the style in chiaroscuro, which is divine.

And there was infused in that brain such grace from God, and a power of expression in such sublime accord with the intellect and memory that served it, and he knew so well how to express his conceptions by draughtmanship, that he vanquished with his discourse, and confuted with his reasoning, every valiant wit. And he was continually making models and designs to show men how to remove mountains with ease, and how to bore them in order to pass from one level to another; and by means of levers, windlasses, and screws, he showed the way to raise and draw great weights, together with methods for emptying harbors, and pumps for removing water from low places, things which his brain never ceased from devising.

It is clear that Leonardo, through his comprehension of art, began many things and never finished one of them, since it seemed to him that the hand was not able to attain to the perfection of art in carrying out the things which he imagined; for the reason that he conceived in idea difficulties so subtle and so marvelous, that they could never be expressed by the hands, be they ever so excellent. And so many were his caprices, that, philosophizing of natural things, he set himself to seek out the properties of herbs, going on even to observe the motions of the heavens, the path of the moon, and the courses of the sun.

He also painted in Milan a Last Supper, a most beautiful and marvelous thing; and to the heads of the Apostles he gave such majesty and beauty, that he left the head of Christ unfinished, not believing that he was able to give it that divine air which is essential to the image of Christ. This work, remaining thus all but finished, has ever been held by the Milanese in the greatest veneration, and also by strangers as well; for Leonardo imagined and succeeded in expressing that anxiety which had seized the Apostles in wishing to know who should betray their Master. For which reason in all their faces are seen love, fear, and wrath, or rather, sorrow, at not being able to understand the meaning of Christ; which thing excites no less marvel than the sight, in contrast to it, of obstinacy, hatred, and treachery in Judas; not to mention that every least part of the work displays an incredible diligence, seeing that even in the tablecloth the texture of the stuff is counterfeited in such a manner that linen itself could not seem more real.

161

It is said that the Prior of that place kept pressing Leonardo, in a most importunate manner, to finish the work; for it seemed strange to him to see Leonardo sometimes stand half a day at a time, lost in contemplation, and he would have like him to go on like the laborers hoeing in his garden, without ever stopping his brush. And not content with this, he complained of it to the Duke, and that so warmly, that he was constrained to send for Leonardo and delicately urged him to work, contriving nevertheless to show him that he was doing all this because of the importunity of the Prior. Leonardo, knowing that the intellect of that Prince was acute and discerning, was pleased to discourse at large with the Duke on the subject, a thing which he had never done with the Prior; and he reasoned much with him about art, and made him understand that men of lofty genius sometimes accomplish the most when they work the least, seeking out inventions with the mind, and forming those perfect ideas which the hands afterwards express and reproduce from the images already conceived in the brain. And he added that two heads were still wanting for him to paint; that of Christ, which he did not wish to seek on earth; and he could not think that it was possible to conceive in the imagination that beauty and heavenly grace which should be the mark of God incarnate. Next, there was wanting that of Judas, which was also troubling him, not thinking himself capable of imagining features that should represent the countenance of him who, after so many benefits received, had a mind so cruel as to resolve to betray his Lord, the Creator of the world. However, he would seek out a model for the latter; but if in the end he could not find a better, he should not want that of the importunate and tactless Prior. This thing moved the Duke wondrously to laughter, and he said that Leonardo had a thousand reasons on his side. And so the poor Prior, in confusion, confined himself to urging on the work in the garden, and left Leonardo in peace, who finished only the head of Judas, which seems the very embodiment of treachery and inhumanity; but that of Christ, as has been said, remained unfinished.

Leonardo undertook to execute, for Francesco del Giocondo, the portrait of Mona Lisa, his wife; and after toiling over it for four years, he left it unfinished; and the work is now in the collection of King Frances of France, at Fontainebleau. In this head, whoever wished to see how closely art could imitate nature, was able to comprehend it with ease; for in it were counterfeited all the minutenesses that with subtlety are able to be painted, seeing that the eyes had that lustre and watery sheen which are always seen in life, and around them were all those rosy and pearly tints, as well as the lashes, which cannot be represented without the greatest subtlety. The eyebrows, through his having shown the manner in which the hairs spring from the flesh, here more close and here more scanty, and curve according to the pores of the skin, could not be more natural. The nose, with its beautiful nostrils, rosy and tender, appeared to be alive. The mouth, with its opening, and with its ends united by the red of the lips to the flesh-tints of the face, seemed, in truth, to be not colors but flesh. In the pit of the throat, if one gazed upon it intently, could be seen the beating of the pulse. And, indeed, it may be said that it was painted in such a manner as to make every valiant craftsman, be he who he may, tremble and lose heart. He made use, also, of this device: Mona Lisa being very beautiful, he always employed, while he was painting her portrait, persons to play or sing, and jesters, who might make her remain merry, in order to take away that melancholy which painters are often wont to give to the portraits that they paint. And in this work of Leonardo's there was a smile so pleasing, that it was a thing more divine than human to behold; and it was held to be something marvelous, since the reality was not more alive.

There was very great disdain between Michelangelo Buonarroti and him, on account of which Michelangelo departed from Florence, with the excuse of Duke Giuliano, having been summoned by the Pope to the competition for the facade of S. Lorenzo. Leonardo, understanding this, departed and went into France, where the King, having had works by his hand, bore him great affection; and he desired that he should color the cartoon of S. Anne, but Leonardo, according to his custom, put him off for a long time with words.

Finally, having grown old, he remained ill many months, and, feeling himself near to death, asked to have himself diligently informed of the teaching of the Catholic faith, and of the good way and holy Christian religion; and then, with many moans, he confessed and was penitent; and although he could not raise himself well on his feet, supporting himself on the arms of his friends and servants, he was pleased to take devoutly the most holy Sacrament, out of his bed. The King, who was wont often and lovingly to visit him, then came into the room; wherefore he, out of reverence, having raised himself to sit upon the bed, giving him an account of his sickness and the circumstances of it, showed withal how much he had offended God and mankind in not having worked at his art as he should have done. Thereupon he was seized by a paroxysm, the messenger of death; for which reason the King having risen and having taken his head, in order to assist him and show him favor, to then end that he might alleviate his pain, his spirit, which was divine, knowing that it could not have any greater honor, expired in the arms of the King, in the seventy-fifth year of his age.

The loss of Leonardo was mourned out of measure by all who had known him, for there was none who had done such honor to painting. The splendor of his great beauty could calm the saddest soul, and his words could move the most obdurate mind. His great strength could restrain the most violent fury, and he could bend an iron knocker or a horseshoe as if it were lead. He was liberal to his friends, rich and poor, if they had talent and worth; and indeed as Florence had the greatest of gifts in his birth, so she suffered an infinite loss in his death.

Niccolo Machiavelli, *The Prince*, 1513 CE

Reading and Discussion Questions
1. What does Machiavelli say is the one thing a ruler should be well educated about and why?
2. How should a ruler behave toward his subjects according to Machiavelli?
3. Is it better for a ruler to be feared or loved, according to Machiavelli? Explain.
4. What, if any, virtues does Machiavelli say a ruler should have? Explain.
5. Is Machiavelli's advice to rulers good advice, in your opinion? Explain.

In 1513, a mid-level bureaucrat in the Florentine government wrote a book that would become a cornerstone of western political thought and one of the most hotly debated books ever written. The man was Niccolo Machiavelli and his book was The Prince. *Machiavelli was alive during a period of political turmoil in Florence and all the Italian city-states. Machiavelli watched as the seemingly all-powerful Medici family was chased out of Florence into exile and he also observed the ruthless and cunning tactics of Italy's other most notorious family, the Borgias. The Borgia family held control of the papacy itself during Machiavelli's lifetime and it was widely believed that the Borgia lied, stole, bribed and even murdered to make a member of their family pope. Cesare Borgia used ruthless tactics to assume control over most of the northern Italian city-states and he almost succeeded. In Machiavelli's view, only Cesare Borgia's unexpected illness undid his plans for total domination in Italy. Cesare Borgia is believed to be the main subject of study in* The Prince, *which is a brutally frank analysis of what it takes to win and maintain power. It was dedicated to Lorenzo di Medici, who was struggling to regain his power in Florence at the time.*

Lorenzo never read the book and The Prince *was never published in Machiavelli's lifetime. When printed copies became widely available after 1532, the Catholic Church banned it as an evil work. The word Machiavellian itself has come to mean evil or underhanded, not to be trusted. Machiavelli analyzed the often unpleasant realities of politics and the nature of power, and it struck people as terribly cynical. Machiavelli said things in his book like it is better to be feared than loved, and that a ruler should use any means necessary to achieve the desired outcome. This was a very unvirtuous view of leadership in an era when the illusion of virtue was still important.*

Over time, The Prince *has been recognized as a work of political genius and it marks the birth of political science. Like Da Vinci and Michelangelo dissected all the gruesome parts of the human body to understand how they worked, Machiavelli dissects politics and looked at all the ugly bits to gain understanding.* The Prince *painted a realistic picture for the first time of what politics is, and not what politics and politicians should be.*

That Which Concerns a Prince on the Subject of the Art of War

The Prince ought to have no other aim or thought, nor select anything else for his study, than war and its rules and discipline; for this is the sole art that belongs to him who rules, and it is of such force that it not only upholds those who are born princes, but it often enables men to rise from a private station to that rank. And, on the contrary, it is seen that when princes have thought more of ease than of arms they have lost their states. And the first cause of your losing it is to neglect this art; and what enables you to acquire a state is to be master of the art. Francesco Sforza, though being martial, from a private person became Duke of Milan; and the sons, through avoiding the hardships and troubles of arms, from dukes became private persons. For among other evils which being unarmed brings you, it causes you to be despised, and this is one of those ignominies against which a prince ought to guard himself, as is shown later on.

Concerning Things for Which Men, and Especially Princes, are Blamed

It remains now to see what ought to be the rules of conduct for a prince toward subject and friends. And it being my intention to write a thing which shall be useful to him to apprehends it, it appears to me more appropriate to follow up the real truth of a matter than the imagination of it; for many have pictured republics and principalities which in fact have never been known or seen, because how one lives is so far distant from how one ought to live, that he who neglects what is done for what ought to be done, sooner effects his ruin than his preservation; for a man who wishes to act entirely up to his professions of virtue soon meets with what destroys him among so much that is evil.

Hence, it is necessary for a prince wishing to hold his own to know how to do wrong, and to make use of it or not according to necessity. Therefore, putting on one side imaginary things concerning a prince, and discussing those which are real, I say that all men when they are spoken of, and chiefly princes for being more highly placed, are remarkable for some of those qualities which bring them either blame or praise; and thus it is that one is reputed liberal, another miserly...; one is reputed generous, one rapacious; one cruel, one compassionate; one faithless, another faithful.... And I know that every one will confess that it would be most praiseworthy in a prince to exhibit all the above qualities that are considered good; but because they can neither be entirely possessed nor observed, for human conditions do not permit it, it is necessary for him to be sufficiently prident that he may know how to avoid the reproach of those vices which would lose him his state...

Concerning Cruelty and Clemency, and Whether it is Better to be Loved than Feared

Upon this a question arises: whether it is better to be loved than feared or feared than loved? It may be answered that one should wish to be both, but, because it is difficult to unite them in one person, it is much safer to be feared than loved, when, of the two, either must be dispensed with. Because this is to be asserted in general of men, that they are ungrateful, fickle, false, cowardly, covetous, and as long as you successed they are yours entirely; they will offer you their blood, property, life, and children, as is said above, when the need is far distant; but when it approaches they turn against you. And that prince who, relying entirely on their promises, has neglected other precautions, is ruined; because friendships that are obtained by payments, and not by nobility or greatness of mind, may indeed be earned, but they are not secured, and in time of need cannot be relied upon; and men have less scruple in offending one who is beloved than one who is feared, for love is preserved by the link of obligation which, owing to the baseness of men, is broken at every opportunity for their advantage; but fear preserved you by a dread of punishment which never fails.

Nevertheless a prince ought to inspire fear in such a way that, if he does not win love, he avoids hatred; because he can endure very well being feared whilst he is not hated, which will always be as long as he abstains from the property of his citizens and subjects and from their women.

The Way Princes Should Keep Their Word

Everyone understands how praiseworthy it is for a prince to remain true to his word and to live with complete integrity without any scheming. However, we've seen through experience how many princes in our time have achieved great things who have little cared about keeping their word and have shrewdly known the skill of tricking the minds of men; these princes have overcome those whose actions were founded on honesty and integrity.

It should be understood that there are two types of fighting: one with laws and the other with force. The first is most suitable for men, the second is most suitable for beasts, but it often happens that the first is not enough, which requires that we have recourse to the second. Therefore, it is necessary for a prince to know how to act both as a man and as a beast. This was signified allegorically to princes by the ancient writers: they wrote that Achilles and many other ancient princes were given to be raised and tutored by the centaur Chiron, who took custody of them and disciplined them. This can only mean, this trainer who was half beast and half man, that a prince needs to know how to use either one or the other nature, and the one without the other will never last.

Since it is necessary for the prince to use the ways of beasts, he should imitate the fox and the lion, because the lion cannot defend himself from snares and the fox cannot defend himself from wolves. Therefore, it is important to be a fox in order to understand the snares and a lion in order to terrify the wolves. Those who choose only to be a lion do not really understand. Therefore, a prudent leader will not and should not observe his promises, when such observance will work against him and when the reasons for making the promise are no longer valid. If all men were good, this precept would not be good; but since men are evil and will not keep their word with you, you shouldn't keep yours to them. Never has a prince lacked legitimate reasons to break faith. I could give you an infinite number of examples from modern times, and show you numerous peace treaties and promises that have been broken and made completely empty by the faithlessness of princes: these knew well how to use the ways of the fox, and they are the ones who succeed. But it is necessary to know how to hide this nature and to simulate a good character and to dissimulate: for the majority of men are simple and will only follow the needs of the present, so that the deceiver can always find someone he can deceive.

Sir Thomas More, *Utopia*, 1516 CE

Reading and Discussion Questions

1. Describe Utopians' attitude towards wealth.
2. During the story of the visit to Utopia from the Anemolians, why are these visitors seen as ridiculous by the Utopians?
3. What is the process by which people in Utopia choose spouses? How are adulterers punished in Utopia?
4. Based on the excerpts you read, how "perfect" a society is Utopia? What elements seem ideal? What elements of Utopian society, if any, seem less than perfect to you?
5. What do you think Thomas More was trying to saying in writing *Utopia*?

Sir Thomas More was a trusted advisor to King Henry VIII of England during a time when England was making a controversial transition from Catholicism to Protestantism as a result of the Protestant Reformation. Thomas More was a devout Catholic and he served King Henry VIII well for many years, as Henry too was a dedicated Catholic. But in 1532, Henry VIII broke with the Catholic Church, partly in order to win a divorce from his first wife and marry the younger and more desirable Ann Boleyn. In order to achieve this new marriage, Henry declared England a Protestant nation and enraged English Catholics, including Thomas More. More was defiant in his refusal acknowledge the king's marriage and was executed by Henry VIII for treason. But More was not just a tragic figure in English political history, he was also the author of one of the great works of Renaissance literature, called Utopia.

In the 1500s the world was in the middle of a revolutionary change, and not just in the realm of religion. The Protestant Reformation, which you will learn more about in the next chapter, happened at the same time as the Renaissance was starting in Florence and the Age of Exploration was beginning in nations like Spain and Portugal. Whole new worlds were being discovered, both literally and figuratively. It was in this climate that More wrote Utopia, which, though fictional, was set in the middle of some very real events of the age. In his book, More describes a perfect world, called "Utopia" which comes from the Greek prefix "ou-"(ou), meaning "not," and topos (τόπος), "place;" hence the name literally means "nowhere." More's Utopia is a strictly ruled society that suppresses individualism and private property ownership to achieve the greatest amount of happiness for the greatest number of people.

Utopia criticized many aspects of society in the 1500s like the monarchy, the church, the world of business professionals and wealth in general but it does so cleverly through a fictitious narrator and a satirical tone. As a result, we do not know which criticism is from the narrator and which is from the author. This is a useful writing device, especially in a time before authors could freely criticize their society or its rulers. The man who tells the audience about this perfect place, Utopia, is called Dr. Hythloday, whose name literally means nonsense. So the reader is not sure whether to believe the truth as Hythloday tells it or to reject everything he says as nonsense. Utopia, the place, seems absurd to some readers while others believe it is ideal. Utopia, the novel, created a new genre of literature, the utopian novel, which has been the foundation for later classics of utopian literature, including Brave New World, 1984, Fahrenheit 451 and The Giver, among countless others.

On Utopian Dining

At the hours of dinner and supper, the whole syphogranty [community] being assembled by trumpet, they meet and eat together, excepting only those who are in the hospitals or lie sick at home. Yet after the halls are supplied, no man is hindered from carrying home provision from the marketplace, for they know that no one doth it except for some good reason. For, though any one who pleaseth may eat at home, no one doth it from inclination, it being absurd to prepare a bad dinner at home, when a much more plentiful one is ready for him so near his residence. The unpleasant and sordid services about these halls, are performed by their slaves. But dressing their meat and ordering their tables belong to the women, every family taking it by rotation. They sit at three or more tables according to their number, the men toward the wall, the women on the outside. Thus, if any of the women be taken suddenly ill (which is not uncommon when they are in a state of pregnancy), she may, without disturbing the rest, rise and go to the nursery, where are nurses with the unweaned infants, clean water, cradles, and a fire. Every child is nursed by its own mother, unless death or sickness prevent. In that case the syphogrants' wives quickly provide a nurse, which is no difficulty, as any woman who can do it, offereth herself cheerfully. And, to make her amends, the child she nurseth considereth her as its mother. The children under five sit among the nurses.

The other young of either sex, until marriageable, serve those who sit at table, or, if unequal to that in strength, stand by them in silence and eat what is given them. Nor have they any other particular form at their dinners. In the middle of the first table, which standeth across the upper end of the hall, sit the syphogrant and his wife, that being the most conspicuous place. Next to him sit two of the oldest, there being throughout four in a mess. If there be a temple within that syphogranty, the priest and his wife sit with the syphogrant above the rest. Next to them come a mixture of old and young, so distributed, that though near to others of their own age, they are mingled with the elders. This, they say, was so instituted, that the gravity of the old, and the respect due to them, might restrain the young from all indecent words and gestures.

The dishes are not served to the whole table at first, but the best are set before the old (whose seats are distinguished from the young), and after them all the rest are served alike. The elders distribute to the young any choice meats which happen to be set before them, if there be not such an abundance of them that the whole company may share them alike. Thus the aged are honoured with particular marks of respect, and yet all the rest fare as well as they do. Dinner, as well as supper, is begun with some moral lecture which is read to them, but which is so short that it cannot be deemed tedious. Hence, the old take occasion to entertain those about them with some useful and amusing amplifications. Yet they engross not the whole conversation, but rather engage the young in it, that they may discover their spirit and temper. They dispatch their dinners quickly, but sit long at supper, for they go to work after the one, and sleep after the other; and sleep they think promotes digestion. They never sup without music, and fruit is ever served up after their meat. While they are at table, perfumes are burned, and fragrant ointments and sweet waters sprinkled about the room. In short, they want nothing which may cheer their spirits; and allow themselves great latitude this way.

All things appear incredible to us, as they differ more or less from our own manners. Yet one who can judge aright will not wonder, that since their constitution differeth so materially from ours, their value of gold and silver also, should be measured by a very different standard. Having no use for money among themselves, but keeping it as a provision against events which seldom happen, and between which are generally long intervals, they value it no farther than it deserves, that is, in proportion to its use. Thus it is plain, they must prefer iron to either silver or gold. For we want iron nearly as much as fire and water, but nature hath marked out no use so essential for the other metals, that they may not easily be dispensed with. Man's folly hath enhanced the value of gold and silver because of their scarcity; whereas nature, like a kind parent, hath freely given us the best things, such as air, earth, and water, but hath hidden from us those which are vain and useless. Were these metals to be laid-up in a tower, it would give birth to that foolish mistrust into which the people are apt to fall, and create suspicion that the prince and senate designed to sacrifice the public interest to their own advantage. Should they work them into vessels or other articles, they fear that the people might grow too fond of plate, and be unwilling to melt it again, if a war made it necessary.

To prevent all these inconveniencies, they have fallen upon a plan, which agrees with their other policy, but is very different from ours; and which will hardly gain belief among us who value gold so much and lay it up so carefully. They eat and drink from earthen ware or glass, which make an agreeable appearance though they be of little value; while their chamber-pots and close-stools are made of gold and silver; and this not only in their public halls, but in their private houses. Of the same metals they also make chains and fetters for their slaves; on some of whom, as a badge of infamy, they hang an ear-ring of gold, and make others wear a chain or a coronet of the same metal. And thus they take care, by all possible means, to render gold and silver of no esteem.

Hence it is, that while other countries part with these metals as though one tore-out their bowels, the Utopians would look upon giving-in all they had of them, when occasion required, as parting only with a trifle, or as we should esteem the loss of a penny. They find pearls on their coast, and diamonds and carbuncles on their rocks. They seek them not, but if they find them by chance, they polish them and give them to their children for ornaments, who delight in them during their childhood. But when they come to years of discretion, and see that none but children use such baubles, they lay them aside of their own accord; and would be as much ashamed to use them afterward, as grown children among us would be of their toys.

I never saw a more remarkable instance of the opposite impressions which different manners make on people, than I observed in the Anemolian ambassadors, who came to Amaurot when I was there. Coming to treat of affairs of great consequence, the deputies from several cities met to await their coming. The ambassadors of countries lying near Utopia, knowing their manners,—that fine clothes are in no esteem with them, that silk is despised, and gold a badge of infamy,—came very modestly clothed. But the Anemolians, who lie at a greater distance, having had little intercourse with them, understanding they were coarsely clothed and all in one dress, took it for granted that they had none of that finery among them, of which they made no use. Being also themselves a vain-glorious rather than a wise people, they resolved on this occasion to assume their grandest appearance, and astonish the poor Utopians with their splendour.

169

Thus three ambassadors made their entry with 100 attendants, all clad in garments of different colours, and the greater part in silk. The ambassadors themselves, who were of the nobility of their country, were in clothes of gold, adorned with massy chains and rings of gold. Their caps were covered with bracelets, thickly set with pearls and other gems. In a word, they were decorated in those very things, which, among the Utopians, are either badges of slavery, marks of infamy, or play-things for children. It was pleasant to behold, on one side, how big they looked in comparing their rich habits with the plain clothes of the Utopians, who came out in great numbers to see them make their entry; and on the other, how much they were mistaken in the impression which they expected this pomp would have made. The sight appeared so ridiculous to those who had not seen the customs of other countries, that, though they respected such as were meanly clad (as if they had been the ambassadors), when they saw the ambassadors themselves, covered with gold and chains, they looked upon them as slaves, and shewed them no respect. You might have heard children, who had thrown away their jewels, cry to their mothers, *see that great fool, wearing pearls and gems as if he was yet a child;* and the mothers as innocently replying, *peace, this must be one of the ambassador's fools.*

Others censured the fashion of their chains, and observed, they were of no use. For their slaves could easily break them; and they hung so loosely, that they thought it easy to throw them away. But when the ambassadors had been a day among them, and had seen the vast quantity of gold in their houses, as much despised by them as esteemed by others; when they beheld more gold and silver in the chains and fetters of one slave, than in all their ornaments; their crests fell, they were ashamed of their glory, and laid it aside; a resolution which they took, in consequence of engaging in free conversation with the Utopians, and discovering their sense of these things, and their other customs.

The Utopians wonder that any man should be so enamoured of the lustre of a jewel, when he can behold a star or the sun; or that he should value himself upon his cloth being made of a finer thread. For, however fine this thread, it was once the fleece of a sheep, which remained a sheep notwithstanding it wore it. They marvel much to hear, that gold, in itself so useless, should be everywhere so much sought, that even men, for whom it was made, and by them hath its value, should be less esteemed. That a stupid fellow, with no more sense than a log, and as base as he is foolish, should have many wise and good men to serve him because he possesseth a heap of it. And that, should an accident, or a law-quirk (which sometimes produceth as great changes as chance herself), pass this wealth from the master to his meanest slave, he would soon become the servant of the other, as if he was an appendage of his wealth, and bound to follow it. But they much more wonder at and detest the folly of those, who, when they see a rich man, though they owe him nothing, and are not in the least dependent on his bounty, are ready to pay him divine honours because he is rich; even though they know him at the same time to be so covetous and mean-spirited, that notwithstanding all his wealth, he will not part with one farthing of it to them as long as he liveth.

Euthanasia and Suicide

I have already related to you with what care they look after their sick, so that nothing is left undone which may contribute either to their health or ease. And as for those who are afflicted with incurable disorders, they use all possible means of cherishing them, and of making their lives as comfortable as possible; they visit them often, and take great pains to make their time pass easily. But if any have torturing, lingering pain, without hope of recovery or ease, the priests and magistrates repair to them and exhort them, since they are unable to proceed with the business of life, are become a burden to themselves and all about them, and have in reality outlived themselves, they should no longer cherish a rooted disease, but choose to die since they cannot live but in great misery; being persuaded, if they thus deliver themselves from torture, or allow others to do it, they shall be happy after death. Since they forfeit none of the pleasures, but only the troubles of life by this, they think they not only act reasonably, but consistently with religion; for they follow the advice of their priests, the expounders of God's will. Those who are wrought upon by these persuasions, either starve themselves or take laudanum. But no one is compelled to end his life thus; and if they cannot be persuaded to it, the former care and attendance on them is continued. And though they esteem a voluntary death, when chosen on such authority, to be very honourable, on the contrary, if any one commit suicide without the concurrence of the priests and senate, they honour not the body with a decent funeral, but throw it into a ditch.

Marriage and Divorce

Their women are not allowed to marry before eighteen, and their men not before twenty-two. If any of them be guilty of unlawful intercourse before marriage, they are severely punished, and they are not allowed to marry unless they can obtain an especial warrant from the prince. Such disorderly conduct also bringeth a severe reproach on the master and mistress of the family in which it happened; for it is concluded that they have been negligent in their duty. Their reason for punishing this so severely is, because they think, were they not strictly restrained from all vagrant appetites, very few would engage in a state, in which they hazard the peace of their whole lives by being tied to one person, and are obliged to endure all the inconveniences with which that state is accompanied.

In matching, they adopt a plan which appears to us very extravagant, yet is constantly observed among them and accounted very wise. Before marriage, a grave matron presenteth the bride (be she virgin or widow) naked, to the bridegroom; and after that, some grave man presenteth the bridegroom naked to the bride. We laughed at this, and condemned it as very indecent. They, on the other hand, wondered at the folly of mankind in all other countries; who, if they buy but an inferior horse, examine him all over and take off his trappings; yet a wife, on whom dependeth the happiness of the remainder of life, they take upon trust, regarding only her face, and leaving the rest of her body covered, where contagious and loathsome disorders may lie concealed. All men are not so wise as to choose a woman only for her good qualities; and even the wise consider the body as adding not a little to the mind. It is certain the clothes may conceal some deformity which may alienate a man from his wife when it is too late to part with her. If such a thing be discovered after marriage, he hath no remedy but patience. They therefore think it reasonable, that good care should be taken to guard against such mischievous deception.

There was the more reason for this regulation among them, because they are the only people of those parts who allow not polygamy or divorce, except in case of adultery or insufferable perverseness. In these cases the senate dissolveth the marriage, and granteth the injured leave to marry again; but the guilty are made infamous and never allowed the privilege of a second marriage. No one is suffered to put away his wife against her inclination, on account of any misfortune which may have befallen her person. They esteem it the height of cruelty and treachery to abandon either of the married pair, when they most need the tenderness of their partner; especially in the case of old age, which bringeth many diseases with it, and is itself a disease.

But it often happens, that, when a married pair do not agree, they separate by mutual

171

consent, and find others with whom they hope to live more happily. Yet this is not done without leave from the senate, which never alloweth a divorce without a strict inquiry, by the senators and their wives, into the grounds on which it is desired. Even when they are satisfied as to the reasons of it, the matter proceedeth but slowly, for they are persuaded that a too ready permission of new marriages, would greatly impair the kind intercourse of the married.   They severely punish those who defile the marriage-bed. If both the offenders be married, they are divorced, and the injured may intermarry, or with whom else they please; but the adulterer and adultress are condemned to slavery. Yet if the injured cannot conquer the love of the offender, they may still live together, the partner following to the labour to which the slave is condemned; and sometimes the repentance of the condemned, and the unaltered kindness of the injured, have prevailed with the prince to take off the sentence. But who relapse after they are once pardoned, are punished with death.

Desiderus Erasmus, *In Praise of Folly*, 1511 CE

Reading and Discussion Questions
  1. Who are the "illuminated divines" that Folly discusses in the first oration below? What things do they claim to know and what do you think Erasmus' critique is of them?
  2. How do these "illuminated divines" treat Holy Scripture, according to Folly? And what is the role of the people in receiving the teachings of the Bible?
  3. In her oration on monks, why does Folly say the people hate and fear monks?
  4. In the last oration, who are the people Folly refers to as "The lights of the world?" Why do you think these people are given this label?
  5. Why does Folly say these people have been reduced to "mere wallets?" Are they acting in the way they should as spiritual leaders? Why or why not?
  6. Based on your understanding of the reading, what are Erasmus' critiques of the Catholic Church?

Desiderus Erasmus was a Dutch writer and theologian. Erasmus was great friends with Sir Thomas More, and both men shared a love of dark wit and biting humor as a tool to critique elements of the status quo. The use of humor and sarcasm to point out flaws in a system is a literary device known as satire. Erasmus was a satirical genius. In his book, In Praise of Folly, *Erasmus cleverly critiques a wide variety of practices and institutions of the European world in 1500.*

The main character of In Praise of Folly *is Folly herself, who is the daughter of the Greek gods of Wealth and Youth. In the book's opening, she introduces herself arrogantly, saying that she was nursed by the gods of Drunkenness and Ignorance and raised with the help of Self-Love, Laziness and Pleasure. Much like Dr. Hytholoday in Thomas More's* Utopia, *the reader is rightfully skeptical about whether what Folly says is to be trusted. But she delivers her defense of flawed practices so convincingly that the reader cannot help but see the absurdity in the things she passionately defends as a good idea.* In Praise of Folly *provides commentary on everything from marriage laws and rituals to rulers to the need or usefulness of wisdom. In the following excerpt, Folly is discussing religion and specifically, the role of clergy. This section is viewed as some of the most biting criticism of the corrupt practices of the Catholic Church in the 1500s.*

172

ORATION: GREAT ILLUMINATED DIVINES But perhaps I had better pass over our divines in silence and not stir this pool or touch this fair but unsavory plant, as a kind of men that are supercilious beyond comparison, and to that too, implacable; lest setting them about my ears, they attack me by troops and force me to a recantation sermon, which if I refuse, they straight pronounce me a heretic. For this is the thunderbolt with which they fright those whom they are resolved not to favor. And truly, though there are few others that less willingly acknowledge the kindnesses I have done them, yet even these too stand fast bound to me upon no ordinary accounts; while being happy in their own opinion, and as if they dwelt in the third heaven, they look with haughtiness on all others as poor creeping things and could almost find in their hearts to pity them; while hedged in with so many magisterial definitions, conclusions, corollaries, propositions explicit and implicit. Besides, while they explicate the most hidden mysteries according to their own fancy- as how the world was first made; how original sin is derived to posterity; in what manner, how much room, and how long time Christ lay in the Virgin's womb; how accidents subsist in the Eucharist without their subject.

But these are common and threadbare; these are worthy of our great and illuminated divines, as the world calls them! At these, if ever they fall athwart them, they prick up- as whether there was any instant of time in the generation of the Second Person; whether there be more than one filiation in Christ; whether it be a possible proposition that God the Father hates the Son; or whether it was possible that Christ could have taken upon Him the likeness of a woman, or of the devil, or of an ass, or of a stone, or of a gourd; and then how that gourd should have preached, wrought miracles, or been hung on the cross; and what Peter had consecrated if he had administered the Sacrament at what time the body of Christ hung upon the cross; or whether at the same time he might be said to be man; whether after the Resurrection there will be any eating and drinking, since we are so much afraid of hunger and thirst in this world. There are infinite of these subtle trifles.

Paul knew what faith was, and yet when he said, "Faith is the substance of things hoped for, and the evidence of things not seen," he did not define it doctor-like.

They knew the mother of Jesus, but which of them has so philosophically demonstrated how she was preserved from original sin as have done our divines? Peter received the keys, and from Him too that would not have trusted them with a person unworthy; yet whether he had understanding or no, I know not, for certainly he never attained to that subtlety to determine how he could have the key of knowledge that had no knowledge himself. They baptized far and near, and yet taught nowhere what was the formal, material, efficient, and final cause of baptism, nor made the least mention of delible and indelible characters. They worshiped, 'tis true, but in spirit, following herein no other than that of the Gospel, "God is a Spirit, and they that worship, must worship him in spirit and truth"; yet it does not appear it was at that time revealed to them that an image sketched on the wall with a coal was to be worshiped with the same worship as Christ Himself, if at least the two forefingers be stretched out, the hair long and uncut, and have three rays about the crown of the head. For who can

173

conceive these things, unless he has spent at least six and thirty years in the philosophical and supercelestial whims of Aristotle and the Schoolmen?

In like manner, the apostles press to us grace; but which of them distinguishes between free grace and grace that makes a man acceptable? They exhort us to good works, and yet determine not what is the work working, and what a resting in the work done. They incite us to charity, and yet make no difference between charity infused and charity wrought in us by our own endeavors. Nor do they declare whether it be an accident or a substance, a thing created or uncreated. They detest and abominate sin, but let me not live if they could define according to art what that is which we call sin.

Although yet the gentlemen are so modest that if they meet with anything written by the apostles not so smooth and even as might be expected from a master, they do not presently condemn it but handsomely bend it to their own purpose As if Holy Scripture were a nose of wax, they fashion and refashion it according to their pleasure; while they require that their own conclusions, subscribed by two or three Schoolmen, be accounted greater than Solon's laws and preferred before the papal decretals; while, as censors of the world, they force everyone to a recantation that differs but a hair's breadth from the least of their explicit or implicit determinations. And those too they pronounce like oracles. This proposition is scandalous; this irreverent; this has a smack of heresy; this no very good sound: so that neither baptism, nor the Gospel, nor Paul, nor Peter, nor St. Jerome, nor St. Augustine, no nor most Aristotelian Thomas himself can make a man a Christian, without these bachelors too be pleased to give him his grace.

Nay, I have sometimes laughed myself to see them so tower in their own opinion when they speak most barbarously; and when they humh and hawh so pitifully that none but one of their own tribe can understand them, they call it heights which the vulgar can't reach; for they say 'tis beneath the dignity of divine mysteries to be cramped and tied up to the narrow rules of grammarians: from whence we may conjecture the great prerogative of divines, if they only have the privilege of speaking corruptly, in which yet every cobbler thinks himself concerned for his share.

ORATION: MONKS And next these come those that commonly call themselves the religious and monks, most false in both titles, when both a great part of them are farthest from religion, and no men swarm thicker in all places than themselves. Nor can I think of anything that could be more miserable did not I support them so many several ways. For whereas all men detest them to the height, that they take it for ill luck to meet one of them by chance, yet such is their happiness that they flatter themselves. For first, they reckon it one of the main points of piety if they are so illiterate that they can't so much as read. And yet, like pleasant fellows, with all this vileness, ignorance, rudeness, and impudence, they represent to us, for so they call it, the lives of the apostles.

And yet these monks, no man dares despise because they are privy to all men's secrets by means of confessions, as they call them. Which yet were no less than treason to discover, unless, being got drunk, they have a mind to be pleasant, and then all comes out, that is to say by hints and conjectures but suppressing the names. But if anyone should anger these wasps, they'll sufficiently revenge themselves in their public sermons and so point out their enemy by circumlocutions that there's no one but understands whom 'tis they mean, unless he understand nothing at all; nor will they give over their barking till you throw the dogs a bone.

They erect their theological crests and beat into the people's ears those magnificent titles of illustrious doctors, subtle doctors, most subtle doctors, seraphic doctors, cherubin doctors, holy doctors, unquestionable doctors, and the like; and then throw abroad among the ignorant people syllogisms, majors, minors, conclusions, corollaries, suppositions, and those so weak and foolish that they are below pedantry.

ORATION: LIGHTS OF THE WORLD Whereas now they do well enough while they feed themselves only, and for the care of their flock either put it over to Christ or lay it all on their suffragans, as they call them, or some poor vicars. Nor do they so much as remember their name, or what the word bishop signifies, to wit, labor, care, and trouble. But in racking to gather money they truly act the part of bishops, and herein acquit themselves to be no blind seers.

In like manner cardinals, if they thought themselves the successors of the apostles, they would likewise imagine that the same things the other did are required of them, and that they are not lords but dispensers of spiritual things of which they must shortly give an exact account. If they did but duly consider their actions, they would willingly abandon their obsession with the material world and live a laborious, careful life, such as was that of the ancient apostles.

And for popes, that supply the place of Christ, if they should endeavor to imitate His life, to wit His poverty, labor, doctrine, cross, and contempt of life, or should they consider what the name pope, that is father, or holiness, imports, who would live more unhappy than themselves? Or who would purchase that chair (of the papacy] with all his fortune? or defend it, so purchased, with swords, poisons, and all force imaginable?

A most inhuman and abominable thing, and more to be execrated, that those great princes of the Church and true lights of the world should be reduced to a staff and a wallet. Whereas now, if there be anything that requires their pains, they leave that to Peter and Paul that have leisure enough; but if there be anything of honor or pleasure, they take that to themselves. By which means it is, yet by my courtesy, that scarce any kind of men live more voluptuously or with less trouble; as believing that Christ will be well enough pleased if in their mystical and almost mimical pontificality, ceremonies, titles of holiness and the like, and blessing and cursing, they play the parts of bishops. To work miracles is old and antiquated, and not in fashion now; to instruct the people, troublesome; to interpret the Scripture, pedantic; to pray, a sign one has little else to do; to shed tears, silly and womanish; to be poor, base; to be vanquished, dishonorable and little becoming him that scarce admits even kings to kiss his slipper; and lastly, to die, uncouth; and to be stretched on a cross, infamous.

Theirs are only those weapons and sweet blessings which Paul mentions, and of these truly they are bountiful enough: as interdictions, hangings, heavy burdens, reproofs anathemas, executions in effigy, and that terrible thunderbolt of excommunication, with the very sight of which they sink men's souls beneath the bottom of hell: which yet these most holy fathers in Christ and His vicars hurl with more fierceness against none than against such as, by the instigation of the devil, attempt to lessen or rob them of Peter's patrimony. When, though those words in the Gospel, "We have left all, and followed Thee," were his, yet they call his patrimony lands, cities, tribute, imposts, riches; for which, being enflamed with the love of Christ, they contend with fire and sword, and not without loss of much Christian blood, and believe they have then most apostolically defended the Church, the spouse of Christ, when the enemy, as they call them, are valiantly routed. As if the Church had any deadlier enemies than wicked prelates, who not only suffer Christ to run out of request for want of preaching him, but hinder his spreading by their multitudes of laws merely contrived for their own profit, corrupt him by their forced expositions, and murder him by the evil example of their pestilent life.

Nay, further, whereas the Church of Christ was founded in blood, confirmed by blood, and augmented by blood, now, as if Christ, who after his wonted manner defends his people, were lost, they govern all by the word. And whereas war is so savage a thing that it rather befit beasts than men, so outrageous that the very poets feigned it came from the Furies, so pestilent that it corrupts all men's manners, so unjust that it is best executed by the worst of men, so wicked that it has no agreement with Christ; and yet, omitting all the other, they make this their only business.

But this they have in common with those of the heathens, that they are vigilant enough to the harvest of their profit, nor is there any of them that is not better read in those laws than the Scripture. Whereas if there be anything burdensome, they prudently lay that on other men's shoulders and shift it from one to the other, as men toss a ball from hand to hand, following herein the example of lay princes who commit the government of their kingdoms to their grand ministers, and they again to others, and leave all study of piety to the common people. In like manner the common people put it over to those they call ecclesiastics, as if themselves were no part of the Church, or that their vow in baptism had lost its obligation.

In like manner the popes, the most diligent of all others in gathering in the harvest of money, refer all their apostolical work to the bishops, the bishops to the parsons, the parsons to the vicars, the vicars to their brother mendicants, and they again throw back the care of the flock on those that take the wool.

But it is not my business to sift too narrowly the lives of prelates and priests for fear I seem to have intended rather a satire than an oration, and be thought to tax good princes while I praise the bad. And therefore, what I slightly taught before has been to no other end but that it might appear that there's no man can live pleasantly unless he [take folly as his master].

CHAPTER 7–
THE PROTESTANT REFORMATION
(1500 to 1650 CE)

GUIDING QUESTIONS
- What are some examples of the corruption that was prevalent among Catholic Church clergy by 1500?
- Was Luther the first to criticize the church for its abuses? Explain.
- What were Luther's specific complaints about the Church and what did he hope would happen by writing the 95 Theses?
- Luther has sometimes been called an "accidental revolutionary." Do you agree or disagree with that label? Explain.
- What was the political impact of Luther's work? How did the Protestant Reformation impact the Holy Roman Empire? France? England?

The 16th century, as we have seen, was a time of unprecedented change in every area of life. Students sometimes ask, if I could go back to any time in history, when would it be and why? My answer is always the same: I would time travel back to Florence in 1519 and I would have a huge dinner party. I would invite a number of artists, including Michelangelo, Leonardo da Vinci, Raphael and Titian and writers too, like Niccolo Machiavelli and Sir Thomas More. I think it would be nice to have a politician at the table so I would also invite King Henry VIII and his troublesome wife, Ann Boleyn. To keep things intellectually stimulating, I would add Nicholas Copernicus to my guest list as well. To share stories of their grand adventures, I hope Christopher Columbus, Jacques Cartier, Hernan Cortez, Vasco de Gama and Ferdinand Magellan might come as well (though Magellan may or may not be a no show!) Finally, I would add Martin Luther to my list to give the evening a little fire. Imagine it. To my knowledge, nowhere before or since has there been a larger collection of geniuses and revolutionaries alive at one time than there were in the early 1500s in Europe. It is important for us to stop and ask "Why?" Why, after a thousand years of men who's names we do not remember and whose achievements we cannot recall, was there such a high concentration of ambition and genius in the 16th century?

One answer is Humanism. Humanism inspired acts of imagination, self-expression and genius amongst Renaissance artists and writers and the Humanist love of logic and reason gave rise to modern science in the same century. As you will learn, Humanist curiosity and the quest for knowledge also caused the Age of Discovery and Conquest and the colonization of the Americas. It should come as no surprise then that religion was also radically changed by the Humanist philosophy. Remember, a key characteristic of Humanists is reason over faith. In other words, Humanists did not take anyone's word for anything, even if that someone was the pope himself. Humanism is all about self-reliance and the power of the individual. Many people questioned why they needed a priest to communicate with God, to be granted forgiveness or to get into Heaven. One such person was a German monk named Martin Luther.

Martin Luther was, in 1517, a rebellious young monk who was appalled by the abuses he saw among Catholic church clergy. He was so outraged by the corruption he witnessed in Rome and in his home city of Wittenberg that he decided to write a very angry letter. It was his list of complaints about the corruption of the Catholic Church.

Luther had 95 specific complaints, that have become known at the *Ninety-Five Theses*, that he angrily nailed to the door of the church in Wittenberg, Germany. This seemingly simple act set the world on fire, created a permanent split within the Catholic Church and resulted in several deadly wars that lasted decades and killed millions. The firestorm ignited by Luther is the event known as the Protestant Reformation.

Luther fiercely objected to the church practice of selling of indulgences, which promised that people could shorten their time in purgatory or win immediate entrance into Heaven with money. The selling of indulgences was not a new practice for the Catholic Church, which believes that people can get into Heaven through a combination of faith and good works. The church considered charitable donations to the church a kind of "good work," and the selling of indulgences to remorseful Christians had long been a part of church practices. During Luther's life, the selling of indulgences became more about raising money for the church than it was about getting people into Heaven. And the priests who were selling indulgences were notoriously corrupt.

Many people are surprised to learn an unusual connection between the actions of Martin Luther and the life of Michelangelo but the two men's lives are strangely intertwined. At the end of Michelangelo's life, he was asked by the pope to design plans for an elaborate cathedral in Rome that would be the heart of the Catholic Church. The church he designed would become St. Peter's Basilica, the largest Catholic Church in the world. The design was a masterpiece, but a very, very expensive masterpiece. Church leaders began an aggressive fundraising campaign to raise the money to make Michelangelo's vision a reality and this is where the indulgence-sellers came in. Priests were encouraged to be aggressive in their sale of new indulgences to finance the construction of St. Peter's. They sometimes preached whole sermons about the reasons for buying these "forgiveness tickets" and made impossible promises about what these tickets could buy for people. In some cases, priests promised forgiveness for future sins, or that a person could shorten the time a deceased loved one spent in Purgatory. The most notorious of all indulgence-sellers was a man named Johannes Tetzel, who was selling indulgences in Luther's town. Tetzel promised that a man could win forgiveness for "violating the Virgin mother herself" with the special indulgence he was offering. Understandably, Luther was enraged at such an immoral and impossible promise. Tetzel was the last straw for Luther, who could no longer watch his townsfolk be preyed upon with such terrible lies. His crusade against the corruption of the Catholic Church began in 1517 in Wittenberg, Germany and had ripple effects around the world.

Luther, however, was not the first man to object to Catholic Church practices. Many had criticized the church before him and paid for their critiques with their lives. Dissatisfaction with the church was not a new thing. Since the time of the Crusades, people had quietly questioned the all-consuming power of the Catholic Church and their own helplessness in winning salvation. But since the church acted as both a political and a religious institution during all of the Middle Ages, to go against the church was a fatal mistake for most. A number of clergy in the 1300s criticized church corruption and were burned at the stake as heretics for their words. The Catholic Church killed thousands of critics who were labeled as heretics and it created a list of books and other works that were banned by the Church because of their "false and lying teaching or doctrine." But try as it did, the Catholic Church could not fully rid the world of these critics or their criticisms.

Though Luther was not first critic of church corruption, he became the most famous and successful of them. There were three factors that allowed Luther to survive for doing the same thing countless others had died for. First, by the 1500s, there was widespread public skepticism about the church and Catholic clergy. In a time when most people had no personal wealth, they resented the opulent palaces, fine velvet robes and jewel-encrusted adornments of the clergy. Why should the church have and display so much wealth and not also help to make its flock more comfortable in their own lives. Second, Luther was alive during the explosion of Humanist philosophy, when people believed more and more in self-sufficiency and the power of the individual. It made less sense by 1500 that people should need a go-between to communicate with God or to read the Bible to them. If humans were wise and capable, as Humanists believed they were, why couldn't they be trusted with their own spiritual matters? Why should they have to depend on a corrupt priest to get into Heaven? To many 16th-century Humanists, this idea simply did not make sense. Finally, Luther was born after the invention of the printing press. His *Ninety-Five Theses* were printed and reprinted thousands of times in just a few days and were circulated across Europe within weeks. The printing press made Martin Luther a celebrity and celebrities are harder to kill or to make disappear, much to the dismay of the Catholic Church. So instead of simply killing Luther, they had to deal with him.

What was it, exactly, that Luther said in his famous *Ninety-Five Theses* that caused such an uproar? He had three basic points, which have become the foundation of the Protestant branch of Christianity. He said: 1. Christians can get into Heaven through faith alone; 2. Christians do not need a priest to communicate with God; and 3. People should read and interpret the Bible themselves, rather than relying on a second-hand interpretation from clergy. That's it. His words and teachings were simple but the reaction to them was swift and severe.

Luther posted his *Ninety-Five Theses* in Wittenberg, Germany in the fall of 1517. By the spring of 1518, his words had been read by hundreds of thousands of European Christians and the church realized Luther posed a huge problem. He was ordered to officially recant, or take back, the things he had said but he refused and was brought to trial for heresy. While he awaited trial, Luther preached against church corruption but never advocated or wanted a split from the church. What Luther wanted was meaningful reforms from the church, of which he was a devoted clergyman and theologian. The church was unwilling to see any truth in what Luther had said and refused to admit any wrongdoing. Luther stood trial in 1521. He was found guilty of crimes against the church, excommunicated and labeled an outlaw, which meant there was a price on his head. In addition, all of his writings were ordered to be burned and it was a crime to read anything Luther had written. Pope Leo X was the head of the church at the time and he issued a Papal Bull, or official order, condemning Luther and his works.

Adhering to what he believed was the truth as revealed in the Bible, Luther continually refused to take back what he had written and preached. Before he could be captured and sentenced for his crimes, Luther was hidden away by a German Prince named Prince Frederick of Saxony, who supported Luther. Luther remained in hiding for a full year after his trial. Prince Frederick almost certainly saved Luther's life. During

179

Luther's year in hiding, two very important things occurred: First, he translated the Bible into German, marking the first time the Bible had been written in a language of the common people. Before this, the Bible was only written in Latin, Greek or Hebrew so common people had to rely on scholars to read the Bible and tell them what it said. Having access to the Bible in a common language radically transformed how people experienced Christianity and substantially lessened the power of church leaders. The second thing that happened was the creation of the Protestant branch of Christianity. Remember, Luther himself never called for a split from the Catholic Church. He simply wanted the church to reform its corrupt practices. In Luther's absence, a group of enthusiastic supporters of Luther declared themselves separate from Catholicism, as a *protest* for centuries of church abuses of power. Hence the name *Protestant*. When Luther emerged from his seclusion he was horrified at the split that had occurred without his knowledge or approval. He was especially appalled at the violence that had broken out amongst those who claimed to be fighting in defense of Luther's teachings.

The violence that erupted in Germany in 1524, known as the German Peasants' War, highlighted the broad political and economic conflict caused by Luther's teachings. The Catholic Church represented the status quo. Kings and nobles, along with clergy, were very wealthy while the masses of people were very poor. One of Luther's main objections to the selling of indulgences had been that they preyed on the ignorance and desperation of peasants, who spent their meager life savings to buy these promises of forgiveness. This message was interpreted more broadly by Luther's more radical followers as deliberate economic oppression of the poor by the rich. In reality, the turmoil caused by Luther was used as an excuse for rebellion amongst German peasants who had resented their servitude to German nobility for centuries.

The German Peasants' War, though fought largely in the name of religion, had very little to do with religion except that peasants equated wealth with the church, and so when they rebelled against their wealthy oppressors, the church also became a target for their anger. In general, the German Peasants' War was a war against the establishment and the status quo, or a war of the "Haves" versus the "Have Nots." It did not end well for the peasants, who were the "Have Nots" in this story. After receiving word of the uprising and that peasants were committing murder in his name, Luther ruthlessly condemned the violence of the German peasants as a dangerous distortion of his teachings. The much better organized German nobility raised armies to ruthlessly end the rebellion, and killed as many as 300,000 German peasants before the war's end. As ghastly as these death tolls were, they only hinted at the more widespread violence that would result from Luther and the Protestant Reformation.

The region of modern-day Germany was known as the Holy Roman Empire during the time of the Protestant Reformation. The Holy Roman Empire was ruled by an Emperor, named Charles V at the time and within the Holy Roman Empire were numerous German kingdoms ruled by princes. German princes had very little control over their own lands and people because they answered to the Emperor, who was devoutly Catholic. Many German princes, including Prince Frederick of Saxony, embraced Luther's ideas because they presented an opportunity to gain more power. If German princes severed their allegiance to Catholicism and embraced Protestantism, they could also sever their allegiance to the Holy Roman Emperor and become true rulers on their own. In 1530, a majority of German princes did exactly this at a meeting called the Peace of Augsburg. In defiance of the Holy Roman Emperor and the pope himself. German princes demanded the freedom to choose Protestantism or Catholicism for their kingdoms, marking an important move toward the freer exercise of religion. It was also a shrewd political move on the part of the German princes who could then choose whatever religion would personally benefit them the most. The Protestant Reformation is most important perhaps because it gave people, or actually forced people to make, a choice. Since a person cannot be both Catholic and Protestant, people and nations had to decide to which group they would give their allegiance. And for nations like England and France, this was a very important choice.

In 1509, eight years before Luther wrote the *Ninety-Five Theses*, Henry VIII became the king of England. He was a devout Catholic. Henry VIII, a member of the Tudor Dynasty, was married to Catherine of Aragon, the daughter of King Ferdinand and Queen Isabella of Spain. You will learn much more about both of these powerful families during the Age of Absolutism but their story is closely tied to religious events during the Reformation. The marriage of Catherine and Henry created a powerful Catholic alliance between powerful Spain and less powerful England. Catherine and Henry were happily married for 20 years but Catherine failed to produce a male heir and Henry grew anxious. During this time, Henry also grew resentful of the immense power the Catholic Church had over his kingdom. The church took a huge portion of England's taxes for itself, controlled vast regions of territory and required that Henry be under the constant counsel of church advisors. Henry yearned for more freedom and more power. The birth of Protestantism promised to give him both of these things, and the chance to have a male heir. In a now infamous story, Henry VIII converted to Protestantism in order to divorce his Catholic wife, Catherine, and take a younger wife named Ann Boleyn. As the story is often told, Henry tore his country from its Catholic roots and forced it to become Protestant so he could have a younger, more fertile wife. But this is only part of the story. He did get a younger (though not more fertile) wife and he also got more control over his own country. By severing ties with Rome, Henry became more powerful but he also created more than a century of conflict in England, as it struggled to find its true religious identity. It will not be until 1688 that the battle between Protestants and Catholics will finally be brought to an end during the enlightened reign of King William and Queen Mary.

In England, Protestantism was originally forced on the people by their king but in France the opposite was true. Protestantism was popular among the French people but it was brutally suppressed by the French monarchy for most of the 16 century. Between 1562 and 1598, there were at least nine wars and even more public uprisings and massacres in France which are collectively called the French Wars of Religion. In the 1500s, Protestantism spread into France without much objection from the monarchy. However, by 1550 some more radical Protestants began protesting the corruption of the Catholic Church and the French crown viewed this as a threat to their power. The French monarchy passed laws limiting the freedoms of French Protestants, known as Huguenots, which only increased religious tension. Further complicating matters, many French nobles converted to Protestantism for the same reason the German princes did. They saw political advantage in Protestantism. For thirty years, France was immersed in religious conflict. By 1598, as many as four million people had been killed in the French Wars of Religion. In that year, tensions between Protestants and Catholics were finally eased when the French King Henry IV, passed the Edict of Nantes. The law granted religious tolerance to French Huguenots after decades of persecution. Henry IV, known as Good King Henry, was a Huguenot himself but for the good of his country, he converted to Catholicism, reportedly saying of his conversion, "Paris is well worth a mass."

Though religious tensions settled out considerably by the middle of the 1600s, the battle for supremacy of the Catholic Church was far from settled. One of the driving forces behind the Age of Exploration and Conquest was the desire to make the world Catholic. It seemed that if Catholics had temporarily lost the battle for souls in Europe, they would aggressively take their campaign to the Americas in the Age of Discovery and Conquest. The global impact of Luther and the Protestant Reformation, in spite of Catholic push back, have been profound. There are about 2.2 billion Christians in the world today--1.2 billion of those are Catholic; 400 million are Orthodox Christians; and 800 million are Protestant.

Early Church Critics, 14th and 15th Centuries CE

Reading and Discussion Questions

1. How can you broadly summarize the complaints that all three men had about the Catholic Church?
2. What specific types of corruption of abuses did each man write about?
3. What was the response of the church to each man's writings? What happened to each man?
4. It has been said of Luther's actions against the Catholic Church that, "The egg had been laid. All Luther had to do was incubate and hatch it." What does this quote mean in light of the writings of the earlier critics of church abuses? Consider also the critiques found in *In Praise of Folly* from the chapter on the Renaissance.

Martin Luther is credited with starting the Protestant Reformation, which did technically begin with his posting of the Ninety-Five Theses in 1517. However, for more than two centuries before Martin Luther, a handful of brave men were already speaking out about the abuses of the church. Three of the most noteworthy early critics were Francesco Petrarch, John Wycliffe and Jan Hus.

Francesco Petrarch, 1358 CE

By now we know that Francesco Petrarch was the Father of Humanism and one of the intellectual sparks that led to the Renaissance. But Petrarch was also outspoken in his criticisms against the Catholic Church. Because he was a man of the church himself, he was not punished for his criticisms, which inspired generations of other, more outspoken reformers. Below is an excerpt from a letter Petrarch wrote after witnessing the lifestyle of Pope and the Catholic clergy during the Avignon papacy.

Instead of holy solitude we find a criminal host and crowds of the most infamous satellites; instead of soberness, licentious banquets; instead of pious pilgrimages, preternatural and foul sloth; instead of the bare feet of the apostles, the snowy coursers of brigands fly past us, the horses decked in gold and fed on gold, soon to be shod with gold, if the Lord does not check this slavish luxury. In short, we seem to be among the kings of the Persians or Parthians, before whom we must fall down and worship, and who cannot be approached except presents be offered. O ye unkempt and emaciated old men, is it for this you labored? Is it for this that you have sown the field of the Lord and watered it with your holy blood? But let us leave the subject.

I have been so depressed and overcome that the heaviness of my soul has passed into bodily affliction, so that I am really ill and can only give voice to sighs and groans.

John Wycliffe , 1380 CE

John Wycliffe was an Oxford professor, scholar, and theologian who wrote the first hand-written English language Bibles in the late 1380 CE He was an outspoken critic of the teachings of the Catholic Church, which he said were largely inconsistent with what the Bible actually said. They were translated out of the Latin Vulgate, which was the only source text available to Wycliffe. The Pope was so infuriated by his teachings and his translation of the Bible into English, that 44 years after Wycliffe had died, he ordered the bones to be dug-up, crushed, and scattered in the river! Below are some of the criticisms that Wycliffe had about church practices.

5. That if a man has been truly repentant, all external confession is superfluous to him or useless.

8. That if the pope is fore-ordained to destruction and a wicked man, and therefore a member of the devil, no power has been given to him over the faithful of Christ by any one, unless perhaps by the Emperor.

11. That no prelate ought to excommunicate any one unless he first knows that the man is excommunicated by God.

12. That a prelate thus excommunicating is thereby a heretic or excommunicate.

18. That tithes are purely charity, and that parishoners may, on account of the sins of their curates, detain these and confer them on others at their will.

Jan Huss , 1415

One of Wycliffe's followers, John Hus, actively promoted Wycliffe's ideas: that people should be permitted to read the Bible in their own language, and they should oppose the tyranny of the Roman church that threatened anyone possessing a non-Latin Bible with execution. Hus was burned at the stake in 1415, with Wycliffe's manuscript Bibles used as kindling for the fire. The last words of John Hus were that, "in 100 years, God will raise up a man whose calls for reform cannot be suppressed." Almost exactly 100 years later, in 1517, Martin Luther nailed his famous 95 Theses onto the church door at Wittenberg. Below are some of the criticisms that Huss wrote about the Church.

--No pope or bishop has the right to take up the sword in the name of God.

--True men of God should pray for their enemies and not condemn them.

--Man obtains forgiveness of sins through real repentance, not through money.

Johannes Tetzel, Sermon on Indulgences, 1517 CE

Reading and Discussion Questions
1. What are the "letters of safe conduct" to which Tetzel is referring?
2. According to Tetzel, how long does it take to work off a single sin in Purgatory?
3. In your opinion, does Tetzel make a convincing case for people to purchase the indulgence he was selling? If you were in his audience, would you have been convinced?

Though the practice of selling indulgences was not new and was widespread by the 1500s, a German priest named Johann Tetzel became the most infamous indulgence seller. More than any other person, it was Tetzel and his impossible promises about indulgences that prompted Martin Luther to write his 95 Theses. Tetzel was given the task of selling a special indulgence to help finance the construction of St. Peter's in Rome. He was very good at raising funds because of his charismatic manner and his promises about what an indulgence might buy for its purchaser. Indulgences were usually sold just to shorten one's time in Purgatory for sins already committed, but Tetzel promised his indulgence could win people forgiveness for future sins and could even rescue dead loved ones from their time in Purgatory. Below is an excerpt from one of Tetzel's speeches on indulgences.

I pray you that you may be pleased to make use of such words as shall serve to open the eyes of the mind and cause your hearers to consider how great a grace and gift they have had and now have at their very doors. Blessed eyes indeed, which see what they see, because already they possess letters of safe conduct by which they are able to lead their souls through that valley of tears, through that sea of the mad world, where storms and tempests and dangers lie in wait, to the blessed land of Paradise. Know that the life of man upon earth is a constant struggle. We have to fight against the flesh, the world and the devil, who are always seeking to destroy the soul. In sin we are conceived, alas! what bonds of sin encompass us, and how difficult and almost impossible it is to attain to the gate of salvation without divine aid; since He causes us to be saved, not by virtue of the good works which we accomplish, but through His divine mercy ; it is necessary then to put on the armor of God.

You may obtain letters of safe conduct from the vicar of our Lord Jesus Christ, by means of which you are able to liberate your soul from the hands of the enemy, and convey it by means of contrition and confession, safe and secure from all pains of Purgatory, into the happy kingdom. For know that in these letters are stamped and engraven all the merits of Christ's passion there laid bare. Consider, that for each and every mortal sin it is necessary to undergo seven years of penitence after confession and contrition, either in this life or in Purgatory.

How many mortal sins are committed in a day, how many in a week, how many in a month, how many in a year, how many in the whole course of life ! They are well-nigh numberless, and those that commit them must needs suffer endless punishment in the burning pains of Purgatory.

Do you not know that when it is necessary for anyone to go to Rome, or undertake any other dangerous journey, he takes his money to a broker and gives a certain per cent in order that at Rome or elsewhere he may receive again his funds intact, by means of the letter of this same broker? Are you not willing, then, for a small fee, to obtain these letters, by virtue of which you may bring, not your money, but your divine and immortal soul safe and sound into the land of Paradise?

Martin Luther, *The Ninety-Five Theses*, 1517 CE

Reading and Discussion Questions
1. What are Luther's main criticisms of the church as outlined in this document?
2. Instead of buying indulgences, how should Christians should try to win salvation, according to Luther?
3. Instead of selling indulgences, what does Luther say church officials should be doing to help the people and to pay for their church?
4. What do you think of Luther's tone in this document? How would you have reacted to this document if you had been a church official in 1517?

Below are excerpts of the famous Ninety-Five Theses *that Martin Luther wrote and nailed to the church door in 1517. When he wrote the* Ninety-Five Theses, *Luther insisted that he only wanted the Catholic Church to reform its corrupt practices. He claimed he never envisioned a split from the church as a result of what he wrote. But because of the printing press and the inflammatory nature of what Luther said, an entire religious revolution resulted in the creation of the Protestant branch of Christianity. The foundations of Protestantism are found in this document.*

1. When our Lord and Master Jesus Christ said, "Repent" (Mt 4:17), he willed the entire life of believers to be one of repentance.
2. This word cannot be understood as referring to the sacrament of penance, that is, confession and satisfaction, as administered by the clergy.
3. Yet it does not mean solely inner repentance; such inner repentance is worthless unless it produces various outward mortification of the flesh.
4. The penalty of sin remains as long as the hatred of self (that is, true inner repentance), namely till our entrance into the kingdom of heaven.
7. God remits guilt to no one unless at the same time he humbles him in all things and makes him submissive to the vicar, the priest.
21. Thus those indulgence preachers are in error who say that a man is absolved from every penalty and saved by papal indulgences.
27. They preach only human doctrines who say that as soon as the money clinks into the money chest, the soul flies out of purgatory.
32. Those who believe that they can be certain of their salvation because they have indulgence letters will be eternally damned, together with their teachers.
36. Any truly repentant Christian has a right to full remission of penalty and guilt, even without indulgence letters.
42. Christians are to be taught that the pope does not intend that the buying of indulgences should in any way be compared with works of mercy.
43. Christians are to be taught that he who gives to the poor or lends to the needy does a better deed than he who buys indulgences.

44. Because love grows by works of love, man thereby becomes better. Man does not, however, become better by means of indulgences but is merely freed from penalties.

45. Christians are to be taught that he who sees a needy man and passes him by, yet gives his money for indulgences, does not buy papal indulgences but God's wrath.

46. Christians are to be taught that, unless they have more than they need, they must reserve enough for their family needs and by no means squander it on indulgences.

48 Christians are to be taught that the pope, in granting indulgences, needs and thus desires their devout prayer more than their money.

50. Christians are to be taught that if the pope knew the exactions of the indulgence preachers, he would rather that the basilica of St. Peter were burned to ashes than built up with the skin, flesh, and bones of his sheep.

51. Christians are to be taught that the pope would and should wish to give of his own money, even though he had to sell the basilica of St. Peter, to many of those from whom certain hawkers of indulgences cajole money.

53. They are the enemies of Christ who forbid altogether the preaching of the Word of God in some churches in order that indulgences may be preached in others.

75. To consider papal indulgences so great that they could absolve a man even if he had done the impossible and had violated the mother of God is madness.

76. We say on the contrary that papal indulgences cannot remove the very least of venial sins as far as guilt is concerned.

77. To say that even St. Peter if he were now pope, could not grant greater graces is blasphemy against St. Peter and the pope.

82. Why does not the pope empty purgatory for the sake of holy love and the dire need of the souls that are there if he redeems an infinite number of souls for the sake of miserable money with which to build a church?

86. Why does not the pope, whose wealth is today greater than the wealth of the richest Crassus, build this one basilica of St. Peter with his own money rather than with the money of poor believers?

94. Christians should be exhorted to be diligent in following Christ, their Head, through penalties, death and hell.

95. And thus be confident of entering into heaven through many tribulations rather than through the false security of peace (Acts 14:22).

Pope Leo X, *Exsurge Domine*, 1520 CE

Reading and Discussion Questions

1. How is Martin Luther described by Pope Leo X? What specific language in his description of Luther do you find most powerful and why?
2. Based on your understanding of the reading, what is the purpose of this document?
3. What is Martin Luther being commanded to do in this document? What is his punishment if he refuses?
4. What is to be done with Luther's writings? What is to be done to anyone who is caught reading his writings or spreading his teachings?
5. Based on the tone of the language of the 95 Theses, are you surprised by the severity of the church's response to Martin Luther? Why or why not?

Martin Luther and his Ninety-Five Theses became an overnight sensation as a result of the printing press. Within weeks, his writings had spread throughout the German states. Within a couple of months, copies of the Ninety-Five Theses had spread to every country in Europe and had been read by hundreds of thousands of people. Because of his fame, Luther was a very big problem for the Catholic Church and they were determined to put a stop to his teachings before the problem got any worse. The following "Papal Bull" or official order from Pope Leo X contains the Catholic Church's official condemnation of Martin Luther and their plan for stomping out his troublesome teachings.

Arise, O Lord, and listen to our prayers, for foxes have arisen seeking to destroy the vineyard whose winepress you alone have trod. The wild boar from the forest seeks to destroy it and every wild beast feeds upon it. Against the Roman Church, lying teachers are rising, introducing ruinous sects, and drawing upon themselves speedy doom. Their tongues are fire, a restless evil, full of deadly poison.

Let all this holy Church of God, I say, arise, and with the blessed apostles intercede with almighty God to purge the errors of His sheep, to banish all heresies from the lands of the faithful, and be pleased to maintain the peace and unity of His holy Church. In virtue of our spiritual office committed to us by the divine favor we can under no circumstances tolerate or overlook any longer the pernicious poison of the above errors without disgrace to the Christian religion and injury to orthodox faith.

No one of sound mind is ignorant how destructive, pernicious, scandalous, and seductive to pious and simple minds are the teachings of Martin Luther, how opposed they are to all charity and reverence for the holy Roman Church who is the mother of all the faithful and teacher of the faith; how destructive they are of the vigor of ecclesiastical discipline, namely obedience. This virtue is the font and origin of all virtues and without it anyone is readily convicted of being unfaithful.

We wish to proceed with great care as is proper, and to cut off the advance of this plague and cancerous disease so it will not spread any further in the Lord's field as harmful thornbushes.

With the advice and consent of these our venerable brothers, with mature deliberation on each and every one of the above theses, and by the authority of almighty God, we condemn, reprobate, and reject completely the teachings of Martin Luther as either heretical, scandalous, false, offensive to pious ears or seductive of simple minds, and against Catholic truth. We decree and declare that all the faithful of both sexes must regard them as condemned, reprobated, and rejected . . . Punishment for failure to comply with this order is automatic excommunication.

Moreover, because the preceding errors and many others are contained in the books or writings of Martin Luther, we likewise condemn, reprobate, and reject completely the books and all the writings and sermons of the said Martin, whether in Latin or any other language, containing the said errors or any one of them; and we wish them to be regarded as utterly condemned, reprobated, and rejected. We forbid each and every one of the faithful of either sex, in virtue of holy obedience and under the above penalties to be incurred automatically, to read, assert, preach, praise, print, publish, or defend them. They will incur these penalties if they presume to uphold them in any way, personally or through another or others, directly or indirectly, tacitly or explicitly, publicly or occultly, either in their own homes or in other public or private places. Indeed immediately after the publication of this letter these works, wherever they may be, shall be sought out carefully and shall be burned publicly and solemnly in the presence of the clerics and people.

As far as Martin himself is concerned, we must, without any further citation or delay, proceed against him to his condemnation and damnation as one whose faith is notoriously suspect and in fact a true heretic with the full severity of each and all of the above penalties and censures. Therefore let Martin himself and all those adhering to him, and those who shelter and support him, know that from our heart we exhort and beseech that he cease to disturb the peace, unity, and truth of the Church for which the Savior prayed so earnestly to the Father. We demand, further, that Martin cease from all preaching or the office of preacher.

And even though the love of righteousness and virtue did not take him away from sin and the hope of forgiveness did not lead him to penance, perhaps the terror of the pain of punishment may move him. Thus we beseech and remind this Martin, his supporters and accomplices of his holy orders and the described punishment. We ask him earnestly that he and his supporters, desist from preaching, both expounding their views and denouncing others, from publishing books and pamphlets concerning some or all of their errors. Furthermore, all writings which contain some or all of his errors are to be burned. Furthermore, Martin is to recant perpetually such errors and views.

If, however, this Martin, his supporters, adherents and accomplices, much to our regret, should stubbornly not comply with the mentioned stipulations within the mentioned period, we shall condemn this Martin, his supporters, adherents and accomplices as barren vines which are not in Christ, preaching an offensive doctrine contrary to the Christian faith and offend the divine majesty, to the damage and shame of the entire Christian Church, and diminish the keys of the Church as stubborn and public heretics.

King Henry VIII, *The Act of Supremacy*, 1534 CE

Reading and Discussion Questions
1. What power, besides becoming the head of the church, did Henry VIII gain as a result of this document?
2. This document gives Henry, among other things "all profits and commodities of the Church." What does that mean?
3. Besides winning a divorce and the ability to remarry, why else would this law have benefitted the reign of Henry VIII?

In 1534, Henry VIII declared a split in England from the Catholic Church in Rome. The document below, called the Act of Supremacy, was the law passed by the British Parliament that made that split possible and legal. Henry's decision to break from the authority of the Roman church caused more than a century of turmoil in England but it provided immediate personal gain for him. The decision to break from Rome and to create a new Protestant faith in England (called the Anglican Church) was motivated partly by Henry's desire to get a divorce from his Catholic wife. But there were also very important political and economic motives for Henry passing the Act of Supremacy and for bringing Protestantism to England.

Albeit the king's Majesty justly and rightfully is and ought to be the supreme head of the Church of England, and so is recognized by the clergy of this realm, be it enacted, by authority of this present Parliament, that the king, our sovereign lord, shall be taken, accepted, and reputed the only supreme head in earth of the Church of England, called *Anglicans Ecclesia;* and shall have and enjoy all honors, dignities, jurisdictions, privileges, authorities, immunities, profits, and commodities of the Church. . . .And that our said sovereign lord, king of this realm, shall have full power and authority from time to time to visit, repress, redress, record, order, correct, restrain, and amend all such errors, heresies, abuses, offenses, contempts and enormities, whatsoever they be, which by any manner of spiritual authority or jurisdiction ought or may lawfully be reformed, repressed, ordered, redressed, corrected, restrained, or amended, most to the pleasure of Almighty God.

Queen Elizabeth I, *Act of Uniformity*, 1559 CE

Reading and Discussion Questions
1. What was the main objective of the Act of Uniformity?
2. What was the punishment for priests who did not use the Book of Common Prayer as required by this act?
3. What was the expectation about people's attendance at church? What happened if people failed to meet these requirements?
4. This Act is considered a great act of diplomacy during the reign of Elizabeth. What is "diplomacy" and why were the Act of Uniformity and Elizabeth's actions in resolving religious conflict considered diplomatic?

After the death of Henry VIII, England was torn apart by religious conflict and was on the verge of a civil war by the time of the reign of Queen Elizabeth I in 1558. Henry was immediately succeeded by his only son, King Edward VI, who ruled England as a Protestant nation like his father before him had done. During his reign, he adopted a Book of Common Prayer, which was to aid England in its transition to Protestantism and was to be used in every church in the realm. These and other efforts to fully "Protestantize" England were slow but were taking hold gradually when, in 1553, Edward died after ruling for only six years. His sister Mary became Queen of England in 1553. Queen Mary I was a fanatic Catholic and declared her sole mission as queen was to return England to Catholicism. In pursuit of that goal, she outlawed the Book of Common Prayer and ruthlessly hunted down and persecuted English Protestants. During her five year reign, she burned more that 400 Protestant "heretics" at the stake, winning her the name Bloody Mary. Mary died in 1558, leaving the throne to her sister, Elizabeth, who would be crowned Queen Elizabeth I.

In order to restore peace in her kingdom, one of the first things Elizabeth did as queen was to create religious unity, which she did largely through the passage of the Act of Uniformity. Elizabeth was a master of diplomacy, which is the art of dealing with people in a sensitive and effective way. Elizabeth knew that the English people took their religion—either Protestant or Catholic—very seriously and she knew she had to tread delicately to resolve the religious tension. Prior to passage of the Act of Uniformity, Elizabeth made clear that she was returning England to Protestantism for the benefit and the peace of the realm and because it was what her father Henry had wanted. The Act of Uniformity ensured that all English people would go to the same kind of church and say the same prayers or they would be punished. But her great diplomatic act was declaring that she had no desire "to make windows into men's souls." By saying this she meant that people could privately, in their hearts, believe in any God or any branch of Christianity that they chose. This gesture granted the English people a kind of freedom of thought that was subtle and brilliantly effective in calming people's nerves. Practice whatever beliefs you want in your heart, was Elizabeth's message to her people. But for the sake of peace and national unity in public, we will all be Protestants . . or else.

Where at the death of our late sovereign lord King Edward VI there remained one uniform order of common service and prayer, and of the administration of sacraments, rites, and ceremonies in the Church of England, which was set forth in one book,

191

entitled: The Book of Common Prayer, and Administration of Sacraments, authorized by Act of Parliament, which was repealed and taken away by Act of Parliament in the first year of the reign of our late sovereign lady Queen Mary, to the great decay of the due honour of God, and discomfort to the professors of the truth of Christ's religion:

Be it therefore enacted by the authority of this present Parliament that the Book of Common shall stand and be, this day forward, in full force and effect, according to the tenor and effect of this statute.

And that if any manner of parson, vicar, or other whatsoever minister, refuse to use the said common prayers, or shall preach, declare, or speak anything in the derogation or depraving of the said book, or anything therein contained, shall be thereof lawfully convicted, according to the laws of this realm, by verdict of twelve men, shall lose and forfeit to the queen, the profit of all his spiritual benefices or promotions coming or arising in one whole year next after his conviction; and also shall suffer imprisonment by the space of six months, without bail.

And that if any such person or persons, after he shall be twice, shall offend against any of the premises the third time, shall suffer imprisonment during his life.

And if any person or persons whatsoever, shall in any interludes, plays, songs, rhymes, or by other open words, declare or speak anything in the derogation, depraving, or despising of the same book shall forfeit to the queen our sovereign lady for the first offence a hundred marks.

And that all and every person within this realm, shall diligently and faithfully, having no lawful or reasonable excuse to be absent, attend their parish church or chapel for common prayer every Sunday and other days used as holy days, and then and there to abide orderly and soberly during the time of the common prayer, preachings, or other service of God upon pain that every person so offending shall pay a fine.

The Council of Trent, *Acts of the Council of Trent*, 1563 CE

Reading and Discussion Questions

1. What teachings or ideas, which were the basis of Protestantism, did this document say were "anathema" or cursed?
2. In what areas did the Catholic Church refuse to make any changes to their practices and beliefs?
3. In what ways do these decrees illustrate the desire for reform within the Catholic Church?
4. How are Catholic clergy advised to live, according to this document and how are they to minster to their congregation? What criticisms about the church do you think these recommendations are a response to?

By the middle of the 1500s, it was clear that Protestantism was not going away, as more and more nations embraced the Protestant faith. It was equally clear to the Catholic Church that they had to do more in response to Luther and his criticisms of the church than ban his writings and label him a heretic. In 1540, the Catholic Church convened a series of meetings, together known as the Council of Trent, to address the widespread allegations of church corruption. The result of those meetings were the Acts of the Council of Trent. Overall, the Acts reaffirmed Catholic beliefs that priests and the sacraments were necessary for salvation. They rejected the ideas of Protestantism. In the Catholic faith even today, priests are viewed as crucial middle men between the common man and God. Also, the practice of the seven sacraments or rituals of Catholicism are still central to Catholic belief, and include Baptism, Confirmation, Eucharist, Penance, Anointing of the Sick, Holy Orders, and Matrimony.

While the Acts of the Council of Trent defended Catholic beliefs against its critics, they did also attempt reform, especially in regard to the extravagant lifestyle of Catholic clergy. The Acts were a smart move on the part of the Catholic Church in the wake of the Protestant Reformation because they did not bend to the will of Protestants. Instead they bolstered Catholicism as a powerful entity based in solid principles. At the same time, they addressed most of the problems common Catholics had with the church in the 1500s. As a result, a great many people who had abandoned Catholicism prior to the Council of Trent returned to their original Christian faith.

The universal Church has always understood that the complete confession of sins was instituted by the Lord, and is of divine right necessary for all who have fallen into sin after baptism; because our Lord Jesus Christ, when about to ascend from earth to heaven, left priests, his own vicars, as leaders and judges, before whom all the mortal offenses into which the faithful of Christ may have fallen should be carried, in order that, in accordance with the power of the keys, they may pronounce the sentence of forgiveness or of retention of sins. For it is manifest that priests could not have exercised this judgment without knowledge of the case....

If anyone says that the New Testament does not provide for a distinct, visible priesthood; or that this priesthood has not any power of consecrating and offering up the true body and blood of the Lord, and of forgiving and retaining sins, but is only an office and bare ministry of preaching the gospel; or that those who do not preach are not priests at all; let him be anathema (cursed)....

If anyone says that in the Catholic Church there is not a hierarchy instituted by divine ordination, consisting of bishops, priests, and ministers; let him be anathema.

If anyone says that the sacraments of the church were not all instituted by Jesus Christ, our Lord; or that they are more or less than seven, to wit, baptism, confirmation, the eucharist, penance, extreme unction, orders, and matrimony; or even that any one of these seven is not truly and properly a sacrament; let him be anathema....

Proper instruction shall be given for each of the sacraments which the bishops shall take care to have faithfully translated into the common language, and to have taught to the people by all parish priests. They shall also explain in the common language the sacred teachings and the truths of salvation; and they shall endeavor to impress them on the hearts of all, and to instruct their hearers in the law of the Lord....

It is to be desired that those who undertake the office of bishop should understand their duty, and comprehend that they are called, not to their own convenience, not to riches or luxury, but to labors and cares, for the glory of God. For it is not to be doubted that the rest of the faithful also will be more easily excited to religion and innocence if they shall see those who are set over them not fixing their thoughts on the things of this world, but on the salvation of souls and on their heavenly country. Clergy should they show themselves as examples by their actual deeds and the actions of their lives; which is a kind of perpetual sermon; but, above all, that they so order their whole conversation that others may thence be able to derive examples of frugality, modesty, and of that holy humility which so much commends us to God.

Wherefore, this Council not only orders that bishops be content with modest furniture, and a frugal table and diet, but that they also give heed that in the rest of their manner of living, and in their whole house, there be nothing seen which is alien to this holy institution, and which does not manifest simplicity, zeal toward God, and a contempt of vanities.

Jacques-Auguste de Thou, St. Bartholomew's Day Massacre, 1572 CE

Reading and Discussion Questions

1. Who is Admiral Coligny? What happened to Coligny in this story?
2. Why was Coligny killed? In whose name was the murder committed?
3. What does this story tell you about the level of religious tension in France in the 1500s?

By the late 1500s, tension between French Catholics and Huguenots had reached a boiling point. The French had been fighting a series of small-scale religious wars called the French Wars of Religion since 1562. Many Huguenots were living in hiding out of fear of persecution or murder by the French King. France was ruled by Charles IX at this time, who had become king at the age of one, leaving his kingdom to be run by his mother, the scheming and deeply Catholic Catherine de Medici.

In 1572, many of the Huguenot nobles came to Paris for a royal wedding, after receiving assurances that religious differences would be put on hold long enough to celebrate the happy marriage. This promise was made and ultimately broken by Charles IX's mother, Catherine de Medici. A few days after the wedding ceremony, a handful of powerful Huguenots who were still in Paris were carefully targeted for assassination. The first man targeted was of Admiral Gaspard de Coligny, the military and political leader of the Huguenots. Coligny was brutally murdered and his body defiled in August of 1572, setting off a string of assassinations of key Huguenot leaders.

These assassinations triggered more widespread violence against Huguenots in France, with estimates ranging from 5000 to as many as 30,000 Huguenots killed in the span of several weeks. The killing of Admiral Coligny and the ensuing violence is known as the St. Bartholomew's Day Massacre because Coligny was killed on a holy day honoring the Catholic Saint Bartholomew. This massacre was a violent escalation of the French Wars of Religion and it signaled that France desperately needed to do something to end the religious conflict that was tearing it apart. The following first-hand account of the murder of Admiral Coligny was recorded by the French historian, Jacques-Auguste de Thou, who bore witness to the gruesome event.

So it was determined to exterminate all the Protestants, and the plan was approved by the queen. The duke of Guise, who was put in full command of the enterprise, summoned by night several captains of the Catholic Swiss mercenaries, and some commanders of French companies, and told them that it was the will of the king that, according to God's will, they should take vengeance on the band of rebels while they had the beasts in the toils. Victory was easy and the booty great and to be obtained without danger. The signal to commence the massacre should be given by the bell of the palace, and the marks by which they should recognize each other in the darkness were a bit of white linen tied around the left arm and a white cross on the hat.

Meanwhile Coligny awoke and recognized from the noise that a riot was taking place. He perceived that the noise increased and that some one had fired an arquebus in the courtyard of his dwelling, and, guessing what it might be, but too late, he arose from his bed and having put on his dressing gown he said his prayers, leaning against the wall. The Swiss who were in the courtyard fled into the house and closed the door, piling against it tables and all the furniture they could find. It was in the first scrimmage that a Swiss was killed with a ball from an arquebus fired by one of Cosseins' people. But the conspirators broke through and mounted the stairway.

After Coligny had said his prayers with Merlin the minister, he said, without any appearance of alarm, to those who were present (and almost all were surgeons, for few of them were of his retinue) : "I see clearly that which they seek, and I am ready steadfastly to suffer that death which I have never feared and which for a long time past I have pictured to myself. I consider myself happy in feeling the approach of death and in being ready to die in God, by whose grace I hope for the life everlasting. I have no further need of human succor. Go then from this place, my friends, as quickly as you may, for fear lest you shall be involved in my misfortune, and that some day your wives shall curse me as the author of your loss. For me it is enough that God is here, to whose goodness I commend my soul, which is so soon to issue from my body. After these words they ascended to an upper room, whence they sought safety in flight here and there over the roofs.

Meanwhile the conspirators, having burst through the door of the chamber, entered, and when Besme, a assassin, sword in hand, had demanded of Coligny, who stood near the door, "Are you Coligny ?" Coligny replied, "Yes, I am he," with fearless countenance. "But you, young man, respect these white hairs. What is it you would do? You cannot shorten by many days this life of mine." As he spoke, the assassin gave him a sword thrust through the body, and having withdrawn his sword, another thrust in the mouth, by which his face was disfigured. So Coligny fell, killed with many thrusts. Others have written that Coligny in dying pronounced as though in anger these words: "Would that I might at least die at the hands of a soldier and not of a butler." But Attin, one of the murderers, has reported as I have written, and added that he never saw any one less afraid in so great a peril, nor die more steadfastly.

Then the duke of Guise inquired of Besme from the courtyard if the thing were done, and when Besme answered him that it was, the duke replied that the Chevalier d'Angouleme was unable to believe it unless he saw it; and at the same time that he made the inquiry they threw the body through the window into the courtyard, disfigured as it was with blood. When the Chevalier d'Angouleme, who could scarcely believe his eyes, had wiped away with a cloth the blood which overran the face and finally had recognized him, some say that he spurned the body with his foot. However this may be, when he left the house with his followers he said: "Cheer up, my friends! Let us do thoroughly that which we have begun. The king commands it." He frequently repeated these words, and as soon as they had caused the bell of the palace clock to ring, on every side arose the cry, "To arms !" and the people ran to the house of Coligny. After his body had been treated to all sorts of insults, they threw it into a neighboring stable, and finally cut off his head, which they sent to Rome. They also shamefully mutilated him, and dragged his body through the streets to the bank of the Seine, a thing which he had formerly almost prophesied, although he did not think of anything like this.

As some children were in the act of throwing the body into the river, it was dragged out and placed upon the gallows, where it hung by the feet in chains of iron; and then they built a fire beneath, by which he was burned without being consumed; so that he was, so to speak, tortured with all the elements, since he was killed upon the earth, thrown into the water, placed upon the fire, and finally put to hang in the air. After he had served for several days as a spectacle to gratify the hate of many and arouse the fury of many others, who reckoned that this fury of the people would cost the king and France many a sorrowful day, François de Montmorency, who was nearly related to the dead man, and still more his friend, and who moreover had escaped the danger in time, had him taken by night from the gibbet by trusty men and carried to Chantilly, where he was buried in the chapel.

Henry IV, *The Edict of Nantes*, 1598 CE

Reading and Discussion Questions
1. What is the stated overall purpose of this document as outlined in the first two paragraphs of this Edict?
2. What right is granted to Huguenots by provision #6 of the Edict?
3. What right is granted to Huguenots by provision #7 of the Edict and how is it different from what is accomplished in provision #6?
4. What right is granted to Huguenots in provision #16?
5. What right is granted to Huguenots in provision #27?
6. Do you think the Edict of Nantes was a good work of "diplomacy" in France? Explain your answer. (Review the definition of that word in the section on Elizabeth's Act of Uniformity.)

King Henry IV was more familiar than anyone in France with the turmoil caused by the split between French Catholics and Huguenots. It was for his wedding that French Huguenots had traveled to Paris, having been promised protection by the French crown. It was in the days after his own wedding that the St. Bartholomew's Day Massacre began. Henry was himself a Huguenot, and in the years before he became king himself, he was married to the sister then-King Charles IX to forge a delicate alliance between Huguenots and Catholics. Such an alliance proved impossible and the French Wars of Religion raged on for 27 years after the St. Bartholomew's Day Massacre.

Henry had become an heir to the French throne through is marriage to the king's sister and in 1589 he was crowned King Henry IV of France. He ruled until his death in 1610. Henry was the founder of a new dynasty in France, called the Bourbon dynasty, which is the most infamous and long-ruling monarchy in French history. Henry was a capable and well-liked king who was said to have deep concern for the well-being of his people. He was jovial and wise. The most lasting legacy of Henry IV was his passage of the Edict of Nantes, which granted religious toleration to Huguenots and ended the long and bloody Wars of Religion in 1598. Though neither Huguenots or Catholics were fully satisfied with the terms of the Edict, it did bring peace to the realm, earning Henry IV the title of "Good King Henry."

Henry, By the Grace of God, King of France, has given us Power and Strength not to yield to the dreadful Troubles, Confusions, and Disorders, which were found throughout this Kingdom, divided into so many Parties and Factions, enabling us with to oppose the Storm, and in the end to surmount it.

For this cause, acknowledging this affair to be of the greatest importance, and worthy of the best consideration, after having considered the papers of complaints of our Catholic subjects, and having also permitted to our Subjects of the Reformed Religion (Protestantism) to assemble themselves for framing their complaints, and making a collection of all their grievances; we have upon the whole judged it necessary to give to all our said Subjects one general Law, Clear, Pure, and Absolute, by which they shall be regulated in all differences which have heretofore risen among them, or may hereafter rise, having had no other regard in this deliberation than solely the Zeal we have to the service of God, praying that he would henceforward render to all our subjects a durable and Established peace.

6. We have permitted and do permit to those of the Reformed Religion, to live and dwell in all the Cities and places of this our Kingdom, without being inquired after, vexed, molested, or compelled to do any thing in Religion, contrary to their Conscience, nor by reason of the same be searched after in houses or places where they live.

7. We also permit to all Lords, Gentlemen and other Persons, as well inhabitants as others, making profession of the Reformed Religion, the free exercise of the said Religion.

16. We further grant to those of the Reformed Religion power to build Places for the Exercise of the same, in Cities and Places where it is granted them. . . .

27. To the end of reuniting the minds and good will of our Subjects, as is our intention, and to take away all complaints for the future; We declare that all those who make or shall make profession of the said Reformed Religion, are capable of holding and exercising all Estates, Dignities, Offices, and public charges whatsoever.

CHAPTER 8—
THE SCIENTIFIC REVOLUTION (1600 to 1750 CE)

GUIDING QUESTIONS
- What is "science" and has it always been an area of study? If not, why not?
- How was the Scientific Revolution influenced by Humanism?
- How did the way we think change as a result of the Scientific Revolution?
- Is inductive or deductive reasoning more reliable in the pursuit of truth?
- How do you think life changed as an immediate result of the Scientific Revolution? How has life changed since the Scientific Revolution?
- In your opinion, do you have to believe in either religion or science? Explain.

According to the dictionary, science is "the systematic study of the structure and behavior of the physical and natural world through observation and experiment." In more basic language, science is how we study and understand the world and everything in it. In the world today, science is everything. Yes, it is biology and chemistry class, and--insofar as math is an extension of scientific thinking--geometry and calculus are also science. Our lives are completely dictated by scientific technology, from our smart phones that wake us up in the morning to our laptops that house every shred of information we have ever processed. Our weather is tracked by scientific satellites, our homes are powered by the science of electricity. We can actually Google questions about almost any conceivable phenomenon--from the nature and causes of cancer to the diets of howler monkey--and we can get answers instantaneously. Heck, Google itself is science. Is it even possible for you to imagine a life without science? I kind of doubt it, but let's try. . .

In the Medieval world there was no science. There was only God and the miracle of his creation. People in the Middle Ages did not ask questions like, "Why?" because they already knew the answer. "God." And if they asked "How?", the answer to that question was also, "God." To push the issue farther would be to risk condemnation by the church, so no one for a thousand years asked any questions, or at least not out loud. But as we have already learned, Humanism was transforming the world by 1500. The whole point of Humanist existence was to understand things deeply. Many Humanists during the 16th and 17th centuries were still deeply religious and believed that God created man and the cosmos but they were only partly satisfied with "God" as an explanation. They had a follow up to this answer which was "Yes, but HOW?" How does it all work? How do we work? And what are the laws and truths that govern all of God's creation? These were the probing questions that the first modern scientists asked. And they were not satisfied until they found answers.

Another hallmark of the Humanist movement was a heavy reliance of old wisdom, from Greece and Rome primarily but also from Middle Eastern cultures. Humanists embraced true knowledge from any source. Ancient scientists like Aristotle, Ptolemy, Hippocrates, Euclid and Pythagoras heavily influenced scientifically-minded scholars in the 1500s and they learned all that they could from these ancient sources. But old knowledge could only take them so far. Do you remember how, at the beginning of the Renaissance, people liked to gather at the Medici palace to marvel over old works of Greek and Roman art but then they decided to start creating art of their own? The same progression occurred in the birth of modern science. After studying all the best classical scientific wisdom, men like Nicholas Copernicus, Rene Descartes and Isaac

Newton recognized there was much work still to do in understanding creation. Humanist curiosity was as much at work in the Scientific Revolution as in any other realm of 15th century life. The insatiable curiosity of minds like Leonardo da Vinci's and hundreds of others' helped to unlock the mysteries of the universe and bring science to the world for the first time in a millennium.

Leonardo da Vinci is remembered as a lot of things in history—a great artist, a genius, a true Renaissance man. Perhaps most important, he is also considered the father of modern science. Da Vinci had an insatiable curiosity about everything, including the workings of the human body. He was notorious, along with Michelangelo, for dissecting dead bodies to understand human anatomy. He was also a brilliant engineer and inventor and as a result there was hardly a scientific process that he did not explore during his lifetime.

At almost the same time that Da Vinci was uncovering the workings of the human body and painting masterpieces like the Last Supper, a Polish mathematician named Nicholas Copernicus was unveiling the secrets of the universe. Since ancient Greek times, it had been accepted truth that the earth was the center of the universe. This view of the universe was called the Ptolemaic view because it was created by the Greek astronomer Ptolemy and had been the established view for more than 2000 years. But Copernicus had a problem with this idea, known as the geocentric theory. His problem was that it just did not make sense. Through mathematical calculations and observation with the naked eye, Copernicus concluded that the sun could not revolve around the earth. The math did not support that position and math does not lie, he said. Copernicus proposed that the sun, not the earth, was the center of the (known) universe. This sun-centered theory, known as Heliocentricism, was laid out by Copernicus in his book *On the Revolution of Heavenly Bodies*, published in 1543. When he first put forth the Heliocentric theory, Copernicus' ideas were largely rejected by scientists of the day, but by the early 1600s, his ideas had won quite a following. This new "Copernican science" was objectionable to the Catholic Church, which preferred the earth-centered view of things because it was more consistent with the Biblical story of creation. In 1616, *On the Revolution of Heavenly Bodies* was added to the list of books banned by the Catholic Church because of its controversial theories.

At the time of Copernicus' death, the proper tools did not yet exist to prove what he had theorized to be true. But by the early 1600s, analytical methods and mathematics evolved rapidly, as did scientific technology. It was during this time that an Italian astronomer and mathematician named Galileo Galilei perfected a technology that would definitively and indisputably prove what Copernicus had theorized. Among his many other considerable contributions to science and math, Galileo perfected the telescope, which made observation of the cosmos possible for the first time. Galileo saw with his own eyes the truth of what Copernicus had hypothesized: that the planets orbit around the sun and not the earth. Galileo published his still controversial findings in *Starry Messenger* in 1610. Even though what he had written was proven with math and direct observation, he still faced the wrath of the Catholic Church who labeled his work as heretical and forced him to stand trial. Galileo was found guilty of heresy for his work in astronomy but he nonetheless marked a turning point in science and scientific discovery. The church could continue to claim that what he said was false but Galileo relied on facts to support his work, and facts do not lie. That is the beauty of science.

Over the next half-century, profound improvements continued to be made in fields of mathematics and physics but more important than the advances in any particular field of the sciences was the development of a universal scientific method that could be used in every discipline, in every language, in every corner of the world. Just as math is a universal language, so too would be the scientific method developed by men like Francis Bacon and Rene Descartes. Scientists during this period created a revolution in the way we think. Bacon and Descartes valued reason and proof, as well as method, above all things. Just as will later be discovered about physics and the workings of the universe, early thinkers in the Scientific Revolution said that there were universal truths and methodologies in the way the natural world should be studied. Interestingly, during the 1700s, the term "science" was not used to explain natural phenomenon or the study of the natural world. What we today call "science" was labeled "natural philosophy" until the Scientific Revolution, because scientific ideas were largely theoretical and were not yet based on hard, empirical fact.

The work of Bacon and Descartes taught us a new way of thinking and a method of uncovering truth. Bacon warned against ever making assumptions when looking for scientific explanations. He explained that men are naturally influenced by our biases, superstitions and opinions on things and those biases can interfere with finding scientific truth. He said that the only language that can be trusted is math, a fact that was universally supported by every scientist from this age forward. The great minds of this age were Empiricists, who believed that man can only truly know something through direct experimentation or observation, not through an innate sense of things and because of a feeling. There was no room for feeling in the minds of the scientists of this period. The only thing that mattered was facts. But they went beyond just saying that facts mattered. They taught us how to find facts and to analyze those facts to reach important conclusions or universal truths.

Key figures in the Scientific Revolution favored a process called inductive reasoning over its opposite, called deductive reasoning. Using inductive reasoning, a scientist studies small parts and tiny details to reach big truths. Deductive reasoning, which had been the scientific standard until the 1700s, began with the big idea and then looked for smaller details to support that idea as true. It really is a question of whether small parts explain the whole or whether the whole explains the parts. Scientists in the 1700s preferred inductive reasoning because it left less room for bias or preconceived ideas about a subject. If you go into an experiment with an idea in mind already about what you think or hope the outcome will be, you are likely to tweak your research to support what you hope, or already believe is true. This is the problem with deductive reasoning. In inductive reasoning, you let the parts speak for themselves. It is sort of like solving a puzzle.

Imagine you have 1000 pieces of a puzzle laying on the table. Using deductive reasoning, you may assume that when completed, you will have a picture of hundreds of cats, because the three puzzles you did last week were all pictures of hundreds of cats. It would be logical to assume, looking at the pile of puzzle pieces and based on your experience with your last puzzles, that this puzzle too would produce a picture of cats. This is deductive reasoning. You deduce that since the last puzzle was of cats, the logical probability is that this puzzle is also a cat puzzle. But you would be wrong, because you were made biased by past experience and failed to study the evidence. If you were to study each of the 1000 tiny pieces of the puzzle without making any assumptions at the beginning, you would realize this *cannot* be a cat puzzle. First, the colors of the pieces are not cat colors. There are purples and vibrant blues, pinks and greens. Those would be strange cat colors, indeed. Now you are a little closer to the truth of the puzzle because you are using inductive reasoning. Further investigation reveals that a lot of the pieces are blue, and you begin lumping and connecting many blue pieces together. A vague picture begins to emerge. It is a blue sky, perhaps? There are no billowy white, cloud-like pieces so a sky scene is unlikely. Your investigation of the pieces continues. To your surprise, many of the brightly colored pieces have eyes, or fins or rough surfaces that might be scales. You piece some of those together and discover fish. Your evidence is beginning to give you a truer picture of what you have before you. You have an ocean scene, or at least you have a hypothesis that this is an ocean scene. As you work methodically to complete your work, you discover that not only do you have an ocean scene but draw the conclusion that you have a detailed picture of a red coral reef teeming with ocean life that includes anemones, barracudas, nurse sharks and rainbow fish. How silly you would feel if you had undertaken this project believing and telling all your friends you were working on a cat puzzle. But instead, you let the facts of the evidence speak for themselves and reveal the truth of what they are—a picture of ocean life.

Inductive reasoning allows small facts to reveal big truths. This idea was used extensively by 17th century scientists. They even used inductive reasoning to prove what was, in their eyes, the biggest truth of all—God. Men like Blaise Pascal and even Sir Isaac Newton came to believe that by studying the infinitesimally small details in the natural world, God revealed himself. They did not set out searching for God or using science as a tool to find God. They studied science like we might study puzzle pieces and they had no idea what they might find. But when they laid out all the tiny pieces of nature and nature's laws, there was only one truth that made sense. There was a master creator that perfectly ordered all the tiny pieces in the only way they could possibly work. The natural world was perfect and universal, and this perfection and universality was not an accident. It was *designed*, in the view of many scientists in this era. After centuries of conflict between science and religion and a sense that one must believe in one or the other, the great triumph for scientists during the 17th century was that science, they believed, proved that there was a divine architect that gave perfect, scientific order to everything.

Nicholas Copernicus, *On the Revolutions of Heavenly Bodies*, 1543 CE

Reading and Discussion Questions
1. Why do you think Copernicus felt he needed to write a letter of explanation to Pope Paul III at the beginning of his book?
2. How does he explain why he decided to go ahead with the work he did on understanding the universe?
3. Copernicus outlines in this introduction all the major ideas he covers in his book. What ideas does he reveal that are included in the larger work?
4. Why did Copernicus dedicate his book to the Pope, according to what he wrote?

In 1543, Polish astronomer Nicholas Copernicus had completed work on his book, On the Revolution of Heavenly Bodies. In it, Copernicus outlined his theories for why the sun, not the earth, was the center of the known universe. This view was in direct conflict with the accepted views of the Catholic Church at the time. Copernicus probably finished work on his book much earlier than 1543 but intentionally waited until the end of his life to make it public. He clearly understood that the reaction to his work would be negative and he would be labeled as a liar and a heretic. After all, his new heliocentric view of the universe was only theory at the time and could therefore be easily dismissed as false. But Copernicus knew it was true because his mathematical calculations suggested that it must be true. Nonetheless, Copernicus was right to fear the reaction of the church. On the Revolution of Heavenly Bodies was quickly added to the Catholic Church's list of banned books, and his ideas were labeled heretical. Copernicus hoped that, by writing the following letter to Pope Paul III and by dedicating his book to him, he could avoid some of the church's wrath. He tried to explain that, in his findings, he had no intention of challenging church supremacy or established church beliefs. He was simply pursuing the truth and that pursuit, he said, led him to discover the findings that were presented in his book. Despite his efforts to protect his reputation and the validity of his work, he was condemned by the Catholic Church just as he feared he would be.

To His Holiness, Pope Paul III, I can readily imagine, Holy Father, that as soon as some people hear that in this volume, which I have written about the revolutions of the spheres of the universe, I ascribe certain motions to the terrestrial globe, they will shout that I must be immediately repudiated together with this belief. For I am not so enamored of my own opinions that I disregard what others may think of them. I am aware that a philosopher's ideas are not subject to the judgment of ordinary person's, because it is his endeavor to seek the truth in all things, to the extent permitted to human reason by God. Yet I hold that completely erroneous views should be shunned.

Those who know that the consensus of many centuries has sanctioned the conception that the earth remains at rest in the middle of the heaven as its center would, I reflected, regard it as an insane pronouncement if I made the opposite assertion that the earth moves. Therefore I debated with myself for a long time whether to publish the volume which I wrote to prove the earth's motion or rather to follow the example of the Pythagoreans and certain others, who used to transmit philosophy's secrets only to kinsmen and friends, not in writing but by word of mouth.... And they did so, it seems to me, not, as some suppose, because they were in some way jealous about their teachings, which would be spread around; on the contrary, they wanted the very beautiful thoughts attained by great men of deep devotion not to be ridiculed by those who are reluctant to assert themselves vigorously in any literary pursuit unless it is lucrative; or if they are stimulated to the nonacquisitive study of philosophy by the exhortation and example of others, yet because of their dullness of mind they play the same part among philosophers as drones among bees. When I weighed these considerations, the scorn which I had reason to fear on account of the novelty and unconventionality of my opinion almost induced me to abandon completely the work which I had undertaken.

But while I hesitated for a long time and even resisted, my friends [encouraged me]. . . . Foremost among them was the cardinal of Capua, Nicholas Schönberg, renowned in every field of learning. Next to him was a man who loves me dearly, Tiedemann Giese, bishop of Chelmno, a close student of sacred letters as well as of all good literature. For he repeatedly encouraged me and, sometimes adding reproaches, urgently requested me to publish this volume and finally permit it to appear after being buried among my papers and lying concealed not merely until the ninth year but by now the fourth period of nine years. The same conduct was recommended to me by not a few other very eminent scholars. They exhorted me to no longer refuse, on account of the fear which I felt, to make my work available for the general use of students of astronomy. The crazier my doctrine of the earth's motion now appeared to most people, the argument ran, so much the more admiration and thanks would it gain after they saw the publication of my writings dispel the fog of absurdity by most luminous proofs. Influenced therefore by these persuasive men and by this hope, in the end I allowed my friends to bring out an edition of the volume, as they had long besought me to do. . . .

But you are rather waiting to hear from me how it occurred to me to venture to conceive any motion of the earth, against the traditional opinion of astronomers and almost against common sense. . . .

For a long time, then, I reflected on this confusion in the astronomical traditions concerning the derivations of the motions of the universe's spheres. I began to be annoyed that the movements of the world machine, created for our sake by the best and most systematic Artisan of all, were not understood with greater certainty by the philosophers, who otherwise examined so precisely the most insignificant trifles of this world. For this reason I undertook the task of rereading the works of all the philosophers which I could obtain to learn whether anyone had ever proposed other motions of the universe's spheres than those expounded by the teachers of astronomy in the schools. And in fact first I found in Cicero that Hicetas supposed the earth to move. Later I also discovered in Plutarch that certain others were of this opinion. . . .

Therefore, having obtained the opportunity from these sources, I too began to consider the mobility of the earth. . . . I thought that I too would be readily permitted to ascertain whether explanations sounder than those of my predecessors could be found for the revolution of the celestial spheres on the assumption of some motion of the earth.

Having thus assumed the motions which I ascribe to the earth later on in the volume, by long and intense study I finally found that if the motions of the other planets are correlated with the orbiting of the earth, and are computed for the revolution of each planet, not only do their phenomena follow therefrom but also the order and size of all the planets and spheres, and heaven itself is so linked together that in no portion of it can anything be shifted without disrupting the remaining parts and the universe as a whole. Accordingly in the arrangement of the volume too I have adopted the following order. In the first book I set forth the entire distribution of the spheres together with the motions which I attribute to the earth, so that this book contains, as it were, the general structure of the universe.

Then in the remaining books I correlate the motions of the other planets and of all the spheres with the movement of the earth so that I may thereby determine to what extent the motions and appearances of the other planets and spheres can be saved if they are correlated with the earth's motions. I have no doubt that acute and learned astronomers will agree with me if, as this discipline especially requires, they are willing to examine and consider, not superficially but thoroughly, what I adduce in this volume in proof of these matters. However, in order that the educated and uneducated alike may see that I do not run away from the judgment of anybody at all, I have preferred dedicating my studies to Your Holiness rather than to anyone else. For even in this very remote corner of the earth where I live you are considered the highest authority by virtue of the loftiness of your office and your love for all literature and astronomy too. Hence by your prestige and judgment you can easily suppress calumnious attacks although, as the proverb has it, there is no remedy for a backbite.

Perhaps there will be babblers who claim to be judges of astronomy although completely ignorant of the subject and, badly distorting some passages of Scripture to their purpose, will dare to find fault with my undertaking and censure it. I disregard them even to the extent of despising their criticism as unfounded. Astronomy is written for astronomers. To them my work too will seem, unless I am mistaken, to make some contribution.

Galileo Galilei, *Starry Messenger*, 1610 CE

Reading and Discussion Questions

1. What is the "spyglass" that Galileo is referring to and how did he improve upon it, based on his explanation?
2. With his improved instrument, what was he able to observe about the moon?
3. What did Galileo observe about Jupiter and what conclusions did these observations cause him to make?
4. Galileo uses a persuasive, almost apologetic, tone in his writing. Who do you think he is trying to persuade and why?

Building on the work of Nicholas Copernicus, Galileo Galilei set out to prove what Copernicus had only been able to hypothesize. He was determined to prove that the sun was the center of the solar system and that the planets, including the earth, revolve around it. Nearly seventy years had passed between the time of Copernicus' On the Revolution of Heavenly Bodies and the work of Galileo. By then, the truth of what Copernicus had hypothesized had become widely accepted as true within the scientific community. But the Catholic Church still refused to accept the Copernican view because it had not been proven with indisputable data. Galileo's work provided the proof that had been missing.

Galileo was an Italian mathematician, philosopher and astronomer and he was a man of many talents. He made important contributions to the study of gravity and to the establishment of rules for scientific experimentation and discovery. He is most well-known, however, for perfecting the telescope and for proving the Copernican (heliocentric) theory. Many people wrongly assume that Galileo invented the telescope. He did not. But he did improve upon and perfect existing technology that made direct observation of the universe possible for the first time. While we recognize Galileo's work as a crucial evolution of tools for scientific understanding, the Catholic Church saw it as heresy. The telescope caused two very big problems for the church. First, the universe or the heavens was where God lived and to observe close-up what happens in the heavens was viewed as an intrusion into God's realm. The second problem was that the telescope was a tool that could definitively disprove the geocentric view, despite the church defense of it.

Nonetheless, Galileo used his telescope to see the truth of the universe for the first time and he recorded these observations and indisputable truths in his work, Starry Messenger. *His work represented a turning point in science and in the field of astronomy, in particular, because things that had previously been only educated guesses could now be factually, empirically proven.*

About ten months ago a report reached my ears that a certain Flemish man had constructed a spyglass by means of which visible objects, though very distant from the eye of the observer, were distinctly see as if nearby. Of this truly remarkable effect several experiences were related, to which some persons gave credence while others denied them. A few days later the report was confirmed to me in a letter from a noble Frenchman at Paris, which caused me to apply myself wholeheartedly to inquire into the means by which I might arrive at the invention of a similar instrument. This I did shortly afterwards, my basis being the theory of refraction. First I prepared a tube of lead, at the ends of which I fitted two glass lenses, both plane on one side while on the other side was one spherically convex and the other concave. Then placing my eye near the concave lens I perceived objects satisfactorily large and near, for they appeared three times closer and nine times larger than when see with the naked eye alone. Next I constructed another one, more accurate, which represented objects as enlarged more than sixty times. Finally, sparing neither labor nor expense, I succeeded in constructing for myself so excellent an instrument that objects seen by means of it appeared nearly one thousand times larger and over thirty times closer than when regarded with our natural vision.

It would be superfluous to enumerate the number and importance of the advantages of such an instrument at sea as well as on land. But forsaking terrestrial observations, I turned to celestial ones, and first I saw the moon from as near at hand as if it were scarcely two terrestrial radii away. After that I observed often with wondering delight both the planets and the fixed stars, and since I saw these latter to be very crowded, I began to seek (and eventually found) a method by which I might measure their distances apart . . . .

Now let us review the observations made during the past two months, once more inviting the attention of all who are eager for true philosophy to the first steps of such important contemplations. Let us speak first of that surface of the moon which faces us. For greater clarity I distinguish two parts of this surface, a lighter and a darker; the lighter part seems to surround and to pervade the whole hemisphere, while the darker part discolors the moon's surface like a kind of cloud, and makes it appear covered with spots. Now those spots which are fairly dark and rather large are plain to everyone and have been seen throughout the ages; these I shall call the "large" or "ancient" spots, distinguishing them from others that are smaller in size but so numerous as to occur all over the lunar surface, and especially the lighter part. The latter spots had never been seen by anyone before me. From observations of these spots repeated many times I have been led to the opinion and conviction that the surface of the moon is not smooth, uniform, and precisely spherical as a great number of philosophers believe it (and the other heavenly bodies) to be, but is uneven, rough, and full of cavities and prominences, being not unlike the face of the earth, relieved by chains of mountains and deep valleys . . . .

On the seventh day of January in this present year 1610, at the first hour of night, when I was viewing the heavenly bodies with a telescope, Jupiter presented itself to me; and because I had prepared a very excellent instrument for myself, I perceived (as I had not before, on account of the weakness of my previous instrument) that beside the planet there were three starlets, small indeed, but very bright. Though I believed them to be among the host of fixed stars, they aroused my curiosity somewhat by appearing to lie in an exact straight line parallel to the ecliptic, and by their being more splendid than others of their size. . . . There were two stars on the eastern side and one to the west. The most easterly star and the western one appeared larger than the other. I paid no attention to the distances between them and Jupiter, for at the outset I thought them to be fixed stars, as I have said. But returning to the same investigation on January eight -- led by what, I do not know -- I found a very different arrangement. The three starlets were now all to the west of Jupiter, closer together, and at equal intervals from one another . . . .

On the tenth of January . . . there were but two of them, both easterly, the third (as I supposed) being hidden behind Jupiter . . . . There was no way in which such alterations could be attributed to Jupiter's motion, yet being certain that these were still the same stars I had observed . . . my perplexity was now transformed into amazement. I was sure that the apparent changes belonged not to Jupiter but to the observed stars, and I resolved to pursue this investigation with greater care and attention . . . .

I had now decided beyond all question that there existed in the heavens three stars wandering about Jupiter as do Venus and Mercury about the sun, and this became plainer than daylight from observations on similar occasions which followed. Nor were there just three such stars; four wanderers complete their revolution about Jupiter . . . .

Here we have a fine and elegant argument for quieting the doubts of those who, while accepting with tranquil mind the revolutions of the planets about the sun in the Copernican system, are mightily disturbed to have the moon alone revolve about the earth and accompany it in annual rotation about the sun. Some have believed that this structure of the universe should be rejected as impossible. But now we have not just one planet rotating about another while both run through a greater orbit around the sun; our eyes show us four stars which wander about Jupiter as does the moon around the earth, while all together trace out a grand revolution about the sun in the space of twelve years.

The Trial of Galileo, 1633 CE

<u>Reading and Discussion Questions</u>
1. What crimes is Galileo accused of? (Hint: There are five of them.)
2. What was Galileo found guilty of and what was the punishment for his crime?
3. In order to return to good standing in the eyes of the church, what was Galileo told to do?
4. Did Galileo do what he was ordered to do by the church? Why do you think he made the decision that he made? Does this change your opinion of Galileo or his achievements? Explain.

As you read in the previous passage, Galileo's findings in Starry Messenger *and his work with other scientists and students on astronomy was considered heresy by the Catholic Church. The following passage is the transcript of Galileo's trial for his crimes in 1633. It also contains Galileo's response to the sentence he received.*

Whereas you, Galileo, son of the late Vincenzio Galilei, of Florence, aged seventy years, were denounced in 1615, to this Holy Office, for holding as true a false doctrine taught by many, namely, that the sun is immovable in the center of the world, and that the earth moves, and also with a diurnal motion; also, for having pupils whom you instructed in the same opinions; also, for maintaining a correspondence on the same with some German mathematicians; also for publishing certain letters on the sun-spots, in which you developed the same doctrine as true; also, for answering the objections which were continually produced from the Holy Scriptures, by glozing the said Scriptures according to your own meaning; and whereas thereupon was produced the copy of a writing, in form of a letter professedly written by you to a person formerly your pupil, in which, following the hypothesis of Copernicus, you include several propositions contrary to the true sense and authority of the Holy Scriptures;

Therefore by the desire of his Holiness and the Most Emminent Lords, the proposition that the sun is in the center of the world and immovable from its place is absurd, philosophically false, and formally heretical; because it is expressly contrary to Holy Scriptures.

The proposition that the earth is not the center of the world, nor immovable, but that it moves, and also with a diurnal action, is also absurd, philosophically false, and, theologically considered, at least erroneous in faith.

Therefore . . . ., invoking the most holy name of our Lord Jesus Christ and of His Most Glorious Mother Mary, We pronounce this Our final sentence: We pronounce, judge, and declare, that you, the said Galileo . . . have rendered yourself vehemently suspected by this Holy Office of heresy, that is, of having believed and held the doctrine (which is false and contrary to the Holy and Divine Scriptures) that the sun is the center of the world, and that it does not move from east to west, and that the earth does move, and is not the center of the world;

Also, that an opinion can be held and supported as probable, after it has been declared and finally decreed contrary to the Holy Scripture, and, consequently, that you have incurred all the censures and penalties due to delinquents of this description.

"And to the end that this thy grave error and transgression remain not entirely unpunished, and that thou may be more cautious in the future, and an example to others to abstain from and avoid similar offences,

"We order that by a public edict the book of DIALOGUES OF GALILEO GALILEI be prohibited, and We condemn thee to the prison of this Holy Office during Our will and pleasure; and as a salutary penance We enjoin on thee that for the space of three years thou shalt recite once a week the Seven Penitential Psalms.

It is Our pleasure that you should be absolved of these crimes, provided that with a sincere heart and unfeigned faith, in Our presence, you abjure, curse, and detest, the said error and heresies, and every other error and heresy contrary to the Catholic and Apostolic Church of Rome.

GALILEO'S ABJURATION
I, Galileo Galilei, son of the late Vincenzio Galilei of Florence, aged 70 years, swear that I have always believed, I believe now, and with God's help I will in future believe all which the Holy Catholic and Apostolic Church doth hold, preach, and teach.

But since I, after having been admonished by this Holy Office entirely to abandon the false opinion that the Sun was the centre of the universe and immoveable, and that the Earth was not the centre of the same and that it moved, and that I was neither to hold, defend, nor teach in any manner whatever, either orally or in writing, the said false doctrine; and after having received a notification that the said doctrine is contrary to Holy Writ, I did write and cause to be printed a book in which I treat of the said already condemned doctrine, and bring forward arguments of much efficacy in its favour, without arriving at any solution: I have been judged vehemently suspected of heresy, that is, of having held and believed that the Sun is the centre of the universe and immoveable, and that the Earth is not the centre of the same, and that it does move.

Nevertheless, wishing to remove from the minds of your Eminences and all faithful Christians this vehement suspicion reasonably conceived against me, I abjure with sincere heart and unfeigned faith, I curse and detest the said errors and heresies, and generally all and every error and sect contrary to the Holy Catholic Church. And I swear that for the future I will neither say nor assert in speaking or writing such things as may bring upon me similar suspicion; and if I know any heretic, or one suspected of heresy, I will denounce him to this Holy Office, or to the Inquisitor and Ordinary of the place in which I may be.

I also swear and promise to adopt and observe entirely all the penances which have been or may be by this Holy Office imposed on me. And if I contravene any of these said promises, protests, or oaths, (which God forbid!) I submit myself to all the pains and penalties which by the Sacred Canons and other Decrees general and particular are against such offenders imposed and promulgated. So help me God and the Holy Gospels, which I touch with my own hands.

I Galileo Galilei aforesaid have abjured, sworn, and promised, and hold myself bound as above; and in token of the truth, with my own hand have subscribed the present schedule of my abjuration, and have recited it word by word.

Sir Francis Bacon, *Novum Organum*, 1620 CE

Reading and Discussion Questions

1. According to Bacon, what are the two ways of discovering truth?
2. What are the dangers of superstition or the "zeal of religion" and how do they interfere with the discovery of the truth?
3. Toward the end of this passage, Bacon says some people "seek to gratify God with a lie." What is he talking about here? What lie are they telling?
4. Why do men fear science and why does Bacon believe that natural philosophy (a.k.a. science) is the "most faithful handmaiden" to religion?

Francis Bacon was a true Renaissance man. He was an English scientist as well as a philosopher, a lawyer, an orator and a politician. More than any other person in this period, he valued the Humanist idea of reason over faith. Bacon is most important for his work in creating the scientific method, which is a universal system of inquiry that requires only the use of hard facts to discover scientific truths. Bacon is indispensable for his work in re-teaching Europeans how to think. His master work was entitled Novum Organum, *which both acknowledges and rejects the science of Aristotle that had been accepted as truth for more than 2000 years. One of Aristotle's great works was called* Organon, *which is Greek for "tool." Aristotle's Organon was his explanation of how to use logic and deductive reasoning as a tool for understanding. As a Humanist, Bacon was intimately knowledgeable of the work of Aristotle but he viewed much of his methodology as outdated and needing to be evolved to keep pace with modern science. So he called his book* Novum Organum, *or "new tools," to indicate that he was building on the work of Greek pioneers like Aristotle.*

Bacon realized that the emerging science of his day was still feared as a crime against the church because it challenged church teachings. And Bacon did not try to reject religion; he instead tried to make it so the two could co-exist. But he had no patience for people who claimed something was true because it was what they believed, or had been taught or sensed instinctively. Bacon was a dedicated Empiricist. Nothing, he said, can be known without experiencing the cold, hard, factual realities of the thing. He also rejected the idea of using prior knowledge in the discovery of truths. What you think you know, Bacon reasoned, gets in the way of actually knowing something. He supported aporoaching scientific discovery with fresh, unbiased eyes. He also believed there should be a universal system for scientific experimentation that could not be twisted by an individual's biases or wishes for what they want to be true. In the following excerpt from Novum Organum, *Bacon urged the use of inductive reasoning to find truth. In order to do this, he said, superstition and bias must be utterly excluded from the process.*

The discoveries which have hitherto been made in the sciences are [too simple], scarcely beneath the surface. In order to penetrate into the inner and further recesses of nature, it is necessary that both notions and truths [be] derived from things by a more sure and guarded way, and that a method of intellectual operation be introduced altogether better and more certain . . . There is no soundness in our notions, whether logical or physical. Substance, quality, action, passion, essence itself are not sound notions; much less are heavy, light, dense, rare, moist, dry, generation, corruption, attraction, repulsion, element, matter, form, and the like; but all are fantastical and ill-defined. ...

There are and can be only two ways of searching into and discovering truth. The one flies from the senses and particulars to the most general axioms, and from these principles, the truth of which it takes for settled and immovable, proceeds to judgment and the discovery of middle axioms. And this way is now in fashion. The other derives axioms from the senses and particulars, rising by a gradual and unbroken ascent, so that it arrives at the most general axioms last of all. This is the true way, but as yet untried. ...

It is not to be forgotten that in every age natural philosophy has had a troublesome adversary and hard to deal with,—namely, superstition and the blind and immoderate zeal of religion. For we see among the Greeks that those who first proposed to man's uninitiated ears the natural causes for thunder and for storms were thereupon found guilty of impiety. Nor was much more forbearance shown by some of the ancient fathers of the Christian Church to those who, on most convincing grounds (such as no one in his senses would now think of contradicting), maintained that the earth was round and, of consequence, asserted the existence of the antipodes.

Moreover, as things now are, to discourse of nature is made harder and more perilous by the summaries and systems of the schoolmen; who, having reduced theology into regular order as well as they were able, and fashioned it into the shape of an art, ended in incorporating the contentious and thorny philosophy of Aristotle, more than was fit, with the body of religion. ...

Lastly, some are weakly afraid lest a deeper search into nature should transgress the permitted limits of sobermindedness; wrongfully wresting and transferring what is said in Holy Writ against those who pry into sacred mysteries to the hidden things of nature, which are barred by no prohibition. Others, with more subtlety, surmise and reflect that if secondary causes are unknown everything can be more readily referred to the divine hand and rod,—a point in which they think religion greatly concerned; which is, in fact, nothing else but to seek to gratify God with a lie. Others fear from past example that movements and changes in philosophy will end in assaults on religion; and others again appear apprehensive that in the investigation of nature something may be found to subvert, or at least shake, the authority of religion, especially with the unlearned.

But these two last fears seem to me to savor utterly of carnal wisdom; as if men in the recesses and secret thoughts of their hearts doubted and distrusted the strength of religion, and the empire of faith over the senses, and therefore feared that the investigation of truth in nature might be dangerous to them. But if the matter be truly considered, natural philosophy is, after the word of God, at once the surest medicine against superstition and the most approved nourishment for faith; and therefore she is rightly given to religion as her most faithful handmaid, since the one displays the will of God, the other his power. ...

Rene Descartes, *Discourse on Method*, 1637 CE

Reading and Discussion Questions

1. Descartes wrote about the value of a "single master" or one architect to oversee a whole project. What is the analogy he is making here? Who do you think the architect is?

2. Descartes says that people who live in poorly built houses sometimes start over and rebuild. Why does he say they do this? And what is his analogy here in relation to scientific knowledge and discovery?

3. Descartes presents four laws that he believes should be universally used in the discovery of scientific truths. Summarize each of the laws in your own words.

4. The last paragraph has a very Humanist tone. Based on your understanding of Humanism, what parts of the last paragraph, specifically, embody Humanist ideals?

Rene Descartes was one of the most brilliant minds to come out of the Scientific Revolution, though his influence extends well beyond the natural sciences. Descartes was a French philosopher and mathematician as well as a scientist and he is considered both the father of modern western philosophy and of modern analytical geometry. He refused to believe anything he did not see and experience for himself, and he refused even to accept the work of previous scientists and philosophers because the flaws in their beliefs might muddle his own pursuit of the truth. Descartes believed that man's ability to find truth was what made him special and Descartes is most famous as the man who said, "I think, therefore, I am."

Among his many other contributions to philosophy, math and science is Descartes' book Discourse on Method, *written in 1637. The full name of the book is* Discourse on the Method of Rightly Conducting One's Reason and of Seeking Truth in the Sciences *and that name gives us a fuller picture of what the book is about. In* Discourse, *Descartes is teaching how to think in order to find truth. In the passage from Descartes below, he advises truth-seekers to begin by doubting everything and never, ever assuming something is true because someone else said it was. He compared the idea of believing someone else's view of things to building your home on a shaky foundation. No matter how strong your own structure is, if your foundation is weak, the structure will not stand. Descartes gave readers four rules to use whenever seeking truth. He believed fundamentally that, if methodical tools were used for inquiry, there was nothing that the human mind could not know.*

I was then in Germany, attracted thither by the wars in that country, which have not yet been brought to a termination; and as I was returning to the army from the coronation of the Emperor, the setting in of winter arrested me in a locality where, as I found no society to interest me, and was besides fortunately undisturbed by any cares or passions, I remained the whole day in [a stove-heated room,] with full opportunity to occupy my attention with my own thoughts. Of these one of the very first that occurred to me was, that there is seldom so much perfection in works composed of many separate parts, upon which different hands have been employed, as in those completed

213

by a single master. Thus it is observable that the buildings which a single architect has planned and executed, are generally more elegant and commodious than those which several have attempted to improve, by making old walls serve for purposes for which they were not originally built. Thus also, those ancient cities which, from being at first only villages, have become, in course of time, large towns, are usually but ill laid out compared with the regularly constructed towns which a professional architect has freely planned on an open plain; so that although the several buildings of the former may often equal or surpass in beauty those of the latter, yet when one observes their indiscriminate juxtaposition, there a large one and here a small, and the consequent crookedness and irregularity of the streets, one is disposed to allege that chance rather than any human will guided by reason, must have led to such an arrangement. ...

It is true ... that it is not customary to pull down all the houses of a town with the single design of rebuilding them differently, and thereby rendering the streets more handsome; but it often happens that a private individual takes down his own with the view of erecting it anew, and that people are even sometimes constrained to this when their houses are in danger of falling from age, or when the foundations are insecure. With this before me by way of example, I was persuaded that it would indeed be preposterous for a private individual to think of reforming a state by fundamentally changing it throughout, and overturning it in order to set it up amended; and the same I thought was true of any similar project for reforming the body of the Sciences, or the order of teaching them established in the Schools [scholastic philosophy]: but as for the opinions which up to that time I had embraced, I thought that I could not do better than resolve at once to sweep them wholly away, that I might afterwards be in a position to admit either others more correct, or even perhaps the same when they had undergone the scrutiny of Reason. I firmly believed that in this way I should much better succeed in the conduct of my life, than if I built only upon old foundations, and leant upon principles which, in my youth, I had taken upon trust. ...

Among the branches of Philosophy, I had, at an earlier period, given some attention to Logic, and among those of the Mathematics to Geometrical Analysis and Algebra,- three arts or Sciences which ought, as I conceived, to contribute something to my design. But, on examination, I found that, as for Logic, its syllogisms and the majority of its other precepts are of avail rather in the communication of what we already know ... than in the investigation of the unknown; and although this Science contains indeed a number of correct and very excellent precepts, there are, nevertheless, so many others, and these either injurious or superfluous, mingled with the former, that it is almost quite as difficult to effect a severance of the true from the false as it is to extract a Diana or a Minerva from a rough block of marble. ... By these considerations I was induced to seek some other Method which would comprise [their] advantages ... and be exempt from their defects. And as a multitude of laws often only hampers justice, so that a state is best governed when, with few laws, these are rigidly administered; in like manner, instead of the great number of precepts of which Logic is composed, I believed that the four following would prove perfectly sufficient for me, provided I took the firm and unwavering resolution never in a single instance to fail in observing them.

The *first* was never to accept anything for true which I did not clearly know to be such; that is to say, carefully to avoid precipitancy and prejudice, and to comprise nothing more in my judgment than what was presented to my mind so clearly and distinctly as to exclude all ground of doubt.

214

The *second*, to divide each of the difficulties under examination into as many parts as possible, and as might be necessary for its adequate solution.

The *third*, to conduct my thoughts in such order that, by commencing with objects the simplest and easiest to know, I might ascend by little and little, and, as it were, step by step, to the knowledge of the more complex; assigning in thought a certain order even to those objects which in their own nature do not stand in a relation of antecedence and sequence.

And the *last*, in every case to make enumerations so complete, and reviews so general, that I might be assured that nothing was omitted.

The long chains of simple and easy reasonings by means of which geometers are accustomed to reach the conclusions of their most difficult demonstrations, had led me to imagine that all things, to the knowledge of which man is competent, are mutually connected in the same way, and that there is nothing so far removed from us as to be beyond our reach, or so hidden that we cannot discover it, provided only we abstain from accepting the false for the true, and always preserve in our thoughts the order necessary for the deduction of one truth from another. ...

Blaise Pascal, *Pensées*, 1670 CE

Reading and Discussion Questions

1. What does Pascal explain as the condition of men? Why is this frightening to him?
2. In the passage marked 229 what does Pascal say troubles him? What is he uncertain about?
3. What makes men great, according to Pascal? Does this sound like anything that Descartes said? Explain.
4. Pascal says all men must wager on God's existence. How does he believe we should wager? Should we say "Yes, God does exist," or "No, God does not exist?" Explain why Pascal advises us to wager the way he does.

Blaise Pascal was a French physicist, mathematician and philosopher during the Scientific Revolution. He made important contributions to the creation of the scientific method as well as the development of branches of analytical geometry. He is also believed to be the inventor of the first mechanical calculator. Pascal had a powerful religious experience at some point in his life that turned him deeply religious, and he devoted much of his life to wrestling with metaphysical questions, including whether or not God exists. Pascal's life's work is contained in a book called Pensées, *which literally means "thoughts." It is a loosely organized collection of Pascal's philosophical ideas. In* Pensées *we find what is known as "Pascal's Wager," in which Pascal tried to determine whether God existed or not by weighing the probability on both sides. His rationale for God's existence was based largely on mathematical calculations, and he sought to understand God through reason rather than through blind faith.*

199. Let us imagine a number of men in chains, and all condemned to death, where some are killed each day in the sight of the others, and those who remain see their own fate in that of their fellows, and wait their turn, looking at each other sorrowfully and without hope. It is an image of the condition of men. ...

205. When I consider the short duration of my life, swallowed up in the eternity before and after, the little space which I fill, and even can see, engulfed in the infinite immensity of spaces of which I am ignorant, and which know me not, I am frightened, and am astonished at being here rather than there; for there is no reason why here rather than there, why now rather than then. Who has put me here? By whose order and direction have this place and time been allotted to me?

206. The eternal silence of these infinite spaces frightens me. ...

229. This is what I see and what troubles me. I look on all sides, and I see only darkness everywhere. Nature presents to me nothing which is not matter of doubt and concern. If I saw nothing there which revealed a Divinity, I would come to a negative conclusion; if I saw everywhere the signs of a Creator, I would remain peacefully in faith. But, seeing too much to deny and too little to be sure, I am in a state to be pitied; wherefore I have a hundred times wished that if a God maintains nature, she should testify to Him unequivocally, and that, if the signs she gives are deceptive, she should suppress them altogether; that she should say everything or nothing, that I might see which cause I ought to follow. Whereas in my present state, ignorant of what I am or of what I ought to do, I know neither my condition nor my duty. My heart inclines wholly to know where is the true good, in order to follow it; nothing would be too dear to me for eternity.

I envy those whom I see living in the faith with such carelessness, and who make such a bad use of a gift of which it seems to me I would make such a different use.

230. It is incomprehensible that God should exist, and it is incomprehensible that He should not exist; that the soul should be joined to the body, and that we should have no soul; that the world should be created, and that it should not be created, etc.; that original sin should be, and that it should not be. ...

346. Thought constitutes the greatness of man.

347. Man is but a reed, the most feeble thing in nature; but he is a thinking reed. The entire universe need not arm itself to crush him. A vapour, a drop of water suffices to kill him. But, if the universe were to crush him, man would still be more noble than that which killed him, because he knows that he dies and the advantage which the universe has over him; the universe knows nothing of this.

All our dignity consists, then, in thought. By it we must elevate ourselves, and not by space and time which we cannot fill. Let us endeavour, then, to think well; this is the principle of morality.

348. *A thinking reed.*–It is not from space that I must seek my dignity, but from the government of my thought. I shall have no more if I possess worlds. By space the

universe encompasses and swallows me up like an atom; by thought I comprehend the world.

... If there is a God, He is infinitely incomprehensible, since, having neither parts nor limits, He has no affinity to us. We are then incapable of knowing either what He is or if He is. This being so, who will dare to undertake the decision of the question? Not we, who have no affinity to Him. ...

... But you must wager. It is not optional. You are embarked. Which will you choose then? Let us see. Since you must choose, let us see which interests you least. You have two things to lose, the true and the good; and two things to stake, your reason and your will, your knowledge and your happiness; and your nature has two things to shun, error and misery. Your reason is no more shocked in choosing one rather than the other, since you must of necessity choose. This is one point settled. But your happiness? Let us weigh the gain and the loss in wagering that God is. Let us estimate these two chances. If you gain, you gain all; if you lose, you lose nothing. Wager, then, without hesitation that He is.-"That is very fine. Yes, I must wager; but I may perhaps wager too much."-Let us see. Since there is equal risk of gain and loss, if you had only to gain two lives, instead of one, you might still wager. But if there were three lives to gain, you would have to play (since you are under the necessity of playing), and you would be imprudent, when you are forced to play, not to chance your life to gain three at a game where there is an equal risk of loss and gain. But there is an eternity of life and happiness. And this being so, if there were an infinity of chances, of which one only would be for you, you would still be right in wagering one to win two, and you would act stupidly, being obliged to play, by refusing to stake one life against three at a game in which out of an infinity of chances there is one for you, if there were an infinity of an infinitely happy life to gain. But there is here an infinity of an infinitely happy life to gain, a chance to gain against a finite number of chances of loss, and what you stake is finite. It is all divided; wherever the infinite is and there is not an infinity of chances of loss against that of gain, there is no time to hesitate, you must give all. And thus, when one is forced to play, he must renounce reason to preserve his life, rather than risk it for infinite gain, as likely to happen as the loss of nothingness.

Isaac Newton, *Principia*, 1687 CE

Reading and Discussion Questions
1. Summarize each of Newton's Laws on Motion in your own words.
2. According to Newton, how does he know that God exists?
3. For Newton, what is God's relationship to the universe?
4. How does Newton argue against those that say there is no God?

Isaac Newton is widely and rightfully considered the most influential scientists in history for his work in physics and the understanding of gravitational forces, as well as the creation of calculus. Born in England in 1642, Newton dedicated his life to solving the riddles of the universe by building on the knowledge and methods developed by earlier scientists. Newton is famous for the quotation, "If I have seen further than others, it is because I have stood on the shoulders of giants." Newton recognized science could only advance if it consistently and continually built on past discoveries and achievements. Most of modern science is built on the laws and truths discovered by Isaac Newton. Newton's master work, and a book which is considered the most important book written in modern European history, is called Mathematical Principals of Natural Philosophy, *or* Principia *for short. In this work, Newton unveils his Three Laws of Motion which every student in the world at some point learns in science class. Also included in* Principia *are rules that Newton says must be followed in order to find indisputable scientific truths. In the final section of his work, Newton does something that is unexpected by some readers. He uses his knowledge of science to defend the existence of God. Many during the Scientific Revolution, felt that one had to choose between believing in God or accepting modern science. This was certainly the position of the Catholic Church at the time. But Newton used the mathematical perfection of the universe and the complex organization of natural systems as proof that God exists. Perfection, Newton argued, cannot be an accident.*

LAWS OF MOTION

LAW I.
Every body perseveres in its state of rest, or of uniform motion in a right line, unless it is compelled to change that state by forces impressed thereon.

PROJECTILES persevere in their motions, so far as they are not retarded by the resistance of the air, or impelled downwards by the force of gravity. A top, whose parts by their cohesion are perpetually drawn aside from rectilinear motions, does not cease its rotation, otherwise than as it is retarded by the air. The greater bodies of the planets and comets, meeting with less resistance in more free spaces, preserve their motions both progressive and circular for a much longer time.

LAW II.
The alteration of motion is ever proportional to the motive force impressed; and is made in the direction of the right line in which that force is impressed.

If any force generates a motion, a double force will generate double the motion, a triple force triple the motion, whether that force be impressed altogether and at once, or gradually and successively. And this motion (being always directed the same way with the generating force), if the body moved before, is added to or subducted from the former motion, according as they directly conspire with or are directly contrary to each other; or obliquely joined, when they are oblique, so as to produce a new motion compounded from the determination of both.

LAW III.

To every action there is always opposed an equal reaction: or the mutual actions of two bodies upon each other are always equal, and directed to contrary parts.

Whatever draws or presses another is as much drawn or pressed by that other. If you press a stone with your finger, the finger is also pressed by the stone. If a horse draws a stone tied to a rope, the horse (if I may so say) will be equally drawn back towards the stone: for the distended rope, by the same endeavour to relax or unbend itself, will draw the horse as much towards the stone, as it does the stone towards the horse, and will obstruct the progress of the one as much as it advances that of the other. If a body impinge upon another, and by its force change the motion of the other, that body also (because of the equality of the mutual pressure) will undergo an equal change, in its own motion, towards the contrary part. The changes made by these actions are equal, not in the velocities but in the motions of bodies; that is to say, if the bodies are not hindered by any other impediments. For, because the motions are equally changed, the changes of the velocities made towards contrary parts are reciprocally proportional to the bodies.

ON GOD AND THE UNIVERSE

This most beautiful system of the sun, planets, and comets could only proceed from the counsel and dominion of an intelligent and powerful Being. And if the fixed stars are the centers of other like systems, these, being formed by the like wise counsel, must be all subject to the dominion of One, especially since the light of the fixed stars is of the same nature with the light of the sun and from every system light passes into all the other systems; and lest the systems of the fixed stars should, by their gravity, fall on each other mutually, he hath placed those systems at immense distances from one another.

This Being governs all things not as the soul of the world, but as Lord over all; and on account of his dominion he is wont to be called "Lord God" . . . or "Universal Ruler." . . . It is the dominion of a spiritual being which constitutes a God. . . . And from his true dominion it follows that the true God is a living, intelligent and powerful Being. . . . he governs all things, and knows all things that are or can be done. . . . He endures for ever, and is every where present; and by existing always and every where, he constitutes duration and space. . .

In him are all things contained and moved; yet neither affects the other: God suffers nothing from the motion of bodies; bodies find no resistance from the omnipresence of God. . . . As a blind man has no idea of colors so we have no idea of the manner by which the all-wise God preserves and understands all things. He is utterly void of all body and bodily figure, and can therefore neither be seen, nor heard, nor touched; nor ought to be worshipped under the representation of any corporeal thing.

We have ideas of his attributes, but what the real substance of any thing is we know not. . . . Much less, then, have we any idea of the substance of God. We know him only by his most wise and excellent contrivances of things. . . . [W]e reverence and adore him

219

as his servants; and a god without dominion, providence, and final causes, is nothing else but Fate and Nature. Blind metaphysical necessity, which is certainly the same always and everywhere, could produce no variety of things.

All the diversity of natural things could arise from nothing but the ideas and will of a Being necessarily existing. . . .

CHAPTER 9–
THE AGE OF DISCOVERY AND CONQUEST
(1500 to 1650 CE)

<u>GUIDING QUESTIONS</u>
- Should we celebrate Columbus Day? Why or why not?
- What is the Columbian Exchange and how has it changed the world?
- Did Columbus' voyages add to or detract from human happiness?
- What attitudes or beliefs makes it possible for humans to justify the conquest, massacre and enslavement other humans?
- Is imperialism ever justified? Does might equal right?

"In fourteen hundred and ninety-two, Columbus sailed the ocean blue." This is a rhyme we learn as school children to celebrate the importance of Christopher Columbus discovering America. 1492 was undoubtedly a year that changed history, and our history in particular, quite radically. As kids, we learn about the courageous voyage of the Nina, the Pinta and the Santa Maria and the brave souls who charged into the unknown on a voyage of great discovery. Columbus, in our first learning about his accomplishments, is a great hero in the Age of Discovery.

But there is another side to the story and a much more complicated one. When we study the lives of explorers like Columbus as children, it is in a unit called "The Age of Discovery" or "The Explorers." These names themselves are misleading about what this time in history was all about. "The Age of Discovery" suggests that people happened upon new places quite by accident and they were delighted at the surprise of stumbling upon something new. In most cases, however, the explorers or conquistadors knew where they were headed and what they expected to find. And while it is true that once they arrived in new places like Africa or the Americas there was a lot of exploring to be done, there was a lot more to the story of this era.

The extent of our geographic knowledge increased dramatically during the period between 1450 and 1650 because explorers traveled with cartographers or map makers who meticulously chronicled every step of these exploratory journeys. The work of the explorers made our world much bigger and more mysterious and much more interesting. Stories of exotic animals, places and people captivated the imaginations of the Europeans of the 16th and 17th centuries. And in this way, the Age of Discovery and Exploration is a fitting name. But have you ever asked yourself what happened *after* the discovery? Did the explorers take good notes, make good maps and record good stories and then return home again, leaving everything just as they found it? Unfortunately, they did not. The story of this period is much, much more complicated than the way we first learn it. Some say a better name for this period might be the Age of Discovery, Exploration and Conquest. Is that a cynical view of things? Perhaps. But is it a more accurate view? You decide.

All of the men (there were no known female explorers) who sailed into uncharted waters looking for golden cities or resource-rich lands worked for powerful nations. And these powerful nations wanted to become more powerful. As we know from ancient civilizations like the Romans', the quickest way to increase power is to increase land through imperialism. Imperialism is the process of building an empire and is a fancy term for conquest. An imperialist conquers vast amounts of territory and peoples and rules them. During the 1500s in Europe, intense rivalries developed between of the monarchs of places like Spain, England, France and Portugal. These rulers competed for power in Europe through seemingly endless wars and they began competing for territory outside of Europe, as well. The unspoken motto of the rulers of this time was, "He who dies with the biggest empire wins." And this was the real reason the discovery of Columbus was so important. It created an opportunity for power.

Like the other revolutionary eras we have discussed, the Age of Discovery and Conquest was also made possible by Humanism and technology. If you recall, Humanists have a deep curiosity about the world and they value reason over faith. They also have a deep knowledge of classical wisdom. The Humanist in this part of the story is a Portuguese noble known as Prince Henry the Navigator. Prince Henry was a very well-educated man who was insatiably curious about the world. He studied old maps obsessively. He had a number of cartographers who worked for him and they tried to make better maps of known places by studying details in written accounts of far away lands. Henry also financed a number of expeditions to the northwest coast of Africa. The knowledge gained on those expeditions improved the understanding of the northern Atlantic Ocean. And they paved the way for more ambitious exploration. Prince Henry died in 1460 but he had launched a new era in history that would transform human existence and result in the birth of globalization.

Prince Henry's explorations and those that came after would not have been possible without the creation of three new pieces of nautical technology that were invented in the 1400s. The first technological innovation that revolutionized nautical exploration was the compass. A compass is an instrument used for navigation and orientation that shows direction relative to the geographic "cardinal directions," or "points." The compass was invented by the Chinese several hundred years before it was introduced to European navigators. Prior to the compass, navigation was done by referencing landmarks along a voyage which would require a ship to always stay within sight of the coastline. The compass made longer journeys possible. It also made cartography much more accurate.

The second innovation that led to the age of conquest was the caravel, or an easily maneuverable ship with interchangeable sails. Before the 1500s, ships had only one large square sail, a design that had not changed since ancient times. The problem with a square-sailed ship is that it can only sail when the wind is blowing from behind. In a caravel, however, the sails are interchangeable and movable about the mast so it can capture and harness wind coming from any direction. This important innovation made sailing possible in what were previously considered unfavorable conditions.

The final innovation that made exploration possible in the 1400s was the astrolabe. The mariner's astrolabe was an adaptation of an ancient invention which helped sailors to measure the distance from the horizon to either the sun or the stars to determine direction and orientation. Among other things, the astrolabe allowed sailors to navigate at night. Armed with these three new powerful nautical innovations, would-be explorers and conquerors had all the tools they needed at their disposal.

In the beginning, the Age of Discovery and Conquest was not about discovering new lands at all. It was about economics. From the time of the Crusades, eastern trade goods were in high demand in Europe. Crusaders had been exposed to eastern luxuries like silk and tea from China, and spices from India and the Middle East. All these goods made dull Medieval life far more colorful, flavorful and *interesting*. Until the 1400s, European traders traveled to Asia using land routes, primarily along the famous Silk Road. But by the 1400s, land travel had become dangerous and merchant caravans were frequently raided by bandits. As a result, land travel had become less profitable. Middle Eastern traders had become competitors with Europeans in the sale of eastern goods. These traders bought supplies of spices and tea from farmers and merchants before the Europeans could and then resold them to Europeans at inflated prices. A number of enterprising Europeans decided to cut out the middleman by finding a sea route to Asia, thus keeping all the profits for themselves. And with this idea, the race to India was on. It would be easy, reasoned European explorers of the time, to simply sail around Africa to India in far less time than it took to walk there. The only problem with this theory was that no one yet realized that Africa is *huge*.

The Portuguese seemed the likely candidates to reach India first by sea, since their own Prince Henry was the original mastermind of nautical exploration. In 1467, a Portuguese explorer named Bartolomeu Dias was the first to attempt a sea voyage to India around Africa. Based on earlier exploration done by Prince Henry's expeditions, it was well known that, after sailing south along the western coast of Africa for several hundred miles, it was possible to begin sailing east. The belief was that once sailors turned east, it was a short and straight shot to India. When Dias set out to chart this course, however, he was shocked at what he discovered. He did in fact make an eastward journey for several hundred miles and believed he would continue east until reaching Asia. To his surprise, he instead had to begin sailing south again for several hundred miles before he finally reached the southern tip of Africa. He named the southern tip of Africa the Cape of Torment because of his perilous, miserable journey. Then he turned around and headed home. Dias had failed to reach India but he had succeeded in discovering the actual size of Africa.

Realizing that an eastward voyage to India would take much longer than expected, Christopher Columbus proposed a radical alternative to the rulers of Spain. In 1492, Spain was under the rule of devout Catholics, King Ferdinand and Queen Isabella. In addition to ridding Spain of non-Catholics at home, Ferdinand and Isabella were determined to spread the global reach of Catholicism. For this reason, they financed the first voyage of Christopher Columbus, who claimed he could get to India faster by sailing west instead of east. Intrigued by Columbus' proposal, the Spanish king and queen gave money to Columbus for his three boats, crew and other supplies for his journey. After two months at sea, Columbus' expedition made landfall on October 12th, 1492, believing they had reached the islands known as the East Indies in Asia. What we all know is that he had actually landed in the Bahamas, and had accidentally discovered the Americas. ("Rediscovered" would be a more accurate word for Columbus' achievement, since the Vikings had discovered and colonized North America 500 years earlier.)

In 1499 another Portuguese explorer, Vasco de Gama, successfully completed the first sea voyage to India. He did it by sailing east around Africa. And Columbus' error about having reached Asia by a westward route was corrected by an Italian explorer named Amerigo Vespucci. In 1502, Vespucci made his own westward voyage of exploration and realized that the land Columbus had reached was not the outskirts of Asia but an entirely new massive landmass (which we now know are two!). Vespucci's

223

discoveries were reflected in a groundbreaking new map by cartographer Martin Waldseemuller in 1507, which became known as the Waldseemuller map. These newly discovered landmasses on that map were called "America" in honor of Amerigo Vespucci.

Even though Columbus was wrong about what he had found in 1492, the impact of his discovery was tremendous. He wrote a letter to Ferdinand and Isabella, which was reproduced by the printing press hundreds of thousands of times, which painted a picture of a world that was intriguing and ripe for the taking. 1492 marks the birth of a period in history that is more controversial in its positives and negatives than any other time before or since. In less than 200 years, after Columbus' first voyage, almost every corner of North and South America had been conquered by a European power and incorporated into its empire. Spain, Portugal, France and England built huge colonial empires and even nations like the Netherlands, Denmark and Russia took chunks of the Americas for themselves. In each instance of conquest, there were large and well-established indigenous groups that were conquered and subjugated as part of the imperialist process. The history and the struggles of these indigenous people have been overlooked until very modern times.

The popular depiction of the indigenous populations of the Americas was as a single group of godless savages. But this view was entirely wrong. There were many different civilizations, many of which were more advanced than late Medieval societies of Europe at the time. The better known civilizations are the Aztec, the Inca and the Maya, but there were at least a dozen smaller civilizations during the same period including the Olmec, the Toltec, the Teotihuacano, the Zapotec, the Mixtec, the Moche and the Chibcha. All of these groups were ultimately destroyed by the conquistadors, which was the name given to Spanish explorers who conquered the native people in the Americas. The conquest of the Aztec in Mexico and the Inca in Peru were both unimaginably horrific and efficient. Hernan Cortez completed his conquest of the Aztec in Mexico in less than two years, and Francisco Pizzaro defeated the Inca and became the ruler of Peru in less than a year. The conquest of the Americas is the first modern example of the power of modern weapons of war in building global empires. Modern weapons, combined with diseases the Europeans brought to the Americas, resulted in the near eradication of indigenous civilizations by the early 1600s.

One of the darkest elements of the Age of Discovery and Conquest was the birth of the Trans-Atlantic slave trade. Trans-Atlantic slavery was a legal practice for nearly 400 years, from the 1400s to the 1800s, and during that time between 10 million and 12 million Africans were forced into slavery. The journey of slaves, known as the Middle Passage, from Africa to the Americas is one of the most brutal events ever recorded. We have excruciatingly detailed accounts of how Africans were treated worse than livestock and they were only as important as the price they would bring at the slave market. Economies boomed in the Americas and came to depend on slave labor and so slavery, in the minds of many in the Americas, had become a necessary evil by 1700. Abolitionists worked for nearly a century to convince people of the inhumanity of slavery but it was not until 1833 that the British became the first nation to outlaw the slave trade. By the late 1800s, most nations had passed laws abolishing slavery.

When people highlight the positives of the Age of Discovery and Conquest, they point to the birth of global trade. By the mid-1500s, European countries had colonies in the

Americas and trade relations with Africa. Thus they had established what was called The Columbian Exchange or Triangular Trade. Europeans took goods they manufactured, like guns, and traded them in Africa for slaves. Those slaves were then transported to the Americas where they were used for the harvesting of raw materials, including cotton and tobacco that were sold in Europe. In addition to trade goods, raw materials and slaves, something else equally important was being traded on these transatlantic voyages—ideas.

The Spaniards came to the New World to increase the power of their king and queen and to spread the Catholic faith. France created its empire almost entirely for economic and political power. English monarchs also established colonies to stay in the race for global empires. But the colonists who came to the Americas came for very different reasons. In North America, British colonists left England during very specific periods of religious and political turmoil. During the reign of Henry VIII (1509-1547), England became a Protestant nation but much of its population remained openly or secretly Catholic. And much of England's royalty and nobility also remained loyal to Catholicism so England suffered a religious identify crisis for more than 100 years. Some rulers reigned as Protestants and persecuted Catholics, who then fled to colonies in the America. Other rulers reigned as Catholics and persecuted Protestants, and then they fled to North America. Maryland, for instance, was founded as a Catholic colony but Massachusetts was strictly a Protestant settlement. Regardless of religious beliefs, though, all colonists came here with ideas of what a better life looked like. Their dreams of democracy and free-market economies were as much a part of what they brought with them as the physical things they packed for the journey. So what can be said in truth about Columbus' journey was that the history of people on four continents was forever changed by it—some for the better and some for the worse.

PRIMARY SOURCES—
AGE OF DISCOVERY AND CONQUEST

Christopher Columbus, Letter to Ferdinand and Isabella, 1493 CE

Reading and Discussion Questions
1. Columbus described the Natives he first encountered as "timid and full of fear." He also explained that they had no weapons. Why do you think he included these details?
2. Imagine the thoughts of the Europeans as they first saw land in the "New World." What do you think would have been their most immediate impression? Explain.
3. How do you think people in Europe reacted when they read Columbus' letter? How would you have reacted? Explain your answer.

Christopher Columbus is one of the most famous figures in history for his accidental discovery of the Americas in 1492. He sought to find a western sea route to India for trade and he sailed for the King and Queen of Spain, Ferdinand and Isabella. Instead, he stumbled on a whole new continent and began a new era in world history. He returned to Spain from his voyage in 1493 and wrote a letter to Ferdinand and Isabella, describing his discoveries. Columbus' letter quickly became one of the most widely read documents around the world, thanks to its reprinting by the printing press. Not only did Columbus' descriptions of what he had found stir the curiosity of would-be conquerors and treasure hunters, it was also seen as a great opportunity by the Catholic Church to spread its influence to new parts of the world. The Catholic Church was very active in the reprinting of Columbus' letter for circulation in both Latin and regional languages.

I have determined to write you this letter to inform you of everything that has been done and discovered in this voyage of mine.

On the thirty-third day after leaving Cadiz I came into the Indian Sea, where I discovered many islands inhabited by numerous people. I took possession of all of them for our most fortunate King by making public proclamation and unfurling his standard, no one making any resistance. The island called Juana, as well as the others in its neighborhood, is exceedingly fertile. It has numerous harbors on all sides, very safe and wide, above comparison with any I have ever seen. Through it flow many very broad and health-giving rivers; and there are in it numerous very lofty mountains. All these island are very beautiful, and of quite different shapes; easy to be traversed, and full of the greatest variety of trees reaching to the stars. . . .

In the island, which I have said before was called Hispana, there are very lofty and beautiful mountains, great farms, groves and fields, most fertile both for cultivation and for pasturage, and well adapted for constructing buildings. The convenience of the harbors in this island, and the excellence of the rivers, in volume and salubrity, surpass human belief, unless one should see them. In it the trees, pasture-lands and fruits different much from those of Juana. Besides, this Hispana abounds in various kinds of species, gold and metals.

The inhabitants . . . are all, as I said before, unprovided with any sort of iron, and they are destitute of arms, which are entirely unknown to them, and for which they are not adapted; not on account of any bodily deformity, for they are well made, but because they are timid and full of terror. . . . But when they see that they are safe, and all fear is banished, they are very guileless and honest, and very liberal of all they have. No one refuses the asker anything that he possesses; on the contrary they themselves invite us to ask for it. They manifest the greatest affection towards all of us, exchanging valuable things for trifles, content with the very least thing or nothing at all. . . .

I gave them many beautiful and pleasing things, which I had brought with me, for no return whatever, in order to win their affection, and that they might become Christians and inclined to love our King and Queen and Princes and all the people of Spain; and that they might be eager to search for and gather and give to us what they abound in and we greatly need.

Pope Alexander VI, *The Doctrine of Discovery*, 1493 CE

Reading and Discussion Questions

1. By what authority did Pope Alexander VI claim the power to give Spain nearly exclusive possession of the New World?
2. Why do you think Spain wanted exclusive rights to the New World?
3. Along with the right to possess the land, the Doctrine also indicated that Spain had specific responsibilities. List and explain these duties.
4. How did the Doctrine of Discovery impact other nations immediately after it was written? How did it impact nations later in history?
5. How did the Doctrine impact indigenous populations in the Americas?

After Columbus' letter was widely circulated thanks to the printing press, it was clear that there would be a global race to colonize this newly discovered territory. As you have read, the Catholic Church was very determined that the New World be under its control. So in 1493, Pope Alexander VI wrote a Papal Bull, known as the Doctrine of Discovery, that would determine how the Americas would be conquered and colonized and by whom. In 1493, Ferdinand and Isabella of Spain were the most powerful rulers in the world and they were the ultimate defenders of Catholicism. It made perfect sense then for the Catholic Church to do everything in its power to see that the New World ended up under Spanish control. Spanish conquest equaled Catholic conquest. And Catholic conquest was the primary goal of the Doctrine of Discovery.

The Doctrine of Discovery created a very detailed geographic line, known as the Line of Demarcation, which established that nearly all of the land discovered in the New World would belong to Spain. Not only did the Doctrine say that this territory belonged to Spain, but it went on to say that no other group or nation could use the land, colonize it or trade on it without the permission of Spain. This prohibition included the indigenous people inhabiting the Americas in 1493 and with the stroke of a pen, civilizations like the Aztec, Inca and Mayans were suddenly trespassers in their own homelands. The Doctrine of Discovery was the justification for the later conquest of the Americas by the conquistadors, who claimed it was their legal right to take what

227

was theirs, even if they had to take it by force. This same Doctrine was used later by Americans to defend American westward expansion, since the land controlled by the United States by 1800 had been rightfully won from Spain and property ownership had been legally transferred or given "with Spain's permission," per the terms of the Doctrine of Discovery.

Wherefore, you have managed with the favor of divine clemency to bring under your sway the said mainlands and islands with their residents and inhabitants and to bring them to the Catholic faith. Hence, heartily commending in the Lord this your holy and praiseworthy purpose, and desirous that it be duly accomplished, and that the name of our Savior be carried into those regions, we exhort to lead the peoples dwelling in those islands and countries to embrace the Christian religion; nor at any time let dangers or hardships deter you therefrom, with the stout hope and trust in your hearts that Almighty God will further your undertakings. And, in order that you may enter upon so great an undertaking with greater readiness and, we, of our own accord, do give, grant, and assign to you and your heirs all islands and mainlands found and to be found, discovered and to be discovered towards the west and south, by drawing and establishing a line from the Arctic pole, namely the north, to the Antarctic pole, namely the south, no matter whether the said mainlands and islands are found and to be found in the direction of India or towards any other quarter, the said line to be distant one hundred leagues towards the west and south from any of the islands commonly known as the Azores and Cape Verde.

And we make, appoint, and depute you with full and free power, authority, and jurisdiction of every kind; Moreover we command you to appoint to the mainlands and islands worthy, God-fearing, learned, skilled, and experienced men, in order to instruct the aforesaid inhabitants and residents in the Catholic faith and train them in good morals. Furthermore, under penalty of excommunication, we strictly forbid all persons of whatsoever rank or nation, or of whatsoever estate, degree, order, or condition, to dare without your special permit, to go for the purpose of trade or any other reason to the islands or mainlands, found and to be found, discovered and to be discovered, towards the west and south, by drawing and establishing a line from the Arctic pole to the Antarctic pole, no matter whether the mainlands and islands, found and to be found, lie in the direction of India or toward any other quarter whatsoever, the said line to be distant one hundred leagues towards the west and south, as is aforesaid, from any of the islands commonly known as the Azores and Cape Verde.

We trust in Him from whom empires and governments and all good things proceed, that, should you, with the Lord's guidance, pursue this holy and praiseworthy undertaking, in a short while your hardships and endeavors will attain the most joyful result, to the happiness and glory of all Christendom.

Two Accounts of the Conquest of the Americas, 1500s CE

Reading and Discussion Questions

1. In both readings, how were the conquistadors originally treated and welcomed by the natives? Reference specific details from each reading in your answer.
2. What things did the conquistadors do to win the trust of the natives? Again, cite details from each reading in your response.
3. What were the natives like, according to the account of De Las Casas in particular?
4. From the De Las Casas reading, why did he call the Spaniards "ravening wild beasts?" What "beastly" things did they do, specifically?
5. In your opinion, why did the Spaniards treat the indigenous people as less than human? How do you think they justified their actions to themselves? How could they live with what they did?

By the early 1500s, hundreds of conquistadors and their armies had flooded the Americas and made shockingly short work of subduing or massacring indigenous populations. While conquistadors had steel weapons and horses, native people had only rudimentary weapons to defend themselves. Perhaps more important, the native civilizations were caught completely by surprise by the violence of the Spaniards. The natives welcomed the Spaniards as guests and the Spaniards responded with savage violence. Traveling with the conquistadors or sometimes even coming before them were Christian missionaries, who provide us with some of the most detailed, and horrifying, accounts of the Spanish conquest of the Americas. Two of those accounts are recorded here. The first chronicles the conquest of Mexico by Hernan Cortez in 1519 and the second documents the Spanish conquest of the Caribbean Islands, including Cuba and Puerto Rico, as well as dozens of smaller islands.

An Aztec Account of the Conquest of Mexico

Speeches of Motecuhzoma and Cortés

When Motecuhzoma [Montezuma] had given necklaces to each one, Cortés asked him: "Are you Motecuhzoma? Are you the king? Is it true that you are the king Motecuhzoma?"

And the king said: "Yes, I am Motecuhzoma." Then he stood up to welcome Cortés; he came forward, bowed his head low and addressed him in these words: "Our lord, you are weary. The journey has tired you, but now you have arrived. Rest now, and take comfort. Welcome, my lords!"

When Motecuhzoma had finished, La Malinche translated his address into Spanish so that the Captain could understand it. Cortés replied in his strange and savage tongue, speaking first to La Malinche: "Tell Motecuhzoma that we are his friends. There is nothing to fear. We have wanted to see him for a long time, and now we have seen his face and heard his words. Tell him that we love him well and that our hearts are contented."

Then he said to Motecuhzoma: "We have come to your house in Mexico as friends. There is nothing to fear."

La Malinche translated this speech and the Spaniards grasped Motecuhzoma's hands and patted his back to show their affection for him....

Massacre in the Main Temple

During this time, the people asked Motecuhzoma how they should celebrate their god's fiesta. He said: "Dress him in all his finery, in all his sacred ornaments."

During this same time, the Spaniards commanded that Motecuhzoma and Itzcohuatzin, the military chief of Tlatelolco, be made prisoners. The Spaniards hanged a chief from Acolhuacan named Nezahualquentzin. They also murdered the king of Nauhtla, Cohualpopocatzin, by wounding him with arrows and then burning him alive.

For this reason, our warriors were on guard at the Eagle Gate. The sentries from Tenochtitlan stood at one side of the gate, and the sentries from Tlatelolco at the other. But messengers came to tell them to dress the figure of Huitzilopochtli. They left their posts and went to dress him in his sacred finery: his ornaments and his paper clothing.

When this had been done, the celebrants began to sing their songs. That is how they celebrated the first day of the fiesta. On the second day they began to sing again, but without warning they were all put to death. The dancers and singers were completely unarmed. They brought only their embroidered cloaks, their turquoises, their lip plugs, their necklaces, their clusters of heron feathers, their trinkets made of deer hooves. Those who played the drums, the old men, had brought their gourds of snuff and their timbrels.

The Spaniards attacked the musicians first, slashing at their hands and faces until they had killed all of them. The singers-and even the spectators- were also killed. This slaughter in the Sacred Patio went on for three hours. Then the Spaniards burst into the rooms of the temple to kill the others: those who were carrying water, or bringing fodder for the horses, or grinding meal, or sweeping, or standing watch over this work.

The king Motecuhzoma, who was accompanied by Itzcohuatzin and by those who had brought food for the Spaniards, protested: "Our lords, that is enough! What are you doing? These people are not carrying shields or macanas. Our lords, they are completely unarmed!" The Spaniards had treacherously murdered our people on the twentieth day after the captain left for the coast. We allowed the Captain to return to the city in peace. But on the following day we attacked him with all our might, and that was the beginning of the war .

* * * * * * * * *

Bartoleme de Las Casas, The Devastation of the Indies, 1542 CE

The Indies were discovered in the year one thousand four hundred and ninety-two. In the following year a great many Spaniards went there with the intention of settling the land. Thus, forty-nine years have passed since the first settlers penetrated the land, and claimed many islands. All of them were, as we saw with our own eyes, densely populated with native peoples called Indians. The land so far discovered is a beehive of people; it is as though God had crowded into these lands the great majority of mankind.

And of all the infinite universe of humanity, these people are the most guileless, the most devoid of wickedness and duplicity, the most obedient and faithful to their native masters and to the Spanish Christians whom they serve. They are by nature the most humble, patient, and peaceable, holding no grudges, free from embroilments, neither excitable nor quarrelsome. These people are the most devoid of rancors, hatreds, or desire for vengeance of any people in the world. And because they are so weak and complaisant, they are less able to endure heavy labor and soon die of no matter what malady. They are also poor people, for they not only possess little but have no desire to possess worldly goods. For this reason they are not arrogant, embittered, or greedy.

As to their dress, they are generally naked, with only their pudenda covered somewhat. And when they cover their shoulders it is with a square cloth no more than two varas in size. They have no beds, but sleep on a kind of matting or else in a kind of suspended net called bamacas. They are very clean in their persons, with alert, intelligent minds, docile and open to doctrine, very apt to receive our holy Catholic faith, to be endowed with virtuous customs, and to behave in a godly fashion.

Yet into this land there came some Spaniards who immediately behaved like ravening wild beasts, wolves, tigers, or lions that had been starved for many days. And Spaniards have behaved in no other way during the past forty years, down to the present time, for they are still acting like ravening beasts, killing, terrorizing, afflicting, torturing, and destroying the native peoples, doing all this with the strangest and most varied new methods of cruelty, never seen or heard of before, and to such a degree that this Island of Hispaniola once so populous (having a population that I estimated to be more than three million), has now a population of barely two hundred persons.

The island of Cuba is now almost completely depopulated. San Juan [Puerto Rico] and Jamaica are two of the largest, most productive and attractive islands; both are now deserted and devastated. All the people were slain or died after being taken into captivity and brought to the Island of Hispaniola to be sold as slaves. More than thirty other islands in the vicinity of San Juan are for the most part and for the same reason depopulated, and the land laid waste.

As for the vast mainland, we are sure that our Spaniards, with their cruel and abominable acts, have devastated the land and exterminated the rational people who fully inhabited it. We can estimate very surely and truthfully that in the forty years that have passed, with the infernal actions of the Christians, there have been unjustly slain more than twelve million men, women, and children. In truth, I believe without trying to deceive myself that the number of the slain is more like fifteen million.

The common ways mainly employed by the Spaniards who call themselves Christian and who have gone there to extirpate those pitiful nations and wipe them off the earth is by unjustly waging cruel and bloody wars. Then, when they have slain all those who fought for their lives or to escape the tortures they would have to endure, that is to say, when they have slain all the native rulers and young men (since the Spaniards usually spare only the women and children, who are subjected to the hardest and bitterest servitude ever suffered by man or beast), they enslave any survivors. With these infernal methods of tyranny they debase and weaken countless numbers of those pitiful Indian nations.

Their reason for killing and destroying such an infinite number of souls is that the Christians have an ultimate aim, which is to acquire gold, and to swell themselves with riches in a very brief. It should be kept in mind that their insatiable greed and ambition, the greatest ever seen in the world, is the cause of their villainies. And also, those lands are so rich and felicitous, the native peoples so meek and patient, so easy to subject, that our Spaniards have no more consideration for them than beasts. And I say this from my own knowledge of the acts I witnessed. And never have the Indians in all the Indies committed any act against the Spanish Christians, until those Christians have first and many times committed countless cruel aggressions against them or against neighboring nations. For in the beginning the Indians regarded the Spaniards as angels from Heaven. Only after the Spaniards had used violence against them, killing, robbing, torturing, did the Indians ever rise up against them....

And the Christians attacked them with buffets and beatings, until finally they laid hands on the nobles of the villages. Then they behaved with such temerity and shamelessness that the most powerful ruler of the islands had to see his own wife raped by a Christian officer. From that time onward the Indians began to seek ways to throw the Christians out of their lands. They took up arms, but their weapons were very weak and of little service in offense and still less in defense. (Because of this, the wars of the Indians against each other are little more than games played by children.) And the Christians, with their horses and swords and pikes began to carry out massacres and strange cruelties against them. They attacked the towns and spared neither the children nor the aged nor pregnant women nor women in childbed, not only stabbing them and dismembering them but cutting them to pieces as if dealing with sheep in the slaughter house.

After the wars and the killings had ended, when usually there survived only some boys, some women, and children, these survivors were distributed among the Christians to be slaves. The distribution was made according to the rank and importance of the Christian to whom the Indians were allocated, one of them being given thirty, another forty, still another, one or two hundred. The pretext was that these allocated Indians were to be instructed in the articles of the Christian Faith. As if those Christians who were as a rule foolish and cruel and greedy and vicious could be caretakers of souls! And the care they took was to send the men to the mines to dig for gold, which is intolerable labor, and to send the women into the fields of the big ranches to hoe and till the land, work suitable for strong men. Nor to either the men or the women did they give any food except herbs and legumes, things of little substance. And since men and women were separated, there could be no marital relations. And the men died in the mines and the women died on the ranches from the same causes, exhaustion and hunger. And thus was depopulated that island which had been densely populated.

Two Accounts of the Trans-Atlantic Slave Trade, 18th and 19th Centuries

Reading and Discussion Questions

1. After reading both passages below, describe what conditions were like for slaves on the Middle Passage. Cite specific details from each reading in your answer.

2. In the first passage, were all the black people on board captives like Equiano himself? Explain.

3. In the second passage, describe the scene when the captives were allowed on deck. Why were they allowed to come up and what happened when they were returned to the belly of the boat?

4. In your opinion, how is it that humans can treat other humans like animals? How do you think the slave masters justified their actions to themselves? How could they live with what they did?

The following two passages are some of the most detailed and painful descriptions that exist about the horrors of the journey known as the Middle Passage. The Middle Passage was the journey that captured Africans were forced to make from their homelands in Africa to their new homes as slaves on plantations in the Americas.

The first passage is written by a freed slave named Olaudah Equiano, who had been captured in Africa and sold into slavery when he was eleven. Ultimately, Equiano was able to purchase his freedom from his American slave master, and he moved to England were he became active in efforts to abolish the slave trade. He wrote his autobiography, The Interesting Narrative of the Life of Olaudah Equiano, which is considered a major factor in passage of the Slave Trade Act which ended slave trading for Britain and its colonies.

The second passage is from an Irish priest named Robert Walsh whose writings were also important in the eventual abolition of the slave trade. Walsh was active in the Irish Catholic Church and was given an important position within the church in the newly colonized region of Brazil. When Walsh arrived in Brazil, he was horrified by the widespread practice of slavery there, and he worked tirelessly to raise awareness about the inhumane practices that were common. On one occasion, he came across a slave ship, which he managed to board. Walsh wrote about what he saw once onboard.

Ultimately, it was descriptions like these two that led to the abolition of slavery in Britain in 1833, when public outcry against the inhumanity of the slave trade finally became too loud to ignore. By that time, the Trans-Atlantic slave trade had been going on for nearly four centuries and had claimed the lives of more than 12 million men, women and children. Many of those died during the horrors of the Middle Passage.

Olaudah Equiano, *The Interesting Narrative of the Life of Olaudah Equiano, or Gustavus Vassa, the African*, 1745 CE

The first object which saluted my eyes when I arrived on the coast was the sea, and a slave ship, which was then riding at anchor, and waiting for its cargo. These filled me with astonishment, which was soon converted into terror when I was carried on board. I was immediately handled and tossed up to see if I were sound by some of the crew; and I was now persuaded that I had gotten into a world of bad spirits, and that they were going to kill me.

Their complexions were different from ours, their long hair, and the language they spoke, (which was very different from any I had ever heard) united to confirm me in this belief. Indeed such were the horrors of my views and fears at the moment, that, if ten thousand worlds had been my own, I would have freely parted with them all to have exchanged my condition with that of the meanest slave in my own country. When I looked round the ship too and saw a multitude of black people of every description chained together, every one of their countenances expressing dejection and sorrow, I no longer doubted of my fate; and, quite overpowered with horror and anguish, I fell motionless on the deck and fainted.

When I recovered a little I found some black people about me, who I believed were some of those who brought me on board, and had been receiving their pay; they talked to me in order to cheer me, but all in vain. I asked them if we were not to be eaten by those white men with horrible looks, red faces, and loose hair. They told me I was not; and one of the crew brought me a small portion of spirituous liquor in a wine glass; but, being afraid of him, I would not take it out of his hand. One of the blacks therefore took it from him and gave it to me, and I took a little down my palate, which, instead of reviving me, as they thought it would, threw me into the greatest consternation at the strange feeling it produced, having never tasted any such liquor before.

Soon after this the blacks who brought me on board went off, and left me abandoned to despair. I now saw myself deprived of all chance of returning to my native country, or even the least glimpse of hope of gaining the shore, which I now considered as friendly; and I even wished for my former slavery in preference to my present situation, which was filled with horrors of every kind.

I was not long suffered to indulge my grief; I was soon put down under the decks, and there I received such a salutation in my nostrils as I had never experienced in my life: so that, with the loathsomeness of the stench, and crying together, I became so sick and low that I was not able to eat, nor had I the least desire to taste any thing. I now wished for the last friend, death, to relieve me; but soon, to my grief, two of the white men offered me food; and, on my refusing to eat, one of them held me fast by the hands, and laid me across I think the windlass, and tied my feet, while the other flogged me severely. I had never experienced any thing of this kind before; and although, not being used to the water, I naturally feared that element the first time I saw it, yet nevertheless, could I have got over the nettings, I would have jumped over the side, but I could not; and, besides, the crew used to watch us very closely who were not chained down to the decks, lest we should leap into the water: and I have seen some of these poor African prisoners most severely cut for attempting to do so, and hourly whipped for not eating.

* * * * * * *

Robert Walsh, *Notices of Brazil*, 1829 CE

She (the ship) had taken in, on the coast of Africa, three hundred and thirty-six males, and two hundred and twenty-six females, making in all five hundred and sixty-two, and had been out seventeen days. The slaves were all enclosed under grated hatchways, between decks. The space was so low that they sat between each other's legs, and were stowed so close together that there was no possibility of their lying down, or at all changing their position, by night or day. As they belonged to, and were shipped on account of different individuals, they were all branded, like sheep, with the owners' marks. These were impressed under their breasts, or on their arms, and, as the mate informed me, with perfect indifference, 'Burnt with red-hot iron.'

What struck me most forcibly, was how it was possible for such a number of human beings to exist, packed up and wedged together as tight as they could cram, in low cells, three feet high, the greater part of which, except that immediately under the grated hatchway, was shut out from light, or air, and this when the thermometer, exposed to the open sky, was standing, in the shade on our deck, at 89°. The space between decks was divided into two compartments, three feet three inches high; the size of one was sixteen feet by eighteen, and of the other forty by twenty-one; into the first were crammed the women and girls; into the second the men and boys. Two hundred and twenty-six fellow creatures were thus thrust into one space two hundred and eighty-eight feet square, and three hundred and thirty-six into another space eight hundred feet square, giving to the whole an average of twenty-three inches, and to each of the women not more than thirteen inches, although many of them were pregnant.

We also found chains and shackles of different kinds; but it appears that they had all been taken off before we boarded. The heat of these horrid places was so great, and the odor so offensive, that it was quite impossible to enter there, even had there been room. They were measured, as above, when the slaves left them. The officers insisted that the poor suffering creatures should be admitted on deck, to get air and water. This was opposed by the mate of the slaver, who, from a feeling that they deserved it, declared that they would murder them all. The officers, however, persisted, and the poor beings were all turned up together. It is impossible to conceive the effect of this eruption; five hundred and seven fellow creatures, of all ages and sexes, some children, some adults, some old men and women, all in a state of total nudity, scrambling out together to taste the luxury of a little fresh air and water.

They came swarming up, like bees from the aperture of a hive, till the whole deck was crowded to suffocation, from stem to stern; so that it was impossible to imagine where they could all have come from, or how they could all have been stowed away. On looking into the places where they had been crammed, there were found some children, next to the side of the ship, in the places most remote from light and air; they were lying nearly in a torpid state, after the rest had turned out. The little creatures seemed indifferent as to life or death, and when they were carried on deck, many of them could not stand.

After enjoying for a short time the unusual luxury of air, some water was brought; it was then that the extent of their sufferings was exposed in a fearful manner. They all rushed like maniacs towards it. No entreaties, or threats, or blows could restrain them; they shrieked, and struggled, and fought with one another for a drop of this precious

235

liquid, as if they grew rabid at the sight of it. There is nothing from which slaves, in the mid-passage, suffer so much, as want of water.

When the poor creatures were ordered down again, several of them came and pressed their heads against our knees, with looks of the greatest anguish, at the prospect of returning to the horrid place of suffering below.

William Wilberforce, On the Abolition of Slavery, 1795 CE

Reading and Discussion Questions

1. The key to an effective speech is to know one's audience. Wilberforce was addressing members of the British Parliament, who were well-educated and rational men for the most part. What do you think of the effectiveness of Wilberforce's tone in this speech? Did he effectively craft his remarks to meaningfully impact his audience? Explain your answer.
2. What is the most persuasive part of Wilberforce's argument against slavery, in your opinion?
3. How does Wilberforce respond to the claims of those who support the continued practice of slavery? What arguments does he make to counter their positions? Are these arguments effective, in your opinion?

William Wilberforce was an English politician who was instrumental in the abolition of the slave trade and of slavery in the 1800s. By the late 1700s, there was growing evidence of the horror of the slave trade, thanks to accounts including the autobiography of Olaudah Equiano and others. But supporters of efforts to end the slave trade needed a powerful ally in British government, which they found in Wilberforce. Wilberforce was a member of the British Parliament, and this speech made before Parliament in 1795 is considered a turning point in the abolitionist movement. In 1807, the British government passed the Slave Trade Act *which outlawed the Trans-Atlantic slave trade, that is the buying and selling of African slaves. At that time, it was still legal to own slaves that had been purchased before 1807. In 1833, the British government passed the* Slavery Abolition Act *which finally ended the entire institution of slavery, including the ownership of slaves purchased prior to 1807. Wilberforce was also instrumental in the passage of that law. He died just three days after hearing of the passage of the* Slavery Abolition Act *by Parliament.*

When I consider the magnitude of the subject which I am to bring before the House - a subject, in which the interests, not of this country, nor of Europe alone, but of the whole world, and of posterity, are involved: and when I think, at the same time, on the weakness of the advocate who has undertaken this great cause - when these reflections press upon my mind, it is impossible for me not to feel both terrified and concerned at my own inadequacy to such a task. But when I reflect, however, on the encouragement which I have had, through the whole course of a long and laborious examination of this question, and how much candour I have experienced, and how conviction has increased within my own mind, in proportion as I have advanced in my labours; - when I reflect, especially, that however averse any gentleman may now be, yet we shall all be of one opinion in the end; - when I turn myself to these thoughts, I take courage - I determine to forget all my other fears, and I march forward with a firmer step in the full assurance that my cause will bear me out, and that I shall be able to justify upon the clearest principles, every resolution in my hand, the avowed end of which is, the total abolition of the slave trade.

I wish exceedingly, in the outset, to guard both myself and the House from entering into the subject with any sort of passion. It is not their passions I shall appeal to - I ask only for their cool and impartial reason; and I wish not to take them by surprise, but to deliberate, point by point, upon every part of this question. I mean not to accuse any one, but to take the shame upon myself, in common, indeed, with the whole parliament of Great Britain, for having suffered this horrid trade to be carried on under their authority.

We are all guilty - we ought all to plead guilty, and not to exculpate ourselves by throwing the blame on others; and I therefore deprecate every kind of reflection against the various descriptions of people who are more immediately involved in this wretched business.

In opening the nature of the slave trade, I need only observe, that it is found by experience to be just as every man, who uses his reason, would infallibly conclude it to be. For my own part, so clearly am I convinced of the mischiefs inseparable from it, that I should hardly want and farther evidence than my own mind would furnish, by the most simple deductions. Facts however, are now laid before the House. A report has been made by his majesty's privy council, which, I trust, every gentleman has read, and which ascertains the slave trade to be just such in practice as we know, from theory, it must be.

What should we suppose must naturally be the consequence of our carrying on a slave trade with Africa? With a country which was in its extent, not utterly barbarous, but civilized in a very small degree? Does anyone suppose a slave trade would help their civilization? Is it not plain, that she must suffer from it? That civilization must be checked; that her barbarous manners must be made more barbarous; and that the happiness of her millions of inhabitants must be prejudiced with her intercourse with Britain? Does not everyone see that a slave trade, carried on around her coasts, must carry violence and desolation to her very center?

The slave trade, in its very nature, is the source of such kind of tragedies; nor has there been a single person, almost, before the privy council, who does not add something by his testimony to the mass of evidence upon this point. Some, nay most, I believe, have admitted the slave trade to be the chief cause of wars in Africa. It is a trade in its principle most inevitable calculated to spread disunion among the African princes, to sow the seeds of every mischief, to inspire enmity, to destroy humanity; and it is found in practice, by the most abundant testimony to have had the effect in Africa of carrying misery, devastation and ruin wherever its baneful influence has extended.

Having now disposed of the first part of this subject, I must speak of the transit of the slaves in the West Indies. This I confess, in my own opinion, is the most wretched part of the whole subject. So much misery condensed in so little room, is more than the human imagination had ever before conceived. I believe, if the wretchedness of any one of the many hundred Negroes stowed in each ship could be brought before your view, that there is no one among you whose heart would bear it. Let any one imagine to himself 600 or 700 of these wretches chained two and two, surrounded with every object that is nauseous and disgusting, diseased, and struggling under every kind of wretchedness! How can we bear to think of such a scene as this? One would think it had been determined to heap upon them all the varieties of bodily pain, for the purpose of blunting the feelings of the mind; and yet, in this very point (to show the power of human prejudice) the situation of the slaves has been described in a manner which, I am sure will convince the House how interest can draw a film over the eyes, so thick, that total blindness could do no more; and how it is our duty therefore to trust not to the reasonings of interested men, or to their way of colouring a transaction.

"Their apartments", says the slave trade, "are fitted up as much for their advantage as circumstances will admit. The right ankle of one, indeed is connected with the left ankle of another by a small iron fetter, and if they are turbulent, by another on their wrists. They have several meals a day; some of their own country provisions, with the best sauces of African cookery; and by way of variety, another meal of pulse, according to European taste. After breakfast they have water to wash themselves, while their apartments are perfumed with frankincense and lime-juice. Before dinner, they are amused after the manner of their country. The song and dance are promoted," and, as if the whole was really a scene of pleasure and dissipation it is added, that games of chance are furnished. "The men play and sing, while the women and girls make fanciful ornaments with beads, which they are plentifully supplied with." Such is the sort of story the slave trader tells. What will the House think when, by the concurring testimony of other witnesses, the true history is laid open.

The slaves who are sometimes described as rejoicing at their captivity, are so wrung with misery at leaving their country, that it is the constant practice to set sail at night, lest they should be sensible of their departure. The pulse which Mr. Norris talks of are horse beans; and the scantiness, both of water and provision, was suggested by the very legislature of Jamaica in the report of their committee, to be a subject that called for the interference of parliament. Mr. Norris talks of frankincense and lime juice; when surgeons tell you the slaves are stowed so close, that there is not room to tread among them; and when you have it in evidence from Sir George Yonge, that even in a ship which wanted 200 of her complement, the stench was intolerable. The song and the dance, says Mr. Norris, are promoted. It had been more fair, perhaps, if he had explained that word promoted. The truth is, that for the sake of exercise, these miserable wretches, loaded with chains, oppressed with disease and wretchedness, are forced to dance by the terror of the lash, and sometimes by the actual use of it

In order, however, not to trust too much to any sort of description, I will call the attention of the House to one species of evidence which is absolutely infallible. Death, at least, is a sure ground of evidence, and the proportion of deaths will not only confirm, but if possible will even aggravate our suspicion of their misery in the transit. It will be found, upon an average of all the ships, not less than $12\frac{1}{2}$ per cent perish in the passage. Besides these, the Jamaica report tells you, that not less than $4\frac{1}{2}$ per cent die on shore before the day of sale, which is only a week or two from the time of landing. One third more die in the seasoning, and this in a country exactly like their own, where they are healthy and happy as some of the evidences would pretend. The diseases, however, which they contract on shipboard, the astringent washes which are to hide their wounds, and the mischievous tricks used to make them up for sale, are, as the Jamaica report says, one principle cause of this mortality. Upon the whole, however, here is a mortality of about 50 percent. How then can the House deny the savage treatment of the negroes in the middle passage? Nay, indeed, what need is there of any evidence? The number of deaths speaks for itself, and makes all such enquiry superfluous.

As soon as ever I had arrived thus far in my investigation of the slave trade, I confess to you sir, so enormous, so dreadful, so irremediable did its wickedness appear that my own mind was completely made up for the abolition. A trade founded in iniquity, and carried on as this was, must be abolished, let the policy be what it might, let the consequences be what they would. I from this time determined that I would never rest till I had effected its abolition.

How strange it was that divine providence, however mysterious in its ways, should so have constituted the world, as to make one part of it depend for its existence on the depopulation and devastation of another. This cannot be the way of it. I could not help but distrust the arguments of those who insisted that the plundering of Africa was necessary for the cultivation of the West-Indies. I could not believe that the same Being who forbids pillaging and bloodshed, had made pillaging and bloodshed necessary to the well-being of any part of his universe. I felt a confidence in this principle, and took the resolution to act upon it: soon, indeed, the light broke in upon me.........

Having heard all of this you may choose to look the other way but you can never again say that you did not know.

PART FOUR –
TYRANNY AND TRIUMPH

One of the enduring themes of Western Civilization is the struggle of the individual and of individuals within a society to overcome oppression and tyranny. The ancient Greeks ended centuries of monarchial rule with the creation of democracy in Athens and battled empires in defense of their liberty. The very foundation of the Roman Republic was the concept of "no kings allowed." The story of the Rape of Lucretia was taught to Roman children the way we learn of George Washington and the cherry tree. It was a cautionary tale meant to remind Romans that absolute power corrupts absolutely and cannot be tolerated. And yet, in spite of these inspirational triumphs of the people to win liberty in government, absolute rulers emerge again and again in history. Why?

Some cynical thinkers believe history cannot rid itself of absolute rulers because, at our core, an absolute ruler is what our nature demands. Others argue that this is just one side of a two-sided coin or one part of an ongoing cycle. Perhaps it is true that periods of dictatorship and tyranny are inevitable. But the rest of the story is that nearly every period of absolute oppression in history is followed by an effort by the people to throw off their oppressors. Sometimes these are periods of level-headed negotiations resulting in a peaceful settlement of grievances and sometimes they are periods of radical reform and widespread violence. Often, they are a combination of talk and action. Regardless of their nature, though, the history of civilizations is largely a history of people struggling against, and often triumphing over, the cruel force of tyranny. While it can cynically be said that governments always resort to absolute rule, it can also more optimistically be posed that people always triumph over tyrants. It's all a matter of perspective.

CHAPTER 10–
THE AGE OF ABSOLUTISM (1550 - 1800 CE)

GUIDING QUESTIONS

- What is "absolutism?"
- What is "Divine Right of Kings" and how is it used to justify absolutism?
- Why is hereditary succession a critical element of absolute rule?
- What were the ruling dynasties in Europe during the Age of Absolutism and what were the major impacts or influences?
- What are the benefits and dangers of absolute rule?
- Is absolutism the natural form of government for man?

I like to think of the Age of Absolutism as "The Era of Kings Behaving Badly—Part II." Can you remember what the first era of kings behaving badly was? Think way, way back to 509 BC and the actions of an immoral youth called Sextus Tarquinius. Ringing any bells?

Sextus Tarquinius, you will recall, was the son of the last king of Rome, Tarquinius Superbus. It was Sextus Tarquinius who raped the virtuous Lucretia and led to the founding of the mighty Roman Republic. I hope you remember that the point of that story was to demonstrate that absolute power, like the kind that Roman kings had in ancient times, corrupts absolutely. Brutus swore by the blood of Lucretia that there would never be another king of Rome. To honor this promise, the descendant of Brutus and many Roman patricians murdered Julius Caesar on the floor of the Roman Senate several hundred years after the Republic's founding. Caesar showed signs of craving absolute power and the Romans absolutely could not allow him to become a tyrant. "Caesar must die so that the Republic can live." That was the slogan that justified Caesar's death. During the Roman Republic, Romans feared absolute power more than anything and went to great trouble to protect against anyone seizing it. That is until Augustus took absolute power in Rome with the approval of the people by cleverly disguising himself as "first citizen" and not "imperator."

For nearly 1700 years after Augustus' rule, Westerners seemed to have virtually forgotten their ancient legacy of liberty. The Greeks, who founded democracy, believed it was a natural right for men to be self-governing. The Romans declared loudly with the creation of the Republic that man himself is the best architect of his own future and the Roman motto SPQR was the ultimate nod to the power of self-governance. Then, in 27 BCE, along came Augustus who wrote the book on how to seize absolute power. For the next 1700 years, people in Europe were nearly powerless under the yoke of absolutism.

There are many types of absolute rulers and many names for them. But an absolute ruler is simply one person who exercises power over a large population, whose actions are restricted neither by written law nor by custom. Emperors, kings, dictators, czars, and even popes can be absolute rulers. They are just different names for the same absolute use of authority. The Roman Empire was ruled by, you guessed it, emperors. During the early Middle Ages, Europeans were under the nearly dictatorial leadership of the pope. By the late Middle Ages, powerful kings exerted total control over their subjects. But in no other period in history did so few men hold so much power as they did in Europe between 1550 and 1800. Never before or since was the saying more true: "Absolute power corrupts absolutely." Though there had been kings ruling Europe for millennia, the kings and queens of Europe beginning in the 16th century ruled flamboyantly and with the claim that God willed them to rule with absolute authority. Hence, this unique period is called the Age of Absolutism.

In the Age of Absolutism, rulers were called "monarchs" and their form of rule was called absolute monarchy. Monarchies were powerful families, or dynasties, where rule was passed down through the family from one generation of male heir to the next. This practice is called *hereditary succession*. During this era, only males were seen as fit to rule (with a few notable exceptions) so the production of male heirs was the main priority of rulers. If a king died without a son to succeed him, another male relative was often chosen, like a brother or a cousin. However, these claims to the throne by distant relatives were considered weak. Power struggles and even civil wars could be the result of no hereditary heir. Consequently, male children were the ultimate prize for absolute monarchs, who tried to "keep power in the family" at all costs.

In 1469 Europe's first power couple was born with the marriage of Ferdinand II of Aragon and Isabella I of Castile. Their marriage united the Kingdom of Spain and together they were known as Ferdinand and Isabella, King and Queen of the Spanish Empire. It was during the reign of Ferdinand and Isabella that Columbus stumbled upon the new world which led to Spanish colonization of the Americas. It was also during the reign of Ferdinand and Isabella that the 700-year Muslim occupation of Spain was ended by the ruthless campaign against Muslims known as the Reconquista. The Reconquista was a series of wars that ultimately resulted in the expulsion of Muslims from Spain in 1492, but Muslims were not the only enemy of Ferdinand and Isabella. The long term goal of the king and queen of Spain was to make Catholicism the only religion in Spain and her colonies.

To this end, Ferdinand and Isabella began the infamous Spanish Inquisition, which began in 1480. The Inquisition was a group of Catholic agents or spies whose job it was to hunt down "conversos" or Jews and Muslims who converted to Catholicism but who might not be true converts at heart. The Inquisition is remembered in history as a period of ruthless torture and murder of suspected heretics and enemies of the Catholic faith. Much of this violence is exaggerated. It is true, however, that Ferdinand and Isabella forcibly removed or ordered the expulsion of all Jews, Muslims and Protestants from Spain. They also heavily censored information to ensure people had little to no access to information which was in conflict with Catholic doctrine. By the time of the death of Isabella in 1504, Spain had achieved its goal of a fully unified and a fully Catholic nation. It was also the wealthiest and most powerful country in the world because of the unimaginable import of gold from its colonies in the Americas.

Ferdinand and Isabella were the founders of the all-powerful Hapsburg dynasty that would eventually have members of its family on the thrones of Austria and the Holy Roman Empire as well as Spain. The grandson of Ferdinand and Isabella was King Phillip II of Spain, who ruled Spain during the height of its power and was also largely responsible for its demise. Phillip II exercised tyrannical power over his Spanish subjects at home and in his country's colonies in the New World. He was determined to continue the mission of his grandparents to bring the whole world under Spanish Catholic rule, which he tried to achieve in a number of ways. First, Phillip hoped to add England to the territory under his rule and did so for a time through an arranged marriage to his cousin, Mary Tudor (who would become Queen Mary I of England in 1553). During their marriage, Phillip was the King of Spain and England but Mary died unexpectedly in 1558, leaving the throne in England to her Protestant half-sister Elizabeth. Phillip wrongly assumed that Elizabeth would continue the alliance between her country and the more powerful Spain because she was, after all, only a woman. But much to Phillip's surprise, Elizabeth refused his proposal for marriage because she was unwilling to marry her power away. Elizabeth remained unmarried her entire life, earning her the title of "the virgin queen." She also became one of the most successful and well-loved rulers in English history. When she became queen in 1558, England was almost bankrupt and on the verge of a civil war. By the time of her death in 1603, England was the most powerful nation in the world.

England's rise to power came in part because of its victory over Spain and its king, Phillip II. When it became clear to Phillip II that he would not rule England through marriage, he decided to take it by force. He built what he called the "Invincible Armada," the largest navy that had ever been constructed. He invested a huge fortune into the construction of his Spanish navy, believing that victory over England would repay his investment and then some. In 1588, he launched full-scale naval invasion of England, almost assured of victory over the ill-equipped British navy. But nature, or some would say God, was on the side of the English on that day in 1588, because the entire fleet of Phillip's invincible Armada was destroyed in a storm at sea. The English had defeated Spain without ever fighting a battle. The defeat of Spain happened during the reign of Elizabeth, and it won her the undying adoration of her subjects. Spain never recovered from the loss of the Spanish Armada or from the debt it incurred from its construction. Spain had been the most powerful nation in the world at the beginning of 1588 but lost much of its power in that same year. Since that date, Spain has never again been at the top or near the top of the power hierarchy among the nations of Europe.

The rise of Queen Elizabeth I, and of England to unrivaled power in Europe, had been a long one. Elizabeth was part of the Tudor dynasty, which came to power after nearly three decades of civil war in England. In 1485, England was nearing the end of a bloody civil war called the War of the Roses. Two powerful families, the Lancasters and the Yorks, were engaged in a ruthless and bloody war over which family would be the next ruling dynasty in England. Each family's crest bore the rose as their family symbol, hence the name, War of the Roses. By 1485, members of both families had been murdered in such numbers that a lesser family, the Tudors, rose out of the destruction of the bloody war. Margaret Tudor believed that her son, Henry, was destined by God to rule England some day, and she spent her life brokering deals and maneuvering her family into a position of high standing. In the wake of the turmoil of the War of the Roses and because of his mother's unyielding ambition, Henry Tudor, a little known English noble, was married to a York princess, giving Henry a claim to the disputed throne. He was crowned King Henry VII of England in 1485. The Tudor dynasty ruled England until 1603.

Though the rise of Henry VII was full of drama, his story paled in comparison to the drama that surrounded his son, King Henry VIII, who became King of England in 1509. Henry is the infamous English king who had six wives, two of whom he beheaded. But Henry began his reign as a devout Catholic, a capable ruler and a good husband to his Spanish wife, Catherine of Aragon. Catherine was the daughter of Ferdinand and Isabella, and the marriage of Henry and Catherine created an important alliance between powerful Spain and the less powerful England. Henry and Catherine were married for 20 years and were happy by all accounts, except for the fact that Catherine never bore Henry a son. You may recall that, as dynasties go, the most important priority is to have one, or many sons to carry on the family's rule. Henry VIII was particularly aware of the need for a male heir, because he had seen how hard his father had fought to win the crown for his family. Also, the War of the Roses was a power struggle that arose from the failure of the last ruling family, the Plantagenets, to leave a male heir to succeed the throne. In the politics of absolutism, a male heir is everything.

Henry VIII had been king for only eight years when Martin Luther posted his *Ninety-Five Theses* and sparked the Protestant Reformation. Initially, upon hearing reports from Germany about Luther's actions, Henry condemned Luther's teachings as heretical. But by 1525, Henry had grown impatient in his quest for an heir. A young daughter of noble birth named Ann Boleyn had been sent to the court of Henry and Catherine to be a lady-in-waiting to the queen. During her time at the palace, Ann caught Henry's eye and he became obsessed with her. He pursued her relentlessly and unlike almost every other woman in England, she refused his advances. The more Ann refused him, the more determined Henry was in his pursuit. Ann insisted that the only way the two would ever be together was as man and wife. But Henry was a Catholic and the Catholic Church did not permit divorce. It seemed that Ann would be forever off limits to him--*unless* he became a Protestant. Henry's pursuit of Ann Boleyn lasted nearly ten years. Finally, he agreed to marry her and to convert to Protestantism, thus nullifying his marriage to Catherine of Aragon. In 1533, Henry VIII and Ann Boleyn were married, and England was plunged into a firestorm that would last for the next seventy years.

Henry's decision to split with Catholicism, though largely motivated by lust, had political advantages. First, it freed him from the tight control of the Catholic leaders in Rome. Second, it allowed him keep the tax money he had been sending to the church in Rome for use in England. But his split with the Catholic faith enraged Henry's subjects and brought England to the brink of civil war. Spain, too, was furious about the split from Catholicism and the treatment of Catherine of Aragon, the princess of Spain. When Henry married Ann, he sent Catherine and their daughter, Mary, home to Spain, humiliated. This was an insult the Spanish would not soon forget.

Ann Boleyn's youth represented great hope for Henry that he would have many sons, which she often promised him. But those promises were empty ones. Ann became pregnant soon after their marriage and had a daughter, the Princess Elizabeth. She became pregnant several more times but all those pregnancies ended in miscarriage or stillbirth. The more Ann failed to produce a son, the more erratic and troublesome her behavior became. She was said to nag at Henry constantly and often embarrassed him at official functions. Henry lost interest in Ann within two years of their marriage and he began to see her as the root of all his political problems. Ann was the most hated woman in England and rumors of all kinds surrounded her, including rumors about her infidelity. Though there has never been any proof that Ann was unfaithful to the king, he had her arrested and tried as a traitor, because cheating on the King of England is treason. Having been found guilty of all charges, Ann Boleyn was publicly beheaded in May of 1536, leaving her daughter Elizabeth in the care of the king.

Two weeks after the execution of Ann Boleyn, Henry married his third wife, Jane Seymour. Jane produced one child, a boy, for the king. She died of complications of childbirth two weeks later. The son of Henry and Jane was Prince Edward. Henry married three more times in an effort to have more sons but none of his later wives bore him any children. Henry divorced his fourth wife, beheaded his fifth (also on charges of adultery) and was outlived by his sixth wife. By the time of his death in 1547, Henry had three children—Mary, Elizabeth and Edward. Each would rule England for a time.

At the time of Henry's death, England was in a full-blown religious identity crisis. Henry had declared the nation Protestant but most of his subjects still clung to Catholicism. There was political pressure from Spain to revert to the Catholic faith while the Germanic states, including Austria and Prussia, urged England to remain Protestant. Henry's son, Edward, was the first to rule after Henry's death and during his reign, England remained Protestant. But Edward was crowned king at the age of nine and died six years later. The throne then passed to Edward's oldest sister, Mary. Mary was the child of Henry and the Spanish Catholic princess Catherine of Aragon, and Mary was raised as a devout Catholic. She was also raised to despise Protestantism because it was, in her mind, the thing that ruined her parents' marriage and her childhood happiness. Consequently, when Mary became Queen Mary I of England in 1553, she immediately declared England would return to Catholicism. She solidified her allegiance to the Catholic Church by marrying her cousin, King Phillip II of Spain. Most of her short five-year reign was devoted to a merciless war on Protestants, during which time she burned nearly 300 Protestants at the stake, earning her the name "Bloody Mary." Mary died in 1558 of a stomach tumor (she wrongly believed and proclaimed that she was pregnant) and the throne of England passed to her Protestant half-sister, Elizabeth, the daughter of Henry and the slain Ann Boleyn.

Queen Elizabeth I ruled England from 1558 until 1603. When she was crowned queen, England was bankrupt and on the verge of civil war. By the time of Elizabeth's death, England was the wealthiest and most powerful country in the world and had been set on a path to becoming the largest empire in world history. This was due in part to her miraculous defeat of the Spanish Armada, which ended Spanish supremacy in Europe and the New World. But because Elizabeth never married, she did not have a hereditary heir and so she named her nephew, James Stewart of Scotland as her successor. While Elizabeth was level-headed and worked tirelessly to meet the needs of her people, James ruled England with a firm belief in divine right, the idea that God had chosen him to be king. James I's reign marked the beginning of the Stuart dynasty in England, and under the Stuart kings, England would be torn apart by a civil war that Elizabeth had worked so hard to avoid.

Although James I was a bad leader, his son, Charles I was much, much worse. Charles believed even more firmly that God had chosen him and him alone to rule England. Charles dismissed the British Parliament in 1629 and refused to convene them for the next 13 years. In 1642, the English started a war against the king for his refusal to give them their voice in Parliament. The English Civil War raged for seven years before ending in 1649, with the defeat and the beheading of Charles I. It seemed after the English Civil War that the people and their love of liberty had prevailed. They established a new government, called the English Commonwealth, which was meant to have no king and to include more liberties for the people.

What had started out hopefully in the English Commonwealth ended in disaster. The Commonwealth was overseen by a ruthless military tyrant named Oliver Cromwell, who called himself "Lord Protector" but he ruled like a king in every way but name. Life under the English Commonwealth was so bad that in 1661, the English people actually asked for the Stuart monarchy to be restored. Imagine that. They fought a war to rid themselves of the king and then begged for the return of a king. During the Restoration of the Stuart monarchy, two more Stuart kings ruled England and they were almost as out of touch with their subjects as the earlier two Stuarts had been. Charles II took the throne in 1661 and his son James II succeeded him in 1685. Things under Charles II and James II were so insufferable that the people were once again talking about war but they were desperate to find some other non-violent solution. They found their solution in James II's daughter, Mary, and her husband, William of Orange.

After much negotiation and persuasion, Mary Stuart agreed to assume the throne of England with her husband if her father would agree to the transfer of power. James II really had no choice in the matter because if he did not step down from the throne he would have been killed. In 1688, in what became known as the Glorious Revolution, William and Mary became the new and enlightened rulers of England. William and Mary rejected the divine right of kings, acknowledging that royal power came from the consent of the people and not from God. As a promise to their people upon their coronation that they would serve the people rather than being served by them, William and Mary signed the English Bill of Rights into law. This document reaffirmed many of the basic rights guaranteed by the Magna Carta in 1215 but this time those rights applied to all citizens, not just nobles. It also contained many new rights, including the right to free speech in Parliament and some right to bear arms. The liberties guaranteed in the English Bill of Rights would become the basis for the United States Bill of Rights nearly 100 years later.

In England, the people's struggle against absolutism ended well in 1688. But the story of absolutism in France is much more complicated. France, like Spain during this period, was dominated by the reign of one very powerful dynasty. If you recall from the chapter on the Early Middle Ages, the first dynasty or ruling family in France dating back to 486 CE was the Merovingian dynasty. The Merovingians were overthrown by Pepin the Short who founded the Carolingian dynasty, which is the family of Charlemagne. The Carolingian dynasty was the ruling dynasty from 486 to 987 CE. In 987, there was no male heir to the Carolingian dynasty. An ambitious French noble named Hugh Capet founded the Capetian dynasty which ruled France almost continuously from 987 until 1848. The Capetian dynasty was the most influential family in French history and one particular branch of the Capetian dynasty was the most influential and extravagant of all—the Bourbon dynasty.

In 1589, Henry IV became the first Bourbon king of France. Known as "Good King Henry," he tried to spare France the turmoil that other nations like Spain were enduring because of the Protestant Reformation. Unlike Ferdinand and Isabella who ruthlessly persecuted non-Catholics, Henry passed the Edict of Nantes in 1598 which granted religious tolerance to French Protestants called Huguenots. He was generally loved by his subjects because he was a wise ruler, but he was assassinated by a Catholic extremist in 1610 and was succeeded by his son, Louis XIII, who was nine years old.

As a boy-king, Louis' reign lacked the wisdom of his father, and France was ruled mainly by Louis' mother, Marie de Medici. (Does that family name sound familiar?) During Louis' 33-year reign, the religious toleration that defined his father's reign deteriorated. France was deeply divided between Protestants and Catholics by the time of Louis XIII's death in 1643. He was succeeded by his son, Louis XIV, the most flamboyant king in history.

Like his father before him, Louis XIV became king of France as a child. He was five years old at his coronation. But Louis XIV reigned for 72 years, making him the longest ruling monarch in history. Also like his father, France was ruled by his mother until he reached adulthood. Louis XIV's mother, Queen Ann, believed in the divine right of kings. Because Ann believed that her son had divine blessing to rule, she devoted herself to eliminating any challenges to his power and to establishing a position of absolute power for him. This made her, and Louis, many enemies. Before Louis reached adulthood, Louis was almost killed in an uprising of angry French subjects called Le Fronde. This traumatic event made a lasting impression on Louis XIV, who had a permanent suspicion of the masses of French citizens. He wanted to stay as far away from them as possible, and he did just that.

Since the late 14th century, French kings lived in the Louvre Palace in Paris. The Louvre (now the most famous art museum in the world) was an elaborate palace in the heart of Paris. It was seen as inadequate accommodations for a king as majestic as King Louis XIV, and Louis began constructing a new palace at Versailles. Versailles was a small hunting village 12 miles outside of Paris where the king had a small hunting lodge; Louis began its conversion into a massive palace in 1661. The palace was completed in 1682, and Louis relocated to Versailles permanently. By the end of his reign, he had also relocated the entire bureaucracy of the French government to Versailles so that he would never again have to see Paris, or his poor and unhappy French subjects.

Versailles was a paradise for the rich and famous of France. Think of it as Las Vegas and Disneyland all in one opulent, over-the-top setting. Versailles was the most elaborate palace every built. It has more than 700 rooms, 2000 windows, 1250 fireplaces, 67 staircases. It also has eleven fountains (a marvel of the age), one grand canal, two guest lodges, a church, a theater, and more than 1800 acres of park that were stocked with every kind of animal for Versailles' infamous hunting parties. It could accommodate 5000 guests at any one time and much of the palace's furniture was solid silver. In a single year, there were 36,000 people and 6000 horses employed on its construction. The chateau is one of the largest palaces in the world and it is estimated that the palace cost about $4 billion (in today's currency). Versailles was entirely paid for by taxes from the French people.

Louis XIV lived the last 32 years of his life at Versailles, dying in 1715 at the age of 77. By the time of his death, all the power in France lay in his hands. Louis XIV gave himself the name "the Sun King" because everything quite literally revolved around him. He is most famous for saying, "L'etat c'est moi" or "I am the state." He was the embodiment of absolutism, believing that God had chosen him and his descendants to rule France for their own benefit. The Bourbon dynasty was immensely rich and powerful, to be sure, but their extravagant lives came at the expense of the French people, who were struggling to survive. Ultimately, the Bourbon kings would pay for their excesses. Louis XVI, the Sun King's great-grandson, would lose his head to settle

248

the debt during the French Revolution, which began in 1789.

In the 15th and 16th centuries, Spain, France and England ruled the world. But three new powers were emerging in Europe, and all three were also ruled by powerful and ambitious dynasties. In Austria, the Hapsburg family was maneuvering its way to dominance in European affairs. In Russia, a new family of nobles assumed power with visions for westernizing and modernizing their country. That family was the Romanov dynasty. And one of the least known and most important players in European history until the First World War was a Germanic state called Prussia. Prussia was ruled by the Hohenzollern family and, under their leadership, Prussia became one of the most powerful kingdoms in the world by 1750. In every nation in Europe, the people lived under or struggled against the oppression of absolutism, with the exception of England, which enjoyed a limited monarchy by 1700. So the question must be asked, "Is monarchy the most natural and inevitable form of government?" A cynical Englishman named Thomas Hobbes said absolutely "yes."

Thomas Hobbes was a product of the age and the events he lived through. He was an English philosopher who was born in 1588, the same year as the invasion of the Spanish Armada. His mother supposedly went into premature labor when she learned of the Spanish invasion. From the very beginning, Hobbes lived in a world of uncertainty and conflict. These experiences powerfully impacted his views on human nature and of how men should be governed. Hobbes' most famous work is a book entitled *Leviathan*, a name taken from a mythological sea monster. Hobbes chose this name for his work because he believed that man, without a strong ruler to control him, was monstrous and destructive. Hobbes was a vehement defender of absolute monarchy as the natural and appropriate form of government to keep in check the savage nature of humans. Hobbes lived through the English Civil War and fought for Charles I. He was devastated by the execution of his king, and was not surprised when the English Commonwealth was a disaster. He believed that the Restoration of the Stuart monarchy proved that absolute monarchy was the right way to maintain peace and security. He wrote *Leviathan* to elaborate on these beliefs.

Hobbes began his work by explaining that men flattered themselves in assuming they were highly complex beings, but in reality they were only complicated animals. He said that all men were governed by animal instincts to seek pleasure and avoid pain. For this reason, men pursued their own needs and self-interests and inevitably came into conflict with other self-interested men. This clash of self-interests led to a "war of every man against every man" and peace could only be established by giving control to an absolute ruler. He said that men gladly gave over control, and freedom, in exchange for protection. Hobbes has been harshly judged as overly cynical in his views and a big portion of the Enlightenment in the 1700s centered on proving Hobbes wrong. But he is very hard to prove entirely wrong if judged by the history of human experience.

The Expulsion of Jews from Spain, 1492 CE

<u>Reading and Discussion Questions</u>
1. How much time was given to Jews to leave Spain? What could they take with them? What could they not take?
2. Based on your reading, can you see any ways in which the expulsion of the Jews from Spain was bad for Spain?
3. Where did Spanish Jews go when the fled from Spain? Overall, how were they received or treated in the places they traveled to?
4. Summarize your understanding of the overall impact of the expulsion of the Jews from Spain.

1492 was an eventful and, in many ways, horrifying year in Spanish history. This year included a powerful display of the total power of Ferdinand and Isabella. While Columbus was landing in the New World, Ferdinand and Isabella were completing their reconquest of Spain for Catholicism, which was known as the Reconquista. Spanish monarchs had been fighting to drive Muslims from Spain for centuries, which they finally achieved in 1492. In that same year, Ferdinand and Isabella expelled a massive population of Jews from their country, with some estimates suggesting as many as a million people were forced to flee from Spain. The following is an account of the expulsion of the Jews described by a Jew who was part of the expulsion in 1492.

And in the year 1492, in the days of King Ferdinand, the Lord visited the Jews a second time and exiled them. After the King had captured the city of Granada from the Moors, and it had surrendered to him on the 7th of January of the year just mentioned, he ordered the expulsion of all the Jews in all parts of his kingdom. Even before that the Queen had expelled them from the kingdom of Andalusia [1483]

The King gave them three months' time in which to leave. It was announced in public in every city on the first of May. About their number there is no agreement, but, after many inquiries, I found that the most generally accepted estimate is 50,000 families, or, [This would be about 250,000 persons. Other estimates run from 100,000 to 800,000.] They had houses, fields, vineyards, and cattle, and most of them were artisans. At that time there existed many Jewish academies in Spain, and in the last named city there was a great expert in mathematics, and whenever there was any doubt on mathematical questions in the Christian academy of that city they referred them to him. His name was Abraham Zacuto.

Three months is little time, and they [the Jews] had to hasten their exodus from Spain. They sold their houses, their landed estates, and their cattle for very small prices, to save themselves. The King did not allow them to carry silver and gold out of his country, so that they were compelled to exchange their silver and gold for merchandise of cloths and skins and other things.

Many of the exiled Spaniards went to Muslim countries, to Fez, Tlemçen, and the Berber provinces. On account of their large numbers the Moors [Muslims] did not allow them into their cities, and many of them died in the fields from hunger, thirst, and lack of everything. The lions and bears, which are numerous in this country, killed some of them while they lay starving outside of the cities.

When the edict of expulsion became known in the other countries, vessels came from Genoa to the Spanish harbors to carry away the Jews. The crews of these vessels, too, acted maliciously and meanly toward the Jews, robbed them, and delivered some of them to the famous pirate of that time who was called the Corsair of Genoa. To those who escaped and arrived at Genoa the people of the city showed themselves merciless, and oppressed and robbed them, and the cruelty of their wicked hearts went so far that they took the infants from the mothers' breasts.

Many ships with Jews, especially from Sicily, went to the city of Naples on the coast. The King of this country was friendly to the Jews, received them all, and was merciful towards them, and he helped them with money. The Jews that were at Naples supplied them with food as much as they could, and sent around to the other parts of Italy to collect money to sustain them. On account of their very large number, all this was not enough. Some of them died by famine, others sold their children to Christians to sustain their life. Finally, a plague broke out among them, spread to Naples, and very many of them died, so that the living wearied of burying the dead.

Part of the exiled Spaniards went over sea to Turkey. Some of them were thrown into the sea and drowned, but those who arrived, there the King of Turkey received kindly, as they were artisans. He lent them money and settled many of them on an island, and gave them fields and estates.

He who said unto His world, Enough, may He also say Enough unto our sufferings, and may He look down upon our helplessness. May He turn again, and have compassion upon us, and hasten out salvation. Thus may it be Thy will!

Lope de Aguirre, Letter to King Philip of Spain, 1561 CE

Reading and Discussion Questions
1. Who is Lope de Aguirre and why is he writing to the king?
2. What does this letter suggest to you about the reign of King Phillip II? Was he a good king? Why or why not?
3. What is your overall reaction to this letter?

By the mid-1500s, King Phillip II had a massive empire under his control that included all of Spain as well as most of Central and South America. Spanish colonies were ruled primarily by governors and Phillip II had no immediate involvement in the colonies' governance. Ultimately, however, the management or mismanagement of colonial territories was Phillip's responsibility. Accounts of Spanish atrocities committed against indigenous populations are well documented but what is less well known is Spain's neglect of its own citizens in the colonies. Provincial governors took advantage of Spanish citizens living abroad as ruthlessly as they did the natives and this provoked no response from King Phillip II. The following letter was written by one Spanish subject of Phillip II. The level of his anger is clear, as he threatens outright rebellion against the king. This letter summarized a pretty common sentiment among Spanish subjects; that the king was concerned about the interests of the king and believed his subjects existed solely to serve him.

To King Philip, the Spaniard,

In my youth I crossed the sea to the land of Peru to gain fame, lance in hand, and to fulfill the obligation of all good men. In 24 years I have done you great service in Peru, in conquests of the Indians, in founding towns, and especially in battles and encounters fought in your name, always to the best of my power and ability, without requesting of your officials pay nor assistance, as can be seen in your royal records.

I firmly believe, most excellent King and lord, that to me and my companions you have been nothing but cruel and ungrateful. I also believe that those who write to you from this land deceive you, because of the great distance.

I demand of you, King, that you do justice and right by the good vassals you have in this land, even though I and my companions, unable to suffer further the cruelties of your judges, viceroy, and governors, have resolved to obey you no longer. Denaturalizing ourselves from our land, Spain, we make the most cruel war against you that our power can sustain and endure. Believe, King and lord, we have done this because we can no longer tolerate the great oppression and unjust punishments of your ministers who have usurped and robbed our fame, life, and honor. It is a pity, King, the bad treatment you have given us.

Look here, King of Spain! Do not be cruel and ungrateful to your subjects, because while your father and you stayed in Spain without the slightest bother, your subjects, at the price of their blood and fortune, have given you all the kingdoms and holding you have in these parts. Beware, King and lord, that you cannot take, under the title of legitimate king, any benefit from this land where you risked nothing, without first giving due gratification to those who have labored and sweated in it.

I am certain there are few kings in hell because there are few kings, but if there were many none would go to heaven. Even in hell you would be worse than Lucifer, because you all thirst after human blood.

Oh, how sad that a great ruler, your father, should conquer with the power of Spain the great Germany, and should spend so much money from these Indies discovered by us, and that you should not concern yourself with our old age and weariness enough to provide for our daily bread. God grant that we might obtain with our arms the reward by right due us, but which you have denied.

I, rebel until death against you for your ingratitude.

Lope de Aguirre, the Wanderer

Queen Elizabeth I, Speech to the Troops at Tilbury, 1588 CE

Reading and Discussion Questions

1. During this speech, how does Elizabeth describe herself in relation to her people?
2. Elizabeth was beloved by her people. Does this speech give you any hints as to why that was true?
3. What is your reaction to this speech? Is your reaction at all influenced by the fact that this speech is being delivered by a woman? Why or why not?

*As you read in this chapter introduction, **King Phillip II of Spain launched a naval invasion of England using his "Invincible Armada" in 1588**. The English troops were outnumbered and their chance of victory was slim. As the Armada approached English shores, Queen Elizabeth I rode out to her troops, who were waiting on the coast to meet the coming Spanish invasion. The following is the speech she gave to her troops to rally them for the battle ahead.*

My loving people, we have been persuaded by some that are careful of our safety to take heed how we commit ourself to armed multitudes for fear of treachery; but I assure you, I do not desire to live to distrust my faithful and loving people. Let tyrants fear. I have always so behaved myself that, under God, I have placed my chiefest strength and safe guard in the loyal hearts and good will of my subjects; and therefore I am come amongst you, as you see, at this time, not for my recreation and disport, but being resolved, in the midst and heat of the battle, to live or die amongst you all, to lay down my life for my God and for my kingdom and for my people, my honour, and my blood, even in the dust. I know I have the body of a weak and feeble woman, but I have the heart and stomach of a king, and a king of England too, and think foul scorn that Parma or Spain, or any prince of Europe should dare to invade the borders of my realm; the which, rather than any dishonour shall grow by me, I myself will take up arms, I myself will be your general, judge, and rewarder of every one of your virtues in the field. I know, already for your forwardness, you have deserved rewards and crowns; and we do assure you, in the word of a prince, they shall be duly paid you. In the meantime my lieutenant-general shall be in my stead, than whom never prince commanded a more noble or worthy subject, not doubting but by your obedience to my general, by your concord in the camp, and your valour in the field, we shall shortly have a famous victory over those enemies of my God, of my kingdom, and of my people.

King James I, In Defense of Divine Right, 1610 CE

Reading and Discussion Questions

1. Compare this speech to the one given by Elizabeth to her troops in 1588. How does this tone differ? What does this speech indicate about James I's relationship with his subjects?

2. What right do the people have to question decisions of the king or to express their grievances? Why is this the case?

3. According to this document, what are the people ordered not to do in relation to their government? There are two things.

4. How do you think the English people felt about James I, based on this speech?

James I was the successor of Elizabeth I. Elizabeth was a master of diplomacy and of winning the support of conflicting groups with her carefully chosen thoughts, words and actions. James enjoyed almost none of the same restraint or the same skill at diplomacy that Elizabeth had. He often ranted about the inconvenience of having to work with Parliament, since he had been given the right to rule by God himself. The following is one of his frequent speeches about Divine Right and the role the English people should, and should not have, in government.

. . .The state of monarchy is the supremest thing upon earth, for kings are not only God's lieutenants upon earth and sit upon God's throne, but even by God himself they are called gods. There be three principal [comparisons] that illustrate the state of monarchy: one taken out of the word of God, and the two other out of the grounds of policy and philosophy. In the Scriptures kings are called gods, and so their power after a certain relation compared to the Divine power. Kings are also compared to fathers of families; for a king is *truly parens patriae* [parent of the country], the politic father of his people. And lastly, kings are compared to the head of this microcosm of the body of man . . .

I that to dispute what God may do is blasphemy . . . so is it sedition in subjects to dispute what a king may do in the height of his power. But just kings will ever be willing to declare what they will do, if they will not incur the curse of God. I will not be content that my power be disputed upon, but I shall ever be willing to make the reason appear of all my doings, and rule my actions according to my laws . . .

Now the second general ground whereof I am to speak concerns the matter of grievances . . . First then, I am not to find fault that you inform yourselves of the particular just grievances of the people; nay I must tell you, ye can neither be just nor faithful to me or to your countries that trust and employ you, if you do it not . . . But I would wish you to be careful to avoid [these] things in the matter of grievances.

First, do not meddle with the main points of government; that is my craft . . . to meddle with that, were to lessen me. I am now an old king . . . I must not be taught my office.

Secondly, I would not have you meddle with such ancient rights of mine as I have received from my predecessors, possessing them *more* (as ancestral customs); such things I would be sorry should be accounted for grievances. All novelties are dangerous as well in a politic as in a natural body, and therefore I would be loath to be quarreled in my ancient rights and possessions: for that were to judge me unworthy of that which my predecessors had and left me.

English Bill of Rights, 1689 CE

Reading and Discussion Questions
1. What abuses of power was King James II guilty of, according to this document?
2. What liberties, rights or protections were guaranteed to the English people as a result of this document?
3. Looking at your list of rights from Question 2, which of these are rights that were originally guaranteed by the Magna Carta? Which of them are new rights?
4. Are the rights guaranteed in this document similar to any of the rights we enjoy as Americans? If so, which ones? Why do you think that is?

William and Mary became the King and Queen of England in 1688 after the bloodless overthrow of Mary's father, the tyrannical King James II. As a promise of their commitment to serving the English people, William and Mary signed the English Bill of Rights and presented it as a gift to their subjects shortly after their coronation in 1688. The English Bill of Rights reaffirmed many of the rights originally put forth by the Magna Carta and expanded those rights to include new liberties. This document set the example for countless other governments who sought to limit the power of rulers and to provide basic protections for its citizens.

William and Mary, prince and princess of Orange, being present in their proper persons solemnly declare before Parliament:

Whereas the late King James the Second did endeavour to subvert and extirpate the Protestant religion and the laws and liberties of this kingdom;

By assuming and exercising a power of dispensing with and suspending of laws and the execution of laws without consent of Parliament;

By committing and prosecuting divers worthy prelates for humbly petitioning to be excused from concurring to the said assumed power;

By levying money [taxes] without the consent of Parliament;

By raising and keeping a standing army within this kingdom in time of peace without consent of Parliament, and quartering soldiers contrary to law;

By causing several good subjects being Protestants to be disarmed at the same time when papists were both armed and employed contrary to law;

By violating the freedom of election of members to serve in Parliament;

And whereas of late years partial corrupt and unqualified persons have been returned and served on juries in trials;

And excessive bail hath been required of persons committed in criminal cases to elude the benefit of the laws made for the liberty of the subjects;

And excessive fines have been imposed;

And illegal and cruel punishments inflicted;

And several grants and promises made of fines and forfeitures before any conviction or judgment against the persons upon whom the same were to be levied;

And whereas the said late King James the Second having abdicated the government and the throne being thereby vacant, his Highness the prince of Orange [assumes all the powers of the English crown and swears that henceforth] the religion, laws and liberties [of the English people] might not again be in danger of being subverted;

And thereupon King William solemnly declares:

That the pretended power of suspending the laws or the execution of laws by regal authority without consent of Parliament is illegal;

That the pretended power of dispensing with laws or the execution of laws by regal authority, as it hath been assumed and exercised of late, is illegal;

That levying money [taxing] for or to the use of the Crown, without grant of Parliament, is illegal;

That it is the right of the subjects to petition the king, and all commitments and prosecutions for such petitioning are illegal;

That the raising or keeping a standing army within the kingdom in time of peace, unless it be with consent of Parliament, is against law;

That the subjects which are Protestants may have arms for their defense suitable to their conditions and as allowed by law;

That election of members of Parliament ought to be free;

That the freedom of speech and debates or proceedings in Parliament ought not to be impeached or questioned in any court or place out of Parliament;

That excessive bail ought not to be required, nor excessive fines imposed, nor cruel and unusual punishments inflicted;

That jurors ought to be duly impanelled and returned, and jurors which pass upon men in trials for high treason ought to be freeholders;

That all grants and promises of fines and forfeitures of particular persons before conviction are illegal and void;

And that for redress of all grievances, and for the amending, strengthening and preserving of the laws, Parliaments ought to be held frequently.

And they do claim, demand and insist upon all and singular the premises as their undoubted rights and liberties, and that no declarations, judgments, doings or proceedings to the prejudice of the people in any of the said premises ought in any wise to be drawn hereafter into consequence or example; to which demand of their rights they are particularly encouraged by the declaration of his Highness the prince of Orange as being the only means for obtaining a full redress and remedy therein. Having therefore an entire confidence that his said Highness the prince of Orange will perfect the deliverance so far advanced by him, and will still preserve them from the violation of their rights which they have here asserted, and from all other attempts upon their religion, rights and liberties.

Louis XIV, Revocation of the Edict of Nantes, 1685 CE

Reading and Discussion Questions
1. Why did Louis XIV claim the Edict of Nantes was no longer necessary?
2. What happened to Protestant churches as a result of this revocation?
3. What happened to Protestant schools as a result of revoking the Edict of Nantes? How were French children to be educated in the future, according to this order?
4. What happened to Protestant ministers who continued to preach Protestantism after the Edict of Nantes was revoked?
5. What happened to the property of Protestants as a result of this order?

As you learned from your study of the Protestant Reformation, many nations in Europe were torn apart by religious conflict between Protestants and Catholics. France, you will recall, fought a series of bloody religious wars, called the French Wars of Religion, which were only brought to an end by the passage of the Edict of Nantes in 1598. The Edict of Nantes granted religious freedom to Huguenots and peace was reestablished in the realm. The decision to pass the Edict was smart diplomacy on the part of Good King Henry IV. Much like James I lacked the diplomatic judgment of Elizabeth I in England, so too King Louis XIV lacked the wisdom of his predecessor Henry VI to keep the peace among rival religious factions. In 1685, Louis XIV made the fateful decision to revoke the Edict of Nantes. He did this, he said, because so many Protestants had returned to Catholicism in France that the Edict was no longer necessary.

There was some truth to this statement but it only tells half the story. In the years after Henry IV's reign, there continued to be hostility against Huguenots. Sometimes it was subtle alienation and sometimes it was blatant persecution. Huguenots by the mid-1600s were strongly encouraged, some would say forced, to reconvert to Catholicism or flee. This was not dissimilar to the events of the Reconquista in Spain at the end of the 1400s. As a result of the emigration out of France of many Huguenots and the conversion to Catholicism of others, France had a smaller Protestant population. Louis XIV was a devout Catholic and he viewed Protestants as heretics. Louis liked everything to be just the way he liked it, and he liked France to be Catholic. To that end, he revoked the Edict of Nantes in 1685 and ended the religious freedom that had been enjoyed in France for the last 90 years. The French people were outraged.

Louis, by the grace of God king of France and Navarre, to all present and to come, greeting:

King Henry the Great, our grandfather of glorious memory, being desirous that the peace which he had procured for his subjects after the grievous losses they had sustained in the course of domestic and foreign wars, should not be troubled on account of the Reformed Protestant Religion (R.P.R.), as had happened in the reigns of the kings, his predecessors, by his edict, granted at Nantes in the month of April, 1598, regulated the procedure to be adopted with regard to those of the said religion, and the places in which they might meet for public worship, established extraordinary judges to administer justice to them, and, in fine, provided in particular articles for whatever could be thought necessary for maintaining the tranquility of his kingdom and for diminishing mutual aversion between the members of the two religions.

And now we perceive, with thankful acknowledgment of God's aid, that our endeavors have attained their proposed end, inasmuch as the better and the greater part of our subjects of the said R.P.R. have embraced the Catholic faith. And since by this fact the execution of the Edict of Nantes and of all that has ever been ordained in favor of the said R.P.R. has been rendered nugatory, we have determined that we can do nothing better than entirely to revoke the said Edict of Nantes.

I. Be it known that we have, by this present perpetual and irrevocable edict, suppressed and revoked, and do suppress and revoke, the edict of our said grandfather, given at Nantes in April, 1598, in its whole extent; we declare it null and void, together with all concessions, of whatever nature they may be, made by them as well as by other edicts, declarations, and orders, in favor of the said persons of the R.P.R; and in consequence we desire, and it is our pleasure, that all the temples of those of the said R.P.R. situate in our kingdom, countries, territories, and the lordships under our crown, shall be demolished without delay.

II. We forbid our subjects of the R.P.R. to meet any more for the exercise of the said religion in any place or private house, under any pretext whatever, . . .

III. We likewise forbid all noblemen to hold such religious exercises in their houses or fiefs, under penalty to be inflicted upon all our said subjects who shall engage in the said exercises, of imprisonment and confiscation.

IV. We enjoin all ministers of the said R.P.R., who do not choose to become converts and to embrace the Catholic, apostolic, and Roman religion, to leave our kingdom and the territories subject to us within a fortnight of the publication of our present edict, without leave to reside therein beyond that period, or, during the said fortnight, to engage in any preaching, exhortation, or any other function, on pain of being sent to the galleys. . . .

VII. We forbid private schools for the instruction of children of the said R.P.R., and in general all things what ever which can be regarded as a concession of any kind in favor of the said religion.

VIII. As for children who may be born of persons of the said R.P.R., we desire that from henceforth they be baptized by the parish priests. We enjoin parents to send them to the churches for that purpose, under penalty of five hundred livres fine; and thereafter the children shall be brought up in the Catholic, apostolic, and Roman religion, which we expressly enjoin the local magistrates to see done.

IX. And in the exercise of our clemency towards our subjects of the said R.P.R. who have left our kingdom, lands, and territories subject to us, previous to the publication of our present edict, it is our will and pleasure that in case of their returning within the period of four months from the day of the said publication, they may, and it shall be lawful for them to, again take possession of their property, and to enjoy the same as if they had all along remained there: on the contrary, the property abandoned by those who, during the specified period of four months, shall not have returned into our kingdom, lands, and territories subject to us, shall remain and be confiscated in consequence of our declaration.

X. We repeat our most express prohibition to all our subjects of the said R.P.R., together with their wives and children, against leaving our kingdom, lands, and territories subject to us, or transporting their goods and effects therefrom under penalty, as respects the men, of being sent to the galleys, and as respects the women, of imprisonment and confiscation of property.

Given at Fontainebleau in the month of October, in the year of grace 1685, and of our reign the forty-third.

Duc de Saint-Simon, The Court of Louis XIV, 1695 CE

Reading and Discussion Questions
  1. What was the personality of Louis XIV? What did he have a passion for, according to the author?
  2. How did members of Louis' court take advantage of his weaknesses to increase their own power?
  3. What was life like in the court of Louis XIV? What did Louis require from the people in his court in their service to him?
  4. How did Louis cause the members of his court to become totally dependent on him for their financial survival? Why does the author call this practice a "plague" and a "scourge on the whole country?"

King Louis XIV was the epitome of absolutism and the belief that the people were put on earth for the service and enjoyment of the king. Louis' life at the Palace of Versailles was absurd in its extravagance, especially at a time when the French people were struggling to survive. The excesses that Versailles was known for are well documented and the lavish lifestyle of King Louis XIV and his court are one of the main causes of the discontent of the French people during this era. The following is one of the many accounts of the extravagance of the court of Louis XIV.

THE COURT

Louis' natural talents were below mediocrity; but he had a mind capable of improvement, of receiving polish, of assimilating what was best in the minds of others without slavish imitation; and he profited greatly throughout his life from having associated with the ablest and wittiest persons, of both sexes, and of various stations.

Glory was his passion, but he also liked order and regularity in all things; he was naturally prudent, moderate, and reserved; always master of his tongue and his emotions. Will it be believed? he was also naturally kind-hearted and just. God had given him all that was necessary for him to be a good King, perhaps also to be a fairly great one. All his faults were produced by his surroundings. In his childhood he was so much neglected that no one dared go near his rooms. He was often heard to speak of those times with great bitterness; he used to relate how, through the carelessness of his attendants, he was found one evening in the basin of a fountain in the Palais-Royal gardens....

His Ministers, generals, mistresses, and courtiers soon found out his weak point, namely, his love of hearing his own praises. There was nothing he liked so much as flattery, or, to put it more plainly, adulation; the coarser and clumsier it was, the more he relished it. That was the only way to approach him; if he ever took a liking to a man it was invariably due to some lucky stroke of flattery in the first meeting....

His mind was occupied with small things rather than with great, and he delighted in all sorts of petty details, such as the dress and drill of his soldiers; and it was just the same with regard to his building operations, his household, and even his cookery. He always thought he could teach something of their own craft even to the most skillful professional men; and they, for their part, used to listen gratefully to lessons which they had long ago learnt by heart. He imagined that all this showed his indefatigable industry; in reality, it was a great waste of time, and his Ministers turned it to good account for their own purposes, as soon as they had learnt the art of managing him; they kept his attention engaged with a mass of details, while they contrived to get their own way in more important matters.

His vanity, which was perpetually nourished - for even preachers used to praise him to his face from the pulpit - was the cause of the aggrandisement of his Ministers. He imagined that they were great only through him, mere mouthpieces through which he expressed his will; consequently he made no objection when they gradually [took more power for themselves] . .

But for the fear of the devil, he would have caused himself to be worshipped as a deity. He would not have lacked worshippers....

LIFE AT VERSAILLES

Very early in the reign of Louis XIV the Court was removed from Paris, never to return. The troubles of the minority had given him a dislike to that city; his enforced and surreptitious flight from it still rankled in his memory; he did not consider himself safe there. No doubt that he was also influenced by the feeling that he would be regarded with greater awe and veneration when no longer exposed every day to the gaze of the multitude.

The Court was moved to Versailles in 1682. [He expanded the palace and accompanying buildings to include an elaborate guest lodge among other things.] The new building contained an infinite number of rooms for courtiers, and the King liked the grant of these rooms to be regarded as a coveted privilege.

He held frequent festivities at Versailles, and went on excursions to other places, to make the courtiers devoted in their attendance and anxious to please him; for he nominated beforehand those who were to take part in them, and could thus gratify some and inflict a snub on others. He was conscious that the substantial favours he had to bestow were not nearly sufficient to produce a continual effect; he had therefore to invent imaginary ones, and no one was so clever in devising petty distinctions and preferences which aroused jealousy and emulation.

Not only did he expect all persons of distinction to be in continual attendance at Court, but he was quick to notice the absence of those of inferior degree; When he woke up, when he retired for the night, at his meals, in the gardens of Versailles-- he used to cast his eyes to right and left; nothing escaped him, he saw everybody. If any one was absent he insisted on knowing the reason. If asked to bestow a favour on such person who was often absent he would reply haughtily: "I do not know him;" or "He is a man I never see;" and from these judgments there was no appeal.

He always took great pains to find out what was going on in public places, in society, in private houses, even family secrets, and maintained an immense number of spies and tale-bearers. Many a man in all ranks of life was ruined by these methods, often very unjustly, without ever being able to discover the reason; and when the King had once taken a prejudice against a man, he hardly ever got over it....

He loved splendour, magnificence, and profusion in all things, and encouraged similar tastes in his Court; to spend money freely on equipages and buildings, on feasting and at cards, was a sure way to gain his favour. Motives of policy had something to do with this; by making expensive habits the fashion, and, for people in a certain position, a necessity, he compelled his courtiers to live beyond their income, and gradually reduced them to depend on his bounty for their survival.

This was a plague which, once introduced, became a scourge to the whole country, for it did not take long to spread to Paris, and thence to the armies and the provinces; so that a man of any position is now estimated entirely according to his expenditure on his table and other luxuries. This folly, sustained by pride and ostentation, has already produced widespread confusion; it threatens to end in nothing short of ruin and a general overthrow.

Thomas Hobbes, *Leviathan*, 1651 CE

Reading and Discussion Questions
1. What does Hobbes say life will be like for men who live without a "common power?" Why does he say it will be so?
2. According to Hobbes, why is war undesirable and unproductive? What things can man not do when in a state of war?
3. Hobbes says that we "accuse mankind by our actions" of being untrustworthy and brutish. What does he mean when he says this?
4. Why is there no peace or justice among men in nature?
5. Why would men ever choose peace, according to Hobbes?
6. Do you think Hobbes' views of human nature are overly cynical or are they true, in your opinion? Explain your answer.

Thomas Hobbes was an English philosopher in the mid-1600s whose name has become synonymous with "cynical." He had a dark view of human nature and, consequently, he believed that men needed to be governed like the animals that they are. Hobbes was the original supporter of absolute monarchy as a natural condition and he outlined his ideas on absolutism in his book, Leviathan, in 1651 CE.

Hereby it is manifest, that during the time men live without a common power to keep them all in awe, they are in that condition which is called war; and such a war, as is of every man, against every man. For war, consists not in battle only, or the act of fighting; but in a tract of time, wherein the will to contend by battle is sufficiently known: and therefore the notion of *time,* is to be considered in the nature of war; as it is in the nature of weather. For as the nature of foul weather, lies not in a shower or two of rain; but in an inclination thereto of many days together: so the nature of war, consists not in actual fighting; but in the known disposition thereto, during all the time there is no assurance to the contrary. All other time is peace.

262

Whatsoever therefore is consequent to a time of war, where every man is enemy to every man; the same is consequent to the time, wherein men live without other security, than what their own strength, and their own invention shall furnish them withal. In such condition, there is no place for industry; because the fruit thereof is uncertain: and consequently no culture of the earth; no navigation, nor use of the commodities that may be imported by sea; no commodious building; no instruments of moving, and removing, such things as require much force; no knowledge of the face of the earth; no account of time; no arts; no letters; no society; and which is worst of all, continual fear, and danger of violent death; and the life of man, solitary, poor, nasty, brutish, and short.

It may seem strange to some man, that has not well weighed these things; that nature should thus dissociate, and render men apt to invade, and destroy one another: and he may therefore, not trusting to this inference, made from the passions, desire perhaps to have the same confirmed by experience. Let him therefore consider with himself, when taking a journey, he arms himself, and seeks to go well accompanied; when going to sleep, he locks his doors; when even in his house he locks his chests; and this when he knows there be laws, and public officers, armed, to revenge all injuries shall be done him; what opinion he has of his fellow-subjects, when he rides armed; of his fellow citizens, when he locks his doors; and of his children, and servants, when he locks his chests. Does he not there as much accuse mankind by his actions, as I do by my words? But neither of us accuse man's nature in it. The desires, and other passions of man, are in themselves no sin. No more are the actions, that proceed from those passions, till they know a law that forbids them: which till laws be made they cannot know: nor can any law be made, till they have agreed upon the person that shall make it.

It may peradventure be thought, there was never such a time, nor condition of war as this; and I believe it was never generally so, over all the world: but there are many places, where they live so now. For the savage people in many places of America, except the government of small families, the concord whereof dependeth on natural lust, have no government at all; and live at this day in that brutish manner, as I said before. Howsoever, it may be perceived what manner of life there would be, where there were no common power to fear, by the manner of life, which men that have formerly lived under a peaceful government, use to degenerate into, in a civil war.

But though there had never been any time, wherein particular men were in a condition of war one against another; yet in all times, kings, and persons of sovereign authority, because of their independency, are in continual jealousies, and in the state and posture of gladiators; having their weapons pointing, and their eyes fixed on one another; that is, their forts, garrisons, and guns upon the frontiers of their kingdoms; and continual spies upon their neighbours; which is a posture of war. But because they uphold thereby, the industry of their subjects; there does not follow from it, that misery, which accompanies the liberty of particular men.

To this war of every man, against every man, this also is consequent; that nothing can be unjust. The notions of right and wrong, justice and injustice have there no place. Where there is no common power, there is no law: where no law, no injustice. Force, and fraud, are in war the two cardinal virtues. Justice, and injustice are none of the faculties neither of the body, nor mind. If they were, they might be in a man that were alone in the world, as well as his senses, and passions. They are qualities, that relate to men in society, not in solitude. It is consequent also to the same condition, that there be no propriety, no dominion, no *mine* and *thine* distinct; but only that to be every man's, that he can get; and for so long, as he can keep it. And thus much for the ill condition, which man by mere nature is actually placed in; though with a possibility to come out of it, consisting partly in the passions, partly in his reason.

The passions that incline men to peace, are fear of death; desire of such things as are necessary to commodious living; and a hope by their industry to obtain them. And reason suggesteth convenient articles of peace, upon which men may be drawn to agreement. These articles, are they, which otherwise are called the Laws of Nature ...

CHAPTER 11—
THE AGE OF ENLIGHTENMENT
(1700-1800 CE)

GUIDING QUESTIONS
- Define "revolution." What kinds of revolutions have there been in history?
- What is the Enlightenment? Why is it considered the ultimate Humanist revolution?
- How did the ideas of the following people influence our founders' creation of the United States—John Locke, Montesquieu, Voltaire?
- Who is Adam Smith and how did his ideas influence our founders?
- Explain the statement "America is a product of the Enlightenment."
- Was America a success from the beginning? Why or why not? Explain.

Humanists—The modern world was created by them. In the mid-1300s, Francesco Petrarch challenged Medieval minds to shake off the stupor of the Middle Ages. He lamented the stagnation of the times and longed for a return of the glory of the classical era. "Time once smiled and will again, but in this middle age, time's dregs swirl around us and we beneath a heavy load of vice." He illuminated the dangers of being ruled by sloth and apathy and called 14-century Europeans to action: "Shameful vision this. We must awake or die!" Petrarch wrote obsessively to people living and dead about the need for wisdom and the light of the past to point the way forward. Centuries before George Santayana said, "Those who do not remember the past are condemned to repeat it," Petrarch was spreading this message. One of Petrarch's greatest influences was the Roman statesman Cicero who said the same sentiment a different way: "To be ignorant of the past is to remain a child." Petrarch's voice echoed into nothing at first, or so it seemed.

Over time, Petrarch's ideas took hold. Slowly and over many decades and even centuries, people began to awaken. And very, very slowly a new way of living replaced the darkness and helplessness that characterized life under the Augustinian worldview. Augustine, you may recall, taught that all life is a preparation for death and that too much pleasure on earth can jeopardize true happiness in the hereafter. Petrarch fundamentally rejected that idea. He said we must live *now*, as fully and as deeply as we can. But if you recall, Petrarch was not unreligious. In fact, he believed that the best way to glorify God was to maximize every gift bestowed upon us by our creator and to live every blessed moment of our lives with purpose because as humans, God made us and our lives special. God gave us *power* to improve our lives and help ourselves. To squander those gifts would be a great sin, Petrarch said. Out of his writings, the humanist philosophy was born. And Humanists changed everything. Humanists were revolutionaries.

As we have discussed, a "revolution" sometimes involves weapons and power struggles. When we think of revolutions we think "American Revolution" or "Russian Revolution." Usually in our minds, some ruler gets killed or overthrown, the people win power and everyone celebrates the triumph of the human spirit. But the word "revolution" simply means "radical change." The Humanist life philosophy has sparked more revolutions or radical changes than any other set of ideas in human history. The first Humanist revolution was the Renaissance, as we have discussed. During this era,

265

brave pioneers transformed the way we expressed ourselves in painting, literature and sculpture. The Protestant Reformation was a Humanist revolution too. Martin Luther was a fierce defender of the Humanist concept of reason over faith. For this reason, Luther translated the Bible into German so that Germans could read it and would no longer be forced to blindly accept what the church told them. The Age of Exploration was fueled by Humanist curiosity to know all that was not known. And the Scientific Revolution was also a Humanist movement. Building on the knowledge of the past, men like Galileo, Newton, Kepler and others gave us proof of things that we were asked to blindly believe in before. By 1700, science, art, geography and even religion had been transformed or revolutionized because of Humanism. *Society* itself, however, was still unchanged. But around 1700 in Paris, a group of Humanists who called themselves *philosophes* began to radically reimagine the world as they knew it. And this revolutionary period of reimagining is what we call the Age of Enlightenment.

No one knows the precise moment the Enlightenment began or the exact question or discussion that sparked a new age. I like to think the question that birthed a new era was something like, "Why can't we change the world?" or maybe something less romantic like "I wonder if my life could be better?" Perhaps the question was simpler still, like "Why don't I have enough to eat?" Though no one knows how the philosophical dialogue of the Enlightenment started, there is no question that it began with a series of questions about the human condition and the quality of life. By 1700, people had probably been wondering for centuries why they were hungry, or why society was unequal or why the rules were unfair. But before the Enlightenment, these questions didn't seem much worth pondering because they were not likely to produce any answers. By 1700, though, attitudes had changed. Humanists had proved that change is possible. Also by 1700, the Scientific Revolution had created tools for examining the inner-workings of complicated natural systems like the universe, physics and anatomy. Machiavelli had shown the world that politics, too, could be dissected and analyzed scientifically. It seemed only logical that social structures and even governments could also be studied and understood scientifically. In this way the social sciences were born.

No single question was more on the minds of Enlightenment philosophers than the question, "How should man be governed?" To answer the question of governance, one must first tackle the question, "What is the nature of man?" Political science and psychology became intertwined at this moment in history. Men like Thomas Hobbes believed that the exercise of absolute power was both inevitable and appropriate because of our self-interested nature as complex animals. Men like John Locke, by contrast, believed that absolute power was absolutely unnatural. He believed that all men were born with three natural rights—the right to life, the right to liberty and the right to property. Absolute rulers, by their nature, violate these rights, said Locke. He instead advocated a government created by the "will of the governed" because he believed humans were rational beings capable of creating a government that would meet the needs of the many and not the few. Still others, like Jean Jacques Rousseau, were convinced that only a true democracy would keep people in check.

There were many different schools of thought during the Enlightenment about the best form of government. There were also many great thinkers who opted not to prescribe the best form of government but the best function of the government. An influential thinker named Baron de Montesquieu said that any good government should be balanced and that there should be separate branches of government to serve as checks on one another. Sound familiar? Montesquieu was one of the main influences on our founders when crafting our Constitution. Another powerful voice of the Enlightenment was a sharp-witted man named Voltaire. Voltaire was an advocate of equality and human rights and the right to free expression or speech more than anything. He is famous for his quotation, "I despise what you say but I will defend with my life your right to say it." Voltaire's ideas were also profoundly influential in shaping American liberties.

The British colonists came to North America seeking freedom, mainly from religious and political persecution. But they were also seeking more economic opportunity, and when they arrived they enjoyed tremendous freedom to pursue their fortunes. A man by the name of Adam Smith may have influenced our founders and the direction of our nation more than any other Enlightenment figure, even though none of his ideas are directly included in our founding documents. Adam Smith is the father of an economic system called capitalism and he wrote about all his economic ideas in a book called *The Wealth of Nations*. Smith was puzzled by what he saw in countries like France, where the nation itself was quite rich but the people were disturbingly poor. "Why did this wealth gap exist?" Smith asked. The answer he found was in the economic system of the day called *mercantilism*. Mercantilism is an economic system that is heavily regulated by the government for the enrichment of the government.

Smith believed that natural laws governed all things, including economics. Humans, he said, are instinctively motivated to pursue their self interest and to accumulate wealth. Therefore, he said, it is not necessary for governments to regulate commerce or trade because it will happen naturally. Smith supported what is called a *laissez faire* (French for "leave it alone") style of government and believed that governments should not involve themselves in the regulation of economics. This idea of a free market economy or an economic system where the government does not regulate the economy is *capitalism*. In a capitalist system, Smith said that three laws of economics are true all the time in all places for all people. Those laws are: the law of self-interest; the law of competition; and the law of supply and demand. Quite simply, Smith said people's self-interests will cause them to become smart competitors in business, and the flow and supply of trade goods will naturally be set by the demand for those products. Smith saw economics as a natural system which works when left alone and fails only when the government tries to over-complicate it. Our founders agreed.

The American Revolution and the founding of the United States were products of the Enlightenment. Many of our founders were Enlightenment thinkers themselves, including Thomas Jefferson and Benjamin Franklin. They were deeply familiar with the ideas of natural rights, the dangers of absolutism and the need for protection of our precious liberties. So when King George III of England began to violate colonists' sacred rights as promised by the English Bill of Rights, they were inspired by Enlightenment ideals to take action. In their view, the excessive taxation of the colonists violated the promise of no taxation without consent. They believed that their right to petition when wronged had been taken away and they loudly declared the transgressions of King George III in the Declaration of Independence. Brilliant in its brevity, the Declaration of Independence is largely a combination of the style and ideas of the English Bill of Rights with the philosophies of John Locke. Our founders knew their history and they drew on all the best from history in stating the reasons for war against England. Locke said that when people's natural rights are violated by a government, the people *must* rebel and our founders agreed. And so the Declaration of Independence was a statement of cherished principles which were the justification for the American Revolution.

In history, as we have discussed, armed revolution is hard. Rising up against a government and putting lives on the line for the hope of a better life is a great sacrifice. But often what is even harder than the rebellion is figuring out what the new world will look like when the fighting is done. Our founding fathers had a clear idea of what they did not want in a government: an absolute ruler or anyone who could steal away absolute power. And they were armed with all the best wisdom from the Enlightenment and the span of history. Even then, they did not easily create a new nation. Their first attempt at a national government was collected in a document called the Articles of Confederation and it was a disaster. Within a few years of the end of the Revolutionary War, the new America was almost at war with itself because the Articles of Confederation were so full of unforeseen mistakes and pitfalls. America almost fell apart before it ever really came together.

But our founders did not simply give up and decide that Thomas Hobbes was right. They were unwilling to accept defeat after their hard-fought victory over the British, so they came back together at the Constitutional Convention in 1789 to try again to capture the sprit of balance and liberty in a workable government "of the people, by the people and for the people." Inspired this time by the ideas of balanced government put forth by Montesquieu, the U.S. Constitution created the United States of America as it is today. Some of the debates at the Constitutional Convention would have made the political fights of today look like child's play because even wise and inspired men disagreed ferociously about what this nation should look like. It took two years to win final approval or ratification of the Constitution and our government was only made official after adding crucial protections for citizens, which channeled the voice of Voltaire and many of the rights first promised by the English Bill of Rights more than 100 years before.

PRIMARY SOURCES – THE ENLIGHTENMENT

Immanuel Kant, *What Is Enlightenment?*, 1784 CE

Reading and Discussion Questions

1. According to Kant, why do some people choose to "remain minors all their lives?" What do people like about remaining child-like even after they are grown?
2. Why does Kant believe it is more possible for the public to become enlightened than the individual?
3. How does Kant answer the question "Are we living in an enlightened age?"
4. Would you rather have the grown-up power of knowledge or the ease of ignorant youth? Explain your answer.

In 1784, the German philosopher Immanuel Kant wrote the following essay for a German newspaper in response to the question, "What is Enlightenment?" Kant's essay became a famous declaration of the period known as the Enlightenment because it captures the spirit of the age. Kant was a product of both the Scientific Revolution and the Enlightenment. His most influential work, Critique of Pure Reason, *builds on the work of earlier empiricists and marries ideas about rational thought and philosophy to further hone the way Europeans thought about human existence.*

Kant shared the views of men like Rene Descartes who believed that it is man's ability to reason that makes him divinely human. "I think, therefore I am," said Descartes. While Kant agreed that man's intellect is what makes him sublime, he observed that most men choose not to think and instead prefer the state of ignorant bliss, which he calls "nonage." He believed that by choosing to remain intellectually childlike, humanity could not ever realize its full potential. He issued this challenge to humanity – Sapere aude! ("Dare to Know"). It is easier to remain children, but it is empowering to be wise.

Enlightenment is man's emergence from his self-imposed nonage [immaturity]. Nonage is the inability to use one's own understanding without another's guidance. This nonage is self-imposed if its cause lies not in lack of understanding but in indecision and lack of courage to use one's own mind without another's guidance. Dare to know! (Sapere aude.) "Have the courage to use your own understanding," is therefore the motto of the enlightenment.

Laziness and cowardice are the reasons why such a large part of mankind gladly remain minors all their lives, long after nature has freed them from external guidance. They are the reasons why it is so easy for others to set themselves up as guardians. It is so comfortable to be a minor. If I have a book that thinks for me, a pastor who acts as my conscience, a physician who prescribes my diet, and so on--then I have no need to exert myself. I have no need to think, if only I can pay; others will take care of that disagreeable business for me. Those guardians who have kindly taken supervision upon themselves see to it that the overwhelming majority of mankind--among them the entire fair sex--should consider the step to maturity, not only as hard, but as extremely dangerous. First, these guardians make their domestic cattle stupid and carefully prevent the docile creatures from taking a single step without the leading-strings to which they have fastened them. Then they show them the danger that would threaten them if they should try to walk by themselves. Now this danger is really not very great; after stumbling a few times they would, at last, learn to walk. However, examples of such failures intimidate and generally discourage all further attempts.

Thus it is very difficult for the individual to work himself out of the nonage which has become almost second nature to him. He has even grown to like it, and is at first really incapable of using his own understanding because he has never been permitted to try it. It is more nearly possible, however, for the public to enlighten itself; indeed, if it is only given freedom, enlightenment is almost inevitable. There will always be a few independent thinkers, even among the self-appointed guardians of the multitude. Once such men have thrown off the yoke of nonage, they will spread about them the spirit of a reasonable appreciation of man's value and of his duty to think for himself.

This enlightenment requires nothing but freedom--and the most innocent of all that may be called "freedom": freedom to make public use of one's reason in all matters. Now I hear the cry from all sides: "Do not argue!" The officer says: "Do not argue-- drill!" The tax collector: "Do not argue--pay!" The pastor: "Do not argue--believe!" The ruler says: "Do not argue--obey!" We find restrictions on freedom everywhere. But which restriction is harmful to enlightenment? Which restriction is innocent, and which advances enlightenment? I reply: the public use of one's reason must be free at all times, and this alone can bring enlightenment to mankind.

A man may postpone his own enlightenment, but only for a limited period of time. And to give up enlightenment altogether, either for oneself or one's descendants, is to violate and to trample upon the sacred rights of man..

When we ask, Are we now living in an enlightened age? the answer is, No, but we live in an age of enlightenment. As matters now stand it is still far from true that men are already capable of using their own reason confidently and correctly without external guidance. Still, we have some obvious indications that the field of working toward the goal [of religious truth] is now opened. What is more, the hindrances against general enlightenment or the emergence from self-imposed nonage are gradually diminishing. In this respect this is the age of the enlightenment.

Denis Diderot, *Encyclopédie*, 1751 CE

Reading and Discussion Questions
  1. What is the aim of this work, according to the author?
  2. What are the dangers of fanaticism?
  3. How is history useful, according to the reading?
  4. Why was the publication of the Encyclopedia such a vital step in the philosophes' hopes for reform?
  5. What political ideals are reflected in the Encyclopedia?
  6. Why was freedom of the press of such significance to the philosophes?

Denis Diderot took on and oversaw one of the most ambitious intellectual works ever undertaken. As he said in his own words, he wanted to "change the way people think" by presenting them with the full collection of human knowledge. He was the Editor-in-Chief and the primary author of the world's first Encyclopédie. *Unlike encyclopedias of today that present unbiased, factual information about everything from aardvarks to zeppelins, Diderot's* Encyclopédie *included lengthy intellectual essays on topics like "Fanaticism" and "Intolerance," and they advanced Enlightenment viewpoints on government, humanity and education. The production of* Encyclopédie *was put on hold on several occasions for fear that it included dangerous, anti-government ideas that might influence the people against their rulers. The first volume of the work was completed in 1751 and represented the most comprehensive collection of human wisdom ever attempted. Of the final work Diderot said, "This work will surely produce in time a revolution in the minds of man, and I hope that tyrants, oppressors, fanatics, and the intolerant will not gain thereby. We shall have served humanity."*

Encyclopedia . . . In truth, the aim of an encyclopedia is to collect all the knowledge scattered over the face of the earth, to present its general outlines and structure to the men with whom we live, and to transmit this to those who will come after us, so that the work of past centuries may be useful to the following centuries, that our children, by becoming more educated, may at the same time become more virtuous and happier, and that we may not die without having deserved well of the human race. . . . We have seen that our Encyclopedia could only have been the endeavor of a philosophical century. . . I have said that it could only belong to a philosophical age to attempt an encyclopedia; and I have said this because such a work constantly demands more intellectual daring than is commonly found in [less courageous periods]. All things must be examined, debated, investigated without exception and without regard for anyone's feelings. . . .

Fanaticism . . . is blind and passionate zeal born of superstitious opinions, causing people to commit ridiculous, unjust, and cruel actions, not only without any shame or remorse, but even with a kind of joy and comfort. Fanaticism, therefore, is only superstition put into practice. . . .Fanaticism has done much more harm to the world than impiety. What do impious people claim? To free themselves of a yoke, while fanatics want to extend their chains over all the earth. Infernal zealomania! . . .

Government . . . The good of the people must be the great purpose of the government. The governors are appointed to fulfill it; and the civil constitution that invests them with this power is bound therein by the laws of nature and by the law of reason, which has determined that purpose in any form of government as the cause of its welfare. The greatest good of the people is its liberty. Liberty is to the body of the state what health is to each individual; without health man cannot enjoy pleasure; without liberty the state of welfare is excluded from nations. A patriotic governor will therefore see that the right to defend and to maintain liberty is the most sacred of his duties. . . .

History . . . On the usefulness of history. The advantage consists of the comparison that a statesman or a citizen can make of foreign laws, morals, and customs with those of his country. This is what stimulates modern nations to surpass one another in the arts, in commerce, and in agriculture. The great mistakes of the past are useful in all areas. We cannot describe too often the crimes and misfortunes caused by absurd quarrels. It is certain that by refreshing our memory of these quarrels, we prevent a repetition of them. . . .

Humanity . . . is a benevolent feeling for all men, which hardly inflames anyone without a great and sensitive soul. This sublime and noble enthusiasm is troubled by the pains of other people and by the necessity to alleviate them. With these sentiments an individual would wish to cover the entire universe in order to abolish slavery, superstition, vice, and misfortune. . . .

Intolerance . . . Any method that would tend to stir up men, to arm nations, and to soak the earth with blood is impious. It is impious to want to impose laws upon man's conscience: this is a universal rule of conduct. People must be enlightened and not constrained. . . .

Peace . . . War is the fruit of man's depravity; it is a convulsive and violent sickness of the body politic. . . .If reason governed men and had the influence over the heads of nations that it deserves, we would never see them inconsiderately surrender themselves to the fury of war; they would not show that ferocity that characterizes wild beasts. . .

Political Authority . . .No man has received from nature the right to command others. Liberty is a gift from heaven, and each individual of the same species has the right to enjoy it as soon as he enjoys the use of reason. . . .The prince owes to his very subjects the authority that he has over them; and this authority is limited by the laws of nature and the state. The laws of nature and the state are the conditions under which they have submitted or are supposed to have submitted to its government. . . .Moreover the government, although hereditary in a family and placed in the hands of one person, is not private property, but public property that consequently can never be taken from the people, to whom it belongs exclusively, fundamentally, and as a freehold. Consequently it is always the people who make the lease or the agreement: they always intervene in the contract that adjudges its exercise. It is not the state that belongs to the prince, it is the prince who belongs to the state. . . .

The Press . . . ask if freedom of the press is advantageous or prejudicial to a state. The answer is not difficult. It is of the greatest importance to conserve this practice in all states founded on liberty. I would even say that the disadvantages of this liberty are so inconsiderable compared to its advantages that this ought to be the common right of the universe, and it is certainly advisable to authorize its practice in all governments. . . .

John Locke, *Second Treatise on Government*, 1690 CE

Reading and Discussion Questions

1. According to Locke, what was the consequence of entering into a social contract?
2. According to Locke, what is the difference between civil society and the state of nature?
3. Why did Locke believe that absolute monarchy was not a legitimate form of government?
4. According to Locke, what circumstances give people the right to revolt and overthrow a government or ruler?
5. How did Locke's views differ from those of Thomas Hobbes on man in a state of nature and on the ideal form of government?

John Locke is one of the most influential philosophers of the Enlightenment. He was an empiricist, like many scientists of the age, and believed that all knowledge comes from direct experience. Locke was influential in shaping ideas of the 18th century on things like human nature and identity, and came up with the idea of the tabula rasa ("blank slate"), which is the idea that men are born as blank canvases and become a product of their life experiences. This was a new idea and a departure from existing thought at the time which said that all humans came into the world with certain pre-formed or innate ideas. Locke was also one of the most important political philosophers of the age. He is one of the most important influences on Enlightenment thinkers like Voltaire and Jean Jacques Rousseau. Perhaps his most powerful influence, though, was on the founders of the United States, including Thomas Jefferson, who included much of Locke's philosophy in writing the Declaration of Independence.

Chapter II. Of the State of Nature.

Sec. 4. TO understand political power right, and derive it from its original, we must consider, what state all men are naturally in, and that is, a state of perfect freedom to order their actions, and dispose of their possessions and persons, as they think fit, within the bounds of the law of nature, without asking leave, or depending upon the will of any other man.

A state also of equality, wherein all the power and jurisdiction is reciprocal, no one having more than another; there being nothing more evident, than that creatures of the same species and rank, promiscuously born to all the same advantages of nature, and the use of the same faculties, should also be equal one amongst another without subordination or subjection, unless the lord and master of them all should, by any manifest declaration of his will, set one above another, and confer on him, by an evident and clear appointment, an undoubted right to dominion and sovereignty.

Sec. 7. And that all men may be restrained from invading others rights, and from doing hurt to one another, and the law of nature be observed, which willeth the peace and preservation of all mankind, the execution of the law of nature is, in that state, put into every man's hands, whereby every one has a right to punish the transgressors of that law to such a degree, as may hinder its violation: for the law of nature would, as all

273

other laws that concern men in this world 'be in vain, if there were no body that in the state of nature had a power to execute that law, and thereby preserve the innocent and restrain offenders. And if any one in the state of nature may punish another for any evil he has done, every one may do so: for in that state of perfect equality, where naturally there is no superiority or jurisdiction of one over another, what any may do in prosecution of that law, every one must needs have a right to do.

Sec. 8. And thus, in the state of nature, one man comes by a power over another; but yet no absolute or arbitrary power, to use a criminal, when he has got him in his hands, according to the passionate heats, or boundless extravagancy of his own will; but only to retribute to him, so far as calm reason and conscience dictate, what is proportionate to his transgression, which is so much as may serve for reparation and restraint: for these two are the only reasons, why one man may lawfully do harm to another, which is that we call punishment. In transgressing the law of nature, the offender declares himself to live by another rule than that of reason and common equity, which is that measure God has set to the actions of men, for their mutual security; and so he becomes dangerous to mankind, the tye, which is to secure them from injury and violence, being slighted and broken by him. Which being a trespass against the whole species, and the peace and safety of it, provided for by the law of nature, every man upon this score, by the right he hath to preserve mankind in general, may restrain, or where it is necessary, destroy things noxious to them, and so may bring such evil on any one, who hath transgressed that law, as may make him repent the doing of it, and thereby deter him, and by his example others, from doing the like mischief. And in the case, and upon this ground, every man hat a right to punish the offender and be executioner of the law of nature.

CHAP. VII. Of Political or Civil Society.

Sec. 87. Man being born, as has been proved, with a title to perfect freedom, and an uncontrolled enjoyment of all the rights and privileges of the law of nature, equally with any other man, or number of men in the world, hath by nature a power, not only to preserve his property, that is, his life, liberty and estate, against the injuries and attempts of other men; but to judge of, and punish the breaches of that law in others, as he is persuaded the offence deserves, even with death itself, in crimes where the heinousness of the fact, in his opinion, requires it. But because no political society can be, nor subsist, without having in itself the power to preserve the property, and in order thereunto, punish the offences of all those of that society; there, and there only is political society, where every one of the members hath quitted this natural power, resigned it up into the hands of the community in all cases that exclude him not from appealing for protection to the law established by it.

And thus all private judgment of every particular member being excluded, the community comes to be umpire, by settled standing rules, indifferent, and the same to all parties; and by men having authority from the community, for the execution of those rules, decides all the differences that may happen between any members of that society concerning any matter of right; and punishes those offences which any member hath committed against the society, with such penalties as the law has established: whereby it is easy to discern, who are, and who are not, in political society together. Those who are united into one body, and have a common established law and judicature to appeal to, with authority to decide controversies between them, and punish offenders, are in civil society one with another: but those who have no such common appeal, I mean on earth, are still in the state of nature, each being, where there is no other, judge for himself, and executioner; which is, as I have before shown it, the perfect state of nature.

Sec. 90. Hence it is evident, that absolute monarchy, which by some men is counted the only government in the world, is indeed inconsistent with civil society, and so can be no form of civil-government at all: for the end of civil society, being to avoid, and remedy those inconveniencies of the state of nature, which necessarily follow from every man's being judge in his own case, by setting up a known authority, to which every one of that society may appeal upon any injury received, or controversy that may arise, and which every one of the* society ought to obey; where-ever any persons are, who have not such an authority to appeal to, for the decision of any difference between them, there those persons are still in the state of nature; and so is every absolute prince, in respect of those who are under his dominion.

CHAP. XIX. Of the Dissolution of Government.

Sec. 222. The reason why men enter into society, is the preservation of their property; and the end why they choose and authorize a legislative, is, that there may be laws made, and rules set, as guards and fences to the properties of all the members of the society, to limit the power, and moderate the dominion, of every part and member of the society: for since it can never be supposed to be the will of the society, that the legislative should have a power to destroy that which every one designs to secure, by entering into society, and for which the people submitted themselves to legislators of their own making; whenever the legislators endeavor to take away, and destroy the property of the people, or to reduce them to slavery under arbitrary power, they put themselves into a state of war with the people, who are thereupon absolved from any farther obedience, and are left to the common refuge, which God hath provided for all men, against force and violence.

Whensoever therefore the legislative shall transgress this fundamental rule of society; and either by ambition, fear, folly or corruption, endeavor to grasp themselves, or put into the hands of any other, an absolute power over the lives, liberties, and estates of the people; by this breach of trust they forfeit the power the people had put into their hands for quite contrary ends, and it devolves to the people, who have a right to resume their original liberty, and, by the establishment of a new legislative, (such as they shall think fit) provide for their own safety and security, which is the end for which they are in society.

Jean Jacques Rousseau, *The Social Contract*, 1762 CE

Reading and Discussion Questions
1. What did Jean Jacques Rousseau mean by the "general will?" What function did it serve in his political theory?
2. What is the "social compact" or the social contract as Rousseau explains it?
3. What is "civil liberty" and how is it different than "natural liberty?"
4. What does man get when he leaves his natural state and enters into civil society?
5. Rousseau talks about the dangers of factions or what he calls partial associations in decision-making. What do these groups sound like in the modern sense, and why are they a hindrance to sound decision-making?
6. Based on your understanding of this reading, what type of government did Rousseau support and why?

Jean-Jacques Rousseau was an influential Enlightenment philosopher from Geneva, Switzerland but he spent all his time in France and is often mistaken, in history, as a Frenchman. He wrote extensively on everything from the right kind of education, in his famous book Emile, *to the best form of government, in works like* Discourse on Inequality *and the* Social Contract. *It is in the* Social Contract *that we see Rousseau's most enduring contributions to social and political theory, which is his idea of the "general will." This concept is most easily understood as the "common interest" or the "general welfare" which he said should be both the means and the ends of good government. Like Hobbes, Rousseau believed that men worked in their own self-interest and that those self-interests caused conflict. Hobbes and he disagreed on how to prevent such conflict, which was basic to human nature. Hobbes said one man should force us all into obedience. Rousseau disagreed.*

He believed it was unnatural for one self-interested ruler to economically enslave all other self-interested humans for his own benefit. Instead, he believed that all men should make up the political body to create the "general will." He proposed that each man give up an equal share of his natural freedom to the larger group and, thus, would enjoy different freedoms because of the security and collective will of the group. Men must sometimes be "forced to be free" he argued, and he said that the only check on one man's self-interest is that he knows he benefits more from the general will than he would benefit from his own individual pursuits. In the end, it is in man's self-interest to be part of the collective governing group.

[To rulers who argued that they provided security for their subjects, Rousseau responded as follows:]

It will be said that the despot assures his subjects civil tranquility. Granted; but what do they gain, if the wars his ambition brings down upon them, his insatiable avidity, and the vexatious conduct of his ministers press harder on them than their own dissensions would have done? What do they gain, if the very tranquility they enjoy is one of their miseries? Tranquility is found also in dungeons; but is that enough to make them desirable places to live in? The Greeks imprisoned in the cave of the Cyclops lived there very tranquilly, while they were awaiting their turn to be devoured. . . .

To renounce liberty is to renounce being a man, to surrender the rights of humanity and even its duties. Such a renunciation is incompatible with man's nature; to remove all liberty from his will is to remove all morality from his acts. I suppose men to have reached the point at which the obstacles in the way of their preservation in the state of nature [are] greater than the resources at the disposal of each individual for his maintenance in that state. That primitive condition can then subsist no longer; and the human race would perish unless it changed its manner of existence. . . .

This sum of forces can arise only where several persons come together; but, as the force and liberty of each man are the chief instruments of his self-preservation, how can he pledge them without harming his own interests, and neglecting the care he owes to himself? This difficulty, in its bearing on my present subject, may be stated in the following terms: "The problem is to find a form of association which will defend and protect with the whole common force the person and goods of each associate, and in which each, while uniting himself with all, may still obey himself alone, and remain as free as before." This is the fundamental problem of which the Social Contract provides the solution.

The clauses of this contract . . . properly understood, may be reduced to one—the total alienation of each associate, together with all his rights, to the whole community; for, in the first place, as each gives himself absolutely, the conditions are the same for all; Each man, in giving himself to all, gives himself to nobody; and as there is no associate over which he does not acquire the same right as he yields others over himself, he gains an equivalent for everything he loses, and an increase of force for the preservation of what he has.

If then we discard from the social compact what is not of its essence, we shall find that it reduces itself to the following terms: "Each of us puts his person and all his power in common under the supreme direction of the general will, and, so joined personality of each contracting party, this act of association creates a moral and collective body, composed of as many members as the assembly contains voters, and receiving from this act its unity, its common identity, its life, and its will. . . .

In order then that the social compact may not be an empty formula, it tacitly includes the undertaking, which alone can give force to the rest, that whoever refuses to obey the general will shall be compelled to do so by the whole body. This means nothing less than that he will be forced to be free; for this is the condition which, by giving each citizen to his country, secures him against all personal dependence. In this lies the key to the working of the political machine; this alone legitimizes civil undertakings, which, without it, would be absurd, tyrannical, and liable to the most frightful abuses.

The passage from the state of nature to the civil state produces a very remarkable change in man, by substituting justice for instinct in his conduct, and giving his actions the morality they had formerly lacked. Then only, when the voice of duty takes the place of physical impulses and right of appetite, does man, who so far had considered only himself, find that he is forced to act on different principles, and to consult his reason before listening to his inclinations.

Let us draw up the whole account in terms easily commensurable. What man loses by the social contract is his natural liberty and an unlimited right to everything he tries to get and succeeds in getting; what he gains is civil liberty. If we are to avoid mistake in weighing one against the other, we must clearly distinguish natural liberty, which is bounded only by the strength of the individual, from civil liberty, which is limited by the general will. We might, over and above all this, add, to what man acquires in the civil state, moral liberty, which alone makes him truly master of himself; for the mere impulse of appetite is slavery, while obedience to a law which we prescribe to ourselves is liberty. . . . The first and most important deduction from the principles we have so far laid down is that the general will alone can direct the State according to the object for which it was instituted, i.e. the common good.

It follows from what has gone before that the general will is always right and tends to the public advantage; but it does not follow that the deliberations of the people are always equally correct. Our will is always for our own good, but we do not always see what that is; the people is never corrupted, but it is often deceived, and on such occasions only does it seem to will what is bad.

If, when the people, being furnished with adequate information, held its deliberations, the citizens had no communication one with another, the grand total of the small differences would always give the general will, and the decision would always be good. But when factions arise, and partial associations are formed at the expense of the great association, the will of each of these associations becomes general in relation to its members, while it remains particular in relation to the State: it may then be said that there are no longer as many votes as there are men, but only as many as there are associations. The differences become less numerous and give a less general result. Lastly, when one of these associations is so great as to prevail over all the rest, the result is no longer a sum of small differences, but a single difference; in this case there is no longer a general will, and the opinion which prevails is purely particular.

It is therefore essential, if the general will is to be able to express itself, that there should be no partial society [factions] within the State, and that each citizen should think only his own thoughts. . . . But if there are partial societies, it is best to have as many as possible and to prevent them from being unequal. . . . These precautions are the only ones that can guarantee that the general will shall be always enlightened, and that the people shall in no way deceive itself.

Montesquieu, *The Spirit of the Laws*, 1748 CE

Reading and Discussion Questions
   1. Why does Montesquieu think it is dangerous for legislative and executive power to be combined or held by one person?
   2. Why did Montesquieu think the legislature should not assemble itself? Who should convene it and why?
   3. What are the natural limits on executive power, according to Montesquieu, or why was he less concerned with limiting executive power than legislative power?
   4. Why should the army be commanded by the executive and not the legislature, according to Montesquieu?
   5. According to this document, what government does Montesquieu most admire as a model for other nations?

Charles de Secondat, Baron de Montesquieu was a French nobleman and one of the most influential political thinkers in history. He did extensive research on political theory and studied different political systems throughout history and in his own time. He presented his ideas for the most workable form of government in his book, The Spirit of the Laws, *which was published in 1748.*

Montesquieu's ideas for the best form of government have been embraced in nations around the world, including the United States. One of Montesquieu's most influential ideas was that of a balance of powers, and he said that a government with three branches was the most likely to succeed. He said governments serve three types of functions—legislative, executive and judicial, and in order to avoid corruption or abuse of power, these powers should never be in the hands of one man or one group. He proposed three distinct branches of government, and it was Montesquieu's ideas more than any other that guided our Founding Fathers when they were crafting the U.S. Constitution in 1787.

In every government there are three sorts of power: the legislative, the executive and the judicial.

The first power, the legislature, enacts temporary or perpetual laws, and amends or repeals those that have been already enacted. The second power makes peace or war, sends or receives embassies; establishes the public security, and provides against invasions. The third power punishes criminals, or determines the disputes that arise between individuals. The latter we shall call the judiciary power, and the second simply the executive power of the state.

The political liberty of the subject is a tranquility of mind, arising from the opinion each person has of his safety. In order to have this liberty, it is required that the government be so constituted as one man need not be afraid of another.

When the legislative and executive powers are united in the same person, or in the same body of magistrates, there can be no liberty; because apprehensions may arise, lest the same monarch or senate should enact tyrannical laws, to execute them in a tyrannical manner.

Again, there is no liberty, if the power of judging be not separated from the legislative and executive powers. Were it joined with the legislative, the life and liberty of the subject would be exposed to arbitrary control, for the judge would then be the legislator. Were it joined to the executive power, the judge might behave with all the violence of an oppressor.

There would be an end of every thing were the same man to exercise those three powers that of enacting laws, that of executing the public resolutions, and that of judging the crimes or differences of individuals.

Many of the princes of Europe, who want absolute power, have constantly set out to unite in their own persons, all the branches of government and all the great offices of state.

The executive power ought to be in the hands of a monarch; because this branch of government, which has always need of expedition, is better administered by one than by many: Whereas, whatever depends on the legislative power, is oftentimes better regulated by many than by a single person.

When different legislative bodies succeed one another, the people who have a bad opinion of that which is actually sitting, may reasonably entertain some hopes of the next: But were it to be always the same body, the people, upon seeing it once corrupted, would no longer expect any good from its laws; and of course they would either become desperate, or fall into a state of indolence.

The legislative body should not assemble of itself. For a body is supposed to have no will but when it is assembled; and besides, were it not to assemble unanimously, it would be impossible to determine which was really the legislative body, the part assembled, or the other. And if it had a right to prorogue itself, it might happen never to be prorogued; which would be extremely dangerous, in case it should ever attempt to encroach on the executive power. Besides, there are seasons, some of which are more proper than others, for assembling the legislative body: It is fit therefore that the executive power should regulate the time of convening, as well as the duration of those assemblies, according to the circumstances and exigencies of state known to itself.

Were the executive power not to have a right of putting a stop to the encroachments of the legislative body, the latter would become despotic; for as it might arrogate to itself what authority it pleased, it would soon destroy all the other powers.

But it is not proper, on the other hand, that the legislative power should have a right to stop the executive. For as the execution has its natural limits, it is useless to confine it; besides, the executive power is generally employed in momentary operations.

But if the legislative power in a free government ought to have no right to stop the executive, it has a right, and ought to have the means of examining in what manner its laws have been executed.

The legislative body ought not to have a power of judging the person, nor of course the conduct of him who is entrusted with the executive power. His person should be sacred, because as it is necessary for the good of the state to prevent the legislative body from rendering themselves arbitrary, the moment he is accused or tried, there is an end of liberty.

To prevent the executive power from being able to oppress, it is requisite, that the armies, with which it is entrusted, should consist of the people, and have the same spirit as the people, as was the case at Rome.

When once an army is established, it ought not to depend immediately on the legislative, but on the executive power, and this from the very nature of the thing; its business consisting more in action than in deliberation.

From a manner of thinking that prevails amongst mankind, they set a higher value upon courage than timorousness, on activity than prudence, on strength than counsel. Hence, the army will ever despise a senate, and respect their own officers. They will naturally slight the orders sent them by a body of men, whom they look upon as cowards, and therefore unworthy to command them.

Whoever shall read the admirable treatise of Tacitus on the manners of the Germans, will find that it is from them the English have borrowed the idea of their political government. This beautiful system was invented first in the woods.

As all human things have an end, the state we are speaking of will lose its liberty, it will perish. Have not Rome, Sparta, and Carthage perished? It will perish when the legislative power shall be more corrupted than the executive.

It is not my business to examine whether the English actually enjoy this liberty, or not. It is sufficient for my purpose to observe, that it is established by their laws; and I inquire no further.

Voltaire, *A Treatise on Toleration, 1763 CE*

Reading and Discussion Questions

1. What did Voltaire mean by the line, "If you have two religions in your countries, they will cut each other's throat; if you have thirty religions, they will dwell in peace."

2. What does Voltaire mean by the following passage: "Of all religions, the Christian is without doubt the one which should inspire tolerance most, although up to now the Christians have been the most intolerant of all men."

3. Which is more natural to Voltaire, tolerance or intolerance?

4. Does Voltaire make a convincing argument for tolerance? Why or why not?

François-Marie Arouet, or Voltaire, was born in 1694 in Paris, France, and lived and worked there for his entire life. Throughout his 83 years of life, Voltaire wrote numerous philosophical works, works in history, plays, and is considered one of the greatest minds of the French Enlightenment. He is known as a defender of religious freedom, self-expression, civil liberties and social reform. He was also fighting against the limitations of censorship, religious dogma, intolerance, and the institutions of his time. His works heavily influenced both the French and the American revolutions. Voltaire's writings were widely embraced by revolutionary thinkers because they challenged the common beliefs of the age.

Voltaire was a fierce critic of religious traditions but that does not mean he was unreligious. He asserted that the existence of God was a question of reason and observation rather than of faith. In his words, "It is perfectly evident to my mind that there exists a necessary, eternal, supreme, and intelligent being. This is no matter of faith, but of reason." He therefore favored an understanding of God beyond institutionalized religion. In A Treatise on Toleration, Voltaire said that all men are brothers, regardless of religion, as they are the same creature created by the same God.

WHAT is tolerance? It is the consequence of humanity. We are all formed of frailty and error; let us pardon reciprocally each other's folly--that is the first law of nature.

It is clear that the individual who persecutes a man, his brother, because he is not of the same opinion, is a monster. That admits of no difficulty. But the government! But the magistrates! But the princes! How do they treat those who have another worship than theirs?

Madmen, who have never been able to give worship to the God who made you! You have been told it already, and there is nothing else to tell you-if you have two religions in your countries, they will cut each other's throat ; if you have thirty religions, they will dwell in peace.

Of all religions, the Christian is without doubt the one which should inspire tolerance most, although up to now the Christians have been the most intolerant of all men. The Christian Church was divided in its cradle, and was divided even in the persecutions which under the first emperors it sometimes endured.

This horrible discord, which has lasted for so many centuries, is a very striking lesson that we should pardon each other's errors; discord is the great ill of mankind; and tolerance is the only remedy for it.

There is nobody who is not in agreement with this truth, whether he meditates soberly in his study, or peaceably examines the truth with his friends. Why then do the same men who admit in private indulgence, kindness, justice, rise in public with so much fury against these virtues? Why? It is that their own interest is their god, and that they sacrifice everything to this monster that they worship.

And today when so many sects make a balance of power, what course to take with them? Every sect, as one knows, is a ground of error; there are no sects of geometers, algebraists, arithmeticians, because all the propositions of geometry, algebra and arithmetic are true. In every other science one may be deceived. What Christian theologian would dare say seriously that he is sure of his case?

If it were permitted to reason consistently in religious matters, it is clear that we all ought to become Jews, because Jesus Christ our Saviour was born a Jew, lived a Jew, died a Jew, and that he said expressly that he was accomplishing, that he was fulfilling the Jewish religion. But it is clearer still that we ought to be tolerant of one another, because we are all weak, inconsistent, liable to fickleness and error. Shall a reed laid low in the mud by the wind say to a fellow reed fallen in the opposite direction: "Crawl as I crawl, wretch, or I shall petition that you be torn up by the roots and burned? "

Natural law is that indicated to men by nature. You have reared a child; he owes you respect as a father, gratitude as a benefactor. You have a right to the products of the soil that you have cultivated with your own hands. You have given or received a promise; it must be kept.

Human law must in every case be based on natural law. All over the earth the great principle of both is: Do not unto others what you would that they do not unto you. Now, in virtue of this principle, one man cannot say to another: "Believe what I believe, and what thou canst not believe, or thou shalt perish." Thus do men speak in Portugal, Spain, and Goa. In some other countries they are now content to say: "Believe, or I detest thee; believe, or I will do thee all the harm I can. Monster, thou sharest not my religion, and therefore hast no religion; thou shalt be a thing of horror to thy neighbours, thy city, and thy province."

The supposed right of intolerance is absurd and barbaric. It is the right of the tiger; nay, it is far worse, for tigers do but tear in order to have food, while we destroy each other for words.

Cesare Beccaria, *On Crimes and Punishments*, 1764 CE

Reading and Discussion Questions
1. What is the intent or purpose of laws, according to Beccaria?
2. How are Beccaria's ideas related to those of Montesquieu? What task did Montesquieu fail to do in his own writings, according to Beccaria?
3. Why do rulers punish?
4. How does Beccaria define justice?
5. What is the purpose of punishments, according to Chapter XII?
6. Why did Beccaria say it was more important for punishments to be certain than to be severe?
7. Do you agree or disagree with Beccaria's ideas on crime and punishment? Explain.

Cesare Beccaria was an Italian politician and legal philosopher who is considered the father of modern criminal justice. He was an enthusiastic student of the Enlightenment and was particularly fond of the work of Baron de Montesquieu. He believed that Montesquieu had proposed solid ideas for the most workable political system but believed that he had overlooked a crucial element in his plans for the ideal government—the relationship between crime and punishment. The lack of solid theory on punishment and justice in previous work by Enlightenment philosophers prompted Beccaria to write On Crimes and Punishments, *which has become a cornerstone of criminal justice and penology, or the study of punishments. His work heavily influenced the founders of the United States and the creation of other criminal justice systems around the world.*

In every human society, there is an effort continually tending to confer on one part the height of power and happiness, and to reduce the other to the extreme of weakness and misery. The intent of good laws is to oppose this effort, and to diffuse their influence universally, and equally. But men generally abandon the care of their most important

concerns to the uncertain prudence and discretion of those, whose interest it is to reject the best, and wisest institutions; and it is not till they have been led into a thousand mistakes in matters, the most essential to their lives and liberties, and are weary of suffering, that they can be induced to apply a remedy to the evils, with which they are oppressed.

The art of printing has diffused the knowledge of those philosophical truths, by which the relations between sovereigns and their subjects, and between nations, are discovered. By this knowledge, commerce is animated, and there has sprung up a spirit of emulation, and industry, worthy of rational beings. These are the produce of this enlightened age; but the cruelty of punishments, and the irregularity of proceeding in criminal cases, has hardly ever been called in question.

Surely, the groans of the weak, sacrificed to the cruel ignorance, and indolence of the powerful; the barbarous torments lavished, and multiplied with useless severity, for crimes either not proved, or in their nature impossible; the filth and horrors of a prison, increased by the most cruel tormentor of the miserable, uncertainty, ought to have roused the attention of those whose business is to direct the opinions of mankind. The immortal Montesquieu has but slightly touched on this subject. Truth, which is eternally the same, has obliged me to follow the steps of that great man.

Chapter II: Of the Right to Punish

Every punishment, which does not arise from absolute necessity, says the great Montesquieu, is tyrannical. A proposition which may be made more general, thus. Every act of authority of one man over another, for which there is not an absolute necessity, is tyrannical. It is upon this then, that the ruler's right to punish crimes is founded: that is, upon the necessity of defending the public liberty from the abuses of individuals.

Observe, that by justice I understand nothing more, than that bond, which is necessary to keep the interest of individuals united: without which, men would return to their original state of barbarity. All punishments which exceed the necessity of preserving this bond, are in their nature unjust. . . .

Chapter VI: Of the Proportion between Crimes and Punishments

It is not only the common interest of mankind, that crimes should not be committed, but that crimes of every kind should be less frequent, in proportion to the evil they produce to society. Therefore, the means made use of by the legislature to prevent crimes, should be more powerful, in proportion as they are destructive of the public safety and happiness, and as the inducements to commit them are stronger. Therefore there ought to be a fixed proportion between crimes and punishments.

Chapter XII: Of the Intent of Punishments

From the foregoing considerations it is evident, that the intent of punishments, is not to torment a sensible being, nor to undo a crime already committed. Is it possible that torments and useless cruelty, the instrument of furious fanaticism, or the impotency of tyrants, can be authorized by a political body? Which, so far from being influences by passion, should be the cool moderator of the passions of individuals. Can the groans of a tortured wretch recall the time past, or reverse the crime he has committed?

The end of punishment, therefore, is no other, than to prevent the criminal from doing further injury to society, and to prevent others from committing the like offence. Such punishments, therefore, and such a mode of inflicting them, ought to be chosen, as will make the strongest and most lasting impression on the minds of others, with the least torment to the body of the criminal.

Chapter XIX: Of the Advantage of Immediate Punishment

The more immediately after the commission of a crime, a punishment is inflicted, the more just and useful it will be. It will be more just, because it spares the criminal the cruel and superfluous torment of uncertainty: and because the loss of liberty, being a punishment, ought to be inflicted before condemnation, but for as short a time as possible. . . . An immediate punishment is more useful: because the smaller the interval of time between the punishment and the crime, the stronger and more lasting will be the association of the two ideas of Crime and Punishment: so that they may be considered, one as the cause, and the other as the unavoidable and necessary effect.

285

Chapter XXVII: Of the Mildness of Punishments

Crimes are more effectively prevented by the certainty, than the severity of punishment. The certainty of small punishment will make a stronger impression, than the fear of one more severe.

If punishments be very severe, men are naturally led to the perpetration of other crimes, to avoid the punishment due to the first. The countries and times most notorious for severity of punishments, were always those in which the most bloody and inhuman actions and most atrocious crimes were committed; for the hand of the legislator and the assassin were directed by the same spirit of ferocity. In proportion as punishments become more cruel, the minds of men, as a fluid rises to the same height with that which surrounds it, grow hardened and insensible. That a punishment may produce the effect required, it is sufficient that the evil it occasions should exceed the good expected from the crime. All severity beyond this is superfluous, and therefore tyrannical.

Madame du Châtelet, *An Appeal for Female Education*, 1741 CE

Reading and Discussion Questions
1. What is the author's criticism about the status quo at the time she wrote this appeal?
2. What is the author's appeal or wish? What does she want to be different in the world in the future?

Gabrielle Emilie Le Tonnelier de Breteuil du Châtelet was the daughter of a Parisian nobleman and one of the few women in 18th century France who had a high level of education. She was known by most simply as Madame du Chatelet. Because women were not allowed to have a formal education, her father hired private tutors for her to cultivate what he recognized as her superior intelligence. Madam du Chatelet participated in the intellectual conversations of the Enlightenment, which was rare for a woman. She made friends with many of the key figures of the Enlightenment, including Voltaire, with whom she was rumored to have had an affair. Of Madame du Chatelet and her intellectual strength, Voltaire was rumored to have said that she was "a great man whose only fault was being a woman." Chatelet became an outspoken supporter of women's education during the 18th Century.

I feel the full weight of prejudice that excludes us [women] so universally from the sciences, this being one of the contradictions of this world, which has always astonished me, as there are great countries whose laws allow us to decide their destiny, but none where we are brought up to think.

Let us reflect briefly on why for so many centuries, not one good tragedy, one good poem, one esteemed history, one beautiful painting, one good book of physics, has come from the hands of women. Why do these creatures whose understanding appears in all things equal to that of men, seem, for all that, to be stopped by an invincible force on this side of a barrier, let someone give me some explanation, if there is one. I leave it to naturalists to find a physical explanation, but until that happens, women will be entitled to protest against their education. As for me, I confess that if I were king I would wish to make this scientific experiment. I would reform an abuse that cuts out

286

half of humanity. I would allow women to share in all the rights of humanity, and most of all those of the mind.

The new system of education that I propose would in all respects be beneficial to the human species. Women would be more valuable beings, men would thereby gain a new object of emulation, and our social interchanges which, in refining women's minds in the past, too often weakened and narrowed them, would now only serve to extend their knowledge.

My [system of education] will perhaps seem difficult to put into practice, even though it is reasonable. I am convinced that many women are either ignorant of their talents, because of the flaws in their education, or because of a lack of a bold spirit. What I have experienced myself confirms me in this opinion. Chance led me to become acquainted with educated men, I gained their friendship, and I saw with extreme surprise that they valued this friendship.

I began to believe that I was a thinking creature. But I only glimpsed this, and the world has carried away all my time and all my soul. I only believed in earnest in my capacity to think at an age when there was still time to become reasonable, but when it was too late to acquire talents. Nonetheless, I hold myself quite fortunate to have renounced in mid-course frivolous things that occupy most women all their lives, and I want to use what time remains to cultivate my soul.

Mary Wollstonecraft, *A Vindication of the Rights of Woman*, 1792 CE

Reading and Discussion Questions
1. Based on your reading, how are women viewed in society during this time?
2. According to the author, how are women raised and for what purpose?
3. What kind of education does Wollstonecraft support and for whom?
4. Why is Wollstonecraft critical of love? Why does she say that a woman's focus on love does her a disservice?
5. What is your understanding of Wollstonecraft's vision for women? What is her "Utopian dream," as she calls it?

Mary Wollstonecraft was an English philosopher during a time when there were no female philosophers and she is considered by many as the first feminist. Wollstonecraft wrote extensively during her short life and penned novels, travel narratives and even children's books. But her most important contribution to literature and to women's rights was her work, A Vindication of the Rights of Women, *in which she disputes the popular notion of the age that women were naturally inferior to men. As a gifted intellectual herself, Wollstonecraft observed that women were not less capable of education and virtue than men; they simply were not given the opportunities that were available to men and so they never had the chance to become anything more than silly, flirtatious slaves to their husbands. Wollstonecraft died at the age of 38 after complications from childbirth. It was not until after her death that she was fully recognized for her contributions to the women's movement. By the 20th century, she was rightfully viewed as the first real advocate for women's rights and her book is considered essential reading for every modern feminist or student of feminist history.*

THE CHARACTER AND EDUCATION OF WOMEN

To account for, and excuse the tyranny of men [over women], many ingenious arguments have been brought forward to prove that the two sexes, in the acquirement of virtue, ought to aim at attaining a very different character: or, to speak explicitly, women are not allowed to have sufficient strength of mind to acquire what really deserves the name of virtue. Yet it should seem, allowing them to have souls, that there is but one way appointed by Providence to lead mankind to either virtue or happiness.

If then women are not a swarm of [mindless and valueless insects], why should they be kept in ignorance under the specious name of innocence? The mind will ever be unstable that has only prejudices to rest on, and the current will run with destructive fury when there are no barriers to break its force. Women are told from their infancy, to develop a softness of temper, outward obedience, and a childlike manner, so that they may obtain the protection of man; and, should they be beautiful, every thing else is needless.

How grossly do they insult us who thus advise us only to render ourselves gentle, domestic brutes! Children, I grant, should be innocent; but when the epithet is applied to men, or women, it is but a polite term for weakness. But if it be allowed by

God for women to acquire human virtues and stability of character, they must be permitted to turn to the fountain of light, and not forced to shape their course by the twinkling of a mere satellite. In treating, therefore, of the manners of women, let us, disregarding sensual arguments, trace what we should endeavor to make them in order to co-operate, if the expression be not too bold, with the supreme Being.

By individual education, I mean, for the sense of the word is not precisely defined, such an attention to a child as will slowly sharpen the senses, form the temper, regulate the passions as they begin to ferment, and set the understanding to work before the body arrives at maturity; so that the man may only have to proceed, not the begin, the important task of learning to think and reason.

To prevent any misunderstanding, I must add that I do not believe that a private education can work the wonders which some sanguine writers have attributed to it. Men and women must be educated, in a great degree, by the opinions and manners of the society they live in. In every age there has been a stream of popular opinion that has carried all before it, and given a family character, as it were, to the century. It may then fairly be inferred, that, till society be differently constituted, much cannot be expected from education. It is, however, sufficient for my present purpose to assert, that, whatever circumstances have on the abilities, every being may become virtuous by the exercise of its own reason.

Consequently, the most perfect education, in my opinion, is such an exercise of the understanding as is best calculated to strengthen the body and form the heart. Or, in other words, to enable the individual to attain such habits of virtue as will render it independent. In fact, it is a farce to call any being virtuous whose virtues do not result from the exercise of its own reason. But for this epoch we must wait--wait, perhaps, till kings and nobles, enlightened by reason, and, preferring the real dignity of man, throw off their gaudy hereditary trappings. But if women do not give up their obsession with the power of beauty, they will prove that they have less mind than man.

Women should be considered either as moral beings, or so weak that they must be entirely subjected to the superior faculties of men.

Let us examine this question. Rousseau declares that a woman should never, for a moment, feel herself independent, that she should be governed by fear to exercise her natural cunning, and made a flirtatious slave in order to render her a more alluring object of desire, a sweeter companion to man, whenever he chooses to relax himself. He carries the arguments, which he pretends to draw from the indications of nature, still further, and insinuates that truth and fortitude, the corner stones of all human virtue, should be cultivated with certain restrictions, because, with respect to the female character, obedience is the grand lesson which ought to be impressed with unrelenting rigor. What nonsense!

ON LOVE AND MARRIAGE

I cannot discover why females should always be degraded by being made subservient to love or lust. To speak disrespectfully of love is, I know, high treason against sentiment and fine feelings; but I wish to speak the simple language of truth, and rather to address the head than the heart.

Youth is the season for love in both sexes; but in those days of thoughtless enjoyment provision should be made for the more important years of life, when reflection takes place of sensation. But Rousseau, and most of the male writers who have followed his steps, have warmly inculcated that the whole tendency of female education ought to be directed to one point:--to render them pleasing in their youth. But what about afterward?

The woman who has only been taught to please will soon find that her charms cannot have much effect on her husband's heart when they are seen every day, when the summer is passed and gone. Will she then have sufficient native energy to look into herself for comfort, and cultivate her dormant faculties? or, is it not more rational to expect that she will try to please other men; and, in the emotions raised by the expectation of new conquests, endeavor to forget the hurt her love or pride has received? When the husband ceases to be a lover--and the time will inevitably come, her desire of pleasing will then grow languid, or become a spring of bitterness; and love, perhaps, the most evanescent of all passions, is replaced by jealousy or vanity.

Surely no woman can live her life solely for the purpose of adorning her person, that she may amuse the languid hours, and soften the cares of a man who is willing to be enlivened by her smiles and tricks, when the serious business of his life is over.

The woman who strengthens her body and exercises her mind will, by managing her family and practicing various virtues, become the friend, and not the humble dependent of her husband. This is, must be, the course of nature and marriage.— Either friendship or indifference inevitably succeeds love. In order to fulfill the duties of life, and to be able to pursue with vigor the various employments which form the moral character, a husband and wife of a family ought not to continue to love each other with passion. I mean to say, that they ought not to indulge those emotions which disturb the order of society, and distract the mind that should be focused on [adult responsibilities].

If all the faculties of woman's mind are only to be cultivated as they respect her dependence on man; if, when a husband be obtained, she have arrived at her goal, and meanly proud rests satisfied with such a paltry crown, let her grovel contentedly, scarcely better than other beasts of the animal kingdom; but, if, struggling for the prize of her high calling, she look beyond the present scene, let her cultivate her understanding without stopping to consider what character the husband may have whom she is destined to marry. Let her only determine, without being too anxious about present happiness, to acquire the qualities that ennoble a rational being, and a rough inelegant husband may shock her taste without destroying her peace of mind. She will not model her soul to suit the frailties of her companion, but to bear with them: his character may be a trial, but not an impediment to virtue.

If, as I believe is true, women really are capable of acting like rational creatures, let them not be treated like slaves; or, like the brutes who are dependent on the reason of man. Let them attain conscious dignity by feeling themselves only dependent on God.

These may be termed Utopian dreams.--Thanks to that Being who impressed them on my soul, and gave me sufficient strength of mind to dare to exert my own reason, till, becoming dependent only on him for the support of virtue, I view, with indignation, the mistaken notions that enslave my sex.

I love man as my fellow; but his power, real, or usurped, extends not to me.

I shall not pursue this argument any further than to establish an obvious inference, that the more widely liberty is made available to all mankind, including women, the wiser and more virtuous we shall all be.

Adam Smith, *Wealth of Nations*, 1776 CE

Reading and Discussion Questions
1. What is the organizational innovation of the pin factory and what, according to Smith, is its significance for society?
2. How is Smith both praiseworthy and suspicious of businessmen's ability to serve the public good?
3. What did Adam Smith mean by the metaphor of the "invisible hand?"
4. What were Adam Smith's objections to the policy of mercantilism?
5. What did Smith say were the results of a laissez-faire policy?
6. What were the duties/responsibilities of a government that cannot be done by an individual or a business?
7. What is the "real price" of a good or service?

No one man, it can be argued, has impacted the modern world more than the Scottish economist Adam Smith. Smith is considered the father of capitalism, which is an economic system free from government interference or regulation. Today we call this type of capitalist system a "free market economy" but Smith called it a "laissez-faire" system. "Laissez-faire" literally means "leave it alone" and Smith believed that many of the problems of economies of his age were caused by unnecessary and unnatural interference in financial business by governments. He is famous for saying "the government which governs least governs best" and he supported a government system that created peace, stability and other conditions necessary for Capitalism to flourish and to leave the rest to the self-interested nature of men. Most of Smith's ideas can be found in his master work, An Inquiry into the Nature and Causes of the Wealth of Nations, *or simply* Wealth of Nations. *Though Smith's ideas were not included in the founding documents of the United States as were the ideas of Locke, Montesquieu, Voltaire and others, his attitudes about economic freedom were at the heart of what our founders wanted for the future of their new nation.*

Of the Division of Labor
THE greatest improvement in the productive powers of labor, and the greater part of the skill, dexterity, and judgment with which it is anywhere directed, or applied, seem to have been the effects of the division of labor....To take an example, therefore, the trade of the pin-maker: a workman not educated to this business, nor acquainted with the use of the machinery employed in it, could scarce, perhaps, with his utmost industry, make one pin in a day, and certainly could not make twenty. But in the way in which this business is now carried on, not only the whole work is a peculiar trade, but it is divided into a number of branches, of which the greater part are likewise peculiar

trades. One man draws out the wire, another straights it, a third cuts it, a fourth points it, a fifth grinds it at the top for receiving, the head; to make the head requires two or three distinct operations; to put it on is a peculiar business, to whiten the pins is another; it is even a trade by itself to put them into the paper; and the important business of making a pin is, in this manner, divided into about eighteen distinct operations, which, in some factories, are all performed by distinct hands, though in others the same man will sometimes perform two or three of them. I have seen a small manufactory of this kind where ten men only were employed, and where some of them consequently performed two or three distinct operations. But though they were very poor, and therefore but indifferently accommodated with the necessary machinery, they could, when they exerted themselves, make among them about twelve pounds of pins in a day. There are in a pound upwards of four thousand pins of a middling size. Those ten persons, therefore, could make among them upwards of forty-eight thousand pins in a day. Each person, therefore, making a tenth part of forty-eight thousand pins, might be considered as making four thousand eight hundred pins in a day.

But if they had all wrought separately and independently, and without any of them having been educated to this peculiar business, they certainly could not each of them have made twenty, perhaps not one pin in a day; that is, certainly, not the two hundred and fortieth, perhaps not the four thousand eight hundredth part of what they are at present capable of performing, in consequence of a proper division and combination of their different operations....

The division of labor, so far as it can be introduced, occasions, in every art, a proportionable increase of the productive powers of labor. The separation of different trades and employments from one another seems to have taken place in consequence of this advantage. This separation, too, is generally called furthest in those countries which enjoy the highest degree of industry and improvement; what is the work of one man in a rude state of society being generally that of several in an improved one.....This great increase of the quantity of work which, in consequence of the division of labor, the same number of people are capable of performing, is owing to three different circumstances; first, to the increase of dexterity in every particular workman; secondly, to the saving of the time which is commonly lost in passing from one species of work to another; and lastly, to the invention of a great number of machines which facilitate and abridge labor, and enable one man to do the work of many....

It is the great multiplication of the productions of all the different arts, in consequence of the division of labor, which occasions, in a well-governed society, that universal opulence which extends itself to the lowest ranks of the people. Every workman has a great quantity of his own work to dispose of beyond what he himself has occasion for; and every other workman being exactly in the same situation, he is enabled to exchange a great quantity of his own goods for a great quantity, or, what comes to the same thing, for the price of a great quantity of theirs. He supplies them abundantly with what they have occasion for, and they accommodate him as amply with what he has occasion for, and a general plenty diffuses itself through all the different ranks of the society....

On Tariffs and the Regulation of Trade
By restraining, either by high duties, or by absolute prohibitions, the importation of such goods from foreign countries as can be produced at home, the monopoly of the home-market is more or less secured to the domestic industry employed in producing them. Thus the . . . high duties upon the importation of corn, which in times of

moderate plenty amount to a prohibition, give a like advantage to the growers of that commodity. The prohibition of the importation of foreign woolens is equally favorable to the woolen manufacturers. The silk manufacture, though altogether employed upon foreign materials, has lately obtained the same advantage. The linen manufacture has not yet obtained it, but is making great strides towards it. Many other sorts of manufacturers have, in the same manner, obtained in Great Britain, either altogether, or very nearly a monopoly against their countrymen. . . .

That this monopoly of the home-market frequently gives great encouragement to that particular species of industry which enjoys it . . . cannot be doubted. But whether it tends either to increase the general industry of the society, or to give it the most advantageous direction, is not, perhaps, altogether so evident. . . .

The natural advantages which one country has over another in producing particular commodities are sometimes so great, that it is acknowledged by all the world to be in vain to struggle with them. By means of glasses, hotbeds, and hotwalls, very good grapes can be raised in Scotland, and very good wine too can be made of them at about thirty times the expense for which at least equally good can be brought from foreign countries. Would it be a reasonable law to prohibit the importation of all foreign wines, merely to encourage the making of claret and burgundy in Scotland? But if there would be a manifest absurdity in turning towards any employment, thirty times more of the capital and industry of the country, than would be necessary to purchase from foreign countries an equal quantity of the commodities wanted, there must be an absurdity, though not altogether so glaring, yet exactly of the same kind, in turning towards any such employment a thirtieth, or even a three hundredth part more of either. . . . As long as the one country has those advantages, and the other wants (them, it will always be more advantageous for the latter, rather to buy of the former than to make. It is an acquired advantage only, which one artificer has over his neighbor, who exercises another trade; and yet they both find it more advantageous to buy of one another, than to make what does not belong to their particular trades.

Merchants and manufacturers are the people who derive the greatest advantage from this monopoly of the home market. The prohibition of the importation of foreign cattle, and of salt provisions, together with the high duties upon foreign corn, which in times of moderate plenty amount to a prohibition, are not near so advantageous to the graziers and farmers of Great Britain, as other regulations of the same kind are to its merchants and manufacturers. Manufacturers, those of the finer kind especially, are more easily transported from one country to another than corn or cattle. It is in the fetching and carrying manufacturers, accordingly, that foreign trade is chiefly employed. In manufactures, a very small advantage will enable foreigners to undersell our own workmen, even in the home market. It will require a very great one to enable them to do so in the rude produce of the soil. If the free importation of foreign manufacturers were permitted, several of the home manufactures would probably suffer, and some of them, perhaps, go to ruin altogether, and a considerable part of the stock and industry at present employed in them, would be forced to find out some other employment. But the freest importation of the rude produce of the soil could have no such effect upon the agriculture of the country.

On Self-Interest

Every individual is continually exerting himself to find out the most advantageous employment for whatever capital he can command. It is his own advantage, indeed, and not that of the society, which he has in view. But the study of his own advantage, naturally, or rather necessarily, leads him to prefer that employment which is most advantageous to the society....

As every individual, therefore, endeavors as much as he can both to employ his capital in the support of domestic industry, and so to direct that industry that its produce may be of the greatest value, every individual necessarily labors to render the annual revenue of the society as great as he can. He generally, indeed, neither intends to promote the public interest, nor knows how much he is promoting it. By preferring the support of domestic to that of foreign industry, he intends only his own security; and by directing that industry in such a manner as its produce may be of the greatest value, he intends only his own gain, and he is in this, as in many other cases, led by an invisible hand to promote an end which was no part of his intention. Nor is it always the worse for the society that it was no part of it.

By pursuing his own interest he frequently promotes that of the society more effectually than when he really intends to promote it. I have never known much good done by those who affected to trade for the public good....

....The statesman who should attempt to direct private people in what manner they ought to employ their capitals, would not only load himself with a most unnecessary attention, but assume an authority which could safely be trusted, not only to no single person, but to no council or senate whatever, and which would nowhere be so dangerous as in the hands of a man who had folly and presumption enough to fancy himself fit to exercise it....

It is thus that every system which endeavors, either by extraordinary encouragements to draw towards a particular species of industry a greater share of the capital of the society than would naturally go to it, or, by extraordinary restraints, force from a particular species of industry some share of the capital which would otherwise be employed in it, is in reality subversive to the great purpose which it means to promote. It retards, instead of accelerating, the progress of the society towards real wealth and greatness; and diminishes, instead of increasing, the real value of the annual produce of its land and labor.

All systems either of preference or of restraint, therefore, being thus completely taken away, the obvious and simple system of natural liberty establishes itself of its own accord. Every man, as long as he does not violate the laws of justice, is left perfectly free to pursue his own interest his own way, and to bring both his industry and capital into competition with those of any other man, or order of men. The sovereign is completely discharged from a duty, in the attempting to perform which he must always be exposed to innumerable delusions, and for the proper performance of which no human wisdom or knowledge could ever be sufficient; the duty of superintending the industry of private people, and of directing it towards the employments most suitable to the interest of the society. According to the system of natural liberty, the sovereign has only three duties to attend to; three duties of great importance, indeed, but plain and intelligible to common understandings: first, the duty of protecting the society from the violence and invasion of other independent societies; secondly, the duty of protecting, as far as possible, every member of the society from the injustice or oppression of every other member of it, or the duty of establishing an exact administration of justice; and thirdly, the duty of erecting and maintaining certain public works and certain public institutions which it can never be for the interest of any individual, or small number of individuals, to erect and maintain; because the profit could never repay the expense to any individual or small number of individuals, though it may frequently do much more than repay it to a great society....

It is not from the benevolence of the butcher, the brewer, or the baker, that we expect our dinner, but from their regard to their own interest. We address ourselves, not to their humanity but to their self-love, and never talk to them of our necessities but of their advantages.

On Valuation

The real price of everything, what everything really costs to the man who wants to acquire it, is the toil and trouble of acquiring it. What everything is really worth to the man who has acquired it, and who wants to dispose of it or exchange it for something else, is the toil and trouble which it can save to himself, and which it can impose upon other people. What is bought with money or with goods is purchased by labor as much as what we acquire by the toil of our own body. That money or those goods indeed save us this toil. They contain the value of a certain quantity of labor which we exchange for what is supposed at the time to contain the value of an equal quantity. Labor was the first price, the original purchase-money that was paid for all things. It was not by gold or by silver, but by labor, that all the wealth of the world was originally purchased; and its value, to those who possess it, and who want to exchange it for some new productions, is precisely equal to the quantity of labor which it can enable them to purchase or command.

The Declaration of Independence, 1776 CE

1. Identify two phrases or concepts in *The Declaration of Independence* where the author referenced the theories of John Locke or used his ideas to justify the split from England.
2. Summarize in your own words five grievances or complaints that the colonists make against England and King George III.
3. In your opinion, did Jefferson succeed in adequately justifying a revolution? Why or why not?
4. Define equality. Do you think Jefferson's idea that "all men are created equal" matches with the modern definition of equality? Why or why not?
5. To what extent does this document embody the ideals of the Enlightenment as you understand them? Explain your answer.

Below is the full text of the Declaration of Independence, ratified by the Second Continental Congress in 1776. Many believe that the Declaration is what started the Revolutionary War but in truth, the war had started two years earlier in 1774. The real purpose of the Declaration of Independence was to explain and justify the war that had already started to a world audience who deemed the acts of the British colonists as unjustified treason. Thomas Jefferson was given the job of giving the cause of the colonists legitimacy, by explaining exactly what had been done to them by King George III and why they were in the midst of armed rebellion. Jefferson summoned all the best wisdom from history in crafting this short document, and its structure and tone are modeled in part after the English Bill of Rights. The justification that Jefferson uses in defense of the rebellion, however, almost entirely comes from John Locke. If you recall, Locke believed that a government's primary function was to protect the life, liberty and property of its subjects and that if a government fails to fulfill its function, the people have an obligation to rebel. Jefferson and the other founders of the United States wholeheartedly agreed.

IN CONGRESS, July 4, 1776.

The unanimous Declaration of the thirteen united States of America,

When in the course of human events, it becomes necessary for one people to dissolve the political bands which have connected them with another, and to assume among the powers of the earth, the separate and equal station to which the Laws of Nature and of Nature's God entitle them, a decent respect to the opinions of mankind requires that they should declare the causes which impel them to the separation.

We hold these truths to be self-evident, that all men are created equal, that they are endowed by their Creator with certain unalienable Rights, that among these are Life, Liberty and the pursuit of Happiness.--That to secure these rights, Governments are instituted among Men, deriving their just powers from the consent of the governed, – That whenever any Form of Government becomes destructive of these ends, it is the Right of the People to alter or to abolish it, and to institute new Government, laying its foundation on such principles and organizing its powers in such form, as to them shall seem most likely to effect their Safety and Happiness. Prudence, indeed, will dictate that Governments long established should not be changed for light and transient causes; and accordingly all experience hath shown, that mankind are more disposed to suffer, while evils are sufferable, than to right themselves by abolishing the forms to which they are accustomed.

But when a long train of abuses and usurpations, pursuing invariably the same Object evinces a design to reduce them under absolute Despotism, it is their right, it is their duty, to throw off such Government, and to provide new Guards for their future security.--Such has been the patient sufferance of these Colonies; and such is now the necessity which constrains them to alter their former Systems of Government. The history of the present King of Great Britain is a history of repeated injuries and usurpations, all having in direct object the establishment of an absolute Tyranny over these States. To prove this, let Facts be submitted to a candid world.

He has refused his Assent to Laws, the most wholesome and necessary for the public good.

He has forbidden his Governors to pass Laws of immediate and pressing importance, unless suspended in their operation till his Assent should be obtained; and when so suspended, he has utterly neglected to attend to them.

He has refused to pass other Laws for the accommodation of large districts of people, unless those people would relinquish the right of Representation in the Legislature, a right inestimable to them and formidable to tyrants only.

He has called together legislative bodies at places unusual, uncomfortable, and distant from the depository of their public Records, for the sole purpose of fatiguing them into compliance with his measures.

He has dissolved Representative Houses repeatedly, for opposing with manly firmness his invasions on the rights of the people.

He has refused for a long time, after such dissolutions, to cause others to be elected; whereby the Legislative powers, incapable of Annihilation, have returned to the People at large for their exercise; the State remaining in the mean time exposed to all the dangers of invasion from without, and convulsions within.

He has endeavoured to prevent the population of these States; for that purpose obstructing the Laws for Naturalization of Foreigners; refusing to pass others to encourage their migrations hither, and raising the conditions of new Appropriations of Lands.

He has obstructed the Administration of Justice, by refusing his Assent to Laws for establishing Judiciary powers.

He has made Judges dependent on his Will alone, for the tenure of their offices, and the amount and payment of their salaries.

He has erected a multitude of New Offices, and sent hither swarms of Officers to harrass our people, and eat out their substance.

He has kept among us, in times of peace, Standing Armies without the Consent of our legislatures.

He has affected to render the Military independent of and superior to the Civil power.

He has combined with others to subject us to a jurisdiction foreign to our constitution, and unacknowledged by our laws; giving his Assent to their Acts of pretended Legislation:

For Quartering large bodies of armed troops among us:

For protecting them, by a mock Trial, from punishment for any Murders which they should commit on the Inhabitants of these States:

For cutting off our Trade with all parts of the world:

For imposing Taxes on us without our Consent:

For depriving us in many cases, of the benefits of Trial by Jury:

For transporting us beyond Seas to be tried for pretended offences:

For abolishing the free System of English Laws in a neighbouring Province, establishing therein an Arbitrary government, and enlarging its Boundaries so as to render it at once an example and fit instrument for introducing the same absolute rule into these Colonies:

For taking away our Charters, abolishing our most valuable Laws, and altering fundamentally the Forms of our Governments:

For suspending our own Legislatures, and declaring themselves invested with power to legislate for us in all cases whatsoever.

He has abdicated Government here, by declaring us out of his Protection and waging War against us. He has plundered our seas, ravaged our Coasts, burnt our towns, and destroyed the lives of our people. He is at this time transporting large Armies of foreign Mercenaries to complete the works of death, desolation and tyranny, already begun with circumstances of Cruelty & perfidy scarcely paralleled in the most barbarous ages, and totally unworthy the Head of a civilized nation.

He has constrained our fellow Citizens taken Captive on the high Seas to bear Arms against their Country, to become the executioners of their friends and Brethren, or to fall themselves by their Hands.

He has excited domestic insurrections amongst us, and has endeavored to bring on the inhabitants of our frontiers, the merciless Indian Savages, whose known rule of warfare, is an undistinguished destruction of all ages, sexes and conditions.

In every stage of these Oppressions We have Petitioned for Redress in the most humble terms: Our repeated Petitions have been answered only by repeated injury. A

Prince whose character is thus marked by every act which may define a Tyrant, is unfit to be the ruler of a free people.

Nor have We been wanting in attentions to our British brethren. We have warned them from time to time of attempts by their legislature to extend an unwarrantable jurisdiction over us. We have reminded them of the circumstances of our emigration and settlement here. We have appealed to their native justice and magnanimity, and we have conjured them by the ties of our common kindred to disavow these usurpations, which, would inevitably interrupt our connections and correspondence. They too have been deaf to the voice of justice and of consanguinity. We must, therefore, acquiesce in the necessity, which denounces our Separation, and hold them, as we hold the rest of mankind, Enemies in War, in Peace Friends.

We, therefore, the Representatives of the United States of America, in General Congress, Assembled, appealing to the Supreme Judge of the world for the rectitude of our intentions, do, in the Name, and by Authority of the good People of these Colonies, solemnly publish and declare, That these United Colonies are, and of Right ought to be Free and Independent States; that they are Absolved from all Allegiance to the British Crown, and that all political connection between them and the State of Great Britain, is and ought to be totally dissolved; and that as Free and Independent States, they have full Power to levy War, conclude Peace, contract Alliances, establish Commerce, and to do all other Acts and Things which Independent States may of right do. And for the support of this Declaration, with a firm reliance on the protection of divine Providence, we mutually pledge to each other our Lives, our Fortunes and our sacred Honor.

The Articles of Confederation, 1777 CE

Reading and Discussion Questions
1. What is the role of the state governments or what powers do states have under the Articles? What specific things can the state governments NOT do, according to the Articles of Confederation?
2. What are the responsibilities of Congress under the Articles of Confederation? What are the specific powers of Congress?
3. What is the process for voting on resolutions or laws in Congress?
4. What is the procedure by which Congress was to raise funds?
5. What problems can you identify in the Articles of Confederation that might make a unified national government difficult?

Work began in 1777 on crafting a new government, in the hope that the British colonists' efforts in the Revolutionary War might actually succeed. The result of that work was The Articles of Confederation, which was the name of the document that created our first government in this country. The men at the Second Continental Congress were guided by one all-important principle in their deliberations in 1777: No kings allowed. They were determined that, in this new country they were creating, it would be impossible for one man to ever win absolute and tyrannical power of his subjects. So fearful were they of absolutism that the Founding Fathers gave almost no power to the federal government and did not create an executive branch of government. Their reasoning was that if there was no executive power, there could be no abuse of executive power. They were right and they did avoid abuses of this sort in the person of an executive leader, but they failed to see a myriad of other problems and abuses that would become huge problems as a result of the system they had created. The Articles of Confederation were ratified in 1781 and were discarded in 1787, after their flaws had brought the fledgling United States to the brink of armed rebellion.

Articles of Confederation and perpetual Union between the states of New Hampshire, Massachusetts bay Rhode Island and Providence Plantations, Connecticut, New York, New Jersey, Pennsylvania, Delaware, Maryland, Virginia, North Carolina, South Carolina and Georgia.

Article I. The Stile of this Confederacy shall be "The United States of America".

Article II. Each state retains its sovereignty, freedom, and independence, and every power, jurisdiction, and right, which is not by this Confederation expressly delegated to the United States, in Congress assembled.

Article III. The said States hereby severally enter into a firm league of friendship with each other, for their common defense, the security of their liberties, and their mutual and general welfare, binding themselves to assist each other, against all force offered to, or attacks made upon them, or any of them, on account of religion, sovereignty, trade, or any other pretense whatever...

Article V. For the most convenient management of the general interests of the United States, delegates shall be annually appointed in such manner as the legislatures of each

State shall direct, to meet in Congress on the first Monday in November, in every year, with a power reserved to each State to recall its delegates, or any of them, at any time within the year, and to send others in their stead for the remainder of the year.

No State shall be represented in Congress by less than two, nor more than seven members; and no person shall be capable of being a delegate for more than three years in any term of six years; nor shall any person, being a delegate, be capable of holding any office under the United States, for which he, or another for his benefit, receives any salary, fees or emolument of any kind.

Each State shall maintain its own delegates in a meeting of the States, and while they act as members of the committee of the States. In determining questions in the United States in Congress assembled, each State shall have one vote...

Article VI. No State, without the consent of the United States in Congress assembled, shall send any embassy to, or receive any embassy from, or enter into any conference, agreement, alliance or treaty with any King, Prince or State; nor shall any person holding any office of profit or trust under the United States, or any of them, accept any present, emolument, office or title of any kind whatever from any King, Prince or foreign State; nor shall the United States in Congress assembled, or any of them, grant any title of nobility.

No two or more States shall enter into any treaty, confederation or alliance whatever between them, without the consent of the United States in Congress assembled, specifying accurately the purposes for which the same is to be entered into, and how long it shall continue...

No vessel of war shall be kept up in time of peace by any State, except such number only, as shall be deemed necessary by the United States in Congress assembled, for the defense of such State, or its trade; nor shall any body of forces be kept up by any State in time of peace, except such number only, as in the judgment of the United States in Congress assembled, shall be deemed requisite to garrison the forts necessary for the defense of such State; but every State shall always keep up a well-regulated and disciplined militia, sufficiently armed and accoutered, and shall provide and constantly have ready for use, in public stores, a due number of filed pieces and tents, and a proper quantity of arms, ammunition and camp equipage.

No State shall engage in any war without the consent of the United States in Congress assembled, unless such State be actually invaded by enemies...

Article VIII. All charges of war, and all other expenses that shall be incurred for the common defense or general welfare, and allowed by the United States in Congress assembled, shall be defrayed out of a common treasury, which shall be supplied by the several States in proportion to the value of all and within each State, granted or surveyed for any person, as such land and the buildings and improvements thereon shall be estimated according to such mode as the United States in Congress assembled, shall from time to time direct and appoint.

The taxes for paying that proportion shall be laid and levied by the authority and direction of the legislatures of the several States within the time agreed upon by the United States in Congress assembled.

Article IX. The United States in Congress assembled, shall have the sole and exclusive right and power of determining on peace and war, except in the cases mentioned in the sixth article -- of sending and receiving ambassadors -- entering into treaties and alliances...

The United States in Congress assembled shall have authority to...ascertain the necessary sums of money to be raised for the service of the United States, and to appropriate and apply the same for defraying the public expenses -- to borrow money, or emit bills on the credit of the United States, transmitting every half-year to the respective States an account of the sums of money so borrowed or emitted -- to build and equip a navy -- to agree upon the number of land forces, and to make requisitions from each State for its quota, in proportion to the number of white inhabitants in such State; which requisition shall be binding, and thereupon the legislature of each State shall appoint the regimental officers, raise the men and cloath, arm and equip them in a solid-like manner, at the expense of the United States...

The United States in Congress assembled shall never engage in a war, nor grant letters of marque or reprisal in time of peace, nor enter into any treaties or alliances, nor coin money, nor regulate the value thereof, nor ascertain the sums and expenses necessary for the defense and welfare of the United States, or any of them, nor emit bills, nor borrow money on the credit of the United States, nor appropriate money, nor agree upon the number of vessels of war, to be built or purchased, or the number of land or sea forces to be raised, nor appoint a commander in chief of the army or navy, unless nine States assent to the same: nor shall a question on any other point, except for adjourning from day to day be determined, unless by the votes of the majority of the United States in Congress assembled...

Article XIII. Every State shall abide by the determination of the United States in Congress assembled, on all questions which by this confederation are submitted to them. And the Articles of this Confederation shall be inviolably observed by every State, and the Union shall be perpetual; nor shall any alteration at any time hereafter be made in any of them; unless such alteration be agreed to in a Congress of the United States, and be afterwards confirmed by the legislatures of every State...

The United States Constitution, 1787 CE

Reading and Discussion Questions
1. What are the powers of Congress? Does the Senate have any special additional powers?
2. What are the powers of the Executive Branch? How are these powers checked by the other branches?
3. Compare the list of the powers of Congress to the list of Executive powers. Does one branch have more power than the other? If so, why is this?
4. What is the primary function of the Supreme Court? In what ways is it a check on the power of other branches?
5. After analyzing the Constitution for its individual parts, look at it again as a whole document. What Enlightenment ideals and beliefs does it contain? Make note of specific Enlightenment thinkers whose ideas are included here.

In 1787, it was clear that the Articles of Confederation were a disaster, as the newly formed nation of the United States was on the brink of collapse. States exercised almost unchecked power and the federal government had virtually no power to require the states to do anything. The Articles of Confederation had failed to create any "glue" to hold the states together or unify them in cause and action. Instead, the Articles actually encouraged competition between states, which is a recipe for trouble in a supposedly united nation. The Constitutional Convention was convened in Philadelphia in 1787 to try and fix the problems the Articles had created. The hope in the beginning was that perhaps the Articles could be amended to make them workable but it became clear almost immediately that there was nothing in the Articles of Confederation worth saving. Instead, our founders scrapped their first government altogether and started over. Governed more fully by wisdom from the Enlightenment in their second try, the result of discussions in 1787 was the U.S. Constitution and a well-balanced new government for the United States. The U.S. Constitution was ratified in 1791.

We the People of the United States, in Order to form a more perfect Union, establish Justice, insure domestic Tranquility, provide for the common defense, promote the general Welfare, and secure the Blessings of Liberty to ourselves and our Posterity, do ordain and establish this Constitution for the United States of America.

Article. I.

Section. 1.
All legislative Powers herein granted shall be vested in a Congress of the United States, which shall consist of a Senate and House of Representatives.

Section. 2.
The House of Representatives shall be composed of Members chosen every second Year by the People of the several States, and the Electors in each State shall have the Qualifications requisite for Electors of the most numerous Branch of the State Legislature.

No Person shall be a Representative who shall not have attained to the Age of twenty five Years, and been seven Years a Citizen of the United States, and who shall not, when elected, be an Inhabitant of that State in which he shall be chosen.

Representatives and direct Taxes shall be apportioned among the several States which may be included within this Union, according to their respective Numbers, which shall be determined by adding to the whole Number of free Persons, including those bound to Service for a Term of Years, and excluding Indians not taxed, three fifths of all other Persons.

The House of Representatives shall choose their Speaker and other Officers; and shall have the sole Power of Impeachment.

Section. 3.
The Senate of the United States shall be composed of two Senators from each State, chosen by the Legislature thereof, for six Years; and each Senator shall have one Vote.

Elections for Senators will be held every two years, on a rotating basis, with one third of the Senate being up for reelection during each election cycle.

No Person shall be a Senator who shall not have attained to the Age of thirty Years, and been nine Years a Citizen of the United States, and who shall not, when elected, be an Inhabitant of that State for which he shall be chosen.

The Vice President of the United States shall be President of the Senate, but shall have no Vote, unless they be equally divided. The Senate shall choose their other Officers, and also a President pro tempore, in the Absence of the Vice President, or when he shall exercise the Office of President of the United States.

The Senate shall have the sole Power to try all Impeachments. When sitting for that Purpose, they shall be on Oath or Affirmation. When the President of the United States is tried, the Chief Justice shall preside: And no Person shall be convicted without the Concurrence of two thirds of the Members present.

Section. 4.
The Congress shall assemble at least once in every Year, and such Meeting shall be on the first Monday in December, unless they shall by Law appoint a different Day.

Section. 6.
The Senators and Representatives shall receive a Compensation for their Services, to be ascertained by Law, and paid out of the Treasury of the United States. They shall in all Cases, except Treason, Felony and Breach of the Peace, be privileged from Arrest during their Attendance at the Session of their respective Houses, and in going to and returning from the same; and for any Speech or Debate in either House, they shall not be questioned in any other Place.

No Senator or Representative shall, during the Time for which he was elected, be appointed to any civil Office under the Authority of the United States, which shall have been created, or the Emoluments whereof shall have been increased.

Section. 7.
All Bills for raising Revenue shall originate in the House of Representatives; but the Senate may propose or concur with Amendments as on other Bills.

Every Bill which shall have passed the House of Representatives and the Senate, shall, before it become a Law, be presented to the President of the United States; If he approve he shall sign it, but if not he shall return it, with his Objections to that House in which it shall have originated, who shall enter the Objections at large on their Journal, and proceed to reconsider it. If after such Reconsideration two thirds of that House shall agree to pass the Bill, it shall be sent, together with the Objections, to the other House, by which it shall likewise be reconsidered, and if approved by two thirds of that House, it shall become a Law. But in all such Cases the Votes of both Houses shall be determined by yeas and Nays, and the Names of the Persons voting for and against the Bill shall be entered on the Journal of each House respectively. If any Bill shall not be returned by the President within ten Days (Sundays excepted) after it shall have been presented to him, the Same shall be a Law, in like Manner as if he had signed it, unless the Congress by their Adjournment prevent its Return, in which Case it shall not be a Law.

Section. 8.
The Congress shall have Power:

To lay and collect Taxes, Duties, Imposts and Excises, to pay the Debts and provide for the common Defense and general Welfare of the United States; but all Duties, Imposts and Excises shall be uniform throughout the United States;

To borrow Money on the credit of the United States;

To regulate Commerce with foreign Nations, and among the several States, and with the Indian Tribes;

To establish an uniform Rule of Naturalization, and uniform Laws on the subject of Bankruptcies throughout the United States;

To coin Money, regulate the Value thereof, and of foreign Coin, and fix the Standard of Weights and Measures;

To provide for the Punishment of counterfeiting the Securities and current Coin of the United States;

To establish Post Offices and post Roads;

To promote the Progress of Science and useful Arts, by securing for limited Times to Authors and Inventors the exclusive Right to their respective Writings and Discoveries;

To constitute Tribunals inferior to the supreme Court;

To define and punish Piracies and Felonies committed on the high Seas, and Offences against the Law of Nations;
To declare War, grant Letters of Marque and Reprisal, and make Rules concerning

305

Captures on Land and Water;

To raise and support Armies, but no Appropriation of Money to that Use shall be for a longer Term than two Years;

To provide and maintain a Navy;

To make Rules for the Government and Regulation of the land and naval Forces;

To provide for calling forth the Militia to execute the Laws of the Union, suppress Insurrections and repel Invasions;

To provide for organizing, arming, and disciplining, the Militia, and for governing such Part of them as may be employed in the Service of the United States, reserving to the States respectively, the Appointment of the Officers, and the Authority of training the Militia according to the discipline prescribed by Congress;

To exercise exclusive Legislation in all Cases whatsoever, over such District (not exceeding ten Miles square) as may, by Cession of particular States, and the Acceptance of Congress, become the Seat of the Government of the United States, and to exercise like Authority over all Places purchased by the Consent of the Legislature of the State in which the Same shall be, for the Erection of Forts, Magazines, Arsenals, dock-Yards, and other needful Buildings;—And

To make all Laws which shall be necessary and proper for carrying into Execution the foregoing Powers, and all other Powers vested by this Constitution in the Government of the United States, or in any Department or Officer thereof.

ARTICLE II

Section. 1.
The executive Power shall be vested in a President of the United States of America. He shall hold his Office during the Term of four Years, and, together with the Vice President, chosen for the same Term, be elected, as follows

Each State shall appoint, in such Manner as the Legislature thereof may direct, a Number of Electors, equal to the whole Number of Senators and Representatives to which the State may be entitled in the Congress: but no Senator or Representative, or Person holding an Office of Trust or Profit under the United States, shall be appointed an Elector.

No Person except a natural born Citizen, or a Citizen of the United States, at the time of the Adoption of this Constitution, shall be eligible to the Office of President; neither shall any Person be eligible to that Office who shall not have attained to the Age of thirty five Years, and been fourteen Years a Resident within the United States.

In Case of the Removal of the President from Office, or of his Death, Resignation, or Inability to discharge the Powers and Duties of the said Office, the Same shall devolve on the Vice President, and the Congress may by Law provide for the Case of Removal, Death, Resignation or Inability, both of the President and Vice President, declaring what Officer shall then act as President, and such Officer shall act accordingly, until the Disability be removed, or a President shall be elected.

The President shall, at stated Times, receive for his Services, a Compensation, which shall neither be increased nor diminished during the Period for which he shall have been elected, and he shall not receive within that Period any other Emolument from the United States, or any of them.

Before he enter on the Execution of his Office, he shall take the following Oath or Affirmation:—"I do solemnly swear (or affirm) that I will faithfully execute the Office of President of the United States, and will to the best of my Ability, preserve, protect and defend the Constitution of the United States."

Section. 2.
The President shall be Commander in Chief of the Army and Navy of the United States, and of the Militia of the several States, when called into the actual Service of the United States;

He may require the Opinion, in writing, of the principal Officer in each of the executive Departments, upon any Subject relating to the Duties of their respective Offices, and

He shall have Power to grant Reprieves and Pardons for Offences against the United States, except in Cases of Impeachment.

He shall have Power, by and with the Advice and Consent of the Senate, to make Treaties, provided two thirds of the Senators present concur; and

He shall nominate, and by and with the Advice and Consent of the Senate, shall appoint Ambassadors, other public Ministers and Consuls, Judges of the supreme Court, and all other Officers of the United States, whose Appointments are not herein otherwise provided for, and which shall be established by Law: but the Congress may by Law vest the Appointment of such inferior Officers, as they think proper, in the President alone, in the Courts of Law, or in the Heads of Departments.

The President shall have Power to fill up all Vacancies that may happen during the Recess of the Senate, by granting Commissions which shall expire at the End of their next Session.

Section. 3.
He shall from time to time give to the Congress Information of the State of the Union, and recommend to their Consideration such Measures as he shall judge necessary and expedient; he may, on extraordinary Occasions, convene both Houses, or either of them, and in Case of Disagreement between them, with Respect to the Time of Adjournment, he may adjourn them to such Time as he shall think proper; he shall receive Ambassadors and other public Ministers; he shall take Care that the Laws be faithfully executed, and shall Commission all the Officers of the United States.

Section. 4.
The President, Vice President and all civil Officers of the United States, shall be removed from Office on Impeachment for, and Conviction of, Treason, Bribery, or other high Crimes and Misdemeanors.

ARTICLE III

Section. 1.
The judicial Power of the United States, shall be vested in one Supreme Court, and in such inferior Courts as the Congress may from time to time ordain and establish. The Judges, both of the supreme and inferior Courts, shall hold their Offices during good Behaviour, and shall, at stated Times, receive for their Services, a Compensation, which shall not be diminished during their Continuance in Office.

Section. 2.
The judicial Power shall extend to all Cases, in Law and Equity, arising under this Constitution, the Laws of the United States, and Treaties made, or which shall be made, under their Authority;
—to all Cases affecting Ambassadors, other public Ministers and Consuls;
—to all Cases of admiralty and maritime Jurisdiction;
—to Controversies to which the United States shall be a Party;
—to Controversies between two or more States;
— between a State and Citizens of another State,
—between Citizens of different States,
—between Citizens of the same State claiming Lands under Grants of different States, and between a State, or the Citizens thereof, and foreign States, Citizens or Subjects.

In all Cases affecting Ambassadors, other public Ministers and Consuls, and those in which a State shall be Party, the supreme Court shall have original Jurisdiction. In all the other Cases before mentioned, the supreme Court shall have appellate Jurisdiction, both as to Law and Fact, with such Exceptions, and under such Regulations as the Congress shall make.

The Trial of all Crimes, except in Cases of Impeachment, shall be by Jury; and such Trial shall be held in the State where the said Crimes shall have been committed; but when not committed within any State, the Trial shall be at such Place or Places as the Congress may by Law have directed.

Section 3.
Treason against the United States, shall consist only in levying War against them, or in adhering to their Enemies, giving them Aid and Comfort. No Person shall be convicted of Treason unless on the Testimony of two Witnesses to the same overt Act, or on Confession in open Court.

The Congress shall have Power to declare the Punishment of Treason, but no Attainder of Treason shall work Corruption of Blood, or Forfeiture except during the Life of the Person attainted.

ARTICLE IV

Section. 1.
Full Faith and Credit shall be given in each State to the public Acts, Records, and judicial Proceedings of every other State. And the Congress may by general Laws prescribe the Manner in which such Acts, Records and Proceedings shall be proved, and the Effect thereof.

Section. 2.

The Citizens of each State shall be entitled to all Privileges and Immunities of Citizens in the several States.

A Person charged in any State with Treason, Felony, or other Crime, who shall flee from Justice, and be found in another State, shall on Demand of the executive Authority of the State from which he fled, be delivered up, to be removed to the State having Jurisdiction of the Crime.

No Person held to Service or Labour in one State, under the Laws thereof, escaping into another, shall, in Consequence of any Law or Regulation therein, be discharged from such Service or Labour, but shall be delivered up on Claim of the Party to whom such Service or Labour may be due.

Section. 3.

New States may be admitted by the Congress into this Union; but no new State shall be formed or erected within the Jurisdiction of any other State; nor any State be formed by the Junction of two or more States, or Parts of States, without the Consent of the Legislatures of the States concerned as well as of the Congress.

The Congress shall have Power to dispose of and make all needful Rules and Regulations respecting the Territory or other Property belonging to the United States; and nothing in this Constitution shall be so construed as to Prejudice any Claims of the United States, or of any particular State.

Section. 4.

The United States shall guarantee to every State in this Union a Republican Form of Government, and shall protect each of them against Invasion; and on Application of the Legislature, or of the Executive (when the Legislature cannot be convened), against domestic Violence.

ARTICLE V

The Congress, whenever two thirds of both Houses shall deem it necessary, shall propose Amendments to this Constitution, or, on the Application of the Legislatures of two thirds of the several States, shall call a Convention for proposing Amendments, which, in either Case, shall be valid to all Intents and Purposes, as Part of this Constitution, when ratified by the Legislatures of three fourths of the several States, or by Conventions in three fourths thereof, as the one or the other Mode of Ratification may be proposed by the Congress; Provided that no Amendment which may be made prior to the Year One thousand eight hundred and eight shall in any Manner affect the first and fourth Clauses in the Ninth Section of the first Article; and that no State, without its Consent, shall be deprived of its equal Suffrage in the Senate.

ARTICLE VI

All Debts contracted and Engagements entered into, before the Adoption of this Constitution, shall be as valid against the United States under this Constitution, as under the Confederation.

This Constitution, and the Laws of the United States which shall be made in Pursuance thereof; and all Treaties made, or which shall be made, under the Authority of the United States, shall be the supreme Law of the Land; and the Judges in every State shall be bound thereby, any Thing in the Constitution or Laws of any State to the Contrary notwithstanding.

The Senators and Representatives before mentioned, and the Members of the several State Legislatures, and all executive and judicial Officers, both of the United States and of the several States, shall be bound by Oath or Affirmation, to support this Constitution; but no religious Test shall ever be required as a Qualification to any Office or public Trust under the United States.

Article. VII.

The Ratification of the Conventions of nine States, shall be sufficient for the Establishment of this Constitution between the States so ratifying the Same.

The United States Bill of Rights, 1789 CE

Reading and Discussion Questions
1. Why was the Bill of Rights added to the Constitution?
2. Summarize the rights guaranteed to American citizens by the Bill of Rights.
3. What is the origin of these rights? Most of these protections for citizens were not new ideas but were influenced by other ideas in history. Trace the origin of these rights by looking at documents like the Magna Carta and the English Bill of Rights and at ideas from Enlightenment philosophers. Write an analysis of where our rights come from, including an identification of at least three sources from which these rights were drawn.
4. Are there any entirely new rights in the Bill of Rights that did not originate from other documents or philosophies?

Creating a new government is easy. As we have seen, governments are created and destroyed throughout history. People get angry. They overthrow their ruler. They demand people's rights. And things often end badly. Even for our Founding Fathers, their first attempt at a new government failed. Creating a new government is easy, but creating a good, balanced government is hard. In 1787, the Constitutional Convention had successfully created the structure and function of the new United States government. It had three clear branches of government and an intricate system of checks and balances. It was a very good government.

But there was a concern among many of the representatives at the Constitutional Convention. They were concerned that, while the Constitution was full of things the government could do, it said nothing about what the government could not do. This group of people who feared an overly strong federal government were called Anti-federalists. They demanded that a list be added to the Constitution that guaranteed certain limits on the government's power and included sacredly protected rights for individuals. On the other side of this argument were people known as the Federalists, who said that it was implied that the powers of the government would be needed and it was unnecessary to spell out those limits. But the Anti-Federalists remembered their

English history and the repeated moments when kings had abused their power in ways that had been unanticipated by the people and so they were not satisfied with implied limits. They wanted written limits on the government and written and public declarations of individual liberties. Ultimately, the Anti-Federalists refused to ratify or approve the Constitution without an added list of protections, which we know today as the American Bill of Rights.

THE Conventions of a number of the States, having at the time of their adopting the Constitution, expressed a desire, in order to prevent misconstruction or abuse of its powers, that further declaratory and restrictive clauses should be added: And as extending the ground of public confidence in the Government, will best ensure the beneficent ends of its institution.

RESOLVED by the Senate and House of Representatives of the United States of America, in Congress assembled, two thirds of both Houses concurring, that the following Articles be proposed to the Legislatures of the several States, as amendments to the Constitution of the United States, all, or any of which Articles, when ratified by three fourths of the said Legislatures, to be valid to all intents and purposes, as part of the said Constitution; viz.

ARTICLES in addition to, and Amendment of the Constitution of the United States of America, proposed by Congress, and ratified by the Legislatures of the several States, pursuant to the fifth Article of the original Constitution.

Amendment I
Congress shall make no law respecting an establishment of religion, or prohibiting the free exercise thereof; or abridging the freedom of speech, or of the press; or the right of the people peaceably to assemble, and to petition the Government for a redress of grievances.

Amendment II
A well regulated Militia, being necessary to the security of a free State, the right of the people to keep and bear Arms, shall not be infringed.

Amendment III
No Soldier shall, in time of peace be quartered in any house, without the consent of the Owner, nor in time of war, but in a manner to be prescribed by law.

Amendment IV
The right of the people to be secure in their persons, houses, papers, and effects, against unreasonable searches and seizures, shall not be violated, and no Warrants shall issue, but upon probable cause, supported by Oath or affirmation, and particularly describing the place to be searched, and the persons or things to be seized.

Amendment V
No person shall be held to answer for a capital, or otherwise infamous crime, unless on a presentment or indictment of a Grand Jury, except in cases arising in the land or naval forces, or in the Militia, when in actual service in time of War or public danger; nor shall any person be subject for the same offence to be twice put in jeopardy of life or limb; nor shall be compelled in any criminal case to be a witness against himself, nor be

deprived of life, liberty, or property, without due process of law; nor shall private property be taken for public use, without just compensation.

Amendment VI

In all criminal prosecutions, the accused shall enjoy the right to a speedy and public trial, by an impartial jury of the State and district wherein the crime shall have been committed, which district shall have been previously ascertained by law, and to be informed of the nature and cause of the accusation; to be confronted with the witnesses against him; to have compulsory process for obtaining witnesses in his favor, and to have the Assistance of Counsel for his defense.

Amendment VII

In Suits at common law, where the value in controversy shall exceed twenty dollars, the right of trial by jury shall be preserved, and no fact tried by a jury, shall be otherwise re-examined in any Court of the United States, than according to the rules of the common law.

Amendment VIII

Excessive bail shall not be required, nor excessive fines imposed, nor cruel and unusual punishments inflicted.

Amendment IX

The enumeration in the Constitution, of certain rights, shall not be construed to deny or disparage others retained by the people.

Amendment X

The powers not delegated to the United States by the Constitution, nor prohibited by it to the States, are reserved to the States respectively, or to the people.

CHAPTER 12 —
THE FRENCH REVOLUTION AND NAPOLEON
(1789-1815 CE)

GUIDING QUESTIONS
- What was the mood in France in the 1780s and why?
- What was the Ancien Regime in France?
- What were the causes of the French Revolution? Explain four.
- What was the impact of the American Revolution on France?
- How did the French Revolution shift from a moderate to a radical revolution?
- What was the Reign of Terror? Why did it begin and how did it end?
- How did Napoleon rise to power in France? Does his rise remind you of any other dictators in history? Explain.

France in the late 1700s was a mix of many emotions. On one hand, the people of France suffered tremendously under the oppression and extravagance of the Bourbon dynasty. The vast majority of people struggled for survival under a government that scarcely ever considered the plight of its citizens. On the other hand, few places in history were more alive with enthusiasm and optimism than France in the 1780s. The human spirit was triumphing over tyranny in America and England and Enlightenment ideals were alive and well. In 1789, the French deeply believed their nation would be the home of the next and most glorious triumph. They had plenty of reasons to be optimistic. One hundred years earlier the English had triumphed over the divine right of kings in the Glorious Revolution. The English Bill of Rights was a beacon to all who dreamt of a society where people's liberties were protected by government. An English minister named Richard Price, on the 100-year anniversary of the Glorious Revolution, had this to say of the example set by England for freedom-loving people the world over:

What an eventful period this is! I am thankful that I have lived to see it; and I could almost say, Lord, now lettest thou thy servant depart in peace, for mine eyes have seen thy salvation. I have lived to see a diffusion of knowledge, which has undermined superstition and error -- I have lived to see the rights of men better understood than ever; and nations panting for liberty, which seem to have lost the idea of it. I have lived to see 30 MILLIONS of people, indignant and resolute, spurning at slavery, and demanding liberty with an irresistible voice; their king led in triumph, and an arbitrary monarch surrendering himself to his subjects. -- After sharing in the benefits of one revolution, I have been spared to be witness to two other revolutions, both glorious. And now methinks I see the love for liberty catching and spreading, a general amendment beginning in human affairs; the dominion of kings changed for the dominion of laws, and the dominion of priests giving way to the dominion of reason and conscience.

Be encouraged, all ye friends of freedom, and writers in its defense! The times are auspicious. Your labours have not been in vain. Behold kingdoms, admonished by you, starting from sleep, breaking their fetters, and claiming justice from their oppressors! Behold, the light you have struck out, after setting America free, reflected to France, and there kindled into a blaze that lays despotism in ashes, and warms and illuminates EUROPE!

Tremble all ye oppressors of the world! Take warning all ye supporters of slavish governments. . . . Call no more reformation, innovation. You cannot hold the world in darkness. Struggle no longer against increasing light and liberality. Restore to mankind their rights; and consent to the correction of abuses, before they and you are destroyed together.

"Tremble all ye oppressors of the world!" That is a powerful warning and it was on the minds and lips of citizens from France to the Carribbean. By 1900, dozens of nations staged their own revolutions and threw off their imperialist oppressors. The revolutionary fire, first fanned by the English Civil War and its aftermath, erupted full blaze after the American Revolution and was afterwards uncontainable.

The writer Thomas Carlyle wrote about the powerful example set in France by the American Revolution:

The world is all so changed; so much that seemed vigorous has sunk decrepit, so much that was not is beginning to be!--Borne over the Atlantic, to the closing ear of Louis, King by the Grace of God, what sounds are these; muffled ominous, new in our centuries? Boston Harbour is black with unexpected Tea: behold a Pennsylvanian Congress gather; and ere long, on Bunker Hill, DEMOCRACY announcing, in rifle-volleys death-winged, under her Star Banner, to the tune of Yankee-doodle-doo, that she is born, and, whirlwind-like, will envelope the whole world!

Such were the sentiments that were brewing in France by the summer of 1789. Life if France by the 1780s was very, very hard for the common French citizen. But a new world seemed possible for the first time. All that had to be done was topple the old world, which the French called the *Ancien Regime*. The French were empowered by the English and American examples of winning rights for citizens in government. But what the French envisioned was a much more radical overhaul than had been achieved in either America or England. England and America changed their governments substantially but much of the social structure, including the consolidation of wealth and power into the hands of the few, did not change. The French wanted social equality as well as political liberty. They wanted a truly radical reimagining of French society, which was encapsulated in the slogan of the French Revolution—"Liberty, Equality, Fraternity."

The problem with ending the Ancien Regime is that it was a very, very old and very firmly established regime or system. French civilization was the oldest in Europe. If you will recall, it was the Merovingian kings dating back to the 5th century that conquered and unified what is France today. France had been run both politically and economically by a king and powerful land-owning nobles for nearly twelve centuries by the time of the French Revolution. And 1200 years of history is very hard to undo. France was still rigidly divided into three social classes, or estates. The First Estate was made of the clergy. The Second Estate was made up of nobles. Both groups exercised tremendous political power and owned most of the land in France yet they paid little to no taxes. Together, the First and Second Estates consisted of about 500,000 people. The Third Estate in France was made up of "everyone else" and consisted of about 25 million French citizens.

Though the Third Estate was by far the largest segment of French society, they had virtually no political power and paid the majority of the taxes. The French legislative body was called the Estates General and was made up of representatives from each of the three estates. While this was a noble concept in theory, each estate only got one vote in the Estates' General, and the First and Second Estates almost always voted together on laws. Typically they voted against change and for the maintenance of the status quo. Therefore, change within the existing French government was all but impossible. As the economic situation in France grew increasingly bad, so did the quality of life for the members of the Third Estate. And they grew increasingly frustrated with their inability to improve things.

There is a tendency when explaining the causes of revolutions to simply say "oppression." To be sure, oppression of the French people by the 1780s was extreme. The Bourbon dynasty had been the reigning family in France for 200 years by the eve of the revolution and they lived lives completely out of touch with their subjects. Louis XIV, the Sun King, was the epitome of absolutism and is most famous for using the people's tax dollars to build the most elaborate palace ever imagined. By the late 1700s, France had suffered through the tyranny of three Louis'—Louis XIII, Louis XIV and Louis XV. They were living under the despotism of Louis XVI by the beginning of the Revolution and with every king's reign, the spending became more extravagant and the suffering of the people grew more intense. As you have read, the Third Estate, which was made up of peasants and unskilled laborers as well as the educated middle class known as the bourgeoisie, paid all the taxes in France. And as kings grew more in debt, the tax burden on the Third Estate grew. This taxation without true representation was a major cause of the French Revolution. But there were many others.

The price of grain skyrocketed in France in the 1780s and so did the price of bread. Bread was the staple of the French diet and the average person ate as many as three loaves of bread a day, and sometimes nothing else. By 1789, a single loaf of bread cost an entire day's wages and consequently the people of France were starving. The French government did little to alleviate this problem. Amidst this great suffering, the Enlightenment was in full swing. As people toiled and died, men like Voltaire, Rousseau, Adam Smith and others grappled with the question of "Why?" Why in a land of plenty was there so little bounty for the common man? Was this not against man's very nature as equal and freedom-loving creatures? Enlightenment ideals like liberty, equality and the brotherhood of all humanity took hold in France more powerfully than anywhere else. While American colonists dreamt of a new political identity separate from England, the French dreamt of a great leveling of all that was unlevel or unequal in the world. They wanted to tear down the existing world brick by brick and build something entirely new based on the ideals of the Enlightenment. In their minds, the English and the American successes over tyranny were all the proof they needed that their dreams were achievable. But what they envisioned was far more extreme and sweeping than what had been accomplished in either England or the colonies.

1789 was the year the French Revolution began. In the summer of that year, a united group of Third Estate representatives drafted and presented a set of ideals that they were fighting for. That document was called the Declaration of the Rights of Man and the Citizen and it was a moderate but sweeping embodiment of enlightened ideas about government. For the first three years of the fighting against the reign of Louis

315

XVI and the French nobility, the principles of this document were largely agreed to be the ones for which they were fighting. But something went wrong and things became much more extreme in 1792, the year that King Louis XVI and his wife, Marie Antoinette, were executed. A more radical leader of the revolution, Maximilian Robespierre, came to the forefront and demanded more radical action in pursuit of more radical change. Robespierre was a charismatic speaker who capitalized on the anger the French people felt at the time. Under his leadership, moderate leaders were swept aside, even killed, in favor of more violent and universal change. Over the next two years, more than 40,000 declared "enemies" of the Revolution were executed by the guillotine at the order of Robespierre. Robespierre created what he called "the Republic of Virtue" with himself as the chairman of the Committee on Public Safety, a heavy-handed organization that censored ideas and searched for suspected opponents of this radical change. It became clear very quickly that what Robespierre was creating with his "Reign of Terror" was decidedly *not* what the French had started the Revolution to achieve. Robespierre was arrested and sentenced to death, proving true the saying, "Revolutions devour their own children."

A period of chaotic reordering followed the end of the Reign of Terror and several different new governments were tried, all of which failed. As France was trying to put itself back together again after the Reign of Terror, France's neighbors were growing very nervous. Kings and queens of Europe began to fear the spread of revolutionary ideas beyond France and began raising armies to contain France's radical revolutionary spirit. In response to the militarization of France's neighbors, France felt compelled to raise its own force to defend itself and to counter-balance the war-like spirit gripping the continent. They sought the best military leaders to lead their armies. And in their talent search, the came across an ambitious young Corsican man named Napoleon Bonaparte who seemed to be an answer to their prayers. The men who hired Napoleon could not have foreseen, however, that in this supposed savior of France was the man who would be their next absolute ruler and the conqueror of all of Europe.

Napoleon Bonaparte, the most famous figure in French history, was not even French. He was from a small Mediterranean island called Corsica that had been conquered by France in Napoleon's youth. Napoleon had no love for France early in his life. However, Napoleon's ambition was more powerful than his devotion to his homeland, and when he saw that France was in chaos, he quickly recognized that France would be the place where he would achieve his rise to power. Napoleon rose quickly through the ranks of the French military and had a way of making even his defeats look like great victories. Napoleon achieved his first set of major victories in Italy in 1795. By 1799, he orchestrated a coup d'etat in which he overthrew the French Directory which had hired him and created a new government which he called the Consulate. Napoleon was one of three consuls in a triumvirate, meaning he technically shared power with two other men. Before the end of 1799, Napoleon assumed the title of First Consul, giving him more power than his counterparts. You may remember the term "consul" and "triumvirate" from our study of the Roman Republic, which appointed co-consuls as the executive powers in Roman government. Napoleon carefully and deliberately choose the term consul instead of king, president or emperor. The French had just fought a bloody revolution to end the tyranny of the French monarchy so Napoleon was careful not to make himself look too much like a king—at first.

Once in power, Napoleon quickly took over control of France in subtle but effective ways. In 1802 he was elected Consul for Life (much like Julius Caesar had been in 44 BCE). He achieved this seizure of unchecked power by rewriting the French Constitution to make his new position legal. Roughly 99% of the French people voted to approve the new Constitution and the power it gave to Napoleon. After the strife they had lived through in the preceding decades, Napoleon represented the promise of stability and a better future. He did make many substantial improvements to life in France; however, the reforms and other changes were carefully calculated for maximum benefit to Napoleon himself as he continued his meteoric rise to the top of the power hierarchy in Europe. For instance, Napoleon brought public education to France, making it the first country in the Western world to have such a system. But he did this largely to increase the quality of recruits he had working under him in the government and the military. Napoleon also streamlined and modernized the French legal code, which became known as the Napoleonic Code, and did away with thousands of outdated and contradictory laws in France. This was good for the people but it was also good for Napoleon because clear and consistent laws are easy to enforce and help to maintain law and order. The Roman Emperor Augustus was also well known for making reforms that won the respect of the people, but which actually benefitted him more than they benefitted his unsuspecting subjects.

While Napoleon brought a high degree of peace and stability to France, he continued his conquest of his European neighbors. In 1804, Napoleon had himself crowned Emperor of France and made clear his intentions of creating a French Empire. Between 1804 and 1812, Napoleon nearly succeeded in conquering all of Europe. Only England stood in his way of complete domination. Since early in Napoleon's military career, he had been frustrated by his attempts to defeat Britain in battle. He had lost to Britain in Egypt and knew he could not beat Britain in a naval battle because the British had the most powerful navy in the world by 1800. Napoleon resolved that if he could not defeat Britain by force he would destroy them economically. Unfortunately, it was his obsession with conquering Britain that would lead to his downfall.

By 1806, Napoleon had either conquered or created alliances with every nation in Europe except Britain. In that year, he decreed that any country that was under his control or allied with him was forbidden from trading with Britain or her colonies. This prohibition on trade between Britain and the continent of Europe was known as the Continental System. Far from having the desired result of crushing Britain's economy, the Continental System turned many of his allies against him and caused his empire to unravel as quickly as it has been assembled. Britain was the most powerful trade empire in the world in 1800 and forcing nations to cut off trade with Britain was economically devastating. At first, most nations tried to be compliant, fearing war with Napoleon if they were not. But as the economic toll became unbearable, many of those same nations first secretly and then openly began trading with Britain again. To do otherwise, they argued, was economic suicide.

Russia was one of the nations that violated the Continental System. Napoleon was enraged. In 1812, he vowed to make an example of Russia to show what happened when a nation defied Napoleon. He assembled an army of more than 700,000 men in 1812 and launched a full-scale invasion of Russia. It was a disaster. Undeterred by the coming of the Russian winter, Napoleon forced his troops to march deeper and deeper into Russia. The Russian army refused to engage Napoleon in any significant battle, choosing instead to let the Russian weather wreak havoc on the French forces. Their plan worked. Napoleon marched into Russia in the summer of 1812 with 700,000 men. When he retreated out of Russia again in the winter of that same year, he had less than 25,000 men at his side.

Napoleon never recovered from the disaster of his Russian Campaign. He did rebuild his army and continued to fight against a growing coalition of European nations who had grown tired of his rule of the continent. In 1814, Napoleon was soundly defeated by the Grand Coalition of European nations and was forced to surrender. As a result of his surrender, he was exiled to a small Mediterranean island called Elba, where he was to live out the remainder of his life in peace. But Napoleon refused to give up all he had won. For a short 100 days in 1815, Napoleon once again ruled in France, after having been smuggled back into Paris by loyal supporters. He raised an army of more than 200,000 men but he was once again defeated, this time at the Battle of Waterloo in June of 1815. This would be Napoleon's final defeat. Not wanting to take any chances with another return to power from Napoleon, this time he was exiled to a tiny, desolate island called St. Helena which was 1200 miles of the western coast of Africa. Napoleon died there in 1821, almost completely alone.

With Napoleon finally out of the picture, the other nations of Europe had to figure out how to repair the damage Napoleon had caused across Europe. In 1815 they convened a meeting, called the Congress of Vienna, in 1815 to craft a lasting peace. The mastermind of those meetings was an Austrian diplomat named Klemens von Metternich. Metternich was determined that the negotiations in Vienna not be dominated by vengeance but instead by a spirit of reconciliation. With that in mind, his goals were: to restore the legitimate royals to their positions in nations conquered by Napoleon; to restore prewar borders so that countries that lost territory to France were made whole again; and to strengthen France's neighbors so that small nations would not be susceptible to easy conquest in the future. Metternich's goals were met and implemented nearly exactly as he had envisioned and the peace agreement that came out of the Congress of Vienna achieved 99 years of peace in Europe. The great genius of the deliberations in Vienna in 1815 is that they did not set out to punish France for the actions of Napoleon. The goal was to make things right; not to punish, humiliate or destroy. As a result of these level-headed negotiations, there would not be major war in Europe until 1914, which is the year that World War I began.

Arthur Young, *Travels in France*, 1787 CE

Reading and Discussion Questions
1. Who is Arthur Young and what perspective does he offer on conditions in France?
2. What is Paris like and how does it compare to London, in the writer's opinion?
3. Based on this document of Arthur Young's travels, explain two reasons the French peasants were dissatisfied with their life during this period of French history.

France by the mid-1700s was full of suffering and unhappiness. The level of poverty and misery in Paris had prompted Adam Smith to write his book, Wealth of Nations, to see why some countries and its people are prosperous and others are not. Smith looked at the suffering in France from a purely economic perspective but others chronicled the suffering of the French people as more of an analysis of the human condition. One of the best accounts we have of the widespread misery of the French people in the 1780s comes from a young Englishman named Arthur Young, who traveled through France at the end of the 18 Century. He was an English farmer and writer, known for his honesty and forthrightness. The following are excerpts from his book about his journey and the suffering he witnessed, entitled Arthur Young's Travels in France during the Years 1787, 1788, 1789

This great city [Paris] appears to be in many respects the most ineligible and inconvenient for the residence of a person of small fortune of any that I have seen, and vastly inferior to London. The streets are very narrow, and many of them crowded, nine tenths dirty, and all without foot pavements. Walking, which in London is so pleasant and so clean that ladies do it every day, is here a toil and a fatigue to a man, and an impossibility to a well-dressed woman. The coaches are numerous, and, what is much worse, there are an infinity of one-horse cabriolets, which are driven by young men of fashion and their imitators, alike fools, with such rapidity as to be real nuisances, and render the streets exceedingly dangerous, without an incessant caution. I saw a poor child run over and probably killed, and have been myself many times blackened with the mud of the kennels. This beggarly practice, of driving a one-horse booby hutch about the streets of a great capital, flows either from poverty or wretched and despicable economy; nor is it possible to speak of it with too much severity. If young noblemen at London were to drive their chaises in streets without footways, as their brethren do at Paris, they would speedily and justly get very well threshed or rolled in the kennel. This circumstance renders Paris an ineligible residence for persons, particularly families that cannot afford to keep a coach, - a convenience which is as dear as at London. The fiacres - hackney coaches - are much worse than at that city; and chairs there are none, for they would be driven down in the streets. To this circumstance also it is owing that all persons of small or moderate fortune are forced to dress in black, with black stockings.

[handwritten: Paris - dirty / London - nice]

Of his encounter with a French peasant he writes:

Walking up a long hill, to ease my mare, I was joined by a poor woman, who complained of the times, and that it was a sad country; demanding her reasons, she said her husband had but a morsel of land, one cow, and a poor little horse, yet they had a franchar (42lb.) of wheat, and three chickens, to pay as a quit-rent to one Seigneur [noble]; and four franchar of oats, one chicken and 1 sou [small unit of money] to pay to another, besides very heavy tailles [taxes on the land and its produce] and other taxes. She had seven children, and the cow's milk helped to make the soup. But why, instead of a horse, do not you keep another cow? Oh, her husband could not carry his produce so well without a horse; and asses are little used in the country. It was said, at present, that something was to be done by some great folks for such poor ones, but she did not know who nor how, but God send us better, car les tailles & les droits nous ecrasent [because the taxes and laws are crushing us]. —This woman, at no great distance, might have been taken for sixty or seventy, her figure was so bent, and her face so furrowed [wrinkled] and hardened by labour, — but she said she was only twenty-eight. An Englishman who has not travelled, cannot imagine the figure made by infinitely the greater part of the countrywomen in France; it speaks, at the first sight, hard and severe labour: I am inclined to think, that they work harder than the men, and this, united with the more miserable labour of bringing a new race of slaves into the world, destroys absolutely all symmetry of person [balanced proportions] and every feminine appearance. To what are we to attribute this difference in the manners of the lower people in the two kingdoms? To Government . . . .

Joseph Emmanuel Sieyès, What Is the Third Estate?, 1789 CE

<u>Reading and Discussion Questions</u>
1. According to Sieyès, what function does the Third Estate serve in society? Why does he say the Third Estate is a complete nation?
2. Why does Sieyes argue that the French nobles are not a part of the nation?
3. What does the Third Estate want and why does Sieyes say they deserve it?

The Abbe Emmanuel Joseph Sieyes was a French priest who was an outspoken supporter of social and political reform in France. He wrote pamphlets in support of the French Revolution and made passionate speeches about the rights of the silent majority in France. His most famous pamphlet was entitled "What is the Third Estate?" In it he eloquently spelled out the ways in which the common people of France were being denied a voice in or protections from the government. Sieyes was not only an important voice in the early days of the French Revolution but he remained influential and held various government positions during the various phases of the French Revolution, which dragged on until the early 1800s. Sieyes even became a member of the five-man executive body in France called the Directory, which governed France after the Reign of Terror. Sieyes, in his role as a member of the Directory, also helped to launch the career of Napoleon Bonaparte.

What is the Third Estate?

The plan of this work is quite simple. We have three questions to consider: (1) What is the third estate? Everything. (2) What has it been in the political order up to the present? Nothing. (3) What does it demand? To become something....

The Third Estate is a Complete Nation

What is necessary that a nation should subsist and prosper? Individual effort and public functions.

All individual efforts may be included in four classes: (1) Since the earth and the waters furnish crude products for the needs of man, the first class, in logical sequence, will be that of all families which devote themselves to agricultural labor. (2) Between the first sale of products and their consumption or use, a new manipulation, more of less repeated, adds to these products a second value more or less composite. In this manner human industry succeeds in perfecting the gifts of nature, and the crude product increases twofold, tenfold, one hundred-fold in value. Such are the efforts of the second class. (3) Between production and consumption, as well as between the various stages of production, a group of intermediary agents establish themselves, useful both to producers and consumers; these are the merchants and brokers: the brokers who, comparing incessantly the demands of time and place, speculate upon the profit of retention and transportation; merchants who are charged with distribution, in the last analysis, either at wholesale or at retail. This species of utility characterizes the third class. (4) Outside of these three classes of productive and useful citizens, who are occupied with real objects of consumption and use, there is also need in a society of a series of efforts and pains, whose objects are directly useful or agreeable to the individual. This fourth class embraces all those who stand between the most distinguished and liberal professions and the less esteemed services of domestics.

Such are the efforts which sustain society. Who puts them forth? The Third Estate.

Public functions may be classified equally well, in the present state of affairs, under four recognized heads: the sword, the robe, the church, and the administration. It would be superfluous to take them up one by one, for the purpose of showing that everywhere the Third Estate attends to nineteen-twentieths of them, with this distinction; that it is laden with all that which is really painful, with all the burdens which the privileged classes refuse to carry. Do we give the Third Estate credit for this? That this might come about, it would be necessary that the Third Estate should refuse to fill these places, or that it should be less ready to exercise their functions. The facts are well known. Meanwhile they have dared to impose a prohibition upon the order of the Third Estate. They have said to it: "Whatever may be your services, whatever may be your abilities, you shall go thus far; you may not pass beyond!" Certain rare exceptions, properly regarded, are but a mockery, and the terms which are indulged in on such occasions, one insult the more.

Who then shall dare to say that the Third Estate has not within itself all that is necessary for the formation of a complete nation? It is the strong and robust man who has one arm still shackled. If the privileged order should be abolished, the nation would be nothing less, but something more. Therefore, what is the Third Estate? Everything; but an everything shackled and oppressed. What would it be without the privileged order? Everything, but an everything free and flourishing. Nothing can succeed without it, everything would be infinitely better without the others.

What is a nation? A body of associates, living under a common law, and represented by the same legislature, etc.

It is not evident that the noble order has privileges and expenditures which it dares to call its rights, but which are apart from the rights of the great body of citizens? It departs there from the common order, from the common law. So its civil rights make of it an isolated people in the midst of the great nation. This is truly imperium in imperio.

In regard to its political rights, these also it exercises apart. It has its special representatives, which are not charged with securing the interests of the people. The body of its deputies sit apart; and when it is assembled in the same hall with the deputies of simple citizens, it is none the less true that its representation is essentially distinct and separate: it is a stranger to the nation, in the first place, by its origin, since its commission is not derived from the people; then by its object, which consists of defending not the general, but the particular interest.

The Third Estate embraces then all that which belongs to the nation; and all that which is not the Third Estate, cannot be regarded as being of the nation. What is the Third Estate? It is the whole.

What Does the Third Estate Demand? To Become Something.

It is not necessary to judge its demands on the basis of the isolated observations of a few authors more or less informed about the rights of man. The third estate is still very backward in this respect, not only with regard to the insights of those who have studied the social order, but also with regard to that mass of common ideas which constitutes public opinion. The true petitions of this estate cannot be appreciated except in terms of the authentic protests which the great municipalities of the kingdom have addressed to the government. What do these show? That the people want to be something, and in truth the least possible. It wants to have genuine representatives in the Estates General, that is to say, deputies drawn from its own ranks, who are capable of being the interpreters of its desire and the protectors of its interests. But of what use is it to this estate to be present in the Estates General if the interest contrary to its own predominates there! It would only serve to give sanction by its presence to the oppression of which it is the eternal victim.

Therefore it is quite certain that it cannot come to vote at the Estates General if it ought not to have there an influence which is as least equal to that of the privileged classes, and it demands a number of representatives equal to the number of the two other orders together. Finally, this equality of representation would become completely illusory if every chamber had its separate voice. The third estate demands therefore that the votes be taken by heads and not by order. These protests which have created such alarm in the circles of the privileged amount to this, because it is only from this that the reform of abuses would follow. The true intention of the third estate is to have in the Estates General an influence equal to that of the privileged. I repeat, can it ask less? And is it not clear that if its influence there is not equal, one cannot hope that it will leave its state of political nullity and become something?

Declaration of the Rights of Man and Citizen, 1789 CE

Reading and Discussion Questions
1. Analyze the tone of this document. What is the mood or emotional feel here? Compare it to the tone of the Declaration of Independence.
2. Summarize in your own words the rights that the French people are demanding.
3. How many of these rights are similar to rights Americans fought for in their revolution? What differences, if any, do you see in the rights the French were fighting for and the ones that America fought for in won a decade earlier?

In 1789, a collection of members from the Third Estate in France left a meeting of the Estates General which had been convened by King Louis XVI. As the majority of the population in France, the Third Estate declared themselves a new government called the National Assembly. The Declaration of the Rights of Man and Citizen was their proclamation of the principles upon which their new institution was founded.

The representatives of the French people, organized as a National Assembly, believing that the ignorance, neglect, or contempt of the rights of man are the sole cause of public calamities and of the corruption of governments, have determined to set forth in a solemn declaration the natural, unalienable, and sacred rights of man, in order that this declaration, being constantly before all the members of the Social body, shall remind them continually of their rights and duties; in order that the acts of the legislative power, as well as those of the executive power, may be compared at any moment with the objects and purposes of all political institutions and may thus be

323

more respected, and, lastly, in order that the grievances of the citizens, based hereafter upon simple and incontestable principles, shall tend to the maintenance of the constitution and redound to the happiness of all. Therefore the National Assembly recognizes and proclaims, in the presence and under the auspices of the Supreme Being, the following rights of man and of the citizen:

1. Men are born and remain free and equal in rights. Social distinctions may be founded only upon the general good.

2. The aim of all political association is the preservation of the natural and imprescriptible rights of man. These rights are liberty, property, security, and resistance to oppression.

3. The principle of all sovereignty resides essentially in the nation. No body nor individual may exercise any authority which does not proceed directly from the nation.

4. Liberty consists in the freedom to do everything which injures no one else; hence the exercise of the natural rights of each man has no limits except those which assure to the other members of the society the enjoyment of the same rights. These limits can only be determined by law.

5. Law can only prohibit such actions as are hurtful to society. Nothing may be prevented which is not forbidden by law, and no one may be forced to do anything not provided for by law.

6. Law is the expression of the general will. Every citizen has a right to participate personally, or through his representative, in its foundation. It must be the same for all, whether it protects or punishes. All citizens, being equal in the eyes of the law, are equally eligible to all dignities and to all public positions and occupations, according to their abilities, and without distinction except that of their virtues and talents.

7. No person shall be accused, arrested, or imprisoned except in the cases and according to the forms prescribed by law. Any one soliciting, transmitting, executing, or causing to be executed, any arbitrary order, shall be punished. But any citizen summoned or arrested in virtue of the law shall submit without delay, as resistance constitutes an offense.

8. The law shall provide for such punishments only as are strictly and obviously necessary, and no one shall suffer punishment except it be legally inflicted in virtue of a law passed and promulgated before the commission of the offense.

9. As all persons are held innocent until they shall have been declared guilty, if arrest shall be deemed indispensable, all harshness not essential to the securing of the prisoner's person shall be severely repressed by law.

10. No one shall be disquieted on account of his opinions, including his religious views, provided their manifestation does not disturb the public order established by law.

11. The free communication of ideas and opinions is one of the most precious of the rights of man. Every citizen may, accordingly, speak, write, and print with freedom, but shall be responsible for such abuses of this freedom as shall be defined by law.

12. The security of the rights of man and of the citizen requires public military forces. These forces are, therefore, established for the good of all and not for the personal advantage of those to whom they shall be entrusted.

13. A common contribution is essential for the maintenance of the public forces and for the cost of administration. This should be equitably distributed among all the citizens in proportion to their means.

14. All the citizens have a right to decide, either personally or by their representatives, as to the necessity of the public contribution; to grant this freely; to know to what uses it is put; and to fix the proportion, the mode of assessment and of collection and the duration of the taxes.

15. Society has the right to require of every public agent an account of his administration.

16. A society in which the observance of the law is not assured, nor the separation of powers defined, has no constitution at all.

17. Since property is an inviolable and sacred right, no one shall be deprived thereof except where public necessity, legally determined, shall clearly demand it, and then only on condition that the owner shall have been previously and equitably indemnified.

Olympe de Gouges, *Declaration of the Rights of Women*, 1791 CE

Reading and Discussion Questions

1. This document begins as a call to action. Who is de Gouges calling to action and what is she calling on them to do?

2. In what ways is de Gouges accusing French men of being hypocrites in their revolutionary struggle for equality?

3. What are de Gouges' criticisms about marriage? In what ways does she propose to change the relationship between men and women, and husbands and wives?

4. What are the terms of the marriage contract the author proposes? What does it do in relation to wealth and property?

5. What does de Gouges propose in regard to prostitutes? Why do you think she included this part?

6. Why do you think de Gouges was executed during the French Revolution? Does anything in this document come across as treasonous? Why was it decided she was an enemy of France?

Olympe de Gouges was a middle-class French activist during the French Revolution. Before the outbreak of the Revolution, she championed many other humanitarian causes, including the abolition of the slave trade or at least the more humane treatment of slaves. She fought for equality of all those who were denied it, including women. In 1789, the French National Assembly passed the Declaration of the Rights of Man and Citizen. This document was a declaration of principles for the protection of all French citizens in a brotherhood of man. Presumably, the drafters of the Declaration of the Rights of Man meant the word "man" to represent all of humanity but de Gouges read this title literally and believed it represented the continued exclusion of women from political and social equality. In response to the Declaration of the Rights of Man, she wrote the infamous Declaration of the Rights of Woman. In it she pointed out the unbalanced nature of relations between men and women and called on womankind to use the energy of the Revolution to win rights of their own. De Gouges was passionate in the language she used and she directly challenged many powerful people in France with her criticisms. Ultimately, the power and passion of her words brought her to the attention of radical revolutionaries in France, who viewed her writings as treasonous. She was tried and convicted of treason in 1793 and was executed by guillotine in that same year.

Woman, wake up; the tocsin of reason is being heard throughout the whole universe; discover your rights. The powerful empire of nature is no longer surrounded by prejudice, fanaticism, superstition, and lies. The flame of truth has dispersed all the clouds of folly and usurpation. Enslaved man has multiplied his strength and needs recourse to yours to break his chains. Having become free, he has become unjust to his companion. Oh, women, women! When will you cease to be blind? What advantage have you received from the Revolution? A more pronounced scorn, a more marked disdain. French legislators, correctors of that morality, long ensnared by political practices now out of date, will only say again to you: women, what is there in common between you and us? Everything, you will have to answer. If they persist in their weakness of contradicting their principles, courageously oppose the force of reason to the empty pretentions of superiority; unite yourselves beneath the standards of philosophy; deploy all the energy of your character, and you will soon see these haughty men, not groveling at your feet as servile adorers, but proud to share with you the treasures of the Supreme Being. Regardless of what barriers confront you, it is in your power to free yourselves; you have only to want to....

Marriage is the tomb of trust and love. The married woman can with impunity give bastards to her husband, and also give them the wealth which does not belong to them. The woman who is unmarried has only one feeble right; ancient and inhuman laws refuse to her for her children the right to the name and the wealth of their father; no new laws have been made in this matter. If it is considered a paradox and an impossibility on my part to try to give my sex an honorable and just consistency, I leave it to men to attain glory for dealing with this matter; but while we wait, the way can be prepared through national education, the restoration of morals, and conjugal conventions.

Form for a Social Contract Between Man and Woman
We, _____ and _____, moved by our own will, unite ourselves for the duration of our lives, and for the duration of our mutual inclinations, under the following conditions: We intend and wish to make our wealth communal, meanwhile reserving to ourselves the right to divide it in favor of our children and of those toward whom we might have a particular inclination, mutually recognizing that our property belongs directly to our children, from whatever bed they come, and that all of them without distinction have the right to bear the name of the fathers and mothers who have acknowledged them, and we are charged to subscribe to the law which punishes the renunciation of one's own blood. We likewise obligate ourselves, in case of separation, to divide our wealth and to set aside in advance the portion the law indicates for our children, and in the event of a perfect union, the one who dies will divest himself of half his property in his children's favor, and if one dies childless, the survivor will inherit by right, unless the dying person has disposed of half the common property in favor of one whom he judged deserving.

That is approximately the formula for the marriage act I propose for execution. Upon reading this strange document, I see rising up against me the hypocrites, the prudes, the clergy, and the whole infernal sequence. But how it [my proposal] offers to the wise the moral means of achieving the perfection of a happy government! . . .

Moreover, I would like a law which would assist widows and young girls deceived by the false promises of a man to whom they were attached; I would like, I say, this law to force an inconstant man to hold to his obligations or at least [to pay] an indemnity equal to his wealth. Again, I would like this law to be rigorous against women, at least those who have the effrontery to have recourse to a law which they themselves had violated by their misconduct, if proof of that were given. At the same time, prostitutes should be placed in designated quarters. It is not prostitutes who contribute the most to the depravity of morals, it is the women of society. In regenerating the latter, the former are changed. This link of fraternal union will first bring disorder, but in consequence it will produce at the end a perfect harmony.
I offer a foolproof way to elevate the soul of women; it is to join them to all the activities of man; if man persists in finding this way impractical, let him share his fortune with woman, not at his caprice, but by the wisdom of laws. Prejudice falls, morals are

purified, and nature regains all her rights. Add to this the marriage of priests and the strengthening of the king on his throne, and the French government cannot fail.

Maximilien Robespierre, On Virtue and Terror, 1794 CE

Reading and Discussion Questions
1. How does Robespierre define "virtue?" What happens when a group or a nation loses its virtue?
2. What is the great weakness of the Revolution, according to Robespierre?
3. Analyze the quote, "We must smother the internal and external enemies of the Republic or perish with it." Who are the internal and external enemies? What must be done with them, according to Robespierre?
4. According to Robespierre, what is "terror" and what is its relationship to "virtue?"
5. What is your reaction to this speech? Is there any truth to the points Robespierre makes? Why or why not? Explain your answer.

Maximilien Robespierre was the mouthpiece of the radical phase of the French Revolution and the most outspoken member of the radical revolutionaries called the Jacobins. Robespierre seemed to reinvent himself as the tides changed in France. In the beginning, he was a defender of Louis XVI but later he became one of the loudest voices in support of Louis' execution. Robespierre was a lawyer and a gifted orator. He realized during the early years of the revolution that he had a great power to move people with his words. Over time his beliefs and his words grew more and more radical. After the execution of the king in 1792, the Jacobins created the twelve-man Committee of Public Safety and Robespierre was the leader of that group.

The Committee of Public Safety was notorious for hunting down suspected opponents of the radical Revolution and executing them. During a period of exceptional violence, called the Reign of Terror, more than 40,000 people were executed by guillotine, most at the order of Robespierre. When challenged about his use of widespread and ruthless violence in the name of the Revolution, Robespierre argued that terror was sometimes necessary to achieve virtue. First war, then peace, was the logic that Robespierre used to justify his actions. Eventually, Robespierre became a casualty of his own Reign of Terror. By 1794, Robespierre had grown too radical even for his radical friends and he was arrested as an enemy of the Revolution. He was executed by guillotine in July of 1794 and his death marked the end of the Reign of Terror.

But, to found and consolidate democracy, to achieve the peaceable reign of the constitutional laws, we must end the war of liberty against tyranny and pass safely across the storms of the revolution: such is the aim of the revolutionary system that you have enacted. Your conduct, then, ought also to be regulated by the stormy circumstances in which the republic is placed; and the plan of your administration must result from the spirit of the revolutionary government combined with the general principles of democracy.

Now, what is the fundamental principle of the democratic or popular government-that is, the essential spring which makes it move? It is virtue; I am speaking of the public virtue which effected so many prodigies in Greece and Rome and which ought to

328

produce much more surprising ones in republican France; of that virtue which is nothing other than the love of country and of its laws.

But as the essence of the republic or of democracy is equality, it follows that the love of country necessarily includes the love of equality.

It is also true that this sublime sentiment assumes a preference for the public interest over every particular interest; hence the love of country presupposes or produces all the virtues: for what are they other than that spiritual strength which renders one capable of those sacrifices? And how could the slave of avarice or ambition, for example, sacrifice his idol to his country?

Not only is virtue the soul of democracy; it can exist only in that government ....

Republican virtue can be considered in relation to the people and in relation to the government; it is necessary in both. When only the government lacks virtue, there remains a resource in the people's virtue; but when the people itself is corrupted, liberty is already lost.

Fortunately virtue is natural to the people, notwithstanding aristocratic prejudices. A nation is truly corrupted when, having by degrees lost its character and its liberty, it passes from democracy to aristocracy or to monarchy; that is the decrepitude and death of the body politic....

But when, by prodigious efforts of courage and reason, a people breaks the chains of despotism to make them into trophies of liberty; when by the force of its moral temperament it comes, as it were, out of the arms of the death, to recapture all the vigor of youth; when by turns it is sensitive and proud, intrepid and docile, and can be stopped neither by impregnable ramparts nor by the innumerable armies of the tyrants armed against it, but stops of itself upon confronting the law's image; then if it does not climb rapidly to the summit of its destinies, this can only be the fault of those who govern it.. . .

From all this let us deduce a great truth: the characteristic of popular government is confidence in the people and severity towards itself.

The whole development of our theory would end here if you had only to pilot the vessel of the Republic through calm waters; but the tempest roars, and the revolution imposes on you another task.

This great purity of the French revolution's basis, the very sublimity of its objective, is precisely what causes both our strength and our weakness. Our strength, because it gives to us truth's ascendancy over imposture, and the rights of the public interest over private interests; our weakness, because it rallies all vicious men against us, all those who in their hearts contemplated despoiling the people and all those who intend to let it be despoiled with impunity, both those who have rejected freedom as a personal calamity and those who have embraced the revolution as a career and the Republic as prey. Hence the defection of so many ambitious or greedy men who since the point of departure have abandoned us along the way because they did not begin the journey with the same destination in view. The two opposing spirits that have been represented in a struggle to rule nature might be said to be fighting in this great period of human history to fix irrevocably the world's destinies, and France is the scene of this fearful combat. Without, all the tyrants encircle you; within, all tyranny's friends conspire; they will conspire until hope is wrested from crime. We must smother the internal and external enemies of the Republic or perish with it; now in this situation, the first maxim of your policy ought to be to lead the people by reason and the people's enemies by terror.

If the spring of popular government in time of peace is virtue, the springs of popular government in revolution are at once virtue and terror: virtue, without which terror is fatal; terror, without which virtue is powerless. Terror is nothing other than justice, prompt, severe, inflexible; it is therefore an emanation of virtue; it is not so much a special principle as it is a consequence of the general principle of democracy applied to our country's most urgent needs.

It has been said that terror is the principle of despotic government. Does your government therefore resemble despotism? Yes, as the sword that gleams in the hands of the heroes of liberty resembles that with which the henchmen of tyranny are armed. Let the despot govern by terror his brutalized subjects; he is right, as a despot. Subdue by terror the enemies of liberty, and you will be right, as founders of the Republic. The government of the revolution is liberty's despotism against tyranny. Is force made only to protect crime? And is the thunderbolt not destined to strike the heads of the proud?

Indulgence for the royalists, cry certain men, mercy for the villains! No! mercy for the innocent, mercy for the weak, mercy for the unfortunate, mercy for humanity.

Society owes protection only to peaceable citizens; the only citizens in the Republic are the republicans. For it, the royalists, the conspirators are only strangers or, rather, enemies. This terrible war waged by liberty against tyranny- is it not indivisible? Are the enemies within not the allies of the enemies without? The assassins who tear our country apart, the intriguers who buy the consciences that hold the people's mandate; the traitors who sell them; the mercenary pamphleteers hired to dishonor the people's cause, to kill public virtue, to stir up the fire of civil discord, and to prepare political counterrevolution by moral counterrevolution-are all those men less guilty or less dangerous than the tyrants whom they serve?

The Napoleonic Code, 1804 CE

Reading and Discussion Questions
1. What is meant by the opening statement of Book I: "The exercise of civil rights is independent of the quality of citizen?"
2. In relation to marriage, what responsibilities does a wife owe to her husband? What responsibilities to a husband owe to his wife?
3. What were some of the laws that were passed under the Napoleonic Code that show that Napoleon was influenced by the Enlightenment?
4. In what ways might some of the laws and reforms in this reading have benefitted Napoleon, as ruler of France?

Napoleon Bonaparte is judged by history as a tyrant whose ambition threatened every nation of Europe by the early 1800s. But even tyrants can make improvements to their realm during their reign and often do, because law and order benefit the tyrant. Recall that during the reign of Augustus that the emperor made many positive reforms for Rome and the Roman people. This is good business for an absolute ruler because if the people are happy under the illusion of law and order, they are more likely to be obedient. One of the most beneficial things Napoleon accomplished during his reign was the creation of the Napoleonic Code. The Napoleonic Code streamlined Napoleon's ability to control his empire through the guise of law and order; but it also benefitted the people of Europe who had been living under outdated and often conflicting laws that had been put in place a thousand years earlier.

From the collapse of the Roman Empire until the 16th and 17th Centuries, Europeans had lived under the feudal system, in which feudal lords ruled over their realms and created laws that were specific to those regions. These laws were designed to benefit the nobility in the feudal system, often at the expense of the peasantry and the common people. One of the primary goals of the French Revolution was to end feudalism and all laws and practices associated with it. The main complaint of the Third Estate was that they were still treated as nothing by the men of influence in France, which was a holdover from old feudal practice. The French Revolution demanded an end to the old world and the creation of a new one which was based on equality and the rule of law. The problem was that there had not been a uniform system of law since the time of the Emperor Justinian in the 6 Century. Since that time, new laws had been created in different realms for different people to address circumstances specific to the age they were written. By the time of Napoleon's reign, there were tens of thousands of pages of laws in France which were nearly impossible to make sense of, even to the most experienced legal minds. Napoleon and his ministers decided to create a thoroughly modern, and streamlined set of laws called the Napoleonic Code. The Napoleonic Code was not perfect in correcting the errors of the past, including the fact that it still placed females under the control of their father or husband. However, it made substantial leaps forward in advancing the ideas of equal protection by law and equal access to a uniform system of justice for all [male] citizens. The Napoleonic Code became the model for the modernization legal codes around the world soon after its completion in 1804.

The laws are binding throughout the whole French territory. They shall be executed in every part of the Republic. The law ordains for the future only; it has no retrospective operation.

The laws of police and public security bind all the inhabitants of the territory. Immovable property, although in the possession of foreigners, is governed by the French law. The laws relating to the condition and privileges of persons govern Frenchmen, although residing in a foreign country.

Private agreements must not contravene the laws which concern public order and good morals.

On Civil Rights
The exercise of civil rights is independent of the quality of citizen, which is only acquired and preserved conformably to the constitutional law. Every Frenchman shall enjoy civil rights.

On Property
Property is the right of enjoying and disposing of things in the most absolute manner, provided they are not used in a way prohibited by the laws or statutes.

No one can be compelled to give up his property except for the public good, and for a just compensation.

On the Respective Rights and Duties of Married Persons
Married persons owe to each other fidelity, succor, assistance.

The husband owes protection to his wife, the wife obedience to her husband.

The wife is obliged to live with her husband, and to follow him to every place where he may judge it convenient to reside: the husband is obliged to receive her, and to furnish her with every necessity for the wants of life, according to his means and station.

A wife cannot give, pledge, or acquire by free or chargeable title, without the concurrence of her husband in the act, or his consent in writing.

When the husband is subjected to a condemnation, carrying with it an afflictive or infamous punishment, although it may have been pronounced merely for contumacy, the wife, though of age, cannot, during the continuance of such punishment, plead in her own name or contract, until after authority given by the judge, who may in such case give his authority without hearing or summoning the husband. The wife may make a will without the authority of her husband.

On Divorce
The provisional management of the children shall rest with the husband, petitioner, or defendant, in the suit for divorce, unless it be otherwise ordered for the greater advantage of the children, on petition of either the mother, or the family, or the government commissioner.

On Paternal Power

A father who shall have cause of grievous dissatisfaction at the conduct. of a child, shall have the following means of correction.

If the child has not commenced his sixteenth year, the father may cause him to be confined for a period which shall not exceed one month; and to this effect the president of the court of the circle shall be bound, on his petition, to deliver an order of arrest.

From the age of sixteen years commenced to the majority or emancipation, the father is only empowered to require the confinement of his child during six months at the most; he shall apply to the president of the aforesaid court, who, after having conferred thereon with the commissioner of government, shall deliver an order of arrest or refuse the same, and may in the first case abridge the time of confinement required by the father.

The father is always at liberty to abridge the duration of the confinement by him ordered or required. If the child after his liberation fall into new irregularities, his confinement may be ordered anew, according to the manner prescribed in the preceding articles.

On Family Property and Inheritance

The husband alone administers the property of the community. He may sell it, alienate and pledge it without the concurrence of his wife.

The wife cannot bind herself nor engage the property of the community, even to free her husband from prison, or for the establishment of their children in case of her husband's absence, until she shall have been thereto authorized by the law.

The husband has the management of all the personal property of the wife. He may prosecute alone all possessory actions and those relating to movables, which belong to his wife. He is responsible for all waste in the personal goods of his wife, occasioned by the neglect of conservatory acts.

The husband alone has the management of the property in dowry, during the marriage. He has alone the right to use the debtors and detainers thereof, to enjoy the fruits and interest thereof, and to receive reimbursements of capital. Nevertheless it may be agreed, by the marriage contract, that the wife shall receive annually, on her single acquaintance, a part of her revenues for her maintenance and personal wants.

Napoleon Bonaparte, The Establishment of a National Education System, 1802 CE

Reading and Discussion Questions
1. What types of schools were established by Napoleon? How do these compare to the public school system in the United States?
2. What types of schools were the Lycee, and what was studied there?
3. What were "special schools"? What types of these schools were there and what was studied in them?
4. Why did Napoleon create a national school system? How would these schools have benefitted Napoleon, personally, as the leader of France?

In addition to overhauling the existing legal code in France to modernize laws concerning civil rights, property and marriage, Napoleon also made many new laws that he believed were necessary for the health of France. Among the new laws he created was a law to create the world's first public school system. Below are excerpts from the law which created the new national education system in France. Napoleon is praised for his far-sightedness in seeing the need for education but Napoleon never did anything that did not in some way benefit Napoleon. Napoleon benefitted by establishing a uniform system of education for all his citizens in a curriculum overseen by his own government ministers. It raised the general education level in France and gave him a more qualified pool from which to draw government advisors and military leaders.

Title I. Division of the Instruction.
Instruction shall be given: 1st. In the primary schools established by the communes; 2d. In the secondary schools established by the communes or kept by private masters; 3d. In the lycées and the special schools maintained at the expense of the public treasury.

Title II. Of the Primary Schools.
The instructors shall be chosen by the mayors and tile municipal councils; their stipend shall consist of: 1st, the dwelling provided by tile communes; 2d, a fee paid by the parents, and fixed by tile municipal councils.

The municipal councils shall exempt from the fee those of the parents who may be unable to pay it; nevertheless, this exemption cannot exceed a fifth of the children received into the primary schools.

Title III. Of Secondary Schools
Every school established by the communes or kept by individuals, in which instruction is given in tile Latin and French languages, the first principles of geography, history, and mathematics, shall be considered a secondary school.

The government encourages the establishment of secondary schools and will compensate good instruction which shall be given there, either by the grant of a habitation or by the distribution of gratuitous places in the *lycées* to those of the pupils of each department who shall most distinguish themselves, and by the bounties granted to the fifty masters of those schools which shall have had the most pupils admitted to the *lycées*.

Secondary schools cannot be established without the authorisation of the government. The secondary schools, as well as all the private schools whose instruction shall be higher than that of the primary schools, shall be placed under the special surveillance and inspection of the prefects.

Title IV: Of the Lycee

Lycées shall be established for instruction in letters and the sciences. There shall be at least one *lycée* for each tribunal of appeal district.

Instruction shall be given in the *lycées* in the ancient languages, rhetoric, logic, ethics, and the elements of the mathematical and physical sciences.

The number of professors in the *lycée* shall never be less than eight; but it can be increased by the government, as well as the number of the subjects of instruction, according to the number of pupils who shall attend the *lycées*.

There shall be in the *lycées*, study masters, and masters of drawing, military exercises, and of accomplishments, [i.e. music and dancing].

Instruction shall be given there: To pupils whom the government shall place there; To the pupils of the secondary schools who shall be admitted there by a competition; To pupils whose parents shall have placed them there to board; To day scholars.

The administration of each *lycée* shall be confided to a principal; he shall have immediately under him a study-critic and a proctor conducting the affairs of the school.

The First Consul shall appoint three inspectors-general of studies who shall visit the *lycées* at least once a year, shall definitely settle their accounts, shall examine all parts of the instruction and administration, and shall render an account thereof to the government.

Title V: Of Special Schools

The last grade of instruction shall include in the special schools the complete and profound study of the sciences and the useful arts, as well as the perfecting thereof.

The special schools now in existence shall be preserved, without prejudice to the modifications which the government believes that it must order for the economy and the welfare of the service. When the place of a professor shall become vacant, including the school of law which shall be established at Paris, it shall be filled by the First Consul from three candidates who shall be presented the first by one of the classes of the national institute, the second by the inspectors-general of studies, and the third by the professors of the school in which the place shall be vacant.

335

The following new special schools shall be instituted:

1st. Ten law schools can be established: each, of them shall have four professors at most;

2d. Three new schools of medicine can be created, which shall have at most eight professors each, and one of which shall be devoted especially to the study and treatment of the diseases of the troops of the army and navy;

3d. There shall be four schools of natural history, physics, and chemistry, with four professors in each;

4th. The mechanical and chemical arts shall be taught in two special schools; there shall be three professors in each of these schools;

5th. A school of transcendental mathematics shall have three professors;

6th. A special school of geography, history, and public economy shall be composed of four professors;

7th. In addition to the schools of the arts of design existing at Paris, Dijon, and Toulouse, there shall be formed a fourth one with four professors;

8th. The observatories in operation at present shall each have a professor of astronomy;

9th. There shall be in several *lycées* professors of the living languages;

10th. There shall be appointed eight professors of music and composition.

PART FIVE—
CONFLICT AND CONQUEST

By the 1800s, Enlightenment ideals had helped to topple old monarchies and old social orders. The modern era had begun and with it, the Industrial Age. In less than 100 years, life changed radically from the way it had been for the last 1000 years. Monarchies were replaced by people's governments, mercantilist economies were rejected in favor of capitalist ideals, quiet lives in pastoral villages were replaced with face-paced lives in bustling cities. Change was everywhere and hope inspired the young dreamer to aspire to better than their parents could ever have imagined. Just as the changes to western lives happened quickly, so did life itself by the mid-1800s. The phrase "time is money" became the motto of the new world and many men made great fortunes during this industrial boom time. But for many the promise of a better life never came true and so a great many grew disillusioned.

Capitalism, or free-market economy, coupled with rapid industrialization, caused competition between people and between nations that is unrivalled in history. Industrialization fueled the need for natural resources, which fueled a second age of conquest. This time, Africa and Asia were almost entirely carved up and devoured by the European powers. The competition for territory and power both in Europe and across the globe fueled tensions among old nations like France and Britain but also among new ambitious powers like Prussia and Russia. The world had grown too small by 1900 for the ambitions of all the would-be empires and a global clash was inevitable.

The first industrialized war, known as World War I, was called "the war to end all wars" because the devastation was unimaginable in scope. For a moment, it seemed that the horrors of war had become so clear that no one would ever fight a war like that again. Unfortunately, bitterness and vengeance as a result of that hellish war fueled a Second World War, even more deadly than the first.

CHAPTER 13—
THE INDUSTRIAL REVOLUTION (1750-1900)

GUIDING QUESTIONS
- Why did the Industrial Revolution start in England?
- What agricultural innovations led to the birth of industry?
- How did the Industrial Revolution change the way man lived and worked?
- What is the "commodification of man?"
- What were the political and economic responses to industrialized Capitalism?
- What was the response in literature to the Industrial Revolution?
- How did the Industrial Revolution change man's relationship with nature?
- Was the Industrial Revolution the most significant event in western history?

Think of all the eras in history that we have covered since you began working your way through this book. We have covered a *lot* of history so far and we have studied monumental changes in every facet of life. Our story began in the city-states of Greece which included the founding of the world's first democracy, as well as a cultural explosion that witnessed the birth of modern architecture, philosophy and history itself. We were then transported to the mighty Roman Republic and the birth of a balanced people's government. The Romans mastered miraculous feats of engineering and created a global empire that shaped the world of today on every imaginable level. Those are pretty impressive achievements, wouldn't you agree? We have studied moments of profound intellectual darkness; but also the ways in which brave men ushered in new eras by reimagining what the world could be like. We have immersed ourselves in new political ideas and modes of self-expression and have witnessed the power of belief in human potential to transform human existence. We have toiled alongside revolutionaries who staked everything on a belief that all men were created equal and should be treated accordingly. On our voyage through history we have crossed oceans, toppled tyrants and demanded progress and a better life. The story of western civilization is a magnificent journey where no obstacle cannot be surmounted.

Take a moment to decide what you think the biggest change has been that you have learned about from ancient Greece through the 1800s. Have you got your answer? There are almost too many pivotal moments from which to choose. But what if I told you the most monumental change of all is still ahead. Hard to believe, right? But many historians argue that, in the history of humankind, there has not been a more profound change in the way humans think, work, live and are governed than the change that began in the late 1700s and was complete by 1900. The change I am speaking of was a result of a seemingly simple period that was in reality very complex. That period was the Industrial Revolution.

Industrialization has a simple definition—the process of replacing man power with machine power. So what's the big deal about that? Shirts that had been made by hand were now made by machines. Fields that had been planted and sown by manpower were now planted and harvested by machines. Cool, but no big deal, right? Wrong. The technology that sparked the Industrial Revolution was relatively simply and the reason they were invented was also easy to understand—to make life easier. Since the beginning of time, humans have been working to make their lives easier. We inherently want to spend less time working and more time doing things we enjoy. This progress toward more leisure and less work is what we call innovation or progress. And progress is always good, right? As it turns out, not always.

In order to understand the radical changes caused by the Industrial Revolution we must first understand how, when and where it started. The Industrial Revolution began in around 1750 in England. England in 1750 enjoyed many of the same characteristics of a peaceful and stable society that Florence had in 1400s which made the Renaissance possible. In the 1700s, England had political stability. After the Glorious Revolution in 1688, England ended its age of absolutism and oppression. The liberties guaranteed to the English by William and Mary created an environment of progressive thinking and a high degree of intellectual and economic freedom (at least considerably more than any other nation in Europe during the same period). As we have seen throughout history, nations that do not spend all their time and money on wars have time to invest their energies in moving forward. The great leap forward in England during the dawn of the Industrial Age was actually started by an earlier agricultural revolution. Inspired by the more methodical thinking of the Scientific Revolution, English farmers began learning about the science of farming and agriculture. Important scientific advances in farming included improving soil quality through the use of fertilizers and crop rotation to prevent depletion of minerals from the soil. Healthier soil meant higher crop yields which meant more food.

But even with improved soil and plant yields, the farming system in England was still inefficient. In 1700, the vast majority of English people—upwards of 80% of the population—made their living through farming. They worked on small family or community farms and produced a wide variety of crops, which was great for sustaining the local population with all the food they needed, but it was not great for producing large amounts of food for large populations at maximum profit. Each farmer might grow apples, wheat and pumpkins, and also raise dairy cows for milk and pigs for meat. This meant that each farmer had to tend the different crops and livestock, know their soil requirements for each type of plant and the right times for the harvest of each and also be an expert in the best diets for the animals and the proper ways to slaughter hogs and cure meat. Every farmer was a expert in many things, but was not efficient in the production of his commodities.

Efficiency in farming was improved dramatically by the invention of the enclosure system. Dating back to the reign of Queen Elizabeth a century earlier, efforts were being made to improve agricultural efficiency. This was accomplished by consolidating many small farms into larger farms that specialized in the production of one or a handful of crops instead of many. These large farms were enclosed by fences and that is where the name enclosure system comes from. The enclosure system marks the beginning of the *business* of farming, where profits and productivity mattered. The enclosure system had a significant impact on the way people lived in England. In 1700, the majority of the people in England farmed for a living. By 1800, less than half of English citizens, roughly 40%, earned income from farming. The enclosure system made farming much more efficient, which meant that fewer people were needed to work the fields. A large farm that produced only wheat could be farmed much more efficiently with fewer people than a number of small farms that produced a wide variety of crops and other commodities. If you have been paying attention to the numbers associated with the enclosure system, you will have noticed that half of the people who used to support themselves and their families through farming were no longer needed in the field of agriculture. The result was that these people had to find a new way and usually a new place to make a living. It may sound like a joy to be freed from the grueling labor of farming but for many people it meant losing their family homes and farms, and along with it, their identities. The vast majority of displaced farmers made their way to cities, found work in factories and became a part of the faceless army of industrialized workers that was forming by 1800.

Innovation typically leads to more innovation and the Industrial Age was no exception to this rule. Farmers who used to produce their own food also used to produce their own clothing from fabric made from wool they sheered from their own sheep. They had been utterly self-sufficient. But families displaced from their farms had none of the tools or materials to make their own clothes. They had to purchase clothing and other necessities from others. As a result, the next area to be revolutionized by the agricultural revolution was the textile industry. Textiles simply means cloth or woven fabric. When crops were harvested faster, including wool and cotton, they also needed to be made into something faster. This is why technological innovations like the cotton gin, the spinning jenny and the water frame were invented. Cotton is a tricky material to work with, as it is full of seeds. Picking out the seeds from a cotton ball was painstaking work. Eli Whitney invented a handy little contraption called the cotton gin that made quick work of the labor-intensive process. Another problem in the production of cotton cloth and clothing was the process of spinning cotton into yarn. In 1765 James Hargreaves invented his cotton-spinning jenny to speed up this process. At almost the same time, Richard Arkwright invented another kind of spinning device, the water frame. Thanks to these two innovations, ten times as much cotton yarn had been manufactured in 1790 than had been possible just twenty years earlier. The technical details of these machines are less important than the impact they had, which was substantial. First, cotton goods became much cheaper and could be afforded by all social classes. Plus, it was breathable, lightweight, comfortable and easy to clean. This resulted in a huge leap forward in the quality of life for people around the world because, for the first time, they had underwear! Imagine how much happier people were when they no longer had to wear wool pants with no undergarments. This innovation alone might have made the Industrial Revolution worth it!

It might appear that the agricultural and industrial advances during the 1700s brought only positive changes to people's lives. After all, who could hope for more than cheap food, city life and underwear? For young people especially, this was an exciting time. Since feudal times, boys and girls were raised on family farms, which they worked all their lives. They grew up and married the boy or girl from the neighboring farm, whether they liked them or not. They lived and died in the same few square miles where they were born, sewing their own clothes, harvesting their own food, building their own homes. With all this work to be done, there was little time for leisure. Life was all laid out before them, with little hope of adventure or excitement or change from the lives of their parents and their parents' parents. So the changes that came about in England in 1750 held the promise of excitement and change for young people in Europe for the first time in centuries. And things changed to be sure, but they did not, for most people, change for the better.

As textile factories began to pop up across England and later across all of Europe, the innovations continued. Textile machines grew larger and larger and they needed more power to run them. The steam engine further increased the productivity of new machinery in factories but would soon spark the development of transportation technology as well. The steam locomotive meant that travel was possible across long

340

distances for the first time, as was the mass transportation of goods for sale. Innovation leads to innovation. Steam power was replaced in 1800 with coal and coal-fired factories, and their smoke-belching stacks soon dominated the skylines of nearly every town and city in England. You know the rest of the story. The way we traveled changed. The way we communicated would soon change as well. The telegraph and the telephone made it possible to maintain relationships and do business over long distances. Electricity made it possible to stay up, and to be productive, well after dark. Everything was faster, bigger and more powerful. And this was exciting. But faster, bigger and more powerful, it turns out, can also be exhausting. If more is better, then musn't we always be making more, doing more, being more?

The idea of "More is Better" led to a dehumanizing phenomenon known as the "commodification of man." More dresses, shoes, cuckoo clocks, and children's toys were what everyone wanted, which meant more workers in more factories to produce more goods over longer hours. The "More is Better" mentality bled into ideas about workers. Working a man for eight hours is good, but working him for twelve hours is better. I cannot help but think of the book, *The Lorax*, when I imagine this age. When The Onecler told his tale about how he came to know The Lorax, he said it was because he just could not help himself from "Biggering, and Biggering and Biggering." He tells the tale of how people needed more and more of his Thneeds ("because Thneeds are something that everyone needs . ."). The demand for more thneeds meant more workers, which meant more factories. For the Onecler this all meant more money, and how can that be bad? It was actually very bad, for the trees, for the workers and ultimately for The Onecler himself. The lesson of *The Lorax* seems to be that at some point, the Bigger-ing must stop. Either the resources run out or the people revolt. A system of perpetual Bigger-ing is unsustainable on both a human and an environmental level. But no one in 1800 was willing or able to believe that this was true.

People swarmed into to industrial cities in the 1800s like a plague of Biblical proportions. More jobs, more opportunities, more fun, more stuff, more romance was what everyone wanted. These were the things they sought ravenously. And there were jobs that needed filling and there was fun to be had, there were men and women from strange places who were fun to date and sometimes to marry. But there were also many more pitfalls to life in industrial cities than could have ever been imagined. As people flooded into cities by the tens and then hundreds of thousands, the cities themselves could not keep up with the growth. There was not enough housing for all the people who arrived day after day. Homes were literally built on top of each other and the first apartments were born. They were tenements, actually, where men and women lived, packed like livestock into apartments with paper-thin walls and no running water. The close quarters in which most people lived were breeding grounds for disease because there was little or no sanitation. Human waste was tossed into the streets and mixed with the toxic runoff from factories in the middle of town. Cities became sewers. Living conditions were so deplorable that countless philosophers and writers chronicled the horrors in hopes that awareness would bring change. Men like Fredrick Engels and others were so shocked by the quality of life in industrial cities like Manchester, England that they wrote whole books about them. Their hope was that someone, somewhere would do something.

Because of the "commodification of man," men were seen as just another resource to be used for profit. Consequently, little thought was given to the treatment of these human resources. Working conditions during the Industrial Age were no better than the living conditions. Men, women and children were worked for twelve, fourteen, nineteen hours at a time, with no breaks or proper nourishment and for a pitiful amount of money. Factory accidents were common and people were permanently disfigured or killed from malfunctioning equipment, collapsed mines or exhaustion from being overworked.

I hope that you are asking yourself at this point, "Why was all this happening?" How could the human condition ever sink so low when just a minute ago life seemed so promising? The answer is a vindication of the often-criticized cynic, Thomas Hobbes. The suffering of the Industrial Age was a product of unchecked, self-interested greed. People greedily demanded the newest products to impress their friends. Greedy factory owners were all too happy to meet this demand. They filled their factories with men and women who answered the siren's call of cities and needed work, any work, to survive. If a man or woman chose not to take a job that was too grueling or demeaning for them, there were a hundred more in line behind them who would jump at the chance for work. Workers worked as the factory owners demanded or did not work at all. And so the industrial capitalists in the 1800s just kept Bigger-ing and Bigger-ing and Bigger-ing because more is better and because they could.

Cities grew as ambition grew. Living and working conditions continued to deteriorate and death tolls among the working poor climbed to alarming rates. Even for those who did not die in a factory or mining accident, the life expectancy was shocking. The average life expectancy of a man in the industrial city of Liverpool, England in 1860 was twenty-seven. *Twenty-seven!* It was not much better in other cities, where the average man lived to roughly thirty-six years of age. An increasing number of people began to recognize that things could not go on like this. Something had to change. From the suffering and misery of industrialized capitalism emerged a radical new ideology that sought to undo all the inhumanity wrought by capitalist greed. This new ideology was Socialism.

Ben Franklin once said, "Time is money." This meant in essence, that every hour of the day was an opportunity to make money and that the more time men invested in work, the more money could be made. Man was viewed in the late 1800s as another commodity to be bought and sold, like pork or sweaters or clocks. This "commodification" of man bothered many people so much as the decades of industrialism progressed that they began to envision different ways of living that went beyond just basic survival. One group, called the Utopian Socialists, believed that men were a product of their environment and if a better environment could be created, life would inevitably be better. One such Utopian Socialist named Robert Owen proposed and actually created a Utopian Socialist community based on cooperation and reeducation and focused more on what man *was* than what he *owned*. This new community, called New Harmony, Indiana, lasted about two years before it was dissolved. Owen's failed experiment seemed to prove that a perfect world was not possible. Or at least this was the conclusion reached by men like Frederick Engels and Karl Marx.

Marx agreed with Owen that humans had totally lost their humanity in the industrialized capitalist world of the 1800s but he radically disagreed with Owen on the solution to this problem. Karl Marx was heavily influenced by Engels' work on the conditions of the working class and together the two created an alternative to industrialized capitalist society. They wrote their ideas in their book, *The Communist*

Manifesto, that would change the world forever, though not exactly in the way that the two men envisioned. Marx predicted that, over time, industrial wage slaves, whom he called the Proletariat, would rise up in a global revolution to overthrow their oppressive Capitalist masters. He said that after the worker's revolution, there would be a period of reorganizing and reeducation that would result in a new Communist system. In this new system, property and the means of production would be owned collectively, or in *common*, by the community and the old oppressive systems and the conflicts those systems created would disappear. *The Communist Manifesto*, written in 1848, inspired disgruntled revolutionaries everywhere. Over the next 100 years, Communist revolutions would take place in both Russia and China that resulted in an end to the old monarchical systems in both nations. The new governments that were created in Russia and China, however, did not look much at all like the society that Marx had envisioned.

Just as man's relationship with other men changed radically as a result of industrialization, another relationship was also radically altered during this period — man's relationship with nature. It became a source of pride that man, by the 1800s, had completely conquered nature. All of the seemingly infinite resources that nature provided, from water and coal, to cotton and timber, were harnessed for the benefit of man with astounding quickness and efficiency. For centuries, even millennia, humans had lived as a part of nature, living off the land. But the Industrial Revolution changed all that. Men and women did everything the could to be apart from nature, from the creation of artificial light with the light bulb, to spending most of their time indoors instead of out. It even became fashionable to have pale skin during the 18th century because only farm laborers had tans. Pale skin said to the world "Look how infrequently I have to go outside. Isn't it wonderful! I'm rich (or at least I am trying to look that way)!" But there was a movement that stirred as passionately as that of Socialism in rejection of the lifestyle of the Industrial Age. It was called Romanticism.

Socialism tried to change the economic practices of the era to create a more equitable existence for all. Romanticism, however, had nothing to do with economics. Romantics were concerned with human priorities about how people lived their lives and what they valued. Romantics got their name because they romanticized the past. To *romanticize* means to glorify something or make it seem more appealing than it may in reality be. Much like Petrarch romanticized the civilizations of Greece and Rome, so did the Romantics glorify a simpler era when men lived on and with the land. The ideals of Romanticism produced great literary genius in the works of men like William Wordsworth, John Keats, Victor Hugo and Edgar Allen Poe and women like Mary Shelly and Emily Dickenson. Though Romantics varied widely in the topics they wrote about and in the style of their writing, they shared a common belief that life had become too hard and unfeeling. In their mind, Rousseau's quote, "Men are born free but are everywhere in chains" had never been more true. Men were slaves to their work and to the cold hard facts of scientific empiricism. In an attempt to move away from ignorance and toward truth, man had almost left no room for feelings, human imagination and a connection with nature. To Romantics, the world had turned hard and cruel. British poet John Keats captured the essence of Romanticism when he said, "Beauty is truth, truth beauty -that is all ye know on earth, and all ye need to know." Romantics believed that nature revealed truth and even revealed God, and to destroy nature was to destroy oneself. A particular offshoot of the Romantics, called the Transcendentalists, worshipped nature as God himself. They raged in their writings against industrialism, and grieved for what industrialized capitalism was doing to nature and to humans as part of the natural world. The work of some of the most passionate Transcendentalists—men like Henry David Thoreau, Ralph Waldo Emerson and John Muir—helped to create some of the first laws for environmental protection. Their commitment to preserving nature also resulted in the creation of a national and global park system which protects animals and habitats around the world.

Socialists, Romantics and Transcendentalists all rejected the values of industrialized life for different reasons. And they were far from the only groups who questioned whether or not the world was changed for the better by the Industrial Revolution. There were, no doubt, many things about industrialization that improved the global quality of life. Enterprising businessmen and inventors could amass limitless fortunes in a capitalist system, where the only limit to a man's success is his own determination and luck. The self-made man and the rags to riches story were products of this period. Agricultural innovations made food more widely available which led to an eventual rise in life expectancy, as did life-saving medicine and better medical technology by the end of the industrial age. Transportation opened up a wider world to people and opened people's minds in the process. Over time, labor laws were put into place that protected workers from exploitation. Wages increased as did home sizes. Life in many ways got exponentially better and lives, thankfully have gotten much longer. But the cost of this progress was, and continues to be, substantial.

Chadwick's Report on Sanitary Conditions, 1842 CE

Reading and Discussion Questions

1. Summarize three of the findings on sanitary conditions that Chadwick published in his report. Which of these, if any, do you find shocking or alarming?
2. What did Chadwick assess was the impact of these conditions on the population in the cities he investigated? Analyze his statistics on life expectancy as well as widowhood and the number of orphans in your answer.
3. What impact did Chadwick say these sanitary conditions had on the moral and intellectual health of people in industrial cities?
4. To what extent did Chadwick say that existing laws about sanitation and management of industrial cities were working?
5. What did Chadwick recommend to fix the problems he identified?

Edwin Chadwick was an English social reformer who was instrumental in raising awareness about the deplorable living and working conditions of factory workers in 19 century England. In 1832, Chadwick was hired by the British government to investigate allegations of unsanitary conditions of industrial factories and towns. Part of his task was also to see how effectively England's Poor Law was being put to use in the towns and cities. The Poor Law was a rudimentary welfare system in England that provided small relief to men, women and children who were injured as a result of industrial labor or who were unemployed. At the time of Chadwick's inquiries, the Poor Law was being enforced sporadically at best, and corruption by Poor Law agents was rampant. As a result, none of the problems the Poor Law was meant to alleviate were being addressed to any degree of satisfaction. The following is an excerpt from Chadwick's report on his findings of the sanitary conditions in industrial England. His work opened the eyes of many to the realities of industrialized life and was an important step toward the eventual passage of the Public Health Act of 1848 in England. Though that act did not cure many of the ills of industrial towns, it did implement more strict sanitary requirements across England, including proper disposal of sewage and access to clean drinking water.

After as careful an examination of the evidence collected as I have been enabled to make, I summarize my findings here:

First, the extent and operation of the evils which are the subject of this inquiry: –

That the various forms of epidemic, endemic, and other disease caused, or aggravated, by atmospheric impurities produced by decomposing animal and vegetable substances, by damp and filth, and close and overcrowded dwellings prevail amongst the population in every part of the kingdom, whether dwelling in separate houses, in rural villages, in small towns, in the larger towns.

That such disease, wherever its attacks are frequent, is always found in connection with the physical circumstances above specified, and that where those circumstances are removed by drainage, proper cleansing, better ventilation, and other means of diminishing atmospheric impurity, the frequency and intensity of such disease is abated; and where the removal of the noxious agencies appears to be complete, such disease almost entirely disappears.

Contaminated London drinking water containing various micro-organisms, refuse, and the like.

That the formation of all habits of cleanliness is obstructed by defective supplies of water.

That the annual loss of life from filth and bad ventilation are greater than the loss from death or wounds in any wars in which the country has been engaged in modern times.

That of the 43,000 cases of widowhood, and 112,000 cases of destitute orphanage relieved from the poor's rates in England and Wales alone, it appears that the greatest proportion of deaths of the heads of families occurred from the above causes; that their ages were under 45 years on average.

That the public loss from the premature deaths of the heads of families is greater than can be represented by any enumeration of the monetary burdens caused by their sickness and death.

That in the districts where the mortality is greatest the births are not only sufficient to replace the numbers removed by death, but to add to the population.

That the younger population, bred up under noxious physical agencies, is inferior in physical organization and general health to a population [which is not exposed to such conditions].

That the population so exposed is less susceptible of moral influences, and the effects of education are more transient than with a healthy population.

That these adverse circumstances tend to produce an adult population short-lived, improvident, reckless, and intemperate, and with habitual avidity for sensual gratifications.

That these habits lead to the abandonment of all the conveniences and decencies of life, and especially lead to the overcrowding of their homes, which is destructive to the morality as well as the health of large classes of both sexes.

That defective town cleansing fosters habits of the most abject degradation and tends to the demoralization of large numbers of human beings, who subsist by means of what they find amidst the noxious filth accumulated in neglected streets and bye-places.

That the existing law for the protection of the public health have fallen into disuse.

Secondly. the means by which the present sanitary may be improved:--

The primary and most important measures, and at the same time the most practicable, and within the recognized province of public administration, are drainage, the removal of all refuse of habitations, streets, and roads, and the improvement of the supplies of water.

That for all these purposes, as well as for domestic use, better supplies of water are absolutely necessary.

That for the prevention of the disease occasioned by defective ventilation and other causes of impurity in places of work and other places where large numbers are assembled, and for the prevention of disease, that it would be wise to appoint a district medical officer independent of private practice, and with the securities of special qualifications and responsibilities to initiate sanitary measures and reclaim the execution of the law.

That by the combinations of all these arrangements, it is probable that life expectancy in these areas would increase by 13 years at least.

And that the removal of harmful physical circumstances, and the promotion of civic, household, and personal cleanliness, are necessary to the improvement of the moral condition of the population; for that sound morality and refinement in manners and health are not long found co-existent with filthy habits amongst any class of the community.

347

Three Readings on Life in the Industrial Age

Reading and Discussion Questions
1. For each of the three readings, write a two or three sentence summary of what life and living conditions were like in each of the cities discussed in the excerpts. Make particular note of the worst elements in each description.
2. Which of the three authors does the best job of conveying the horrors of life in industrial cities and towns?
3. Which of the three towns below, Manchester, Coketown or Marney, would you choose to live in if you had to live in one of the three and why?

The Industrial Age (1750-1850) is often portrayed as a time when men made unbelievable fortunes and the American "rags to riches" story was available to every hardworking man and woman. But the realities of life during the industrial revolution were very different, and often very harsh. The first nations to be thrust into the Industrial Age were England, Prussia (Germany) and the United States and writers in all three of those places wrote about the miserable living conditions of the new class known as the "urban poor" or the "wage slaves." Below are excerpts from three different works on life in the Industrial Age.

Charles Dickens, *Hard Times*, 1854 CE

Hard Times - For These Times (commonly known as Hard Times) is the tenth novel by Charles Dickens, first published in 1854. The book analyzes industrial English society in the 1800s and tried to highlight the social and economic problems of the times. The story is set in the industrial town of Coketown, a fictional Northern English mill-town, which was a lot like the industrial city of Manchester, England. Dickens hoped his novel would help in the fight for reform of industrial working conditions. Dickens had visited factories in Manchester as early as 1839, and was appalled by the environment in which workers toiled. Drawing upon his own childhood experiences, Dickens resolved to "strike the heaviest blow in my power" for those who lived in those horrific conditions.

It [Coketown] was a town of machinery and tall chimneys, out of which interminable serpents of smoke trailed themselves for ever and ever, and never got uncoiled. It had a black canal in it, and a river that ran purple with ill-smelling dye, and vast piles of building full of windows where there was a rattling and a trembling all day long, and where the piston of the steam-engine worked monotonously up and down, like the head of an elephant in a state of melancholy madness. It contained several large streets all very like one another, and many small streets still more like one another, inhabited by people equally like one another, who all went in and out at the same hours, with the same sound upon the same pavements, to do the same work, and to whom every day was the same as yesterday and to-morrow, and every year the counterpart of the last and the next....

Time went on in Coketown like its own machinery: so much material wrought up, so much fuel consumed, so many powers worn out, so much money made. But, less inexorable than iron, steel, and brass, it brought its varying seasons even into that

348

wilderness of smoke and brick, and made the only stand that ever was made in the place against its direful uniformity....

In the hardest working part of Coketown; in the innermost fortifications of that ugly citadel, where Nature was as strongly bricked out as killing airs and gases were bricked in; at the heart of the labyrinth of narrow courts upon courts, and close streets upon streets, which had come into existence piecemeal, every piece in a violent hurry for some one man's purpose, and the whole an unnatural family, shouldering, and trampling, and pressing one another to death; in the last close nook of this great exhausted receiver, where the chimneys, for want of air to make a draught, were built in an immense variety of stunted and crooked shapes, as though every house put out a sign of the kind of people who might be expected to be born in it; among the multitude of Coketown, generically called 'the Hands,' – a race who would have found more favour with some people, if Providence had seen fit to make them only hands, or, like the lower creatures of the seashore, only hands and stomachs.

Day after day, "the Hands" toiled as such people must toil, whatever their anxieties. The smoke-serpents were indifferent who was lost or found, who turned out bad or good; the melancholy mad elephants, like the Hard Fact men, abated nothing of their set routine, whatever happened. Day and night again, day and night again. The monotony was unbroken.

* * * * * * *

Friedrick Engels, *The Conditions of the Working Class in England, 1844 CE*

Friedrick Engels grew up in Prussia (Germany) and was the son of a wealthy German cotton manufacture. As a radical journalist and critic of industrialization, he sought to make the public aware of the poor conditions of workers and the negative effects of industrialization. His parents sent him to work in a factory in Manchester, England, hoping it would change his radical thoughts. It had the opposite effect. Engels later partnered with Karl Marx to write The Communist Manifesto *in 1848.*

Manchester proper lies on the left bank of the Irwell, between that stream and the two smaller ones, the Irk and the Medlock, which here empty into the Irwell. . . . The whole assemblage of buildings is commonly called Manchester, and contains about four hundred thousand inhabitants, rather more than less.

I may mention just here that the mills [factories] almost all adjoin the rivers or the different canals that ramify throughout the city, before I proceed at once to describe the living quarters. First of all, there is the old town of Manchester, which lies between the northern boundary of the commercial district and the Irk. Here the streets, even the better ones, are narrow and winding, as Todd Street, Long Millgate, Withy Grove, and Shude Hill, the houses dirty, old, and tumble-down, and the construction of the side streets utterly horrible. Going from the Old Church to Long Millgate, the stroller has at once a row of old-fashioned houses at the right, of which not one has kept its original level; these are remnants of the old pre-manufacturing Manchester, whose former inhabitants have removed with their descendants into better built districts, and have left the houses, which were not good enough for them, to a population strongly mixed with Irish blood. Here one is in an almost undisguised working-men's quarter,

349

for even the shops and beer houses hardly take the trouble to exhibit a trifling degree of cleanliness. But all this is nothing in comparison with the courts and lanes which lie behind, to which access can be gained only through covered passages, in which no two human beings can pass at the same time. Of the irregular cramming together of dwellings in ways which defy all rational plan, of the tangle in which they are crowded literally one upon the other, it is impossible to convey an idea. And it is not the buildings surviving from the old times of Manchester which are to blame for this; the confusion has only recently reached its height when every scrap of space left by the old way of building has been filled up and patched over until not a foot of land is left to be further occupied.

Right and left a multitude of covered passages lead from the main street into numerous courts, and he who turns in thither gets into a filth and disgusting grime, the equal of which is not to be found – especially in the courts which lead down to the Irk, and which contain unqualifiedly the most horrible dwellings which I have yet beheld. In one of these courts there stands directly at the entrance, at the end of the covered passage, a privy (outhouse) without a door, so dirty that the inhabitants can pass into and out of the court only by passing through foul pools of stagnant urine and excrement. Below it on the river there are several tanneries which fill the whole neighbourhood with the stench of animal putrefaction. Below Ducie Bridge the only entrance to most of the houses is by means of narrow, dirty stairs and over heaps of refuse and filth. The first court below Ducie Bridge, known as Allen's Court, was in such a state at the time of the cholera that the sanitary police ordered it evacuated, swept, and disinfected with chloride of lime. . . . At the bottom flows, or rather stagnates, the Irk, a narrow, coal-black, foul-smelling stream, full of debris and refuse, which it deposits on the shallower right bank.

In dry weather, a long string of the most disgusting, blackish-green, slime pools are left standing on this bank, from the depths of which bubbles of miasmatic gas constantly arise and give forth a stench unendurable even on the bridge forty or fifty feet above the surface of the stream. But besides this, the stream itself is checked every few paces by high weirs, behind which slime and refuse accumulate and rot in thick masses. Above the bridge are tanneries, bone mills, and gasworks, from which all drains and refuse find their way into the river, which receives further the contents of all the neighbouring sewers and privies. It may be easily imagined, therefore, what sort of residue the stream deposits. Below the bridge you look upon the piles of debris, the refuse, filth, and offal from the courts on the steep left bank; here each house is packed close behind its neighbor and a piece of each is visible, all black, smoky, crumbling, ancient, with broken panes and window frames. The background is furnished by old barrack-like factory buildings.

Everywhere heaps of debris, refuse, and offal; standing pools for gutters, and a stench which alone would make it impossible for a human being to live in such a district. . . . Passing along a rough bank, among stakes and washing-lines, one penetrates into this chaos of small one-storied, one-roomed huts, in most of which there is no artificial floor; kitchen, living and sleeping-room all in one. In such a hole, scarcely five feet long by six broad, I found two beds – and such bedsteads and beds! – which, with a staircase and chimney-place, exactly filled the room. In several others I found absolutely nothing, while the door stood open, and the inhabitants leaned against it. Everywhere before the doors refuse and offal; that any sort of pavement lay underneath could not be seen but only felt, here and there, with the feet. This whole collection of cattle-sheds for human beings was surrounded on two sides by houses and a factory, and on the third by the river, and besides the narrow stair up the bank, a narrow doorway alone led out into another almost equally ill-built, ill-kept labyrinth of dwellings....

Such is the Old Town of Manchester, and on re-reading my description, I am forced to admit that instead of being exaggerated, it is far from black enough to convey a true impression of the filth, ruin, and uninhabitableness of this single district, containing at least twenty to thirty thousand inhabitants. And such a district exists in the heart of the second city of England, the first manufacturing city of the world. If any one wishes to see in how little space a human being can move, how little air - and such air! - he can breathe, it is only necessary to travel hither. True, this is the Old Town, and the people of Manchester emphasize the fact whenever anyone mentions to them the frightful condition of this Hell upon Earth; but what does that prove? Everything which here arouses horror and indignation is of recent origin, belongs to the industrial epoch.

* * * * * * *

Benjamin Disraeli, *Sybil*, 1845 CE

Sybil, or The Two Nations *is an 1845 novel by Benjamin Disraeli. Sybil traces the plight of the working classes of England. Disraeli was interested in dealing with the horrific conditions of England's working class. In the excerpt below, two noblemen from a castle in the region visit the industrial town of Marney and describe and discuss what they find upon their arrival.*

The location of the rural town of Marney was one of the most delightful easily to be imagined. In a spreading valley, contiguous to the margin of a clear and lively stream, surrounded by meadows and gardens, and backed by lofty hills, undulating and richly wooded, the traveller would often stop to admire the merry prospect of such a well situated village.

Beautiful illusion! For behind that laughing landscape, penury and disease fed upon the vitals of a miserable population!

The contrast between the interior of the town and its external aspect, was as striking as it was full of pain. With the exception of the dull high street, which had the usual characteristics of a small agricultural market town, some mansions and a dingy inn, Marney mainly consisted of a variety of narrow and crowded lanes formed by cottages built of rubble, or unhewn stones without cement, and from age, or badness of the material, looking as if they could scarcely hold together. The gaping chinks admitted every blast; the leaning chimneys had lost half their original height; the rotten rafters were evidently misplaced; while in many instances the thatch, yawning in some parts to admit the wind and wet, and in all utterly unfit for its original purpose of giving protection from the weather, looked more like the top of a dunghill than a cottage. Before the doors of these dwellings, and often surrounding them, ran open drains full of animal and vegetable refuse, decomposing into disease, or sometimes in their imperfect course filling foul pits or spreading into stagnant pools, while a concentrated solution of every species of dissolving filth was allowed to soak through and thoroughly impregnate the walls and ground adjoining.

These wretched tenements seldom consisted of more than two rooms, in one of which the whole family, however numerous, were obliged to sleep, without distinction of age, or sex, or suffering. With the water streaming down the walls, the light distinguished through the roof, with no hearth even in winter, the virtuous mother in the sacred pangs of childbirth, gives forth another victim to our thoughtless civilization; surrounded by three generations whose inevitable presence is more painful than her sufferings in that hour of travail; while the father of her coming child, in another corner of the sordid chamber, lies stricken by that typhus which his contaminated dwelling has breathed into his veins, and for whose next prey is perhaps destined, his new-born child. These swarming walls had neither windows nor doors sufficient to keep out the weather, or admit the sun or supply the means of ventilation; the humid and putrid roof of thatch exhaling malaria like all other decaying vegetable matter.

These slums were in many instances not provided with the commonest conveniences of the rudest police; contiguous to every door might be observed the dung-heap on which every kind of filth was accumulated, for the purpose of being disposed of for manure, so that, when the poor man opened his narrow habitation in the hope of refreshing it with the breeze of summer, he was met with a mixture of gases from reeking dunghills.

One of the two noblemen commented on what he observed: "In industrial towns such as these, men are brought together by the desire of gain. They are not in a state of co-operation, but of isolation, as to the making of fortunes; and for all the rest they are careless of neighbours. Christianity teaches us to love our neighbors as ourselves; modern society acknowledges no such law."

"Well, we live in strange times," said Egremont, struck by the observation of his companion, and relieving a perplexed spirit by an ordinary exclamation, which often denotes that the mind is more stirring than it cares to acknowledge, or at the moment is capable to express.

"When the infant begins to walk, it also thinks that it lives in strange times," said his companion.
"Your inference?" asked Egremont.
"That society, still in its infancy, is beginning to feel its way."
"This is a new reign," said Egremont, "perhaps it is a new era.
"I think so," said the younger stranger.
"I hope so," said the elder one.
"Well, society may be in its infancy," said Egremont slightly smiling; "but, say what you like, our Queen reigns over the greatest nation that ever existed."
"Which nation?" asked the younger stranger, "for she reigns over two."
The stranger paused; Egremont was silent, but looked inquiringly.
"Yes," resumed the younger stranger after a moment's interval. "Two nations; between whom there is no intercourse and no sympathy; who are as ignorant of each other's habits, thoughts, and feelings, as if they were dwellers in different zones, or inhabitants of different planets; who are formed by a different breeding, are fed by a different food, are ordered by different manners, and are not governed by the same laws."
"You speak of—" said Egremont, hesitatingly.
"THE RICH AND THE POOR."

Thomas Malthus, *An Essay on the Principle of Population*, 1798 CE

Reading and Discussion Questions

1. According to Malthus, how are populations of species kept from growing too large in the natural world?
2. Among humans, why is managing population not as simple? In what ways does Malthus say man tries to alter his situation in order to reproduce without consequence?
3. How do the poor suffer in relation to population? What happens to the urban poor and their children when food resources grow scarce?
4. What do you think of Malthus' ideas on population? Are they overly harsh? True? Explain your reaction to this reading.

Reverend Thomas Malthus was and English clergyman and philosopher whose work on population during the Industrial Age has influenced scientists, capitalists, reformers and humanitarians alike. Living in England during the Industrial Revolution, Malthus saw first-hand the suffering and death of a great many industrial workers. In England during his lifetime, some efforts were being made to ease the suffering of the urban poor. One particular problem was the high number of children being born to poor families, who had trouble feeding them and relied on government assistance. Malthus argues that welfare measures like England's Poor Act, were well-intentioned but unnatural. He observed that, in nature, more plants and animals are born than can survive. He considered two elements necessary for survival of any species—the availability of food and the urge to procreate for continuation of the species. He said that, in nature, when there is not enough food to feed all living things, some of those things naturally die. Then there will be only enough members of a species left living to match the available food supply, which Malthus called the "means of subsistence."

In society, Malthus observed that among poor populations there was a particular problem in that the urge to procreate and reproduce was very strong, and that more children were born than could be fed by the existing food supply. The natural cycle would naturally fix this problem, Malthus argued, because after some or many of the weaker humans die, there would again be a balance between food supply and population. He wrote all of his ideas on population in his book, An Essay on the Principles of Population. Malthus was one of the main influences on Charles Darwin and the development of his theory on the Survival of the Fittest. Of Malthus' influence on his ideas, Darwin wrote the following in his autobiography: I happened to read for amusement Malthus On Population, and being well prepared to appreciate the struggle for existence which everywhere goes on, it at once struck me that under these circumstances favorable variations [among species] would tend to be preserved, and unfavorable ones to be destroyed. The results of this would be the formation of a new species. Here, then I had at last got a theory by which to work."

On the question of population, and whether it can be maintained or will inevitably grow until it is checked by nature:

I think I may fairly make two assumptions of fact: First, That food is necessary to the existence of man. Secondly, that the passion between the sexes is necessary, and will remain nearly in its present state.

It seems a natural instinct among all living things to perpetuate the species, whether plants or animals. Among plants and animals the view of the subject is simple. They are all impelled by a powerful instinct to the increase of their species; and this instinct is interrupted by no reasoning, or doubts about providing for their offspring. Wherever therefore there is liberty, the power of increase is exerted; and the superabundant populations [of these species] are decreased afterwards by want of space and nourishment, which is common to animals and plants; and among animals, by becoming the prey of others.

The effects of this check on man are more complicated.

Impelled to the increase of his species by an equally powerful instinct, reason interrupts his career, and asks him whether he may not bring beings into the world, for whom he cannot provide the means of subsistence. In a state of equality, this would be the simple question. In the present state of society, other considerations occur. Will he not lower his rank in life? Will he not subject himself to greater difficulties than he at present feels? Will he not be obliged to labor harder? And if he has a large family, will his utmost exertions enable him to support them? May he not see his offspring in rags and misery, and clamoring for bread that he cannot give them? And may he not be reduced to the grating necessity of forfeiting his independence, and of being obliged to the sparing hand of charity for support?

These considerations are calculated to prevent, and certainly do prevent, a very great number in all civilized nations from pursuing the dictate of nature in an early attachment to one woman. And this restraint almost necessarily, though not absolutely so, produces vice. Yet in all societies, even those that are most vicious, the tendency to a virtuous attachment is so strong, that there is a constant effort towards an increase of population. This constant effort as constantly tends to subject the lower classes of the society to distress, and to prevent any great permanent amelioration of their condition.

The way in which these effects are produced seems to be this.

We will suppose the means of survival in any country just equal to the easy support of its inhabitants. The constant effort towards population, which is found to act even in the most vicious societies, increases the number of people before the means of subsistence are increased. The food therefore which before supported seven millions, must now be divided among seven millions and a half or eight millions.

The poor consequently must live much worse, and many of them be reduced to severe distress. The number of labourers also being above the proportion of the work in the market, the price of labour must tend toward a decrease; while the price of provisions would at the same time tend to rise. The labourer therefore must work harder to earn the same as he did before. During this season of distress, the discouragements to marriage, and the difficulty of rearing a family are so great, that population is at a stand. In the mean time the cheapness of labour, the plenty of labourers, and the necessity of

354

an increased industry amongst them, encourage cultivators to employ more labour upon their land; to turn up fresh soil, and to manure and improve more completely what is already in tillage; till ultimately the means of subsistence become in the same proportion to the population as at the period from which we set out. The situation of the labourer being then again tolerably comfortable, the restraints to population are in some degree loosened; and the same retrograde and progressive movements with respect to happiness are repeated....

The theory, on which the truth of this position depends, appears to me so extremely clear; that I feel at a loss to conjecture what part of it can be denied.

Population cannot increase without the means of survival, namely, food.

That population does invariably increase, where there are the means of survival, the history of every people that have ever existed will abundantly prove.

And, that the superior power of population [and the need to procreate] cannot be checked, without producing misery or vice, the ample portion of these too bitter ingredients in the cup of human life, and the continuance of the physical causes that seem to have produced them bear too convincing a testimony.

Herbert Spencer, *Social Statics*, 1851 CE

Reading and Discussion Questions
1. According to Spencer, why should the state not provide charity to the poor?
2. Why does Spencer say that the way nature manages populations is "a little cruel so that it may be very kind?" What does he mean by this?
3. What similarities do you see between the theories of Thomas Malthus and Herbert Spencer? Are they convincing arguments in support of Capitalism and the survival of the economically fittest? Why or why not?

As you have learned from your reading of Thomas Malthus, concepts about evolution and the struggle for survival were well established before Charles Darwin published his findings in 1859. One of the great minds and philosophical geniuses of the 19 century, a man named Herbert Spencer, contributed significantly to ideas about survival of the species. Like Malthus, Spencer was interested in whether or not financial assistance to the poor helped or hurt them and the wider community. In Spencer's view, it was the natural order for the weak to be pushed aside in favor of the strong. He believed this was true of plants and animals and also true of humans. Spencer wrote about these ideas in his book Social Statics, or The Conditions Essential to Happiness Specified, and the First of Them Developed. *Spencer's ideas of the survival of the fittest in society have come to be known as Social Darwinism but that name gets the chronology of events backwards. Darwin solidified his scientific ideas from reading men like Spencer and Malthus.*

A government cannot rightly do anything more than protect [its people]. In taxing citizens for the mitigation of distress the state is reversing its function. Possibly, some will assert that by satisfying the wants of the poor man, a government is extending his liberty to exercise his abilities. But this statement implies a confounding of two widely different things. To enforce the fundamental law–to take care that every man has freedom to do all that he wills––this is the special purpose for which the civil power exists. Now insuring to each man has the right to pursue his desires without hindrance, is quite a separate thing from insuring him satisfaction.

In all of nature we see at work a stern discipline, which is a little cruel that it may be very kind. That state of universal warfare maintained throughout the lower creation, to the great perplexity of many worthy people, is at bottom the most merciful provision which the circumstances admit of. The poverty of the incapable, the distresses that come upon the imprudent, the starvation of the idle, and those shoulderings aside of the weak by the strong, which leave so many "in shallows and in miseries," are the decrees of a large, farseeing benevolence. It seems hard that a laborer incapacitated by sickness from competing with his stronger fellows, should have to bear the resulting sufferings. It seems hard that widows and orphans should be left to struggle for life or death. Nevertheless, when regarded not separately, but in connection with the interests of universal humanity, these harsh fatalities are seen to be full of the highest beneficence–the same beneficence which brings to early graves the children of diseased parents, and singles out the low-spirited, the intemperate, and the debilitated as the victims of an epidemic.

Robert Owen, *A New View on Society*, 1813 CE

Reading and Discussion Questions
1. Why does Owen think it is a mistake to punish a man for behaving like an animal in a system that treats him like an animal?
2. What wrong assumptions does Owen say most societies are based on? What are the right assumptions on which to build a society?
3. What are the "vital machines" that Owen talks about? Why should people invest more in "vital machines" than in "inanimate machines"?
4. To whom does Owen think his proposals would be appealing? Who would not be interested in the society he is proposing?
5. Are any of Owen's proposals appealing to you? Why or why not?

Men like Malthus and Spencer were defenders of Capitalism and the harsh conditions of industrialized life as natural and appropriate for the evolution of society. But there were others who thought a different kind of existence could provide greater happiness for more people. One of those men was Robert Owen. In his work, A New View of Society, Owen argued that the current system of business, government and justice created environments where it was impossible for men to thrive and then punished them for not thriving. Owen believed that it was the system, and not man, that was broken and so he proposed a new system, which came to be known as Utopian Socialism. Owen argued that just as men can be educated to value wealth, competition and cunning, so too they could be educated to value equality, bounty and virtue. Virtuous environments produce virtuous humans, and flawed systems produce flawed humans, according to Owen's ideas. Owen proposed, and actually created, new societies where there was no private ownership of property and where people were educated to value cooperation for mutual benefit. The focus of these communities was investment in the individual as the most important "commodity". Owen explained that not everyone would want to live in the kinds of communities that he proposed but he said that men who had been nearly destroyed by industrialized capitalism would jump at the chance to be part of the new world he envisioned.

During his lifetime, Owen created a new Utopian Socialist community in New Harmony, Indiana after doing a lot of experimenting with his Socialist concepts at home in Britain. The experiment was a failure and the community disbanded after two years. Owen blamed this on the "motley" members who had joined his community and on the fact that the project was not given time to succeed. Reeducation on the value of cooperation took a generation to take hold, said Owen, not just a few years. Owen's failure was proof to men like Karl Marx that a Utopian world was mere fantasy, and that in order to embrace new social and political systems, a period of violent upheaval is often necessary.

Man's Character is Formed For Him

From the earliest ages it has been a practice of the world to act on the supposition that each individual man forms his own character, and that therefore he is accountable for all his sentiments and habits, and consequently merits reward for some and punishment for others. Every system which has been established among man has been founded on these erroneous principles. When, however, they should be brought to the test of fair examination, they will be found not only unsupported, but in direct opposition to all experience, and to the evidence of our senses.

This is not a slight mistake, which involves only trivial consequences; it is a fundamental error of the highest possible magnitude, it enters into all our proceedings regarding man from his infancy; and it will be found to be the true and sole origin of evil. It generates a perpetual ignorance, hatred and revenge, where, without such error, only intelligence, confidence, and kindness would exist. It has hitherto been the Evil Genius of the world. It severs man from man throughout the various regions of the earth; and it makes enemies of those who, but for this gross error, would have enjoyed each other's kind offices and sincere friendship. It is, in short, an error which carries misery in all its consequences.

This error cannot much longer exist; for every day will make it more evident that the character of man is, without a single exception, always formed for him; and that it may be, and is, chiefly created by his predecessors that they give him, or may give him, his ideas and habits, which are the powers that govern and direct his conduct. Man, therefore, never did, nor is it possible that he ever can, form a his own character.

True and False Principles

Every society which now exists, as well as every society history records, has been formed and governed on a belief in the notions, assumed as *first principles*:

First – that it is in the power of every individual to form his own character. Hence the various systems called by the name of religion, codes of law and punishments. Hence also the angry passions entertained by individuals and nations towards each other.

Second – That the affections are at the command of the individual. Hence insincerity and degradation of character. Hence the miseries of domestic life, and more than one-half of the crimes of mankind.

Third – that it is necessary that a large portion of mankind should exist in ignorance and poverty, in order to secure the remaining part such a degree of happiness as they now enjoy. Hence a system of counteraction in the pursuits of man, a general opposition among individuals to the interests of each other, and the necessary effects of such a system – ignorance, poverty, and vice.

Facts prove, however –

First – that character is universally formed *for*, and not *by* the individual.

Second – that *any* habits and sentiments may be given to mankind.

Third – that the affections are *not* under the control of the individual.

Fourth – that every individual may be trained to produce far more than he can consume, while there is a sufficiency of soil left for him to cultivate.

Fifth - that nature has provided means by which populations may be at all times maintained in the proper state to give the greatest happiness to every individual, without one check of vice or misery.

Sixth - that any community may be arranged, on a due combination of the foregoing principles, in such a manner, as not only to withdraw vice, poverty, and, in a great degree, misery, from the world, but also to place in *every* individual under such circumstances in which he shall enjoy more permanent happiness than can be given to *any* individual under the principles which have hitherto regulated society.

Seventh - that all the assumed fundamental principles on which society has hitherto been founded are erroneous, and may be demonstrated to be contrary to fact. And -

Eighth - that the change which would follow the abandonment of these erroneous maxim which bring misery to the world, and the adoption of principles of truth, unfolding a system which shall remove and for ever exclude that misery, may be effected without the slightest injury to any human being.

Our Society Manufactures Criminals

How much longer shall we continue to allow generation after generation to be taught crime from their infancy, and when so taught, hunt them like beasts of the forest, until they are entangled beyond escape in the toils and nets of law? When, if the circumstances of those poor unpitied sufferers had been reversed with those who are even surrounded with the pomp and dignity of justice, these latter would have been at the bar of the culprit, and the former would have been at the judgment seat.

Men and Machines

Many of you have long experienced in your manufacturing operations the advantages of substantial, well-contrived, and well-executed machinery.

Experience has also show you the difference of the results between mechanism which is neat, clean, well arranged, and always in a high state of repair; and that which is allowed to be dirty, in disorder, and without the means of preventing unnecessary friction, and which therefore becomes, and works, much out of repair.

In the first case the whole economy and management are good, every operation proceeds with ease, order, and success. In the last, the reverse must follow, and dissatisfaction among all the agents and instrument interested or occupied in the general process, which cannot fail to create great loss.

If, then, due care as to the state of your inanimate machines can produce such beneficial results, what may not expected if you devote equal attention to your vital machines [humans], which are far more wonderfully constructed?

When you shall acquire a right knowledge of these, of their curious mechanism, of their self-adjusting powers; when the proper main spring shall be applied to their various movements - you will become conscious of their real value, and you will readily be induced to turn your thoughts more frequently from your inanimate to your living machines; and you will discover that the latter may be easily trained and directed to procure a large increase of pecuniary gain, while you may also derive from them a high and substantial satisfaction.

Will you then continue to expend large sums of money to procure the best devised mechanisms of wood, brass, or iron; to retain it in perfect repair; to provide the best substance for the prevention of unnecessary friction, and to save it from falling into premature decay? Will you not also invest a portion of your time and capital toward improving your living machines? From experience, I venture to assure you, that your time and money so applied, would return you, not five, ten, or fifteen percent, for your capital so expended, but often fifty, and in many cases a hundred percent.

Children Can be Molded

Children are, without exception, passive and wonderfully contrived compounds; which, by an accurate previous and subsequent attention, *founded on a correct knowledge of the subject*, may be formed collectively to have any human character. And although these compounds, like all the other works of nature, possess endless varieties, yet they partake of that plastic quality, which, by perseverance under judicious management, may be ultimately molded into the very image of rational wishes and desires.

To Whom Can My Plans Be Submitted

Not to the children of commerce [Capitalists] who have been trained to direct all their faculties to buy cheap and sell dear; and consequently, those who are the most expert and successful in this wise and noble art, are, in the commercial world, deemed to possess foresight and superior acquirements; while such as attempt to improve the moral habits and increase the comforts of those whom they employ, are termed wild enthusiasts.

Nor yet are they to be submitted to the mere men of the law; for these are necessarily trained to endeavor to make wrong appear right, or to involve both in a maze of intricacies, and to legalized injustice.

Nor to the mere political leaders or their partisans, for they are embarrassed by the trammels of party, which mislead their judgment, and often constrain them to sacrifice the real well-being of the community and of themselves, to an apparent but most mistaken self-interest.

Nor to those termed heroes and conquerors, or to their followers; for their minds have been trained to consider the infliction of human misery, and the commission of military murders, a glorious duty, almost beyond reward.

Nor yet to the fashionable or splendid in their appearance; for these are from infancy trained to deceive and to be deceived, to accept shadows for substances, and to live life of insincerity, and of consequent discontent and misery.

360

Still less are they to be exclusively submitted to the official expounders and defenders of the various opposing religious systems throughout the world; for many of these are actively engaged in propagating imaginary notions, which cannot fail to vitiate the rational powers of man, and to perpetuate his misery.

These principles, therefore, and the practical systems which they recommend, are not to be submitted to the judgment of those with been trained under, and continue in, any of these unhappy combinations of circumstances. But they are to be submitted to the dispassionate and patient investigation and decision of those individuals of every rank and class and denomination of society, who have become in some degree conscious of the errors in which they exist; who have felt the thick mental darkness by which they are surrounded; who are ardently desirous of discovering and following truth wherever it may lead; and who can perceive the inseparable connection which exists between individual and general, between private and public good!

Karl Marx, *Communist Manifesto, 1848 CE*

Reading and Discussion Questions
1. Explain what is meant by the statement: "The history of all hitherto existing society is the history of class struggles." Give two examples from history that support this statement.
2. Who are the bourgeoisie? Discuss three ways in which the Communist Manifesto says that the bourgeoisie exploits or does harm to the rest of society.
3. What is the proletariat? How is the growth of the proletariat directly related to the growth and power of the bourgeoisie?
4. How will the growth of industry increase the power of the proletariat?
5. Explain how, through the proletariat, revolution will inevitably happen.
6. Explain the final passage of *The Communist Manifesto*: "What the bourgeoisie therefore produces, above all, are its own grave-diggers. Its fall and the victory of the proletariat are equally inevitable." In what way does the bourgeoisie produce its own grave-diggers? Why is the victory of the proletariat inevitable?

Karl Marx and his coauthor, Friedrich Engels, begin The Communist Manifesto *with the famous and provocative statement that the "history of all hitherto existing societies is the history of class struggle." They argue that all changes in society, in political institutions and in history itself, are driven by a process of collective struggle by a group with similar economic situations in order to achieve their collective goals. These struggles, occurring throughout history from ancient Rome through the Middle Ages to the present day, have been struggles of economically subordinate classes against economically dominant classes who opposed their economic interests—slaves against masters, serfs against landlords, and so on. The modern industrialized world has been shaped by one such subordinate class—the bourgeoisie, or merchant class—in its struggle against the aristocratic elite of feudal society. Through world exploration, the discovery of raw materials and metals, and the opening of commercial markets across the globe, the bourgeoisie, whose livelihood is accumulation, grew wealthier and politically emboldened against the feudal order, which it eventually managed to sweep away through struggle and revolution. The bourgeoisie have risen to the status of dominant class in the modern industrial world, shaping political institutions and* society according to its own interests. Far from doing away with class struggle, this once subordinate class, now dominant, has replaced one class struggle with another.

The bourgeoisie is a terribly powerful force, according to Marx. The businessman's enthusiasm for wealth has led them to conquer the globe, forcing everyone under his power to submit to capitalism. The bourgeoisie see the world as one big market for business, according to Marx, and this attitude has forever changed every aspect of life. During the Industrial Age, a new class was created that became the "wage slaves" to the bourgeoisie. This class is what Marx calls the Proletariat, or modern working class. These workers have been forced to sell their labor to the bourgeoisie, making their existence one of modern slavery to the factory owner. The Proletariat are forced to compete with one another for ever-shrinking wages as the means of production grow more sophisticated.

Marx predicted that the struggles that were born in factories would spread to broader society. Eventually, workers will recognize how they are being taken advantage of and they will unite to improve their situation, by overthrowing their bourgeoisie masters. All of society will be drawn to one or the other side of the struggle. Like the bourgeoisie before them who threw off the oppressive nobility in their struggle against feudalism, the proletariat and their allies will work together to achieve their goals. Marx predicted a working class revolution and then a temporary new government that he called the Dictatorship of the Proletariat. He believed that it would be necessary for a short time for the Proletariat to take control of all property and production while people learned how to live under the new world order. Eventually, Marx said, the rule of the Proletariat would become unnecessary because people will have mended their old ways and learned to embrace the ideals of the new Communist society, where there is no private ownership of property or the means of production. Then Marx's vision would be complete.

BOURGEOIS AND PROLETARIANS

The history of all hitherto existing society is the history of class struggles.

Freeman and slave, patrician and plebian, lord and serf, guild-master and journeyman, in a word, oppressor and oppressed, stood in constant opposition to one another, carried on an uninterrupted, now hidden, now open fight, a fight that each time ended, either in a revolutionary reconstitution of society at large, or in the common ruin of the contending classes.

In the earlier epochs of history, we find almost everywhere a complicated arrangement of society into various orders, a manifold gradation of social rank. In ancient Rome we have patricians, knights, plebians, slaves; in the Middle Ages, feudal lords, vassals, guild-masters, journeymen, apprentices, serfs; in almost all of these classes, again, subordinate gradations.

The modern bourgeois society that has sprouted from the ruins of feudal society has not done away with class antagonisms. It has but established new classes, new conditions of oppression, new forms of struggle in place of the old ones.

Our epoch, the epoch of the bourgeoisie, possesses, however, this distinct feature: it has simplified class antagonisms. Society as a whole is more and more splitting up into two great hostile camps, into two great classes directly facing each other – bourgeoisie and proletariat.

From the serfs of the Middle Ages sprang the chartered burghers of the earliest towns. From these burgesses the first elements of the bourgeoisie were developed.

The discovery of America, the rounding of the Cape, opened up fresh ground for the rising bourgeoisie. The East-Indian and Chinese markets, the discovery of America, trade with the colonies, the increase in the means of exchange and in commodities generally, gave to commerce, to navigation, to industry, an impulse never before known, and thereby, to the revolutionary element in the tottering feudal society, a rapid development.

The feudal system of industry, in which industrial production was monopolized by closed guilds, now no longer suffices for the growing wants of the new markets. The manufacturing system took its place. The guild-masters were pushed aside by the manufacturing middle class; division of labor between the different corporate guilds vanished in the face of division of labor in each single workshop.

Meantime, the markets kept ever growing, the demand ever rising. Even manufacturers no longer sufficed. Thereupon, steam and machinery revolutionized industrial production. The place of manufacture was taken by the giant, MODERN INDUSTRY; the place of the industrial middle class by industrial millionaires, the leaders of the whole industrial armies, the modern bourgeois.

Modern industry has established the world market, for which the discovery of America paved the way. This market has given an immense development to commerce, to navigation, to communication by land. This development has, in turn, reacted on the extension of industry; and in proportion as industry, commerce, navigation, railways extended, in the same proportion the bourgeoisie developed, increased its capital, and pushed into the background every class handed down from the Middle Ages.

We see, therefore, how the modern bourgeoisie is itself the product of a long course of development, of a series of revolutions in the modes of production and of exchange.

Each step in the development of the bourgeoisie was accompanied by a corresponding political advance in that class. An oppressed class under the sway of the feudal nobility, an armed and self-governing association of medieval commune: here independent urban republic (as in Italy and Germany); there taxable "third estate" of the monarchy (as in France); afterward, in the period of manufacturing proper, serving either the semi-feudal or the absolute monarchy as a counterpoise against the nobility, and, in fact, cornerstone of the great monarchies in general – the bourgeoisie has at last, since the establishment of Modern Industry and of the world market, conquered for itself, in the modern representative state, exclusive political sway. The executive of the modern state is but a committee for managing the common affairs of the whole bourgeoisie.

The bourgeoisie, historically, has played a most revolutionary part.

The bourgeoisie, wherever it has got the upper hand, has put an end to all feudal, patriarchal, idyllic relations. It has pitilessly torn asunder the motley feudal ties that bound man to his "natural superiors", and has left no other nexus between man and man than naked self-interest, than callous "cash payment". It has drowned out the most heavenly exstacies of religious fervor, of chivalrous enthusiasm, of philistine sentimentalism, in the icy water of egotistical calculation. It has resolved personal worth into exchange value, and in place of the numberless indefeasible chartered freedoms, has set up that single, unconscionable freedom – Free Trade. In one word, for exploitation, veiled by religious and political illusions, it has substituted naked, shameless, direct, brutal exploitation.

The bourgeoisie has stripped of its halo every occupation hitherto honored and looked up to with reverent awe. It has converted the physician, the lawyer, the priest, the poet, the man of science, into its paid wage laborers.

The bourgeoisie has torn away from the family its sentimental veil, and has reduced the family relation into a mere money relation.

The bourgeoisie has disclosed how it came to pass that the brutal display of vigor in the Middle Ages, which reactionaries so much admire, found its fitting complement in the most slothful indolence. It has been the first to show what man's activity can bring about. It has accomplished wonders far surpassing Egyptian pyramids, Roman aqueducts, and Gothic cathedrals; it has conducted expeditions that put in the shade all former exoduses of nations and crusades.

The bourgeoisie cannot exist without constantly revolutionizing the instruments of production, and thereby the relations of production, and with them the whole relations of society. Conservation of the old modes of production in unaltered form, was, on the contrary, the first condition of existence for all earlier industrial classes. Constant revolutionizing of production, uninterrupted disturbance of all social conditions, everlasting uncertainty and agitation distinguish the bourgeois epoch from all earlier ones. All fixed, fast frozen relations, with their train of ancient and venerable prejudices and opinions, are swept away, all new-formed ones become antiquated before they can ossify. All that is solid melts into air, all that is holy is profaned, and man is at last compelled to face with sober senses his real condition of life and his relations with his kind.

The need of a constantly expanding market for its products chases the bourgeoisie over the entire surface of the globe. It must nestle everywhere, settle everywhere, establish connections everywhere.

The bourgeoisie has, through its exploitation of the world market, given a cosmopolitan character to production and consumption in every country. To the great chagrin of reactionaries, it has drawn from under the feet of industry the national ground on which it stood. All old-established national industries have been destroyed or are daily being destroyed. They are dislodged by new industries, whose introduction becomes a life and death question for all civilized nations, by industries that no longer work up indigenous raw material, but raw material drawn from the remotest zones; industries whose products are consumed, not only at home, but in every quarter of the globe. In place of the old wants, satisfied by the production of the country, we find new wants, requiring for their satisfaction the products of distant lands and climes. In place of the old local and national seclusion and self-sufficiency, we have intercourse in every direction, universal inter-dependence of nations. And as in material, so also in intellectual production. The intellectual creations of individual nations become common property. National one-sidedness and narrow-mindedness become more and more impossible, and from the numerous national and local literatures, there arises a world literature.

The bourgeoisie, by the rapid improvement of all instruments of production, by the immensely facilitated means of communication, draws all, even the most barbarian, nations into civilization. The cheap prices of commodities are the heavy artillery with which it forces the barbarians' intensely obstinate hatred of foreigners to capitulate. It compels all nations, on pain of extinction, to adopt the bourgeois mode of production; it compels them to introduce what it calls civilization into their midst, i.e., to become bourgeois themselves. In one word, it creates a world after its own image.

The bourgeoisie has subjected the country to the rule of the towns. It has created enormous cities, has greatly increased the urban population as compared with the rural, and has thus rescued a considerable part of the population from the idiocy of rural life. Just as it has made the country dependent on the towns, so it has made barbarian and semi-barbarian countries dependent on the civilized ones, nations of peasants on nations of bourgeois, the East on the West.

The bourgeoisie keeps more and more doing away with the scattered state of the population, of the means of production, and of property. It has agglomerated population, centralized the means of production, and has concentrated property in a few hands. The necessary consequence of this was political centralization. Independent, or but loosely connected provinces, with separate interests, laws, governments, and systems of taxation, became lumped together into one nation, with one government, one code of laws, one national class interest, one frontier, and one customs tariff.

The bourgeoisie, during its rule of scarce one hundred years, has created more massive and more colossal productive forces than have all preceding generations together. Subjection of nature's forces to man, machinery, application of chemistry to industry and agriculture, steam navigation, railways, electric telegraphs, clearing of whole continents for cultivation, canalization or rivers, whole populations conjured out of the ground – what earlier century had even a presentiment that such productive forces slumbered in the lap of social labor?

Into their place stepped free competition, accompanied by a social and political constitution adapted in it, and the economic and political sway of the bourgeois class.

The weapons with which the bourgeoisie felled feudalism to the ground are now turned against the bourgeoisie itself. But not only has the bourgeoisie forged the weapons that bring death to itself; it has also called into existence the men who are to wield those weapons – the modern working class – the proletarians.

In proportion as the bourgeoisie, i.e., capital, is developed, in the same proportion is the proletariat, the modern working class, developed – a class of laborers, who live only so long as they find work, and who find work only so long as their labor increases capital. These laborers, who must sell themselves piecemeal, are a commodity, like every other article of commerce, and are consequently exposed to all the vicissitudes of competition, to all the fluctuations of the market.

Owing to the extensive use of machinery, and to the division of labor, the work of the proletarians has lost all individual character, and, consequently, all charm for the workman. He becomes an appendage of the machine, and it is only the most simple, most monotonous, and most easily acquired knack, that is required of him. Hence, the cost of production of a workman is restricted, almost entirely, to the means of subsistence that he requires for maintenance, and for the propagation of his race. But the price of a commodity, and therefore also of labor, is equal to its cost of production. In proportion, therefore, as the repulsiveness of the work increases, the wage decreases. What is more, in proportion as the use of machinery and division of labor increases, in the same proportion the burden of toil also increases, whether by prolongation of the working hours, by the increase of the work exacted in a given time, or by increased speed of machinery, etc.

Modern Industry has converted the little workshop of the patriarchal master into the great factory of the industrial capitalist. Masses of laborers, crowded into the factory, are organized like soldiers. As privates of the industrial army, they are placed under the command of a perfect hierarchy of officers and sergeants. Not only are they slaves of the bourgeois class, and of the bourgeois state; they are daily and hourly enslaved by the machine, by the overlooker, and, above all, in the individual bourgeois manufacturer himself. The more openly this despotism proclaims gain to be its end and aim, the more petty, the more hateful and the more embittering it is.

The less the skill and exertion of strength implied in manual labor, in other words, the more modern industry becomes developed, the more is the labor of men superseded by that of women. Differences of age and sex have no longer any distinctive social validity for the working class. All are instruments of labor, more or less expensive to use, according to their age and sex.

No sooner is the exploitation of the laborer by the manufacturer, so far at an end, that he receives his wages in cash, than he is set upon by the other portion of the bourgeoisie, the landlord, the shopkeeper, the pawnbroker, etc.

The lower strata of the middle class – the small tradespeople, shopkeepers, and retired tradesmen generally, the handicraftsmen and peasants – all these sink gradually into the proletariat, partly because their diminutive capital does not suffice for the scale on which Modern Industry is carried on, and is swamped in the competition with the large capitalists, partly because their specialized skill is rendered worthless by new methods of production. Thus, the proletariat is recruited from all classes of the population.

The proletariat goes through various stages of development. With its birth begins its struggle with the bourgeoisie. At first, the contest is carried on by individual laborers, then by the work of people of a factory, then by the operative of one trade, in one locality, against the individual bourgeois who directly exploits them. They direct their attacks not against the bourgeois condition of production, but against the instruments of production themselves; they destroy imported wares that compete with their labor, they smash to pieces machinery, they set factories ablaze, they seek to restore by force the vanished status of the workman of the Middle Ages.

At this stage, the laborers still form an incoherent mass scattered over the whole country, and broken up by their mutual competition. If anywhere they unite to form more compact bodies, this is not yet the consequence of their own active union, but of the union of the bourgeoisie, which class, in order to attain its own political ends, is compelled to set the whole proletariat in motion, and is moreover yet, for a time, able to do so. At this stage, therefore, the proletarians do not fight their enemies, but the enemies of their enemies, the remnants of absolute monarchy, the landowners, the non-industrial bourgeois, the petty bourgeois. Thus, the whole historical movement is concentrated in the hands of the bourgeoisie; every victory so obtained is a victory for the bourgeoisie.

But with the development of industry, the proletariat not only increases in number; it becomes concentrated in greater masses, its strength grows, and it feels that strength more. The various interests and conditions of life within the ranks of the proletariat are more and more equalized, in proportion as machinery obliterates all distinctions of labor, and nearly everywhere reduces wages to the same low level. The growing competition among the bourgeois, and the resulting commercial crises, make the

366

wages of the workers ever more fluctuating. The increasing improvement of machinery, ever more rapidly developing, makes their livelihood more and more precarious; the collisions between individual workmen and individual bourgeois take more and more the character of collisions between two classes. Thereupon, the workers begin to form combinations (trade unions) against the bourgeois; they club together in order to keep up the rate of wages; they found permanent associations in order to make provision beforehand for these occasional revolts. Here and there, the contest breaks out into riots.

Now and then the workers are victorious, but only for a time. The real fruit of their battles lie not in the immediate result, but in the ever expanding union of the workers. This union is helped on by the improved means of communication that are created by Modern Industry, and that place the workers of different localities in contact with one another. It was just this contact that was needed to centralize the numerous local struggles, all of the same character, into one national struggle between classes. But every class struggle is a political struggle. And that union, to attain which the burghers of the Middle Ages, with their miserable highways, required centuries, the modern proletarian, thanks to railways, achieve in a few years.

This organization of the proletarians into a class, and, consequently, into a political party, is continually being upset again by the competition between the workers themselves. But it ever rises up again, stronger, firmer, mightier. It compels legislative recognition of particular interests of the workers, by taking advantage of the divisions among the bourgeoisie itself. Thus, the Ten-Hours Bill in England was carried.

Altogether, collisions between the classes of the old society further in many ways the course of development of the proletariat. The bourgeoisie finds itself involved in a constant battle. At first with the aristocracy; later on, with those portions of the bourgeoisie itself, whose interests have become antagonistic to the progress of industry; at all time with the bourgeoisie of foreign countries. In all these battles, it sees itself compelled to appeal to the proletariat, to ask for help, and thus to drag it into the political arena. The bourgeoisie itself, therefore, supplies the proletariat with its own elements of political and general education, in other words, it furnishes the proletariat with weapons for fighting the bourgeoisie.

Further, as we have already seen, entire sections of the ruling class are, by the advance of industry, precipitated into the proletariat, or are at least threatened in their conditions of existence. These also supply the proletariat with fresh elements of enlightenment and progress.

Finally, in times when the class struggle nears the decisive hour, the progress of dissolution going on within the ruling class, in fact within the whole range of old society, assumes such a violent, glaring character, that a small section of the ruling class cuts itself adrift, and joins the revolutionary class, the class that holds the future in its hands. Just as, therefore, at an earlier period, a section of the nobility went over to the bourgeoisie, so now a portion of the bourgeoisie goes over to the proletariat, and in particular, a portion of the bourgeois ideologists, who have raised themselves to the level of comprehending theoretically the historical movement as a whole.

Of all the classes that stand face to face with the bourgeoisie today, the proletariat alone is a genuinely revolutionary class. The other classes decay and finally disappear in the face of Modern Industry; the proletariat is its special and essential product.

The lower middle class, the small manufacturer, the shopkeeper, the artisan, the peasant, all these fight against the bourgeoisie, to save from extinction their existence

367

as fractions of the middle class. They are therefore not revolutionary, but conservative. Nay, more, they are reactionary, for they try to roll back the wheel of history. If, by chance, they are revolutionary, they are only so in view of their impending transfer into the proletariat; they thus defend not their present, but their future interests; they desert their own standpoint to place themselves at that of the proletariat.

The "dangerous class", the social scum, that passively rotting mass thrown off by the lowest layers of the old society, may, here and there, be swept into the movement by a proletarian revolution; its conditions of life, however, prepare it far more for the part of a bribed tool of reactionary intrigue.

In the condition of the proletariat, those of old society at large are already virtually swamped. The proletarian is without property; his relation to his wife and children has no longer anything in common with the bourgeois family relations; modern industry labor, modern subjection to capital, the same in England as in France, in America as in Germany, has stripped him of every trace of national character. Law, morality, religion, are to him so many bourgeois prejudices, behind which lurk in ambush just as many bourgeois interests.

All the preceding classes that got the upper hand sought to fortify their already acquired status by subjecting society at large to their conditions of appropriation. The proletarians cannot become masters of the productive forces of society, except by abolishing their own previous mode of appropriation, and thereby also every other previous mode of appropriation. They have nothing of their own to secure and to fortify; their mission is to destroy all previous securities for, and insurances of, individual property.

All previous historical movements were movements of minorities, or in the interest of minorities. The proletarian movement is the self-conscious, independent movement of the immense majority, in the interest of the immense majority. The proletariat, the lowest stratum of our present society, cannot stir, cannot raise itself up, without the whole superincumbent strata of official society being sprung into the air.

Though not in substance, yet in form, the struggle of the proletariat with the bourgeoisie is at first a national struggle. The proletariat of each country must, of course, first of all settle matters with its own bourgeoisie.

In depicting the most general phases of the development of the proletariat, we traced the more or less veiled civil war, raging within existing society, up to the point where that war breaks out into open revolution, and where the violent overthrow of the bourgeoisie lays the foundation for the sway of the proletariat.

Hitherto, every form of society has been based, as we have already seen, on the antagonism of oppressing and oppressed classes. But in order to oppress a class, certain conditions must be assured to it under which it can, at least, continue its slavish existence. The serf, in the period of serfdom, raised himself to membership in the commune, just as the petty bourgeois, under the yoke of the feudal absolutism, managed to develop into a bourgeois. The modern laborer, on the contrary, instead of rising with the process of industry, sinks deeper and deeper below the conditions of existence of his own class. He becomes a pauper, and pauperism develops more rapidly than population and wealth. And here it becomes evident that the bourgeoisie is unfit any longer to be the ruling class in society, and to impose its conditions of existence upon society as an overriding law. It is unfit to rule because it is incompetent to assure an existence to its slave within his slavery, because it cannot help letting him sink into such a state, that it has to feed him, instead of being fed by him. Society can no longer live under this bourgeoisie, in other words, its existence is no longer compatible with society.

The essential conditions for the existence and for the sway of the bourgeois class is the formation and augmentation of capital; the condition for capital is wage labor. Wage labor rests exclusively on competition between the laborers. The advance of industry, whose involuntary promoter is the bourgeoisie, replaces the isolation of the laborers, due to competition, by the revolutionary combination, due to association. The development of Modern Industry, therefore, cuts from under its feet the very foundation on which the bourgeoisie produces and appropriates products. What the bourgeoisie therefore produces, above all, are its own grave-diggers. Its fall and the victory of the proletariat are equally inevitable.

Karl Marx, *The Communist Manifesto* (Ten Planks), 1848 CE

Reading and Discussion Questions
  1. Summarize in your own words the steps Marx says are necessary for achieving his vision?
  2. Why does Marx say that eventually the Proletariat will have "swept away the conditions for the existence of class antagonisms and of classes generally, and will thereby have abolished its own supremacy as a class?" What does he mean by this statement?

In this section of the Communist Manifesto, Marx outlines the actual steps that will be taken to achieve his vision.

The proletariat will use its political supremacy to wrest, by degree, all capital from the bourgeoisie, to consolidate all instruments of production in the hands of the State, i.e., of the proletariat as the ruling class; and to increase the total productive forces as rapidly as possible.

Of course, in the beginning, this cannot be effected except by means of despotic inroads on the rights of property, and on the conditions of bourgeois production; by means of measures, therefore, which appear economically insufficient and untenable, but which, in the course of the movement, outstrip themselves, necessitate further inroads upon the old social order.

These measures will, of course, be different in different countries.

Nevertheless, in most advanced countries, the following will be pretty generally applicable.

1. Abolition of property in land and application of all rents of land to public purposes.
2. A heavy progressive or graduated income tax.
3. Abolition of all rights of inheritance.
4. Confiscation of the property of all emigrants and rebels.
5. Centralization of credit in the hands of the state, by means of a national bank with State capital and an exclusive monopoly.
6. Centralization of the means of communication and transport in the hands of the

State.

7. Extension of factories and instruments of production owned by the State; the bringing into cultivation of waste-lands, and the improvement of the soil generally in accordance with a common plan.

8. Equal liability of all to work. Establishment of industrial armies, especially for agriculture.

9. Combination of agriculture with manufacturing industries; gradual abolition of all the distinction between town and country by a more equable distribution of the populace over the country.

10. Free education for all children in public schools. Abolition of children's factory labor in its present form. Combination of education with industrial production, etc...

When, in the course of development, class distinctions have disappeared, and all production has been concentrated in the hands of a vast association of the whole nation, the public power will lose its political character. Political power, properly so called, is merely the power of one class for oppressing another. If the proletariat during its contest with the bourgeoisie is compelled, by the force of circumstances, to elevate itself as a class, if, by means of a revolution, it makes itself the ruling class, and, as such, sweeps away by force the old conditions of production, then it will, along with these conditions, have swept away the conditions for the existence of class antagonisms and of classes generally, and will thereby have abolished its own supremacy as a class.

In place of the old bourgeois society, with its classes and class antagonisms, we shall have an association, in which the free development of each is the condition for the free development of all.

Thorstein Veblen, *Conspicuous Consumption*, 1899 CE

Reading and Discussion Questions

1. What is "conspicuous consumption?" How do the social classes relate to each other in regard to conspicuous consumption?
2. What is the role of the middle class housewife in conspicuous consumption?
3. Summarize Veblen's critique of American society as you understand it from your reading?
4. Is there anything about the phenomenon that Veblen discusses that is present in the world today? Explain your answer.

Thorstein Veblen was an American economist and sociologist who studied the lifestyles and habits of those who had become very wealthy during the Industrial Age. In his book, The Theory of the Leisure Class, he noted that these uber-rich set the norms, the trends and the behaviors for the lower social classes. He said that the rich went to extreme measures to display their wealth and to demonstrate that they were wealthier, more interesting and therefore more valuable than their other wealthy friends. Veblen called this extravagant display of wealth "conspicuous consumption." Conspicuous means "clearly visible" and consumption in economic terms means "the utilization of economic goods to satisfy wants or appetites." Simply put, conspicuous consumption was the practice of spending money in such a way that it was widely noticed as a show of one's wealth, power and importance. Veblen argued that never before in history had there been a more elaborate, sometimes absurd and sometimes disgusting, display of wealth than in America in the late 1800s. What was more absurd, Veblen said, was how hard other classes of people tried to create the illusion that they were wealthy and important by mimicking the trends, norms and leisure activities of the upper class. Veblen observed that housewives, more than any other group, devoted their entire existence to creating a physical appearance as well as a matter of behaving, that told the world that she and her family mattered. Middle class women went to elaborate lengths to convince the world they were well-off were. They did so at the expense of the man of the household who had to nearly kill himself with work in order for his wife to keep up appearances of wealth.

Conspicuous consumption of valuable goods is a means of improving one's reputation by assuming the appearances of a gentleman of leisure. As wealth accumulates on his hands, his own unaided effort will not avail to sufficiently put his opulence in evidence by this method. The aid of friends and competitors is therefore brought in by resorting to the giving of valuable presents and expensive feasts and entertainments. Presents and feasts had probably another origin than that of naïve ostentation, but they acquired their utility for this purpose very early, and they have retained that character to the present; so that their utility in this respect has now long been the substantial ground on which these usages rest. Costly entertainments, such as the potlatch or the ball, are peculiarly adapted to serve this end. The competitor with whom the entertainer wishes to institute a comparison is, by this method, made to serve as a means to the end.

As wealth accumulates, the leisure class develops further in function and structure, and there arises a competition within the class. But as we descend the social scale, the point is reached where the duties of leisure and consumption devolve upon the wife alone. In the communities of the Western culture, this point is at present found among the lower middle class. And here occurs a curious phenomenon. In the lower middle class there is no pretense of leisure on the part of the head of the household [man]. The head of the middle-class household has been forced by economic circumstances to pursue a livelihood by occupation, as in the case of the ordinary business man of today. But the leisure and consumption of the wife, remains in vogue. It is by no means an uncommon spectacle to find a man applying himself to work with the utmost effort, in order that his wife may have from him a high degree of leisure which the common sense of the time demands.

Her leisure almost invariably occurs disguised as form of work or household duties or social amenities, which serves little or no purpose except showing that she does not occupy herself with anything that is meaningful or useful. The result of her efforts is usually of a decorative character and take the form of household adornment and tidiness. The effects are pleasing to us chiefly because we have been taught to find them pleasing. In general, the housewife's efforts are guided by the law of conspicuously wasteful use of time and money.

Decency requires the wife to consume some goods conspicuously for the reputability of the household and its head. So that the wife, who was at the outset the servant and property of the man, both in fact and in theory—the producer of goods for him to consume—has become the ceremonial consumer of goods which he produces. But she still quite unmistakably remains his property; for the obsessive display of leisure and consumption is the surest sign of the unfree servant.

This conspicuous consumption practiced by the household of the middle and lower classes is not a direct expression of the leisure-class scheme of life, since the household of this class does not belong within the leisure class. The leisure class stands at the head of the social structure and has the highest reputation; and its manner of life and its standards of worth therefore set the standards of acceptability for the community. The observance of these standards becomes the duty of all classes lower in the scale. In modern civilized communities the lines between social classes have grown vague and transient, and wherever this happens the norms imposed by the upper class extend down through the social structure to the lowest classes. The result is that the members of each class accept as their ideal of decency the scheme of life in vogue in the next higher class, and bend their energies to live up to that ideal. On pain of forfeiting their good name and their self-respect, they must conform to the accepted code of the higher class, at least in appearance.

The basis on which good repute in any highly organized industrial community ultimately rests is wealth; and the means of showing wealth, and so of gaining or retaining a good name, are leisure and a conspicuous consumption of goods. Accordingly, both of these methods are in vogue as far down the scale as it remains possible; and in the lower strata in which the two methods are employed, both offices are in great part delegated to the wife and children of the household. Lower still, where any degree of leisure, even ostensible, has become impracticable for the wife, the conspicuous consumption of goods remains and is carried on by the wife and children.

No class of society, not even the most abjectly poor, forgoes all customary conspicuous consumption. The last items of conspicuous consumption are not given up except under stress of the direst necessity. Very much of squalor and discomfort will be endured before the last trinket or the last pretense of wealth is put away. There is no class and no country that has yielded so abjectly before the pressure of physical want as to deny themselves all gratification of this deep need.

William Wordsworth, *Tintern Abbey*, 1798 CE

Reading and Discussion Questions

1. On the surface, what is the poem about? What is "the plot" so to speak?
2. Analyze the relationship between Wordsworth and the natural environment in *Tintern Abbey*. How does Nature act on him? How does he act on it?
3. How has his relationship with nature changed over time?
4. What are Wordsworth's most powerful passages on nature, in your opinion and why?
5. What is your overall reaction to this poem? Does it speak to you in any way? Why or why not? Explain your answer.

William Wordsworth is the most famous of the British Romantic poets. Wordsworth and other writers of the Romantic period reinvented poetry and literature in general. Poems, before men like Wordsworth, tended to glorify kings and queens or immortalize great heroes on epic journeys. Poems were about things that were larger than life and well beyond the realities of the lives of most people. Wordsworth and the Romantics wrote about common people and everyday life and they made them beautiful. Romantics wrote about shepherds and farmers, mothers and children, even sheep and urns. They found beauty in the ordinary and the real and they immortalized that beauty in their poems. More than anything else, though, Romantics glorified and celebrated nature. One of Wordsworth's most famous poems, Lines Composed a Few Miles above Tintern Abbey (or Tintern Abbey for short) is the final poem, the climax, in his collection of poems called Lyrical Ballads. In the preface of that book, Wordsworth said that he wanted to write "in the real language of men" about real things that might touch real people with their power and beauty. Tintern Abbey is Wordsworth's love poem to nature and it teaches us about the tremendous healing power of nature to restore our life-weary souls.

Five years have past; five summers, with the length
Of five long winters! and again I hear
These waters, rolling from their mountain-springs
With a soft inland murmur.—Once again
Do I behold these steep and lofty cliffs,
That on a wild secluded scene impress
Thoughts of more deep seclusion; and connect
The landscape with the quiet of the sky.
The day is come when I again repose
Here, under this dark sycamore, and view
These plots of cottage-ground, these orchard-tufts,
Which at this season, with their unripe fruits,
Are clad in one green hue, and lose themselves
'Mid groves and copses. Once again I see
These hedge-rows, hardly hedge-rows, little lines
Of sportive wood run wild: these pastoral farms,
Green to the very door; and wreaths of smoke
Sent up, in silence, from among the trees!

With some uncertain notice, as might seem
Of vagrant dwellers in the houseless woods,
Or of some Hermit's cave, where by his fire
The Hermit sits alone.

These beauteous forms,
Through a long absence, have not been to me
As is a landscape to a blind man's eye:
But oft, in lonely rooms, and 'mid the din
Of towns and cities, I have owed to them,
In hours of weariness, sensations sweet,
Felt in the blood, and felt along the heart;
And passing even into my purer mind
With tranquil restoration:—feelings too
Of unremembered pleasure: such, perhaps,
As have no slight or trivial influence
On that best portion of a good man's life,
His little, nameless, unremembered, acts
Of kindness and of love. Nor less, I trust,
To them I may have owed another gift,
Of aspect more sublime; that blessed mood,
In which the burthen of the mystery,
In which the heavy and the weary weight
Of all this unintelligible world,
Is lightened:—that serene and blessed mood,
In which the affections gently lead us on,—
Until, the breath of this corporeal frame
And even the motion of our human blood
Almost suspended, we are laid asleep
In body, and become a living soul:
While with an eye made quiet by the power
Of harmony, and the deep power of joy,
We see into the life of things.

If this
Be but a vain belief, yet, oh! how oft—
In darkness and amid the many shapes
Of joyless daylight; when the fretful stir
Unprofitable, and the fever of the world,
Have hung upon the beatings of my heart—
How oft, in spirit, have I turned to thee,
O sylvan Wye! thou wanderer thro' the woods,
    How often has my spirit turned to thee!

And now, with gleams of half-extinguished thought,
With many recognitions dim and faint,
And somewhat of a sad perplexity,
The picture of the mind revives again:
While here I stand, not only with the sense
Of present pleasure, but with pleasing thoughts
That in this moment there is life and food

For future years. And so I dare to hope,
Though changed, no doubt, from what I was when first
I came among these hills; when like a roe
I bounded o'er the mountains, by the sides
Of the deep rivers, and the lonely streams,
Wherever nature led: more like a man
Flying from something that he dreads, than one
Who sought the thing he loved. For nature then
(The coarser pleasures of my boyish days
And their glad animal movements all gone by)
To me was all in all.—I cannot paint
What then I was. The sounding cataract
Haunted me like a passion: the tall rock,
The mountain, and the deep and gloomy wood,
Their colours and their forms, were then to me
An appetite; a feeling and a love,
That had no need of a remoter charm,
By thought supplied, not any interest
Unborrowed from the eye.—That time is past,
And all its aching joys are now no more,
And all its dizzy raptures. Not for this
Faint I, nor mourn nor murmur; other gifts
Have followed; for such loss, I would believe,
Abundant recompense. For I have learned
To look on nature, not as in the hour
Of thoughtless youth; but hearing oftentimes
The still sad music of humanity,
Nor harsh nor grating, though of ample power
To chasten and subdue.—And I have felt
A presence that disturbs me with the joy
Of elevated thoughts; a sense sublime
Of something far more deeply interfused,
Whose dwelling is the light of setting suns,
And the round ocean and the living air,
And the blue sky, and in the mind of man:
A motion and a spirit, that impels
All thinking things, all objects of all thought,
And rolls through all things. Therefore am I still
A lover of the meadows and the woods
And mountains; and of all that we behold
From this green earth; of all the mighty world
Of eye, and ear,—both what they half create,
And what perceive; well pleased to recognise
In nature and the language of the sense
The anchor of my purest thoughts, the nurse,
The guide, the guardian of my heart, and soul
Of all my moral being.

Nor perchance,
If I were not thus taught, should I the more
Suffer my genial spirits to decay:
For thou art with me here upon the banks
Of this fair river; thou my dearest Friend,
My dear, dear Friend; and in thy voice I catch
The language of my former heart, and read
My former pleasures in the shooting lights
Of thy wild eyes. Oh! yet a little while
May I behold in thee what I was once,
My dear, dear Sister! and this prayer I make,
Knowing that Nature never did betray
The heart that loved her; 'tis her privilege,
Through all the years of this our life, to lead
From joy to joy: for she can so inform
The mind that is within us, so impress
With quietness and beauty, and so feed
With lofty thoughts, that neither evil tongues,
Rash judgments, nor the sneers of selfish men,
Nor greetings where no kindness is, nor all
The dreary intercourse of daily life,
Shall e'er prevail against us, or disturb
Our cheerful faith, that all which we behold
Is full of blessings. Therefore let the moon
Shine on thee in thy solitary walk;
And let the misty mountain-winds be free
To blow against thee: and, in after years,
When these wild ecstasies shall be matured
Into a sober pleasure; when thy mind
Shall be a mansion for all lovely forms,
Thy memory be as a dwelling-place
For all sweet sounds and harmonies; oh! then,
If solitude, or fear, or pain, or grief,
Should be thy portion, with what healing thoughts
Of tender joy wilt thou remember me,
And these my exhortations! Nor, perchance—
If I should be where I no more can hear
Thy voice, nor catch from thy wild eyes these gleams
Of past existence—wilt thou then forget
That on the banks of this delightful stream
We stood together; and that I, so long
A worshipper of Nature, hither came
Unwearied in that service: rather say
With warmer love—oh! with far deeper zeal
Of holier love. Nor wilt thou then forget,
That after many wanderings, many years
Of absence, these steep woods and lofty cliffs,
And this green pastoral landscape, were to me
More dear, both for themselves and for thy sake!

Henry David Thoreau, *Walden*, 1854 CE

Reading and Discussion
1. What does Thoreau mean when he says, "Be a Columbus to whole new continents and worlds within you?"
2. Reflect on your reading on Conspicuous Consumption. What observations does Thoreau make in this reading about the conspicuous consumption of his companions in Boston? How does he react to this?
3. What criticisms does Thoreau have about the way most men live their lives?
4. What do you take from this reading about how Thoreau thinks we should live our lives? What is his advice to you?
5. Find and analyze three passages from this reading that you think are the most powerful. Explain why you picked them and what you understand them to mean.

Henry David Thoreau was an American Transcendentalist in the 1800s who, along with other Transcendentalists, believed that man was moving dangerously far away from nature and was being led astray by the priorities of the Industrial Age. Thoreau withdrew from American city life and lived for two years in a small, Spartan cabin which he built on the shore of Walden pond in rural Massachusetts. There he wrote his most famous book, Walden, which reflected on the spiritual and timeless value of nature in restoring the soul of man. He wrote that "most men live lives of quiet desperation," lost in the sea of faceless industrial life. He encouraged people to rediscover themselves by spending time in the natural world. Like other Romantics, of which Transcendentalism is one branch, Thoreau also believed that man could find God in nature much more easily than in the churches. The following passage is from the conclusion of Walden when Thoreau rejoined the world and his friends in Boston. He shared the same concerns as Thorstein Veblen about the extravagant display of wealth in America and the belief that financial wealth somehow equaled human worth.

The universe is wider than our views of it.

Our voyaging is only great-circle sailing. One hastens to southern Africa to chase the giraffe; but surely that is not the game he would be after. How long, pray, would a man hunt giraffes if he could? Snipes and woodcocks also may afford rare sport; but I trust it would be nobler game to shoot one's self.—

> "Direct your eye right inward, and you'll find
> A thousand regions in your mind
> Yet undiscovered. Travel them, and be
> Expert in home-cosmography."

Be a Columbus to whole new continents and worlds within you, opening new channels, not of trade, but of thought. Every man is the lord of a realm beside which the earthly empire of the Czar is but a petty state, a hummock left by the ice. Yet some can be patriotic who have no self-respect, and sacrifice the greater to the less. They love the soil which makes their graves, but have no sympathy with the spirit which may still animate their clay. Patriotism is a maggot in their heads. What was the meaning of [global exploration], with all its parade and expense, but an indirect recognition of the fact that there are continents and seas in the moral world to which every man is an isthmus or an inlet, yet unexplored by him, but that it is easier to sail many thousand miles through cold and storm and cannibals, in a government ship, with five hundred men and boys to assist one, than it is to explore the private sea, the Atlantic and Pacific Ocean of one's being alone.

I left the woods for as good a reason as I went there. Perhaps it seemed to me that I had several more lives to live, and could not spare any more time for that one. It is remarkable how easily and insensibly we fall into a particular route, and make a beaten track for ourselves. I had not lived there a week before my feet wore a path from my door to the pond-side; and though it is five or six years since I trod it, it is still quite distinct. It is true, I fear, that others may have fallen into it, and so helped to keep it open. The surface of the earth is soft and impressible by the feet of men; and so with the paths which the mind travels. How worn and dusty, then, must be the highways of the world, how deep the ruts of tradition and conformity! I did not wish to take a cabin passage, but rather to go before the mast and on the deck of the world, for there I could best see the moonlight amid the mountains. I do not wish to go below now.

I learned this, at least, by my experiment: that if one advances confidently in the direction of his dreams, and endeavors to live the life which he has imagined, he will meet with a success unexpected in common hours. If you have built castles in the air, your work need not be lost; that is where they should be. Now put the foundations under them.

While England endeavors to cure the potato-rot, will not any endeavor to cure the brain-rot, which prevails so much more widely and fatally?

Why should we be in such desperate haste to succeed and in such desperate enterprises? If a man does not keep pace with his companions, perhaps it is because he hears a different drummer. Let him step to the music which he hears, however measured or far away. It is not important that he should mature as soon as an apple tree or an oak. Shall he turn his spring into summer? If the condition of things which we were made for is not yet, what were any reality which we can substitute? We will not be shipwrecked on a vain reality. Shall we with pains erect a heaven of blue glass over ourselves, though when it is done we shall be sure to gaze still at the true ethereal heaven far above, as if the former were not?

However mean your life is, meet it and live it; do not shun it and call it hard names. It is not so bad as you are. It looks poorest when you are richest. The fault-finder will find faults even in paradise. Love your life, poor as it is. You may perhaps have some pleasant, thrilling, glorious hours, even in a poorhouse. The setting sun is reflected from the windows of the almshouse as brightly as from the rich man's abode; the snow melts before its door as early in the spring. I do not see but a quiet mind may live as contentedly there, and have as cheering thoughts, as in a palace.

Cultivate poverty like a garden herb, like sage. Do not trouble yourself much to get new things, whether clothes or friends. Turn the old; return to them. Things do not change; we change. Sell your clothes and keep your thoughts. God will see that you do not want society.

Humility like darkness reveals the heavenly lights. The shadows of poverty and meanness gather around us, "and lo! Creation widens to our view." It is life near the bone where it is sweetest. You are defended from being a trifler. No man loses ever on a lower level by magnanimity on a higher. Superfluous wealth can buy superfluities only. Money is not required to buy one necessary of the soul.

I live [now, in Boston] in the angle of a leaden wall, into whose composition was poured a little alloy of bell-metal. Often, in the repose of my mid-day, there reaches my ears a confused tintinnabulum from without. It is the noise of my contemporaries. My neighbors tell me of their adventures with famous gentlemen and ladies, what notabilities they met at the dinner-table; but I am no more interested in such things than in the contents of the Daily Times. The interest and the conversation are about costume and manners chiefly; but a goose is a goose still, dress it as you will. I delight to come to my bearings—not walk in procession with pomp and parade, in a conspicuous place, but to walk even with the Builder of the universe, if I may—not to live in this restless, nervous, bustling, trivial Nineteenth Century, but stand or sit thoughtfully while it goes by. What are men celebrating? They are all on a committee of arrangements, and hourly expect a speech from somebody.

Rather than love, than money, than fame, give me truth. I sat at a table where were rich food and wine in abundance, and obsequious attendance, but sincerity and truth were not; and I went away hungry from the inhospitable board. The hospitality was as cold as the ices. I thought that there was no need of ice to freeze them. They talked to me of the age of the wine and the fame of the vintage; but I thought of an older, a newer, and purer wine, of a more glorious vintage, which they had not got, and could not buy. The style, the house and grounds and "entertainment" pass for nothing with me. I called on the king, but he made me wait in his hall, and conducted like a man incapacitated for hospitality. There was a man in my neighborhood who lived in a hollow tree. His manners were truly regal. I should have done better had I called on him.

Consider the pride and stagnant self-complacency of mankind. This generation inclines a little to congratulate itself on being the last of an illustrious line; and in Boston and London and Paris and Rome, thinking of its long descent, it speaks of its progress in art and science and literature with satisfaction. There are the Records of the Philosophical Societies, and the public Eulogies of Great Men! It is the good Adam contemplating his own virtue. "Yes, we have done great deeds, and sung divine songs, which shall never die"—that is, as long as we can remember them. The learned societies and great men of Assyria—where are they? What youthful philosophers and experimentalists we are! There is not one of my readers who has yet lived a whole human life.

Ralph Waldo Emerson , *Blight*, 1904 CE

<u>Reading and Discussion Questions</u>
1. Look up and define blight. What does it mean and why do you think Emerson chose that word as the title for this poem?
2. Define "inanition." What is it and why does Emerson say he is dying of it?
3. We studied the concept of "the lament" when we read the letters of Francesco Petrarch. Review the definition of "lament" now. Does Emerson's poem read like a lament to you? If so, what is he lamenting? If not, why not?
4. How do you interpret this poem? What is Emerson saying, in your opinion?

More than any other Transcendentalist, Ralph Waldo Emerson worshipped nature. And he grieved for its destruction. Emerson was a noted poet but he was also a very successful public speaker and author of countless essays and publications on Romantic and Transcendentalist themes. He was the leader of the Transcendentalist movement in America. He was raised in a deeply religious home and his father was a tyrannically strict minister, which gave Emerson a distaste for organized religion later in his life. He came to discover a new religion for himself in nature, which he believed was the only place God could be really known and understood.

Give me truths;
For I am weary of the surfaces,
And die of inanition.

If I knew
Only the herbs and simples of the wood,
Rue, cinquefoil, gill, vervain and agrimony,
Blue-vetch and trillium, hawkweed, sassafras,
Milkweeds and murky brakes, quaint pipes and sun-dew,
And rare and virtuous roots, which in these woods
Draw untold juices from the common earth,
Untold, unknown, and I could surely spell
Their fragrance, and their chemistry apply
By sweet affinities to human flesh,
Driving the foe and stablishing the friend,--
O, that were much, and I could be a part
Of the round day, related to the sun
And planted world, and full executor
Of their imperfect functions.

But these young scholars, who invade our hills,
Bold as the engineer who fells the wood,
And traveling often in the cut he makes,
Love not the flower they pluck, and know it not,
And all their botany is Latin names.

The old men studied magic in the flowers,
And human fortunes in astronomy,
And an omnipotence in chemistry,
Preferring things to names, for these were men,
Were unitarians of the united world,
And, wheresoever their clear eye-beams fell,
They caught the footsteps of the SAME.

Our eyes
And strangers to the mystic beast and bird,
And strangers to the plant and to the mine.
The injured elements say, 'Not in us;'
And haughtily return us stare for stare.
For we invade them impiously for gain;
We devastate them unreligiously,
And coldly ask their pottage, not their love.

Therefore they shove us from them, yield to us
Only what to our griping toil is due;
But the sweet affluence of love and song,
The rich results of the divine consents
Of man and earth, of world beloved and lover,
The nectar and ambrosia, are withheld;
And in the midst of spoils and slaves, we thieves
And pirates of the universe, shut out
Daily to a more thin and outward rind,
Turn pale and starve.

Therefore, to our sick eyes,
The stunted trees look sick, the summer short,
Clouds shade the sun, which will not tan our hay,
And nothing thrives to reach its natural term;
And life, shorn of its venerable length,
Even at its greatest space is a defeat,
And dies in anger that it was a dupe;
And, in its highest noon and wantonness,
Is early frugal, like a beggar's child;
Even in the hot pursuit of the best aims
And prizes of ambition, checks its hand,
Like Alpine cataracts frozen as they leaped,
Chilled with a miserly comparison
Of the toy's purchase with the length of life.

CHAPTER 14 –
THE AGE OF IMPERIALISM (1750 to 1900 CE)

GUIDING QUESTIONS
- What are the Three Gs of Imperialism and what is The Big G?
- In your opinion, did those who conquered territory in the name of God really do so because of religion or because of some other motive? Explain.
- Why had colonization waned by the 1700s and why did a new era of imperialism begin when it did in the 1800s?
- What was significant about the Opium Wars in terms of the message it sent to other nations?
- What is the Scramble for Africa and how might it have intensified rivalries between European powers?
- Who bears the real burden of imperialism – the white man or someone else? Explain.
- Why was the Age of Imperialism one of the main causes of World War I?

The clever children's rhyme about Columbus in 1492, as we have seen, is an elementary summary and an oversimplification of the impact that Columbus had, especially on the indigenous people and cultures in the Americas. The childhood stories we learn about the explorers like Columbus and the conquistadors who colonized the Americas make these men sound like heroes, but in truth were not always heroic in their actions. Never do we see more clearly that there are two sides to every story than during the period of exploration and conquest. From the perspective of the European Christian, men like Columbus, Cortez and Coronado look like heroes because they spread their religion, culture and power to places previously undiscovered. They ignited the curiosities of young adventurers and would-be conquers because their accomplishments represented a new world of possibilities. But as you learned in your unit on the Age of Discovery and Conquest, there is a much more sinister side of the story that is hard to explain to younger audiences. And too often we just tell the easy part of the story.

Contrary to popular telling of the conquistadors' stories, there were millions of people living in the Americas who had complex civilizations, established traditions and sacred beliefs. What we now understand in our more grown up study of the age of exploration is that European conquerors murdered or enslaved millions of native peoples and wiped out old customs, traditions and beliefs in order to establish new ones. This practice of conquering and ruling (or eradicating) a group of people, as you know, is called imperialism and imperialism is as old as civilization itself. The ancient Persians under Xerxes were the inventors of imperialism, and the Romans were masters of it. Imperialism was not new when Columbus sailed the ocean blue. It was simply that Columbus' discoveries and the discoveries of other explorers revealed whole new regions of the world to be imperialized.

It is important to pause and analyze the causes of imperialism before we take a look at an age named for the practice, which began in the 1800s. Imperialism happens because of a very complex web of human motives. Some would say that imperialism feeds our need to feel superior to others and others would argue that imperialism is in essence the law of the jungle, in which the strongest naturally rule over the weakest. We could delve into a deep psycho-analysis of the imperialist mindset but for our purposes, it is sufficient to look at what I call the "Three Gs of Imperialism"—Gold, God and Glory. The First G, Gold, actually refers to any natural resource that one power wants to take from the land and from the people living there. In the Seven Years' War, coal was the resource that inspired conquest. For the conquistadors in their quest for El Dorado, it was gold that they sought. But by the Industrial Age, there were dozens of resources that the European powers wanted and needed. The need for raw materials is the first driving force behind imperialism.

The Second G is God. During the 1800s and in the earlier age of discovery, "God" is the Christian God, but nations have been conquering in the name of religion since the beginning of time. If you recall, the Persians believed that their Emperor, Xerxes, was a god himself and they conquered for him. The Romans loved to conquer "the godless heathens" like the Germanic tribes because they didn't believe in the Roman pantheon of gods and were therefore deemed less civilized. And in the 1500s and again in the 1800s, vast territories were conquered in the name of the Christian God. King Ferdinand and Queen Isabella of Spain vowed to create "one king, one God, one flag" and to make as much of the world Catholic as possible. And they achieved quite a lot in their mission, converting almost all of Central and South America to Catholicism. Again in the 1800s, there was a widespread sentiment in Europe that it was the duty of European Christians to civilize the Godless savage. Thousands of pure-hearted missionaries traveled to and spent their whole lives in remote places in Asia, Africa and Latin America bringing people into the Christian flock. But Christian armies followed and forced their will, their power and their beliefs on those they called "heathens" and often fought in the name of religion but without true religious motives.

The Third G is glory. Glory has many synonyms—superiority, reputation, power, rank and authority are just a few. To win glory means to prove you are "better than." The unspoken motto of modern Europe during this period seems to have been "the nation with the most territory wins." The Age of Imperialism was frighteningly similar to the board game Risk, where opponents strategize about how to conquer all the space on their board and defeat the other players. The game was originally called "The Game of Global Domination." It is a blast to play and if you win, the glory you feel is fantastic, and you might gloat a little bit for dominating your opponent so completely. But in the game of Risk, no one dies (though the loser's pride does sting a bit!). Would you believe me if I told you that, in real life, a group of men played a very, very high stakes game of Risk once? Would it sound made up if I told you about how these men sat around a table and carved up a real map of the world, giving chunks of land to one another based on the amount of power each man had coming into the game? What if I said that a bunch of people lived in the land being divided up, and the players in this game knew that many of those people would have to die in order for them to have the land? Sounds too crazy to be true, right? Wrong.

By the 1800s, imperialism was considered such a natural right of the European Christian that the real life game of global domination did not even feel wrong to the players. They deserved the glory, they believed, because of the very nature of their birth. Hard to believe that so strange a tale can be true, until you analyze the Big G that rules all the little Gs. The Big G is Greed. Gold, God and Glory are easy ways to remember what causes imperialism but these three "g's" are all really just different forms of greed. The Age of Imperialism was a period of intense competition for territory, resources and power. Nations had insatiable appetites and were motivated by intense greed. But this is not the first time that powerful nations raced to conquer places and people around the globe.

The period we studied as the Age of Discovery and Conquest was the first era of modern imperialism. From 1492 to 1830, the major powers of Europe, and the newly formed United States, conquered, colonized and ruled most of the Americas. They also created the transatlantic slave trade, which supported the triangular trade network between Europe, Africa and the Americas. For more than three centuries, these newly conquered territories were outward displays of the growing power of rival nations like England, France and Spain. The more colonies a nation had and the more subjects it ruled over, the more power a nation had. But conflict is inevitably a part of imperialism. Not only do imperialist nations have to fight and subdue indigenous populations; they must also fight their rival imperialist neighbors. Dozens of wars, including the Seven Years' War, were fought to defend and conquer colonial territory. And wars are very, very expensive.

The Seven Years' War started off as a resource war between Austria and Prussia over coal. Because of delicate alliances, that small war erupted into a global war between England and her allies, and France and her allies. England, who fought with Prussia, was victorious and France was devastated, territorially and economically. Even though England won the war, it still caused significant financial trouble which led to the excessive taxation on the colonists in the 1760s. The debt for both nations as a result of this war led to two revolutions and caused a great deal of political instability. In the minds of some, maintaining imperial empires by the late 1700s was becoming too costly to be worth it.

Also, by the late 1700s, there was growing opposition to the practice of slavery, as more and more detailed accounts of a slave's life were made public. Abolitionist groups in England and elsewhere began to work for the abolition of the slave trade and the practice of owning slaves. Slavery was abolished in Britain in 1833, and that started a domino effect of abolition in other nations, as the slave trade grew to be universally understood as inhumane and evil. It seemed like by the early 1800s that colonization was about to become a thing of the past, since it was not as economically advantageous as it had been. But something happened in the mid-1700s that was fully underway by 1800 that made a new era of imperialism desirable and necessary. The world powers had begun to industrialize.

In some ways, industrialization was a positive thing for the plight of man because machines could now do the jobs that men once did, meaning that less slave labor was necessary. Machines could work faster, cheaper and more efficiently than humans. But what industrial factories and systems do require is natural resources. It requires lots and lots of raw materials, like coal, timber, rubber, iron, lead and cotton. The three leaders of industrialization by 1800 were Britain, Prussia and the United States. The U.S. had a huge territory full of abundant natural resources, which meant that the only territory the U.S. had to conquer was on the North American continent. Most people do not think of America as an imperialist nation because it did not conquer an overseas empire like Great Britain. But America did negotiate uneven treaties with, forcibly relocate and kill the Native Americas in order to fulfill their vision of westward expansion. So, is America an imperialist country? You decide for yourself.

To be certain, Great Britain, France and Prussia were proudly imperialist by the 1800s and made widely known their plans for global conquest. The nations of Europe did not enjoy the benefit of huge amounts of territory at home the way the United States did and so tiny nations like Great Britain were forced to conquer and colonize if they were to have the resources they needed to fuel industrialization. England ultimately gave up or lost all of its territory in North America but they built a much bigger colonial empire in Asia, Africa and the Pacific. By 1900, it was said that the sun never set on the British Empire and more than 25% of the world's population lived under British rule by that time.

Britain's second global empire began with the conquest of India in the mid-1700s. They continued to extend their control over the Indian subcontinent in a series of regional wars into the 1800s. Thereafter, Britain set its sights on the conquest of China, which the British viewed as a huge opportunity to increase its global reach through trade. The British first tried to woo China with diplomacy and promises of favorable trade arrangements if the Chinese agreed to become a robust trade partner of Britain. China, however, was the longest continuous civilization in the world at the time and had withstood unwanted approaches and invasions many times in its 3500 year history. China had even built a very, very large wall 1500 years earlier to keep foreigners out and in the early 1800s, they had no intention of opening to British encroachment into Chinese trade and culture. The Chinese emperor bluntly refused efforts by the British to establish a relationship, perhaps because they saw what Britain had done to their neighbor, India. The British were not planning to take no for an answer; and when it became clear that they would not control China through diplomacy and asking nicely, Britain resolved to take control of China by force.

A series of events called the Opium Wars of 1839 between Britain and China might have been viewed as just another imperialist war in history except that its timing made it a new kind of phenomenon and sent a powerful message to nations around the world. Britain had a very powerful industrialized military by 1839 and China did not. China was untouched by the Industrial Revolution in the 1800s and the Chinese were content to do things the way they had been successfully doing them for the last four millennia. But they were unprepared for a war in the newly industrialized world and they were devastated by the might of the British industrial military. China was forced to sign a humiliating treaty with Britain to end the war, called the Treaty of Nanking. The treaty forced China to pay a huge indemnity, or yearly payment, to Britain for losing the war. It also ceded the island of Hong Kong to Britain. China had to open up its five major port cities to trade with Britain and to grant Britain favorable trade terms. Chinese pride and power was substantially impacted by its defeat in the Opium War. And it served as a warning to other unindustrialized nations of the world— industrialize or die. Eat or be eaten. As a result of the Opium Wars, Asian countries like Japan and Eurasian countries like Russia took heed of the warning and began to conquer territory of their own to gain resources for industrialization. The conflict between Britain and China in the Opium Wars led to more widespread conflicts between Asian and European powers, as the race to be industrialized intensified. Nowhere did the race for colonies play out more savagely than in a ruthless display of imperialism known as the "Scramble for Africa."

In the Age of Discovery, India was the desired prize. If you will recall, nations like Spain and Portugal were competing to see who could reach India first by sea to exploit the rich trade market in spices. During the 1500s, Africa was mainly seen as a gigantic

385

obstacle in the way of getting to India. Over time, explorers established trade forts along the coast of Africa to trade with the African tribes and it was here that the transatlantic slave trade was born. But until the 1800s, the interior of the African continent was almost entirely unexplored and untouched by Europeans. This all changed as the demand for resources grew during the Industrial Revolution. By the 1800s, missionaries seeking to spread the reach of Christianity began venturing into Africa's interior and explorers and map-makers soon followed. The knowledge about the geography of Africa that was gained through these expeditions would be used to organize a massive power grab by European powers in 1885. Anyone up for a game of Risk?

In 1885, a meeting called the Berlin Conference was convened among thirteen European nations, including representatives from Great Britain, France, Germany, Austria-Hungary, Russia, Italy, Denmark and Belgium. The United States also participated in the meeting, though not a single African was invited to discuss the fate of Africa. Prior to 1885, there was a heavy European presence in Africa as competing imperialist nations sought to carve out colonies for themselves in what was known as the "Scramble for Africa." Sensing that conflict among European neighbors was imminent, it was decided that Africa was big enough to share and that it should be carved up in a civilized fashion. But it would be carved up to be sure. The Belgian King Leopold II summed up attitudes towards Africa when, in a letter to a diplomat he wrote, "I do not want to miss a good chance of getting us a slice of this magnificent African cake." This letter was written in 1876 and by 1885, the entire African continent was under the control of eight European nations.

Prior to the Berlin Conference, there were more than 2000 indigenous tribes in Africa who had lived there for thousands of years. These tribes did not have clearly defined borders or territories that they "owned" but there were understood boundaries for each group. This lack of what we would consider firm political boundaries made it easy to assume that no one owned the territory in Africa and that it was there for the taking. This was much the same attitude of Americans in the 1800s about territory taken from Native American tribes. Great Britain took the largest chunk of Africa, fulfilling the vision of the infamous British Imperialist, Cecil Rhodes, whose vision was to walk from the northern tip of Africa to the southernmost point without ever leaving British territory. France won the second biggest chuck of land, claiming ownership of all of western Africa. The remaining powers had to divide up what was left. Ultimately, the only region of Africa that did not fall under European control was Ethiopia. With the stroke of a pen, thousands of years of indigenous traditions, civilizations, were wiped away.

At the Berlin Conference, borders were drawn to distinguish one nation's property from another's. These lines were drawn for the benefit of their new rulers with no regard for old tribal boundaries or the impact on existing communities. Often, tribes were split by new borders, with one part being forced to become French while another part was declared British. The impact of this on the native populations cannot be overstated. As subjects to their new masters, crossing borders into another nation was forbidden, so families were torn apart. Ranchers were separated from their grazing land so they lost their means of making a living. And anyone who was even suspected of objecting to the new order of things was killed as an example of how disobedience is punished. European imperialists systematically and deliberately took away all shreds of an old identity to make sure there was order under the new system. No where was this accomplished with more brutality than in the Belgian Congo.

King Leopold II, who you recall envisioned Africa like a delicious cake, carved out a huge territory in central Africa called the Congo as his colonial territory. The Belgian Congo originally belonged to Leopold personally, and not to the nation of Belgium. Leopold believed that the laws that governed nations did not govern him. Leopold was particularly ruthless in his management of the Congo, essentially enslaving the native populations to increase his personal fortune. At first he made money on the export of ivory but soon changed his focus to the export of rubber, which came from the sap of Hevea Brasilinensis tree (a.k.a. Rubber Tree) which filled the Congo basin. Leopold and his men reportedly enforced impossible quotas for the daily production of rubber from the native workers, and failure to meet a daily quota meant having an arm cut off, either at the wrist or at the elbow. Failure to meet a quota more than once resulted in death. Estimates on the death toll in the Belgian Congo vary widely but it is now believed that Leopold and his private army killed roughly 10 million Congolese people during the two decades when the region was under his control. To this day, the region of central Africa that was under Leopold's control suffers the lasting impact of his reign of terror. Though control of the Congo was handed over to the Belgium government in 1908 because of widespread allegations of Leopold's mismanagement, the Congo did not win its independence from colonial rule until 1960.

The atrocities committed in the Belgian Congo area gross example of the price Africans paid as the result of those "gentlemanly" negotiations in that game of global domination which played out at the Berlin Conference. While the negotiations for carving up Africa might have been viewed as civilized, the establishment of the determined territories was anything but. While the negotiations at the Berlin Conference were "gentlemanly," competition over other territories around the globe was far less cordial.

By the close of the 19th century and the beginning of the 20th century, dozens of wars were fought over imperialism. Russia, Japan and Germany got heavily involved in imperialist conquests, as the new rule seemed to be "Conquer or be conquered." Imperialism pitted old rivals against each other like never before in a ruthless competition for territory. As a result, new rivals were born, as countries that feared being left behind fought ruthlessly to catch up. The world, which had seemed so big and full of possibilities after the Age of Discovery in the 1500s, had quickly grown too small to contain the ambitions of all the old and emerging powers. The game of total world domination would continue to intensify to a breaking point in the early 1900s, as teams chose sides to improve their chances for dominance. Small conflicts escalated into larger and larger conflicts which were complicated by a global entanglement of alliances until 1914, when the entire world erupted into "the war to end all wars."

Rudyard Kipling, *The White Man's Burden*, 1899 CE

Reading and Discussion Questions

1. In your own words, explain what the white man's duty is, according to Kipling?
2. How does Kipling describe indigenous people? Quote at least three passages that use descriptive language about native people. What do you think of Kipling's use of language?
3. What are the hardships or challenges that Kipling says the white man will face in pursuit of his goal?
4. Explain your reaction to this poem. Do you agree with Kipling's sentiments here or any part of them? Why or why not?
5. Does this poem help you to understand the general attitudes at the time about conquest and colonization? Explain your answer.

This famous poem, written by British poet Rudyard Kipling in 1899, was a response to the American take over of the Philippines after the Spanish-American War. It encourages the white man to go boldly on his mission of conquest because he had a duty to do so. It also warns that, though the white man's struggle will not be easy, it will be worth the sacrifice. The poem has come to be seen as the embodiment of attitudes of the supremacy of the white Christian that had been the prevailing view since the fall of the Roman Empire. The ideas in White Man's Burden are not new, but never before had someone said them so publicly, so descriptively and so proudly as Kipling did in 1899. The poem has prompted more reaction than almost any other work in modern literature, with some people embracing it as the great defense of their imperialist cause and others radically rejecting it as a grotesque declaration of racism and violence.

Take up the White Man's burden--
Send forth the best ye breed--
Go bind your sons to exile
To serve your captives' need;
To wait in heavy harness,
On fluttered folk and wild--
Your new-caught, sullen peoples,
Half-devil and half-child.

Take up the White Man's burden--
In patience to abide,
To veil the threat of terror
And check the show of pride;
By open speech and simple,
An hundred times made plain
To seek another's profit,
And work another's gain.

Take up the White Man's burden--
The savage wars of peace--
Fill full the mouth of Famine
And bid the sickness cease;
And when your goal is nearest
The end for others sought,
Watch sloth and heathen Folly
Bring all your hopes to nought.

Take up the White Man's burden--
No tawdry rule of kings,
But toil of serf and sweeper--
The tale of common things.
The ports ye shall not enter,
The roads ye shall not tread,
Go mark them with your living,
And mark them with your dead.

Take up the White Man's burden--
And reap his old reward:
The blame of those ye better,
The hate of those ye guard--
The cry of hosts ye humour
(Ah, slowly!) toward the light:--
"Why brought he us from bondage,
Our loved Egyptian night?"

Take up the White Man's burden--
Ye dare not stoop to less--
Nor call too loud on Freedom
To cloke your weariness;
By all ye cry or whisper,
By all ye leave or do,
The silent, sullen peoples
Shall weigh your gods and you.

Take up the White Man's burden--
Have done with childish days--
The lightly proferred laurel,
The easy, ungrudged praise.
Comes now, to search your manhood
Through all the thankless years
Cold, edged with dear-bought wisdom,
The judgment of your peers!

Lin Tse-Hsu, Letter of Advice to Queen Victoria, 1839 CE

<u>Reading and Discussion Questions</u>
1. What does the author say is the punishment for anyone caught selling, purchasing or using opium in China? Is there any way that someone could avoid this punishment, according to the letter?
2. What does the author have to say about trade relations between Britain and China? Has it historically been a relationship that benefitted both countries equally? Why or why not?
3. What does the author imply might happen to trade relations between Britain and China if opium smuggling is not ended?

Lin Tse-Hsu was a Chinese diplomat before the Opium Wars with England. He wrote the following letter, which has become famous for its frankness, to Queen Victoria of England. The letter outlines new Chinese policy toward punishment for the sale or use of opium in China. For decades before this letter, British smugglers made fortunes smuggling opium into China. The use of opium had become a national epidemic, and the Emperor's own son died of an opium overdose. In addition to severely punishing opium smugglers, this letter subtly threatens a change in trade relations between China and England, which Tse-Hsu argues would be bad for England. Rather than prompting the end of the opium trade in China, this letter led to the British invasion of China and the beginning of the Opium Wars, which lasted from 1839 to 1842.

A communication: magnificently our great Emperor soothes and pacifies China and the foreign countries, regarding all with the same kindness. If there is profit, then he shares it with the peoples of the world; if there is harm, then he removes it on behalf of the world. This is because he takes the mind of heaven and earth as his mind.

After a long and profitable trade relationship, there appear among the crowd of barbarians both good persons and bad, unevenly. Consequently there are those who smuggle opium to seduce the Chinese people and so cause the spread of the poison to all provinces. Such persons who only care to profit themselves, and disregard their harm to others, are not tolerated by the laws of heaven and are unanimously hated by human beings. His Majesty the Emperor, upon hearing of this, is in a towering rage. He has especially sent me, his commissioner, to investigate and settle this matter.

All those people in China who sell opium or smoke opium should receive the death penalty. We trace the crime of those barbarians who through the years have been selling opium, then the deep harm they have wrought and the great profit they have usurped should fundamentally justify their execution according to law.

Fortunately we have received a specially extended favor Born His Majesty the Emperor, who considers that for those who voluntarily surrender there are still some circumstances to lessen their crime, and so for the time being he has magnanimously excused them from punishment. But as for those who again violate the opium prohibition, it is difficult for the law to pardon them repeatedly. Having established new regulations, we presume that the ruler of your honorable country must be able to instruct the various barbarians to observe the law with care. It is only necessary to explain to them the advantages and disadvantages and then they will know that the legal code of the Celestial Court must be absolutely obeyed with awe.

England is far from China. Yet there are barbarian ships that strive to come here for trade for the purpose of making a great profit. The wealth of China is used to profit the barbarians. That is to say, the great profit made by barbarians is all taken from the rightful share of China. By what right do they then in return use the poisonous drug to injure the Chinese people? Even though the barbarians may not necessarily intend to do us harm, yet in coveting profit to an extreme, they have no regard for injuring others. Let us ask, where is your conscience? I have heard that the smoking of opium is very strictly forbidden by your country; that is because the harm caused by opium is clearly understood. Since it is not permitted to do harm to your own country, then even less should you let it be passed on to the harm of other countries -- how much less to China! Of all that China exports to foreign countries, there is not a single thing which is not beneficial to people: they are of benefit when eaten, or of benefit when used, or of benefit when resold: all are beneficial. Is there a single article from China which has done any harm to foreign countries? Take tea and rhubarb, for example; the foreign countries cannot get along for a single day without them. If China cuts off these benefits with no sympathy for those who are to suffer, then what can the barbarians rely upon to keep themselves alive? Moreover the woolens, camlets, and longells [i.e., textiles] of foreign countries cannot be woven unless they obtain Chinese silk. If China, again, cuts off this beneficial export, what profit can the barbarians expect to make? As for other foodstuffs, beginning with candy, ginger, cinnamon, and so forth, and articles for use, beginning with silk, satin, chinaware, and so on, all the things that must be had by foreign countries are innumerable.

On the other hand, articles coming from the outside to China can only be used as toys. We can take them or get along without them. Since they are not needed by China, what difficulty would there be if we closed our frontier and stopped the trade? Nevertheless, our Celestial Court lets tea, silk, and other goods be shipped without limit and circulated everywhere without begrudging it in the slightest. This is for no other reason but to share the benefit with the people of the whole world. The goods from China carried away by your country not only supply your own consumption and use, but also can be divided up and sold to other countries, producing a triple profit. Even if you do not sell opium, you still have this threefold profit. How can you bear to go further, selling products injurious to others in order to fulfill your insatiable desire?

Suppose there were people from another country who carried opium for sale to England and seduced your people into buying and smoking it; certainly your honorable ruler would deeply hate it and be bitterly aroused. Naturally you would not wish to give unto others what you yourself do not want.

Now we have set up regulations governing the Chinese people. He who sells opium shall receive the death penalty and he who smokes it also the death penalty. Now consider this: if the barbarians do not bring opium, then how can the Chinese people resell it, and how can they smoke it? The fact is that the wicked barbarians beguile the Chinese people into a death trap. How then can we grant life only to these barbarians? He who takes the life of even one person still has to atone for it with his own life; yet is the harm done by opium limited to the taking of one life only? Therefore in the new regulations, in regard to those barbarians who bring opium to China, the penalty is

391

fixed at decapitation or strangulation. This is what is called getting rid of a harmful thing on behalf of mankind.

The barbarian merchants of your country, if they wish to do business for a prolonged period, are required to obey our statues respectfully and to cut off permanently the source of opium. They must by no means try to test the effectiveness of the law with their lives. May you, O King, check your wicked and sift your wicked people before they come to China, in order to guarantee the peace of your nation and to let the two countries enjoy together the blessings of peace.

The Treaty of Nanking, 1842 CE

Reading and Discussion Questions
1. What does Provision II of the treaty require China to do?
2. What is accomplished by Provision III?
3. How would the conditions laid forth in this treaty affect the financial health of China? How much money in total was China required to pay to Britain?
4. What lesson do you think other non-industrialized nations learned from China's defeat in the Opium Wars and the humiliating treaty that followed?

In the Opium Wars, China was woefully outmatched. The Chinese military fought with muskets, bows and arrows, and even spears. They had inadequate means for protecting their port cities and towns. The British military, on the other hand, had all the most powerful industrial weapons to use against the Chinese. They had machine guns, steel-sided warships and cannons. The war was an uneven fight and the Chinese were easily defeated by the British. At the war's end, China was forced to agree to the terms of the Treaty of Nanjing, which was humiliating and economically crippling.

HER MAJESTY the Queen of the United Kingdom of Great Britain and Ireland, and His Majesty the Emperor of China, being desirous of putting an end to the misunderstandings and consequent hostilities which have arisen between the two countries, have resolved to conclude a Treaty for that purpose....[and] have agreed upon and concluded the following Articles:

I. ...There shall henceforward be peace and friendship between Her Majesty the Queen of the United Kingdom of Great Britain and Ireland and His Majesty the Emperor of China, and between their respective subjects, who shall enjoy full security and protection for their persons and property within the dominions of the other....

II. His Majesty the Emperor of China agrees, that British subjects shall be allowed to reside, for the purposes of carrying on their mercantile pursuits, without molestation or restraint, at the cities and towns of Guangzhou, Xiamen, Fuzhou, Ningbo, and Shanghai.

III. It being obviously necessary and desirable that British subjects should have some port whereat they may [maintain] and refit their ships when required, and keep stores for that purpose, His Majesty the Emperor of China cedes to Her Majesty the Queen of Great Britain, the Island of Hong-Kong, to be possessed [for the foreseeable future] by Her Britannic Majesty, and to be governed by such laws and regulations as Her

Majesty the Queen of Great Britain shall see fit to direct.

IV. The Emperor of China agrees to pay the sum of 6,000,000 of dollars, as the value of the opium which was surrendered and destroyed at Guangzhou in the month of March, 1839. And it is further stipulated, that interest, at the rate of 5 per cent. per annum, shall be paid by the Government of China on any portion of the above sums that are not punctually discharged at the periods fixed.

V. His Imperial Majesty further agrees to pay to the British Government the sum of 3,000,000 of dollars, on account of debts due to British subjects for other trade transactions which are owed to Britain.

VI. The Government of Her Britannic Majesty having been obliged to send out an expedition to demand and obtain redress for the violent and unjust proceedings of the Chinese High Authorities towards Her Britannic Majesty's officer and subjects, the Emperor of China agrees to pay the sum of 12,000,000 of dollars, on account of the expenses incurred;

VII. stipulated exactly when installments of the total $21 million should be paid.

VIII. The Emperor of China agrees to release, unconditionally, all subjects of Her Britannic Majesty (whether natives of Europe or India), who may be in confinement at this moment in any part of the Chinese empire....

In Defense of Imperialism—Three Western Perspectives

Reading and Discussion Questions
1. What ideas or concepts do all three sets of readings have in common?
2. What is the primary justification for imperialism, based on your reading?
3. Do you think these passages make a strong and convincing case for imperialism? Why or why not?

The following is a collection of writings and excerpts of speeches from German, French and American imperialists in defense of their conquests in Africa and Asia.

French Imperialism

Jules Ferry, On French Colonial Expansion, 1885 CE
"Gentlemen, we must speak more loudly and more honestly! We must say openly that indeed the higher races have a right over the lower races .... I repeat, that the superior races have a right because they have a duty. They have the duty to civilize the inferior races .... In the history of earlier centuries these duties, gentlemen, have often been misunderstood; and certainly when the Spanish soldiers and explorers introduced slavery into Central America, they did not fulfill their duty as men of a higher race .... But, in our time, I maintain that European nations acquit themselves with generosity, with grandeur, and with sincerity of this superior civilizing duty.

393

I say that French colonial policy, the policy of colonial expansion, the policy that has taken us under the Empire [the Second Empire, of Napoleon IIII, to Saigon, to Indochina [Vietnam], that has led us to Tunisia, to Madagascar-I say that this policy of colonial expansion was inspired by... the fact that a navy such as ours cannot do without safe harbors, defenses, supply centers on the high seas .... Are you unaware of this? Look at a map of the world."

German Imperialism

Letter of Dr. Hugenberg, August 1, 1890 CE
There are also still larger territories--one need only think of Central Sudan, the natural hinterland of the Cameroons, the fate of which has not as yet been settled by any treaty. He who seizes these territories quickest and holds fast the most tenaciously will possess them. For the pride of the German people, we must seize the moment to extend German influence to [check the power of Britain's imperial ambitions].

American Imperialism

Josiah Strong, 1885 CE
The two great needs of mankind, that all men may be lifted into the light of the highest Christian civilization, are, first, a pure, spiritual Christianity, and, second, civil liberty....It follows then, that the Anglo-Saxon, as the great representative of these two ideas, the depository of these two great blessings, sustains peculiar relations to the world's future, is divinely commissioned to be, in a peculiar sense, his brother's keeper.

President McKinley on the Philippines, 1899 CE
When next I realized that the Philippines had dropped into our laps I confess I did not know what to do with them....I walked the floor of the White House night after night until midnight; and I am not ashamed to tell you, gentlemen, that I went down on my knees and prayed Almighty God for light and guidance....And one night late it came to me this way...

(1) that we could not give them back to Spain--that would be cowardly and dishonorable;

(2) That we could not turn them over to France or Germany--our commercial rivals in the Orient--that would be bad business and discreditable;

(3) That we could not leave them to themselves--they were unfit for self-government--and they would soon have anarchy and misrule worse than Spain's war;

(4) That there was nothing left for us to do but to take them all, and to educate the Filipinos, and uplift and civilize and Christianize them as our fellow men for whom Christ also died.

Dadabhai Naoroji, The Benefits of British Rule, 1871 CE

Reading and Discussion Questions

1. In what ways has India benefitted from British rule, according to this speech?
2. In what ways has India been harmed by British rule? Specifically, how has India been harmed materially and financially?

As you have seen from your reading of Kipling's White Man's Burden, there was widespread belief among white Christian imperialists that their colonization of every part of the globe was actually benefitting the native people that came under their rule. The British were the first to build their modern global empire and they were also the first to defend the benefits of their colonial rule. Though there were some benefits to British rule in places like India, it also caused considerable hardship.

Dadabhai Naoroji was an Indian subject of Britain who was also the first Indian to become a member of the British Parliament. Naoroji used his position to highlight the negative impacts of British colonialism. In time, Naoroji became very well-known for his idea called the "Drain Theory", which examined how all of India's wealth was being cleverly drained into Britain's economy and harming India in the process. He wrote his ideas in his book, Poverty and Un-British Rule in India. *In the following speech to members of Parliament, Naoroji wisely points out the ways in which British rule has been good for India but then points out all the ways in which it has been harmful.*

The Benefits of British Rule for India:

In the Cause of Civilization: Education, both male and female. Though yet only partial, an inestimable blessing as far as it has gone, and leading gradually to the destruction of superstition, and many moral and social evils. Resuscitation of India's own noble literature, modified and refined by the enlightenment of the West.

Politically: Peace and order. Freedom of speech and liberty of the press. Higher political knowledge and aspirations. Improvement of government in the native states. Security of life and property. Freedom from oppression caused by the caprice or greed of despotic rulers, and from devastation by war. Equal justice between man and man (sometimes vitiated by partiality to Europeans). Services of highly educated administrators, who have achieved the above-mentioned results.

Materially: Loans for railways and irrigation. Development of a few valuable products, such as indigo, tea, coffee, silk, etc. Increase of exports. Telegraphs.

Generally: A slowly growing desire of late to treat India equitably, and as a country held in trust. Good intentions. No nation on the face of the earth has ever had the opportunity of achieving such a glorious work as this. I hope in the credit side of the account I have done no injustice, and if I have omitted any item which anyone may

think of importance, I shall have the greatest pleasure in inserting it. I appreciate, and so do my countrymen, what England has done for India, and I know that it is only in British hands that her regeneration can be accomplished. Now for the debit side.

The Detriments of British Rule:

In the Cause of Civilization: As I have said already, there has been a failure to do as much as might have been done, but I put nothing to the debit. Much has been done, though.

Politically: Repeated breach of pledges to give the natives a fair and reasonable share in the higher administration of their own country, which has much shaken confidence in the good faith of the British word. Political aspirations and the legitimate claim to have a reasonable voice in the legislation and the imposition and disbursement of taxes, met to a very slight degree, thus treating the natives of India not as British subjects, in whom representation is a birthright. Consequent on the above, an utter disregard of the feelings and views of the natives. The great moral evil of the drain of wisdom and practical administration, leaving none to guide the rising generation.

Financially: All attention is engrossed in devising new modes of taxation, without any adequate effort to increase the means of the people to pay; and the oppressiveness of the taxes imposed, imperial and local. Inequitable financial relations between England and India, i.e., the political debt of ,100,000,000 clapped on India's shoulders, and all home charges also, though the British Exchequer contributes nearly ,3,000,000 to the expense of the colonies.

Materially: The political drain, up to this time, from India to England, of above ,500,000,000, at the lowest computation, in principal alone, which with interest would be some thousands of millions. The further continuation of this drain at the rate, at present, of above ,12,000,000 per annum, with a tendency to increase. The consequent continuous impoverishment and exhaustion of the country, except so far as it has been very partially relieved and replenished by the railway and irrigation loans, and the windfall of the consequences of the American war, since 1850.

Even with this relief, the material condition of India is such that the great mass of the poor have hardly tuppence a day and a few rags, or a scanty subsistence. The famines that were in their power to prevent, if they had done their duty, as a good and intelligent government. The policy adopted during the last fifteen years of building railways, irrigation works, etc., is hopeful, has already resulted in much good to your credit, and if persevered in, gratitude and contentment will follow. An increase of exports without adequate compensation; loss of manufacturing industry and skill. Here I end the debit side.

Summary: To sum up the whole, the British rule has been: morally, a great blessing; politically, peace and order on one hand, blunders on the other; materially, impoverishment, relieved as far as the railway and other loans go. The natives call the British system "Sakar ki Churi," the knife of sugar. That is to say, there is no oppression, it is all smooth and sweet, but it is the knife, notwithstanding. I mention this that you should know these feelings. Our great misfortune is that you do not know our wants. When you will know our real wishes, I have not the least doubt that you would do justice. The genius and spirit of the British people is fair play and justice.

Wilfred Scawen Blunt, Britain's Imperial Destiny, 1896-1899 CE

Reading and Discussion Questions

1. Why do you think Blunt said he would be "delighted to see England stripped of her whole foreign possessions?"

2. What does the author say about the imperialist efforts of other European nations? What other nations are building empires and where? How does he describe these efforts?

3. What is Blunt talking about when he discusses "our English sham philanthropy"?

One of the more damning accounts of British imperial ambition comes from the journals of Wilfred Scawen Blunt between the years 1896 and 1899. You may note that his chronicle of British behavior in regard to its colonies begins in the year following the partitioning of Africa at the Berlin Conference. Blunt was a wealthy English writer who traveled frequently to the Middle East, due to his interest in Arabian horses. During one trip to Egypt, he came to know many Egyptians who were in the midst of fighting against British conquest of their homeland. Blunt's time in north Africa made him a vehement opponent of British imperialism, which is evident from his writings during that period.

9th Jan. 1896. We have now managed in the last six months to quarrel violently with China, Turkey, Belgium, Ashanti, France, Venezuela, America, and Germany. This is a record performance, and if it does not break up the British Empire nothing will. For myself I am glad of it all, for the British Empire is the greatest engine of evil for the weak races now existing in the world---not that we are worse than the French or Italians or Americans--indeed, we are less actively destructive---but we do it over a far wider area and more successfully. I should be delighted to see England stripped of her whole foreign possessions. We are better off and more respected in Queen Elizabeth's time, the "spacious days," when we had not a stick of territory outside the British Islands, than now, and infinitely more respectable. The gangrene of colonial rowdyism is infecting us, and the habit of repressing liberty in weak nations is endangering our own. I should be glad to see the end....

17th Oct. 1898. Arrived at Saighton. I have had it out with a companion [about actions in relation to the conquest in Africa]. He states the English case with brutal frankness. "The day of talking," he says, "about legality in Africa is over, all the international law there is there consists of interest and understandings. It is generally agreed by all the powers that the end of African operations is to 'civilize' it in the interests of Europe, and that to gain that end all means are good. One is as good as another to get our end, which is the railway from Cairo to the Cape. We don't care whether the Nile is called English or Egyptian or what it is called, but we mean to have it and we don't mean the French to have it.

15 June 1899. The natives in South Africa will fight [in defense of their homes], and there is some chance of a general war in South Africa, which may alleviate the condition of the only people there whose interests I really care for in the quarrel, namely the blacks. It will also be a beautiful exposure of our English sham philanthropy, if at the very moment the Peace Congress is sitting at The Hague, we

flout its mediation and launch into an aggressive war. Anything is better than the general handshaking of the great white thieves and their amicable division of the spoils....

22nd Dec., 1900. The old century is very nearly out, and leaves the world in a pretty pass, and the British Empire is playing the devil in it as never an empire before on so large a scale. We may live to see its fall. All the nations of Europe are making the same hell upon earth in China, massacring and pillaging and raping in the captured cities as outrageously as in the Middle Ages. The Emperor of Germany gives the word for slaughter and the Pope looks on and approves. The Americans are spending fifty millions a year on slaughtering the Filipinos; the King of the Belgians has invested his whole fortune on the Congo, where he is brutalizing the Negroes to fill his pockets. The French and Italians for the moment are playing a less prominent part in the slaughter, but their inactivity grieves them. The whole white race is reveling openly in violence, as though it had never pretended to be Christian. God's equal curse be on them all! So ends the famous nineteenth century into which we were so proud to have been born....

Gustave Freensen, German South African Army, 1903-1904

Reading and Discussion Questions
1. According to the author, what two conflicting things does Germany hope to achieve in Africa?
2. Of the two things you identified in your answer to Question #1, what do you think is the truer motive for German action in Africa? Explain your answer.

Below is an account from a soldier in the German army telling of his experiences in the German campaign against the indigenous people of southwest Africa in 1903-04.

I used to sit down quietly with the [older soldiers of the German army] and listen with great eagerness to their talk. Sometimes they talked of the wild fifteen years' struggles in the colony, in all or part of which they had shared, and of the fighting in the last three months. They recalled the scene of many a brave deed, and named many a valiant man, dead or living.

They discussed, too, what the Germans really wanted here. They thought we ought to make that point clear. "The matter stood this way: there were missionaries here who said: "You are our dear brothers in the Lord and we want to bring you these benefits; namely, Faith, Love, and Hope.' And there were soldiers, farmers, and traders, and they said: "We want to take your cattle and your land gradually away from you and make you slaves without legal rights.'

Those two things didn't go side by side. It is a ridiculous and crazy project. Either it is right to colonize, that is, to deprive others of their rights, to rob and to make slaves, or it is just and right to Christianize, that is, to proclaim and live up to brotherly love. One must clearly desire the one and despise the other; one must wish to rule or to love, to be for or against Jesus. The missionaries used to preach to them, "You are our brothers,' and that turned their heads. They are not our brothers, but our slaves, whom we must treat humanely but strictly.

398

Edward D. Morel, *The Black Man's Burden*, 1920 CE

Reading and Discussion Questions
  1. How does Morel explain that the burden of imperialism is on the black man entirely?
  2. Why does the author say that for Africans there is no escape "from the evils of capitalist exploitation?"
  3. What does Morel hope that white men will do in time in relation to Africa and their treatment of Africans? Do you think this ever happened or will happen?

Rudyard Kipling's "White Man's Burden" prompted international response from both supporters and opponents of Kipling's viewpoint. No response was more powerful than that of Edward Morel, a British journalist who worked tirelessly to end forced labor and slavery in central Africa. Morel was horrified by the abuses he witnessed in the Congo Free State, under the management of King Leopold II, who Morel claimed had enslaved the Congolese people for his personal profit. Morel's work in exposing the abuses in the Congo led to the transfer of control of the Congo from Leopold personally to the government of Belgium. This curbed the abuses of the native people substantially but oppression in central Africa would remain the norm through the middle part of the 1900s. Morel's response to Kipling was aptly called "The Black Man's Burden" because Morel observed that it was the black man and not the white man who suffered under imperialism and to suggest otherwise was absurd and a grave insult to native people who were being killed in the hundreds of thousands (or millions) by white imperialists.

It is [the Africans] who carry the "Black man's burden." They have not withered away before the white man's occupation. Indeed... Africa has ultimately absorbed within itself every Caucasian... In hewing out for himself a fixed abode in Africa, the white man has massacred the African in heaps. The African has survived, and it is well for the white settlers that he has. In the process of imposing his political dominion over the African, the white man has carved broad and bloody avenues from one end of Africa to the other. The African has resisted, and persisted.

For three centuries the white man seized and enslaved millions of Africans and transported them, with every circumstance of ferocious cruelty, across the seas. Still the African survived and, in his land of exile, multiplied exceedingly. But what the partial occupation of his soil by the white man has failed to do; what the mapping out of European political "spheres of influence" has failed to do; what the Maxim [machine gun] and the rifle, the slave gang, labor in the bowels of the earth and the lash, have failed to do; what imported measles, smallpox and syphilis have failed to do; what even the oversea slave trade failed to do, the power of modern capitalistic exploitation, assisted by modern engines of destruction, may yet succeed in accomplishing.

For from the evils of capitalist exploitation, there is no escape for the African. Its

destructive effects are not spasmodic: they are permanent. In its permanence resides its fatal consequences. It kills not the body merely, but the soul. It breaks the spirit. It attacks the African at every turn, from every point of vantage. It wrecks his polity, uproots him from the land, invades his family life, destroys his natural pursuits and occupations, claims his whole time, enslaves him in his own home...

The African is really helpless against the material gods of the white man, as embodied in the trinity of imperialism, capitalistic-exploitation, and militarism. If the white man retains these gods and if he insists upon making the African worship them as assiduously as he has done himself, the African will go the way of the... Amerindian, ...the aboriginal Australian, and many more. And this would be at once a crime of enormous magnitude, and a world disaster...

The goal [of imperialists] is clear. It is to make of Africans all over Africa a servile race; to exploit African labor, and through African labor, the soil of Africa for their own exclusive benefit...

For a time it may be possible for the white man to maintain a white civilization in the colonizable, or partly colonizable, areas of the African Continent. But even there the attempt can be no more than fleeting. The days of Roman imperialism are done with forever. Education sooner or later breaks all chains, and knowledge cannot be kept from the African... [When] he becomes alive to his power the whole fabric of European domination will fall to pieces in shame and ruin. From these failures the people of Europe will suffer moral and material damage of a far-reaching kind...

Why cannot the white imperial peoples, acknowledging in some measure the injuries they have inflicted upon the African, turn a new leaf in their treatment of him? For nearly two thousand years they have professed to be governed by the teachings of Christ. Can they not begin in the closing century of that era, to practice what they profess – and what their missionaries of religion teach the African? Can they not cease to regard the African as a producer of dividends for a selected few among their number, and begin to regard him as a human being with human rights? Have they made such a success of their own civilization that they can contemplate with equanimity the forcing of all its social failures upon Africa – its hideous and devastating inequalities, its pauperisms, its senseless and destructive egoisms, its vulgar and soulless materialism? It is in their power to work such good to Africa – and such incalculable harm! Can they not make up their minds that their strength shall be used for noble ends? Africa demands at their hands, justice, and understanding sympathy- not ill-informed sentiment.

Joseph Conrad, *Heart of Darkness*, 1899 CE

Reading and Discussion Questions

1. Describe in your own words or draw a picture of the Africa that Conrad describes. What adjectives come to mind after reading the passage below?
2. Explain the way Conrad describes Marlow's reaction to the Africans he encounters. What was Marlow feeling? And what was Conrad trying to say by describing his reaction in this way?

One of the most enduring and powerful images of Africa comes from the book Heart of Darkness, *written by British author Joseph Conrad, which is based on Conrad's real life experiences in central Africa.* Heart of Darkness *is considered one of the most important novels in western literature because it raises controversial questions about imperialism and what it means to be civilized. The story recounts the journey of its main character, Marlow, up the Congo River into the Congo basin, which Conrad labeled the "heart of darkness." He describes an untamable landscape in which maps and other navigation devices did not help the traveler feel any less lost in an infinite jungle wilderness. The deeper Conrad's character Marlow travels into the jungle the more he loses his connection to civilization and what it means to be civilized. Marlow went into the jungle expecting to encounter natives which were only partly human and deeply savage. When he finally sees the indigenous groups he believed to be part animal, part monster, he was surprised by how immediately and how completely he recognized their shared humanity.*

The book's main story line is that of the mad Captain Kurtz, whom Marlow is sent to find and to aid (Kurtz is presumably ill). As he journeys farther into Africa he learns more about Kurtz, who is the ruthless manager of an ivory-harvesting operation that worked Africans to death for the export of ivory. Kurtz was the most captivating character in Conrad's novel; but the most enduring thing that Heart of Darkness *accomplished was to challenge all accepted ideas at the time about Africans being savages who needed saving from the white man. They might be savagely different, Conrad tells us, as they harassed and even attacked Marlow's boat on several occasions but they were no less human. And in some ways Conrad seemed to envy the Africans he met on his journey because they were thoroughly wild and utterly free.*

Going up that river was like traveling back to the earliest beginnings of the world, when vegetation rioted on the earth and the big trees were kings. An empty stream, a great silence, an impenetrable forest. The air was warm, thick, heavy, sluggish. There was no joy in the brilliance of sunshine. The long stretches of the waterway ran on, deserted, into the gloom of overshadowed distances. On silvery sandbanks hippos and alligators sunned themselves side by side. The broadening waters flowed through a mob of wooded islands; you lost your way on that river as you would in a desert, and butted all day long against shoals, trying to find the channel, till you thought yourself bewitched and cut off forever from everything you had known once -- somewhere -- far away -- in another existence perhaps. There were moments when one's past came back to one, as it will sometimes when you have not a moment to spare to yourself; but it came in the shape of an unrestful and noisy dream, remembered with wonder amongst the overwhelming realities of this strange world of plants, and water, and silence. And this stillness of life did not in the least resemble a peace. It was the stillness of an implacable force brooding over an inscrutable intention. It looked at you with a vengeful aspect.

* * * * *

On we went again into the silence, along empty reaches, round the still bends, between the high walls of our winding way, reverberating in hollow claps the ponderous beat of the stern wheel. Trees, trees, millions of trees, massive, immense, running up high; and at their foot, hugging the bank against the stream, crept the little begrimed steamboat, like a sluggish beetle crawling on the floor of a lofty portico. It made you feel very small, very lost, and yet it was not altogether depressing, that feeling. After all, if you were small, the grimy beetle crawled on -- which was just what you wanted it to do.

* * * * *

The reaches opened before us and closed behind, as if the forest had stepped leisurely across the water to bar the way for our return. We penetrated deeper and deeper into the heart of darkness. It was very quiet in there.... The dawns were heralded by the descent of a chill stillness.... We were wanderers on prehistoric earth, and on an earth that wore the aspect of an unknown planet.... The steamer toiled along slowly on the edge of a black and incomprehensible frenzy.... We were cut off from comprehension of our surroundings; we glided past like phantoms, wondering and secretly appalled, as sane men would be before an enthusiastic outbreak in a madhouse. We could not understand because we were too far and could not remember, because we were traveling in the night of first ages, of those ages that are gone, leaving hardly a sign -- and no memories.

The earth seemed unearthly. We are accustomed to look upon the shackled form of a conquered monster, but there -- there you could look at a thing monstrous and free. It was unearthly, and the men were -- No, they were not inhuman. Well, you know, that was the worst of it -- this suspicion of their not being inhuman. It would come slowly to one. They howled and leaped, and spun, and made horrid faces; but what thrilled you was just the thought of their humanity -- like yours -- the thought of your remote kinship with this wild and passionate uproar. Ugly. Yes, it was ugly enough; but if you were man enough you would admit to yourself that there was in your just the faintest trace of a response to the terrible frankness of that noise, a dim suspicion of there being a meaning in it which you -- you so remote from the night of the first ages -- could comprehend.

402

CHAPTER 15—
WORLD WAR I AND ITS AFTERMATH (1914 to 1920 CE)

GUIDING QUESTIONS

- How are "Militarism" and "Alliances" interrelated?
- What is the relationship between "Imperialism" and "Nationalism"? Can a country begin as "Nationalist" and become "Imperialist"? Explain.
- How did the assassination of Franz Ferdinand lead to a global war?
- What is a "war of attrition"? What is "trench warfare"? What impact did these new concepts have on the soldier?
- Why was France angry in 1919? Were they justified in their anger? Why was Germany angry in 1920? Were they justified in their anger?
- What do you think do John Clare meant when he said "in some ways, mankind has never recovered from the horrors of the First World War"?

World War I was one of the most horrific and tragic events in human history. The scale of devastation, both in terms of lives lost and nations physically and psychologically destroyed, had never been seen or even imagined prior to 1914. John D. Clare tries to describe the devastation in his book *First World War:*

"More than 70 million men fought in the First World War; over eight million of them were killed. In addition, another seven million civilians died - from starvation, disease, artillery fire and air raids. Twelve million tons of shipping were sunk. In France and Belgium, where most of the war was fought, 300,000 houses, 6000 factories, 1000 miles of railway, 2000 breweries and 112 coal mines were destroyed. The human cost of the war - in terms of damaged minds and bodies, and ruined lives - was beyond calculation. In some ways, mankind has never recovered from the horrors of the First World War."

In 1919, it was impossible to walk down the street without visible reminders of the devastation of what was then called The Great War. Towns were leveled, veterans bore physical scars from their time on the battlefront and innumerable lives were ripped apart by the astounding loss of human life. There were more than 38 million casualties in World War I, and between fifteen million and seventeen million people killed. A common misconception is that "casualties" is a synonym for "deaths" but a casualty of war is someone who is either killed or seriously wounded in war.

The physical and psychological toll of the war led many, including the poet, T.S. Elliot, to refer to post-war Europe as a wasteland. That description describes both the landscape and the human psyche of Europe in the 1920s—utterly crushed. The devastation was so complete that in the years after the fighting ended, World War I was branded as "the war to end all wars." Happy vision, the end of all wars. But that vision of the future was not to be. In fact, almost exactly 21 years later, all the nations of the world would be engaged in another, even more deadly conflict that too soon came to be called World War II.

Many students have an almost disconcerting excitement about studying World War II and I have often wondered why. But I think what makes people somewhat enjoy studying World War II is the same phenomenon that created hundreds of millions of Star Wars enthusiasts. In World War II, like Star Wars, there is a heroic good guy and a despicable bad guy. Hitler is our Darth Vader and the Allied Forces are the virtuous Jedi. In both stories, good triumphed and evil was vanquished. We like stories like this, maybe because they make great movies. Or perhaps on a deeper level, it makes us feel good to know that, even if there is evil in the world, good does ultimately triumph. We love happy endings.

By contrast, imagine this cinematic experience: After the opening credits, there a sequence in which are a lot of different guys in suits are in fancy rooms whispering a lot. It seems they are making some sort of secret deals but the audience never gets close enough to hear what is being said. The atmosphere seems tense but confused. Then we are taken to a street in a far off city, and some guy and his wife are shot by a stranger while cruising through town in a convertible. We get the sense that the guy in the car was important somehow, but we are never really told why. There is some more increasingly intense whispering among the same suited guys from the first scene and then suddenly the audience is transported to a scene of mass carnage. Men in trenches are ducking from bomb explosions, being ordered to run into enemy fire and choking on poison gas. Many of them are crying for their mother. This unbearable suffering goes on for the next three hours. During the entire movie, no one seems to be gaining any ground or winning in any way. Finally, the fighting just stops, the camera pans back to reveal an infinite sea of devastation and death. Then the credits roll. The end.

How are you feeling about your movie experience? The drama I just described is the movie that no one dares to make, called the First World War. It's a horrifying story, and if anyone were foolish enough to make a movie about it the audience would demand their money back. There is no moral victory in World War I. There is no catharsis. And there is absolutely no clear hero or villain. The heartbreak of World War I was too real, the victories too hollow to make for good Hollywood productions. Just as World War I has no clear cut winners and losers or good guys and bad guys, it also has no clear causes. In order to simplify the causes of this cataclysmic clash, someone figured out to explain them with the acronym M.A.I.N. That seems like a good place for us to start.

The Causes of the War
M is for Militarism. Militarism is defined as "a policy of aggressive military readiness." More simply, it is a stockpiling of weapons and a willingness to use them. As we have discussed, the world was thoroughly industrialized by 1900 and everything that could be made in factories was made in factories. Weapons were no exception. If you could make sweaters in a factory, you could also make bombs. World War I was a product of industrialism and the birth of industrialized warfare. It was the first industrialized war, which is one of the big reasons for the enormous loss of life. And no where was the Industrial Age slogan "More is better" more true than in the weapons race of the late 1800s and early 1900s. Industrialized nations like England and Prussia were amassing huge weapons arsenals which made non-industrialized nations very nervous. And so those nations began stockpiling weapons at an alarming rate. Some countries could not keep pace with the whirlwind industrialization of their rivals and fell behind in the arms race. But they soon realized that if you can't have a terrifying weapons arsenal of your own, it's almost as good to make friends with countries that do.

A is for Alliances. An alliance is defined as "an association or relationship created to further the common interests of the members." Americans begin to form alliances at a very early age when we picked teams for games like Red Rover. We strategically chose our teammates based on who was strong enough to break through the other team's chain or who had the strongest grip. Everyone wanted to be on the team with the toughest guy. No one wanted to be picked last. This is alliance-building for elementary school. And it is shockingly similar to how it happens with leaders of nations. As early as 1887 (27 years before the beginning of the war), Germany had begun negotiating secret, and sometimes conflicting, alliances with the powerful nations of Europe. By 1907, every country in Europe had forged an alliance for the coming conflict. These alliances were formed by nations with only two considerations in mind—1. who had weapons (or who needed them), and 2. who had offended/been offended by another country at some point earlier in history. In other words, alliances were dictated by brute strength and hurt feelings.

By the late 1800s, Germany was forming alliances to get the jump on France, who was sore at Germany for a number of reasons and would surely want revenge. In order to understand the tension between France and Germany, we must first understand German (Prussian) aggression in the late 1800s. Otto von Bismark, the prime minister of Prussia, had a vision of unifying all Germanic people into the nation of Germany. He said this would be accomplished through blood and iron. This was a reference to the fact that Prussia should be the one to unify all the 39 Germanic states because Prussia was an industrialized (iron) military (blood). On the road to German unification, the Prussian army was gobbling up territories to increase its access to coal, the fuel for industrial factories. In 1870, Prussia invaded and occupied a region of France known as Alsace-Lorraine, which was home to France's largest reserves of coal. Much like they had done to begin the Seven Years' War, Prussia took a coal-rich region from a militarily-weak neighbor who could not stage any real military response. Almost immediately after acquiring Alsace-Lorraine, Prussia united all the Germanic states into Germany. Germany anticipated correctly that France would want revenge for Alsace-Lorraine and that, much like Austria had done during the Seven Years' War, France would shop for and win allies by scaring people about German dominance. So this time Germany decided to do the alliance building first, by giving countries like Austria-Hungary, Italy and Russia the choice to be "With us or against us." Since Germany had the most powerful military in the world in 1887, anyone faced with this choice chose "With us".

In 1914 when the war began, there were two sides in the conflict—The Allied Powers and the Central Powers. The Allied Powers included Great Britain, France, Russia and Italy. You may be wondering why Italy and Russia were "with Germany" in the preceding paragraph and are now against them, which is a further complicating factor in the entanglement of alliances. Countries could switch sides at will, depending on which side would be of most benefit, or depending on who had been insulted or alienated along the way. At the beginning of the war, the Central Powers were lead by the nations of Germany, Austria-Hungary and the Ottoman Empire. In total, more than 30 nations (and their colonies) fought in World War I and were members of either the Allied or Central Powers.

Militarism and Alliances help to explain the "how" and the "who" of World War I but to understand "why" the war was fought requires us to look at the I and the N in M.A.I.N. I is for Imperialism, which is defined as "a policy to increase a nation's size or influence, either by forcing (through war) or influencing (through politics) other countries to submit to their rule." Imperialism, as we have discussed is the act of conquering and ruling an empire. Chapter 14 discussed in depth both the motives for and consequences of the Age of Imperialism. Those consequences included causing intense competition for ever scarcer resources and territory to colonize.

N is for Nationalism, and nationalism can be viewed as a reaction to Imperialism. Nationalism is "a desire by a large group of people (such as people who share the same culture, history, language, etc.) to form a separate and independent nation of their own." Imperialists seek to rule over diverse groups as one group and Nationalists seek independence from imperialists. As we have discussed, imperialism or greed for land is as old as humanity itself. But so is the love of freedom. And Nationalism is simply the love of freedom and the desire of people to be self-ruling. As global empires grew and millions of people became subjects of foreign empires in the 1900s, the nationalist spirit grew. Nationalism can take many forms. The unification of Germany in 1871 was the product of nationalism, or a deep need for a people to be one sovereign entity. But German nationalism threatened the security of its neighbors, including Austria-Hungary. In order to increase its territory and in response to German expansion, in 1908 Austria-Hungary annexed two territories, Bosnia and Herzegovina, in a region known as the Balkans. Bosnia and Herzegovina were composed of a large population of Slavs, a distinct European ethnic group. These Slavs did not want to be subjects of Austria-Hungary and had just won their freedom from the Ottoman Empire in the Russo-Turkish War of 1877. Confused yet?

Nationalism is often the push back against imperialism, as was the case with the Slavs after 1908. On the eve of World War I, there were 23 million Slavs in Austria-Hungary (total population of 50 million) and they were treated as second-class citizens. The Slavs wanted their freedom but their pleas for separation or equality were ignored. The struggle for Slavic independence or Pan-Slavism was one of the most immediate causes for The Great War. Terrorist organizations emerged to fight a covert war for independence against Austria-Hungary. They believed that if they put enough pressure on Austria-Hungary, they would have to be granted independence. It was under these circumstances that a group, known as the Black Hand, was created and unknowingly set things into motion for the deadliest war the world had ever seen.

The Outbreak of War
On June 28th of 1914, the archduke Franz Ferdinand of Austria was murdered in Sarajevo along with his wife Sofia. Franz Ferdinand was the nephew of the Austro-Hungarian Emperor Franz Joseph I and heir to the Austro-Hungarian throne. The couple was murdered by the Slavic nationalist group, the Black Hand. It was an act meant to force the freeing of Slavs from Austro-Hungarian rule but instead it was the spark that ignited World War I. The situation in Europe was incredibly tense by 1913, the year before Ferdinand's assassination. A Paris editorial summed up the mood before the war: "All Europe, uncertain and troubled, prepares for an inevitable war, the immediate cause of which is uncertain to us." Even military leaders knew an epic conflict was coming. No one was more pessimistic than German Chief of Staff Helmuth von Moltke, who said, "I am of the persuasion that a European war must come sooner or later." Moltke had no romantic illusions about such a war. It would be, he predicted, "the mutual butchery of the civilized nations of Europe."

The assassination of Franz Ferdinand would have likely not provoked any response at all during normal times, but 1914 was anything but normal. Austria-Hungary was bound to Germany in an alliance and so if Austria-Hungary was at war, so too would be Germany. The Austro-Hungarian response to the assassination was crucial. The

Black Hand was a Slavic nationalist group based in Serbia, a newly formed Slavic nation that won its independence with the help of Russia. Austria-Hungary ultimately decided that the whole nation of Serbia was responsible for the murder of their archduke, and so Austria-Hungary demanded that Serbia turn over control of their country until such time as all the perpetrators and affiliates had been adequately hunted and eliminated or risk war. Serbia, an independent nation, refused to surrender its newly won independence to Austria-Hungary and so war began. This conflict might have stayed isolated as a regional war even then, had it not been for the fact that Russia had sworn to protect the interests of Slavic people worldwide and pledged military support to Serbia. Further complicating matters, if Russia was at war, so were her allies, Britain and France. And just like that, the whole world erupted into war.

The War

World War I began on August 3rd of 1914 and would rage on until the winter of 1918. World War I was a war unlike anyone had ever seen before. Wars before 1914 had clear objectives and clear signs of victory. They were fought for territorial conquest or to vanquish a tyrant; and once the territory was won or the enemy was dead, victory was complete. But how do you know when you have won a war whose goal is simply power? You make the other side lose the will to fight. This new kind of war, known as a *war of attrition*, is defined as "a war where armies gradually and slowly wear down or weaken the opponent's resistance, especially as a result of continuous pressure or harassment" or "a prolonged war or period of conflict during which each side seeks to gradually wear out the other by a series of small-scale actions." In other words, the object of a war of attrition is to make your enemy run out of bullets, soldiers, supplies or morale before you run out. This kind of war is long, demoralizing and miserable. The fighting troops have no way to tell if they are winning or losing because no ground is captured and so their efforts feel useless. Most men who fought in World War I never advanced more than 3 miles in any direction during the entire war because movement was not the objective of attrition; death was.

World War I saw the birth of a new fighting style called trench warfare. Trench warfare was a product of industrialized weapons such as bombs and machine guns in particular. Industrialized weapons were new to the world in 1914 and no one really knew how to fight against them, except to quite literally "hit the dirt." When someone is firing a machine gun at you, the lower you are the safer you are. And when someone is dropping bombs on you, the best you can do is duck and cover. And so this is how trench warfare was born. Opposing sides dug trenches on opposite sides of a battle field where soldiers were stationed. Behind those trenches were the "big guns" that were fired to the enemy trenches with the hopes of high casualties. After a round of mortar shelling, as periods of intensive bombing were called, soldiers were ordered out of their trenches to run across the open field in an attempt to capture the enemy trench during the chaos of the bombing, usually running headlong into machine gun fire as a result. This was how war was fought day after day, and year after year. The day your opponent ran out of ammunition was the day you got to go home. All you had to do was survive until then.

The vast majority of World War I was fought on a 400-mile long stretch of land in France known as the Western Front. There were other battlefronts in Russia and in the Mediterranean region known as the Balkans but France's eastern border was where most World War I soldiers fought and died. The seemingly endless bloodshed of World War I finally did come to an end in 1918 after four brutal years. In the fall of that year, Germany and her allies had lost the will to keep fighting. This was due in part to a successful British naval blockade that starved the Central Forces of crucial food supplies and ammunition to the battlefront. It was also due to the involvement of the United States in the war in the spring of 1917. By 1917, both the Allied and the Central Powers were on the verge of collapse. But a suspicious turn of events drew the U.S. into the conflict in Europe even though it had previously vowed to stay out of the foreign war.

Though it took the Central Powers another year to surrender, it was clear that defeat was imminent by 1917. On the 11th hour, of the 11th day of the 11th month of 1918, Germany and the Central Powers surrendered and signed the armistice ending World War I. They did so based on a promise of fair treatment after the war and saw proof of these promises in a document written by American President Woodrow Wilson called The Fourteen Point Plan for Peace. It promised that no group or nation would be punished for the war and that, like the Congress of Vienna, the goal would be restoration and not revenge. But things went very wrong at the Paris Peace Conference in 1919. Anger, heartbreak and a need for vengeance dominated the discussions in Paris. The result was a very uneven peace treaty and one that severely punished Germany, pushing it to the brink of collapse—and setting the stage for World War II.

Gustave Le Bon, *The Crowd, 1895 CE*

Reading and Discussion Questions
1. According to Le Bon, how are individuals transformed once they become part of a crowd? How does the leader sway the crowd?
2. What role does the unconscious mind play in the development of crowd mentality?
3. What is the role of reason and logic in influencing a crowd? How do leaders win the support of a crowd?
4. Identify at least three instances in recent history or the world today that support Le Bon's insights.
5. What is your reaction to this reading? Do you agree or disagree with the author? Explain.

Gustave Le Bon was a French social psychologist who examined mass psychology as demonstrated in crowd behavior. "The substitution of the unconscious action of crowds for the conscious activity of individuals is one of the principal characteristics of the present age," Le Bon observed in the opening of his book, The Crowd: A Study of the Popular Mind, published in 1895. Le Bon was specifically influenced by the events in France during his lifetime in which large crowds were embracing radical ideologies for no good reason that Le Bon could understand except that the group had powerful influence over the individual mind. He sought to understand this psychological phenomenon. Written a mere 19 years before the beginning of World War I, The Crowd, can help us understand why there was so much enthusiasm for war in 1914, even when there was no clear reason for war. In many places, people were euphoric about the start of World War I, which is hard to understand given the nature of that conflict. The Crowd becomes even more powerful when reread in the context of the rise of Adolf Hitler and other Fascist dictators in the years leading up to World War II. Le Bon seems to have hit on a fundamental truth about the power of the crowd, which can with frightening efficiency undo the rational and logical thought that otherwise governs individual human intellect.

Thousands of isolated individuals may acquire at certain moments, and under the influence of certain violent emotions—such, for example, as a great national event—the characteristics of a psychological crowd. . . . The most striking peculiarity presented by a psychological crowd is the following: Whoever be the individuals that compose it, the fact that they have been transformed into a crowd puts them in possession of a sort of collective mind which makes them feel, think, and act in a manner quite different from that in which each individual of them would feel, think, and act were he in a state of isolation. . . .

To obtain [an understanding of crowds] it is necessary in the first place to call to mind the truth established by modern psychology, that unconscious phenomena play an [a huge part] not only in organic life, but also in the operations of the intelligence. The conscious life of the mind is of small importance in comparison with its unconscious life. . . . Behind the avowed causes of our acts there undoubtedly lie secret causes that we do not avow, but behind these secret causes there are many others more secret still which we ourselves ignore. The greater part of our daily actions are the result of hidden motives which escape our observation. . . .

. . . In the collective mind the intellectual aptitudes of the individuals, and in consequence their individuality, are weakened . . . and the unconscious qualities obtain the upper hand. . . . . . . In a crowd every sentiment and act is contagious, and contagious to such a degree that an individual readily sacrifices his personal interest to the collective interest. This is an aptitude very contrary to his nature, and of which a man is scarcely capable, except when he [is] part of a crowd. . . . . . . [An] individual [immersed] for some length of time in a crowd in action soon finds himself . . . in a special state, which much resembles the state of fascination in which the hypnotized individual finds himself in the hands of the hypnotizer. The activity of the brain being paralyzed in the case of the hypnotized subject, the latter becomes the slave of all the unconscious activities of his spinal cord, which the hypnotizer directs at will. The conscious personality has entirely vanished; will and discernment are lost. All feelings and thoughts are bent in the direction determined by the hypnotizer.

Such also is approximately the state of the individual forming part of a psychological crowd. He is no longer conscious of his acts. In his case, as in the case of the hypnotized subject, at the same time that certain faculties are destroyed, others may be brought to a high degree of exaltation. Under the influence of a suggestion, he will undertake the accomplishment of certain acts with irresistible impetuosity. . . . He is no longer himself, but has become an automaton who has ceased to be guided by his will. Moreover, by the mere fact that he forms part of an organized crowd, a man descends several rungs in the ladder of civilization. Isolated, he may be a cultivated individual; in a crowd, he is a barbarian—that is, a creature acting by instinct. He possesses the spontaneity, the violence, the ferocity, and also the enthusiasm and heroism of primitive beings, whom he further tends to resemble by the facility with which he allows himself to be impressed by words and images—which would be entirely without action on each of the isolated individuals composing the crowd—and to be induced to commit acts contrary to his most obvious interests and his best-known habits. . . .

In consequence, a crowd perpetually hovering on the borderland of unconsciousness, readily yielding to all suggestions, having all the violence of feeling peculiar to beings who cannot appeal to the influence of reason, deprived of all critical faculty, cannot be otherwise than excessively credulous. The improbable does not exist for a crowd, and it is necessary to bear this circumstance well in mind to understand the facility with which are created and propagated the most improbable legends and stories. . . . A crowd thinks in images, and the image itself immediately calls up a series of other images, having no logical connection with the first. . . . Our reason shows us the incoherence there is in these images, but a crowd is almost blind to this truth, and confuses with the real event what the deforming action of its imagination has superimposed thereon. A crowd scarcely distinguishes between the subjective and the objective. It accepts as real the images evoked in its mind. . . .

Whatever be the ideas suggested to crowds they can only exercise effective influence on condition that they assume a very absolute, uncompromising, and simple shape. They present themselves then in the guise of images, and are only accessible to the masses under this form. These image-like ideas are not connected by any logical bond of analogy or succession. . . . . . . A chain of logical argumentation is totally incomprehensible to crowds, and for this reason it is permissible to say that they do not

410

reason or that they reason falsely and are not to be influenced by reasoning. . . . An orator in intimate communication with a crowd can evoke images by which it will be seduced. . . . . . . [The] powerlessness of crowds to reason aright prevents them displaying any trace of the critical spirit, prevents them, that is, from being capable of discerning truth from error, or of forming a precise judgment on any matter. Judgments accepted by crowds are merely judgments forced upon them and never judgments adopted after discussion. . . .

Crowds are to some extent in the position of the sleeper whose reason, suspended for the time being, allows the arousing in his mind of images of extreme intensity which would quickly be dissipated could they be submit to the action of reflection. Crowds, being incapable both of reflection and of reasoning, are devoid of the notion of improbability; and it is to be noted that in a general way it is the most improbable things that are the most striking. This is why it happens that it is always the marvelous and legendary side of events that more specially strike crowds. . . .Crowds being only capable of thinking in images are only to be impressed by images. It is only images that terrify or attract them and become motives of action. . . . How is the imagination of crowds to be impressed?. . . [The] feat is never to be achieved by attempting to work upon the intelligence or reasoning faculty, that is to say, by way of demonstration. . . .Whatever strikes the imagination of crowds presents itself under the shape of a startling and very clear image, freed from all accessory explanation . . . examples in point are a great victory, a great miracle, a great crime, or a great hope. Things must be laid before the crowd as a whole, and their genesis must never be indicated.

A hundred petty crimes or petty accidents will not strike the imagination of crowds in the least, whereas a single great crime or a single great accident will profoundly impress them. . . .When [the convictions of crowds] are closely examined, whether at epochs marked by fervent religious faith, or by great political upheavals such as those of the last century, it is apparent that they always assume a peculiar form which I cannot better define than by giving it the name of a religious sentiment. . . . A person is not religious solely when he worships a divinity, but when he puts all the resources of his mind, the complete submission of his will, toward the whole-souled ardour his thoughts and actions. Intolerance and fanaticism are the necessary accompaniments of the religious sentiment. . . . All founders of religious or political creeds have established them solely because they were successful in inspiring crowds with those fanatical sentiments which have as result that men find their happiness in worship and obedience and are ready to lay down their lives for their idol. This has been the case at all epochs. . . .

We have already shown that crowds are not to be influenced by reasoning, and can only comprehend rough-and-ready associations of ideas. The orators who know how to make an impression upon them always appeal in consequence to their sentiments and never to their reason. The laws of logic have no action on crowds. To bring home conviction to crowds it is necessary first of all to thoroughly comprehend the sentiments by which they are animated, to pretend to share these sentiments. . . . As soon as a certain number of living beings are gathered together, whether they be animals or men, they place themselves instinctively under the authority of a chief. In the case of human crowds the chief is often nothing more than a ringleader or agitator, but as such he plays a considerable part. His will is the nucleus around which the opinions of the crowd are grouped and attain to identity. . . .

411

A crowd is a servile flock that is incapable of ever doing without a master. The leader has most often started as one of the led. He has himself been hypnotized by the idea, whose apostle he has since become. It has taken possession of him to such a degree that everything outside it vanishes, and that every contrary opinion appears to him an error or a superstition. An example in point is Robespierre, hypnotized by the philosophical ideas of Rousseau [an opponent of monarchy and supporter of democracy], and employing the methods of the Inquisition to propagate them. The leaders we speak of are more frequently men of action than thinkers. . . . The multitude is always ready to listen to the strong-willed man, who knows how to impose himself upon it. Men gathered in a crowd lose all force of will, and turn instinctively to the person who possesses the quality they lack. . . When . . . it is proposed to imbue the mind of a crowd with ideas and beliefs . . . the leaders have recourse to different expedients. The principal of them are three in number and clearly defined affirmation, repetition, and contagion. . . .Affirmation pure and simple, kept free of all reasoning and all proof, is one of the surest means of making an idea enter the mind of crowds. The more concise an affirmation is, the more destitute of every appearance of proof and demonstration, the more weight it carries. . . Affirmation, however, has no real influence unless it be constantly repeated, and so far as possible in the same terms. It was Napoleon, I believe, who said that there is only one figure in rhetoric of serious importance, namely, repetition. The thing affirmed comes by repetition to fix itself in the mind in such a way that it is accepted in the end as a demonstrated truth.

The influence of repetition on crowds is comprehensible when the power is seen which it exercises on the most enlightened minds. This power is due to the fact that the repeated statement is embedded in the long run in those profound regions of our unconscious selves in which the motives of our actions are forged. At the end of a certain time we have forgotten who is the author of the repeated assertion, and we finish by believing it. When an affirmation has been sufficiently repeated and there is unanimity in this repetition . . . what is called a current of opinion is formed and the powerful mechanism of contagion intervenes. Ideas, sentiments, emotions, and beliefs possess in crowds a contagious power as intense as that of microbes.

412

German Nationalism—Two Readings

Reading and Discussion Questions
1. In both passages below, what is the German feeling about England?
2. What are both speakers in the passages below suggesting, or demanding that Germany do?
3. How do these documents represent the idea of Nationalism? Explain at least two quotes from your reading that show German Nationalism.
4. Look up the word "anvil" and then analyze what von Bulow meant in the second reading by the statement, "in the coming century the German people with be either the hammer or the anvil." How does this passage and this speech help you to understand the feelings of Germany by 1900? What competition or rivalry does it suggest? Analyze this quote in relation to the broader idea of nationalism.

By the turn of the century, Germany was carving out a place for itself in the world. Having just been made a nation in 1871, there was a general sense that Germany had a lot of catching up to do, especially to England and the British Empire. Both of the following readings capture the growing sense of Nationalism in Germany by 1900. The also clearly show the growing support of war. The first reading is from Heinrich von Treitschke, a member of the German Reichstag (Parliament) and a supporter of a militarily strong Germany. The second reading is from a speech made by Bernhard von Bülow, which has become famously known as the Hammer and Anvil speech. Von Bülow was a powerful German political leader who served first as Secretary of State to the newly formed country and then as Chancellor from 1900 to 1909.

Heinrich von Treitschke, On the Greatness of War, 1890 CE

. . One must say with the greatest determination: War is for an afflicted people the only remedy. When the State exclaims: My very existence is at stake! then social self-seeking must disappear and all party hatred be silent. The individual must forget his own *ego* and feel himself a member of the whole, he must recognize how negligible is his life compared with the good of the whole. Therein lies the greatness of war that the little man completely vanishes before the great thought of the State. The sacrifice of nationalities for one another is nowhere invested with such beauty as in war. At such a time the corn is separated from the chaff. All who lived through 1870 will understand the saying of Niebuhr with regard to the year 1813, that he then experienced the "bliss of sharing with all his fellow citizens, with the scholar and the ignorant, the one common feeling—no man who enjoyed this experience will to his dying day forget how loving, friendly and strong he felt."

It is indeed political idealism which fosters war, whereas materialism rejects it. What a perversion of morality to want to banish heroism from human life. The heroes of a people are the personalities who fill the youthful souls with delight and enthusiasm, and amongst authors we as boys and youths admire most those whose words sound like a flourish of trumpets. He who cannot take pleasure therein, is too cowardly to take up arms himself for his fatherland. All appeal to Christianity in this matter is perverted. The Bible states expressly that the man in authority shall wield the sword; it states likewise that: "Greater love hath no man than this that he giveth his life for his friend." Those who preach the nonsense about everlasting peace do not understand the life of the Aryan race, the Aryans are before all brave. They have always been men enough to protect by the sword what they had won by the intellect....

To the historian who lives in the realms of the Will, it is quite clear that the furtherance of an everlasting peace is fundamentally reactionary. He sees that to banish war from history would be to banish all progress and becoming. It is only the periods of exhaustion, weariness and mental stagnation that have dallied with the dream of everlasting peace.... The living God will see to it that war returns again and again as a terrible medicine for humanity.

* * * * * *

Bernhard von Bülow, Hammer and Anvil Speech, 1899 CE

In our nineteenth century, England has increased its colonial empire -- the largest the world has seen since the days of the Romans -- further and further; the French have put down roots in North Africa and East Africa and created for themselves a new empire in the Far East; Russia has begun its mighty course of victory in Asia, leading it to the high plateau of the Pamir and to the coasts of the Pacific Ocean. Four years ago the Sino-Japanese war, scarcely one and a half years ago the Spanish-American War have put things further in motion; they've led to great, momentous, far-reaching decisions, shaken old empires, and added new and serious ferment. . . .The English prime minister said a long time ago that the strong states were getting stronger and stronger and the weak ones weaker and weaker. . . .We don't want to step on the toes of any foreign power, but at the same time we don't want our own feet tramped by any foreign power and we don't intend to be shoved aside by any foreign power, not in political nor in economic terms.

It is time, high time, that we . . . make it clear in our own minds what stance we have to take and how we need to prepare ourselves in the face of the processes taking place around us which carry the seeds within them for the restructuring of power relationships for the unforeseeable future. To stand inactively to one side, as we have done so often in the past, either from native modesty or because we were completely absorbed in our own internal arguments or for doctrinaire reasons – to stand dreamily to one side while other people split up the pie, we cannot and we will not do that. We cannot for the simple reason that we now have interests in all parts of the world. [...]

The rapid growth of our population, the unprecedented blossoming of our industries, the hard work of our merchants, in short the mighty vitality of the German people have woven us into the world economy and pulled us into international politics. If the English speak of a 'Greater Britain;' if the French speak of a 'Nouvelle France;' if the Russians open up Asia; then we, too, have the right to a greater Germany, not in the sense of conquest, but indeed in the sense of peaceful extension of our trade and its infrastructures.... We cannot and will not permit that the order of the day passes over the German people . . .

There is a lot of envy present in the world against us political envy and economic envy. There are individuals and there are interest groups, and there are movements, and

414

there are perhaps even peoples that believe that the German was easier to have around and that the German was more pleasant for his neighbors in those earlier days, when, in spite of our education and in spite of our culture, foreigners looked down on us in political and economic matters like cavaliers with their noses in the air looking down on the humble tutor.

These times of political faintness and economic and political humility should never return. We don't ever again want to become, as Friedrich List put it, the 'slaves of humanity.' But we'll only be able to keep ourselves at the fore if we realize that there is no welfare for us without power, without a strong army and a strong fleet.

The means, gentlemen, for a people of almost 60 million -- dwelling in the middle of Europe and, at the same time, stretching its economic antennae out to all sides -it is impossible to battle its way through in the struggle for existence without strong armaments on land and at sea. In the coming century the German people will be a hammer or an anvil.

European Reaction to War—Five Perspectives

Reading and Discussion Questions
1. Summarize the reaction of the people in Germany, France and England to the announcement of war in 1914. What was the common man's mood about war, based on your reading?
2. Based on your reading of all the passages in this section, which nation seemed to have the most enthusiasm for war? Why do you think this?
3. In each section, how does the speaker or group defend the actions of their nation and criticize or condemn the actions or accusations of others? Cite specific examples in answering this question.
4. The accounts of the people's enthusiasm were written by people who in some cases did not share that enthusiasm. Which of the authors in this section did not react positively to the enthusiasm for war and why? Look specifically at Bertrand Russell in your analysis.
5. Does any of the behavior recorded below sound like what you read about in Gustave Le Bon's *The Crowd*? Explain.

World War I began in August of 1914 and there are widespread reports from across Europe about the near-hysteria in reaction to the news of war. From France and England to Austria-Hungary and Russia, there seemed to be a deep excitement about the fact that war had finally arrived, a fact that many observers found disturbing. Below are several passages that capture the people's response to World War I. They are mostly from 1914, but also from 1915, when German submarine aggression, including the sinking of the Lusitania, reinforced the zeal for war in countries like England in France.

In Germany

Manifesto of the Ninety-Three, 1914 CE
As representatives of German Science and Art, we [93 scientists of deep intellect] hereby protest to the civilized world against the lies and calumnies with which our

415

enemies are endeavoring to stain the honor of Germany in her hard struggle for existence – in a struggle that has been forced on her.

The iron mouth of events has proved the untruth of the fictitious German defeats; consequently misrepresentation and calumny are all the more eagerly at work. As heralds of truth we raise our voices against these.

It is not true that Germany is guilty of having caused this war. Neither the people, the Government, nor the "Kaiser" wanted war....

It is not true that we trespassed in neutral Belgium. It has been proved that France and England had resolved on such a trespass, and it has likewise been proved that Belgium had agreed to their doing so. It would have been suicide on our part not to have been beforehand.

It is not true that the life and property of a single Belgian citizen was injured by our soldiers without the bitterest defense having made it necessary....

It is not true that our troops treated Louvain brutally. Furious inhabitants having treacherously fallen upon them in their quarters, our troops with aching hearts were obliged to fire a part of the town, as punishment. The greatest part of Louvain has been preserved....

It is not true that our warfare pays no respects to international laws. It knows no undisciplined cruelty. But in the east, the earth is saturated with the blood of women and children unmercifully butchered by the wild Russian troops, and in the west, dumdum bullets mutilate the breasts of our soldiers....

It is not true that the combat against our so-called militarism is not a combat against our civilization, as our enemies hypocritically pretend it is. Were it not for German militarism, German civilization would long since have been extirpated....

We cannot wrest the poisonous weapon – the lie -- out of the hands of our enemies. All we can do is proclaim to all the world, that our enemies are giving false witness against us....

Have faith in us! Believe, that we shall carry on this war to the end as a civilized nation, to whom the legacy of a Goethe, a Beethoven, and a Kant, is just as sacred as its own hearths and homes.

Phillip Schneidermann, The Hour We Have Yearned For, 1914 CE

At express speed I had returned to Berlin. Everywhere a word could be heard the conversation was of war and rumours of war. There was only one topic of conversation—war. The supporters of war seemed to be in a great majority. Were these pugnacious fellows, young and old, bereft of their senses?

Were they so ignorant of the horrors of war? . . . Vast crowds of demonstrators paraded. . . . Schoolboys and students were there in their thousands; their bearded seniors, with their Iron Crosses of 1870-71 on their breasts, were there too in huge numbers.

War supporters seemed to have multiplied a thousandfold. Patriotic demonstrations had an intoxicating effect and excited the war-mongers to excess. "A call like the voice of thunder." Cheers! "In triumph we will smite France to the ground." "All hail to thee in victor's crown." Cheers! Hurrah!

The counter-demonstrations immediately organized by the Berlin Social Democrats were imposing, and certainly more disciplined than the Jingo [extremely nationalistic] processions, but could not outdo the shouts of the fire-eaters. "Good luck to him who cares for truth and right. Stand firmly round the flag." "Long live peace!" "Socialists, close up your ranks." The Socialist International cheer. The patriots were sometimes silenced by the Proletarians; then they came out on top again. This choral contest . . . went on for days.

"It is the hour we yearned for—our friends know that," so the Pan-German papers shouted, that had for years been shouting for war. The Post, conducted by von Stumm, the Independent Conservative leader and big Industrial, had thus moaned in all its columns in 1900, at the fortieth celebration of the Franco-German War: "Another forty years of peace would be a national misfortune for Germany."

Now these firebrands saw the seeds they had planted ripening. Perhaps in the heads of many who had been called upon to make every effort to keep the peace Bernhardi's words, that "the preservation of peace can and never shall be the aim of politics," had done mischief. These words are infernally like the secret instructions given by Baron von Holstein to the German delegates to the first Peace Conference at The Hague:"For the State there is no higher aim than the preservation of its own interests; among the Great Powers these will not necessarily coincide with the maintenance of peace, but rather with the hostile policy of enemies and rivals."

In France

Roland Dorgelès, Paris: That Fabulous Day, 1914 CE

"It's come! It's posted at the district mayor's office," a passerby shouted to me as he ran. I reached the Rue Drouot in one leap and shouldered through the mob that already filled the courtyard to approach the fascinating white sheet pasted to the door. I read the message at a glance, then reread it slowly, word for word, to convince myself that it was true: "the first day of mobilization will be Sunday, august 2."

It was an announcement to a million and a half Frenchmen. The people who had read it moved away, stunned, while others crowded in, but this silent numbness did not last. Suddenly a heroic wind lifted their heads. What? War, was it? Well, then, let's go! Without any signal, the "Marseillaise" poured from thousands of throats, sheafs of flags appeared at windows, and howling processions rolled out on the boulevards. Each column brandished a placard: Alsace volunteers, Jewish volunteers, polish volunteers. They hailed one another above the bravos of the crowd, and this human torrent, swelling at every corner, moved on to circle around the Place de la Concorde, before the statue of Strasbourg banked with flowers, then flowed toward the Place de la République, where mobs from Belleville and the Faubourg St. Antoine yelled themselves hoarse on the refrain from the great days, "aux armes, citoyens!" (To arms, citizens!)

417

But this time it was better than a song. To gather the news for my paper, I ran around the city in every direction. At the Cours la Reine I saw the fabled cuirassiers [cavalry] in their horsetail plumes march by, and at the Rue La Fayette footsoldiers in battle garb with women throwing flowers and kisses to them. In a marshaling yard I saw guns being loaded, their long, thin barrels twined around with branches and laurel leaves, while troops in red breeches piled gaily into delivery vans they were scrawling with challenges and caricatures. Young and old, civilians and military men burned with the same excitement. It was like a Brotherhood Day.

In England

Arthur Winnington-Ingram, 1915 CE
Everyone that loves freedom and honour ... are banded in a great crusade – we cannot deny it – to kill Germans; to kill them, not for the sake of killing, but to save the world; to kill the good as well as the bad, to kill the young as well as the old, to kill those who have shown kindness to our wounded as well as those fiends who crucified the Canadian sergeant, who superintended the Armenian massacres, who sank the Lusitania, and who turned the machine-guns on the civilians of Aerschott and Louvain – and to kill them lest the civilisation of the world itself be killed.

Bertrand Russell, 1914 CE
During the hot days at the end of July, I was at Cambridge, discussing the situation with all and sundry. I found it impossible to believe that Europe would be so mad as to plunge into war, but I was persuaded that, if there was war, England would be involved. I felt strongly that England ought to remain neutral, and I collected the signatures of a large number of professors and Fellows to a statement which appeared in the Manchester guardian to that effect. The day war was declared, almost all of them changed their minds. . . . I spent the evening walking round the streets, especially in the neighbourhood of Trafalgar Square, noticing cheering crowds, and making myself sensitive to the emotions of passers-by.

During this and the following days I discovered to my amazement that average men and women were delighted at the prospect of war. I had fondly imagined what most pacifists contended, that wars were forced upon a reluctant population by despotic and Machiavellian governments. . . .

The first days of the war were to me utterly amazing. My best friends, such as the Whiteheads, were savagely warlike. Men like J. L. Hammond, who had been writing for years against participation in a European war, were swept off their feet by [Germany's invasion of] Belgium.

Meanwhile, I was living at the highest possible emotional tension. Although I did not foresee anything like the full disaster of the war, I foresaw a great deal more than most people did. The prospect filled me with horror, but what filled me with even more horror was the fact that the anticipation of carnage was delightful to something like ninety per cent of the population. I had to revise my views on human nature. At that time I was wholly ignorant of psychoanalysis, but I arrived for myself at a view of human passions not unlike that of the psychoanalysts. I arrived at this view in an endeavour to understand popular feeling about the War. I had supposed until that time that it was quite common for parents to love their children, but the War persuaded me that it is a rare exception. I had supposed that most people liked money better than almost anything else, but I discovered that they like destruction even better. I had supposed that intellectuals frequently loved truth, but I found here again that not ten per cent of them prefer truth to popularity. . . .

. . . As a lover of truth, the national propaganda of all the belligerent nations sickened me. As a lover of civilization, the return to barbarism appalled me. As a man of thwarted parental feeling, the massacre of the young wrung my heart. I hardly supposed that much good would come of opposing the War, but I felt that for the honour of human nature those who were not swept off their feet should show that they stood firm.

. . . Those who saw the London crowds, during the nights leading up to the Declaration of War saw a whole population, hitherto peaceable and humane, precipitated in a few days down the steep slope to primitive barbarism, letting loose, in a moment, the instincts of hatred and blood lust against which the whole fabric of society has been raised. All countries acclaim this brutal orgy as a noble determination to vindicate the right; reason and mercy are swept away in one great flood of hatred; dim abstractions of unimaginable wickedness—Germany to us and the French, Russia to the Germans—conceal the simple fact that the enemy are men, like ourselves, neither better nor worse—men who love their homes and the sunshine, and all the simple pleasures of common lives.

The Black Hand Oath, Constitution and Journals, 1910-1914 CE

Reading and Discussion Questions
1. How serious is the oath for membership to the Black Hand? What do members pledge when they swear their oath?
2. What are the stated goals of the Black Hand and how do they propose to achieve those goals?
3. What can you understand about why Franz Ferdinand was assassinated based on the journal entry of Borijove Jevtic?

In the early 1900s, a group known as "Unification or Death" was formed in the new nation of Serbia. That group was more commonly known as The Black Hand. The Black Hand was a group of radical Slavs in Serbia who were determined to create a Slavic nation, inspired by Nationalist movements that led to the creation of Italy and Germany in 1871. The Black Hand considered themselves a Nationalist group of freedom fighters, who were struggling to win Slavic independence from empires like Austria-Hungary. To the powers of Europe, The Black Hand was a terrorist organization. It was a member of the Black Hand, Gavrilo Princip, who assassinated Archduke Franz Ferdinand in the summer of 1914. The objective of the assassination was to put pressure on Austria-Hungary to free its Slavic population because Franz Ferdinand was heir to the Austro-Hungarian throne. It did not have the desired impact. Instead of Slavic independence, the assassination prompted the beginning of World War I. The following documents are some of the secret documents associated with membership to the Black Hand.

419

Oath sworn by all members of the Black Hand

I, in joining the organization "Union or Death", swear by the Sun that warms me, by the Earth that nourishes me, before God, by the blood of the ancestors, on my honor and on my life, that I will from this moment until my death be faithful to the laws of this organization; and that I will always be ready to make any sacrifice for it.

I swear before God, on my honor and on my life, that I will take all the secrets of this organization into my grave with me.

Constitution of the Black Hand

Article 1. For the purpose of realizing the national ideals - the Unification of Slav-dom - an organization is hereby created, whose members may be any Slavs irrespective of sex, religion, place or birth, as well as anybody else who will sincerely serve this idea.

Article 2. The organization gives priority to the revolutionary struggle rather than relies on cultural striving, therefore its institution is an absolutely secret one for wider circles.

Article 4. In order to carry into effect its task the organization will do the following things:
(a) Following the character of its reason for being it will exercise its influence over all the official factors in Serbia as also over all the strata of the State and over the entire social life in it:
(b) It will carry out a revolutionary organization in all the territories where Slavs are living:
(c) Beyond the frontiers, it will fight with all means against all enemies of this idea:
(d) It will maintain friendly relations with all the States, nations, organizations, and individual persons who sympathize with Serbia and the Slavic race:
(e) It will give every assistance to those nations and organizations who are fighting for their own national liberation and unification.

Borijove Jevtic, Black Hand member in Serbia in 1914

How dared Franz Ferdinand, not only the representative of the oppressor but in his own person an arrogant tyrant, enter Sarajevo on that day? Such an entry was a studied insult. 28 June is a date engraved deeply in the heart of every Slav, so that day has a name of its own. It is called *vidounan*. It is the day on which the old Slavic kingdom was conquered by the Turks at the battle of Amselfelde in 1389. That was no day for Franz Ferdinand, the new oppressor, to venture to the very doors of Serbia for a display of the force of arms which kept us beneath his heel. Our decision was taken almost immediately. Death to the tyrant!

Austria-Hungary's Ultimatum to Serbia, 1914 CE

Reading and Discussion Questions
1. What things did Austria-Hungary accuse Serbia of in this document?
2. What is the first thing that Austria-Hungary is "compelled to demand from the Royal Serbian Government?"
3. What other things did Austria-Hungary demand from Serbia? Why do you think Serbia objected to these demands?
4. What was Serbia's response to this ultimatum?
5. How do ultimatums work? Serbia met some of Austria=Hungary's demands. Was that enough to satisfy Austria-Hungary? Why or why not?

The assassination of Franz Ferdinand did not result in freedom for the Slavs. Instead it resulted in a severe ultimatum from Austria-Hungary to Serbia, who Austria-Hungary believed was responsible for the assassination and for the terrorist plots. The Serbian government claimed that the Black Hand and other Slavic nationalist groups operated without the permission or approval of the Serbian government but Austria-Hungary did not believe them. Franz Ferdinand was killed on July 23 of 1914 and the ultimatum that follows was issued the same day. One week later, the Serbian government gave their reply, which is also included below. On that same day, Austria-Hungary declared war on Serbia, and a chain reaction based on complicated alliances started World War I.

The history of recent years, and in particular the painful events of the 28th of June last, have shown the existence of a subversive movement with the object of detaching a part of the territories of Austria-Hungary from the Monarchy.

The movement, which had its birth under the eye of the Serbian Government, has gone so far as to make itself manifest on both sides of the Serbian frontier in the shape of acts of terrorism and a series of outrages and murders.

The Royal Serbian Government has done nothing to repress these movements. It has permitted the criminal machinations of various societies and associations directed against the Monarchy, and has tolerated unrestrained language on the part of the press, the glorification of the perpetrators of outrages, and the participation of officers and functionaries in subversive agitation.

It has permitted an unwholesome propaganda in public instruction; in short, it has permitted all manifestations of a nature to incite the Serbian population to hatred of the Monarchy and contempt of its institutions.

This culpable tolerance of the Royal Serbian Government had not ceased at the moment when the events of the 28th of June last proved its fatal consequences to the whole world.

It results from the depositions and confessions of the criminal perpetrators of the outrage of the 28th of June that the Serajevo assassinations were planned in Belgrade; that the arms and explosives with which the murderers were provided had been given to them by Serbian officers and functionaries; and finally, that the passage into Bosnia of the criminals and their arms was organized and effected by the chiefs of the Serbian frontier service.

To [right these wrongs] the Imperial and Royal Government of Austria-Hungary is compelled to demand from the Royal Serbian Government a formal assurance that they condemn this dangerous propaganda against the Monarchy; in other words the whole series of tendencies, the ultimate aim of which is to detach from the Monarchy territories belonging to it and that they undertake to suppress by every means this criminal and terrorist propaganda.

In order to give a formal character to this undertaking the Royal Serbian Government shall publish on the front page of their "Official Journal" of the 13-26 of July the following declaration:

"The Royal Government of Serbia condemn the propaganda directed against Austria-Hungary - i.e., the general tendency of which the final aim is to detach from the Austro-Hungarian Monarchy territories belonging to it, and they sincerely deplore the fatal consequences of these criminal proceedings.

The Royal Government regret that Serbian officers and functionaries participated in the above-mentioned propaganda and thus compromised the good neighbourly relations to which the Royal Government were solemnly pledged by their declaration of the 31st of March, 1909.

The Royal Government, who disapprove and repudiate all idea of interfering or attempting to interfere with the destinies of the inhabitants of any part whatsoever of Austria-Hungary, consider it their duty formally to warn officers and functionaries, and the whole population of the Kingdom, that henceforward they will proceed with the utmost rigor against persons who may be guilty of such machinations, which they will use all their efforts to anticipate and suppress."

The Royal Serbian Government shall further undertake:

(1) To suppress any publication which incites to hatred and contempt of the Austro-Hungarian Monarchy and the general tendency of which is directed against its territorial integrity;

(2) To dissolve immediately terrorist organizations and to confiscate all its means of propaganda, and to proceed in the same manner against other societies and their branches in Serbia which engage in propaganda against the Austro-Hungarian Monarchy. The Royal Government shall take the necessary measures to prevent the societies dissolved from continuing their activity under another name and form;

(3) To eliminate without delay from public instruction in Serbia, both as regards the teaching body and also as regards the methods of instruction, everything that serves, or might serve, to foment the propaganda against Austria-Hungary;

(4) To remove from the military service, and from the administration in general, all officers and functionaries guilty of propaganda against the Austro-Hungarian Monarchy whose names and deeds the Austro-Hungarian Government reserve to themselves the right of communicating to the Royal Government;

(5) To accept the collaboration in Serbia of representatives of the Austro-Hungarian Government for the suppression of the subversive movement directed against the territorial integrity of the Monarchy;

(6) To take judicial proceedings against accessories to the plot of the 28th of June who are on Serbian territory; delegates of the Austro-Hungarian Government will take part in the investigation relating thereto;

(8) To prevent by effective measures the cooperation of the Serbian authorities in the illicit traffic in arms and explosives across the frontier;

(9) To furnish the Imperial and Royal Government with explanations regarding the unjustifiable utterances of high Serbian officials, both in Serbia and abroad, who, notwithstanding their official position, have not hesitated since the crime of the 28th of June to express themselves in interviews in terms of hostility to the Austro-Hungarian Government; and, finally,

(10) To notify the Imperial and Royal Government without delay of the execution of the measures comprised under the preceding heads.

The Austro-Hungarian Government expect the reply of the Royal Government at the latest by 5 o'clock on Saturday evening the 25th of July.

The Serbian Reply

Serbia] cannot be held responsible for manifestations of a private character, such as articles in the press and the peaceable work of societies ... [The Serbian government] have been pained and surprised at the statements, according to which members of the Kingdom of Serbia are supposed to have participated in the preparations of the crime...

[However, Serbia is] prepared to hand over for trial any Serbian subject . .of whose complicity in the crime of Sarajevo proofs are forthcoming [as well as officially condemn all propaganda against A-H].

[Serbia will] introduce ... a provision into the press law providing for the most severe punishment of incitement to hatred and contempt of the [A-H] Monarchy...

[Serbia will] eliminate without delay from public instruction ... everything that serves or might serve to foment the propaganda against [A-H], whenever [Austria] furnish them with facts and proofs...

[Serbia] also agree to remove from the military service all such persons as the judicial inquiry may have proved to be guilty of acts directed against the integrity of the territory of [A-H], and they expect [Austria] to communicate ... the names and acts of these officers for the purpose of the proceedings which are to be taken against them.

[The Serbian govt. does] not clearly grasp the meaning or the scope of the demand ... that Serbia shall undertake to accept the collaboration of the representatives of [A-H], but they declare that they will admit such collaboration as agrees with the principle of international law, with criminal procedure, and with good neighborly relations.

As regards the participation in this inquiry [which Serbia intends to hold] of Austro-Hungarian agents... [Serbia] cannot accept such an arrangement, as it would be a violation of the Constitution... [If Austria is not satisfied with the reply] the Serbian government . . are ready . . to accept a pacific understanding, either by referring this question to the decision of the International Tribunal of the Hague [i.e., the World Court], or to the Great Powers...

Edward Thomas, *This is No Case of Petty Right or Wrong*, 1915 CE

Reading and Discussion Questions

1. Based on your reading, how does Thomas feel about the war?
2. Who does Thomas say he does and does not hate? Who do you think he is calling "one fat patriot?"
3. Do you think the feelings reflected in this poem were more common among men and women in Europe than the feeling of excitement that you read about earlier? Why or why not?

Poetry became a powerful outlet for people to express their feelings about World War I and there are some staggering works of poetical genius that emerged from World War I and its aftermath. Most people in the world had strong emotions about the war on one side or another and the young Englishman, Edward Thomas, was no exception. Thomas was believed to have written this poem after a fierce argument with his father about the value of the war. His father was an English patriot who strongly supported the war, whereas Thomas did not understand the point. Ultimately, Thomas gave in to the pressure to enlist in the English army rather than fleeing to safety in America, which he had contemplated. Thomas joined the war effort in 1915 and was killed in action in 1917 at the age of 39.

This is no case of petty right or wrong
That politicians or philosophers
Can judge. I hate not Germans, nor grow hot
With love of Englishmen, to please newspapers.
Beside my hate for one fat patriot
My hatred of the Kaiser is love true: —
A kind of god he is, banging a gong.
But I have not to choose between the two,
Or between justice and injustice. Dinned
With war and argument I read no more
Than in the storm smoking along the wind
Athwart the wood. Two witches' cauldrons roar.
From one the weather shall rise clear and gay;
Out of the other an England beautiful
And like her mother that died yesterday.
Little I know or care if, being dull,
I shall miss something that historians
Can rake out of the ashes when perchance
The phoenix broods serene above their ken.
But with the best and meanest Englishmen
I am one in crying, God save England, lest
We lose what never slaves and cattle blessed.
The ages made her that made us from dust:
She is all we know and live by, and we trust
She is good and must endure, loving her so:
And as we love ourselves we hate our foe.

Erich Maria Remarque, *All Quiet on the Western Front*, 1929 CE

Reading and Discussion Questions

1. In this excerpt, does Remarque refer to the enemy? Is it possible to know just who he is fighting?
2. Who, or what, are the victims of warfare? Explain.
3. What is the most powerful scene or imagery from the passages you read of *All Quiet*?
4. How does this reading make you feel about war? How do you think it made readers in 1930 feel about war?

Erich Maria Remarque was a German soldier during World War I. After the war, his book All Quiet on the Western Front, *presented the war experience from the point of view of a foot-soldier who saw tremendous death and destruction. Before this book, which is considered one of the most important works of western literature, war was highly romanticized. Books told of heroic deeds of heroic men who died heroically for their countries.* All Quiet on the Western Front *is definitely not that kind of book. Published in 1929, it is decidedly an anti-war novel, as it depicts the senseless and unimaginable horrors of life as a soldier. It is based on Remarque's own experiences in World War I.*

The book is the story of Paul Baumer, and his teenage friends, who enlist for the German war effort with great enthusiasm. They were urged to do so by their passionately nationalistic school teacher. Paul, who was 19 when he enlisted, was quickly stripped of any romantic ideas about what war would be like. It was hell. In the novel, we see all in Paul's inner circle die in one manner or another or suffer from permanent mental trauma. After seemingly endless violence throughout the war, one day it just suddenly ends. On that day, a telegraph about the events at the battle front simply read "All Quiet on the Western Front." The war ended just as quickly and without explanation as it had begun; shattered men like Paul Baumer and millions of others were left to wonder what it had all been for.

At last it grows quiet. The fire has lifted over us and is now dropping on the reserves. We risk a look. Red rockets shoot up to the sky. Apparently there's an attack coming.

Where we are it is still quiet. I sit up and shake the recruit by the shoulder. "All over, kid! It's all right this time."

He looks round him dazedly. "You'll get used to it soon," I tell him. . . . .

He goes off. Things become quieter, but the cries do not cease. "What's up, Albert?" I ask.

"A couple of columns over there got it in the neck."

The cries continued. It is not men, they could not cry so terribly.

"Wounded horses," says Kat.

It's unendurable. It is the moaning of the world, it is the martyred creation, wild with anguish, filled with terror, and groaning.

We are pale. Detering stands up. "God! For God's sake! Shoot them."

He is a farmer and very fond of horses. It gets under his skin. Then as if deliberately the fire dies down again. The screaming of the beasts becomes louder. One can no longer distinguish whence in this now quiet silvery landscape it come; ghostly, invisible, it is everywhere, between heaven and earth it rolls on immeasurably. Detering raves and yells out: "Shoot them! Shoot them, can't you? Damn you again!"

"They must look after the men first," says Kat quietly.

We stand up and try to see where it is. If we could only see the animals we should be able to endure it better. Müller has a pair of glasses. We see a dark group, bearers with stretchers, and larger black clumps moving about. Those are the wounded horses. But not all of them. Some gallop away in the distance, fall down, and then run on farther. The belly of one is ripped open, the guts trail out. He becomes tangled in them and falls, then he stands up again.

Detering raises up his gun and aims. Kat hits it in the air. "Are you mad --?"

Detering trembles and throws his rifle on the ground.

We sit down and hold our ears. But this appalling noise, these groans and screams penetrate, they penetrate everywhere.

We can bear almost anything. But now the sweat breaks out on us. We must get up and run no matter where, but where these cries can no longer be heard. And it is not men, only horses.

From the dark group stretchers move off again. Then single shots crack out. The black heap convulses and then sinks down. At last! But still it is not the end. The men cannot overtake the wounded beast which fly in their pain, their wide open mouths full of anguish. One of the men goes down on one knee, a shot -- one horse drops -- another. The last one props itself on its forelegs and drags itself round in a circle like a merry-go-round; squatting, it drags round in circles on its stiffened forelegs, apparently its back is broken. The soldier runs up and shoots it. Slowly, humbly, it sinks to the ground.

We take our hands from our ears. The cries are silenced. Only a long-drawn, dying sigh still hangs on the air.

426

Then only again the rockets, the singing of the shells and the stars there -- most strange.

Detering walks up and down cursing: "Like to know what harm they've done." He returns to it once again. His voice is agitated, it sounds almost dignified as he says: "I tell you it is the vilest baseness to use horses in the war." . . .

* * * * * *

The days go by and the incredible hours follow one another as a matter of course. Attacks alternate with counter-attacks and slowly the dead pile up in the field of craters between the trenches. We are able to bring in most of the wounded that do not lie too far off. But many have long to wait and we listen to them dying.

For one of them we search two days in vain. He must be lying on his belly and unable to turn over. Otherwise it is hard to understand why we cannot find him; for it is only when a man has his mouth close to the ground that it is impossible to gauge the direction of his cry.

He must have been badly hit -- one of those nasty wounds neither so severe that they exhaust the body at once and a man dreams on in a half-swoon, not so light that a man endures the pain in the hope of becoming well again. Kat thinks he has either a broken pelvis or a shot through the spine. His chest cannot have been injured otherwise he would not have such strength to cry out. And if it were any other kind of wound it would be possible to see him moving.

He grows gradually hoarser. The voice is so strangely pitched that it seems to be everywhere. The first night some of our fellows go out three times to look for him. But when they think they have located him and crawl across, next time they hear the voice it seems to come from somewhere else altogether.

We search in vain until dawn. We scrutinize the field all day with glasses, but discover nothing. On the second day the calls are fainter; that will be because his lips and mouth have become dry.

Our Company Commander has promised next turn to leave with three days extra to anyone who finds him. That is a powerful inducement, but we would do all that is possible without that for his cry is terrible. Kat and Kropp even go out in the afternoon, and Albert gets the lobe of his ear shot off in consequence. It is to no purpose, they come back without him.

It is easy to understand what he cries. At first he called only for help -- the second night he must have had some delirium, he talked with his wife and children, we often detected the name Elise. Today he merely weeps. By evening the voice dwindles to a croaking. But it persists still through the whole night. We hear it so distinctly because the wind blows toward our line. In the morning when we suppose he must already have long gone to his rest, there comes across to us one last gurgling rattle.

427

The days are hot and the dead lie unburied. We cannot fetch them all in, if we did we should not know what to do with them. The shells will bury them. Many have their bellies swollen up like balloons. They hiss, belch, and make movements. The gases in them make noises.

The sky is blue and without clouds. In the evening it grows sultry and the heat rises from the earth. When the wind blows toward us it brings the smell of blood, which is very heavy and sweet. This deathly exhalation from the shellholes seems to be a mixture of chloroform and putrefaction, and fills us with nausea and retching. .

* * * * * *

Although we need reinforcement, the recruits give us almost more trouble than they are worth. They are helpless in this grim fighting area, they fall like flies. Modern trench-warfare demands knowledge and experience; a man must have a feeling for the contours of the ground, an ear for the sound and character of the shells, must be able to decide beforehand where they will drop, how they will burst, and how to shelter from them.

The young recruits of course know none of these things. They get killed simply because they hardly can tell shrapnel from high-explosive, they are mown down because they are listening anxiously to the roar of the big coalboxes falling in the rear, and miss the light, piping whistle of the low spreading daisy-cutters. They flock together like sheep instead of scattering, and even the wounded are shot down like hares by the airmen.

Their pale turnip faces, their pitiful clenched hands, the fine courage of these poor devils, the desperate charges and attacks made by the poor brave wretches, who are so terrified that they dare not cry out loudly, but with battered chests, with torn bellies, arms and legs only whimper softly for their mothers and cease as soon as one looks at them.

Their sharp, downy, dead faces have the awful expressionlessness of dead children.

It brings a lump into the throat to see how they go over, and run and fall. A man would like to spank them, they are so stupid, and to take them by the arm and lead them away from here where they have no business to be. They wear grey coats and trousers and boots, but for most of them the uniform is far too big, it hangs on their limbs, their shoulders are too narrow, their bodies too slight; no uniform was ever made to these childish measurements.

Between five and ten recruits fall to every old hand. . . .

* * * * * *

Bombardment, barrage, curtain-fire, mines, gas, tanks, machine-guns, hand-grenades -- words, words, but they hold the horror of the world.

Our faces are encrusted, our thoughts are devastated, we are weary to death; when the attack comes we shall have to strike many of the men with our fists to waken them and make them come with us -- our eyes are burnt, our hands are torn, our knees bleed, our elbows are raw.

How long has it been? Weeks -- months -- years? Only days. We see time pass in the colorless faces of the dying, we cram food into us, we run, we throw, we shoot, we kill, we lie about, we are feeble and spent, and nothing supports us but the knowledge that there are still feebler, still more spent, still more helpless ones there who, with staring eyes, look upon us as gods that escape death many times.

We show them how to take cover from aircraft, how to simulate a dead man when one is overrun in an attack, how to time hand-grenades so that they explode half a second before hitting the ground; we teach them to fling themselves into holes as quick as lightening before the shells with instantaneous fuses; we show them how to clean up a trench with a handful of bombs; we explain the difference between the fuse-length of the enemy bombs and our own; we put them wise to the sound of gas shells; -- show them all the tricks that can save them from death.

They listen, they are docile -- but when it begins again, in their excitement they do everything wrong.

Haie Westhus drags off with a great wound in his back through which the lung pulses at every breath. I can only press his hand; "It's all up, Paul," he groans and he bites his arm because of the pain.

We see men living with their skulls blown open; we see soldiers run with their two feet cut off, they stagger on their splintered stumps into the next shell-hole; a lance-corporal crawls a mile and a half on his hands dragging his smashed knee after him; another goes to the dressing station and over his clasped hands bulge his intestines; we see men without mouths, without jaws, without faces; we find one man who has held the artery of his arm in his teeth for two hours in order not to bleed to death. The sun goes down, night comes, the shells whine, life is at an end. Still the little piece of convulsed earth in which we lie is held. We have yielded no more than a few hundred yards of it as a prize to the enemy. But on every yard there lies a dead man.

Zimmermann Telegram, 1917 CE

By 1917, the European nations had been fighting an epically deadly and destructive war for three years. Both the Central and Allied powers neared exhaustion as neither side had a clear advantage in this war of attrition. Both sides desperately needed something to sustain them. The Germans' best hope for victory was the intensive use of their u-boats to disable the powerful Allied navy. And the Allied Powers hoped that the United States might become involved on their side. But in 1917, the United States remained neutral. In 1916 Woodrow Wilson was elected President for a second term, largely because of the slogan "He kept us out of war." But in 1917, events unfolded that made continued American neutrality impossible.

In January of 1917, British code-breakers intercepted and deciphered a telegram from German Foreign Minister Arthur Zimmermann to the German Minister to Mexico, offering United States territory to Mexico in return for joining the German cause.

In February of 1917, Britain released the Zimmerman telegram to Wilson. On April 6, 1917, the United States Congress formally declared war on Germany and its allies. The Zimmerman telegram clearly had helped draw the United States into the war and thus changed the course of history. Below is the text of the short but war-altering message from Germany.

We intend to begin on the first of February unrestricted submarine warfare. We shall endeavor in spite of this to keep the United States of America neutral. In the event of this not succeeding, we make Mexico a proposal or alliance on the following basis: make war together, make peace together, generous financial support and an understanding on our part that Mexico is to reconquer the lost territory in Texas, New Mexico, and Arizona. The settlement in detail is left to you. You will inform the President of the above most secretly as soon as the outbreak of war with the United States of America is certain and add the suggestion that he should, on his own initiative, invite Japan to immediate adherence and at the same time mediate between Japan and ourselves. Please call the President's attention to the fact that the ruthless employment of our submarines now offers the prospect of compelling England in a few months to make peace." Signed, ZIMMERMANN.

Russian Social Democratic Labour (Bolshevik) Party Platform, 1903 CE

Reading and Discussion Questions

1. Summarize the global state of affairs for workers as described in the first paragraph below.
2. What is the particular state of affairs for workers in Russia? What is the political and economic situation there?
3. What rights does the RSDLP promise that their new constitution will include?
4. What types of things are included in the party's list of demands? Summarize six demands.
5. How does the Party propose to go about making these changes in Russia? What is their plan of action?
6. To what extent do the ideals of the Bolshevik party sound similar to the goals of the French Revolution? In what ways are they different?

By 1917, the Romanov Dynasty had been the ruling family in Russia for almost 300 years. Like other absolute monarchies, the Romanovs ruled with a heavy hand and the lives of average Russians were hard. During the Industrial Age, the suffering of the masses in Russia intensified because Russia was determined to catch up with other industrialized nations at impossible speed, fearing what would happen if they did not. The burdens faced by Russia's industrialized labor force was, therefore, extreme. By 1900, there was widespread discontent among what Karl Marx called the Proletariat in Russia. Marxist ideology and the call for a revolution of the Proletariat was more popular in Russia than anywhere else in the world within a few years of the release of the Communist Manifesto. In 1905, the Russian working class staged it first unsuccessful revolution against the Romanov monarchy. The workers rose up in widespread protests which seemed, at first, to have had the desired result of winning them more representation in government. Bending to political pressure to end the revolts, Czar Nicholas II issued a document called the October Manifesto which promised many reforms to the Russian government including the creating of a Russian parliament called the Duma. With law and order reestablished, Nicholas II failed to make good on many of the promised reforms and dismissed the Duma in 1907. Discontent was once again rampant across Russia.

Political discontent continued to brew in Russia but the outbreak of World War I diverted the attention of many revolutionaries, who were called to fight for Russia in the war. World War I was disastrous for the Russian military which suffered the highest casualties of any nation fighting in the war. But the situation for civilians across Russia was even worse, because all available food and resources were sent to the war effort. Hunger and misery were causing the Russian people to grow more and more desperate. Since the early 1900s, Marxist groups had been organizing for a day when they would make real the Proletariat revolution that Marx had envisioned. 1917 would become the time to make that dream a reality.

The dominant faction of Marxists in Russia were called Bolsheviks. They had begun organizing into a political party in 1898 and had became the dominant revolutionary party in 1903. In that year, they solidified their party principles and their vision for the future of Russia. The Bolsheviks were created and led by a man named Vladimir Lenin. Lenin and the Bolsheviks waited patiently for the time to be right for their Marxist revolution, taking a backseat in the events of 1905. Feeding off the discontent creatd by World War I, Lenin and the Bolshevik party sensed that 1917 was the right time for their revolution.

The event known as the Russian Revolution of 1917 was actually two revolutions rolled into one. There was the February Revolution, which was an uprising of the Russian proletariat that resulted in the abdication of Czar Nicholas II and the creation of a new provisional government in Russia. Then there was the Bolshevik (or October) Revolution which happened in October of that same year. During the Bolshevik Revolution the provisional government was also overthrown and Lenin and his supporters created the Russian Socialist Federative Soviet Republic, the world's first socialist government. This new government would later become the Union of Soviet Socialist Republics or the U.S.S.R. Below is the document upon which the Bolshevik party was founded. It outlines the goals they envisioned for their new government as well as the means they planned to use to achieve those goals. They made no secret of the fact that a violent revolution was likely.

Considering itself one of the detachments of the universal army of the proletariat, Russian social democracy is pursuing the same ultimate goal, as that for which the social democrats in other countries are striving. This ultimate goal is determined by the nature of contemporary bourgeois society and by the course of its development. The main characteristic of such a society is production for the market on the basis of capitalist production relations, whereby the largest and most important part of the means of production and exchange of commodities belongs to a numerically small class of people, while the overwhelming majority of the population consists of proletarians and semi-proletarians who, by their economic conditions, are forced either continuously or periodically to sell their labor power; that is, to hire themselves out to the capitalists, and by their toil to create the incomes of the upper classes of society. The entrepreneurs utilize to an ever greater extent woman and child labour in the process of production and exchange of commodities.

Such a state of affairs in the bourgeois countries, as well as the ever growing competition among those countries on the world market, render the sale of goods which are produced in greater and greater quantities ever more difficult. Overproduction, which manifests itself in more or less acute industrial crises - which in turn are followed by more or less protracted periods of industrial stagnation - is the inevitable consequence of the development of the productive forces in bourgeois society. Crises and periods of industrial stagnation, in their turn, tend to impoverish still further the small producers, to increase still further the dependence of hired labour upon capital and to accelerate still further the relative, and sometimes the absolute, deterioration of the condition of the working class.

With the growth and development of all these [abuses] inherent in bourgeois society, there grows simultaneously dissatisfaction with the present order among the toiling and exploited masses; the number and solidarity of the proletarians increases, and their struggle against the exploiters sharpens.

By replacing private with public ownership of the means of production and exchange, by introducing planned organization in the public process of production so that the well being and the many sided development of all members of society may be ensured, the social revolution of the proletariat will abolish the division of society into classes and thus emancipate all oppressed humanity, and will terminate all forms of exploitation of one part of society by another.

A necessary condition for this social revolution is the dictatorship of the proletariat; that is, the conquering by the proletariat of such political power as would enable it to crush any resistance offered by the exploiters. In its effort to make the proletariat capable of fulfilling its great historical mission, the party of the working class calls upon all levels of the toiling and exploited population to join its ranks insofar as they accept the point of view of the proletariat.

In Russia, where capitalism has already become the dominant mode of production, there are still preserved numerous vestiges of the old pre-capitalist order, when the toiling masses were serfs of the landowners, the state, or the sovereign. Greatly hampering economic progress, these old institutions interfere with the many-sided development of the class struggle of the proletariat, help to preserve and strengthen the most barbarous forms of exploitation by the state and the propertied classes of the millions of peasants, and thus keep the whole people in darkness and subjection. The most outstanding among these relics of the past, the mightiest bulwark of all this barbarism, is the tsarist autocracy. By its very name it is bound to be hostile to any social movement, and cannot but be bitterly opposed to all the aspirations of the proletariat toward freedom.

The Russian Social Democratic Labour Party therefore sets as its immediate political task the overthrow of the tsarist autocracy and its replacement by a democratic republic whose constitution would guarantee:

1. The sovereignty of the people; i.e., the concentration of the supreme power of the state in a unicameral legislative assembly composed of representatives of the people.
2. Universal, equal and direct suffrage for all citizens, male and female, who have reached the age of twenty;...a secret ballot in these elections....
3. Broad local self-government; regional self-government for localities with special conditions of life or a particular make-up of the population.
4. Inviolability of person and dwelling.
5. Unrestricted freedom of conscience, speech, press and assembly; the right to strike and to form trade unions.
6. Freedom of movement and occupation.
7. Elimination of class privileges and the complete equality of all regardless of sex, religion, race or nationality.
8. The right of any person to obtain an education in their native language...;
9. The right of every person through normal channels to prosecute before a jury any official.

433

10. The replacement of the standing army by the general arming of the population (i.e. the formation of a people's militia).
11. Separation of church and state, and of school and church.
12. Free and compulsory general or vocational education for all children of both sexes up to the age of sixteen; provision by the state of food, clothes, and school supplies for poor children.

As a fundamental condition for the democratization of our national economy, the RSDRP demands the abolition of all indirect taxation and the introduction of a graduated tax on incomes and inheritances.

To protect the working class from physical and moral degradation, and also to develop its capacity for the liberation struggle; the party demands:

1. Limitation of the working day to eight hours for all hired workers. ...
2. A complete ban on overtime work.
3. A ban on night work...with the exception of those (industries) which absolutely require it for technical reasons....
4. The prohibition of the employment of children of school age. . . .
5. A ban on the use of female labor in occupations which are harmful to the health of women; maternity leave from four weeks prior to childbirth until six weeks after birth....
6. The provision of nurseries for infants and young children in all ...enterprises employing women.
7. State insurance for workers against old age and partial or complete disability through a special fund supported by a tax on capitalists....
8. The appointment of an adequate number of factory inspectors in all branches of the economy....
9. The supervision by organs of local self-government, together with elected workers' representatives, of sanitary conditions in factory housing....
10. The establishment of properly organized health inspection in all enterprises...free medical services for workers at the employer's expense, with wages to be paid during time of illness.
11. Establishment of criminal responsibility of employers for violations of laws intended to protect workers.
12. The establishment in all branches of the economy of industrial tribunals made up equally of representatives of the workers and of management.
13. Imposition upon the organs of local self-government of the duty of establishing employment agencies (labor exchanges) to deal with the hiring of local and non-local labor in all branches of industry, and participation of workers' and employers' representatives in their administration.

In striving to achieve its immediate goals, the RSDRP will support any opposition or revolutionary movement directed against the existing social and political order in Russia. The RSDRP, for its part, is firmly convinced that the complete, consistent and lasting realization of these political and social changes can only be achieved through the overthrow of the autocracy and the convocation of a constituent assembly freely elected by the entire nation.

Vladimir Lenin, Call to Power Speech, 1917 CE

Reading and Discussion Questions
1. What is Lenin calling on the people of Russia to do in this speech?
2. Why does he have a sense of urgency in his message? "We must not wait!" he said. Why did he say this?

As the leader of the Bolshevik Party in Russia, Vladimir Lenin knew that 1917 was the moment for his party to seize control in Russia. The February Revolution of that year had ended the Romanov rule of Russia and left widespread chaos and uncertainty. Lenin saw that this chaos was the perfect moment for the revolution he and his party had been planning since 1903. Below is Lenin's famous "Call to Power" speech, in which he summoned all his supporters to rise in support of their cause.

The situation is critical in the extreme. In fact it is now absolutely clear that to delay the uprising would be fatal.

With all my might I urge comrades to realize that everything now hangs by a thread; that we are confronted by problems which are not to be solved by conferences or congresses (even congresses of Soviets), but exclusively by peoples, by the masses, by the struggle of the armed people.

The bourgeois onslaught show that we must not wait. We must at all costs, this very evening, this very night, arrest the government, having first disarmed the officer cadets, and so on. We must not wait! We may lose everything! Who must take power?

That is not important at present. Let the Revolutionary Military Committee do it, or "some other institution" which will declare that it will relinquish power only to the true representatives of the interests of the people, the interests of the army, the interests of the peasants, the interests of the starving.

All districts, all forces must be mobilized at once and must immediately send their delegations to the Revolutionary Military Committee and to the Central Committee of the Bolsheviks with the insistent demand that under no circumstances should power be left in the hands of the provisional government. . . .not under any circumstances; the matter must be decided without fail this very evening, or this very night.

History will not forgive revolutionaries for procrastinating when they could be victorious today (and they certainly will be victorious today), while they risk losing much tomorrow, in fact, the risk losing everything.

The seizure of power is the business of the uprising; its political purpose will become clear after the seizure....It would be an infinite crime on the part of the revolutionaries were they to let the chance slip, knowing that the salvation of the revolution, the offer of peace, the salvation of Petrograd, salvation from famine, the transfer of the land to the peasants depend upon them.

The government is tottering. It must be given the death-blow at all costs.

Woodrow Wilson, *Fourteen-Point Plan for Peace*, 1918 CE

<u>Reading and Discussion Questions</u>
1. What are the Fourteen Points and what was the goal of President Wilson's Fourteen Point Plan?
2. Summarize four points from the Fourteen Points that you believe are consistent with President Wilson's goal.
3. Do you think this document is fair in its treatment of the countries that fought in World War I? Why or why not?

Woodrow Wilson (1856-1924) regarded himself as the personal representative of the people of the United States. "No one but the President," he said, "seems to be expected... to look out for the general interests of the country."

He was nominated for President at the 1912 Democratic Convention and campaigned on a program called the New Freedom, which stressed individualism and states' rights. In the three-way election he received only 42 percent of the popular vote but an overwhelming electoral vote and became president in 1912. By virtue of the slogan "he kept us out of war," Wilson narrowly won re-election in 1916. But after the election Wilson concluded that America could not remain neutral in World War I. On April 2, 1917, he asked Congress for a declaration of war on Germany.

American involvement in the war slowly tipped the balance in favor of the Allies. Wilson went before Congress in January 1918 to reveal his plan to end the war—The Fourteen Point Plan for Peace. He believed his plan would help to prevent future conflicts of such magnitude as World War I. One of the centerpieces of his proposal was the creation of "A general association of nations... affording mutual guarantees of political independence and territorial integrity to great and small states alike." After the Germans signed the Armistice in November 1918, Wilson went to Paris to try to build an enduring peace. Negotiations in Paris did not go the way Wilson had hoped and much of what he supported in his Fourteen Points would not be included in the Treaty of Versailles that was presented to Germany in 1919.

Gentlemen of the Congress...

It will be our wish and purpose that the processes of peace, when they are begun, shall be absolutely open and that they shall involve and permit henceforth no secret understandings of any kind. The day of conquest and aggrandizement is gone by; so is also the day of secret covenants entered into in the interest of particular governments and likely at some unlooked-for moment to upset the peace of the world.

It is this happy fact, now clear to the view of every public man whose thoughts do not still linger in an age that is dead and gone, which makes it possible for every nation whose purposes are consistent with justice and the peace of the world to avow now or at any other time the objects it has in view.

We entered this war because violations of right had occurred which touched us to the quick and made the life of our own people impossible unless they were corrected and the world secured once for all against their recurrence. What we demand in this war, therefore, is nothing peculiar to ourselves.

It is that the world be made fit and safe to live in; and particularly that it be made safe for every peace-loving nation which, like our own, wishes to live its own life, determine its own institutions, be assured of justice and fair dealing by the other peoples of the world as against force and selfish aggression. All the peoples of the world are in effect partners in this interest, and for our own part we see very clearly that unless justice be done to others it will not be done to us. The program of the world's peace, therefore, is our program; and that program, the only possible program, as we see it, is this:

I. Open covenants of peace, openly arrived at, after which there shall be no private international understandings of any kind but diplomacy shall proceed always frankly and in the public view.

II. Absolute freedom of navigation upon the seas, outside territorial waters, alike in peace and in war, except as the seas may be closed in whole or in part by international action for the enforcement of international covenants.

III. The removal, so far as possible, of all economic barriers and the establishment of an equality of trade conditions among all the nations consenting to the peace and associating themselves for its maintenance.

IV. Adequate guarantees given and taken that national armaments will be reduced to the lowest point consistent with domestic safety.

V. A free, open-minded, and absolutely impartial adjustment of all colonial claims, based upon a strict observance of the principle that in determining all such questions of sovereignty the interests of the populations concerned must have equal weight with the equitable claims of the government whose title is to be determined.

VI. The evacuation of all Russian territory and such a settlement of all questions affecting Russia as will secure the best and freest cooperation of the other nations of the world in obtaining for her an unhampered and unembarrassed opportunity for the independent determination of her own political development and national policy and assure her of a sincere welcome into the society of free nations under institutions of her own choosing; and, more than a welcome, assistance also of every kind that she may need and may herself desire. The treatment accorded Russia by her sister nations in the months to come will be the acid test of their good will, of their comprehension of her needs as distinguished from their own interests, and of their intelligent and unselfish sympathy.

VII. Belgium, the whole world will agree, must be evacuated and restored, without any attempt to limit the sovereignty which she enjoys in common with all other free nations. No other single act will serve as this will serve to restore confidence among the nations in the laws which they have themselves set and determined for the government of their relations with one another. Without this healing act the whole structure and validity of international law is forever impaired.

VIII. All French territory should be freed and the invaded portions restored, and the wrong done to France by Prussia in 1871 in the matter of Alsace-Lorraine, which has unsettled the peace of the world for nearly fifty years, should be righted, in order that peace may once more be made secure in the interest of all.

IX. A readjustment of the frontiers of Italy should be effected along clearly recognizable lines of nationality.

X. The peoples of Austria-Hungary, whose place among the nations we wish to see safeguarded and assured, should be accorded the freest opportunity of autonomous development.

XI. Rumania, Serbia, and Montenegro should be evacuated; occupied territories restored; Serbia accorded free and secure access to the sea; and the relations of the several Balkan states to one another determined by friendly counsel along historically established lines of allegiance and nationality; and international guarantees of the political and economic independence and territorial integrity of the several Balkan states should be entered into.

XII. The Turkish portions of the present Ottoman Empire should be assured a secure sovereignty, but the other nationalities which are now under Turkish rule should be assured an undoubted security of life and an absolutely unmolested opportunity of an autonomous development, and the Dardanelles should be permanently opened as a free passage to the ships and commerce of all nations under international guarantees.

XIII. An independent Polish state should be erected which should include the territories inhabited by indisputably Polish populations, which should be assured a free and secure access to the sea, and whose political and economic independence and territorial integrity should be guaranteed by international covenant.

XIV. A general association of nations must be formed under specific covenants for the purpose of affording mutual guarantees of political independence and territorial integrity to great and small states alike.

In regard to these essential rectifications of wrong and assertions of right we feel ourselves to be intimate partners of all the governments and peoples associated together against the Imperialists. We cannot be separated in interest or divided in purpose. We stand together until the end.

438

Georges Clemenceau, *Grandeur of Misery and Victory*, 1930 CE

Reading and Discussion Questions
1. What arguments does Clemenceau make for why the Germans were responsible for World War I?
2. Why does Clemenceau mention the Manifesto of the Ninety-Three? Why does he call their document "nothing but denials"?
3. Summarize Clemenceau's main idea here? What are his concrete proofs that Germany caused the war? What are his general criticisms of Germany and German culture?

Woodrow Wilson's Fourteen Point Plan for Peace promised that all sides who fought in World War I would be treated fairly if everyone would agree to end the bloodshed. He promised no blame and collective rebuilding. But these promises were very different than the reality of what Germany received from the Treaty of Versailles in 1919. The question must be asked, "What went wrong?" Why had the spirit of forgiveness and restoration not been honored at the Paris Peace Conference after the war. There are many answers to that question but the dominant reason why things changed so radically was that France wanted to make Germany pay for what it had done to France both in World War I and in the years leading up to the war. France wanted revenge and the security of knowing they would never be threatened by Germany again. Remember, almost all the fighting of the war had taken place in France; its industries and farmlands were destroyed, and millions of French men, women and children had perished. The French negotiator at the Paris Peace Conference was French Premier George Clemenceau, who was called "the Tiger." He had no patience for Wilson's rhetoric about forgiveness and shared blame since the U.S. had not had to suffer the way France had suffered. Ultimately, Clemenceau prevailed and Germany was treated very harshly by the Treaty of Versailles. George Clemenceau talked about his deep hatred and distrust of Germany in his book, Grandeur and Misery of Victory which was written a decade after the Paris Peace Conference.

For the catastrophe of 1914 the Germans are responsible. Only a professional liar would deny this....

What after all is this war, prepared, undertaken, and waged by the German people, who lung aside every scruple of conscience to let it loose, hoping for a peace of enslavement under the yoke of a militarism destructive of all human dignity? It is simply the continuance, the recrudescence, of those never-ending acts of violence by which the first savage tribes carried but their depredations with all the resources of barbarism. The means improve with the ages. The ends remain the same....

Germany, in this matter, was unfortunate enough to allow herself (in spite of her skill at dissimulation) to be betrayed into an excess of candor by her characteristic tendency to go to extremes. Germany above everything! That, and nothing less, is what she asks, and when once her demand is satisfied she will let you enjoy a peace under the yoke.

Not only does she make no secret of her aim, but the intolerable arrogance of the German aristocracy, the servile good nature of the intellectual and the scholar, the gross vanity of the most competent leaders in industry conspire to shatter throughout the world all the time-honoured traditions of individual, as well as international, dignity...

On November 11, 1918, the fighting ceased. It is not I who will dispute the German soldier's qualities of endurance. But he had been promised afresh and frolicsome war, and for four years he had been pinned down between the anvil and the hammer. . . .

Our defeat would have resulted in a relapse of human civilization into violence and bloodshed. . . .

Outrages against human civilization are in the long run defeated by their own excess, and thus I discern in the peculiar mentality of the German soldier, with his "Germany Above Everything" attitude the cause of the premature exhaustion that brought him to beg for an armistice before the French soldier, who was fighting for his independence....

And what is this "Germanic civilization," this monstrous explosion of the will to power, which threatens openly to do away entirely with the diversities established by many evolutions, to set in their place the implacable mastery of a race whose lordly part would be to substitute itself, by force of arms, for all national developments? We need only read [General Friedrich von] Bernhardi's famous pamphlet Our Future, in which it is alleged that Germany sums up within herself, as the historian Treitschke asserts, the greatest manifestation of human supremacy, and finds herself condemned, by her very greatness, either to absorb all nations in herself or to return to nothingness.... Ought we not all to feel menaced in our very vitals by this mad doctrine of universal Germanic Supremacy over England, France, America, and every other country? ...

What document more suitable to reveal the direction of "German culture" than the famous manifesto of the Ninety-Three super intellectuals of Germany,' issued to justify the bloodiest and the least excusable of military aggressions against the great centers of civilization? At that moment ... violated Belgium lay beneath the heel of the malefactor (October 1914) ... [and German troops destroyed great historical buildings and burned down ... libraries. It would need a whole book to tell of the infamous treatment inflicted upon civilians, to reckon up chose who were shot down, or put to death, or deported, or condemned to forced labor.,. . .

Well, this was the hour chosen by German intellectuals to make themselves heard. Let all the nations give ear! ...

... Their learning made of them merely Germans better than all others qualified to formulate, on their own account, the extravagances of Germanic arrogance. The only difference is that they speak louder than the common people, those docile automatons. The fact is that they really believe themselves to be the representatives of a privileged "culture" that sets them above the errors of the human race, and confers on them the prerogative of a superior power....

The whole document is nothing but denials without the support of a single proof. "It is not trite that Germany wanted the War." [Kaiser] William II had for years been "mocked at by his adversaries of today on account of his unshakable love of peace." They neglect to tell us whence they got this lie.

The "intellectuals" take their place in public opinion as the most ardent propagandists of the thesis which makes Germany the very model of the "chosen people." One such man wrote, "Germany has reached a higher stage of civilization than the other peoples, and the result of the War will be an organization of Europe under German leadership."

I have sometimes penetrated into the sacred cave of the Germanic cult, which is, as every one knows, the Bierhaus (beer hall). A great aisle of massive humanity where there accumulate, amid the fumes of tobacco and beer, the popular rumblings of a nationalism upheld by the sonorous brasses blaring to the heavens the supreme voice of Germany, "Deutschland über alles!" Men, women, and children, all petrified in reverence before the divine stoneware pot, brows furrowed with irrepressible power, eyes lost in a dream of infinity, mouths twisted by the intensity of will-power, drink in long draughts the celestial hope of vague expectations. There you have the ultimate frame work of an old but childish race.

Treaty of Versailles, 1919 CE

Reading and Discussion Questions
1. Explain four provisions of the Treaty of Versailles that are different than specific provisions of the Fourteen Points.
2. Why were the terms of the Treaty of Versailles different than those promised by the Fourteen Points?
3. How did Germany react to the Treaty of Versailles? Is their reaction justified? Explain.

On June 28,1919, the Allied powers presented the Treaty of Versailles to Germany for signature. The following are the key territorial and political clauses, which are in some cases very different than what had been promised to Germany prior to the Paris Peace Conference. The Treaty of Versailles was the document that resulted from the Paris Peace Conference that specifically dealt with Germany. Every other country that fought with the Central Powers had its own treaty, including the Treaty of Saint-Germain for Austria and the Treaty of Sevre for the Ottoman Empire. None were as damaging as the Treaty of Versailles was for Germany.

Article 22. Certain communities formerly belonging to the Turkish Empire have reached a stage of development where their existence as independent nations can be provisionally recognized subject to the rendering of administrative advice and assistance by a Mandatory [i.e., a Western power] until such time as they are able to stand alone. The wishes of these communities must be a principal consideration in the selection of the Mandatory.

441

Article 42. Germany is forbidden to maintain or construct any fortifications either on the left bank of the Rhine or on the right bank to the west of a line drawn 50 kilometers to the East of the Rhine.

Article 45. As compensation for the destruction of the coal mines in the north of France and as part payment towards the total reparation due from Germany for the damage resulting from the war, Germany cedes to France in full and absolute possession, with exclusive right of exploitation, unencumbered and free from all debts and charges of any kind, the coal mines situated in the Saar Basin....

Article 49. Germany renounces in favor of the League of Nations, in the capacity of trustee, the government of the territory defined above. At the end of fifteen years from the coming into force of the present Treaty the inhabitants of the said territory shall be called upon to indicate the sovereignty under which they desire to be placed.

Alsace-Lorraine. The High Contracting Parties, recognizing the moral obligation to redress the wrong done by Germany in 1871 both to the rights of France and to the wishes of the population of Alsace and Lorraine, which were separated from their country in spite of the solemn protest of their representatives at the Assembly of Bordeaux, agree upon the following....

Article 51. The territories which were ceded to Germany in accordance with the Preliminaries of Peace signed at Versailles on February 26, 1871, and the Treaty of Frankfort of May 10, 1871, are restored to French sovereignty as from the date of the Armistice of November 11, 1918.

The provisions of the Treaties establishing the delimitation of the frontiers before 1871 shall be restored.

Article 119. Germany renounces in favor of the Principal Allied and Associated Powers all her rights and titles over her overseas possessions.

Article 156. Germany renounces, in favour of Japan, all her rights, title and privileges . . . which she acquired in virtue of the Treaty concluded by her with China on March 6, 1898, and of all other arrangements relative to the Province of Shantung.

Article 159. The German military forces shall be demobilised and reduced as prescribed hereinafter

Article 160. By a date which must not be later than March 31, 1920, the German Army must not comprise more than seven divisions of infantry and three divisions of cavalry. After that date the total number of effectives in the Army of the States constituting Germany must not exceed 100,000 men, including officers and establishments of depots. The Army shall be devoted exclusively to the maintenance of order within the territory and to the control of the frontiers. The total effective strength of officers, including the personnel of staffs, whatever their composition, must not exceed four thousand....

Article 231. The Allied and Associated Governments affirm and Germany accepts the responsibility of Germany and her allies for causing all the loss and damage to which the Allied and Associated Governments and their nationals have been subjected as a consequence of the war imposed upon them by the aggression of Germany and her allies.

Article 232. The Allied and Associated Governments recognize that the resources of Germany are not adequate, after taking into account permanent diminutions of such resources which will result from other provisions of the present Treaty, to make complete reparation for all such loss and damage.

The Allied and Associated Governments, however, require, and Germany undertakes, that she will make compensation for all damage done to the civilian population of the Allied and Associated Powers and to their property during the period of the belligerency of each as an Allied or Associated Power against Germany.

CHAPTER 16—
TOTALITARIANISM AND WORLD WAR II
(1920 to 1945 CE)

<u>GUIDING QUESTIONS</u>
- In what ways is World War II a direct result of World War I?
- What is Fascism? Why and where was it emerging by the 1920s?
- What was the role of Japan in the Age of Imperialism and how does this relate to its involvement in World War II?
- How did Hitler win power in Germany? Was anyone concerned about his rise to power in the years before World War II? Explain.
- How does genocide happen? What are the steps and how did the Nazis execute each of these steps?
- Analyze Gustave Le Bons' *The Crowd* in relation to the rise of the Nazi party in Germany.
- What was the role of Winston Churchill in World War II? Would the outcome of the war have been different, in your opinion, without Churchill? Explain.

The world in 1919 was changed forever by the events of World War I. Anger, heartbreak and resentment permeated every nation that participated in The Great War and millions prayed that another human catastrophe would never happen again. World War I was called "the war to end all wars," as you have learned, but that lofty hope was not to be a reality. World War I actually created many more problems than it solved and it sowed the seeds of a much greater conflict, which would erupt a short 20 years after the Paris Peace Conference in 1919. This conflict was World War II and more than 80 million people died in this conflict in a span of six years from 1939 to 1945.

It is important to pause a moment here and look at the impact of anger, hatred and the need for revenge. We all know these are traits that get us into trouble in our own lives but they have equally catastrophic consequences when they govern the decisions and actions of nations. The devastation of World War I was unimaginable, especially in France, and it was natural and appropriate for the French people to be enraged and emotionally crushed by the massive loss of life, property and hope in humanity. It was normal to feel a need for revenge and for someone to right the wrongs that happened during World War I. This is probably why the other negotiators at the Paris Peace Conference bent to the demands of the French to "make Germany pay." Someone had to pay, after all. Someone had to take responsibility for what had happened, right? Because if people could understand who caused this disaster, another disaster might be avoidable. And people could sleep better at night, knowing there was someone, or some group who did this. The idea that World War I was a combination of confusing causes that had no clear "good guy" and "bad guy" was unsettling and did not give people the closure they needed to begin healing from the horrors of the Great War. And so Germany was made to pay, and she was asked to pay much more than she was capable of. And this decision to make Germany pay, motivated by vengeance and hatred, had the domino effect of causing Germany, too, to want vengeance for what was done to them in 1919.

The Treaty of Versailles was viewed by the German people as an unforgivable betrayal. Germany agreed to surrender in the war in 1918 based on the promise of Woodrow Wilson's *Fourteen Points*. That document promised that all the nations that fought in the war would rebuild after the war. It promised that all nations would pay to fix the damage and it promised that all nations would decrease their militaries so that war on the scale of World War I would not happen again. Finally it promised, or at least implied, that no one county would assume all the blame for the war. In good faith, the German government surrendered and waited. In 1919, Germany was not allowed to participate in the peace talks at Versailles, but they were hopeful that The Big Three—France, Britain and the United States---would keep their word and honor all the terms of the *Fourteen Points* in their final treaty. It is not hard to imagine their shock and dismay when the final terms of the Treaty of Versailles were unveiled. *Only* Germany was forced to dismantle its military. *Only* Germany was forced to pay a massive sum in reparations to the Allied nations. And most humiliating of all, *only* Germany had to take the blame for the war. At the beginning of the Paris Peace Conference, there was only one party—France—who was determined to avenge its treatment by Germany. By the end, Germany too was determined to get revenge for its insufferable humiliation. So it would seem that hatred and the need for vengeance only cause more hatred and the need for vengeance.

Before we turn out attention to Nazi Germany, let us first look at a broader phenomenon that was happening globally after World War I—the rise of totalitarian rulers. Hitler is the most notorious of the dictators of the 1920s and 30s but he was far from the only one. World War I had destabilized most of the nations of Europe and people across the European continent lived in misery. In Italy, this instability gave rise to their dictatorial leader, Benito Mussolini, who promised to make Italy great again and to restore the glory of the old Roman Empire to the Italian people. He promised to do this through the use of a military dictatorship known as Fascism. Fascism is defined as "a government ruled by a dictator who controls the lives of the people and in which people are not allowed to disagree with the government."

In Italy, Mussolini used an armed group of thugs called the Blackshirts to intimidate Italians into supporting him. He overthrew the government of Italy and established a Fascist state with himself at the head. Hitler and Mussolini saw the world in much the same way; a pie to be carved up by the strongest. Mussolini knew that Hitler and Germany were stronger than Italy so he decided that it would be wiser to be friends with Hitler than enemies. In 1939, the two men formed the Pact of Steel, an alliance which pledged mutual military support between Germany and Italy. Mussolini and Hitler agreed that from that time forward, the world would revolve around the Rome-Berlin axis. Ultimately the Pact of Steel would evolve into the Axis Powers, the alliance of nations siding with Hitler in World War II. The other key member of the Axis powers was the small pacific island of Japan.

Most Americans know that the U.S. was attacked at Pearl Harbor in Hawaii by the Japanese in 1941. Most Americans also know that World War II was mostly fought to defeat Hitler. Very few people understand how Germany and Japan are tied together or how that relationship came to be. In order to understand this connection, we must look at Japan's role in World War I and their treatment at the Paris Peace Conference. Japan played a small but important role on the side of the Allies in World War I. That's right. The nation that viciously attacked the American Naval Base at Pearl Harbor in 1941 was actually on our side in World War I. So why the switch?

445

As you read in the chapter on the Age of Imperialism, many nations of the world were expanding and building small empires to aid in industrialization. Japan was one of those countries. It learned from the defeat of the Chinese in the Opium Wars that it must industrialize rapidly or face the same fate as China—domination by a foreign power. Japan is a tiny island nation and so it created plans to build a colonial empire to win the resources it needed to stay competitive in the modern world. The name of its fledgling empire was the Greater East Asia Co-Prosperity Sphere. In the early 1900s, Japan was at war with Russia and China over territorial interests and conquered some small but important islands in the Pacific. When World War I erupted, Japan was asked by the Allied Powers to join in the war effort to help defend against German expansion in Asia, on the promise that if the Allies were successful, Japan would get German land holdings in Asia. Seeing the chance to expand its new empire, Japan agreed. At the Paris Peace Conference, Japan was given most of the territory it had been promised but it was snubbed in another way that it would not forget. The Japanese ambassador to the Conference asked Woodrow Wilson to add a statement of racial equality to the terms of the Treaty of Versailles and other peace settlements to end a feeling of racial bias against east Asians. Wilson flatly refused, signaling to the Japanese that Wilson and other western powers viewed Asians as very unequal. This snub had very negative consequences for European-Asian relations and would signal disaster for the United States.

By 1937, Japan was still pursuing its imperialist goals when it came under the leadership of the Japanese General Hideki Tôjô, who was made Prime Minister of Japan in that year. Tojo is considered a Fascist like Mussolini who believed that the best way to rule was through strength and conquest. Tojo took control of Japanese media and all information, as well as the military to achieve his goals of conquest. A year before Tojo assumed control, Japan had also entered into a pact with Germany, called the Anti-Comintern Pact, which was on it surface created to stop the spread of Communism from Soviet Russia. Its real purpose, though, was for Hitler to further align all those ambitious military dictators of the world into an alliance aimed at global conquest. As part of the anti-western, anti-democratic alliance with Germany (and later, Italy) Japan continued its expansion in the Pacific, with only one hurdle in its way--the United States. The U.S. also had interest in territory in the Pacific and imposed embargoes on Japan for its efforts in the Pacific and threatened to stop its expansion militarily. In an effort to prevent any intervention from the U.S. in Japan's empire-building, the Japanese military attacked the U.S. military base in Hawaii on December 7· of 1941. As you know, the attack of Pearl Harbor failed to from keep the United States out of Japanese affairs and instead prompted American involvement in World War II.

While most of the world feared Hitler by 1939, Hitler feared, and hated, Communists. Much of his alliance-building was aimed at containment of Soviet Russia and the spread of Communist ideals. Under the leadership of another radical totalitarian leader, Joseph Stalin, the USSR was embarking on a breakneck process of industrialization in order for it to be a match, militarily, to Germany. Like most other dictators in history, Stalin too emerged out of the wreckage of the Russian Revolution. Though Stalin is less famous than Hitler, he was equally deadly. During his reign of terror between 1922 and 1945, Stalin was responsible for the deaths of roughly 30 million Russians. Many of those died in the fighting of World War II but millions were killed in Stalin's forced labor camps or were mercilessly starved to death during

446

Stalin's failed attempt at reforming the agricultural system in Soviet Russia. Stalin and the Soviet Union fought on the side of the Allies in World War II, even though it was a Communist nation, because England, France and America feared Hitler more than they hated Communism. This would all change after 1945 and the beginning of the Cold War.

Of all the dictators, kings, czars and emperors in history whose names have become associated with evil and every possible abuse of power, Adolf Hitler is the man who most embodies the idea of a tyrant. Hitler was born in Austria in 1889 to a doting mother and a tyrannical and abusive father, Alois. Hitler was a misfit in his youth, and struggled to find his place in the world. He had dreams of being an artist but was unable to make a living pursuing art and found himself homeless in Vienna, Austria in his early twenties. He wrote in his memoir, *Mein Kampf*, that that period of hardship was the making of his hard character. Hitler left Austria in 1913 and moved to Munich, Germany. It was there that, upon hearing of Germany's declaration of war against the Allied Powers, Hitler volunteered for the German army.

Hitler's involvement in World War I was generally uneventful, as he was reportedly awkward and odd but also brave in the face of danger. He was promoted to Corporal in the German military and won five medals for his service in the war. In 1918, Hitler was temporarily blinded by mustard gas and was in a German military hospital when he got news of the German surrender in November of 1918. He wrote in *Mein Kampf* how he turned toward the wall and wept when he learned of the cowardice of the German government in surrendering. Germany had a new government in 1918 called the Weimar Republic, which was put in place after the forced abdication of Kaiser Wilhelm II of Germany as requirement for ending the war. Hitler's hatred was largely directed toward this new government in 1918. Of the Weimar Republic Hitler wrote "There followed terrible days and even worse nights – I knew that all was lost...in these nights hatred grew in me, hatred for those responsible for this deed. " It was only later that he would refocus his hatred toward the Jewish population, who he viewed as the underlying cause of the war and Germany's cowardly surrender.

In the war and its aftermath, Hitler seems to have found direction for the first time in his life. He continued to work for the German army after the war as a spy whose job it was to hunt down Marxists and Communists and report them. After the Bolshevik Revolution in Russia, there was widespread concern about the spread of Communism beyond the newly formed USSR. In 1919, Hitler was tipped off about a meeting of a group called the German Workers' Party, who were suspected Marxists. Hitler attended the meeting of the GWP, which consisted of about twenty angry men meeting in the basement of a beer hall in Munich. Much to Hitler's surprise, he agreed with what he heard at that meeting, which was a lot of angry rants and a lot of declarations about how to make Germany great again. Hitler even participated in the discussions at the meeting and was asked to come back for another meeting. He wrote about how he was unsure this unorganized group with no direction and no mission deserved his membership. But he also saw an opportunity in the lack of organization in the GWP. He finally decided to become a member of the group, writing, "This absurd little organization with its few members seemed to me to possess the one advantage that it had not frozen into an 'organization,' but left the individual opportunity for real personal activity. Here it was still possible to work, and the smaller the movement, the more readily it could be put into the proper form. Here, the content, the goal, and the road could still be determined..."

447

Hitler had found the vehicle which would make his rise to power possible. By 1920, Hitler had renamed the German Worker's Party to the National Socialist German Workers' Party, which is what we know as the Nazi Party today. He created a founding document for the group called the 25 Point Plan, which was his plan for how to resurrect Germany and restore its former glory. In this document are clear hints at Hitler's anti-semitic agenda as well as his plans to break every provision of the Treaty of Versailles. It was because of his defiance of the Treaty and the promise of better days that people flocked to Hitler and the Nazi party, first in the thousands and then in the millions.

Adolf Hitler is considered the essence of evil and the sole cause of World War II and the Holocaust. And while it is true that Hitler was the mastermind of the horrors of World War II, the Holocaust was largely conceived of and executed by the millions of followers of Adolf Hitler who were determined to make his vision a reality. Hitler's rise to power is an important tool for looking at what people do in desperate times and the dangers of mass hysteria or mob mentality. Much of the hysterical behavior in Nazi Germany in the 1930s was exactly what Gustave Le Bon warned about in his book, *The Crowd*, 25 years before the rise of the Nazis. In the beginning of the Nazi party, there were a few hundred members. By 1920, there were about 3000. Three years later, there were roughly 55,000 Nazi party members, almost all of whom had been drawn to the party by Hitler's charismatic presence and the depths of their own suffering.

The economic and political situation in Germany had grown dire by 1923, and Germans were desperate. In 1921, Germany was required to begin paying reparations to the Allies per the terms of the Treaty of Versailles. The total reparations owed was roughly $33 billion. At first, Germany brazenly refused to pay but the French army occupied a region of Germany in response to the defiance. Germany had no choice but to pay the debt that was owed, which sent the German economy into a tailspin. In 1920, the German currency, called the Deutschmark, was valued at roughly 4 Deutschmarks to the US dollar. As a result of the inflation caused by the debt payments, by 1922 the value had slipped to 400 Deutschmarks to the dollar. By 1923, it was 4 million Deutschmarks to the dollar. German currency was literally worthless. People lost their life savings, were unable to buy groceries or fuel for heat. Germans actually began burning Deutschmarks instead of firewood because that was the only way their money had any value at all. Germans were desperate. And Hitler saw his chance to seize on this desperation.

In 1923, Hitler unsuccessfully tried to overthrow the German government by force and was tried for treason. He was imprisoned for his unsuccessful revolution and it seemed as if his political career was over. As it turned out, 1923 actually marked a new beginning of Hitler's political power in Germany. Hitler's time in prison after the Beer Hall Putsch gave the rising tyrant time to solidify his principles and to learn valuable lessons about how to win and maintain power. During his imprisonment of less than a year, Hitler wrote his infamous autobiography, *Mein Kampf*, which means "my struggle." The book gives highly sensationalized details about Hitler's life and his supposed lifelong yearning to be leader of a unified and unconquerable German race. He also explained what he had learned about taking power and the foolishness in deciding to take it by force in 1923. He realized that using the system to beat the system was a much wiser way to rise to power. He said, "Instead of working to achieve power

448

by an armed coup we shall have to hold our noses and enter the Reichstag against the Catholic and Marxist deputies. If outvoting them takes longer than outshooting them, at least the results will be guaranteed by their own Constitution! Any lawful process is slow. But sooner or later we shall have a majority – and after that Germany." It seemed that Hitler had learned from all the most successful dictators in history that the way to win a position of absolute power over the people is to make them think that it was their idea to give it to you.

When Hitler was released from prison in 1924, the Nazi party seemed to have stagnated and would continue to have a limited membership over the next five years. But in 1929, the American stock market crashed which sent shock-waves through every economy in the world. No nation was more devastated by the Crash of 1929 than Germany. And no man benefitted more from it than Hitler. The German Deutschmark, already almost worthless before the crash, was not worth the paper it was printed on. American loans that had kept Germany afloat were being recalled and Germany went into an economic tailspin. Millions of Germans were unemployed. But Hitler promised a solution to all their problems as well as someone to blame for their immense suffering. These promises made the German people worship Hitler like a god.

In the next three years, Nazi Party membership skyrocketed from the tens of thousands to the millions. Hitler regularly spoke to crowds of 100,000 or more who hung on his every word adoringly. In 1932, Hitler and the Nazi Party won firm control of the government in Germany. In the 1932 Reichstag elections, the people voted and gave the Nazis 13,745,000 votes, 37% of the total, granting them 230 seats in the Reichstag. The Nazi Party was now the largest and most powerful political force in Germany. In that same year, Hitler was made Chancellor (Prime Minister) of Germany. Though Germany was still led by its President, Paul von Hindenberg, who was 85 years old in 1932, Hitler knew it was only a matter of time until he was the most powerful man in Germany.

Hitler's meteoric rise was not solely the result of his charismatic manner or the desperation of the German people. Hitler also had a powerful propaganda machine, led by a man named Joseph Goebbels, who controlled massive channels of information which began programming the way Germans thought. At first, Nazi propaganda was Pro-Hitler but it turned decidedly anti-Jewish by the height of Nazi power. Their propaganda machine was a horrifying instrument for programming generations of Germans to believe that Jews were the enemy and were to blame for all their suffering, from which Hitler promised to save them. In 1933, Hitler made his move to assume unchecked and absolute power in Germany. Hitler's personal bodyguard, called the SS, perpetrated acts of violence and vandalism in Germany and then used the propaganda machine to blame those acts on enemies of the Nazis. Hitler made speech after speech saying everything the German people wanted to hear. His armed thugs made clear that objection to Nazi authority would not be accepted. All these things he did in preparation for his final act on seizing power. In the spring of 1933, Hitler forced the German Reichstag to pass the Enabling Act, which Hitler claimed would enable him to deal with the unrest in Germany more effectively. What it actually did was empower Hitler and the Nazis to make laws without any input from the Reichstag. Hitler had total power in Germany by 1933 and would keep his iron-fisted control of Nazi Germany until 1945. He had used sinister but legal methods to win power in

449

Germany but the measures he would use to keep and increase his power would be too shocking to be believed until it was too late.

Between 1933 and 1936, Hitler and his Nazis systematically and ruthlessly stamped out any opposition or suspected opposition to their rule. Little by little, the Nazis began to marginalize and alienate Germany's Jewish population by requiring boycotts of Jewish businesses, burning Jewish books and infiltrating German minds with anti-Jewish propaganda. But the human tragedy known as the Holocaust, which resulted in the massacre of more than 11 million Jews and other "undesirables" in Europe, really began in 1935 with the passage of the Nuremberg Laws. This set of laws stripped German Jews of their citizenship and prevented marriage between Jews and non-Jews, among other things. Jews were labeled as "aliens" to the Nazi state and every piece of Nazi propaganda reinforced the idea that Jews were outsiders and enemies to German happiness and peace. The Holocaust was a genocide, or an effort aimed at the extermination of an entire group of people based on their race, ethnicity, religion or other shared trait. There are, according to the U.S. State Department, ten stages of genocide and murder is, surprisingly to most people, one of the final stages.

In order to commit genocide against a group of people, that group must first be made to seem less than human. The early stages in genocide all deal with reprogramming how people think about a targeted group by methods like classification, symbolization, discrimination and dehumanization. For the Nazis, they classified Jews as non-citizens or aliens. They symbolized them by requiring Jews to wear arm bands bearing the Star of David so everyone could recognize "the enemy." They discriminated by passing laws like the Nuremberg Laws, which denied Jews privileges in society. And they dehumanized Jews by depicting them in their ever-present propaganda as not human. Between 1933 and 1939, one of the primary functions of the Nazi regime was to turn every Nazi in Germany—all eight million of them—against the Jews. And it worked with terrible efficiency.

The next phases of genocide involve organization, preparation, mobilization and persecution of the targeted group once the mental reprogramming is complete. In order to prepare for "The Final Solution"—the German name for their plan to kill every Jew in Europe—Nazis separated Jews into ghettos, confiscated their homes and belongings and made them all but disappear from German society well before the mass killing began. They had hundreds of organizational meetings, documented thousands of hours of conversations about how to wipe out millions of people. Once Jews were confined into ghettos, they were relocated farther from German life into concentration camps, under the pretense of work. The great lie on the gates of Auschwitz death camp said, "Work will set you free." Only once all these methodical steps were completed did the mass killing of the Holocaust really begin. The concentration camp at Dachau was created in 1933, but it was mainly a camp for political prisoners and other enemies of the state. The Auschwitz death camp was not constructed until 1940, once it was clear that the German population would put up little resistance to the final massacre of the Jews. The brainwashing, intimidation and meticulous reprogramming of the German mind was so complete by 1940 that a plan too sick and inhuman to be true, became a reality. In the next 5 years, more than 3 million Jews would be killed in concentration camps like Auschwitz. Another 3 million were killed by mobile killing units or died in Jewish ghettos or during transport to concentration camps. It is incomprehensible to think that this nightmare was actually reality. It is even more difficult to understand that the massacre of six million Jews and another five million gypsies, intellectuals, disabled persons and Communists was not the most immediate cause for World War II.

Hitler was the clear cause of World War II but in the beginning it was his ambition, and not his anti-Semitism, that scared people the most. As far back as 1920, Hitler had promised to defy every provision of the Treaty of Versailles and this was the promise that won him a massive following. He made good on every promise he made in this regard, from remilitarizing Germany and ending war debt payments to France to reoccupying the Rhineland and creating a union with Austria. He took back territory that he believed belonged to "pure" Germans in small pieces and his conquests went virtually unnoticed. But Sir Winston Churchill noticed.

Winston Churchill was a First Lord of the Admiralty in the British Navy during World War I. After the war, he served in various government posts and as a member of the British Parliament. He spent many of his years in Parliament warning about the dangers that Hitler presented, long before anyone was willing to listen. His warnings about Hitler fell on deaf ears because Britain could not stand the idea of another war. But Churchill was right in every one of his concerns about Hitler, which the rest of Britain and the world, would only realize when it was too late to stop him.

Hitler took territory after territory in Europe without any response from his European neighbors. In fact, England and France gave him a piece of Czechoslovakia, even though it was not theirs to give. Only when Hitler conquered all of Czechoslovakia and invaded its eastern neighbor Poland did France, England and their allies say "Enough." Hitler invaded Poland on September 1st of 1939 and World War II began on September 3 when France, England, Australia and New Zealand declared war on Nazi Germany. By the end of 1940, the Nazis had conquered Belgium, the Netherlands, Denmark, Norway, Lithuania, Latvia, Estonia and France. It appeared that the Nazi war machine was unstoppable.

1940 was a watershed year for World War II and for the history of the world. In that year, of the great powers Britain stood alone against Hitler and Nazi dominion over Europe. Also in that year, Sir Winston Churchill became Prime Minister of Britain. Churchill had been right about Hitler and he seemed to understand him better than anyone. Hitler announced his plans for the conquest of Britain in 1940 and the belief that once Britain belonged to him, so did all the world. And he was probably right. If the British Isles fell to Hitler, so would Britain's global empire. Churchill's resolve to lead the British people in the monumental struggle against Hitler is one of the most inspiring, and terrifying, moments in history. The German air attack of Britain began in 1940 and continued for the next year. Britain was devastated by Nazi air raids but Hitler never successfully invaded Britain by land. This is a very, very hard thing to do as it turns out. Julius Caesar and Napoleon tried it before Hitler and they both failed. Hitler thought that, with his Blitzkrieg-style lightening war, he would be the man who would finally conquer Britain. He was wrong. Britain held out against Hitler until 1941 and sensing his invasion to be a failure, Hitler turned his attention to the defeat of Soviet Russia. This too, would be a failure and by 1942 Hitler was no longer making any forward progress toward his goals of conquest.

World War II raged on until 1945; but the tide began to turn in 1942, thanks in large part to the arrival of American soldiers in Europe. The United States entered the war after the Japanese attack on Pearl Harbor but to declare war on Japan was to declare war on all the Axis Powers, including Germany. By the end of the war, 16 million Americans fought in the Allied war effort, culminating in the massive invasion of Normandy on June 6 of 1944—D-Day. The biggest naval invasion in history led to the reconquering of France from Hitler and began the dismantling of everything that Hitler had so carefully and ruthlessly built. Less than one year late, Hitler would be dead by suicide. It would not be until the total liberation of all the territory that Hitler controlled that the true horrors of his rule would be fully known. All told, Hitler massacred more than 11 million men, women and children in the Holocaust. Another 40 million humans lost their lives in the fighting of World War II. When we add to those numbers the deaths from persecution in countries like Italy and Soviet Russia and from starvation and disease related to the war, roughly 80 million people died in a six year period between 1939 and 1945. Stop and think about that. That is 11.6 million people per year, which means nearly a million people a month. A million people a month. Stupefying. The human brain cannot fully grasp that level of loss. But we must try. In order to avoid a tragedy on the scale of World War II from *ever* happening again, we must face it, acknowledge it and learn from it. We must remember. Or we will forget.

Benito Mussolini, *What is Fascism?*, 1932 CE

Reading and Discussion Questions
1. What is the value of war, according to Mussolini?
2. What is "Fascism," as Mussolini describes it?
3. Why does Mussolini reject democracy?
4. How is Fascism different than Marxist Socialism, according to Mussolini?
5. How does expansion support Fascism, according to this document?
6. Why does Mussolini say Fascism is the right government for Italy at this time?

Benito Mussolini was the Fascist dictator of Italy from 1922 until 1943, and was known simply as "Il Duce" ("the leader") by his Italian subjects. Mussolini began his early political career as a socialist, blaming class struggle for the problems in Italy. By the end of World War I Mussolini began to drift to a much more radical and militaristic ideology, which would come to be known as Fascism. He became critical of socialism as a weak, even dead theory and said that Italy needed someone strong and courageous to lift it to its former glory. He believed he was the man for the job. Mussolini called on people to remember their heritage as descendants of the all-powerful Roman Empire and said that Italy should be an empire once more. In 1919 he put forth the idea "spazio vitale" (vital space) for the Italian people to be fruitful and multiply in their greatness and said that it was natural for a greater nation and its people to dominate over weaker nations and people. Though Mussolini's notion of "spazio vitale" was a not motivated by superiority along racial lines as Hitler's later idea of "lebensraum" (living space) for the Aryan race, Mussolini certainly did believe that some people were inherently better and more equipped to rule over other inferior people. Because Italy lagged far behind other European nations in wealth, industry and influence, the promise of a new era of Italian greatness was appealing to many Italians by 1920.

The Fascist party grew rapidly in Italy in the midst of the suffering after World War I. Mussolini's rise was partly a result of this and his use of a group of armed strong-men called the Blackshirts, who "restored order" in Italy through violence and intimidation. By 1922, Mussolini's support was substantial enough that he and 30,000 of his Blackshirts marched on Rome and demanded that the Prime Minster of Italy, Luigi Facta, step down in favor of Mussolini. Facta stepped down at the urging of Italy's king at the time, Victor Emmanuel III, who believed that Mussolini could be useful in making changes in Italy. Victor Emmanuel failed to realize that what Mussolini desired what absolute control of Italy for himself. In 1922, Mussolini became the new Prime Minister of Italy. By 1925, he would be its dictator.

Under Mussolini's leadership, he progressively passed laws and amended the Italian Constitution so that he took total control legally. First he gave himself emergency dictatorial powers, then made it so that he no longer answered to the Italian Parliament. He established a one-party system in Italy in which only the Fascist Party could have any say in government. Finally, he used the intimidation of his Blackshirts and a powerful propaganda machine to rule over the minds of the Italian people. He rewrote history with himself as the savior of Italy and even had a new encyclopedia written to which he contributed the following explanation of what Fascism was. He developed around himself a cult of personality that worshipped Mussolini and the Fascist Party ideal.

Fascism, believes neither in the possibility nor the utility of perpetual peace. It thus repudiates the doctrine of Pacifism -- born of a renunciation of the struggle and an act of cowardice in the face of sacrifice. War alone brings up to its highest tension all human energy and puts the stamp of nobility upon the peoples who have courage to meet it. All other trials are substitutes, which never really put men into the position where they have to make the great decision -- the alternative of life or death....

The Fascist accepts life and loves it, knowing nothing of and despising suicide: he rather conceives of life as duty and struggle and conquest, but above all for others -- those who are at hand and those who are far distant, contemporaries, and those who will come after...

Fascism is the complete opposite of...Marxian Socialism, which believes the history of human civilization can be explained simply through the conflict of interests among the various social groups and by economic change .... Fascism, now and always, believes in holiness and in heroism; that is to say, in actions influenced by no economic motive, direct or indirect. And if the economic conception of history be denied, it follows that the existence of an unchangeable and unchanging class-war is also denied. And above all Fascism denies that class-war can be the preponderant force in the transformation of society....

Fascism combats the whole complex system of democratic ideology, and rejects it. Fascism denies that the majority, by the simple fact that it is a majority, can direct human society; it denies that numbers alone can govern by means of a periodical consultation, and it affirms the immutable, beneficial, and fruitful inequality of mankind, which can never be permanently leveled through the mere operation of a mechanical process such as universal suffrage....

Fascism denies, in democracy, the absurd untruth of political equality dressed out in the garb of collective irresponsibility, and the myth of "happiness" and indefinite progress.

Given that the nineteenth century was the century of Socialism, of Liberalism, and of Democracy, it does not necessarily follow that the twentieth century must also be a century of Socialism, Liberalism and Democracy: political doctrines pass, but humanity remains, and it may rather be expected that this will be a century of authority...a century of Fascism. For if the nineteenth century was a century of individualism it may be expected that this will be the century of collectivism and hence the century of the State.

The foundation of Fascism is the conception of the State, its character, its duty, and its aim. Fascism conceives of the State as an absolute, in comparison with which all individuals or groups are relative, only to be conceived of in their relation to the State. The conception of the Liberal State is not that of a directing force, guiding the play and development, both material and spiritual, of a collective body, but merely a force limited to the function of recording results: on the other hand, the Fascist State is itself

454

conscious and has itself a will and a personality -- thus it may be called the "ethic" State....

The Fascist State organizes the nation, but leaves a sufficient margin of liberty to the individual; the latter is deprived of all useless and possibly harmful freedom, but retains what is essential; the deciding power in this question cannot be the individual, but the State alone.

For Fascism, the growth of empire, that is to say the expansion of the nation, is an essential manifestation of vitality, and its opposite a sign of decadence. Peoples which are rising, or rising again after a period of decadence, are always imperialist; and renunciation is a sign of decay and of death. Fascism is the doctrine best adapted to represent the tendencies and the aspirations of a people, like the people of Italy, who are rising again after many centuries of abasement and foreign servitude. But empire demands discipline, the coordination of all forces and a deeply felt sense of duty and sacrifice. This fact explains many aspects of the regime and the necessarily severe measures which must be taken against those who would oppose this spontaneous and inevitable movement of Italy in the twentieth century, and would oppose it by recalling the outworn ideology of the nineteenth century. For never before has the nation stood more in need of authority, of direction and order. If every age has its own characteristic doctrine, there are a thousand signs which point to Fascism as the characteristic doctrine of our time. For if a doctrine must be a living thing, this is proved by the fact that Fascism has created a living faith; and that this faith is very powerful in the minds of men is demonstrated by those who have suffered and died for it.

Three Documents on Joseph Stalin, 1922 to 1936 CE

Reading and Discussion Questions
1. Who was Joseph Stalin and why did Lenin consider him dangerous?
2. Who did Lenin support for leadership instead of Stalin and why
3. How did Stalin come to power in the Soviet Union?
4. Why was rapid industrialization such a high priority for Stalin? What was the impact of his Five-Year Plan on the Russian people?
5. What were Stalin's "purges?" What was he purging and why?

Before his death in 1922, Vladimir Lenin was concerned about the succession of leadership in the U.S.S.R. Two of the top men under Lenin were Leon Trotsky and Joseph Stalin and they were the only likely candidates for taking power after Lenin's death. Lenin made his wishes clear that he be succeed by Trotsky and not Stalin because Lenin had serious concerns about Stalin's temperament and personality. Stalin manipulated his way into power in 1927, and forced Trotsky into exile. Stalin would later have Trotsky assassinated.

Upon assuming power, Stalin sent the USSR down a disastrous path between 1928 and 1933. Stalin passed the First and Second Five-Year Plans to achieve his goal of rapid industrialization, which he believed was necessary to make the USSR as powerful as its European neighbors. In many respects he was successful - by 1939 the USSR was behind only the United States and Germany in industrial output. The human costs, however, were enormous. In addition to rapid industrialization, Stalin also collectivized all farm land in the Soviet Union, displacing farmers and changing what, where and how crops were planted. This part of the plan was a disaster that resulted in devastatingly low harvests and the death of millions of Soviets from starvation.

Adding to the suffering caused by implementation of the Five-Year Plan, Stalin was also deeply paranoid and feared conspiracies against him were everywhere. He set up a police state in the USSR, where people had no rights whatsoever and secret police spied around every corner, looking to expose "enemies of the state." Any suspected enemies were imprisoned (often to be worked to death) or executed. Between 1936 and 1939, somewhere between 600,000 and 1.2 million Soviets were murdered during Stalin's purges. In all, between 1927 and 1939, roughly 20 million Soviets died as a result of Stalin's policies. This was all before the USSR became involved in the fighting of World War II. The following sources document suspicions about Stalin before he assumed power, as well as his rash and paranoid acts once he assumed power.

Last Testament of Vladimir Lenin, 1922 CE

Prior to his death, Vladimir Lenin tried to make his wishes for the future of the Bolshevik Party as clear as possible because he feared power falling into the hands of Joseph Stalin. He wrote his wishes in his Last Testament before he died in 1922.

Comrade Stalin, having become Secretary-General, has unlimited authority concentrated in his hands, and I am not sure whether he will always be capable of using that authority with sufficient caution. Comrade Trotsky, on the other hand, is distinguished not only by outstanding ability. He is personally perhaps the most capable man in the present Party, but he has displayed excessive self-assurance and shown excessive preoccupation with the purely administrative side of the work.

Stalin is too rude and this defect, although quite tolerable in our midst and in dealing among us Communists, becomes intolerable in a larger government. That is why I suggest the comrades think about a way of removing Stalin from power and appointing another man in his stead who in all other respects differs from Comrade Stalin and specifically [has qualities that Stalin lacks], namely, that of being more tolerant, more loyal, more polite, and more considerate to the comrades, less volatile and moody, etc. This circumstance may appear to be a negligible detail. But I think for the good of the Party and considering what I wrote above about the relationship between Stalin and Trotsky, it is not a detail merely, but a detail which is of the greatest importance.

* * * * * *

Joseph Stalin, Industrialization of the Country, 1928 CE

Surrounded on all sides by capitalist countries, we must overtake and outstrip the advanced technology of our neighbors. We have overtaken and outstripped the advanced capitalist countries in the sense of establishing a new political system, the

Soviet system. That is good. But it is not enough. In order to secure the final victory of socialism in our country, we must also overtake and outstrip these countries technically and economically. Either we do this, or we shall be forced to the wall.

This applies not only to the building of socialism. It applies also to upholding the independence of our country in the circumstances of the capitalist encirclement. The independence of our country cannot be upheld unless we have an adequate industrial basis for defense. And such an industrial basis cannot be created if our industry is not more highly developed technically.

That is why a fast rate of development of our industry is necessary and imperative.

We must systematically and persistently, place our agriculture on a new technical basis, the basis of large-scale production, and bring it up to the level of socialist industry. Either we accomplish this task-in which case the final victory of socialism in our country will be assured, or we turn away from it and do not accomplish it-in which case a return to capitalism may become inevitable.

*   *   *   *   *   *

Joseph Stalin, On The Purges, 1936 CE

In 1936, Stalin began to attack his political opponents in a series of "purges" aimed at destroying all whom he even suspected of opposing him. Ultimately, Stalin blamed the exiled Leon Trotsky and other rivals for all the suspected plots against him and his Party. The assassination of one of Stalin's most trusted agents caused his paranoia to become more intense. The following document is his official statement justifying his purges, which killed hundreds of thousands of Soviets. Stalin actually had this explanation of his actions written for Soviet school textbooks, because he strictly controlled ever piece of information and propaganda in order to control the Soviet mind completely.

The achievements of Socialism in our country were a cause of rejoicing not only to the Party, and not only to the workers and collective farmers, but also to our Soviet intelligentsia, and to all honest citizens of the Soviet Union.

But they were no cause of rejoicing to the remnants of our enemies [other political parties and group]; on the contrary, they only enraged them the more as time went on. Our victories infuriated the lickspittles of the defeated classes - the puny remnants of the following of Bukharin and Trotsky.

Since the achievements of Socialism in our country meant the victory of the policy of the Party and the utter bankruptcy of the policy [of our opponents], these people began to revenge themselves on the Party and the people for their own failure, for their own bankruptcy; they began to resort to foul play and sabotage the cause of the workers and collective farmers, to blow up pits, set fire to factories, and commit acts of wrecking in collective and state farms, with the object of undoing the achievements of the workers and collective farmers and evoking popular discontent against the Soviet Government. And in order, while doing so, to shield their puny group from exposure and destruction, they simulated loyalty to the Party, fawned upon it, eulogized it, cringed before it more and more, while in reality continuing their underhanded, subversive activities against the workers and peasants.

Speeches were made at the Seventeenth Congress by [the supporters of Trotsky, and others] who praised the Party extravagantly for its achievements. But the congress could not help seeing that both their nauseating self-castigation and their fulsome praise of the party were only meant to hide an uneasy and unclean conscience. However, the Party did not yet know or suspect that while these men were making their cloying speeches at the congress they were hatching a villainous plot against the life of S. M. Kirov [a high-ranking party official].

On December 1, 1934, S. M. Kirov was foully murdered in the Smolny, in Leningrad, by a shot from a revolver. S. M. Kirov was loved by the Party and the working class, and his murder stirred the people profoundly, sending a wave of wrath and deep sorrow through the country.

The investigation found that an underground counter-revolutionary terrorist group had been formed in Leningrad called the "Leningrad Centre." The purpose of this group was to murder leaders of the Communist Party. S. M. Kirov was chosen as the first victim. The exposed members of this organization were sentenced by the Military Court of the U.S.S.R. to the supreme penalty - to be shot.

Soon afterwards the existence of another underground counter-revolutionary organization called the "Moscow Centre" was discovered. The preliminary investigation and the trial revealed that this organization was cultivating the terrorist mentality among their followers, and in plotting the murder of members of the Party Central Committee and of the Soviet Government.

During their trial, [our enemies] simulated remorse in court; but they persisted in their duplicity even in the dock. They concealed their connection with Trotsky. They concealed their spying and wrecking activities. As it later transpired, the murder of Comrade Kirov was the work of this united Trotsky-Bukharin gang....

The chief instigator and ringleader of this gang of assassins and spies was Judas Trotsky. Trotsky and his underlings were preparing to bring about the defeat of the U.S.S.R. in the event of attack by imperialist countries; they had become defeatists with regard to the workers' and peasants' state; they had become despicable tools and agents of the German and Japanese fascists.

The main lesson which the Party organizations had to draw from the trials of the persons implicated in the foul murder of S. M. Kirov was that the Party must put an end to their own political blindness and political heedlessness, and must increase their vigilance and the vigilance of all Party members....

The highest priority of the Party is purging and consolidating its ranks, destroying the enemies of the Party and relentlessly combating distortions of the Party line.

Hymn to Stalin, 1929 CE

Reading and Discussion Questions
1. What types of things is Stalin celebrated for in this document?
2. Are you surprised by the tone of this document in celebration of Stalin? Why or why not?
3. Do you think that people actually loved Stalin, like this hymn proclaims? Why or why not?

Despite Stalin's cruelty, or perhaps because of it, he was worshipped as a hero and savior among many Soviets in the 1930s. It is hard to know whether anyone genuinely liked Stalin or whether they simply pretended to adore him out of fear. Below is an example of the types of praises that were not uncommon in the Soviet Union in the 1930s which show the cult following that emerged around him.

Thank you, Stalin. Thank you because I am joyful. Thank you because I am well. No matter how old I become, I shall never forget how we received Stalin two days ago. Centuries will pass, and the generations still to come will regard us as the happiest of mortals, as the most fortunate of men, because we lived in the century of centuries, because we were privileged to see Stalin, our inspired leader. Yes, and we regard ourselves as the happiest of mortals because we are the contemporaries of a man who never had an equal in world history.

The men of all ages will call on thy name, which is strong, beautiful, wise and marvelous. Thy name is engraven on every factory, every machine, every place on the earth, and in the hearts of all men.

Every time I have found myself in his presence I have been subjugated by his strength, his charm, his grandeur. I have experienced a great desire to sing, to cry out, to shout with joy and happiness. And now see me--me!--on the same platform where the Great Stalin stood a year ago. In what country, in what part of the world could such a thing happen.

I write books. I am an author. All thanks to thee, O great educator, Stalin. I love a young woman with a renewed love and shall perpetuate myself in my children--all thanks to thee, great educator, Stalin. I shall be eternally happy and joyous, all thanks to thee, great educator, Stalin. Everything belongs to thee, chief of our great country. And when the woman I love presents me with a child the first word it shall utter will be : Stalin.

O great Stalin, O leader of the peoples,
Thou who broughtest man to birth.
Thou who fructifies the earth,
Thou who restorest to centuries,
Thou who makest bloom the spring,
Thou who makest vibrate the musical chords...
Thou, splendour of my spring, O thou,
Sun reflected by millions of hearts.

459

The 25-Point Plan of Nazi Party, 1920 CE

<u>Reading and Discussion Questions</u>

1. Based on your understanding of demagogues in history, in what ways does this document represent demagoguery, or telling people what they want to hear?
2. What are some specific things that Hitler proposes to do in his 25 Points? Paint a picture of what Germany looks like under Nazi rule.
3. What specific things are a reaction to or a rejection of the terms of the Treaty of Versailles? Explain them and what they are in reaction to, by referring to your reading on the Treaty of Versailles.
4. Are there any points that reveal Hitler's anti-Semitic agenda and if so, what do those points say or propose?
5. When were the 25 Points written? What is significant about this year?

The National Socialist Programme (aka the 25-point Programme and the 25-point Plan) was the party program of the National Socialist German Workers' Party (NSDAP). Originally the name of the party was the German Workers' Party (DAP) but on the same day of the announced party program it was renamed the NSDAP. This is what we know as the Nazi Party.

The Party Program of the NSDAP was presented by Adolf Hitler in 1920 at the first large Party gathering in Munich. In 1920, there were roughly 3000 Nazis. By the height of Nazi power, the Party had a membership of more than 8 million, all of whom pledged support for the party principles, which are outlined in the 25-Point Plan.

1. We demand the union of all Germans in a Great Germany on the basis of the principle of self-determination of all peoples.

2. We demand that the German people have rights equal to those of other nations; and that the Peace Treaties of Versailles and St. Germain shall be abrogated.

3. We demand land and territory (colonies) for the maintenance of our people and the settlement of our surplus population.

4. Only those who are our fellow countrymen can become citizens. Only those who have German blood, regardless of creed, can be our countrymen. Hence no Jew can be a countryman.

5. Those who are not citizens must live in Germany as foreigners and must be subject to the law of aliens.

6. The right to choose the government and determine the laws of the State shall belong only to citizens. We therefore demand that no public office, of whatever nature, whether in the central government, the province, or the municipality, shall be held by anyone who is not a citizen.

We wage war against the corrupt parliamentary administration whereby men are appointed to posts by favor of the party without regard to character and fitness.

7. We demand that the State shall above all undertake to ensure that every citizen shall have the possibility of living decently and earning a livelihood. If it should not be possible to feed the whole population, then aliens (non-citizens) must be expelled from the Reich.

8. Any further immigration of non-Germans must be prevented. We demand that all non-Germans who have entered Germany since August 2, 1914, shall be compelled to leave the Reich immediately.

9. All citizens must possess equal rights and duties.

10. The first duty of every citizen must be to work mentally or physically. No individual shall do any work that offends the interest of the community to the benefit of all.

Therefore we demand:

11. That all unearned income be abolished.

12. Since every war imposes on the people fearful sacrifices in blood and treasure, all personal profit arising from the war must be regarded as treason. We therefore demand the total confiscation of all war profits.

13. We demand the nationalization of all trusts.

14. We demand profit-sharing in large industries.

15. We demand a generous increase in old-age pensions.

16. We demand the creation and maintenance of a sound middle-class, the immediate communalization of large stores which will be rented cheaply to small tradespeople, and the strongest consideration must be given to ensure that small traders shall deliver the supplies needed by the State, the provinces and municipalities.

17. We demand an agrarian reform in accordance with our national requirements, and the enactment of a law to expropriate the owners without compensation of any land needed for the common purpose. The abolition of ground rents, and the prohibition of all speculation in land.

18. We demand that ruthless war be waged against those who work to the injury of the common welfare. Traitors, usurers, profiteers, etc., are to be punished with death, regardless of creed or race.

19. We demand that Roman law, which serves a materialist ordering of the world, be replaced by German common law.

20. In order to make it possible for every capable and industrious German to obtain higher education, and thus the opportunity to reach into positions of leadership, the

461

State must assume the responsibility of organizing thoroughly the entire cultural system of the people. The curricula of all educational establishments shall be adapted to practical life. The conception of the State Idea (science of citizenship) must be taught in the schools from the very beginning. We demand that specially talented children of poor parents, whatever their station or occupation, be educated at the expense of the State.

21. The State has the duty to help raise the standard of national health by providing maternity welfare centers, by prohibiting juvenile labor, by increasing physical fitness through the introduction of compulsory games and gymnastics, and by the greatest possible encouragement of associations concerned with the physical education of the young.

22. We demand the abolition of the regular army and the creation of a national army.

23. We demand that there be a legal campaign against those who propagate deliberate political lies and disseminate them through the press. In order to make possible the creation of a German press, we demand:

(a) All editors and their assistants on newspapers published in the German language shall be German citizens.

(b) Non-German newspapers shall only be published with the express permission of the State. They must not be published in the German language.

(c) All financial interests in or in any way affecting German newspapers shall be forbidden to non-Germans by law, and we demand that the punishment for transgressing this law be the immediate suppression of the newspaper and the expulsion of the non-Germans from the Reich.

Newspapers transgressing against the common welfare shall be suppressed. We demand legal action against those tendencies in art and literature that have a disruptive influence upon the life of our folk, and that any organizations that offend against the foregoing demands shall be dissolved.

24. We demand freedom for all religious faiths in the state, insofar as they do not endanger its existence or offend the moral and ethical sense of the Germanic race.

The party as such represents the point of view of a positive Christianity without binding itself to any one particular confession. It fights against the Jewish materialist spirit within and without, and is convinced that a lasting recovery of our folk can only come about from within on the principle: COMMON GOOD BEFORE INDIVIDUAL GOOD

25. In order to carry out this program we demand: the creation of a strong central authority in the State, the unconditional authority by the political central parliament of the whole State and all its organizations.

The leaders of the party undertake to promote the execution of the foregoing points at all costs, if necessary at the sacrifice of their own lives.

Adolf Hitler, *Mein Kampf*, 1925 CE

Reading and Discussion Questions
1. Why is a big lie better than a small lie, according to Hitler?
2. In what way does Hitler say the Jews are harming Germany?
3. In order for propaganda to be effective with the masses, how should it be crafted? What does this strategy say about his opinion of the common man?
4. What is the role of repetition in propaganda?
5. Hitler wrote about the value of "the big lie"? Having read that, what portion of his writings or ideas can or should be trusted? Explain your answer.

Mein Kampf ("My Struggle") is the autobiography of Adolf Hitler. Hitler was imprisoned in 1923 after the failed Beer Hall Putsch and served less than a year in prison. While he was in jail, Hitler wrote the story of his life, including his anti-semetic views and his position that the Jews were responsible for all of Germany's problems. In Mein Kampf he also wrote a lot about what he had learned on how to, and how not to seize power. Upon his release from prison, Hitler renewed his quest for total power in Germany but he did it very differently than in 1923. The second time, Hitler created a cult-like following among desperate Germans by manipulating their minds with grand promises and powerful propaganda.

Fighting Jews as Defending God

If the Jew is victorious over the other peoples of the world, his crown will be the funeral wreath of humanity and this planet will, as it did thousands of years ago, move through the cosmos devoid of men.

Hence today I believe that I am acting in accordance with the will of the Almighty Creator: by defending myself against the Jew, I am fighting for the work of the Lord

On the "Big Lie"

In the big lie there is always a certain force of believability; because the broad masses of a nation are always more easily corrupted in the deeper strata of their emotional nature than consciously or voluntarily; and thus in the primitive simplicity of their minds they more readily fall victims to the big lie than the small lie, since they themselves often tell small lies in little matters but would be ashamed to resort to large-scale falsehoods. It would never come into their heads to fabricate colossal untruths, and they would not believe that others could have the impudence to distort the truth so infamously. Even though the facts which prove this to be so may be brought clearly to their minds, they will still doubt and waver and will continue to think that there may be some other explanation.

For the grossly daring lie always leaves traces behind it, even after it has been nailed down, a fact which is known to all expert liars in this world and to all who conspire together in the art of lying. These people know only too well how to use falsehood for the basest purposes. From time immemorial, however, the Jews have known better than any others how falsehood and calumny can be exploited. Is not their very existence founded on one great lie, namely, that they are a religious community, where as in reality they are a race? And what a race! One of the greatest thinkers that mankind has produced has branded the Jews for all time with a statement which is profoundly and exactly true. Schopenhauer (a German psychologist) called the Jew "The Great Master of Lies". Those who do not realize the truth of that statement, or do not wish to believe it, will never be able to lend a hand in helping Truth to prevail.

On the Weapons of the Jews
Since the Jew is not the attacked but the attacker, not only anyone who attacks passes as his enemy, but also anyone who resists him. But the means with which he seeks to break such reckless but upright souls is not honest warfare, but lies and slander.

Here he stops at nothing, and in his vileness he becomes so gigantic that no one need be surprised if among our people the personification of the devil as the symbol of all evil assumes the living shape of the Jew.

The ignorance of the broad masses about the inner nature of the Jew, the lack of instinct and narrow-mindedness of our upper classes, make the people an easy victim for this Jewish campaign of lies. While from innate cowardice the upper classes turn away from a man whom the Jew attacks with lies and slander, the broad masses from stupidity or simplicity believe everything.

With satanic joy in his face, the black-haired Jewish youth lurks in wait for the unsuspecting girl whom he defiles with his blood, thus stealing her from her people. With every means he tries to destroy the racial foundations of the people he has set out to subjugate. Just as he himself systematically ruins women and girls, he does not shrink back from pulling down the blood barriers for others, even on a large scale. It was and it is Jews who bring the Negroes into the Rhineland, always with the same secret thought and clear aim of ruining the hated white race by the necessarily resulting bastardization, throwing it down from its cultural and political height, and himself rising to be its master.

For a racially pure people which is conscious of its blood can never be enslaved by the Jew. In this world he will forever be master over bastards and bastards alone. And so he tries systematically to lower the racial level by a continuous poisoning of individuals.

In the political field he refuses the state the means for its self-preservation, destroys the foundations of all national self-maintenance and defense, destroys faith in the leadership, scoffs at its history and past, and drags everything that is truly great into the gutter.

Culturally, he contaminates art, literature, the theater, makes a mockery of natural feeling, overthrows all concepts of beauty and sublimity, of the noble and the good, and instead drags men down into the sphere of his own base nature. Religion is ridiculed, ethics and morality represented as outmoded, until the last props of a nation in its struggle for existence in this world have fallen.

On the Use of Propaganda
The function of propaganda does not lie in the scientific training of the individual, but in calling the masses' attention to certain facts, processes, necessities, etc., whose significance is thus for the first time placed within their field of vision ...

All propaganda must be popular and its intellectual level must be adjusted to the most limited intelligence among those it is addressed to. Consequently, the greater the mass it is intended to reach, the lower its purely intellectual level will have to be. But if, as in propaganda for sticking out a war, the aim is to influence a whole people, we must avoid excessive intellectual demands on our public, and too much caution cannot be extended in this direction.

The more modest its intellectual level, and the more it takes into consideration the emotions of the masses, the more effective it will be. And this is the best proof of the soundness or unsoundness of a propaganda campaign, and not success pleasing a few scholars or young aesthetes.

The art of propaganda lies in understanding the emotional ideas of the great masses and finding, through a psychologically correct form, the way to the attention and thence to the heart of the broad masses. The fact that our bright boys do not understand this merely shows how mentally lazy and conceited they are.

The receptivity of the great masses is very limited, their intelligence is small, but their power of forgetting is enormous. In consequence of these facts, all effective propaganda must be limited to a very few points and must harp on these in slogans until the last member of the public understands what you want him to understand by your slogan. As soon as you sacrifice this slogan and try to be many-sided, the effect will piddle away, for the crowd can neither digest nor retain the material offered. In this way the result is weakened and in the end entirely cancelled out.

Thus we see that propaganda must follow a simple line and correspondingly the basic tactics must be psychologically sound ...

The function of propaganda is, for example, not to weigh and ponder the rights of different people, but exclusively to emphasize the one right which it has set out to argue for. Its task is not to make an objective study of the truth, in so far as it favors the enemy, and then set it before the masses with academic fairness; its task is to serve our own right, always and unflinchingly.

Joseph Goebbels, *The Jew*, 1929 CE

Reading and Discussion Questions
1. What emotions are this document trying to stir up in the German people? Cite specific examples from the text that are meant to provoke an emotional response and what the desired response would be.
2. To what extent does this piece adhere to the standards of "good propaganda" that Hitler outlined in *Mein Kampf* (dumbing down the message, repeating key ideas, making big lies. . .) Cite examples from the text of each of these techniques.
3. What percentage of Goebbels' audience do you think actually believed his anti-Semitic messages? Explain your answer.

Joseph Goebbels was one of Hitler's most trusted advisors and the Minister of Propaganda for the Nazi Party. Goebbels joined the Nazi party in 1924 and quickly rose to prominence because of his powerful speaking ability and passion for the success of the Nazis in Germany. While Hitler knew the value of propaganda, as evidenced in Mein Kampf, Goebbels took propaganda to a whole new terrifying level. Goebbels had total control of all art, media and other information in Nazi Germany, including educational material used in German schools for the indoctrination of the Hitler Youth and a whole generation of zealous Nazis. Goebbels bombarded the airways with anti-Jewish propaganda on the radio and he even created a Nazi newspaper called Der Angriff for the spreading of his hateful propaganda. Goebbels was such a devoted follower of Hitler that he and his wife committed suicide with Hitler at the end of World War II. The following article is a typical attack on Jews that Goebbels specialized in manufacturing. He was the master of "the big lie."

Everything is discussed openly in Germany and every German claims the right to have an opinion on any and all questions. One is Catholic, the other Protestant, one an employee, the other an employer, a capitalist, a socialist, a democrat, an aristocrat. There is nothing dishonorable about choosing one side or the other of a question. Discussions happen in public and where matters are unclear or confused one settles it by argument and counter argument. But there is one problem that is not discussed publicly, one that it is delicate even to mention: the Jewish question. It is taboo in our republic.

The Jew is immunized against all dangers: one may call him a scoundrel, parasite, swindler, profiteer, it all runs off him like water off a raincoat. But call him a Jew and you will be astonished at how he recoils, how injured he is, how he suddenly shrinks back: "I've been found out."

One cannot defend himself against the Jew. He attacks with lightning speed from his position of safety and uses his abilities to crush any attempt at defense.

Quickly he turns the attacker's charges back on him and the attacker becomes the liar, the troublemaker, the terrorist. Nothing could be more mistaken than to defend oneself. That is just what the Jew wants. He can invent a new lie every day for the enemy to respond to, and the result is that the enemy spends so much time defending himself that he has no time to do what the Jew really fears: to attack. The accused has become the accuser, and loudly he shoves the accuser into the dock. So it always was in the past when a person or a movement fought the Jew. That is what would happen to us as well were we not fully aware of his nature, and if we lacked the courage to draw the following radical conclusions:

1. One cannot fight the Jew by positive means. He is a negative, and this negative must be erased from the German system or he will forever corrupt it.

2. One cannot discuss the Jewish question with the Jews. One can hardly prove to a person that one has the duty to render him harmless.

3. One cannot allow the Jew the same means one would give an honest opponent, for he is no honorable opponent. He will use generosity and nobility only to trap his enemy.

4. The Jew has nothing to say about German questions. He is a foreigner, an alien, who only enjoys the rights of a guest, rights that he always abuses.

5. The so-called religious morality of the Jews is no morality at all, rather an encouragement to betrayal. Therefore, they have no claim to protection from the state.

6. The Jew is not smarter than we are, rather only cleverer and craftier. His system cannot be defeated economically — he follows entirely different moral principles than we do. It can only be broken through political means.

7. A Jew cannot insult a German. Jewish slanders are but badges of honor for a German opponent of the Jews.

8. The more a German person or a German movement opposes the Jew, the more valuable it is. If someone is attacked by the Jews, that is a sure sign of his virtue. He who is not persecuted by the Jews, or who is praised by them, is useless and dangerous.

9. The Jew evaluates German questions from the Jewish standpoint. As a result, the opposite of what he says must be true.

10. One must either affirm or reject anti-Semitism. He who defends the Jews harms his own people. One can only be a Jewish lackey or a Jewish opponent. Opposing the Jews is a matter of personal hygiene.

These principles give the anti-Jewish movement a chance of success. Only such a movement will be taken seriously by the Jews, only such a movement will be feared by them.

The fact that he shouts and complains about such a movement therefore is only a sign that it is right. We are therefore delighted that we are constantly attacked in the Jewish gazettes. They may shout about terror. We answer with Mussolini's familiar words: "Terror? Never! It is social hygiene. We take these individuals out of circulation just as a doctor does to a bacterium."

Heinrich Himmler, The Master Race Must Procreate & Adopt, 1936 CE

Reading and Discussion Questions
  1. How many children was each Nazi family to have?
  2. If a Nazi couple could not have their own children, what were they to do and what measures were in place to allow them to do this?
  3. What was the purpose of "the Spring of Life" organization, according to Himmler?
  4. What is your reaction to this document? Explain.

Heinrich Himmler was a member of Hitler's inner circle and was one of the most powerful men in Nazi Germany. Himmler became a member of the Nazi party in 1923 and was one of its earliest members. He was responsible for helping Hitler to create the SS ("Schutzstaffel", which is German for personal guard). The SS would be the most powerful arm of the Nazi military and it answered directly to and directly served Hitler. Himmler was most personally responsible for the events of the Holocaust. Hitler said he dreamt of a Germany free of Jews. It was Himmler who most directly worked to make Hitler's vision a reality.

Himmler was responsible for the creation of the first Nazi concentration camp at Dachau as early as 1933 and for the creation of the Einsatzgruppen, or mobile killing units, which were responsible for the mass slaughter of Jews, gypsies, intellectuals, the disabled and elderly in the years before concentration camps became the primary method of extermination of all "undesirables" in Germany. Late in the war, Himmler fell out of favor with Hitler after a series of military misjudgments and Himmler was demoted from his high positions. Himmler fled, fearing he would be killed by Hitler, and was captured by British forces in 1945. He committed suicide while in prison before he could stand trial for war crimes at the end of World War II. Himmler was key to advancing the ideas of racial purity in Nazi Germany, both by exterminating non-Aryans and by encouraging "pure Germans" to reproduce in large numbers to ensure the dominance of the Aryan race. The following document is from Himmler to Nazi leaders about the Nazi policy on reproduction and racial purity.

As early as December 13, 1934, I wrote to all SS leaders and declared that we have fought in vain if political victory was not to be followed by victory of births of good blood. The question of multiplicity of children is not a private affair of the individual, but his duty towards his ancestors and our people.

The SS has taken the first step in this direction long ago with the engagement and marriage decree of December 1931. However, the existence of sound marriage is futile if it does not result in the creation of numerous descendants.

I expect that here, too, the SS and especially the SS leader corps, will serve as a guiding example.

The minimum amount of children for a good sound marriage is four. Should unfortunate circumstances deny a married couple their own children, then every SS leader should adopt racially and hereditarily valuable children, educate them in the spirit of National Socialism, let them have education corresponding to their abilities.

The organization "Lebensborn eingetragener Verein [Spring of Life, registered society]" serves the SS leaders in the selection and adoption of qualified children. The organization "Lebensborn e. V." is under my personal direction, is part of the Central Office for Race and Resettlement bureau of the SS, and has the following obligations:

1. Support racially, biologically, and hereditarily valuable families with many children.

2. Place and care for racially and biologically and hereditarily valuable pregnant women, who, after thorough examination of their and the progenitor's families by the Central Office for Race and Resettlement central bureau of the SS, can be expected to produce equally valuable children.

3. Care for the children.

4. Care for the children's mothers.

It is the honorable duty of all leaders of the central office to become members of the organization "Lebensborn e. V." The application for admission must be filed prior to September 23, 1936.

I shall personally keep myself informed of the success of my appeal.

Let me remind every SS leader once more that only sacrifices of a personal and material nature have brought us success in the times of the battle, and that the further construction of Germany, to last hundreds and thousands of years, will not be possible unless each and every one of us is ready to keep doing his share in the fulfillment of his obvious duty.

Reichsfuhrer SS H. HIMMLER

Nuremberg Laws, 1935 CE

Reading and Discussion Questions
   1.   According to this document, who is and is not a citizen of the German Reich?
   2.   How did these laws change relationships between Jews and non-Jews in Germany?
   3.   What do you think was the motive behind Article 3 of the Law for the Protection of German Blood and German Honor?
   4.   What was the goal of the Nuremberg Laws, based on your understanding of the reading?

By 1933, the Nazi Party was in firm control of the German government. In that year, they began an organized campaign against Jews in Germany. Hitler required a boycott of Jewish businesses, burned books by Jewish authors and prevented Jews from holding any position in German government. But the Nazi program of alienation and removal of Jews from German society was made part of German law in 1935, with the passage of a set of anti-Jewish laws called the Nuremberg Laws. 1935 and the Nuremberg Laws mark the beginning of heightened persecution of Jews and was seen as a critical turning point in the evolution of the Holocaust.

Reich Citizenship Law of September 15, 1935

The Reichstag has unanimously enacted the following law:

Article 1
1. A subject of the state is a person who enjoys the protection of the German Reich and who in consequence has specific obligations toward it.

Article 2
1. A Reich citizen is a subject of the state who is of German or related blood, and proves by his conduct that he is willing and fit to faithfully serve the German people and Reich.
2. Reich citizenship is acquired through the granting of a Reich citizenship certificate.
3. The Reich citizen is the sole bearer of full political rights in accordance with the law.

Law for the Protection of German Blood and German Honor

Moved by the understanding that purity of German blood is the essential condition for the continued existence of the German people, and inspired by the inflexible determination to ensure the existence of the German nation for all time, the Reichstag has unanimously adopted the following law, which is promulgated herewith:

Article 1
1. Marriages between Jews and subjects of the state of German or related blood are forbidden. Marriages nevertheless concluded are invalid, even if concluded abroad to circumvent this law.

Article 2

Extramarital relations between Jews and subjects of the state of German or related blood are forbidden.

Article 3

Jews may not employ in their households female subjects of the state of German or related blood who are under 45 years old.

Article 4

1. Jews are forbidden to fly the Reich or national flag or display Reich colors.
2. They are, on the other hand, permitted to display the Jewish colors. The exercise of this right is protected by the state.

Article 5

1. Any person who violates the prohibition under Article 1 will be punished with a prison sentence.
2. A male who violates the prohibition under Article 2 will be punished with a prison sentence.
3. Any person violating the provisions under Articles 3 or 4 will be punished with a jail term of up to one year and a fine, or with one or the other of these penalties.

Winston Churchill, Two Speeches

Reading and Discussion Questions

1. What is Churchill's feeling about the Munich Agreement and the treatment of Czechoslovakia, based on your reading of the first speech?
2. What does Churchill have to say about Chamberlain in the first speech? Summarize Churchill's feelings about him.
3. How does Churchill say that Britain will respond to Hitler's planned invasion of the British Isles?
4. What is your opinion of Winston Churchill, based on your reading of these two speeches? Was he the right man to lead Britain in World War II or should Chamberlain have retained control? Explain your answer.

Sir Winston Churchill was the Prime Minister of Britain during World War II and is widely believed to be one of the main reasons that Nazi Germany was ultimately defeated. But in the 1930s, Winston Churchill was viewed by most people in Britain as a washed-up old man and a war-monger who was trying to get Britain into another unnecessary war. They believed this because Churchill was one of the only men in Britain and the world who saw how dangerous Hitler really was. And he spoke passionately to everyone who would listen about stopping Hitler before it was too late. But no one listened in time.

Almost immediately after seizing control in Germany in 1933, Hitler began abrogating or breaking the terms of the Treaty of Versailles. He began an aggressive campaign of rebuilding the German military, which was forbidden by the Treaty of Versailles. He reoccupied the Rhineland in eastern Germany which was also forbidden. And he created a union between Austria and Germany in 1938. Hitler violated provision after provision of the Treaty of Versailles and the world did nothing. Everyone was too afraid of another global war.

In September of 1938, then-British Prime Minister Neville Chamberlain met with Adolf Hitler to discuss Hitler's plans. At that meeting, which was described as cordial and agreeable, Hitler explained that he was simply trying to unify all German people into his German nation. This, he explained was why he annexed Austria early in 1938 and why he wanted to incorporate a tiny sliver of western Czechoslovakia into German territory. This part of Czechoslovakia was called the Sudetenland and there were German people living there, said Hitler, who wanted to be part of Germany. At the end of the meeting, Chamberlain, Hitler and representatives from France and Italy signed a document called the Munich Agreement, which gave the Sudetenland to Hitler. In return, Hitler promised not to take any more territory or to pursue any broader military action. The people of Czechoslovakia were not included in the meeting where their country was cut apart and so they felt betrayed by France and England. This policy of giving someone something they want to avoid a conflict is called appeasement.

Neville Chamberlain has become infamous for his decision to appease Hitler. When he returned from his visit with Hitler, Chamberlain declared, "I have achieved peace for our time." In March of 1939, Hitler invaded and occupied all of Czechoslovakia. In September of 1939 he invaded Poland, and prompted the beginning of World War II. It was not until 1939 that people began to realize that Churchill had been right but by then, it was too late. In 1940, Chamberlain stepped down as Prime Minister, largely because his gross misjudgment of Hitler and his policy of appeasement. Winston Churchill became Prime Minister of Britain in 1940 and led Britain in that capacity until the war's end in 1945. When he was made Prime Minister, he said all he had to offer was "blood, toil, tears and sweat." And when many in government celebrated his becoming Prime Minister he reportedly said, "Poor people, poor people. They trust me, and I can give them nothing but disaster for quite a long time."

The Shame of Munich, 1938 CE

I will begin by saying the most unpopular and most unwelcome thing. I will begin by saying what everybody would like to ignore or forget but which must nevertheless be stated, namely--we have sustained a total and unmitigated defeat [in conceding to Hitler's demands].

All that Chamberlain has been able to secure by all his immense exertions, by all the great efforts and mobilization which took place in this country, and by all the anguish and strain through which we have passed in this country, the utmost he has been able to gain for Czechoslovakia has been that the German dictator, instead of snatching his victuals from the table has been content to have them served to him course by course.

There never can be any absolute certainty that there will be a fight if one side is determined that it will give way completely. ...

All is over. Silent, mournful, abandoned, broken, Czechoslovakia recedes into the darkness. She has suffered in every respect by her association with the Western democracies and with the League of Nations, of which she has always been an obedient servant. ... We in this country, as in other liberal and democratic countries, have a perfect right to exalt the principle of self-determination, but it comes ill out of the mouths of those in totalitarian states who deny even the smallest element of toleration to every section and creed within their bounds. But, however you put it, this particular block of land, this mass of human beings to be handed over, has never expressed the desire to go into the Nazi rule. I do not believe that even now–if their opinion could be asked, they would exercise such an option. ...

I venture to think that in the future the Czechoslovak state cannot be maintained as an independent entity. You will find that in a period of time which may be measured by years, but may be measured only by months, Czechoslovakia will be engulfed in the Nazi regime. ... It is the most grievous consequence which we have yet experienced of what we have done and of what we have left undone in the last five years: five years of futile good intention, five years of eager search for the line of least resistance, five years of uninterrupted retreat of British power, five years of neglect of our air defenses. . . .

We are in the presence of a disaster of the first magnitude which has befallen Great Britain and France. Do not let us blind ourselves to that...I do not grudge our loyal, brave people, who were ready to do their duty no matter what the cost...the natural, spontaneous outburst of joy and relief when they learned that the hard ordeal would no longer be required of them at the moment; but they should know the truth. They should know that there has been gross neglect and deficiency in our defenses; they should know that we have sustained a defeat without a war...And do not suppose that this is the end. This is only the beginning of the reckoning. This is only the first sip, the first foretaste of a bitter cup which will be proffered to us year by year unless by a supreme recovery of moral health and martial vigor, we arise again and take our stand for freedom as in the olden time.   Chamberlain had the choice between war and shame. Now he has chosen shame – he'll get war later.

* * * * * *

We shall Fight on the Beaches, 1940 CE

In June of 1940 the Allied war effort was nearly crushed in what became known as the Battle of Dunkirk. With an Allied force of around 300,000 men surrounded by German soldiers, it appeared that total defeat in that battle was inevitable. But the British navy, and thousands of British civilians, crossed the English Channel in any boat they could find to rescue the stranded troops before they could be killed. It was one of the most miraculous and heroic military rescues in history. It was on that occasion that Churchill made the speech below. He celebrated the courage and commitment of every British citizen but then he called them to rise to an even bigger challenge–the invasion of Britain. Hitler had made clear his intention to crush Britain and the following is Churchill's response.

We are told that Herr Hitler has a plan for invading the British Isles. This has often been thought of before. When Napoleon lay at Boulogne for a year with his flat-bottomed boats and his Grand Army, he was told by someone. "There are bitter weeds in England." There are certainly a great many more of them since the British Expeditionary Force returned.

On the question of invasion, I would observe that there has never been a period in all these long centuries of which we boast when an absolute guarantee against invasion, still less against serious raids, could have been given to our people. In the days of Napoleon the same wind which would have carried his transports across the Channel might have driven away the blockading fleet. There was always the chance, and it is that chance which has excited and befooled the imaginations of many Continental tyrants. Many are the tales that are told. We are assured that novel methods will be adopted, and when we see the originality of malice, the ingenuity of aggression, which our enemy displays, we may certainly prepare ourselves for every kind of novel stratagem and every kind of brutal and treacherous maneuver. I think that no idea is so outlandish that it should not be considered and viewed with a searching, but at the same time, I hope, with a steady eye. We must never forget the solid assurances of sea power and those which belong to air power if it can be locally exercised.

I have, myself, full confidence that if all do their duty, if nothing is neglected, and if the best arrangements are made, as they are being made, we shall prove ourselves once again able to defend our Island home, to ride out the storm of war, and to outlive the menace of tyranny, if necessary for years, if necessary alone. At any rate, that is what we are going to try to do. That is the resolve of His Majesty's Government-every man of them. That is the will of Parliament and the nation. The British Empire and the French Republic, linked together in their cause and in their need, will defend to the death their native soil, aiding each other like good comrades to the utmost of their strength. Even though large tracts of Europe and many old and famous States have fallen or may fall into the grip of the Gestapo and all the odious apparatus of Nazi rule, we shall not flag or fail. We shall go on to the end, we shall fight in France, we shall fight on the seas and oceans, we shall fight with growing confidence and growing strength in the air, we shall defend our Island, whatever the cost may be, we shall fight on the beaches, we shall fight on the landing grounds, we shall fight in the fields and in the streets, we shall fight in the hills; we shall never surrender, and even if, which I do not for a moment believe, this Island or a large part of it were subjugated and starving, then our Empire beyond the seas, armed and guarded by the British Fleet, would carry on the struggle, until, in God's good time, the New World, with all its power and might, steps forth to the rescue and the liberation of the old.

Rudolf Hoess, Testimony at Nuremburg, 1946 CE

Reading and Discussion Questions
1. Approximately how many people were killed under the supervision of Rudolph Hoess?
2. What do you think the punishment should be for people who confess to crimes of the magnitude of those committed by Hoess?
3. Is there anything about this testimony that sounds remorseful or sorry for the actions described?
4. What is your reaction to this document? Explain.

Rudolf Hoess was one of the most powerful officers in the Nazi regime. He was one of the earliest members of the Nazi Party, joining its ranks in 1922. He got his start as a Nazi officer working for Henirich Himmler, who was in charge of "the final solution," which is what the Nazis called their plan to exterminate the Jewish population of Europe. Hoess worked first as an officer at Dachau concentration camp and ultimately became the Commandant of Auschwitz death camp. Hoess was captured by Allied Forces one year after the war in 1946 and was brought to trial in Nuremberg that same year. His testimony at that trial is one of the most horrifying, cold and unemotional accounts of the unimaginable acts that took place at Auschwitz. Hoess was found guilty of major war crimes and was executed in 1947.

I, RUDOLF FRANZ FERDINAND HOESS, being first duly sworn, depose and say as follows:

1. I am forty-six years old, and have been a member of the NSDAPI since 1922; a member of the SS since 1934; a member of the WaffenSS since 1939. I was also a member of the SS Guard Unit, the so-called Deathshead Formation.

2. I have been constantly associated with the administration of concentration camps since 1934, serving at Dachau until 1938 when I was appointed Commandant of Auschwitz. I commanded Auschwitz until 1 December,1943, and estimate that at least 2,500,000 victims were executed and exterminated there by gassing and burning, and at least another half million succumbed to starvation and disease, making a total dead of about 3,000,000. This figure represents about 70% or 80% of all persons sent to Auschwitz as prisoners, the remainder having been selected and used for slave labor in the concentration camp industries.

Included among the executed and burnt were approximately 20,000 Russian prisoners of war who were delivered at Auschwitz in Wehrmacht transports operated by regular Wehrmacht officers and men. The remainder of the total number of victims included about 100,000 German Jews, and great numbers of citizens (*mostly* Jewish) from Holland, France, Belgium, Poland, Hungary, Czechoslovakia, Greece, or other countries. We executed about 400,000 Hungarian Jews alone at Auschwitz in the summer of 1944.

4. Mass executions by gassing commenced during the summer 1941 and continued until fall 1944. I personally supervised executions at Auschwitz until the first of December 1943 and know by reason of my continued duties in the Inspectorate of Concentration Camps that these mass executions continued as stated above.

6. The "final solution" of the Jewish question meant the complete extermination of all Jews in Europe. I was ordered to establish extermination facilities at Auschwitz in June 1941. At that time there were already in the general government three other extermination camps; BELZEK, TREBLINKA and WOLZEK. These camps were under the command of the Security Police and SD. I visited Treblinka to find out how they carried out their exterminations. The Camp Commandant at Treblinka told me that he had liquidated 80,000 in the course of one-half year. He was principally concerned with liquidating all the Jews from the Warsaw Ghetto. He used monoxide gas and I did not think that his methods were very efficient. So when I set up the extermination building at Auschwitz, I used Cyclon B, which was a crystallized Prussic Acid which we dropped into the death chamber from a small opening. It took from 3 to 15 minutes to kill the people in the death chamber depending upon climatic conditions. We knew when the people were dead because their screaming stopped. We usually waited about one-half hour before we opened the doors and removed the bodies. After the bodies were removed our special commandos took off the rings and extracted the gold from the teeth of the corpses.

7. Another improvement we made over Treblinka was that we built our gas chambers to accommodate 2,000 people at one time, whereas at Treblinka their 10 gas chambers only accommodated 200 people each. The way we selected our victims was as follows: we had two SS doctors on duty at Auschwitz to examine the incoming transports of prisoners. The prisoners would be marched by one of the doctors who would make spot decisions as they walked by. Those who were fit for work were sent into the Camp. Others were sent immediately to the extermination plants. Children of tender years were invariably exterminated since by reason of their youth they were unable to work.

Still another improvement we made over Treblinka was that at Treblinka the victims almost always knew that they were to be exterminated and at Auschwitz we endeavored to fool the victims into thinking that they were to go through a delousing process. Of course, frequently they realized our true intentions and we sometimes had riots and difficulties due to that fact. Very frequently women would hide their children under the clothes but of course when we found them we would send the children in to be exterminated. We were required to carry out these exterminations in secrecy but of course the foul and nauseating stench from the continuous burning of bodies permeated the entire area and all of the people living in the surrounding communities knew that exterminations were going on at Auschwitz .

8. We received from time to time special prisoners from the local Gestapo office. The SS doctors killed such prisoners by injections of benzine. Doctors had orders to write ordinary death certificates and could put down any reason at all for the cause of death.

9. From time to time we conducted medical experiments on women inmates, including sterilization and experiments relating to cancer. Most of the people who died under these experiments had been already condemned to death by the Gestapo.

476

I understand English as it is written above. The above statements are true; this declaration is made by me voluntarily and without compulsion; after reading over the statement, I have signed and executed the same at Nurnberg, Germany on the fifth day of April 1946.

Adolf Hitler, *Last Testament*, 1945 CE

Reading and Discussion Questions

1. Should Hitler be blamed for the war, according to him? Explain why or why not. If not, who should be blamed?
2. What does Hitler say should become of the Nazi war efforts after his death?
3. Does he sound sorry or remorseful about anything that he had done?
4. What is Hitler's final wish, as expressed in this document? Are you surprised by what he chooses as his final words? Why or why not?

In 1945, Hitler knew the war was lost. The Russian army was within miles of Berlin and Hitler had no intention of being taken prisoner by the Allied Forces to stand trial. On April 30, 1945, Hitler gathered with his new wife and several men from his inner circle in his underground bunker beneath Berlin. There he and his closest friends committed suicide by ingesting cyanide poison. Before his suicide, Hitler wrote his last testament to tell his story the way he wanted it to be told. The following is the Last Testament of Adolf Hitler.

More than thirty years have passed since 1914 when I made my modest contribution as a volunteer in the First World War, which was forced upon the Reich.

In these three decades love and loyalty to my people have guided all my thoughts, actions and my life. They gave me the strength to make the most difficult decisions ever to confront mortal man. In these three decades I have spent my strength and my health.

It is untrue that I or anyone else in Germany wanted war in 1939. It was wanted and provoked solely by international statesmen either of Jewish origin or working for Jewish interests. I have made too many offers for the limitation and control of armaments, which posterity will not be cowardly enough always to disregard, for responsibility for the outbreak of this war to be placed on me. Nor have I ever wished that, after the appalling First World War, there would ever be a second against either England or America. Centuries will go by, but from the ruins of our towns and monuments the hatred of those ultimately responsible will always grow anew against the people whom we have to thank for all this: international Jewry and its henchmen.

I have left no one in doubt that if the people of Europe are once more treated as mere blocks of shares in the hands of these international money and finance conspirators, then the sole responsibility for the massacre must be borne by the true culprits: the Jews. Nor have I left anyone in doubt that this time millions of European children of Aryan descent will starve to death, millions of men will die in battle, and hundreds of thousands of women and children will be burned or bombed to death in our cities without the true culprits being held to account, albeit more humanely.

After six years of war which, despite all setbacks, will one day go down in history as the most glorious and heroic manifestation of the struggle for existence of a nation, I cannot abandon the city which is the capital of this Reich. Since our forces are too meager to withstand the enemy's attack and since our resistance is being debased by creatures who are as blind as they are lacking in character, I wish to share my fate with that which millions of others have also taken upon themselves by remaining in this city. Further, I shall not fall into the hands of the enemy who requires a new spectacle, presented by the Jews, for the diversion of the hysterical masses.

I have therefore decided to stay in Berlin and there to choose death voluntarily when I determine that the position of the Fuhrer and the Chancellery itself can no longer be maintained. I die with a joyful heart in the knowledge of the immeasurable deeds and achievements of our peasants and workers and of a contribution unique in the history of our youth which bears my name.

That I am deeply grateful to them all is as self-evident as is my wish that they do not abandon the struggle but that, no matter where, they continue to fight the enemies of the Fatherland. Through the sacrifices of our soldiers and my own fellowship with them unto death, a seed has been sown in German history that will one day grow to usher in the glorious rebirth of the National Socialist movement in a truly united nation.

Many of our bravest men and women have sworn to bind their lives to mine to the end. I have begged, and finally ordered, them not to do so but to play their part in the further struggle of the nation. I ask the leaders of the Army, the Navy and the Air Force to strengthen the National Socialist spirit of resistance of our soldiers by all possible means, with special emphasis on the fact that I myself, as the founder and creator of this movement, prefer death to cowardly resignation or even to capitulation.

May it become a point of honor of future German army officers, as it is already in our Navy, that the surrender of a district or town is out of the question and that, above everything else, the commanders must set a shining example of faithful devotion to duty unto death.

Before my death, I expel former Reichs-Marshal Hermann Goring from the party and withdraw from him all the rights that were conferred upon him by the decree of 29 June, 1941 and by my Reichstag statement of 1 September, 1939. In his place I appoint Admiral Donitz as President of the Reich and Supreme Commander of the Armed Forces.

Before my death, I expel the former Reichsfuhrer of the S.S. and the Minister of the Interior Heinrich Himmler from the party and from all his state officers. In his place I appoint Gauleiter Karl Hanke as Reichsfuhrer of the S.S. and Head of the German Police, and Gauleiter Paul Giesler as Minister of the Interior.

Apart altogether from their disloyalty to me, Goring and Himmler have brought irreparable shame on the whole nation by secretly negotiating with my enemy without my knowledge and against my will, and also by attempting illegally to seize control of the State.

A number of men, including Martin Bormann, Dr Goebbels and others together with their wives have joined me of their own free will, not wishing to leave the capital under any circumstances and are prepared to die with me. But I implore them to grant my request that they place the welfare of the nation above their own feelings. By their work and loyal companionship they will remain as close to me after my death as I hope my spirit will continue to dwell among them and accompany them always. Let them be severe but never unjust and let them never, above all, allow fear to preside over their actions, placing the honor of the nation above everything that exists on earth. May they, finally, always remember that our task, the consolidation of a National Socialist state, represents the work of centuries to come, so that every individual must subordinate his own interest to the common good. I ask of all Germans, of all National Socialists, men and women and all soldiers of the Wehrmacht, that they remain faithful and obedient unto death to the new government and its President.

Above all, I enjoin the government and the people to uphold the race laws to the limit and to resist mercilessly the poisoner of all nations, international Jewry.

Berlin, 29 April, 1945, 4 a.m.

Adolf Hitler

Albert Camus, *Letters to a German Friend*, 1943 CE

Reading and Discussion Questions
1. How does Camus explain the background and the purpose of his letters?
2. How is Camus' vision of Europe different that that of his friend?
3. What does Camus describe as "our best weapon" in letter Four?
4. There is an element of hope in Camus' letters about life after war. Why does he have hope for the future, according to your understanding of the reading?
5. Do these letters give you a sense of hope for the future and for humanity? Do they impact your view on life and human existence in any way?

Albert Camus was a French philosopher and author who lived through World War II. He was the second youngest person to ever win a Nobel Prize for Literature for his extensive writing of novels, plays and essays. During the war, Camus was a member of the French Resistance and he wrote many subversive essays and articles against the Nazis during the Nazi occupation of France. Camus is most noted as the creator of a branch of philosophy known as Absurdism. Absurdism explores the contradiction in human existence—that men spend their whole lives looking for truth and meaning when truth and meaning are impossible to find. Camus' writings were characterized by an acceptance of life on life's terms and that what is, is. This acceptance is seen by some as a hopeless outlook on life, and yet, in acceptance, peace can be found. And the promise of peace brings hope.

In 1943, Camus wrote a series of letters to a German Friend, which were never intended for a specific person. They were his letters to Germans generally, many of whom were his friends before the war. In these letters, Camus explores the difference views on life and power between the Nazi Germans and men like himself. His Letters have come to be seen as a valuable philosophical reflection on war and the senselessness of struggling against the agelessness of history. I think they are a fitting way to end our journey through history together because, as Camus said, history was here long before us and will be here long after we are gone.

From the Preface:

I cannot let these pages be reprinted without saying what they are. They were written and published clandestinely during the Occupation. They had a purpose, which was to throw some light on the blind battle we were then waging and thereby to make our battle more effective. They are topical writings and hence they may appear unjust. ... When the author of these letters says "you", he means not "you Germans" but "you Nazis". When he says "we", this signifies not always "we Frenchmen" but sometimes "we free Europeans". I am contrasting two attitudes, not two nations, even if, at a certain moment in history, these two nations personified two enemy attitudes. To repeat a remark that is not mine, I love my country too much to be a nationalist. ... I loath none executioners. Any reader who reads the *Letters to a German Friend* in this ective – in other words, as a document emerging from the struggle against – will see how I can say I don't disown a single word I have written here.

From the third letter (April 1944):

That idea of Europe that you took from the best among us and distorted has consequently become hard for us to keep alive in all its original force. ... Your speak of Europe but the difference is that for you Europe is a property, whereas we feel that we belong to it. ... You say "Europe", but you think in terms of potential soldiers, granaries, industries brought to heel, intelligence under control. Am I going too far? But at least I know that when you say "Europe", even in your best moments, when you let yourselves be carried away by your own lies, you cannot keep yourselves from thinking of a cohort of docile nations led by a lordly Germany toward a fabulous and bloody future. I should like you to be fully aware of the difference. For you Europe is an expanse encircled by seas and mountains, dotted with dams, gutted with mines, covered with harvests, where Germany is playing a game in which her fate alone is at stake. But for us Europe is a home of the spirit where for the last twenty centuries the most amazing adventure of the human spirit has been going on. It is the privileged arena in which Western man's struggle against the world, against the gods, against himself is today reaching its climax. As you see, there is no common denominator. ...

Your Europe is not the right one. There is nothing there to unite or inspire. Ours is a joint adventure that we shall continue to pursue, despite you, with the inspiration of intelligence.

Sometimes on a street corner, in the brief intervals of the long struggle that involves us all, I happen to think of all those places in Europe I know well. It is a magnificent land molded by suffering and history. All those flowers and stones, those hills and those landscapes where men's time and the world's time have mingled old trees and monuments! My memories has fused together such superimposed images to make a single face, which is the face of my true native land. ... It never occurred to me that someday we should have to liberate them from you. And even now, at certain moments of rage and despair, I am occasionally sorry that the roses continue to grow in the cloister of San Marco and the pigeons drop clusters from the Cathedral of Salzburg, and the red geraniums grow tirelessly in the little cemeteries of Silesia.

But at other moments, and they are the only ones that count, I delight in this. For all those landscapes, those flowers and those plowed fields, the oldest of lands, show every spring that there are things you cannot choke in blood. ... So I know that everything in Europe, both landscape and spirit, calmly negates you without feeling any rash hatred, but with the calm strength of victory. The weapons the European spirit can use against you are the same as reside in this soil constantly reawakening in blossoms and harvests. The battle we are waging is sure victory because it is as obstinate as spring.

And, finally, I know that all will not be over when you are crushed. Europe will still have to be established. It always has to be established.

From the fourth letter (July, 1944):
For a long time we both thought that this world had no ultimate meaning and that consequently we were cheated. I still think so in a way. But I came to different conclusions from the ones you used to talk about, which, for so many years now, you have been trying to introduce into history. I tell myself now that if I had really followed your reasoning, I ought to approve what you are doing. And this is so serious that I

481

must stop and consider it, during this summer night so full of promises for us and threats for you.

You never believed in the meaning of this world, and you therefore deduced the idea that everything was equivalent and that good and evil could be defined according to one's wishes. You supposed that in the absence of any human or divine code the only values were those of the animal world – in other words, violence and cunning. Hence you concluded that man was negligible and that his soul could be killed, that in the maddest of histories the only pursuit for the individual was the adventure of power and his own morality, the realism of conquests. And, to tell the truth, I, believing I thought as you did, saw no valid argument to answer you except a fierce love of justice which, after all, seemed to me as unreasonable as the most sudden passion.

Where lay the difference? Simply that you readily accepted despair and I never yielded to it. Simply that you saw the injustice of our condition to the point of being willing to add to it, whereas it seemed to me that man must exalt justice in order to fight against eternal injustice, create happiness in order to protest against the universe of unhappiness. ...

I continue to believe that this world has no ultimate meaning. But I know that something in it has a meaning and that is man, because he is the only creature to insist on having one. This world has at least the truth of man, and our task is to provide its justification against fate itself. And it has no justification but man; hence he must be saved if we want to save the idea we have of life. ...

Our difficult achievement consisted in following you into war without forgetting happiness. And despite the clamors and the violence, we tried to preserve in our hearts the memory of a happy sea, of a remembered hill, the smile of a beloved face. For that matter, this was our best weapon, the one we shall never put away. For as soon as we lost it we should be as dead as you are. But we now know that the weapons of happiness cannot be forged without considerable time and too much blood. ...

You are the man of injustice and, and there is nothing in the world that my heart loathes so much. But now I know the reasons for what was once only passion. I am fighting you because your logic is as criminal as your heart. This is why my condemnation will be sweeping; you are already dead as far as I am concerned. But at the very moment when I am judging your horrible behavior, I shall remember that you and we started from the same solitude, that you and we, with all Europe, are caught in the same tragedy of intelligence. And, despite yourselves, I shall still apply to you the name of man. ... I can tell you that at the very moment when we are going to destroy you without pity, we still feel no hatred for you. ...

Hundreds of thousands of men assassinated at dawn, the terrible walls of prisons, the soil of Europe reeking with millions of corpses of its sons – it took all that to pay for the acquisition of two or three slight distinctions which may have no other value than to help some among us to die more nobly. Yes, that is heart-breaking. ... The dawn about to break will mark your final defeat. I know that heaven, which was indifferent to your h   ctories, will be equally indifferent to your defeat. Even now I expect nothing n. But we shall at least have helped save man from the solitude to which you elegate him. Because you scorned such faith in mankind, you are the men sands, are going to die solitary. Now, I can say farewell to you.

482

EPILOGUE

To The Reader,

As I conclude the writing of this book, I wonder what impression you will be left with about history. Will you worry? Will you be afraid? History is full of dark moments and heartbreaking suffering that has made this book, at points, very hard to write. Delving into the horrifying psychology of monstrous men has kept me up at night, because I cannot understand how hate and ignorance can consume some people so completely. World War II in particular is a dark spot on the history of humankind that we can never erase. And it hurts me to my core. But I have devoted my life to the study and teaching of history not because of the darkness, but because of the light. And I hope that you, too, will see that out of unimaginable sadness comes the most sublime beauty and hope. When I study history, I feel hopeful. I hope you will, too.

Almost every belief system and philosophy in the world has at its foundation the idea of two opposing forces fighting for control. Life and death. Joy and sorrow. Wisdom and ignorance. Good and evil. War and peace. Victory and defeat. Some people call this universal phenomenon yin and yang. Others call it God and the Devil. Whatever we call it, the idea is that something cannot exist without its opposite also existing. Yes, there is sorrow. But because there is sorrow, there is also joy. And sorrow makes the joy so much sweeter. In history, times of ignorance make life seem impossible, but they also make the reemergence of wisdom a celebration. Power-hungry men crush people for their ambition. But then evil is vanquished and hope is restored.

Thomas Hobbes said that man's struggles against other men proves that we are brutish, simple and selfish. But I believe Thomas Hobbes was entirely wrong about humanity. In studying all the ways we hurt each other, he entirely overlooked the fact that every single time in history that a tyrannical man has tried to crush humanity, humanity has resisted. Not once, in our thousands of years of living, have we ever given up. We make mistakes. We fall flat on our faces. We give up and even lie down, for a moment, a century or an age. But we *always* get up. When I study history, I *hate* the moments when we fall down. I grieve every time I remember someone who was hurt by ignorance, cruelty or greed. But I love, no I *live for*, the moments when we get up again. As Winston Churchill urged us to do when all hope seemed lost to the Nazis, we never, ever, ever give up. And that is why history is a story of hope to me.

For several days at the end of this project, the final stanza of a poem by Dylan Thomas ran through my mind continuously. It sums up to me what I believe is the song of the ages, a hymn to the men and women who refused to accept failure or defeat and a challenge to us as we march into the future. Thomas wrote: "Do not go gentle into that good night. Rage, rage against the dying of the light." Remember, darkness cannot prevail unless we extinguish the light.

483

83779342R00274

Made in the USA
Middletown, DE
15 August 2018